A
Theory
of Discourse

PRENTICE-HALL INTERNATIONAL, INC., *London*
PRENTICE-HALL OF AUSTRALIA, PTY. LTD., *Sydney*
PRENTICE-HALL OF CANADA, LTD., *Toronto*
PRENTICE-HALL OF INDIA PRIVATE LIMITED, *New Delhi*
PRENTICE-HALL OF JAPAN, INC., *Tokyo*

A
Theory
of Discourse

The Aims of Discourse

James L. Kinneavy
The University of Texas at Austin

Prentice-Hall, Inc., Englewood Cliffs, N.J.

Current printing (last number):
10 9 8 7 6 5 4 3 2 1

Library of Congress Catalog Card No.: 74–133573

13–913582–0

Printed in the United States of America.

ACKNOWLEDGEMENTS

Alfred A. Knopf, Inc.: for materials and quotations from THE DECLARATION OF INDEPENDENCE: A Study in the History of Political Ideas, by Carl Becker, copyright 1933. Reprinted by permission of the publisher.

Alfred A. Knopf, Inc.: for materials and quotations from THE REBEL by Albert Camus, translated by Anthony Bower, published in 1954. Copyright © 1956 by Alfred A. Knopf, Inc. Reprinted by permission of the publisher.

Alsop, Stewart: for the article "The Meaning of the Dead" by Stewart Alsop, in the SATURDAY EVENING POST, April 24, 1965. Reprinted by permission of the author.

Bar-Hillel, Yehoshua: for material and quotations from LANGUAGE AND INFORMATION by Yehoshua Bar-Hillel, copyright 1964. Reprinted by permission of the author.

The Catholic University Press: for material and quotations from A STUDY OF THREE CONTEMPORARY THEORIES OF THE LYRIC by James L. Kinneavy, copyright 1956. Reprinted by permission of the publisher.

Charles Scribner's Sons, Publishers: for material and quotations from A TRANSACTION OF FREE MEN, THE BIRTH AND COURSE OF THE DECLARATION OF INDEPENDENCE by David Hawke, copyright 1964. Reprinted by permission of the publisher.

D. Reidel Publishing Company: for material and quotations from THE METHODS OF CONTEMPORARY THOUGHT by I. M. Bocheński, copyright 1965. Reprinted by permission of the publisher.

Encyclopaedia Britannica, Inc.: for material and quotations from "Philosophy and Religion" by John E. Smith in THE GREAT IDEAS TODAY, 1965, edited by R. M. Hutchins and M. J. Adler, copyright 1965. Reprinted by permission of the publisher.

Encyclopaedia Britannica, Inc.: for material and quotations from "The Year's Development in the Arts and Sciences: Literature" by Susan Sontag in THE GREAT IDEAS TODAY, 1966, edited by R. M. Hutchins and M. J. Adler, copyright 1966. Reprinted by permission of the publisher.

iv

George Allen & Unwin Ltd.: for material and quotations from HUMAN KNOWL-
EDGE: ITS SCOPE AND LIMITS by Bertrand Russell. Reprinted by permission
of the publisher.

The Glencoe Press: for material and quotations from STATISTICS, A NEW
APPROACH by Wilson Allen Wallis and Harry V. Roberts, copyright 1956 by The
Free Press of Glencoe, a Corporation. Reprinted by permission of the publisher.

Hamish Hamilton Ltd.: for material and quotations from THE REBEL by Albert
Camus, translated by Anthony Brown. Copyright © 1952 Editions Gallimard, copyright © 1956 by Alfred A. Knopf, Inc. Reprinted by permission of the publisher.

Harvard University Press: for material and quotations from THE NEW AMERICAN
LIBRARY edition of ORATOR by Cicero, translated by H. M. Hubbell, copyright
1952. Reprinted by permission of the publisher.

Harvard University Press: for material and quotations from THE NEW AMERICAN
LIBRARY edition of PHILOSOPHY IN A NEW KEY by Susanne Langer, copy-
right 1942, 1951, 1957 by the President and Fellows of Harvard College; 1970 by
Susanne Knauth Langer. Reprinted by permission of the publisher.

Hillary House, Ltd.: for material and quotations from THE PHILOSOPHY OF
SCIENCE by Stephen E. Toulmin, copyright 1953. Reprinted by permission of the
publisher.

Humanities Press, Inc.: for material and quotations from THE PHENOMENOLOGY
OF PERCEPTION by Maurice Merleau-Ponty, translated by Collin Smith, copyright 1962. Reprinted by permission of the publisher.

Hutchinson & Co. (Publishers) Ltd.: for material and quotations from THE PHI-
LOSOPHY OF SCIENCE by Stephen Toulmin. Reprinted by permission of the
publisher.

Indiana University Press: for material and quotations from THE WELL-TEMPERED
CRITIC by Northrop Frye. Copyright © 1963 by Indiana University Press. Reprinted by permission of the publisher.

Literary Masterworks, Inc.: for material and quotations from BEING AND NOTH-
INGNESS, AN ESSAY ON PHENOMENOLOGICAL ONTOLOGY by Jean Paul
Sartre, translated by Hazel E. Barnes, copyright 1953. Reprinted by permission of
the publisher.

M.I.T. Press: for material and quotations from THE LANGUAGE OF POLITICS by
Harold D. Lasswell and Nathan Leites and Associates, copyright 1965 by Massachusetts Institute of Technology. Reprinted by permission of the publisher.

Morris, Charles W.: for material and quotations from SIGNS, LANGUAGE AND
BEHAVIOR by Charles W. Morris, published by Prentice-Hall, Inc., in 1946. A
second printing by George Braziller, Inc., 1955. Reprinted by permission of the author.

Northwestern University Press: for material and quotations from SPEAKING (LA
PAROLE) by Georges Gusdorf, translated by Paul T. Brockelman, copyright 1965.
Reprinted by permission of the publisher.

Penguin Books, Inc.: for material and quotations from TECHNIQUES OF PER-
SUASION, FROM PROPAGANDA TO BRAINWASHING by J. A. C. Brown,
copyright 1963. Reprinted by permission of the publisher.

Oxford University Press: for material and quotations from THE MIRROR AND
THE LAMP by M. H. Abrams, copyright 1953. Reprinted by permission of the
publisher.

Oxford University Press: for material and quotations from GERARD MANLEY HOPKINS, A STUDY OF POETIC IDIOSYNCRASY IN RELATION TO POETIC TRADITION by W. H. Gardner, copyright 1949. Reprinted by permission of the publisher.

Oxford University Press: for material and quotations from "On Defining Style: An Essay in Applied Linguistics" by Nils Erik Enkvist in LINGUISTICS AND STYLE, John Spencer, Ed., copyright 1964. Reprinted by permission of the publisher.

Oxford University Press: for material and quotations from THE PARTIAL CRITICS by Lee T. Lemon, copyright 1965. Reprinted by permission of the publisher.

Oxford University Press: for the poem THAT NATURE IS A HERACLITEAN FIRE AND OF THE COMFORT OF THE RESURRECTION, by Gerard Manley Hopkins, edited by W. H. Gardner and N. H. Mackenzie, 4th edition, 1967, copyright held by the Reverend F. Vavasour, S. J., and the Society of Jesus. Reprinted by permission of the publisher.

Oxford University Press: for material and quotations (page 570) from A STUDY OF HISTORY, Abridgement of Volumes I-VI by Arnold J. Toynbee, abridged by D. C. Somervell, copyright 1947 by Oxford University Press. Reprinted by permission of the publisher.

Princeton University Press: for material and quotations from THE DEHUMANIZA-TION OF ART AND OTHER ESSAYS ON ART, CULTURE AND LITERA-TURE, by José Ortega y Gasset, Princeton Paperback, 1968 (copyright 1948 © 1968 by Princeton University Press). Reprinted by permission of the publisher.

Random House, Inc.: for the first inaugural address and explanatory notes from THE PUBLIC PAPERS AND ADDRESSES OF FRANKLIN D. ROOSEVELT, WITH A SPECIAL INTRODUCTION AND EXPLANATORY NOTES BY PRESIDENT ROOSEVELT. Volume II: THE YEAR OF CRISIS, 1933, by Franklin D. Roosevelt, copyright 1938. Reprinted by permission of the publisher.

Richard D. Irwin, Inc.: for material and quotations from ADVERTISING THEORY AND PRACTICE by Charles H. Sandage and Vernon Fryburger, copyright 1963. Reprinted by permission of the publisher.

Routledge & Kegan Paul Ltd.: for material and quotatioins from THE PHENOME-NOLOGY OF PERCEPTION by Maurice Merleau-Ponty, translated by Collin Smith, copyright 1962. Reprinted by permission of the publisher.

Simon & Schuster, Inc.: for material and quotations from HUMAN KNOWLEDGE, ITS SCOPE AND LIMITS by Bertrand Russell, copyright 1948. Reprinted by permission of the publisher.

Yale University Press: for material and quotations from AN ESSAY ON MAN by Ernst Cassirer, copyright 1944. Reprinted by permission of the publisher.

Yale University Press: for material and quotations from THE MYTH OF THE STATE by Ernst Cassirer, copyright 1946. Reprinted by permission of the publisher.

Yale University Press: for material and quotations from THE PHILOSOPHY OF SYMBOLIC FORMS by Ernst Cassirer, translated by Ralph Manheim, copyright 1953. Reprinted by permission of the publisher.

Yale University Press: for material and quotations from COMMUNICATIONS AND PERSUASION by Carl I. Hovland, Irving R. Janis, and Harold H. Kelley, copyright 1953. Reprinted by permission of the publisher.

Preface

This book attempts to bring together, in a systematic framework, various approaches to the teaching of composition from classical and contemporary sources. It is intended to give the reader a comprehensive coverage of the various kinds of oral and written themes which students are expected to engage in at the college and secondary level in composition and speech courses.

By drawing on some hitherto untapped sources, an attempt is made to present a coherent and unified view of the field of English. The system used is no doubt imperfect in many respects, but it at least pretends to an internal consistency. In addition, it presents a hierarchy of importance for matters in the field of composition around which considerable debate has raged traditionally and recently.

The book is directed to several divergent audiences. It could serve as a basic text for courses in advanced composition and rhetoric at the upper class and graduate levels. It should prove quite useful for in-service courses for teaching assistants who are handling typical freshman composition courses. It can serve as a basic or optional text for courses training student teachers to teach composition at the secondary and primary levels. It could profitably be used for in-service courses in composition teaching and for summer institutes for teachers. Because of its comprehensive framework, it has close affinities with some texts currently being used in departments of speech, communications, and philosophy at the upper class and graduate levels.

I should like to express my gratitude to many colleagues, students, staff members, and editors, without whose assistance this book would have been impossible. In particular, I should like to offer special thanks to Robert Anderson, University of Kansas, who assisted me in establishing some of the basic philosophic foundations of composition embodied in the text; Wayne N. Thompson, University of Houston, who made several useful suggestions for the chapter on persuasion; Richard S. Beal, Boston University, who offered needed encouragement at the outset of this project; Edward P. J. Corbett, Ohio State University, for many suggestions and encouragement; W. Ross Winterowd, University of Southern California, for valuable critical comments; Thomas D. Horn, University of Texas, for patience with a piece of scholarship that took many years to come to fruition; Geneva H. Pilgrim, University of Texas, for forcing me to recognize the distinctiveness and importance of expression as an aim of discourse; Francis Christensen, University of Southern Illinois, for friendly support; Frank M. Jackson, Genesee Community College, for invaluable suggestions and reactions; and my wife, who has been, in Shakespeare's words, across the years "a wench of excellent discourse."

James L. Kinneavy
Austin, Texas

Contents

xi

A
Theory
of Discourse

1

Discourse and the Field of English

Introduction

Need for a Theory of Discourse

The present anarchy of the discipline of what is commonly categorized as "composition," both in high schools and colleges, is so evident as scarcely to require proof.

Composition is so clearly the stepchild of the English department that it is not a legitimate area of concern in graduate studies, is not even recognized as a subdivision of the discipline of English in a recent manifesto put out by the major professional association (MLA) of college English teachers (Thorpe, a)[1], in some universities is not a valid area of scholarship for advancement in rank, and is generally the teaching province of graduate assistants or fringe members of the department.

The present chaotic subsistence of freshman and upper-division courses in composition underscores their precarious claim to existence. The agenda of freshman composition vary from nothing to everything. Some colleges are seeking to banish the subject from the college curriculum entirely, taking away even its service department birthright and relegating it to the high school. Others feel that nothing human is foreign to composition, that its business is the instant humanizing of the incoming barbarian through an eclectic look at science, popular and esoteric arts, psychology, and sociology. In between, such governing concepts as expository reading

[1] References given are to items in the bibliography at the end of the chapter.

1

and writing, a survey of logic, new rhetoric, grammar (traditional, structural, or generative), reading in linguistics, semantics, beginning literary analysis structure all or part of the course. The internal structures of most of these courses and the texts constructed to accomodate them are more varied than the courses themselves. The upper-division courses in composition, except technical writing, are usually upgraded versions of the same heterogeneity of courses in creative, i.e., literary writing—though these are not nearly so popular in some quarters as they were fifteen years ago.

Such a rich variety on the surface might suggest an underlying poverty. It does suggest one clear hypothesis: there is no definite concept of what the basic foundations of composition are. There is even the uneasy suspicion that there is nothing more to composition *as* composition than what could and should be covered in an adequate high school course.

On the contrary, it is the thesis of this work that the field of composition—or discourse as it will presently be termed—is a rich and fertile discipline with a worthy past which should be consulted before being consigned to oblivion, an exciting present, and a future that seems as limitless as either linguistics or literature.

This is not meant to imply that the theory of discourse is a settled issue. Indeed, the tentative nature of the present work is reflected in the title chosen—this is in large measure only "theory." Like much in the new linguistics and most of the new criticism, little experimental evidence can be cited as conclusive. There are subdivisions of the theory which could profitably be made the subject of graduate and postgraduate research, there are histories to be written, there are theories to be evaluated, there are many important questions to be raised and answered.

But, by synthesizing some of the neglected areas of the past and much going on in the present within a framework suggested by modern philosophy and linguistics, it is believed that composition can very legitimately carve out a respectable domain in the field of English.

The advantages of such a theory seem immeasureable. By constructing norms parallel in a sense to the techniques of new criticism, the analysis of writing other than literary and the composition of such works also can be improved. Teachers for freshman composition and high schools can be trained more efficiently. Literature itself can emerge more intelligible in its own right.

The field of discourse is still in what Kuhn, a notable historian of science, has called the preparadigm period (Kuhn, f, 354). That is, there has not yet been erected a comprehensive system of the discipline which has received some general acceptance and which could serve as a framework for research, further speculation, innovation, even repudiation. Kuhn sketches the pattern of development of some other disciplines before the advent of a workable paradigm, and the sketch looks very much like a portrait of the field of composition at the present time. Each person begins his work anew from different foundations, the same ground is covered again and again with inconclusive results, there is no way to discriminate among research "accidents" and "essential novelties" (Kuhn, f, 355–56), and there are no systematic commitments which can motivate serious innovation (Kuhn, f, 349).

The case of electricity is typical, says Kuhn:

> During the first half of the eighteenth century there was no way for electricians to distinguish consistently between electrical and nonelectrical effects, between laboratory accidents and essential novelties, or between striking demonstrations and experiments which revealed the essential nature of electricity (f, 356).

If, in this quotation, the appropriate substitutions are made, the author could be talking about literary criticism or composition theory today. But the picture for electricity changed after 1740, as it had changed for other disciplines:

> Some time between 1740 and 1780 electricians, as a group, gained what astronomers had achieved in Antiquity, students of motion in the Middle Ages, of physical optics in the late seventeenth century, and of historical geology in the early nineteenth. They had, that is, achieved a paradigm, possession of which enabled them to take the foundation of their field for granted and to push on to more concrete and recondite problems.... Except with the advantage of hindsight, it is hard to find another criterion that so clearly proclaims a field of science (Kuhn, f, 357).

No paradigm is looked upon as irrevocable; in fact, the later development of the sciences is from paradigm to paradigm, often within the same generation. But some initial order seems essential if a discipline is to emerge from folk wisdom. Francis Bacon's methodological dictum seems appropriate: "Truth emerges more readily from error than from confusion" (quoted in Kuhn, f, 357).

Terminology

Four possible terms are mildly competitive currently as referends (referring words) to the kind of reality envisaged in this text: rhetoric, composition, communication, and discourse. Because of customarily associated connotations, none is entirely satisfactory.

"Rhetoric," especially in speech, in the usage of people talking of a "new rhetoric" (e.g., Fogarty, r), and traditionally for over a century in English departments, often refers to the whole field of the uses of language.

But there are quite divergent and narrower meanings of the term, also sanctioned by traditions of long standing. Because, in this text, "rhetoric" is given a precise and restricted meaning, for important reasons advanced later (see Chapter IV), "rhetoric" will not be used in the sense of a general science or art of communication.

"Communication" itself readily comes to mind. However, because of the preempting of this term by departments whose main concerns are with mass media; and because of the fact that certain of the uses of language are not really *communicative;* and because the term has connotations connected with an important theory of electric and electronic signal transmission (Bar-Hillel, 1, 22, 291); and because the "communications" movement in freshman composition often is associated with a stress on skills *as* skills (of speaking, listening, writing, and reading), an emphasis this text strongly decries, the term will generally be avoided. However, some of the general framework of this text does come from communication and information theory.

"Composition" is undoubtedly the term which is most frequently given to the consideration of many of the kinds of problems treated in the sequence. Yet, too many undesirable connotations also crowd this word. It rarely refers to oral communication and this book intends no such exclusion; in etymology and in practical usage it embodies almost solely a "process" connotation which is not desirable in this instance; and unfortunately it is frequently associated with the too sterile and static disciplines of high school and freshman composition courses; finally, the term is not used in the frameworks of philosophy and linguistics which structure the present approach.

"Discourse" finally seems the last recourse. Historically, the term has meant several things: a coherent and reasoned treatment of a subject or merely an extended treatment of a subject (though not necessarily rational), and conversation. In modern linguistics the term has come to mean any utterance larger than the sentence; in this sense it may or may not comprise the full text in a given situation. The concept adhered to here is a composite of some of the traditional and the linguistic meanings.

Generally discourse here refers to the full text (when feasible) of an oral or written situation; it does not denote necessarily a rational or logically coherent content; the discourse can be directed to any aim of language or refer to any kind or reality; it can be a poem, a conversation, a tragedy, a joke, a seminar discussion, a full-length history, a periodical article, an interview, a sermon, a TV ad. The precise meaning of "full" text in a given situation will be given below.

A theory of discourse will then comprise an intelligible framework of different types of discourse with a treatment of the nature of each type, the underlying logic(s), the organizational structure of this type, and the stylistic characteristics of such discourse.

Method of Approach

In order to construct an intelligible framework of various types of discourse, and the relation of such a framework to the other parts of the field of English, one has not at one's command all of the desirable materials which could conceivably justify on empirical grounds a given classificatory system. Consequently, the history of theory and practice and a survey of current theory and practice seem the only available criteria for erecting a framework. Therefore a short historical sketch of composition theory and practice, followed by a brief survey of what seem to be the best current theoretical tools at hand will be made. After this, a comprehensive synthesis of the valid historical and theoretical components of the discipline of English will be attempted. Within this, the specific orb of a theory of discourse will be located.

Brief Historical Sketch
of Discourse Education
in Western Civilization

A brief historical sketch of college education in English discourse, as such, would, comparatively speaking, be a brief history indeed. It is true that the English language has been the vehicle of instruction in English schools for six centuries since *ca.* 1349 when French was discarded (Stevenson, in Skeat, e, 421 ff.) ; but this has not been true of the colleges or the universities. Oxford, for example, got its first professorship in English Literature in 1873, twenty-three years after it was first suggested (Mallet, h, III, 342, 453).

The major trends and important movements in the teaching of discourse are seen in much better perspective, consequently, by taking a more comprehensive look at discourse education in Western culture generally; the sweep is broader but the lines are more distinct. The lines which emerge, it is hoped, are the lines separating various facets of discourse study. No pretense to an exhaustive coverage is suggested in such a brief outline, of course.

*Discourse Education
in Antiquity*

Greece and Rome

In Greece, education in the use of the language came only after physical and musical education. It crystallized fairly early into three distinct stages which can, with some distortion, be roughly paralleled to our elementary, secondary, and college education. Since Rome almost bodily adopted most of this framework—with a few adaptations which will be pointed out—the two will be considered simultaneously.

The focus of elementary education is epitomized rather neatly in the Greek and Latin names for the teacher (*grammatistes, literator*) both of which have the root meaning of "letter" (of the alphabet). Once the student had mastered the mechanics of reading and writing he passed on to the second stage of instruction.

Secondary schools "were essentially literary schools" (Marrou, h, 199) in which the teacher (*grammaticus*) taught the elements of literary analysis—in Greek the secondary teacher was sometimes called a *kritikos* (critic). This literary study was primarily intended as a preparation for the main function of education—the composition and delivery of speeches in rhetoric, the function of higher education. The secondary school was permitted to encroach upon this territory by having the students do some preparatory composition exercises (*progymnasmata*). Only fairly late in Greek culture was what is now called "grammar" put into the secondary curriculum (on all of this, cf. Marrou, h, 160–75).

A quick look at the study of literary interpretation, and a brief sketch of the kind of compositions written by students will be useful because these established some patterns which transferred to college study later on.

The students usually read Homer, Hesiod, Sappho, Callimachus, the tragedians, Aristophanes, Xenophon, and above all, Thucydides. Quintilian summarizes very succinctly the four stages of the analysis (after a summary outline was given). First there was the establishment of the text, a kind of rudimentary "textual" (lower) criticism, necessary because of poor manuscripts. Secondly, an expressive reading—even memorized recitation—of the text followed. Then came the "exposition" (*exegesis*), comprising a word for word vocabulary equivalency and glossing of archaic and poetic terms and a content analysis called *historikon* (i.e., a recognition of geographic or poetic allusions, etc.). Finally came "judgment," the "finest flower of the grammarian's art," according to Plutarch (Marrou, h, 169), which consisted in drawing moral lessons from the reading—esthetic judgments were reserved for college and the rhetor.

The preparatory exercises in composition were rigidly stereotyped. Almost invariably they consisted of story summaries, narratives (of many kinds with elaborate subdivisions), fables, aphorisms to be developed in a rigid format, and confirmations or confutations (Quintilian, i, I, 9, i, 3).

Actually, the Sophists were the beginners of this kind of literary analysis, as well as of the two main streams of higher education: rhetoric and dialectic.

Systematic higher education began as a device for military training around 320 B.C. and continued well into the third century A.D. These colleges (*ephebia*) spread throughout more than 100 Hellenistic cities. The student entered at fourteen or fifteen and continued for several years. Two ideals dominated the college, the speech-maker and the debater. In a real sense they can be said to be the legacies of Isocrates and Plato, respectively. The first dominated all higher education in Greece and Rome. Historians are quite specific on this subject.

> For the vast majority of students [in Greece], higher education meant taking lessons from the rhetor, learning the art of eloquence from him.
> This fact must be emphasized from the start. On the level of history Plato had been defeated; posterity had not accepted his educational ideals. The victor, generally speaking, was Isocrates, and Isocrates became the educator first of Greece and then of the whole ancient world. . . . Rhetoric is the specific object of Greek education and the highest Greek culture (Marrou, h, 194).

Rhetoric here does not mean a general study of communication— as it now often does. As Marrou says of Roman studies, "In practice higher education was reduced to rhetoric, in the strictest sense of the word" (Marrou, h, 285). Rhetoric here means a science of persuasion, academic eloquence. And it was not peculiar to Rome:

> . . . it ran through Hellenistic culture as a whole. For a thousand years— possibly two—from Demetrius Phalerus to Ennodius (later still in Byzantium), this was the standard type of teaching in all higher education (Marrou, h, 287).

The system established by Isocrates continued the study of the kind of preparatory exercises in composition. He added to these some history and mathematics and a little debating. But all of this was a preparation for rhetoric. He developed the set speech and the imitation of models, as an essential part of his technique, and this has continued down to our own day.

These models were exemplars of the kinds of composition to be found in speeches. Consequently, the preparatory exercises in composition of secondary education were continued and others were added: eulogies and censures, character sketches, comparisons, descriptions, theses (e.g. "Should one marry?") and legal stands (matters of definition, of fact, etc.; cf. Quintilian, i, III, 6). These led immediately to the various kinds of declamations—legal, political, fictional, historical, mythological, etc. The traditional arrangement of the classical rhetorical speech was carefully followed.

The main difference between the Greek and the Roman approach to rhetoric was that the Roman insisted more on the practical, whereas the Greek moved sometimes to the rhetoric that practicing sophists sarcastically called poetry (Marrou, h, 85).

The alternative to a higher education in rhetoric was one in dialectic. This was the residue of the Platonic and Aristotelian tradition of philosophy. Its influence as a pervading dominant force was to come only with the Middle Ages. But, of course, it existed both at the "college" level and in the university equivalents of Antiquity (Monroe, t, 169, 164–65). Even the universities, however, stressed rhetoric and law and medicine more than philosophy (Monroe, t, 204).

In summary it might be pointed out that in Antiquity, three main aims of language structured the training in the art of discourse: the literary, the persuasive (rhetorical), and the pursuit of truth (dialectical). The analysis of literary texts was the province of the secondary school: the other two aims were "collegiate" and university concerns. In composition, which was directed to a preparation for rhetoric, certain forms or modes were thought to be basic to all composition (narrative, description, eulogy, and definition) and structured the composition program.

Discourse Education
in the Middle Ages

The ingredients for the medieval framework of the study of discourse are already present in Antiquity, but there was some repatterning. The three aims of language—literary, rhetorical, and dialectical—came to be called the trivium of the seven liberal arts. The distinction between these "language" arts and the others had been made by Plato and others after him, and many important figures helped to coagulate the tradition— Quintilian, Varro, Augustine, Alcuin, Martianus Capella, and Cassiodorus.

At any rate the trivium continued to be the foundation of the secondary and the college curriculum, as it had in Antiquity. In the Middle Ages, however, grammar included as its main concern the reading and analysis of literary texts and also more of the systematic study of the language, usually in Priscian's grammatical work.

But the main business of the college and university shifted radically from rhetoric to dialectic (Monroe, t, 324). In a real sense, then, the Middle Ages can be regarded as the delayed educational triumph of Plato over Isocrates. Whereas, in Antiquity, the main determinant of academic success was delivery of the set speech (the declamation), in the Middle Ages, each stage of progress in the academic world was determined by the ability to engage in dialectical debate. This concept in college and university education actually permeated higher education till the nineteenth century. Thus, if Isocrates and rhetoric can be said to rule over the first thousand years of higher education in Western civilization, Plato and dialectic can be said to preside over the next thousand.

Although in Antiquity the literary analyses (grammar) and preparatory composition exercises were all oriented to the ultimate delivery of the well-prepared speech, from the Middle Ages till the eighteenth century, all studies were oriented to a defense of ideas in a debate with one's colleagues or with one's masters.

The medieval debate was practically coextensive with education, for around the successive debate exercises was organized the student's progress through the school system. As Pellegrini says, "It is impossible to overestimate the importance of what we now call debate in the medieval university" (Pellegrini, r, 15).

The initial two-year course during which dialectic was thoroughly studied led to the student's receiving the title of "General Sophister." A full year of organized *disputationes* followed. The fourth year was a preparation for the "Responsions," a dispute with a master in grammar and logic. If the student surmounted this important stage, he was qualified to prepare for the "determination," a disputation with four masters. The determination was an event of great éclat in the life of the student. It began on Ash Wednesday and went on all day long. Success at this juncture often determined the young man's future. Three years more of hard work prepared the student for "Inception," an all-day affair also, from 6:00 a.m. till 6:00 p.m., during the course of which successive opponents relieved each other in facing the student. He was allowed an hour off for lunch (Eby, h, 786).

The usual format of the disputation probably consisted of a preliminary statement of thesis by the Respondent; the opponents were usually four in number and they carried the burden of the proof for the negative. All of this was under the chairmanship of a Moderator (Pellegrini, r, 16).

Compared to dialectic, the roles of grammar and rhetoric in the medieval university were quite minor. Grammar itself was usually studied in Priscian. The usual readings in "literature" consisted in the collections of fables of Aesopus and Aninanus and the collections of proverbs of a certain Cato (Paetow, a, 53–54). The classics were revived in these courses usually after 1300.

Rhetoric was generally a neglected art in the Middle Ages (McKeon, r). It was stressed more in the professional school. The art of letter writing (*ars dictaminis*) was emphasized in the law schools (Paetow, a, 72, 76); and the arts of preaching (*artes praedicandi*) were a part of the training in theology. These two were the main rhetorical media of the Middle Ages. Cicero was revived after 1321 in Bologna and 1350 in Paris.

The composition "modes" of the Middle Ages stressed the kinds of composition which were prerequisites to dialectic—definition, disputation, and determination (solution of a disputed question), just as the preparatory exercises of Antiquity had prepared the student for declamation.

From the Renaissance
to the Nineteenth Century

The Renaissance brought some important changes to the dialectical tradition which had often become so sterile, even farcical, that it was ripe for deemphasis. At Oxford, for example, the oral debate exams (*disputationes*) were often memorized sets of mechanical questions and answers on traditional topics, often unattended by professors (Mallet, h, III, 163).

The advent of printing tended largely to decrease the preponderance of speech and to emphasize written media (Ong, r, 307 ff.). Cambridge went to written exams in 1722 and Oxford added them to the orals (Curtis, h, 137).

But the disputations continued. The B.A. at Oxford still required disputations in grammar and logic three days a week in the fall term (Mallet, h, III, 162). Two years of responding and opposing, with obligatory attendance, were required, and after becoming a General Sophister, disputations once a term and twice in Lent were still required. Disputed questions at Oxford (1609) included the justice of war, the use of poison in war, the character of actors, the superiority of ale to beer, and free will. At Cambridge, mathematical topics came to be more predominant than ethical, logical, or political (Winstanley, u, 44, 49). The M.A. requirements were similar, but, though dialectic still controlled the format, the content of the studies changed radically during the Renaissance.

In England, William Lyly's *Grammar of Latin,* published in final form in 1554, held sway till 1867 (Curtis, h, 85, 86). It was an immediate preparation for Cicero, then Virgil, Terence, Ovid, Caesar, and Livy. Poetry and eloquence were thus reasserted in the Renaissance, and Cicero dethroned Aristotle and Plato.

The modes of discourse stressed in the "secondary" schools were again preparations for rhetoric as they had been in Antiquity. Two of the *progymnasmata,* "theme" or "formulary" rhetorics of Antiquity, those of Hermogenes and Aphthonius, were revived and were known much more to the schoolboys of the Renaissance than they had been to the contemporaries of these writers. They "went through an astounding number of editions, in both Greek and Latin versions" (Corbett, c, 543).

The Nineteenth Century

The disputation system had disappeared at Cambridge in the early eighteenth century; even some American universities (e.g., Columbia) had tempered it with written exams during that century. At Oxford, however, it was only by the middle of the nineteenth century that it had effectively disappeared (Mallet, h, III, 307).

But though the dialectical system of examinations and promotions had disintegrated under the pressure of its own mechanized sterility, the content of the studies did not change so radically. At Oxford, for instance, Robert Peel's first examination was in Homer, Cicero, Quintilian, Sophocles, Aeschyles, Pindar, and Lucretius (Mallet, h, III, 177). In America, at this time (1810) the traditional freshman and sophomore years at college were devoted to translating Latin and Greek classics, rhetoric, mathematics, and some natural science (physics and chemistry). In the latter two years logic, metaphysics, ethics, Christian apologetics, some modern language, zoology, history, and geology were studied (Brickman, c, 52–53).

The nineteenth century also saw the beginnings of the separation of English as a separate discipline from the linguistics and literature of the classics. A professorship in English literature had been suggested in 1850 at Oxford. At first it was proposed to attach it to Modern History, but Dr. Stubbs "objected to hampering the History school with 'dilettante teaching' of that kind" (Mallet, h, III, 453). In 1858 a professorship in Anglo-Saxon, (stressing historical philology), was established (Mallet, h, III, 453); and in 1873 the English professorship was finally admitted, and an honors school was established in 1893 (Mallet, h, III, 454).

The fact that the historical linguist had preceded the literary professor is symptomatic of the early problems of the discipline. In 1885, one distinguished professor deplored "the degrading vassalage of literature to philology" (Mallet, h, III, 453).

In America at about this time, the Modern Language Association was organized, and one of its earliest major concerns was the definition of the field of English. Several articles of the first edition of *PMLA* addressed themselves to the problem. James Morgan Hart, J.U.D., in an article entitled "The College Course in English Literature, How It May Be Improved," illustrates the issues of the day:

> What does *not* rightfully pertain to English literature? Settling this pre-liminary question will help us greatly. The main question resolves itself into three: What are we to do with logic, with rhetoric and with English philology (Anglo-Saxon and Early English)? (Hart, c, 84).

He relegates logic and rhetoric back to philosophy, and wants to retain a little philology. He encourages "original" work in literature, against the practice of Oxford and Cambridge. His idea of original work is illustrated by a study tracing euphuism to the Spaniard Guevara and another "mathematical demonstration" by Kissner that Chaucer had Boccaccio's *Filostrato* before him in composing *Troilus and Criseyde* (Hart, c, 92).

T. W. Hunt in the same issue defines English: "We mean by English—the English language and literature as including also, the subject of English style and criticism" (Hunt, p, 118). Actually the whole paper stresses literature and historical philology.

Possibly the most important contribution of the nineteenth century, as far as a theory of discourse is concerned, was a clearer classification of the modes of discourse. Alexander Bain, philosopher and psychologist, established the modes (then called forms) of discourse as being: narration, exposition, description, argumentation, and persuasion. The first four quickly became the structuring principles of many composition books in the next half century. They are still accepted modes in many high school and college texts, though they are not as influential as determinants of syllabus material as they were for many decades. The coincident occurrence of an accepted classification of the modes with the frequent narrowing of the field of English to literature caused the modes to be given, from the outset, almost solely literary orientations. Thus narrative usually meant literary narrative, and description meant the sort of description one found in the novels of Cooper or the sketches of Washington Irving. Exposition meant the near literary expositions of stylists like Newman or Arnold or Ruskin; and the same writers typified argumentation. This restriction has been somewhat harmful to the development of a full theory of discourse.

One final feature of the nineteenth-century college English program was the appearance of the graduate school. The Ph.D. had been granted at Yale in 1861, but it was at Johns Hopkins from 1876 on that the graduate program received its greatest impetus. Most of the important institutions followed soon after. Under William Rainey Harper at Chicago (1892 on), the stress on research and publication, rather than teaching, for promotion began a trend which still influences the graduate and undergraduate department of English (Brickman, c, 126). This was not only an American phenomenon; in England the functions of the university professor and the college tutor reflected an uneasy compromise solution to the same problem.

Discourse Education
in the Twentieth Century

It is always a little difficult to assess historical changes in proper perspective at close range. At this date, however, some movements in the twentieth century do seem to have had perceptible influence on general discourse education. A brief sketch will be attempted, therefore, of some early movements up to and overlapping into the thirties, then of some of the larger tendencies in the thirties and forties, and finally, of some of the recent orientations.

EARLY MOVEMENTS

The first two decades saw some very violent readjustments, more violent undoubtedly than any before or since in the history of western civilization. Beginning around 1913, the formal divorce of speech from English was sought by people who felt that speech was being neglected in English departments, and the cause was carried on in the *Quarterly Journal of Public Speaking* (Laine, r, 14). Departments of speech were created and courses such as elocution, eloquence, declamation, and rhetoric were popular early. These emphases declined in the twenties, and public speaking, debate, argumentation, and discussion received more emphasis (Laine, r, 44–48). In a sense, the speech people took rhetoric (the art of persuasion) with them; only now is it being invited back.

Secondly, logic also departed and found a haven in philosophy and later—with the marriage of logic and mathematics in Russell and White-head—in departments of mathematics. Only incidentally and haphazardly has logic been related to discourse education in English departments since. However, though English departments formally relinquished logic as a tool, they did not relinquish the kind of discourse for which logic was supposed to be the tool. The training for informative and scientific discourse con-tinued to be viewed as a stepchild responsibility of English departments, at least at the lower levels. This residual inconsistency is still with us.

With the departure of logic and rhetoric, discourse education as the locus of the traditional liberal arts can be said to have effectively ceased. These removals cleared the way for English to be a department of literature and philology, the two components of the remaining liberal art, grammar. And the functions of the English department are usually so restricted from that time on (e.g., Chambers, t, 10).

Philology, mainly in its historical facets, often dominated the litera-ture component of the department in these early decades. Though this was true particularly of graduate study, the tendency even extended sometimes down into the secondary school. Bailey, in 1922, quotes Sir Walter Raleigh, in a typical complaint of the period, "English Literature could be the basis of a liberal education, but needed to be freed from slavery to philology and phonology" (Bailey, t, 31).

Within the shadow of historical philology, several other movements managed to exert some influence on the mainstreams of discourse education within the English department.

Joel Spingarn and others were the transmitters of "The New

Criticism" from Italy to America in the twenties (Spingarn, c). This cult of "expressionism" stressed the intuitive and nonrational aspect of the creative impulse. The movements come from German sources via Croce in Italy and reenforced certain other "expressionistic" tendencies operating at the same time. The heritage of Romanticism (as a doctrine of literary composition) also emphasized the emotive and original characteristics of creativity.

The depth-psychology view of art accentuated much the same features, as did Dewey's theory of art. The confluence of all of these streams of expressionisms produced a view of composition which dominated elementary, secondary, and college writing practice through the thirties. Original and creative narratives and descriptions, in which the student above all expressed himself, made up a large part of the composition work during this period.

In another curious combination, these kinds of composition were often taught by means of imitation of models (a continuing heritage of the formulary rhetoric of Isocrates).

MOVEMENTS IN THE THIRTIES
AND FORTIES

Three important movements in the thirties strongly affected the teaching of discourse: semantics, communications, and a second "new criticism."

Korzybski published his *Science and Sanity* in 1933 and it quickly gave a new twist to semantics, which till that time had been largely a historical study of changes in meaning. Korzybski pointed out the dangers inherent in abstractions, stereotypes, and categorizations. The emotional connotations of many of the stereotypes in languages often led to dangerous generalizations, he pointed out. His disciples (Stuart Chase, S. I. Hayakawa, Irving Lee, Anatol Rapaport, Harry Weinberg and others) popularized his doctrines and evangelically preached the reform of thinking by the new semantics. Courses in semantics (often in English departments) spread throughout many colleges and universities; and sometimes they were compulsory, though the fervor has largely died down now.

In partial alliance with the semanticists were the communicationists. This movement, centered in such institutions as Denver, Iowa, Minnesota, and Florida, stressed the integrated nature of the communication skills of writing, reading, speaking, and listening. Under its influence composition courses were often renamed "communication(s)" courses; sometimes speech was reintegrated into the freshman course. More important, however, was the shift in both semantics and communication theory away from the creative and literary compositions of the expressionistic era to a "workaday" prose.

Whereas semantics stressed the scientific, communication theory stressed the informative, sometimes the persuasive.

The Conference on College Composition and Communication, founded in 1949 through the joint efforts of the Speech Association of America and the National Council of Teachers of English, attempted to make the "communications" approach in the freshman course equivalent in status to the composition course.

At the secondary and elementary levels, the NCTE wholeheartedly adopted the "language arts" approach (speaking, listening, writing, and reading), making these arts the structural core of impressive volumes for each level of the academic ladder. Significantly, perhaps, the term "language arts" was not used in the latest volume of the series published a few years ago, whereas it had been used in all the other volumes published through the forties and fifties.

The third important movement of this period, more influential at the college level than either semantics or communications, was a second variety of "new criticism." Its roots extend back before the turn of the century; and it was nurtured by such writers as T. E. Hulme, T. S. Eliot, and Ezra Pound. But its declaration of independence from historical philology and criticism in literature is often considered to be R. S. Crane's article in *The English Journal,* College Edition, in 1935 (h).

In this article, Crane, a very respected historian of ideas and president of the MLA, in effect turned his back on much of his own previous historical work as largely irrelevant to the business of the study of literature *as* literature. In its place, a careful structural analysis of the work itself was advocated. Soon the new critics were challenging the historians in most of the universities of the country. Cleanth Brooks, Robert Penn Warren, Allen Tate, I. A. Richards, John Crowe Ransom, the neo-Aristotelians at Chicago, and many others have made "New Criticism" possibly the dominant approach to the study of literature in this century, to date.

The new critical approach often effected radical changes in the survey courses, changing the emphasis to a close reading of selected works, and deemphasizing "extensive" readings in most of the anthologized selections of a period. Texts often were written in terms of genres, rather than periods. The close analysis of literary texts has found its way into freshman composition courses. The subjects of compositions in English, some say, should be literature and only literature. This, however, is an extrapolation beyond the forties.

New criticism naturally made courses in literary criticism, sometimes even literary theory, more respectable in the forties, fifties, and sixties. In a large measure the kind of "theme" assignments, from freshman compositions to doctoral dissertations and scholarly books and articles, shifted

violently away from the historical, biographical, or whimsically expressive
to analysis of a poem or a play quite autonomously in its own right.

RECENT MOVEMENTS

Besides "new criticism," which continued into the sixties very
strongly, though possibly with fewer original contributions, some other
significant directions are currently discernible in the study of discourse.

In English, the fifties and sixties witnessed the almost total demise
of the influence of expressionism in its Romantic, Crocean, and Deweyite
presentations—as far as practical conscious influences are concerned. This
withdrawal, plus the scientific "ethos" in education generally and the
determined inroads of the second new criticism have had several momentous
results in composition study.

The most notable effect was the gradual disappearance of a stress
on "creative" writing in composition courses generally—though isolated
courses remain, and even a few degrees are offered in it (e.g., Iowa). This
represents one of the first times in the history of western civilization that the
creative literary or expressive genres have been systematically excluded from
discourse education. Oral dialectical expressive media were exiled in the
1800's, rhetorical media in the early 1900's, and literary media in the 1950's.

As far as discourse education is concerned, the English department
has thus in many places narrowed itself down to two concerns: (1) the
reading and analysis of literary texts, and (2) the writing of "expository"
essays about these literary texts. The concern with "expository" prose is only
now spreading to the high schools (cf. Lynch and Evans, h, 335), though
the Dartmouth conference has had a braking effect on this tendency in some
places.

Certainly the strongest single movement in English departments in
the forties and fifties has been the turn from historical to descriptive linguistics and the exciting advances in phonology and syntax. Only recently,
however, with the work of Christensen, Harris, and Pike have structural
and generative grammars moved into areas relevant to discourse education.

Unfortunately, the advances of linguistics have been so meteoric
and so technically allied with mathematics and computer analysis that they
have sometimes discouraged the average English teacher from keeping
abreast of them, particularly in the last few years. Like logic in the past,
linguistics seems destined to fragment away from English departments and
pursue its way in other departments or its own.

Actually, it is in some of these other departments that some of the
most significant advances in discourse analysis have been made in this
century. As the logician John Venn has said, "No science can be safely
abandoned entirely to its own devotees," (Venn, l, vii). A discipline must

be fertilized from without; otherwise it can become stale and sterile. Certainly, composition theory has been sterile for a long time. Importations from other disciplines can help discourse theory at the present time, as much of this book will attempt to show.

Already, much is being done in discourse analysis in other departments. In speech, for instance, experiments in the effectiveness of different structurings of material in persuasion are under investigation, as well as different kinds of persuaders and persuadees (Hovland, c and o). On a larger cultural scale, political scientists and sociologists are making macroanalyses in similar areas (Lasswell, a). In speech and foreign language departments, the use of the laboratory and the "dialogue" techniques are contributing to discourse analysis at an important level. Many important discoveries about discussion, debating, interviewing, questionnaire construction, and allied topics are being made in speech and psychology.

In departments of philosophy, both the artificial models of language used in information theory and the "realistic" work of analytical philosophers like Austin and Ryle have relevance to discourse analysis, as do the dialectical speculations of Hansen, Perelman, and others. Indeed, most of the work on the nature of science, the nature of argument, the nature of description, the kinds of definitions, the nature of evaluation, and the nature of change (in narration) is not being done in English departments at all, but awaits intelligent importation into a complete theory of discourse analysis. In all of the above areas, the author attempts some of this integration in the following chapters. Similarly, from psychologists and group dynamicists, various models of communications networks await transplantation into a full theory of discourse.

Discourse analysis, however, cannot afford to whimsically drink just anywhere from all of these ancillary streams. It needs a framework of selection. Even if not completely adequate, it needs a theoretical structure for placement and hierarchization.

Comprehensive Theory of the Field of English

Introduction

In the field of English there are many *assumed* frameworks of language study, but there are very few rational attempts to justify total frameworks. The language arts and the communications approaches attempt to structure everything within the various provinces of speaking, listening, writing, and reading (sometimes adding thinking). The Commission on English adopts the linguistics–composition–literature trilogy (*Freedom,* f,

13). Thorpe, for the MLA, outlines textual criticism, literary history, literary criticism, and linguistics as the four fields of English departmental concern (Thorpe, a).

Again, nearly any text attempting to educate future teachers of English outlines a system of some kind. Thus Guth considers: linguistics, semantics, composition, and literature as the basic concern of the high school English teacher (Guth, e, 5 ff.). And there are six or seven competitive books in this field (Hook, Sauer, Loban *et al.,* Lewis and Sisk, Bernstein, Fowler).

These positions are fairly explicit. No less real and operative, though implicit, are the assumed frameworks of anthologies of readings for freshman composition, the structure of offerings in English departments, the schemata behind freshman college and high school or elementary syllabuses, the structure of national conventions of NCTE, CCCC, and MLA. (For a survey of some recent attempts to define the field of English, cf. Grommon, o).

In philosophy and linguistics there are also competitive structurings of the field of language; Katz and Fodor's *The Structure of Language* constructs a system, Morris's *Signs, Language and Behavior* another, Martin's *Towards a Systematic Pragmatics* another, and Pike's *Language in Relation to a Unified Theory of the Structure of Human Behavior* another.

Before assessing the validity of these systems, it seems better to present the structure upon which this book is based. Then, in the light of this structure, the relevance of these alternative systems can be judged.

Foundation for the Structure

The foundation for a structure of English study should be fairly solid. It may be stating the obvious to say that the foundations must be grounded in the very nature of the language process itself. No imported metaphysic of structure would seem as applicable as the nature of the language act. Consequently, one sound foundation for the discipline would be the so-called communication triangle, i.e., the interrelationships of expressor, receptor, and language signs as referring to reality.

It has been pointed out that Aristotle made these factors the basis for his study of rhetoric (Berlo, p, 29).[2] Because of Aristotle's influence, this structure has dominated rhetorical theory for twenty-three centuries. But many other disciplines now look upon this structure as basic. Abrams

---

2 No one, I believe, has pointed out how thoroughly this triangle pervades the structure of the *Rhetoric*. The three proofs (ethical, logical, and pathetic), the three components of ethical proof, the treatment of each emotion in the pathetic proof, and the four qualities of the rhetorical style are all based on the triangle, at different levels of application (see Chapter IV).

(m, Ch. I) and Richards (p, 10 f. and 297 ff.) have used it effectively in literary theory and criticism. Pierce and Morris have used it as the foundation for a general theory of signs (Morris, s, esp. 287, 217–20). Logicians like Carnap and Martin make it central to their treatises on semantics and pragmatics as do Polish logicians like Kotarbiński (Hiz, k) and Grzegorczyk in their theories of pragmatics. Bar-Hillel and Carnap use it to distinguish among three basic theories of information (Bar-Hillel, 1, 305). Shannon's basic monograph on information theory used a version of it (Shannon and Weaver, m). Communicationists generally have adopted it as central to their discipline (cf., e.g. Berlo, p, 29 ff.). Propaganda analysts usually follow Lasswell's basic formulation: "Who says what to whom and why?" (Smith, pr, 121). Katz and Fodor, generative linguists outlining *The Structure of Language,* make it central to their theories of syntax, semantics, and discourse analysis. Some psycholinguists use it to define their discipline (Diebold, p, 205).

The list could be continued. But more than the authorities, the structure speaks for itself. Basic to all uses of language are a person who encodes a message, the signal (language) which carries the message, the reality to which the message refers, and the decoder (receiver of the message). These four components are often represented in a triangle, seen in Figure I, 1.

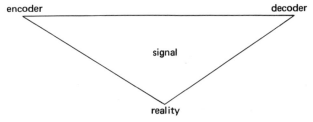

Figure I, 1: The Communication Triangle

These four basic components are actually much more complex. Thus, information theory usually puts the components on a line and distinguishes source and transmitter from encoder, signal from message and channel, and receiver from decoder; and it adds "noise," unintended distortions added to the signal. And for electronic transmission problems, these distinctions are necessary (see Shannon, m, 7, 33–35). In like manner, Morris, a sign theorist, distinguishes the reality referred to (denotatum) from what it means (significatum) to the interpretant (Morris, s, 17 ff.).

Again the terms often differ. Abrams, in literary theory, uses artist, audience, object (of art), universe; communicationists often use speaker, listener, speech, reality; some sign theorists and semanticists use expressor, receptor, referend (referring sign), and referent (object referred to). Since the triangle has many uses at different levels, these variant terminologies will be preserved at their respective places in the general schemata, whenever possible, to avoid ambiguity with another use of the triangle.

A few have objected to the artificial separation of speaker, speech, and reality as if they were three actors in a play (Neurath, r, 11). But this seems to be the danger inherent in any abstraction, and science must abstract. But the warning is salutary and, if abstractions are necessary to distinguish phonological problems from those of syntax, or various uses of languages, or various modes of discourse, it must not be forgotten that these *are* abstractions. This will be a recurrent issue.

More generally, these factors in the process can be viewed as the *components* (signal), the *interpretation* given to the components (reference to reality), and the *use* given the interpreted components by the users (encoder, decoder). Viewed in this general way, the components become similar to what mathematicians or logicians sometimes call a *grammar,* the interpreted components are a *language* and this is used for specific purposes as a *calculus* (Addison, t, 27, n.2). Or the triangle thus becomes what some mathematicians call a "theory," and each interpretation becomes a "model" (cf. Suppes, c, 287 ff.; Tarski, c, 572 ff.).

By taking this general or universal view of the communication factors the *triangle* itself can be given many different *interpretations* for various *purposes* in the sequence. As Weaver puts it, there are technical problems, semantic problems, and effectiveness problems (Shannon, m, 4).

Applications of the Triangle at Level A.
The Three Areas of the Field of English:
√ **Syntactics, Semantics, and Pragmatics (Figure I, 2)**

Given the four basic components of the communication triangle, it is possible to abstract any of them for individual consideration. A study of the characteristics of the signal, as such, is called the *syntactics* of a language. Fundamentally, it is approximately equivalent to the grammar of a language. Grammar, insofar as possible, doesn't concern itself with meanings of words as referrers to reality or the use in actual situations to which words are put. It is true, of course, that grammar has a concern with meanings of a special sort, i.e. grammatical meanings. Thus the sequence of sounds "qu" or "va" in English signals possible "meaningful" sequences to follow, whereas "qr" or "vt" are not "meaningful" initial signals in English. The former are just syntactic meanings, characteristics of the rules of formation of English sounds.

Secondly, it *is* possible to consider the signals of a language as representing or referring to reality. Thus, "dog" refers to a class of objects of reality in a way which "va" does not. "Dog" is a semantic referend,

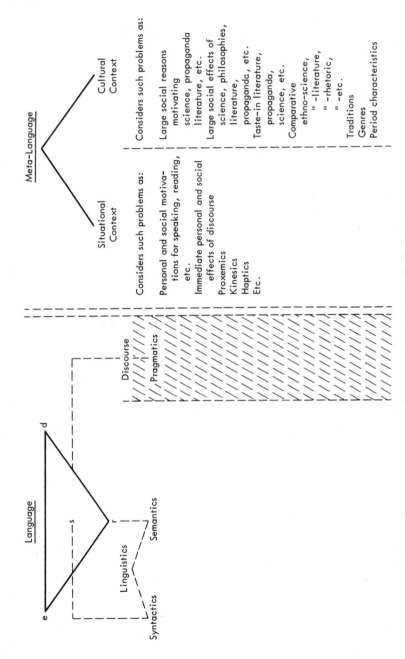

Figure I, 2: The Place of Discourse in Language Study

whereas "va" is not (in English and as so printed). The study of the signals of a language as having meaning in the sense of being referrers to reality is called the semantics of a language.

Finally, these meaningful or interpreted signals can be *used* by the encoder and the decoder in actual speech situations. The study of the *use* of these interpreted signals by encoders and decoders is called *pragmatics* in language study (cf. Morris, s, 217 ff.; Carnap, s, 9).

"The use of interpreted signals by encoder and decoder" is, by itself, a very ambiguous phrase. It is important that use, at this level, be governed by the qualification "actual speech (or written) situations." Otherwise "use" very properly can be given a grammatical or semantic construction.

Since "pragmatics" is sometimes given these latter interpretations, it seems important to clarify the meaning in this context. Taken together, the syntactics and the semantics of the language constitute the language as potential tool. The sounds, morphological units, rules of syntax, the referential qualities of words or other units of language (meanings)—all of these are the potentials which I may marshall into a given speaking or writing situation to serve an ulterior purpose. The study of these potentials is called linguistics. Linguistics is sharply differentiated from the language as put into actual use in real discourse. Discourse study then is the study of the situational uses of the potentials of the language. Discourse is constituted by "text." By way of ostensive definition, "text" means Faulkner's speech of acceptance of the Nobel prize; or Hemingway's *The Old Man and the Sea;* or the twenty-five-minute discussion of the members of the press with Undersecretary of State George W. Ball, on April 10, 1966, 11:30–12:00 (CST); or Shakespeare's *Othello;* or the single sentence "Fire" screamed by a hotel occupant running from a building; or Toynbee's twelve volumes of *A Study of History.*

Discourse, therefore, is characterized by individuals acting in a special time and place (Gardiner, t ,71); it has a beginning, a middle, a closure, and a purpose (cf. Pike, l, I, 9, 39, 44, 64 ff.); it is a language process, not a system, and it has an "undivided and absolute integrity," (Hjelmslev, p, 36–39, 12); it establishes a verbal context and it has a situational context and cultural context (Slama-Cazacu, l, 215–16). These attributes are characteristic of Gardiner's "speech" (as opposed to language), Pike's "uttereme," Hjelmslev's "text" (as opposed to language), Slama-Cazacu's "context." In each case there is the stress on the whole, not just the isolated linguistic part. Slama-Cazacu has traced this emphasis in linguistic theory through history (10 ff., 19 ff., 207 ff.). In linguistics, De Saussure's division of *langage* into *langue* and *parole* represents the most notable attempt to make such a distinction. But this distinction has been given many interpretations (Hjelmslev, 1; Gardiner, t, 71; Slama-Cazacu, 1,

19 ff.; Bally, 1; Pike, 1, III, 52; Sèchehaye, t; Troubetzkoy, p, 2 ff.).[3] In addition, all of these interpretations have been made in order to establish a context which can make more intelligible the linguistic components under analysis. The emphasis here is to establish the text (context) in order to examine the text in its own right. Thus linguistic facts become of interest here only as they clarify the text as a whole.[4]

Discourse, therefore, is determined by the existence of a complete text. Incomplete texts, such as a paragraph or an interrupted conversation, or Keats' *Hyperion,* are incomplete discourses. This definition of discourse, while consistent with the view taken of it by the tradition and some modern philosophers (cf. Cairns, f, Morris, s, 123–53) is larger than that advocated by some linguists, who define discourse in terms of anything beyond the sentence.

Since pragmatics is viewed as the study of complete discourse, it ✓ does not include semantics as such or syntactics as such. These two constitute linguistics; and linguistic analysis is not discourse analysis, though, of course, it can contribute to the understanding of discourse. Consequently, syntactics and semantics are beyond the borders of discourse study.

They establish, therefore, the lower boundaries of discourse. The upper limits must also be defined, since pragmatics for Carnap (Carnap, s, 8–10) and for Morris (Morris, s, 187 ff.) and the somewhat parallel concept of metalinguistics for Trager and Smith and Whorf (Trager, o, 81 ff.) range from the phonological through and beyond the textual into the vast social and cultural effects of language phenomena. In this book pragmatics is limited to text. Beyond text lies the context of the situation of which text is a part. This includes such areas of investigation as psychological and social motivations for speaking and writing or listening and speaking; proxemics, the study of space distances in communication networks (cf. Hall); haptics, the variant uses in different cultures of body contact in communication situations; kinesics, the study of gesture and posture in delivery (cf. Birdwhistell, k). Some anthropologists and linguists have made much of the importance of the context of situation (Malinowski, c, II, 11; Richards, m, 306–16; Pike, I, 2 ff.). Propaganda analysts, as might be expected, have also attempted to see the relation of language use to situational context.

---

3 Hjelmslev translates *langue–parole* into pattern–usage in English (Hjelmslev, 1, 43, n.32); Gardiner and most people translate it language–speech (Gardiner, t, 71); Chomsky changes the concept to what he prefers to call competence–performance (a, 4, 10 ff.). See also Chapter VI.

4 This is not at all to denigrate the part to the whole procedure; both the molecular or meristic and the holistic approaches are complementary (Hjelmslev calls them the synthetic and the analytic, p. 12). But we cannot hold off the building of bridges till the last atom has been smashed.

Lasswell's content analyses in political writings and slogans consistently relate them to the historical events of the time (see, e.g., Lasswell, c, 38 ff.). Advertisers are also continually concerned with the rise-in-sales effects of their promotions as well as the fashions of the day. Literary criticism for a lengthy period in the last century and in this century was heavily preoccupied with the historical and biographical influences on and of literature. Philosophers like Sartre also insist on the crucial importance of the context of situation (see Chapter VI). The denigration of the importance of situational and cultural context was an understandable, but regrettable, offshoot of literary new criticism. And in literary criticism it now seems to be waning.

Beyond the situational context lies the cultural context, the nature and conventions of which make the situational context permissible and meaningful (Sapir, c). It can hardly be denied that cultural context and situational context determine text. In this large sense, no text is autonomous —it exists within a biographical and historical stream. Language is, after all, only a part of life (cf. Figure I, 2).

But the justification for the autonomy of textual study is the same as the justification for any scientific abstraction: by focusing on one aspect of a reality, science can set up tools for isolated analysis which is possible only within this particular vacuum. Then the object of investigation can be reinserted into the stream of life, more intelligible for its academic isolation.

The particular province of discourse study, then, excludes, on the one hand, merely linguistic or semantic analyses and, on the other, aspects of the situational context and cultural context. But whenever either the linguistic or the metapragmatic considerations can throw light on text as such, they become subordinately relevant to discourse analysis. On the one hand, without a linguistic, the text is an undeciphered hieroglyphic. On the other hand, without a situational context and a cultural milieu, the text is a curiosity open to more misinterpretation than interpretation—indeed, sometimes open to interpretation only by chance.

Applications of the Communication Triangle to Level B (Figure I, 3)

At level A, the abstractions from the communication triangle establish three basic areas of study in the field of English: syntactics, having to do with grammar; semantics, having to do with linguistic meaning; and pragmatics, having to do with the study of discourse.

At level B (see Figure I, 3), the main subdivisions of each of these are established.

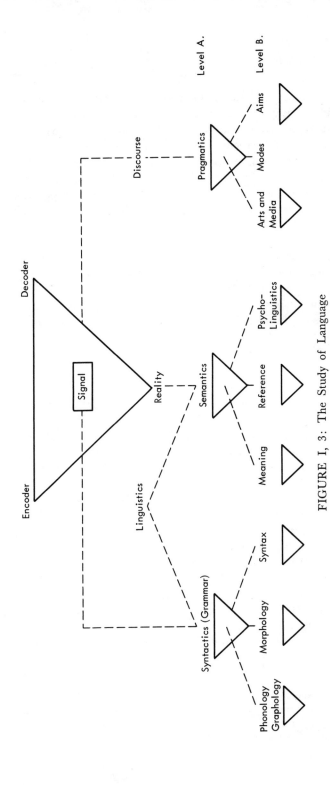

FIGURE I, 3: The Study of Language

SYNTACTICS (GRAMMAR)

Grammar is usually divided into phonology, morphology, and syntax. Even many structural and generative grammarians retain these large traditional divisions (Chomsky, s, 5 ff.; Chomsky, a, 16). Some modern grammarians strongly oriented to the primacy of oral language do not even consider written forms language at all. However, since most do, phonology can be construed to include graphology. Phonology and graphology are the studies of the sounds of the language and their written equivalents. Morphology is often defined as the study of the "meaningful" units of the grammar (cf. Stageberg, i, 85–86). Syntax is usually defined as the study of the structure of the language (Thomas, t, 13; Stageberg, i, 163).

It is easily possible to view the sounds or their written equivalents as the *components* of grammatical study, the meaningful units as the *interpreted components,* and the structures given to these interpreted components as the grammatical *use* to which interpreted components are put.[5] This view of the parts of grammar is, therefore, an application of the communications triangle at a lower level.

SEMANTICS

Semantics proper is not nearly so neat a discipline as either traditional or current grammar. Much informal study in signs and meaning can be seen in Plato, Aristotle, and especially some of the late Scholastics, like John of St. Thomas. However, its formal inauguration with the christening and the customary trappings of a science is usually ascribed to Bréal's *Essay on Semantics* (1897).

Consonant with much philological study in the nineteenth century, Bréal gave semantics an historical orientation, a strong emphasis in the changes in meanings of words through successive ages. And, till the thirties, semantics retained this orientation (cf. Bloomfield, 1, 425 ff.). In the thirties Korzybski and his disciples in "general semantics" gave semantics a critical orientation; i.e., certain kinds of meanings, especially rigid abstractions and categorizations, were severely castigated as distortions of existing reality (Korzybski, s, *passim*). Theoretical or "pure" semantics was a concern, at approximately the same time and later, of logicians like Tarski, Carnap (s), Martin (tr), Russell (m), and others.

Today, there are structural semanticists (cf. Lyons, s; Öhmann, t);

---

5 Chomsky considers both the phonological and the semantic parts of the grammar to be interpretive (Chomsky, a, 16). This is not inconsistent with the present position, for the phonological part does contain an interpretive aspect (here established in the succeeding level).

semanticists (Ziff, s; Ullman, s); linguistic semanticists (Katz and Fodor, s); sign theorists (Morris, s); philosophers who study not artificial systems like Martin's or Carnap's, but "ordinary language" (Austin, h; Ryle, c); and psycholinguists (Diebold, p).

No attempt will be made to structure all of these fragments of a shattered discipline. After considering the modes of discourse, it will be possible to see some patterning among the various parts. For the present let us consider only the divisions of the theory of semantics.

> Positivists usually distinguish between two branches of semantics: theory of meaning and theory of reference. The former is concerned with relations between linguistic entities and the latter with relations between linguistic entities and the world. Such notions as *analycity, significance, synonymity,* and others are basic concepts of theory of meaning, while the basic concepts of theory of reference are naming, truth, extension, and so on (Fodor and Katz, s, 6–7; cf. also Bar-Hillel, 1, 44–45; esp. Quine, f, 11 ff., 22, 48 ff.).

Psycholinguists, aware of these two branches of semantics, usually define their studies of meanings in a way which will not conflict with either "meaning" or "reference." "Psycholinguistics," says Diebold, in a typical definition, "is concerned in the broadest sense with relations between messages and the characteristics of human individuals who select and interpret them" (Diebold, p, 205).

Again, we can see an application of the communications triangle, but this time in the area of semantics. The theory of "meaning" is the study of the significance implied in the relations among the components of the signal, i.e., the significance of predication, modification, conjunction, disjunction, implication, and transformation. The theory of reference is the study of the meanings of terms as explicitly intended to *represent* aspects of the world. It embraces such topics as the kinds of realities referred to (referents), the kinds of referring words (referends), and problems of referral of referend to referent (such as anomaly—null referral—or synonymy, or ambiguity). Notice that the theory of reference is subdivided by another application of the communication triangle.

Finally the field of psycholinguistics considers the psychological problems of the intended meanings and their encoding on the part of the speaker and of the interpreted meaning (appellative) on the parts of different decoders. These variants are called semantic differentials, and attempts are made to measure them (Osgood). Other areas of psycholinguistics consider the different kinds of decoder groups and their variant dialects (social and geographical) of the language, together with their internal semantic implications and the cultural semantic implications when transfer from group to group occurs (cf. Joos, s).

PRAGMATICS

The subdivisions of pragmatics, viewed as the study of texts, are not even as clearly delineated as are the areas of semantics.

Historically, as the survey attempted to bring out, different emphases can be seen in different periods. In Antiquity and the Middle Ages and the Renaissance something like the three liberal arts structured the curriculum. In Antiquity these arts were oriented to rhetoric—the delivery of speeches to persuade. In the Middle Ages, dialectic took over as the dominant art. In both periods grammar, the reading and analysis of literary texts, was secondary. In the Renaissance the literary came to the forefront in many places. The liberal arts represented a stress on aims or uses of language. Logic represented a use of language to demonstrate something as conclusive and certain; dialectic had for its aim the exploration for truth; rhetoric had for its aim the persuasion of an audience; grammar (literature) explored the use of language to delight (cf. La Drière, r, 132 ff.).

The tradition of the liberal arts, therefore, represented an attempt to train people to various and important uses of language, with emphases on one or the other, depending upon the cultural context.

Accompanying these emphases were a set of fairly mechanical "kinds" of compositions. In Antiquity and the Renaissance, these "themes" were the *progymnasmata*. These stressed narratives of different sorts, story summaries, character sketches, aphorisms to be developed, confirmations or confutations, eulogies and censures, definitions, and descriptions. These correspond fairly closely to what later were called the forms of discourse and now are frequently called the modes of discourse.

The Middle Ages had its own stresses on modes too; and the dominant mode of this period (and of the Renaissance) was definition. Determination was a variant of definition, for it consisted in deducing by class logic, and class was established by definition.

The dominance of the modes of discourse over that of the aims of discourse came in the nineteenth century. Now a stress on modes of discourse rather than aims of discourse is a stress on "what" is being talked about rather than on "why" a thing is being talked about. Narrative or definition or description, etc., are determined by a kind of reference, not by an aim of language use. This will be given thorough treatment in Volume II of this study. Narrative, as such, is not necessarily oriented to any aim: there can be scientific or exploratory or persuasive or literary narratives. And the same holds true of descriptions and the other modes.

Therefore the period in which the study of discourse was dominated by modes of discourse (the secondary school in the Renaissance in some places, and secondary school and college in the latter half of the nineteenth century and the first third of the twentieth century in England and America) represents a period in which the kind of thing talked about rather than the purpose in talking structured the curriculum. This is actually a substitution of means for end.

Actually, something is narrated for a reason. Narration, as such, is not a purpose. Consequently, the "modes" periods in history have never lasted very long. Even in the nineteenth and twentieth centuries, the modes were nearly always given a literary purpose. This was a restriction, but it did give the modes a purpose and saved them from pathology.

The twentieth-century stresses on the communication arts in college and the language arts in high school represent a final and very different orientation again. Speech had been stressed in both Antiquity and the Middle Ages, but for *rhetorical* or *dialectical* purposes. It remained for the twentieth century to stress speech *as speech*, listening *as listening*, etc., and to make these predominant in a curriculum. There are reasons for this, no doubt.

But here, our interest is in the kind of emphasis which a stress on *arts* of discourse, rather than *modes* or *aims*, betokens. Arts of discourse—like modes of discourse—are means, not ends. In real life to speak *just* to speak, to listen *just* to listen, etc., would be pathological. In education, training in the mechanics of these skills of reading and speaking is understandable, especially at lower grades, in terms of being able to *use* them for appropriate purposes later on. Such training exercises in skills are not really *uses* of discourse any more than sharpening a knife is using a knife. Here the tool (language) is merely being sharpened for future use. When, as happened in the forties and fifties in secondary schools, arts *as* arts became ultimate aims of English curricula, it is not surprising that the results bordered on the pathological. Certainly it was one of the least fertile and short-lived experiments in the whole history of discourse education.

Any time a means is exalted to an end in the history of discourse education, a similar pattern can be seen. The emphasis is short-lived and it is usually sterile. Aside from the "modes" and the "arts" of discourse periods, the same can be said of the pure formal grammar period in some secondary schools in the first part of this century and the strict "semanticist" approaches in colleges in the forties. These are even more merely instrumental than are the arts or modes of discourse, for syntactics and semantics are always oriented to pragmatics (Carnap, s, 13; Grzegorczyk, p).

However, the historical emphases on arts and modes and aims does call attention to a possible structure of discourse as a discipline. It is possible to view arts and media as the "components" of discourse, modes as the "meanings" as reference of discourse, and aims as the "uses" of discourse. Actually to stand up to give a speech is to *signal* the existence of discourse, just as to turn on the radio and sit back to listen *signals* a commitment to receptive discourse. Similarly, modes of discourse are the interpreted aspects of discourse; for example, narration is constituted by the kind of reality to which reference is made. Both speeches and spoken narratives are determined to specific uses. These constitute the *aims* of language.

Like syntactics and semantics, therefore, the subdivisions of pragmatics are determined by an application of the communication triangle.

Applications of the Communication Triangle to Level C (*Figure I, 4*)

The subdivisions of the major areas of grammar, of semantics, and of pragmatics give Level C in Figure I, 4.

Since the function of this book is exclusively directed to discourse analysis, the main subdivisions of phonology, morphology, and syntax, or theories of meaning, of reference or psycholinguistics will not be structured. Such structurings are the provinces of grammar and semantics, respectively. Some of these subdivisions can use the communications triangle profitably. However, the subdivisions of discourse are the major concern. In other words, what are the basic signals of discourse, the basic kinds of references made by discourse, and the basic uses of discourse?

SIGNALS OF DISCOURSE: ARTS AND MEDIA

Arts of Discourse

The basic signals of discourse are texts which are spoken, listened to, written, or read. These divisions are determined by the kind of sense signal used (oral or written) and the operations of either encoder or decoder. They are, therefore, a partial application of the communications triangle at this level. If one keeps in mind that discourse is text-oriented, one could use the so-called communications arts: speaking, listening, writing, and reading. For normal purposes, these suffice. They do not take into account such discourse texts as articles or books in Braille, semaphore, etc. But if one is willing to accept liberal definitions of "reading" or "speaking," these extrapolations should constitute no problem. They would even allow for the inclusion of "viewing" which some elementary and secondary language arts theorists sometimes include.

But they do not include "thinking," which both communicationists and language arts theorists tend to include (e.g. Berlo, p, 43 ff.). It is true that thinking is involved in communication, but thinking itself is not one of the communication arts nor one of the fine arts nor one of the useful arts. Thinking pervades the whole language and metalanguage process from phonation to situational and cultural uses of language. To reduce it to a skill

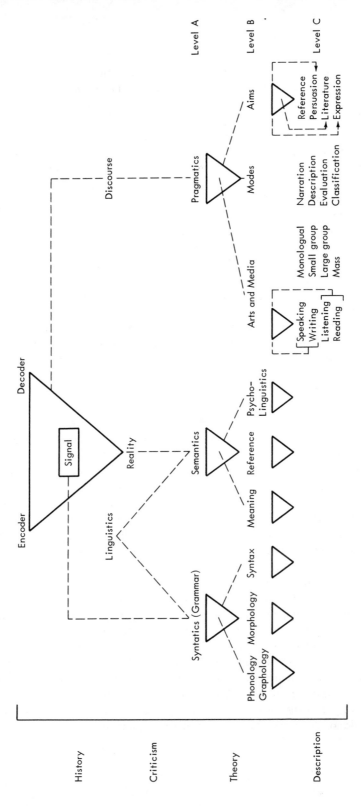

Figure I, 4: The Field of English

coordinate to speaking and the other communication skills is to severely restrict its range of operation. As will be shown in subsequent chapters, different kinds of thinking correlate with each of the aims of discourse and with each of the modes also. Each aim and mode has its correlative logic(s).

Actually, "thinking" was included in the later treatments of the communications arts and the language arts because of the eventual realization by both communicationists and language arts educationists of the merely mechanical interpretation which could be and was given to a pure "arts" orientation. Basically this was an attempt to patch up an inept system— inherently inept because it ignored the more important issues of what the speech referred to and why it was being given at all.

Indeed, the reintegration of thought to expression is one of the major attempts of this book. The segregation of thought from expression by the exile of logic, dialectic, and rhetoric from the field of English is probably the most serious defect of the present composition situation in both college and high school. This divorce is much more serious than the more trumpeted divorce of grammar from expression.

But the integration must be made under the hypothesis that there are different kinds of thinking relevant to different uses of language, not under the dangerous assumption that one kind of thinking can blanket all modes and aims of discourse.

This book, arbitrarily, does not consider the questions involved in discourse study as far as the arts of discourse are concerned. Possibly a later volume can supplement this deficiency. Much of what communication and language arts theorists have written is relevant to the skills peculiar to the specific problems of writing as opposed to speaking, or writing as opposed to reading, or listening as opposed to reading. It is clear that reading involves certain skills which are not germane to the specific problems of writing. And experts in teaching reading have for decades been studying some facets of these concerns. The peculiar concerns of the art of speaking have likewise been given thorough consideration in books and courses and departments of speech for over fifty years in this country. In addition, a considerable portion of the rhetorical tradition has been devoted to these issues. Problems indigenous to the art of listening have, since the early thirties, occupied the attention of educators and psychologists, although it must be admitted that this art is still in what might be considered the folklore stage.

Finally, thousands of books have been written on writing as such. But the distinguishing of the concerns peculiar to the *art* of writing as distinct from the concerns of persuasion or literature or exposition or narration or description have never been carefully made. In other words, the concerns of the *art* of discourse have never been distinguished from those of aims or modes of discourse or even from those peculiar to various media of discourse (such as newspapers, journals, television scripts, film scripts, the stage). Only recently, largely as an outgrowth of linguistic interests, have theorists come to grips with the skills peculiar to writing as such. The work of Francis Christensen on the rhetoric of the sentence and the paragraph (n, *passim*), the work of Pike and his disciples on tagmemics in discourse analysis (cf. *College Composition and Communication,* the issues of May, 1964, October, 1965, December, 1965, May, 1966), and the work of Zelig Harris in discourse analysis (d) all seem to be isolating the problems of the art of writing as such. Of course, traditional methods of teaching paragraph development are germane to this issue also. It seems safe to say that from these movements an intelligent theory of the art of writing will soon evolve. And such a theory, as well as better-developed theories of speaking, listening, and reading, belongs to a full theory of discourse.

Media of Discourse

In addition to the arts of discourse, there are also other signals of discourse. It seems clear that one is in the presence of a signal of discourse if one is confronting a piece which one has just *written,* or if one picks up some *reading* material, or if one is in the process of delivering a *speech,* or if one has settled down in a chair to *listen* to a speech. But one is also in the presence of signals of discourse if one turns on the radio or the television or picks up a telephone, or faces a magazine or newspaper, or joins a club group about to use parliamentary procedure to achieve its aims, or settles down to a conference, or at a convention. In a real sense these latter signals are actually the *channels* of the signals mentioned earlier. The newspaper is the channel which makes possible the transmission of the writing. Similarly, the telephone or the radio are the channels which transmit oral discourse. Similarly, a conversation or a group governed by parliamentary procedure or a counseling occasion are also different kinds of channels for transmission of oral discourse.

In general, therefore, it can be said that arts of discourse and media of discourse can be distinguished by the sort of distinctions made in information theory between signal and channel. In other words, arts of discourse are signals transmitted through various media of discourse. Media of discourse can therefore be generally defined as situations which facilitate the transmission of arts of discourse. It will be noted that this definition avoids the "machine" or hardware associations which the students of media in education give to the concept. In addition, it avoids the notion of media as *self-supporting,* a notion upon which these same groups insist. The Definition and Terminology Commission of the Department of Audio Visual Instruction of the National Educational Association defines instructional media with this insistence:

Devices which present a complete body of information and are largely
self-supporting rather than supplementary in the teaching learning process
[these supplementary devices are called instructional aids] (Ely, c, 54).

The definition of media given in this book does not diverge basically from the
definition of McLuhan which considers media as extensions of human
senses (u, 7, 21). But there is a difference in orientation, the purpose of
which will become clearer immediately in the classification of media.

McLuhan divides media according to the sense which is extended
by the medium. Thus writing is an extension of the visual sense (u, 6–7);
speaking of the auditory sense (u, 7); number of the sense of touch (u, 107);
clothing is the extension of the individual skin and housing of the collective
skin (u, 119 ff. and 123); money is the extension of the climbing, mobility,
and grasping abilities (u, 132–33); photography is the extension of gesture
(u, 195); games are extensions of reactions to the tensions of our inner
lives (u, 237); wheels and roads are extensions of the physical feet (u, 103–
8). The electrical and electronic media are extensions of the central nervous
system (u, 103–4), with the telephone extending the ear and voice, television extending the sense of touch (u, 264–65). Some of these classifications
would seem to need more clarification and justification, possibly even some
revision. Nonetheless, the work of McLuhan is certainly providing a provoca-
tive and fertile paradigm for the study of media.

McLuhan is concerned with all of the extensions of man. Consequently he does not limit his treatment of media to the media of discourse.
His speculations on wheels, roads, money, games, and other nondiscourse
media are as fascinating as his equally interesting observations on books
viewed as private confessional forms or the press viewed as group confessional forms (cf. u, 203–4), or of ads (u, 215 ff., m, *passim*), or of the
styles of various media (u, 206 ff.). Possibly most central (and controversial)
to McLuhan's system of classification of media is his division of media into
hot and cool, according to whether they involve little or much participation
on the part of the decoder (u, 22 ff.). The psychological and cultural effects
of various media provide some of the more exciting aspects of McLuhan's
theory. As with some of McLuhan's other distinctions, the hot-cool differentiation seems to call for further clarification.

In addition to the media considered by McLuhan, some other important channels of discourse must be considered in a comprehensive classification system. With regard to the number of encoders, one could distinguish
monologual situations like lectures or radio speeches from small group
situations like telephone calls, small conversational groups, panels, dramas,
clubs, from large group situations like forums, conventions, and assemblies.

Some of the small group situations have been carefully studied by the students of group dynamics, and the other forms have usually been studied by students of the discipline of speech.

A similar system of classifications can be made if the number of decoders is considered. There would again be the situations that involve the single listener: soliloquy, most counseling situations, the single interviewee, and questionnaire situations. Then there are small group situations often similar to the encoder small groups. There are very common large group decoders: the lecture, and sometimes the conference. Finally, there is the most frequent classification of media, the mass media that use electronic channels to reach thousands or millions.

Thirdly, there are classes of media determined on the basis of how many attitudes to reality are allowed by the structure of the situation. Writers in the field of debate and discussion distinguish these two fields as being bilateral and multilateral, because in debate two sides of the question are heard from, and in discussion many sides of the question are heard from (cf. Chenoweth, d, 8). The distinction can be extended to include unilateral genres, the interview and the questionnaire. Thus, from the standpoint of reality, media are unilateral, bilateral, and multilateral.

It now seems possible to take a comprehensive view of different kinds of media. Certainly an understanding of media from McLuhan's standpoint (the nature of the channel as such) is important. But other classifications of media are also just as important. Certainly, the systematic study of media is presently in its infancy, but it is crucial to a full theory of discourse. Though this volume, dedicated to a consideration of the aims of discourse, does not systematically consider media of discourse, there are sections in each chapter which attempt to investigate the media which seem congenial to a given aim.

THE MODES OF DISCOURSE

The second application of the communications triangle to the field of discourse is that of the meaning of the discourse as reference to reality. In other words, classifications of kinds of realities referred to by full texts constitute the "modes" of discourse.

The "kinds" of realities referred to by full discourses could be grouped by many different principles of classification. The kind of reality to which a discourse refers answers a question like "What is this text about?" The answer to this question could be given by categorizing the subject matter in one of the academic disciplines: "It is about physics, or ethics, or psychology, or linguistics." Such categories would not appreciably help a theory of discourse, for the problems of physics are the concern of physicists. Nevertheless, they have been used as classificational categories in anthologies of readings for freshman courses.

More relevant to the domain of discourse as discourse is an answer to the question of what a thing is about, like the following: "It's a story about the wife of Napoleon's general;" or, "It's a study of the kinds of mental abnormalities;" or, "It's a severe criticism of the Eisenhower administration;" or, "It's a description of the topography of Northern New Mexico." Such formulations would lead to categories like: a narrative, a series of classifications, a criticism or evaluation, and a description.

Actually, these four classes of kinds of referents are the modes of discourse considered here.

Categories like these are significant to a theory of discourse for they are few in number and are therefore more manageable than a whole list of academic disciplines. Further, it can be demonstrated that the problems of narration, classification, evaluation, and description are, unlike the problems of physics or any given subject, the proper province of a theory of discourse. The modes of discourse will be given a fairly thorough historical and theoretical treatment in Volume II. Following the general treatment, several hundred pages are then devoted to the modes in a detailed presentation.

Consequently, only a brief outline of the modes will be presented in this initial chapter. Enough will be given to serve as a skeleton for this aspect of the field of English.

"Modes" of discourse is a fairly recent term. The more traditional eighteenth- and nineteenth-century term was "forms" of discourse (Giovannini, f; Cairns, f); and this is the term often used in German also (Kinneavy, s, 81–83). In literature, where the problem of kind of discourse has been often treated, the dominating terms have been "genre" and "type" (Kinneavy, s, 81 ff.).

In any case, the history of the modes does not reveal a simple classification till the nineteenth century. Bain's *English Composition and Rhetoric* (2nd ed., 1867) established the modes which still prevail today: narration, exposition, argumentation, and description. For reasons given in Volume II, this quartet is shifted to narration, classification, description, and evaluation.

These four modes of discourse are not an application of the communication triangle. They actually are grounded in certain philosophic concepts of the nature of reality considered as being or becoming. This is not surprising. The ultimate attempt of discourse to refer to reality should, as much as possible, be grounded in the nature of reality, not the nature of language.

To each of four modes of discourse there corresponds a principle of thought which permits reality to be considered in this way. Therefore, each of the modes has its own peculiar logic. It also has its own organizational patterns, and, to some extent, its own stylistic characteristics.

Because of these individual modal peculiarities in logic, structure, and style, it is important that the modes be given careful consideration in composition study. At the present time only classification (and consequent definition) is systematically studied in traditional composition courses. Literary narratives are analyzed with no study of the nature of narrative itself, and analyses (descriptions) are made in literature and descriptive linguistics with no attention being given to the nature of description as a kind of discourse. Narrative (as change) is being studied in anthropology, description in philosophy and mathematics, evaluation in sociology and philosophy.

No theory of modes of discourse ever pretends that modes do not overlap. In actuality, it is impossible to have pure narration, description, evaluation, or classification. However, in a given discourse there will often be what Morris calls a "dominant" mode (Morris, s, 75). The same principle will hold in uses of language.

For the whole field of English study the modes are important because when the modes are scientific in aim, narration becomes history, description becomes analysis or description, evaluation becomes criticism, and classification becomes theory. There are, consequently, four basically different scientific approaches to any field of English. That is why, in Figure I, 4, History, Theory, Description, and Criticism are placed at the left of the entire schema to indicate that any aspect of the study of language can be approached in four different ways.

Thus there are: historical linguistics, descriptive linguistics, theoretical linguistics (Chomsky, a, 193–94; c, 53 ff.) and prescriptive linguistics. Similarly there are: historical semantics, pure semantics (Carnap, s, 11), descriptive semantics, and critical semantics; the last, though not a "common" term, is obviously the sort of exercise Korzybski and Hayakawa engage in. In literature, to give a final example, there are: literary history, literary analysis, literary theory, and literary criticism.

The Aims of Discourse

The third application of the triangle at level B results in the *aims* of discourse.

The *aims* of language are the reason for the existence of all the preceding aspects of language. Sounds, morphemes, syntactic patterns, meanings of all kinds, skills in speaking and the other arts of discourse, narratives and other modes of discourse—all of these exist so that humans may achieve certain purposes in their use of language with one another. Both a theory of language and a theory of discourse, then, should be crowned with a viable framework of the uses of discourse.

Educational syllabuses in language from kindergarten through graduate school must make these aims the governing concepts. And, conversely, any comprehensive program in language education must be judged by its account of the fundamental uses of language. All else is in the realm of means.

The next chapter will be entirely devoted to establishing the aims of discourse on solid historical and theoretical foundations. In this chapter, the structure to be arrived at there will be assumed, and only a brief sketch will be made of these aims here.

The structure of the communication process again serves as the theoretical springboard. Clearly, the structure of anything limits the uses to which it may be put. A cup can be used as a container of coffee, or as a paperweight, or as a housewife's defensive tool in a family fight; but it is not suited to serve as a medium of transportation, or as a source of light, because of the inherent limitations of its components and their structure.

Similarly, the process of language, because of its components and structures, lends itself to a variety of uses but is not completely indeterminate to aim. The main components of the process are, as the communication triangle illustrates, an encoder, a language signal, an ability of the signal to refer to reality, and a decoder. The process makes it possible for any or all of these components to be emphasized in a given use situation. Language can therefore be employed with the stress of the process on the *persons* (encoder or decoder), or the *reality* to which reference is made, or on the *product* (the text which the discourse produces). There are, consequently, person discourse, reference discourse, and product discourse.

All of these kinds of discourse always incorporate all of the components of the language process. The different uses of language are, therefore, a matter of which element of the process dominates the particular use under consideration.

Person discourse can stress either encoder or decoder. It seems fairly clear that language can be used as the simple vehicle of expression of some aspect of the personality of the encoder. Such use is called an expressive use of language. Sometimes in these uses the decoder and the referential components of the process become negligible—as with curse words uttered in private. Diaries, journals, certain conversational uses ("I just wanted to talk to you"), cathartic interviews in psychology, some religious and political credos or manifestoes, myths of primitive or sophisticated societies, and value systems are often primarily expressive uses of language whereby an individual or a group expresses its intuitions and emotional aspirations. The expressor dominates the process. Chapter VI considers this use of language in some detail.

Secondly, the discourse may be focused primarily on the decoder, the other person involved in the process. In this use, the encoder may even purposely disguise his own personality and purposely distort the picture of reality which language can paint in order to get the decoder to do something or believe something (as in dishonest advertising or some political speeches). These distortions are not essential to this use of language, however. What is essential is that encoder, reality, and language itself all become instrumental to the achievement of some practical effect in the decoder. Such a use of language is called persuasion or rhetoric. Like expression, it is a very important use of language. It will be treated in Chapter IV.

The reference use of language stresses the ability of the language to designate or reproduce reality, in a manner of speaking. If the reality is conceived as known and the facts about it are simply relayed to the decoder, there is an informative use of language. If this information is systematized and accompanied by demonstrative proof of its validity, there is a scientific use of language. If the reality is not known but being sought, there is an exploratory use of language. Informative uses of language include weather reports, news stories, much conversation, telephone directories. Scientific uses of language include much history, descriptive analysis of anatomy in medicine, taxonomic categories of botany, some literary criticism, etc. Exploratory uses of language include questionnaires, interviews, some seminars, some panel discussions.

All of these are examples of reference discourse. Often they are classed under what is called "expository" writing or speaking. Reference discourse is considered in Chapter III.

Finally, the product or text or work itself may be the focus of the process as an object worthy of being appreciated in its own right. Such appreciation gives pleasure to the beholder. In this use of language, language calls attention to itself, to its own structures, not as references to reality or as expressions of personal aspirations or as instruments of persuasion, but as structures worthy of contemplation in their own right. Of course reference, author personality, and persuasion may and usually are involved. But they are not rigidly relevant. Indeed the reality may be fictional or very distorted; the author may be hidden under dramatic projections; and the persuasions involved may be quite trivial on occasion.

This last use of language is called literature. It appears in such varied forms as the pun, the salacious joke, the sonnet, the novel, the TV drama, and the epic.

Language is like a windowpane. I may throw bricks at it to vent my feelings about something; I may use a chunk of it to chase away an intruder; I may use it to mirror or explore reality; and I may use a stained-glass windowpane to call attention to itself. Windows can be used expressively, persuasively, referentially, and artistically.

Each of these uses of language has its own processes of thought. The ways of thinking of a scientist are not those of an artist, nor of a salesman. Each has its own logic or logics. Each also has its own organizational patterns and stylistic peculiarities. Consequently, it is most essential that each be studied separately. This does not mean to imply that science does not shade into persuasion or that expression is not a component of literature. These aims overlap just as the modes of discourse. But abstracting them for individual consideration is the necessary limitation of any aspect of science. This point will be considered in the next chapter.

EXERCISES

1. Analyze the structure of the offerings in the department of English in your college catalogue. To what extent do historical periods, individuals, genres structure the program? What proportion of the program is given to linguistics, advanced composition or rhetoric, semantics, literary theory? If possible, obtain earlier copies of the catalogue from the thirties, forties, etc., and contrast the structure and emphases.

2. Contrast the structures of the English offerings in your catalogue with other offerings from different institutions, or with the offerings in French in a French institution.

3. Contrast the structure of the English offerings of your department with the structure and implications of a different department, possibly your minor.

4. Analyze a typical high school syllabus from the forties (e.g., the Denver syllabus) or the fifties (e.g., the Minnesota syllabus), or one of the current Project English syllabuses. What structure is given the discipline of English? What of importance seems neglected? What proportions of emphasis are observed? What emphases have changed?

5. If your library has the facilities, do a historical paper on:
   a. The teaching of literary analysis in Greek or Roman schools (start with Quintilian).
   b. A constrast of the teaching of literary analysis in Greek or Roman schools with presentations of literature in college or high schools today.
   c. The medieval readings used in preparation for the university (start with Paetow).

    d. The disputation in the medieval university.

    e. The discipline of rhetoric in the Renaissance (start with Howell).

    f. The separation of speech from English (start with the early issues of the *Quarterly Journal of Speech,* then called the *Quarterly Journal of Public Speaking*).

    g. The reasons for the demise of classical rhetoric and dialectic.

6. What weaknesses do you detect in the structure of the discipline of English proposed in this chapter?

7. Contrast a textbook in English for composition in the earlier decades of this century with a current one (e.g., Cairns, f, with Martin, 1).

8. Make a more thorough critique of Morris, Thorpe, *Freedom and Discipline* (see bibliography).

9. Contrast the expressionistic "new criticism" in the early part of the century with the structural "new criticism" of the forties and fifties (cf. Spingarn, c, vs. Ransom, n, or any other typical new critic).

10. Contrast the historical approach to literature which dominated English graduate study up to the forties in this century with the critical approach which opposed it from the late thirties on (cf. Crane, h).

11. Discuss the implications of an English program for Freshman English or high school based on the communication or language arts (speaking, listening, writing, reading).

12. Discuss the implications for an English program in freshman English or advanced composition or high school English based on creative literary themes or the modes of discourse.

BIBLIOGRAPHY AND FOOTNOTE REFERENCES

Abrams, M. H. *The Mirror and the Lamp.* New York: Oxford University Press, 1953 (m).

Addison, J. W. "The Theory of Hierarchies." In *Logic, Methodology, and Philosophy of Science,* Ernest Nagel, Patrick Suppes, and Alfred Tarski, eds. Stanford, Calif.: Stanford University Press, 1962 (t).

Ajdukiewicz, C. "Sprache und Sinn." *Erkenntnis,* IV (1934), 100–38 (s).

Austin, J. L. *How to Do Things with Words.* Cambridge, Mass.: Harvard University Press, 1962 (h).

Bailey, John. *The Teaching of English in the Universities of England.* Pamphlet No. 53, The English Association, 1922 (t), R. W. Chambers, ed. (t).

Bain, Alexander. *English Composition and Rhetoric.* 2nd American Edition. New York: D. Appleton and Company, 1867 (e).

Bally, Charles. "Langue et parole." *Journal de psychologie,* (XXIII, 1926), 693–702 (l).

Bar-Hillel, Yehoshua. *Language and Information.* Reading, Mass.: Addison-Wesley Publishing Company, Inc., 1964 (l).

Berlo, David K. *The Process of Communication: An Introduction in Theory and Practice.* New York: Holt, Rinehart & Winston, Inc., 1960 (p).

Birdwhistell, Ray L. "Kinesics and Communication." In *Explorations in Communication,* Edmund S. Carpenter and Marshall McLuhan, eds. Boston: Beacon Press, 1960. Pp. 54–64 (k).

Bloomfield, Leonard. *Language.* New York: Henry Holt and Company, 1933 (l).

Bréal, Michel. *Semantics.* Tr. Mrs. Henry Cust. New York: Dover Press, 1964 (s).

Brickman, W. W. and Stanley Lehrer. *A Century of Higher Education.* New York: Society for Advancement of Education, 1962 (c).

Bühler, Karl. "Die Axiomatik der Sprachwissenschaften." *Kant-Studien,* XXXVIII (1933), 19–90 (a).

Cairns, William B. *The Forms of Discourse.* Boston: Ginn and Company, 1902 (f).

Carnap, Rudolf. "Empiricism, Semantics, and Ontology." In Linsky, Leonard, ed., *Semantics and the Philosophy of Language.* Urbana, Ill.: The University of Illinois Press, 1952 (e).

————. "Intellectual Autobiography." In Schilpp, Paul A., ed., *The Philosophy of Rudolf Carnap.* LaSalle, Ill.: Open Court Publishing Co., 1963 (i).

————. *Logical Foundations of Probability.* 2nd Edition. Chicago, Ill.: The University of Chicago Press, 1962 (lo).

————. "On Some Concepts of Pragmatics." In *Meaning and Necessity.* Chicago, Ill.: University of Chicago Press, 1956. Pp. 248–51 (m).

————. *Introduction to Semantics.* Cambridge, Mass.: Harvard University Press, 1942 (s).

————. "Testability and Meaning." *Philosophy of Science,* III, 14 (October, 1936), 419–71 and IV, 1, 166–88 (t).

Chambers, R. W. "The Teaching of English in the Universities of England." *The English Association,* Pamphlet No. 53, 1922 (t).

Chenoweth, Eugene. *Discussion and Debate.* Dubuque, Iowa: William C. Brown Company, 1951 (d).

Cherry, E. C. "A History of Information Theory." *Proceedings of the Institute of Electrical Engineers,* XCVIII (1951), 383–93 (h).

Cherry, Colin. *On Human Communication.* New York: Technology Press of M.I.T. and John Wiley & Sons, Inc., 1952 (o).

Chomsky, Noam. *Aspects of the Theory of Syntax.* Cambridge, Mass.: The M.I.T. Press, 1965 (a).

————. "The Current Scene in Linguistics." *College English,* XXVIII, 8 (May, 1966), 587–95 (c).

————. "A Review of B. F. Skinner's *Verbal Behavior.*" In Fodor and Katz, 547–78 (r).

————. *Syntactic Structures*. The Hague: Mouton & Co., 1964 (s).

Christensen, Francis. *Notes Toward a New Rhetoric: 6 Essays for Teachers*. New York: Harper & Row, Publishers, 1967 (n).

Corbett, Edward. *Classical Rhetoric for the Modern Student*. New York: Oxford University Press, 1965 (c).

Crane, R. S. "History versus Criticism in the University Study of Literature." *English Journal*, College ed., XXIV (1935), 645–67 (h).

Curtis, Stanley J. *History of Education in Great Britain*. 4th Edition. London: University Tutorial Press, Ltd., 1957 (h).

Diebold, Richard, Jr., Osgood, Charles, and Thomas A. Sebeok. *Psycholinguistics: A Survey of Theory and Research Problems*. Bloomington, Ind.: Indiana University Press, 1965 (p).

Eby, F., and C. F. Arrowood. *The History and Philosophy of Education*. New York: Prentice-Hall, Inc., 1940 (h).

Ely, Donald P., ed. *The Changing Role of the Audiovisual Process in Education: A Definition and Glossary of Related Terms. Audiovisual Communication Review*, XI, 1 (Jan.-Feb., 1963). Whole issue (c).

Fodor, Jerry A., and Jerrold J. Katz, eds. *The Structure of Language*. Englewood Cliffs, N. J.: Prentice-Hall, Inc., 1965 (s).

Fogarty, Daniel John. *Roots for a New Rhetoric*. New York: Bureau of Publication, Teachers College, Columbia University, 1959 (r).

Freedom and Discipline in English. Report of the Commission on English. New York: College Entrance Examination Board, 1965 (f).

Gardiner, Alan Anderson. *The Theory of Speech and Language*. Oxford: Clarendon Press, 1932 (t).

Giovannini, Giovanni. "The Four Forms of Composition." *Dictionary of World Literature*. New York: The Philosophical Library, 1943. Pp. 117–18 (f).

Grommon, Alfred H. "Once More—What is English." *English Journal*, XXVIII (March, 1967), 476–80 (o).

Grzegorczyk, A. "The Pragmatic Foundations of Semantics." *Synthese*, VIII (1950–51), 300–24 (p).

Guth, Hans. *English Today and Tomorrow*. Englewood Cliffs, N. J.: Prentice-Hall, Inc., 1964 (e).

Hall, Edward T. *The Silent Language*. Garden City, N. Y.: Doubleday and Company, 1959 (s).

Halle, Morris. "On the Bases of Phonology." In *The Structure of Language*, Jerry A. Fodor and Jerrold J. Katz, eds. Englewood Cliffs, N. J.: Prentice-Hall, Inc., 1965. Pp. 324–33 (b).

Harris, Zelig. "Discourse Analysis." In Jerry A. Fodor and Jerrold J. Katz., eds., *The Structure of Language*. Englewood Cliffs, N. J.: Prentice-Hall, 1964. Pp. 355–83 (d).

————. "Discourse Analysis: A Sample Text." *Language*, XXXVIII, 4 (1952), 474 ff. (di).

Hart, James Morgan, J.U.D. "The College Course in English Literature, How it May Be Improved." *PMLA,* I (1886), 84–94 (c).

Herdan, Gustav. *Quantitative Linguistics.* London: Butterworth & Co. (Publishers) Ltd., 1964 (q).

Hill, Archibald. *An Outline of Linguistic Structure.* New York: Harcourt, Brace, and World, Inc., 1958 (o).

Hiz, H. "Kotarbiński's Praxeology." *Philosophy and Phenomenological Research,* XV (1954), 238–43 (k).

Hjelmslev, Louis. "Langue et parole." *Cahiers Ferdinand de Saussure,* II (1942), 29–44 (1).

———. *Prolegomena to a Theory of Language.* Tr. Francis J. Whitfield. Baltimore: Waverly Press, 1953 (p).

Hovland, C. I., Janis, Irving L., and Harold H. Kelley. *Communication and Persuasion.* New Haven: Yale University Press, 1953 (c).

———, and others. *The Order of Presentation in Persuasion.* New Haven: Yale University Press, 1957 (o).

Howell, Wilbur S. *Logic and Rhetoric in England, 1500–1700.* Princeton, N.J.: Princeton University Press, 1956 (l).

Hunt, T. W. "The Place of English in the College Curriculum." *PMLA,* I (1886), 118–32, (p).

Jakobson, Roman. "Linguistics and Poetics." In *Essays on the Language of Literature,* Seymour Chatman and Samuel R. Levin, eds. Boston: Houghton Mifflin Company, 1967. Pp. 296–322 (l).

———, and Morris Halle. *Fundamentals of Language.* The Hague: Mouton & Company, 1956 (f).

Joos, Martin. *The Five Clocks. International Journal of American Linguistics,* XXXVIII, 2 (April, 1962), 1–62 (f).

Kinneavy, James L. *A Study of Three Contemporary Theories of the Lyric.* Washington, D.C.: Catholic University Press, 1956 (s).

Korzybski, Alfred. *Science and Sanity.* 2nd Edition. Lancaster, Penn.: The International Non-Aristotelian Library Publishing Company, 1941 (s).

Kuhn, Thomas S. "The Function of Dogma in Scientific Research." In *Scientific Change,* A. C. Crombie, ed. New York: Basic Books, Inc., 1963. Pp. 347–69 (f).

La Drière, J. Craig. "Rhetoric and 'Merely Verbal Art.' " *English Institute Essays, 1948,* D. A. Robertson, Jr., ed. New York: Columbia University Press, 1949. Pp. 134–52 (r).

Laine, J. B. *Rhetorical Theory in American Colleges and Universities, 1915–1954.* Dissertation. Evanston, Ill.: Northwestern University, 1958 (r).

Lasswell, Harold D. *The Analysis of Political Behavior.* New York: Oxford University Press, 1948 (a).

———, Lerner, Daniel, and I. de Sola Pool. *The Comparative Study of Symbols,*

An Introduction. Stanford, Calif.: Stanford University Press, 1952 (c).

Lynch, James J., and Bertrand Evans. *High School Textbooks: A Control Examination.* Boston: Little, Brown and Company, 1963 (h).

Lyons, John. *Structural Semantics, An Analysis of Part of the Vocabulary of Plato.* Oxford: Published for the (Philological) Society by B. Blackwell, 1963 (s).

Malinowski, Branislaw. *Coral Gardens and their Magic.* 2 Vols. New York: American Book Company, 1935 (c).

Mallet, C. E. *A History of the University of Oxford.* 3 Vols. London: Methuen & Co., Ltd., 1924 (h).

Marrou, Henry I. *A History of Education in Antiquity.* Tr. George Lamb. London: Sheed and Ward, 1956 (h).

Martin, Harold C., and Richard Ohmann. *The Logic and Rhetoric of Exposition.* New York: Holt, Rinehart, and Winston, Inc., 1963 (l).

Martin, Richard M. *Toward a Systematic Pragmatics.* In Studies in Logic, L. E. J. Brouwer, E. W. Beth, and A. Heyting, eds. Amsterdam: North Holland Publishing Company, 1959 (t).

———. *Truth and Denotation: A Study in Semantical Theory.* Chicago: University of Chicago Press, 1958 (tr).

McKeon, Richard. "Rhetoric in the Middle Ages." *Speculum,* XVII (January, 1942), 1–32 (r).

McLuhan, Marshall. *The Mechanical Bride, Folklore of Industrial Man.* New York: The Vanguard Press, Inc., 1951 (m).

———. *Understanding Media: The Extensions of Man.* New York: McGraw-Hill Book Company, 1965 (u).

Mencken, Henry Louis. *The American Language: An Inquiry into the Development of English in the United States.* 4th Edition. Abridged, annotations, and new material by Raven McDavid. New York: Alfred A. Knopf, Inc., 1963 (a).

Monroe, Paul. *A Textbook in the History of Education.* New York: The Macmillan Company, 1935 (t).

Morris, C. W. *Signs, Language, and Behavior.* Englewood Cliffs, N.J.: Prentice-Hall, Inc., 1946 (s).

Neurath, Otto. "Foundations of the Social Sciences." *International Encyclopedia for Unified Science.* Vol I. Chicago: University of Chicago Press, 1938 (r).

Öhmann, S. "Theories of the Linguistic Field." *Word,* IX (1953), 123–34 (t).

Ong, Walter J. *Ramus: Method, and the Decay of Dialogue.* Cambridge, Mass.: Harvard University Press, 1958 (r).

Osgood, Charles E., Suci, George J., and Percy H. Tannenbaum. *The Measurement of Meaning.* Urbana, Ill.: University of Illinois Press, 1958 (m).

Paetow, Louis J. *The Arts Courses at Medieval Universities with Special Reference to Grammar and Rhetoric.* Champaign: University of Illinois Press, 1910 (a).

Pellegrini, Angelo. "Renaissance and Medieval Antecedents of Debate." *Quarterly Journal of Speech,* XXVIII (1942), 15–17 (r).

Pike, Kenneth. *Language in Relation to a Unified Theory of the Structure of Human Behavior.* 3 Vols. Glendale, Calif.: Summer Institute of Linguistics, 1960 (l).

Quine, W. V. *From a Logical Point of View.* Cambridge, Mass.: Harvard University Press, 1961 (f).

Quintilian. *The Institutio Oratoria.* 4 Vols. Tr. H. E. Butler. London: W. Heinemann, 1921–22 (i).

Ransom, John Crowe. *The New Criticism.* Norfolk, Conn.: New Directions Press, 1941 (n).

Richards, I. A. and C. K. Ogden. *The Meaning of Meaning.* New York: Harcourt, Brace, and World, 1923 (m).

———. *Principles of Literary Criticism.* London: K. Paul, Trench, Trubner and Company, Ltd., 1925 (p).

Russell, Bertrand. *Human Knowledge, Its Scope and Limits.* New York: Simon and Schuster, Inc., 1948 (h).

Ryle, Gilbert. The *Concept of Mind.* New York: Barnes & Noble, Inc., 1949 (c).

Sapir, Edward. *Culture, Language, and Personality.* Berkeley, Calif.: University of California Press, 1961 (c).

Saussure, Ferdinand de. *Course in General Linguistics.* Charles Bally and Albert Sèchehaye, eds., in collaboration with Albert Reidlinger. Tr. Wade Baskin. New York: Philosophical Library, 1959 (c).

Sèchehaye, Charles Albert. "Les trois linguistiques saussuriennes." *Vox Romanica,* V (1940), 1–48 (t).

Shannon, Claude E., and Warren Weaver. *The Mathematical Theory of Communication.* Urbana, Ill.: The University of Illinois Press, 1964 (m).

Skeat, W. W. *An English Miscellany.* Oxford: Clarendon Press, 1901 (e).

Slama-Cazacu, Tatiana. *Langage et contexte.* 'sGravenhage: Mouton & Company, 1961 (l).

Smith, Bruce Lannes, Lasswell, Harold D., and Ralph D. Casey. *Propaganda, Communication and Public Opinion.* Princeton, N. J.: Princeton University Press, 1946 (pr).

Spingarn, Joel E. *Creative Criticism: Essays on the Unity of Genius and Taste.* New York: Henry Holt and Company, 1917 (c).

Stageberg, Norman. *An Introductory English Grammar.* New York: Holt, Rinehart and Winston, Inc., 1965 (i).

Suppes, Patrick. "A Comparison of the Meaning and Use of Models in Mathematics and the Empirical Sciences." *Synthese,* XII (1960), 287–301 (c).

Tarski, Alfred. "Contributions to the Theory of Models." *Indagationes Mathematicae*, XVI (1954), 572–88; XVII (1955), 56–64 (c).

Thomas, Owen. *Transformational Grammar and the Teacher of English*. New York: Holt, Rinehart and Winston, Inc., 1965 (t).

Thorpe, James. *The Aims and Methods of Scholarship in Modern Languages and Literature*. New York: Modern Language Association of America, 1963 (a).

Trager, George L., and Henry Lee Smith. *An Outline of English Structure*. Norman, Okla.: Battenburg Press, 1951 (o).

Troubetskoy, N. S. *Principes de phonologie*. Paris: Librairie C. Klingksieck, 1949 (p).

Ullman, Stephen. *Semantics: An Introduction to the Science of Meaning*. Oxford: B. Blackwell, 1962 (s).

Venn, J. *The Logic of Chance*. London: The Macmillan Company, Ltd., 1888 (l).

Winstanley, D. A. *Early Victorian Cambridge*. Cambridge, England: The University Press, 1940 (e).

———. *The University of Cambridge in the Eighteenth Century*. Cambridge, England: The University Press, 1922 (u).

———. *Unreformed Cambridge: A Study of Certain Aspects of the University in the Eighteenth Century*. Cambridge, England: The University Press, 1935 (ur).

Ziff, Paul. *Semantic Analysis*. Ithaca, N. Y.: Cornell University Press, 1960 (s).

2

The Aims of Discourse

Introduction

Importance of Aim

Despite the ultimate importance to language study of the aims to which discourses are oriented, surprisingly little is made of these aims, in a systematic way, in textbooks teaching language, either native or foreign.

In college and high school textbooks, generally, composition books today usually assume that the student is to be writing serious "expository" prose, as it is usually called. And the literature textbooks, of course, properly assume their function to be taken for granted. The student is to read "litera-ture" and write "expository" themes. Often the functions of language are restricted to these. Grammar textbooks rarely have anything to say about the functions of discourse, nor do grammarians and historical, descriptive and comparative linguists (Gardiner, t, 6; Ogden, m, 226).

Yet purpose in discourse is all important. The aim of a discourse determines everything else in the process of discourse. "What" is talked about, the oral or written medium which is chosen, the words and grammatical patterns used—all of these are largely determined by the purpose of the discourse. In the terminology of the first chapter, mode of discourse, art of discourse, and the semantic and syntactic components of the language are all functions of the aim of discourse.

Concretely, if a salesman wants to sell brooms, his verbal pitch will embody the meanings and grammatical characteristics which will achieve his purpose. Here the aim is persuasive. The art of discourse is speech, the mode of the discourse is partly classification (of the qualities of his broom) and partly evaluation (its alleged superiority over competitive ones); the semantics involve the meanings of the words and grammatical structures used; the syntactics consist of his phonemes and morphemes, and their struc-

48

tured combinations according to the grammatical rules of the dialect of the language he is using. And all of these are determined by aim.

Determination of Aim

How is aim determined? Obviously, it is partly determined by the cultural context and the situational context in both of which the text of the discourse is a part. This means, of course, that the intent of the author of the text partially determines the aim of the discourse.

But it would be dangerous to adduce author intent as the main criterion of the aim of a discourse, for often a discourse does not achieve the author's intent—"That's not what I meant at all," says the character in Eliot's "Prufrock." And, again we may not have the author's intent available to use in recorded form; or, especially in propaganda and literature, the expressed "intent" of the author may not at all be the real intent. The fallacy of judging the intent of a work by the intent of the author has been called the "intentional fallacy" (Wimsatt, v, 3–18).

Nor, from another point of view, is the effect on any given receptor a sure guide. A cloistered teenager may well purchase Joyce's *Ulysses* for pornographic purposes, but this does not make *Ulysses* itself pornographic. The fallacy of judging the intent of a work by the effect upon a given decoder has been called the "affective fallacy," and it parallels the "intentional fallacy" (on the latter, see Wimsatt, v, 21–39).

Rather than encoder or decoder being the determinants of aim, it seems better to find the aim which is embodied in the text itself—given the qualifications of situation and culture mentioned above.

Text here must mean more than the individual sentence or even the individual paragraph or section. An individual sentence without a context is largely indeterminate as to aim (Uhlenbeck, a, 10–12; see also Quine, w, Chapters I and II). Thus, "the train is coming" could function as information in a railroad station, or as entertainment in a comedy routine, or as a warning, or even as a question (given a rising terminal intonation). In like manner, a whole paragraph quoted for purposes of ridicule functions very differently in the quoted context.

This means that a totality of effect is generated by the things talked about, the organization given the materials, the accompanying style, and so on. Other kinds of things talked about, other kinds of organizations, other styles generate other effects, different not only in degree but in kind. The effect of all these means (mode, art, meanings, grammar) is to generate a reaction of some kind of acceptance or rejection on the part of the normal decoder.

The characteristics of the text which generate these effects are the concerns of discourse analysis. They are a major part of language study. They constitute the "intent of the work," to use a venerable philosophic phrase.

The analyses of the actual psychological effects themselves, i.e., the nature of aesthetic pleasure, of the mentality persuaded by propaganda, of the psyche satisfied by its cathartic use of expression, are the concerns of psychologists. Similarly, the mental and emotional processes involved in the generation of a work of art are also the province of psychology. As Jung has said,

> Only that aspect of art which consists in the processes of artistic form can be the object of psychology; whereas that which constitutes the essential nature of art always lies outside its province. This other aspect, namely, the problem what is art in itself, can never be the object of a psychological, but only of an aesthetic-artistic method of approach (Jung, as quoted in Olson, p, 148).

A fortiori, the large social effects of Elizabethan theater, of the naturalistic novel of the nineteenth century, of Newton's *Principia,* of Marx's *The Capital,* or Upton Sinclair's *The Jungle* are all the proper concerns of sociologists and cultural—not literary—historians.

Terminology

With regard to the aims of language, there is a possible confusion in terminology, a problem which will recur in nearly every chapter of this book.

In this chapter heretofore, I have employed "use," "function," "aim," and "purpose" almost interchangeably. Of the group "function" is most liable to misinterpretation. In different linguistic authors "function" can refer to: the kind of reality referred to (cf. Cassirer, e, 171 ff.; Urban, 1, 134 ff.) ; the level of social formality of a given discourse (Kenyon, c, 215 ff.), nonmorphological classes of words in grammar (Fries, s,). Clearly, none of these meanings are intended here.

Traditionally, certain aims of discourse were classified as "arts." Thus rhetoric meant language intended to persuade; logic meant language used to demonstrate; and dialectic—as the etymology indicates—meant language used to explore for truth. In this book the term "arts" has been reserved for the skills of writing, reading, speaking, and listening. Since they are customarily called the communication or language "arts," this term is reserved for these referents.

The determination of the basic aims of language will be achieved by a process similar to that followed in the first chapter in the structuring of the field of English. First, a somewhat comprehensive survey of different views of the aims of language will be given, followed by a theoretical framework to interpret the historical and classificatory coverage.

A Survey of Views
on the Aims of Discourse

For the sake of convenience the views on the functions of language have been arbitrarily divided into the following groups: geneticists, sign theorists, communication theorists, logical positivists, semanticists, educators, metaphysicians, expressionists, and comparative philologists. The divisions are empirically established—these are the major groups concerned with the functions of language. Undoubtedly some important groups are not represented (especially from non-Indo-European cultures).

Geneticists

Possibly the best term for this cluster of theories might be the "genetic procedure," for it attempts to find out the functions of language through investigating the uses to which language has been put in the general evolutionary development of mankind. Four general types of methodologies can be used to meet this problem. First, one can speculate on the origins of language among prehistoric men. Second, one can examine present societies considered "primitive" by Western standards. Third, one can conceive of a child as a primitive and watch the development of various language uses in the growing child. Fourth, one can follow a specific culture with historical records and attempt to determine the emergence of various functions. Several philosophers have approached the uses of language through a genetic methodology (Urban, 1, 74 ff.).

There are many speculative theories of the origin of language in prehistory. Some modern linguists dismiss the question as fruitless. The somewhat irreverent terms which label such attempts occasionally connote the insinuated disrepute which the linguists have for these endeavors.

There is first the interjectional or expressive theory, sometimes called the "ah-ah" or "pooh-pooh" theory. This views language primarily as a vehicle of expressing emotional reactions of approval or disapproval. This is closely allied to the notion that language is a kind of verbal gesture, another theory of some repute.

Then there is the onomatopoetic cluster of speculations, called by Müller the "bow-wow" theory. According to this theory, man tried to represent realities by words that imitate some aspect of the reality.

Third, there are the utilitarian theories. Here language is viewed as a pragmatic symbol in social problems of getting things done. Some gesture theories tend in this direction.

Fourth, there are what might be called the poetic theories of language origin. Jespersen's theory, though it also incorporates an expressionistic component, is representative of this class. (On all of these, cf. Diamond, h, 259 ff.).

Anthropologists usually hold more limited views. Malinowski, for instance, studying the Trobriands in Melanesia, and Doob, studying African cultures, arrive at different conclusions. Malinowski says that language among the Trobriands is not fundamentally expressive or representative, but that language functions primarily in a utilitarian way. This has two large subdivisions, the magical and the pragmatic. The primitive magical use of language he sees as a forerunner of our own rhetorical use of language and the pragmatic as a forerunner of our own scientific use of language. He finds little or no evidence of what he would call an aesthetic use of language, except as involved in ritual or magical contexts (Malinowski, II, 236). Doob's research in Africa leads him to classify uses of language for attaining primary individual food, body, and tool needs, or for achieving social goals. The social goals are ingroup socializing, governing, meeting outlander intrusions, and the expression of emotions (Doob, c, 36 ff.).

Child psychology theories about the origin of language often stress the interjectionist, the utilitarian, and the representative approaches found in the origin or anthropological views. In addition, however, there is much stress on what every parent has undoubtedly noticed, the "play" function of language in children. Some theories consider this the primordial and earliest function of language: for a child, language is first and foremost a toy, later it takes on interjectional and utilitarian functions (Gardiner, t, 63).

Certainly one of the most serious attempts to trace the functions of language genetically has been the historical examination of the functions of language in Western civilization by Cassirer. He finds in Greek culture a movement from the mythological to the metaphysical to the pragmatic use of language. By the first he means an expression of aspirations, by the second a representational mirroring of the world, and by the third the specific rhetorical use of the sophists (Cassirer, e, 111 ff.).

Summarily, then, one might say that the various genetic approaches to the problem of the functions of language yield expressive, representational, pragmatic, and play (or poetic) uses, with varying emphases on primordiality.

Sign Theorists

Possibly the most representative and comprehensive treatment of the functions of language starting with behavioral premises and oriented to sign theory is that of C. W. Morris. Morris' earlier treatment of the problem was subordinated to a general theory of signs itself, but his later treatment applied this general semiotic to language as a special case.

In this latter treatment Morris isolates four primary usages of signs. His initial paragraphs to this section indicate the manner in which he has arrived at his formulation:

> Signs in general serve to control behavior in the way something else would exercise control if it were present. To attain its goals the organism must take account of the environment in which it operates, select for its concerns certain features of this environment, respond by response-sequences which will attain an environment suitable to its needs, and organize its sign-provoked responses into some pattern or other. Each of these stages of its activity may be facilitated by the use of signs, and the primary usages of signs correspond to these four aspects of behavior.
>
> Signs accordingly may be used to inform the organism about something, to aid it in its preferential selection of objects, to incite response-sequences of some behavior family, and to organize sign-produced behavior (interpretants) into a determinate whole. These uses may be called in order the *informative,* the *evaluative,* the *incitive,* and the *systemic* use of signs (his italics, s, 95).

Though the behavioral approach to language has been severely criticized by several symbolists and psycholinguists (Cassirer, e, 116), yet the four usages which Morris arrives at are, with one exception, quite comparable to those arrived at by the geneticists.

Communication Theorists

Closely connected to the sign theorists are the views of many who have investigated general communication theory. As representatives here, I have selected Miller and Britton.

Miller, viewing communication basically from a social psychologist's standpoint, gives four basic reasons for social communication: (1) to increase uniformity of information; (2) to increase uniformity of opinion; (3) to change status in the group; and (4) to express emotion. These are again quite close to the informative, exploratory, instrumental, and emotive uses of language which we have seen in views emanating from the genetic and behavioral systems (Miller, 1, 253).

Britton, a communication theorist, really derives his two basic functions of language from the logical positivist divisions, which will be given more attention in a moment. Britton distinguishes an *informative* use of language which refers to sensations (about which there can be normal agreement) and a *dynamic* use which refers to feelings (about which there cannot be normal universal agreement). The dynamic uses Britton subdivides into that which gives necessary principles, another which refers to moral and ethical judgments, and finally a poetic use of language (Britton, c, 49 ff., 277 ff.).

Logical Positivists

The original purpose of the logical analysis of language by Tarski, Carnap, Russell, and others had to do with the separation of valid scientific statements from any others. The duo of verifiable versus nonverifiable statements thus arose.[1] The former were often called referential (or indicative) and the second emotive (or dynamic). The first could be verified as true or false, and the second (for scientific purposes) were simply meaningless or nonsensical, terms which some logical positivists later regretted. The view that propositions were either referential or emotive made its way into many provinces of thought.

Reichenbach, to take a typical thinker from the school, considers the functions of statements to be cognitive (verifiable as true or false) and instrumental. The latter he subdivides into communicative, suggestive (of emotion or volition—including poetry) and promotive (Reichenbach, i, 17 ff.).

Wittgenstein, Russell, and others later modified the early rigidities of a view that held language to be either scientific or meaningless. As Russell remarks, language is not primarily informative, though philosophers, "being bookish and theoretical folk," have been mainly concerned with this aspect of language (Russell, h, 60). Russell considers the expressive (of emotions) and the communicative uses of language, with the latter being divided into the informative, questioning, and imperative (Russell, h, 58–60). Without attempting to categorize, Wittgenstein points out many non-

---

[1] For a consideration of the origin of the duality, cf. Urban, 1, 68 ff., and Cassirer, e, 30.

scientific but meaningful uses of language—and it is Wittgenstein, possibly more than any other, who forced logical positivists to reconsider Tarski's triad of "true, false, or meaningless" propositions (Wittgenstein, p, I, 11 ff.).

Ogden and Richards, philosophers of language and literary critics, accept the basic dualism of function (scientific and emotive) and distinguish three functions within the emotive. This gives them four basic functions of language: (1) language can refer to reality (science); (2) it can express the attitudes of speaker to listener (feeling); (3) it can express the attitude of speaker to referent (tone); and (4) it can be used to promote some effect (intent). Richards used these "meanings" in a literary critical framework (Ogden, m, 224 ff.).

Later, Richards settled on three uses of language: scientific, rhetorical, poetic. They exist in a continuum with decreasing referential discourse and increasing emotive discourse. Pure referential discourse is science, pure emotive discourse is poetry, and any appreciable mixture of the two is rhetoric. Further subdivisions of the mixed area (rhetoric) are generally useless (Richards, h, 100; p, 261).

Semanticists

The semanticists, as a school, also tend to accept the scientific-emotive distinction. However, like Ogden and Richards and in contrast to most logical positivists, their interests lie in the emotive. Korzybski and his many followers, Stuart Chase, Hugh Walpole, Anatol Rapaport, S. I. Hayakawa, and Harry L. Weinberg preponderantly devote their attention to the distortions of reality which occur in the emotive uses of words. One might say that the semanticists are really more worried about the abuses of words than the uses of words (cf. the title of Chase's *The Tyranny of Words,* or of Hayakawa's *The Use and Abuse of Language*). Certainly in our era of mass propagandizing, such a concern is healthy, though it can become fanatic.

Hayakawa, in a more positive way, does indicate the uses of language. Scientific language is either instrumental and/or informative; affective language is either directive or poetic. He devotes several chapters to these uses (Hayakawa, l, 82 ff.).

Educators

In educational practice, certain trends are noticeable. From the elementary grades through the high school, the concerns of teaching language are considered the province of the "language arts." These are usually listed as speaking, listening, writing, and reading. Occasionally "visual arts" and "thinking" are appended. A typical presentation, the three volumes of the NCTE on the language arts programs, really structures the programs around these "arts," with relatively minor consideration given to the aims for which the arts are used. Municipal, state, and local syllabi, and entire series of textbooks for students and for prospective teachers frequently accept this framework as of primary structural importance. The one recent exception to this trend, which is still unpublished at the time of this writing but which I have seen in mimeograph form, is the ninth-grade syllabus of the Nebraska Project English. Following some of the so-called ordinary language philosophers, the Nebraska syllabus distinguished six basic uses of language: informative, expressive, directive, contractive, imaginative, cohesive.

Probably the best consideration of aims is to be found in the speech sections of these programs, for speech teachers are often trained within a rhetorical tradition which recognizes different purposes of various kinds of speeches. This rhetorical tradition will be discussed in the next section.

A second and occasionally dominant emphasis on the use of language in elementary and high school texts throughout the thirties, forties, and fifties of this century has been the Dewey heritage of language as the medium of self-expression of the individual. The expressionists will be reviewed shortly.

The Liberal Arts Tradition

The rhetorical tradition alluded to above, in which some speech training still operates, is an interpretation of the classical view of the functions of language implicit in Plato and treated by Aristotle in four of his major works. The principle of division here, implicit in Plato and Aristotle and explicitly formulated by Aquinas, Aristotle's most influential medieval disciple, is a scale of probability. Discourse which refers to certainties is *scientific;* discourse used in the pursuit of exploring for the probable is *dialectical;* discourse aimed at persuading others to accept the seemingly probable is *rhetorical;* discourse aimed at pleasing through internal and fictional probabilities is *poetic.*

This tradition can be traced through Plato and Aristotle, the Latin rhetoricians, the trivium of the seven liberal arts in the Schools, the Arabic commentators of Aristotle (Averroës and Avicenna), Aquinas and Albertus Magnus, and many Renaissance thinkers. The basic sources of the tradition can be seen in the first sections of the *Organon* (for scientific discourse), the *Topics* (for dialectical), the *Rhetoric,* and the *Poetics* (La Drière, r, 123 ff.; McKeon, r).

Expressionists

One function of language which received little theoretical attention in Antiquity was the use of language as the basic medium of self-expression of the individual. Yet this function has virtually preempted all others in several modern schools of thought. Crocean expressionism, much in the psychoanalytic treatment of language, and the so-called Dewey school of self-expression tend to view the basic function of language as expressive of inner intuition and emotion.

Croce, pointing out the subtitle of his book on *Aesthetic,* "As Science of Expression and General Linguistic," says,

> Aesthetic and Linguistic, conceived as true sciences, are not two distinct things, but one thing only. Not that there is a special Linguistic: but the much-sought-for science of language, general Linguistic, *in so far as what it contains is reducible to philosophy,* is nothing but Aesthetic (a, 142, his italics).

For Croce, all language functions to enable the individual to express himself—all men are small poets, great works of science are great works of art. Croce views individual expression (of intuition, which is equivalent to emotion) as a form of knowledge parallel to knowledge arrived at by concepts of universals (Croce, a, 15 ff.; 142 ff.).

Croce's expressionism is closely allied to the stream of German expressionism of Wundt, Vossler, and (in some respects) Cassirer. Cassirer's concept of myth is almost that of a pure expressive form of language. Myth is not theoretical or practical, it is quite different from art, nor is it scientific; it is really a basic sentiment of intuitive feeling, a "sentiment of life." At this point Cassirer's position moves very close to the psychoanalytic and psycholinguistic attitude to the functions of language (Cassirer, e, 75 ff.).

Comparative Philologists

The classic comparative philologists of the nineteenth century had little to say about the functions of language. But Joshua Whatmough, sometimes classified as a comparative philologist, has a book devoted to the uses of language; and a very important chapter of his general treatise on language is devoted to the uses of language Whatmough seems to approach this question empirically: there seems to be no framework such as can be seen in thinkers as diverse as Morris and Aquinas. Whatmough lists four basic kinds of language use: informative, dynamic (to persuade to thought), emotive (to persuade to action), and aesthetic (Whatmough, l, 84 ff.).

The Aims of Discourse:
A Theoretical Synthesis

The Communication Process
and the Aims of Discourse

There is much that is common to many of the preceding theories, despite their directly opposing axiomatic commitments. Indeed, to anyone acquainted with similar inquiries in other philosophic areas, there is a surprising degree of concordance.

Most of these common elements can be synthesized within a theoretical framework suggested by the language process itself. Hjelmslev's statement that "in general, language is independent of any specific purpose" (p, 110), is not entirely correct. As was suggested in the last chapter, the purposes to which anything can be directed are necessarily restricted by the structure of the object or the process. Cannot a view of the structure of the language process point out the functions to which it may be adapted?

Many of the previous theories implicitly or explicitly have taken the component of the language process into consideration. Gardiner, a linguist, at the outset of his treatise, lists the four factors of the linguistic process as: speaker, listener, thing referred to, and the linguistic material. He points out that Bühler, Durkheim, Meillet, and others recognize these components (Gardiner, t, 7, n.2.). The many disciplines which now use the communication triangle as a workable model of the language process have already been detailed.

Gardiner believes that, of the four factors, the reality referred to predominates in most linguistic situations (t, 55). Aristotle agrees that there is, as he called it, "a language concerned with things" (*Rhetoric*, 1358 a f.); but he says that there is also a "language directed to the hearer" (*Rhetoric*, 1358 a f.). Indeed, this second kind of language is so common that many have reduced all language uses to it.

These suggestions of Aristotle were carried a step further by the German psychologist Karl Bühler in a lengthy monograph in 1933 (a). In this essay Bühler proposed that not only is there discourse oriented to hearers and to things but that there is also an important use of language fundamentally oriented to the speaker. He called this "expressive discourse." To illustrate these basic foci of speech emphasis, he drew a triangle, presenting the speaker, the hearer, and things as the three vertices of the communication triangle (a, 74). In 1960 Roman Jakobson, acknowledging Bühler as a source, extended the principle of Bühler and pointed out that a focus on the language product as a pleasurable end in itself was a necessary fourth addition to the triangular model of Bühler (l, 299). Jakobson added two other uses: metalanguage, in which language is used to talk about language, and phatic communication, the use of language merely to keep the channel open, as in introductions or some seemingly trivial conversational crutches.

Jakobson's basic model has been adopted by some important anthropologists. Indeed a whole issue of the *American Anthropologist* was devoted almost entirely to an application of this schema to anthropology (LXVI, 6, 1966). Especially the system advocated in this issue by Dell Hymes (22–29) has close parallels with the one proposed in this text. The first version of my system had already been written and copyrighted by that time. And at that time I was not aware of the work of Bühler or Jakobson. The convergence of the work of Aristotle, Gardiner, Bühler, Jakobson, Hymes, and my own is presented in the final column of Figure II, 2, later on in this chapter, in which several systems of aims of discourse are compared.

In other words, the language process seems to be capable of focusing attention on one of its own components as primary in a given situation, with the result that the other components function in a subordinate role. This concept occasionally presents difficulty to someone who says, "But aren't nearly all uses of language directed to hearers?" Except for private exclamations and a few other rare situations, the nature of language presupposes a decoder as the primary element in any communication situation.

In an important sense this is true. Propaganda, science, literature, even expressive utterances are all destined for receptors of some sort. Any theory of discourse must grant this as axiomatic. But the last three, as it were, forget the audience and let the discourse speak for itself. Science achieves its communication successfully by assuming a specific kind of audience and then focusing attention on that which is being talked about— some aspect of reality. Indeed, mechanical rules of scientific writing by some textbooks and some scientific periodicals even forbid the advertence to the addressee within the scientific article. The argument speaks for itself —"*res ipsa loquitur*," says an old legal cliché. Literature, likewise, assumes a reader or a theater-goer and then often seemingly forgets him in the discourse. The reader rarely intrudes into a sonnet, a drama, or even a novel. The addressee within the literary discourse, is, as a matter of fact, often fictional or even nonpersonal. This is even more true of expressive discourse, where, in fact, the addressee may even be missing (diaries, journals, exclamations). But in propaganda and similar kinds of discourse, the addressee is crucial and omnipresent, often explicitly. These variations in the communication framework are treated in the natures of the various types of discourse.

Another way of putting this concept of different dominating components is to suggest that the receptor of the language process is contacted immediately in persuasion and mediately in the other three uses of language. This is to say that different sorts of acceptances (or rejections)—to use Martin's terms (t, 33)—are envisioned in different uses of the communication process. In literary discourse the artifact is presented; in informative and scientific discourse the reality is represented; in expressive discourse the reaction of the self is displayed; but the acceptance of the audience is not directly elicited. Given the proper audience, if the literary structure is adequately presented, the aesthetic pleasure follows without being demanded. If the reality is adequately represented, scientific communication follows almost as a matter of form. If the self has been adequately expurgated, catharsis follows. In persuasion, on the contrary, the acceptance is implicitly or explicitly requested in the text.

As was outlined in Chapter 1, emphasis on the encoder or decoder gives *person* discourse, emphasis on reality to which reference is made gives *reference* discourse, and emphasis on the discourse product itself gives *product* discourse. Since *person* discourse can focus on either the encoder or the decoder, there are two kinds of person discourse; expressive, emphasizing the encoder, and persuasive, emphasizing the decoder. And *reference* discourse must be further subdivided into scientific, informative, and exploratory, as was also pointed out in Chapter 1. These aims of discourse, with some fairly typical examples, are graphically presented in Figure II, 1.

It must be stressed again that in each case there is a question of emphasis on one element, but this does not at all imply exclusion of the others. Failure to recognize this fact can result in a major stumbling block in establishing the aims of discourse.

A Crucial Caution: A Look at Overlap

As far as we know, no one who has ever studied the matter of aims of discourse ever pretended that aims do not overlap. The distinctions which we and others have been making are valid *theoretical* and *practical* distinctions. We have to separate the aims in order to study them in a systematic manner. Any science has to make such abstractions when it studies anything, and the study of discourse is no exception. But it is palpably clear to anyone who takes a look at actual discourses that very few *pure* aims of discourse exist. Persuasion as a matter of course incorporates information about the product, maybe even some valid scientific proof of its superiority, and it may use such literary techniques as rhythm, rhyme, and alliteration in its slogan. Literature incorporates expressive elements and thematic or persuasive components. Scientific prose includes persuasive aspects. The list could go on.

In many cases in these overlaps, one of the aims is dominant and

Figure II, 1: The Aims of Discourse

the other is a means. Information included in an advertisement is there to further the persuasion, so that persuasion is the primary aim. In some literature, it is obvious that persuasion is a secondary motif. Instances of one aim's subsuming another or several as means can be easily multiplied. And it is interesting to see what happens to information in a persuasive context, or to persuasion in a literary context, or to persuasion in an expressive context. This subordination of one or several aims to a dominant aim in a given discourse is the usual pattern that overlap takes.

Overlap of aim can also cause interference. In Macaulay's history, his scientific objectivity is distorted both by his too intrusive persuasive thesis and by his literary techniques of style and dramatic presentation (often rivaling the contemporary novel). His rhetorical and his literary powers make a scientific presentation of history almost impossible. In a converse situation, Sinclair Lewis's persuasive intrusions tend to spoil some of his later novels as literature. And Adlai Stevenson, in the 1952 presidential campaign tended too strongly to the informative and parascientific in his speeches to the extent that his effectiveness as a popular persuader was impaired. Similarly, many present-day campus protests are so expressive that their persuasive intent is not achieved.

Occasionally, it seems possible for a discourse to ride two horses at once, as it were. Some literary satire was also effective persuasion at the time of its appearance. Its survival beyond the situational context is a matter of its literary features in most instances. We read *Absalom and Achitophel* today not because of any great involvement in the contemporary political issues which it embodies. A few rare works can be instanced that seem to combine reference, persuasion, literature, and expression in a fairly proportional combination. *The Diary of a Young Girl,* presumably by Anne Frank, was seemingly written for a primarily expressive, almost therapeutic purpose. Its appearance caused a wave of anti-Nazi feeling in Europe and America. It was quite informative in many areas regarding the lives of the Jewish refugees. It was, and still is, taught in literature classes in high school and college. Apparently it combines all four aims—and it would be difficult to establish one as primary and the others as subordinate. However, this sort of work seems rare. It might be questioned if any great excellence in one aim can be normally achieved in coordination with another or several aims.

But overlap is a hard fact, and any attempt to ignore it can vitiate any theory of discourse. It might be more accurate, in fact, to speak of the scientific, the informative, the exploratory, the persuasive, the expressive, and the literary *aspects* of a discourse. Thus the components of any discourse which are ordered to explanation accompanied with demonstrative logical proof constitute the scientific aspects of the discourse, no matter what its dominant aim might be. Similarly, the components of any discourse which provide comprehensive and new facts to the reader constitute the informative aspects of a discourse, no matter what the dominant aim of the discourse might be. And the principle can be extended to all of the aims.

It is, therefore, quite proper to take a scientific piece of discourse and analyze it for its persuasive features or its expressive features, or to take a dominantly literary work and consider its informative or persuasive features. Kenneth Burke, whose aims of language have a close parallel to the system advocated here, performs interesting analyses of this sort. But the norms of scientific proof are not the norms of information or of persuasion or of literature or of expression. Consequently, it is important to abstract the different norms and consider them in isolation, even if, in practice, aims do overlap.

The establishment of these different norms is the major function of this book. The norms are distinct for the various aims of discourse and the aims are categorized as referential, persuasive, literary, and expressive. The referential are further subdivided into the scientific, the informative, and the exploratory, as was pointed out in Chapter I. The kinds of reference discourse are considered in Chapter III, persuasion is considered in Chapter IV, literature in Chapter V, and expression in Chapter VI. In each of the chapters the distinctive nature, the distinctive logic, the characteristic organizational patterns, and the stylistic features peculiar to the particular aim are discussed. These subdivisions of each chapter derive from the subdivisions of traditional rhetoric and seem very applicable to all kinds of discourse.

To the student accustomed to think only of scientific demonstration as being "logical," this use of the term in each area may seem too generous an extension. But there is need for such a general term; and there is some precedent. Traditionally the methods used to persuade in rhetoric were called "proofs," though none strictly proved anything in a scientific way. And traditionally, certain principles of thought, such as the principle of causality and the principle of finality, were also called "logical" though they also didn't demonstrate anything scientifically. Again, in a literary connection, Aristotle says in the *Poetics* that there must be nothing "illogical" (*alogon*) about the incidents in a plot (1454b 6); here again there is not a question of scientific demonstration. In another area, the modern generative rules of syntax are "logical," but are intended not to demonstrate something scientifically but rather to generate grammatically successful sentences. Careful logicians today write treatises on the logic of the imperative, the logic of the question, the logic of evaluation and so forth. Richards even defines logic as the art of or discipline of systematizing symbols (i, 16). Northrop takes a similar general view of logic (lo, 169–90; 328–98), as does Cassirer (lo, 159–81).

Consequently, the use of the term "logic" in this text will have this general meaning—as in fact, it often does in everyday language. Indeed, each of the examples (except the grammatical) given in the preceding paragraph is incorporated into the logics of one or the other of the aims or modes of discourse in the following chapters. Logics, in each case, will be sets of rules which govern sequential statements significant for a particular aim or mode.

The justification for the various subdivisions of reference discourse will be made in the chapter on *Reference Discourse*. And the justifications for the distinctions among all of the aims of discourse are made at great length in the ensuing chapters. Consequently, the communication framework method of distinguishing aims of discourse is adopted in the text as the basic model.

A Comparison of the Communication Aims of Discourse and Other Systems

The set of aims of discourse adopted in this text and based upon an application of the communications triangle is not at all necessarily competitive or in conflict with other systems of aims of discourse. In fact, different systems can often reinforce each other, as long as they are properly interpreted. And, certainly one of the best means to a proper interpretation of any system must be a consideration of the principle upon which it is based. An examination of these basic principles of division is revealing in that such an examination gives a strong suggestion as to the cluster of general characteristics which determine various aims of discourse.

The principles of division of some of the major groups surveyed in Section II above and the aims of discourse resulting from the application of these principles are charted in Figure II, 2. Some of the major groups outlined above seem to draw their division from empirical generalizations: these are the basic aims of language, regardless of what they are based on theoretically. Such groups are not charted. Whenever possible, similar aims are paralleled. Thus Aristotle's scientific, Cassirer's metaphysical, Morris' informative have much in common; in like manner, Aristotle's dialectical, Miller's opinion, Russell's questioning, and Kinneavy's exploratory have much in common.

It seems from a survey of the various principles of classification that several determinants are at work in the establishment of a given aim or discourse. A level of probability is involved (Aristotle), a stress on one or another capability of the language (Bühler, Jakobson), a social function (Miller), a syntactic differentiation (Russell), a faculty or component of mind (Reichenbach), a preponderance of reference or emotion (Richards). The chart, of course, only reproduces some of the groups. For example, most of the logical positivists somewhat parallel the Richards column.

It is clear also that despite the various principles of classification, the same rough classes reappear in most groupings. This leads to the

SCHOOL	Aristotle and Aquinas	Cassirer	Morris	Miller	Russell	Reichenbach	Richards	Bühler, Jakobson, Kinneavy
PRINCIPLE OF DIVISION	Level of Probability	Historical Sequence in Greece	Behavioral Reactions of Animals to Stimuli	Socio-Psychological Motives for Communications	Grammar (Kinds of Sentences)	Faculty Addressed to	Proportions of Reference and Emotion	Component of Communication Process Stressed
	Scientific—certain	Metaphysical—representative of the world	Informative	Informative—to increase uniformity of information	Informative—declarative	Communicative (thoughts to be believed)	Scientific (Pure reference)	Reference Informative
	Dialectical—probable		Valuative	Opinion—to increase uniformity of opinions	Questioning—interrogative			Scientific Exploratory
	Rhetorical—seemingly probable	Pragmatic—practical use by Sophists	Incitive	Status Change	Imperative—imperative	Promotive (actions to be accomplished)	Rhetorical (mixed reference and emotion)	Persuasive
	Poetic—internally probable		Systemic	Emotive	Expressive (of emotion)—exclamatory	Suggestive (emotions to be aroused)	Poetic (pure emotion)	Literary
		Mythological—expressive of aspirations						Expressive
		Interjectional						

Figure II, 2: A Comparison of Some Systems of Aims of Discourse hypothesis that reference discourse, for example, is characterized by a high level of probability, a declarative sentence orientation, an address to a rational mind, an emphasis on the capability of language to represent reality, and a high degree of strict "reference" and consequent low emotion. What this means, in terms of a theory of discourse, is that these various approaches to aims of discourse are not at all inconsistent with one another but actually reinforce one another by looking at the same kind of discourse from different points of view. A more complete picture of the reality thus emerges. For this reason, tolerance of all points of view is to be advocated— with some limitations to be made shortly. In other words, communication framework, level of probability, basic grammar, social function, and preponderance of reference or emotion have been used as criteria for determination of nature. These factors recur in each chapter. In addition, other criteria might have been used. One could determine the aims of discourse by the kinds of logic which they embody, or the kinds of organizational patterns which they follow, or their variant styles.

In an important sense, then, the view of aims of language taken in this book attempts to synthesize some quite different approaches to language. In a discourse approach to this problem, it seemed appropriate to consider as primary a framework based upon a comprehensive view of the language process. For that reason the communications triangle was adopted. It is also able to absorb the other approaches more readily than some others could.

Another reason why the communications framework seems more serviceable is because of its neutrality. Unlike some of the other systems, it doesn't usually carry connotations of the superiority of one or another aim of discourse. Aristotle's (and even more Plato's) norm of probability sometimes seems to imply a superiority of more probability over less probability, and the consequent superiority of science over dialectic and of both over rhetoric. And the logical positivist norm of referential-emotive has often been interpreted as meaning the superiority of referential over emotive discourse; this is so true that the emotive has been called nonsensical and meaningless by some people using this distinction (mainly scientists, of course). And Morris' norm of behavioral reactions to stimuli carries with it the implication that the informative and valuative are only instrumental to the incitive and systemic. Indeed, in Morris, it is difficult to consider any but the final use (systemic) as an *aim in itself* at all.

In the communications framework, no use of language is considered superior to any other. Information is a good use of language, so is science, and so is persuasion. Simple expression is as good in itself as science. Each achieves a different *and* valid purpose. To achieve a specific purpose a specific aim of language must be used. Persuasion is bad science, but good rhetoric; and science may be good reference discourse but bad literature.

This does mean that one aim may not employ other aims in a subordinate role. Persuasion is used continually in literary structures; thus Iago's successive persuasive machinations structure the plot in *Othello*. And information as theme is also used in nearly all literary structures. Conversely, persuasion uses literary techniques of rhyme, rhythm, imagery structures, and the like for its own purposes.

A few additional reservations are in order. Otherwise a blanket endorsement of all views might be read into this synthesis. Although there are valuable elements in all of the systems analyzed, there are a few serious drawbacks which might briefly be mentioned.

Though Aristotle's divisions are very useful, there are several limitations. His notion of scientific discourse makes no provision for informative discourse, as several critics have pointed out. Second, his concept of science as possessed of absolute certainty is too rigid a norm to be adhered to today. Third,—and this is the most severe restriction—Aristotle's concept of dialectic confused two very distinct aims: the exploration for truth and the successful defeat of an opponent in debate. Only the first is really reference discourse normally. Finally, Aristotle made no provision for expressive discourse.

The framework of Morris does have some parallels with the other systems, but there are two important divergences. His "evaluative" discourse has some affinity to dialectical, opinion-uniformity, questioning, and exploratory uses of language; but it is also quite different from them in important respects. He includes poetry, politics, and rhetoric under this category— inclusions which Aristotle, Miller and Russell would deny. In fact, the basic principle of classification of Morris is suspect. Nor is it really different from his principle of classification of modes (an overlap he acknowledges, s, 96).

Reichenbach's faculty approach, though useful, can be pushed to indefensible positions. Actually, this term used to characterize his approach may conjure up corpses of faculty psychologies, though it is not intended to. But there does seem to be a danger of a compartmentalization of the ego which such a theory might lead one into. I don't believe Reichenbach has been guilty of this—in fact, Reichenbach's concern with aims of discourse is only a tangential interest in his published materials.

Richards' principle of classification is probably the one most frequently employed in discussions of the function of propositions or language, and the like. And it is certainly a useful criterion. Yet, theoretically it is as much a matter of "what" is referred to as it is of "why" something is being talked about. And the failure to distinguish between poetry and other emotive uses of language becomes critical in discussion of the nature of literature. Similarly, the large middle category of rhetoric (mixed reference and emotion) is unwieldly and must include many weird companions.

A few remarks on the general classifications suggested by the chart seem appropriate. At the first level, some distinguish science from exploration, but not all do. Nor does anyone other than the author distinguish science from information, though some mention one or the other. Yet it seems crucial to separate information from scientific and both of these from exploratory discourse, although all three can be included in a large heading (reference discourse).

Second, it is important to distinguish a literary use of language from a simple expressive use. Some, of course, include one in the other (either way). Yet it is clear that emotive language is not limited to poetry or expressive uses of language. Certainly persuasion becomes very emotional at time. And emotion is not entirely excluded from exploratory discourse, e.g. Plato's dialogues.

EXERCISES

1. Take specific examples of similar "content," oriented to various aims and analyze the differences:
   a. Contrast Churchill's persuasive "A Miracle at Dunkirk" with the informative *New York Times* reports, May 27–June 4, 1940, with the scientific (?) Michael Lewis, *The History of the British Navy*, pp. 240–42, or *The Navy of Britain*, pp. 31–32.
   b. Compare and contrast Kenneth Roberts' scientific *March Against Quebec* with literary *Arundel* or *Rabble in Arms* (about Benedict Arnold); or historical *Black Magic* with literary *Lydia Bailey*. Any similar contrasts can be used.
   c. Contrast the battle of Waterloo in Churchill, Thackeray (*Vanity Fair*), and in a French historian, if available.
   d. Contrast the treatments of the conquest of India in Macaulay's *Lord Clive* and in Rajindra Singh, *History of the Indian Army*, pp. 70–72 or Major Mohammed Ibrahim Qureshi, *The First Punjabis, 1759–1956* (for similar encounters).
   e. Get a historical narrative about a city, a treatment in a novel, a chamber of commerce blurb, and an enthusiastic (or the opposite) letter to the editor about a city. Contrast the treatments.
2. Take an issue of a magazine, or some of the articles, or a newspaper, etc., and classify the articles by dominant aims or modes. Make some generalizations about the magazine or the newspaper.
3. Take a piece of obviously persuasive discourse and abstract the scientific and informative components included in it (e.g., Roosevelt's "First Inaugural Address").

4. Take a historical anthology of English or American literature, and classify some of the questionable inclusions by aim (e.g., Lincoln's "Gettysburg Address," Franklin's *Autobiography*, *The Declaration of Independence*). Give detailed evidence from the texts to support your classifications. Discuss the arguments for and against inclusion of such material in a literary text.

5. Take a specific piece of scientific or informative discourse and translate it into a piece of persuasive discourse for a specific audience. Make other similar translations from one aim to another.

6. Analyze the uses to which you put language throughout a day or week by classifying your various uses of language into aims (e.g., reading the news stories in the paper-informative; listening to ads on television-persuasive; going to a play-literary). Determine the percentage of time you devote to each basic aim. Compare or contrast these proportions to the time devoted to the various aims in your high school or college English program.

7. Take two or several of the various approaches to the aims of discourse discussed in the text and contrast and evaluate their treatments (e.g., Morris vs. Aristotle, Richards vs. Whatmough, etc.).

8. Relate the liberal arts tradition to the aims of discourse. Does a stress on the aims of discourse constitute a continuation of the liberal arts tradition?

9. Take the current copy of *TV Guide* and classify the programs for a week according to basic aims. Make some generalizations after your classifications are complete. If possible, compare these to a similar week on the BBC.

   Follow the programs for an evening or two and see how the percentages are affected by the actual time devoted to commercials, preview advertising of upcoming programs, and the like.

10. Take an issue of your local newspaper and consider the proportion of space dedicated to each of the basic aims. If some articles heavily overlap in basic aim, as a column or an editorial may, give fractional credits.

    If possible, contrast two newspapers from different-sized cities or different cultures (French-American, etc.).

11. Contrast the styles of Bertrand Russell in one of his scientific works with one of his exploratory or one of his literary works (e.g., *An Inquiry into Meaning and Truth* with one of his essays on education or marriage or religion and one of his short stories).

    Any other writer will do: e.g., Camus (*The Rebel, The Plague*), Sartre (*Being and Nothingness* and *The Reprieve*).

    Take limited sections for a corpus so that detailed evidence can be given for your assertions.

BIBLIOGRAPHY AND FOOTNOTE REFERENCES

Aristotle. "Rhetoric." Tr. W. Rhys Roberts. In *Aristotle.* New York: Modern Library, 1954 (r).

Britton, Karl. *Communication: A Philosophical Theory of Language.* New York: Harcourt, Brace & World, Inc., 1939 (c).

Bühler, Karl. "Die Axiomatik der Sprachwissenshaften." *Kant-Studien,* XXXVIII (1933), 19–90 (a).

Burrows, Alvina, *et al. They All Want to Write.* 3rd Edition. New York: Holt, Rinehart and Winston, Inc., 1964 (t).

Campbell, George. *The Philosophy of Rhetoric.* New York: Harper & Brothers, 1885 (p).

Cassirer, Ernst. *An Essay on Man.* New Haven: Yale University Press, 1944 (e).

————. *The Logic of the Humanities.* Tr. Clarence Smith Howe. New Haven: Yale University Press, 1961 (lo).

Croce, Benedetto. *Aesthetic.* Tr. Douglas Ainslie. New York: The Macmillan Company, 1922 (a).

Diamond, T. S. *The History and Origin of Languages.* New York: The Philosophical Society, 1959 (h).

Doob, Leonard W. *Communication In Africa: A Search for Boundaries.* New Haven: Yale University Press, 1961 (c).

Fries, Charles Carpenter. *The Structure of English.* New York: Harcourt, Brace & World, Inc., 1952 (s).

Gardiner, Alan Henderson. *The Theory of Speech and Language.* Oxford: The Clarendon Press, 1951 (t).

Hayakawa, S. I. *Language in Thought and Action.* New York: Harcourt, Brace, & World, Inc., 1949 (l).

Hjelmslev, Louis. *Prolegomena to a Theory of Language.* Tr. Francis J. Whitfield. Baltimore: Waverley Press, 1953 (p).

Jakobson, Roman. "Linguistics and Poetics." In *Essays on the Language of Literature.* Seymour Chatman and Samuel R. Levin, eds. Boston: Houghton Mifflin Company, 1967. Pp. 296–322 (l).

Kenyon, John S. "Cultural Levels and Functional Varieties of English." In Harold B. Allen, *Reading in Applied Linguistics.* New York: Appleton-Century-Crofts, Inc., 1958 (c).

La Drière, J. Craig. "Rhetoric and 'Merely Verbal' Art." *English Institute Essays, 1948.* Ed. D. A. Robertson, Jr. New York: Columbia University Press, 1949. Pp. 123–53 (r).

Macaulay, Thomas B. *The Complete Writings of Lord Macaulay.* Vol. II. Ed. Henry D. Sedgwick, Jr. New York: Houghton, Mifflin Company, 1960 (c).

Malinowski, Branislaw. *Coral Gardens and their Magic.* 2 Vols. New York: American Book Company, 1935 (c).

Martin, Richard M. *Toward A Systematic Pragmatics.* Studies in Logic. L. E. J. Brouwer, E. W. Beth, and A. Heyting, eds. Amsterdam: North-Holland Publishing Company, 1959 (t).

McKeon, Richard. "Aristotle's Conception of Language and the Arts of Language." In Ronald S. Crane, ed., *Critics and Criticism.* Chicago: University of Chicago, 1952. Pp. 176–231 (a).

————. "Rhetoric and Poetic in the Philosophy of Aristotle." In Elder Olson, ed., *Aristotle's Poetics and English Literature.* Chicago: University of Chicago Press, 1965. Pp. 201–236 (r).

Miller, George A. *Language and Communication.* New York: McGraw-Hill Book Company, 1951 (l).

Morris, C. W. *Signs, Language and Behavior.* Englewood Cliffs, N. J.: Prentice-Hall, Inc., 1946 (s).

Northrop, F. S. C. *The Logic of the Sciences and the Humanities.* New York: The Macmillan Company, 1948 (l).

Ogden, C. K., and I. A. Richards. *The Meaning of Meaning.* London: K. Paul, Trench, Trubner and Company, Ltd., 1945 (m).

Olson, Elder. *The Poetry of Dylan Thomas.* Chicago: University of Chicago Press, 1954 (p).

Quine, Willard Van Orman. *Word and Object.* Cambridge, Mass.: M.I.T. Press, 1960 (w).

Reinchenbach, Hans. *Experience and Prediction: An Analysis of the Foundations and Structure of Knowledge.* Chicago: University of Chicago Press, 1938 (e).

————. *Introduction to Symbolic Logic.* New York: The Macmillan Company, 1947 (i).

————. *The Rise of Scientific Philosophy.* Berkeley, Calif.: University of California Press, 1958 (r).

————. *The Theory of Probability.* Tr. Ernest H. Hutten and Maria Reichenbach. Berkeley, Calif.: University of California Press, 1949 (t).

Richards, I. A. *How to Read a Page.* London: K. Paul, Trench, Trubner and Company, 1943 (h).

————. *Interpretation in Teaching.* New York: Harcourt, Brace and World, Inc., 1958 (i).

————. *Principles of Criticism.* London: K. Paul, Trench, Trubner and Company, 1925 (p).

Russell, Bertrand. *An Inquiry into Meaning and Truth.* London: George Allen and Unwin Ltd., 1956 (m).

————. *Human Knowledge: Its Scope and Limits.* New York: Simon and Schuster, Inc., 1948 (h).

Uhlenbeck, E. M. "An Appraisal of Transformational Theory." *Lingua,* XII (1963), 1–18 (a).

Urban, Wilbur Marshall. *Language & Reality.* New York: The Macmillan Company, 1939 (1).

Whatmough, Joshua. *Language: A Modern Synthesis.* New York: New American Library of World Literature, Inc., 1956 (1).

————. *Poetic, Scientific, and Other Forms of Discourse.* Berkeley, Calif.: University of California Press, 1956 (p).

Werner, Heinz. *On Expressive Language.* Worcester, Mass.: Clark University Press, 1955 (e).

Wimsatt, W. K., and M. Beardsley. *The Verbal Icon.* Lexington: University of Kentucky Press, 1954. Sections "The Intentional Fallacy," 3–18, "The Affective Fallacy," 21–39 (v).

Wittgenstein, L. *Philosophical Investigations.* Tr. G. E. M. Anscombe. Oxford: Blackwell, 1958 (p).

————. *Tractatus Logico-Philosophicus.* Tr. D. F. Feors and B. I. McGreenness. New York: The Humanities Press, 1961 (t).

3

Reference Discourse

Introduction and Terminology

Introduction

CHOICE OF ANTHOLOGIZED ESSAY

The essay, "Effective Use of Statistics," which is anthologized in the Appendix, was chosen to illustrate reference discourse for several reasons. It is a possibly nontypical conjunction of all three kinds of reference discourse and it is not devoid of a little nonintrusive persuasion. It is the second chapter of a textbook on statistics. After a brief introduction on "Common Sense and Statistics," the chapter pursues its main purpose, which is to inform the neophyte in statistics of the varying uses of statistics in the military, the social, biological, and physical sciences, and even the humanities. This it does by an illustrative survey of these areas in a section of the chapter which has been deleted (pages 19–28). Then it gives three detailed examples of statistical studies, one on the history of mental diseases (29–46), one on vitamins and endurance (46–56), and one on artificial rain-making (56–62). A small conclusion to the chapter follows (62–63).[1] For the purposes of our analysis, the introduction, one of the detailed studies, and the conclusion have been excerpted.

By and large, the main aim of Wallis' and Roberts' chapter is informative. But, because they are summarizing a scientific report, the main scientific components of the experiment on vitamins have been retained. And because the vitamin experiment was precisely that—an experiment—

---

1 Pages given here refer to the original. From now on any quotations from the anthologized sections will follow the paragraph numeration given in the Appendix.

part of the summary records the problems of the erection of a workable hypothesis. As such the discourse in that part of the chapter tends to be typical of some kinds of exploratory discourse. Fortuitously, therefore, the anthologized selection incorporates an interesting amalgam of informative, scientific, and exploratory discourses, the three kinds of reference discourse. Again, partly because the book is a textbook, the authors are at least somewhat interested in selling statistics to the new student—whence the little strand of persuasion.

In addition to the essay's being a happy confluence of several aims, it also vividly illustrates some of the problems of the logics of these aims. Thus, some of the basic issues in inductive reasoning are seen in clear focus; unfortunately, deduction is not crucial in the essay. But the logics of information and of exploration are also clearly posed.

It is hoped that these features of the essay more than compensate for some of the obvious disadvantages of the selections. Chief among these is the fact that the excerpt is only part of a book, and is, consequently, an incomplete discourse. Second, the scientific report is obviously something of a popularization. "It will be impractical to recapitulate the original studies in full detail," remark Wallis and Roberts. This sort of impracticality was also acutely felt by this author in search for an adequate sample to be used to illustrate scientific discourse. After several months of a frustrating and vain quest for a piece of strict scientific prose that would at once be intelligible to the general student for whom this book is intended and that would sacrifice nothing to scientific integrity, I am inclined to agree with J. Robert Oppenheimer, who maintains that the language of science is now "almost impossible to translate" into conventional lay language (Tannenbaum, c, 581).

Oppenheimer's view is seconded by several others (cf. Kuhn, s, 20). Bertrand Russell, with characteristic optimism, takes a different point of view when he maintains that his philosophic works can be read by any educated layman, though his mathematical works cannot. However, I would have high admiration for the "average layman" who could nonchalantly take on *An Inquiry into Meaning and Truth*. Possibly some modern histories which are strictly scientific can be still read by the average educated man, and there are a few beginning sciences which are still nontechnical enough to be read by this same mythical reader. By and large, however, scientific discourse is read by scholars in the same or allied fields and has retreated from the popular world—and this is not necessarily lamentable. In his own field, the average English undergraduate major encounters very little rigid scientific writing, with the possible exception of some embryonic linguistic systems. Nor, conversely, is this same student expected to write on the level of strict scientific discourse either. Consequently, the nontechnical rendition of science here reproduced has at least the merit of representing the type of reading and the level of writing which the users of this book can be expected to engage in.

Finally, it should be understood that neither this anthologized selection nor any other in the book is proposed as a model for imitation. It is offered as a corpus for analysis. I hold no brief for the the style of Wallis and Roberts; I have read many texts which I consider structurally and stylistically superior, but I have also read many, many worse.

Purposes of this Chapter

With the anthologized essay as a focus, then, the characteristics of the various kinds of reference discourse will be examined. Scientific, informative, and exploratory discourse are each considered in isolation, though the anthologized essay combines the three. The abstraction of the problems of each in isolation is necessary, for they are separate problems. This is a common scientific procedure; thus the laws of gravitation and those of air friction are considered separately though in our atmosphere a falling body is subjected at the same time to both forces.

It is hoped that a careful presentation of the theory will enable the student to analyze reference discourse and to produce some such discourse himself. Consequently, the exercises at the end of the chapter provide analytical and original practice for the student.

The decision to treat scientific discourse before either informative or exploratory discourse was prompted by the fact that the logics of information and of exploration are much more understandable against the full background of scientific logic than they would be if treated prior to the latter. Similarly, parts of the logic of persuasion are more intelligible if viewed as watered-down versions of some aspects of scientific logic than they would be if handled in isolation. Consequently, the decision to consider reference discourse before persuasion, and in reference discourse to consider science before information is pedagogically motivated. Psychologically and epistemologically, exploration usually precedes information and both precede scientific demonstration. From the same standpoints, there seem to be no compelling reasons why the treatment of reference discourse should precede expressive or literary or persuasive discourse; indeed one might make a case for the opposite.

Terminology

The use of the term "reference" to cover the three kinds of discourse herein envisaged is somewhat of a departure. It is true that "referential" is used by some writers as opposed to emotive (cf. Urban, 1, 68 ff., and Cassirer, e, 30), and others use "refer" to define the scientific or informative (e.g., Richards). But because few make the distinctions among scientific, informative, and exploratory and then include these in a large category which is differentiated from other uses of language, there has been no general term applied with any consistency to this sort of discourse.

Some implicit attempts have suggested general terms. Some philosophers interested in differentiating discourse which can be scientifically meaningful from discourse not subject to scientific norms have distinguished between propositions which are verifiable (and therefore scientifically meaningful or determinate) and propositions which are nonverifiable by scientific norms (and therefore scientifically meaningless or indeterminate or nonsensical).

Tarski, Ayer, and Carnap are examples of such thinkers (cf. Carnap, lo, 86). The scientifically meaningful propositions are then usually divided into those which can be verified empirically and those which can be verified by pure logic. For these writers five basic kinds of propositions occur (considered from the standpoint of verifiability) : F-true, F-false, L-true, L-false, and meaningless. As it happens, my current pen is blue. Therefore, each of the five kinds of propositions could be exemplified as follows: "My pen is pink" (F–false) ; "My pen is either yellow or not yellow" (L–true) ; "My pen is not a pen" (L–false, contradictory) ; "I love blue pens" (scientifically meaningless, emotive) ; "My pen is blue" (F–true). More or less similar distinctions are drawn up by many philosophers, scientists, high school and college textbook writers.

That these distinctions have such a hardy tradition commends their consideration. Because they will be referred to many times in the remainder of this text, their delineation can serve several useful purposes. In the first place, it seems clear that the range of "verifiable" discourse is certainly included in the range of "reference" discourse. However, to attempt to limit "reference" discourse to propositions which can be either empirically or logically proven true or false is to rule out much that is useful in exploratory and even in scientific discourse.

Thus, questions are ruled out, for a question is neither true nor false. Yet much exploratory work consists in asking intelligent questions. Again, statements about hypothetical models, for example the system of longitudinal and latitudinal lines, can be verified neither by logic nor by fact; but they are certainly scientifically useful and meaningful in some sense, as Toulmin points out (Toulmin, p, 135 ff.). And they certainly, in some way, "refer" to our geographic world.

Consequently, "reference" must be enlarged beyond verifiability to include at least discourse about this kind of construct. Therefore, some senses of the term "opinion" are not ruled out of reference discourse. Nor are most senses of the term "dialectical." The term "judgment" has so many meanings that I shall normally avoid it. It means something very different in traditional logic from its rather idiosyncratic meaning in Kant; and in modern logic "judgment" is spoken of in exactly the opposite sense of something which is not verifiable. An "evaluation," which in some writers means something nonverifiable, is sometimes used in a sense similar to "truth-judgments" by logicians who speak of the "truth-value" of propositions. Again, as the section on the scientific assertion and the considerations of evaluation in Volume II will attempt to show, some evaluations can be scientifically meaningful, even in the sense of "verifiable."

Therefore "reference" can be best understood as comprising scientific, informative, and exploratory discourse. And it is the discourse as a whole, rather than individual propositions, which is considered referential. Quine has stressed this point, and I believe the warning is salutary (f, 42). "Reference" discourse, therefore, comprises these three types of discourse and excludes persuasive, literary, and expressive discourse. It is clear that all three of these latter include much reference to reality, but the reference to subject matter is secondary is each case, whereas in reference discourse it is primary.

The Nature of Referential Discourse

The Nature of Scientific Discourse

TERMINOLOGY

The full definition of scientific discourse will only emerge at the end of this entire chapter, when the nature, logic, structure, and style of scientific discourse has been differentiated generically from persuasive, literary, and expressive discourse and specifically from informative and exploratory discourse. Two introductory cautions must be made about the nature of discourse which purports to be scientific in aim. One caution concerns the "scientific" productions of those who differ from us in time and the other concerns the "scientific" productions of those who differ from us in space.

From the historical point of view, without at all demeaning modern science, it must not be forgotten that we are standing, as Newton once remarked, "on the shoulders of giants," and though we are justly proud of modern science's attainments, yet they have been made possible only through the efforts of some whom we must now disclaim in our attempts to progress. At the same time, it might be properly humbling to reflect that if history pursues its same track, future science may in like manner look upon our own contemporary exploits as childish, amateurish, folklorish, and mythical. In consequence, in the large framework envisaged here, a view must be taken of scientific discourse broad enough to include, at least in a generic way, the attempts of previous eras to represent the universe. Therefore, some myths, legends, folklore, religious cosmologies, and past metaphysics can be valid corpora of scientific discourse.

Similarly, modern anthropology suggests that any given culture's view of science or of a branch of science is often a culturally restricted notion. The term "ethnoscience" has been coined to refer to a given culture's view of science (cf. Sturtevant, s, 99 ff.). For example, it is naive and dangerous to attempt to describe or evaluate all current attempts to make sense of the world by the norms, say, of American positivism.

The corollary of a view of scientific discourse large enough to include all ethnoscience is that, for instance, Russian lexicography, French existentialism, Subanum medicine, Esquimo physics, German literary theory, and Buddhist theology are also bona fide specimens of scientific discourse. This does not mean that all past or cultural scientific discourses are equally true or scientifically relevant in a given situation. It only means that they are all discourse of a certain kind, having in common a serious attempt to represent the universe and to demonstrate, somehow or other, the validity of such a representation.

Of course, many of the terms which are on occasion synonymous with science (and information and exploration) are also frequently ambiguous; i. e., they can refer to discourse which makes no pretense to reporting reality or proving anything. A few other terms are sometimes used in ancillary disciplines which can be synonymous with scientific discourse. In speech textbooks, *demonstrative* speeches are frequently distinguished from informative, persuasive, convincing, and entertaining speeches. In this text, no attempt will be made to preserve the distinction between reference to "process" (often accompanied by a model or illustration) and a speech reporting an event or an idea. Informative or scientific discourse, as here used, can be discourse which refers indiscriminately to process, event, structure, idea, etc. If one were to be consistent, the preservation of this distinction would necessitate the creation of other coordinate and equally justifiable distinctions.

Demonstration, as a process of proof, has a much longer history than the term "demonstrative" speech. The logic of *demonstration,* in the sense of effective proof for a hypothesis, has for a long time been distinguished from the logic of *discovery.* The tradition of such a distinction extends back to Bacon, Descartes, Galileo, and Newton, and is still a very live issue (cf. Carmichael, 1, 2 ff., 15 ff.; Hutchins and Adler, g, 227 ff.). It is the basic distinction between scientific and exploratory discourse. "Demonstration," in this sense, is synonymous with "confirmation" and "justification" (Kuhn, s, 8–9). *Technical writing* or *technical reports* are terms often used in college courses and in research organizations. Normally, this type of writing is both informative and scientific.

Research, as a process, is exploratory, not scientific. But the research report can be an informative paper about research in progress or the reporting of the definitive findings of an experiment and the justification of its findings. *Research papers,* in some textbooks, are occasionally distinguished from personal analyses (for example, in literary criticism courses), the distinction being that the first sort of assignment involves the use of the library, whereas in personal analysis the student faces the autonomous text and comes to his own conclusions without the assistance of secondary services. Though the distinction seems to have a useful pedagogical purpose, nothing will be made of it in this text. As a rule, in the processes of exploration and achieving scientific finality, the restriction of the term "research" to reporting the findings of others seems arbitrary. Nor does the alternative suggestion that one should work in a scientific vacuum seem generally helpful, though it may be temporarily useful as a reaction to a slavish reportorial concept of "research" encountered not infrequently in "controlled" term paper assignments, for example.

The formal essay is sometimes viewed as the equivalent of scientific discourse—though the term is less used now than it was thirty years ago. Unfortunately, the formal essay was never clearly defined in terms of aims, and the formal essayists of the "literary" tradition (e.g. Swift, Hazlitt, Carlyle, Newman, and Arnold) rarely wrote scientific prose in the sense to be defined below. Normally they wrote exploratory or persuasive pieces. The informal essay of the literary tradition (Lamb, Wilde, Thurber) usually *was* a literary essay, though occasionally it was an expressive essay. In educationist circles the informal or personal essay nearly always became an expressive essay, often aformal and intentionally irresponsible.

Expository writing is the most frequent term for informative or scientific discourse currently in use in English departments and texts. As such, it is normally juxtaposed to "creative writing," i.e., the writing of original literary compositions. Though widespread, the usage has its deplorable aspects. First, it fosters the impression that only literary writing is creative. Secondly, it confuses a mode of discourse with an aim of discourse. Exposition, as opposed to narration, is a matter of what is said, not why it is said; the nature of the reference, not the purpose of the reference, constitutes something as expository. Again, expository writing is also, in such contexts, often opposed to narrative writing; the implication in such cases can only be that narrative writing can not be scientific, only literary. For these reasons and others, in this text "expository" will refer only to a mode of discourse. In the sequel, whenever there seems to be danger of misinterpretation, "scientific" will be used for the desired referent, even at the risk of seeming repetitious.

THE GENERAL CHARACTERISTICS
OF SCIENTIFIC DISCOURSE

The Unity of Science

It has been questioned by some authorities that there is such a thing
as "science," in the singular, at all. There are only "sciences," maintains
this position (cf. Scheffler, a, 7 ff.). But a long tradition and several important modern movements, for example, the imposing list of scientists writing
in the *Encyclopedia for Unified Science*, lend support to the opposite view.
The view that there is some kind of unity to scientific discourse is of course
axiomatic to this text, and the axiom is based on the aforementioned tradition and these modern movements.

The Abstractions of Science

This does not at all deny that the various sciences are not distinct in
crucial respects from one another or that there is not a need for many
sciences. Indeed, one of the differentiations of one science from another is
the unique methodology of investigation by which each particular science
analyzes and evaluates some aspect of reality. This particular method of
investigation allows conclusions to be reached which are viewed as more or
less certain and which the methods of investigation of other sciences cannot
attain. Each science, consequently, by reason of its own axioms and methodologies, can analyze only a limited range of realities, and of these realities,
it can consider only a limited number of aspects. The type of reality which a
science can examine was traditionally called the *material object* of the
science; the limited aspects of this object which the science abstracts in its
considerations were called the *formal object* of the science. The sum total
of the axioms, and the investigative and demonstrative procedures of the
science is often called the methodology, the dialectic, or the medium of
analysis of the science (Maritain, i, 105–106; Olson, c, 551–53).

By way of example, a literary critic, a psychologist, and a historian
might each approach the same material object, *The Grapes of Wrath* by
John Steinbeck. Each scientist would then consider the novel from one
limited aspect: the literary critic might consider the symbolism in the novel
as a structural technique; the psychologist might view some of the characters
as illustrations of classical neuroses or psychoses; and the historian might
view the novel as an accurate or distorted picture of a small period in
American history of the 1930's. These aspects would constitute the formal
objects under investigation. The literary critic would chart and explicate
image and symbol recurrences, analyze the relations of these patterns to
other patterns, and pronounce upon the propriety of such relations. The
final evaluation constitutes the terminus of the literary dialectic and it is an
assertion about literature, which should be fairly certain if the procedure

has been conscientious. The psychologist could point out characteristic symptoms of specific psychoses, analyze character actions and reactions, and pronounce upon the presence or absence of psychological disease with a comparable level of competence and certainty, and this statement would be valid psychological evaluation. The historian could compare the panoramic view of Oklahoma and California given in the novel with the actual historical data and pronounce upon coincidence or noncoincidence in a historical pronouncement as valid as the two preceding.

The reporting of these final affirmations and of the procedures which justified them would constitute typical instances of scientific discourse. Ordinarily, the literary critic, the psychologist, and the historian would report their findings in rather esoteric publications, such as *Modern Fiction Studies, American Imago,* and *The Mississippi Valley Historical Review,* which only professors of literature, psychology, and history would normally consult. At more bourgeois levels of popularity, one might encounter their findings in *The Saturday Review,* a freshman reader anthology, or even in summarized form in a textbook.

Each science, therefore, gives only an abstracted and partial picture of a limited chunk of the universe (Carnap, lo, 208 ff., esp. 215 ff.). And the abstraction is usually at a certain stratified level in a full scheme of the sciences. Each stratum accepts as axioms which it does not question some principles which might be analyzed and furnished by another science (Toulmin, p, 81 ff.). The full report on any given phase of reality, say *The Grapes of Wrath,* is never complete. But the reports of the literary critic, the sociologist, the psychologist, the linguist, etc., enable us to know more about the reality than the restricted conclusions of any one science. A grave danger is the application of one methodology to the establishing of conclusions which should be reached by another methodology. A psychologist, for example, is not allowed, because of his inherent limitations *as a psychologist,* to arrive at judgments as to the literary worth of a novel. Unfortunately, some do. And the number of literary critics who pronounce upon psychological validity is probably even greater.

The necessarily abstract and limited nature of scientific discourse has been the occasion of its having been repudiated as furnishing reliable knowledge about reality by some modern existentialists (Sartre, c. 10, 148, and *passim*). No pretense is made here for the sole validity of scientific knowledge. However, the process of abstracting to consider the parts of something separately seems to be indigenous to the human mind—even an existential emotional and intuitive apprehension of reality is abstract since it abstracts at least from the components considered rationally. In any case, whether scientific abstractions are ultimately good or bad is here a moot point. Abstraction is a fact in all scientific discourse and an analysis of the nature of scientific discourse should point it out.

Some of the abstractions made both by Wallis and Roberts in their own chapters on statistics and by the scientists in the included study of vitamins are clearly or at least implicitly indicated in the anthologized selection. At one level of abstraction, it might be said that the material object of the statistician is the kind of reality which can be investigated by their particular methodology (statistical techniques). Some of these material objects are indicated in the deleted section which considers application of statistics in the military, and the social, biological, physical, and humanities areas. In each case, particularly in the humanities, it is implicit that there are some kinds of investigations which are not amenable to statistical treatment. Statistics, therefore, must abstract from these "material objects." Further, even the material objects which are so amenable can sometimes be investigated by nonstatistical means. Statistics abstracts from these treatments.

Of course, a chapter on the "Effective Use of Statistics" abstracts from the misuse of statistics, a problem to which the third chapter in Wallis and Roberts' book is devoted. Similarly, the history of statistics and their uses, the theory of statistics, and similar topics are also abstracted from in the chapter under consideration.

Even more abstract, in the sense of considering only limited aspects of a reality, is the treatment of the scientific analysis of the vitamin study reported by Wallis and Roberts. They stress some of the abstractions: the abstraction from combat activity, from the separate effects of vitamin C and B complex, from a really valid sample of soldiers. Other abstractions might be mentioned: from other vitamin presences or absences, from additional food or drug or other supplements (e.g. leadership, counseling, group dynamics), from many of the psychological dimensions of the problem, from other geographic conditions (not of 8,310 ft. elevation, etc.), from food components other than calories or vitamins (e.g., minerals), and so on.

It is obvious that, with all of these factors not considered, the practical applications of the conclusions of the vitamin study are severely restricted. Any scientific conclusion is limited, in its existential reinsertion into the real situation, by the abstractions from reality which it has made in the scientific process.

The Assertions of Science

The abstractions of science are affirmed to be relevant to reality, that is to say they are *asserted* as *referential*. The kind of referential assertion, however, which science is qualified to make has been the subject of much controversy, particularly in this century. Because this controversy is currently invading even the field of scholarly writing in English, both in linguistics and in literature, a somewhat disproportionate treatment of this problem will be given here. In linguistics for example, there are those in high places who maintain that only descriptive or historical assertions are scientific; they denigrate "theoretical" and "prescriptive" (i.e. evaluative) positions. In literature, there are comrade thinkers who maintain that the business of the literary scholar is either historical, or classificatory, or analytical, but not evaluative (cf. Frye in Thorpe, a, 58–61).

In practice, scientific statements of different kinds are made by many different disciplines. Geographers, geologists, sociologists, physicists, chemists, linguists, literary analysts, for example, all make *descriptive* statements detailing the characteristics respectively of South Africa, the Grand Canyon, Washington, D.C., slums, gravitational attraction, acetylsalicylic acid (aspirin), the "k" sounds in Arabic, and the "gold" images in "Sailing to Byzantium" by Yeats. Biologists, linguists, and astronomers, for example, *classify* respectively floral genera and species, languages, and constellations; and they feel that these are scientific endeavors. Logicians, mechanical engineers, literary critics, and physicians *evaluate* respectively syllogisms, building materials, novels, and new drugs and their evaluations are reported in "scientific" journals. Historians, psychologists, biographers, and meteorologists *narrate* respectively about the Peloponnesian War, a case of paranoia, a life story, and a hurricane's progress.

In practice, therefore, scientific assertions are sometimes descriptive, or classificatory, or evaluative, or narrative. But in theory, exception has been taken to some of these.

THEORY OF SCIENTIFIC ASSERTIONS The two most common positions taken on this issue in this century are: (1) scientific assertions must be only descriptive; (2) scientific assertions can be descriptive or explanatory (cf. Harré, i, Chapters I, III, IV).

In some disciplines, a strong case has been made for the position that only descriptive statements are scientific. Physics, sociology, psychology, linguistics, even literary criticism are a few of the many fields which have been influenced in this regard. The classic presentation of this thesis was made by Ernst Mach, the physicist. In an oft-quoted passage Mach remarks:

> The communication of scientific knowledge always involves description, that is a mimetic reproduction of facts in thought the object of which is to replace and save the trouble of new experience. That is all that natural laws are (Mach, s, 192–93, quoted in Harré, i, 45).

Pearson, Comte, and others take similar stands (Pearson, g, 12). In such a view, even explanation is a form of description. Mach, for instance, maintains that Galileo's "explanation" of equilibrium on an inclined plane in terms of the principle of the lever is really just another description —in this case, of the principle of the lever (see Nagel, s, 27, n. 2).

Despite the fact that this position was endorsed and accepted in some disciplines by several generations of scholars (some educators, physicists, psychologists, and others), it was soon attacked by many important physicists, philosophers of science, and others. These writers pointed out that it is really impossible to translate scientific language into terms which merely designate observables (Carnap, i, 78; and t, 419 ff.; Scheffer, a, 178 ff.); that description is usually done in terms of classes of properties and that classes are not mere descriptions (Quine, f, 18; Carnap, e, 208 ff.; Alexander, s, 122 ff.); that pure description is really impossible (cf. Alexander, s, 79 ff.); that pure description would rule out logic, whether deductive or inductive, from the realm of scientific statements (Day, i, 21); that mere descriptions of phenomena can never be systematic, and science erects systems (Alexander, s, 109).

Finally, nearly all later writers on this subject recognize: (1) that description must be distinguished from explanation and, (2) that explanation is an integral function of science. Their views on explanation will be outlined below. For reasons like these Toulmin concludes, "In any case, the premise that all sciences are alike descriptive is hardly acceptable any more" (p, 55). Bar-Hillel is more emphatic:

> Today we know that no science worth its salt at all could possibly stick to observation exclusively. Whoever is out to describe and nothing else will not describe at all. *Theorizare necesse est.* Though I don't think it necessary, or even helpful, to say that *every* description already contains theoretical elements—as some recent methodologists are fond of stressing—it must be said that theorophobia is a disease, fashionable as it might be (1, 207).

Actually, much of the disillusionment with mere description came from the attempts to discuss scientific explanation. Chomsky, a linguist, typifies this general direction:

> It is hardly open to question that natural sciences are concerned precisely with the problems of explaining phenomena, and have little use for accurate description that is unrelated to problems of explanation (a, 589).

And he specifies this in linguistics:

> But this is just another way of saying that "pure descriptivism" is not fruitful, that progress in linguistics, as in any other field of inquiry, requires that at every stage of our knowledge and understanding we pursue the search for a deeper explanatory theory (a, 593).

In everyday language, explanatory assertions are of several types. Thus there is explanation by indication of cause or agency: the vase fell because he jostled it; he wore that horrible tie because his wife likes it. And there is explanation by categorization or classification: he gestures with his hands because he is Italian; she is so defensive because she is really paranoic. Then there is explanation by purpose: he is willing to take all that abuse from the dean because he wants a promotion. And, of course, there is explanation by description: he was able to make the trip in four hours because Denver is, after all, only 200 miles from Gunnison.

It is not surprising that these common-sense notions of explanation have their sophisticated counterparts. Probably the most frequent definition of explanation is in terms of cause or agency. Popper, Hempel, Scheffler, Harré and Oppenheim are some of the thinkers who advocate this position (cf. Scheffler, a, 19–25; Harré, i, 26). In history and psychology, for example, an explanation such as this might be given, "The Conservatives won the recent election in Britain because Labour stressed nationalization" (Scheffler, a, 79).

Sometimes causal explanation comes to be stated in terms of a general principle of which the event to be explained is an example (Scheffler, a, 25). This is sometimes called deductive explanation. It actually establishes the thing to be explained, the explicandum, as a member of a class, the general law or principle. So that the general law or principle becomes the explaining device, the explicatum (Hempel, p, 49 ff., Oppenheim, s, 137–8, Alexander, s, 118 ff.). In actuality, this is explanation by classification, and the explaining class may even be a mere theoretical construct, like a "light ray," not an actual existent (Toulmin, p, 69).

Quite a few important writers make provision for a teleological explanation, or an explanation in terms of purpose or goal or aim or motive. Occasionally there are attempts to reduce this to cause or deductive explanation (Ryle, c, 89; Scheffler, a, 92). But others (Rosenblueth, Wiener, Bigelow, Braithwaite) do not think that teleological explanation can be reduced in this manner and make a special category of it (cf. Scheffler, a, 88 ff.; Braithwaite, s, 328 ff.)

If the pursuit of a goal is successful, a process is usually considered valuable. Consequently, the teleological concept of explanation is closely allied to the evaluative (cf. Volume II). And there is an important school of explanation theory which distinguishes it from descriptive theory by noting the presence in an explanatory theory of an *evaluation procedure* (Chomsky, a, 34). By this Chomsky means a rule of preference of one system over another (a, 30–31). The preference rule, in his case, becomes one of empirical simplicity and one that is measurable (a, 43–44).

This last component is related to Carnap's concept of "exactness' in explanation (cf. lo, 3–8). In practice, Carnap moves from the explicandum to explicatum (the terms are Carnap's) when he has established a satisfactory measuring device (measure function) which enables him to quantify the thing to be explained. Thus, in information theory, after several presystematic examinations of the concepts of semantic information, content, and amount of information (Bar-Hillel, 1, 227 ff., 231 ff., and 233 ff.), he arrives at the explicata of these terms when he has established measure functions for them (Bar-Hillel, 1, 236 ff.). A measure function is obviously a classificatory device.

In summary, then, there are responsible advocates of scientific explanations which describe, classify, indicate cause or agency or goal, evaluate, and quantify. These positions are not necessarily theoretically incompatible with each other; all are exemplified in respectable practice by people who call themselves scientists; and they correspond to common-sense notions of explanation. For these reasons, in this text, descriptive, classificatory and relational, narrative (corresponding to cause and effect), and evaluative propositions are all viewed as capable of being scientific assertions. In other words, there can be scientific description, classifications, narratives, and evaluations. It is not the kind of reference that establishes something as scientific or not; any of the modes of discourse can be scientific.

THE ASSERTIONS OF SCIENCE IN "VITAMINS AND ENDURANCE" The assertions in "Vitamins and Endurance" may or may not be statistically typical of the language of scientific or informative reports—indeed there are reasons that might indicate they could be atypical. In any case, a brief examination of the kinds of assertions made in the report reveals some interesting and possibly surprising features.

Wallis and Roberts, near the end of the chapter, refer to their report as a "description of the experiment" (paragraph 38). And many, maybe most, of their assertions have been descriptive. Perhaps, if one wished to distinguish between descriptive and narrative, one would have to say that the report is preponderantly narrative. For example, typical paragraphs from the planning, execution, and analysis sections of the report reveal a preponderance of narrative sentences. Thus the four paragraphs on "issues" in the planning section (paragraphs 21–24), all of the paragraph in the execution section (paragraph 25), and the quoted material on Test Subject No. 311 (paragraph 30) include many narrative or descriptive statements. This is what could have been expected.

Yet evaluations occur in practically every paragraph of the report. In the discussion of "The Problem," for example, all three paragraphs are evaluative at crucial points. Of the six sentences of paragraph 9, five contain evaluations: "better to withstand," "enhanced," "less conclusive evidence," "somewhat expensive," "care, persistence, and ingenuity needed." And these evaluations are central to the themes of each sentence. The reader can pursue the evaluations present in the next two paragraphs. The paragraphs on "Statistical Planning" also contain evaluations in heavy doses. Even the very descriptive paragraph 13 has some evaluations: "insubstantial barracks," "clothing. . .inadequate," "caloric total was ample." In the "Execution of the Experiment" (paragraph 25), every section contains an important evaluative component and the reiterated grammatical patterns ("was needed," "had to be devised, prepared, sorted, given, scheduled," etc.) show this by indicating the *normativity* of the executions (they *had* to be done in special ways).

In the basic paragraph describing the findings (paragraph 27) the evaluative components strike the reader in the face: "had improved steadily," "continued to show improvement," "unanticipated improvement," "better physical condition." Finally, in the "conclusions" quoted in full from the original report (paragraph 38), it is interesting to note that three of the five statements are evaluations basically. Only two could be called preponderantly narrative or descriptive. And of course, the recommendations resulting from the study are normative (i.e., prescriptive), and therefore evaluative.

Finally, of course, many of the assertions are classificatory. Indeed, given the nature of language, classification is involved in most assertions. Even a descriptive statement like "This ashtray is crystal, colorless, and hexagonal" contains four classifications (ashtray, crystal, colorless, hexagonal). This is one of the reasons given by some authors who maintain that all description is theory-laden (cf. Alexander, s, 79 ff.).

But beyond this, classifications are very important in this discourse, both in the entire chapter and in the report on "Vitamins and Endurance," with which we are more specifically concerned here. The example was chosen to illustrate the use of statistics in the biological sciences (paragraph 6), and belongs to a class of statistical studies similar to the next example given. The previous evidence seemed fairly conclusive for the class of animals, but less conclusive for humans (paragraph 9). The class of combat-type activities is contrasted to that of high-activities (paragraph 10). The class of vitamin C was to be separated from that of the vitamin B complex. Each aspect of the statistical design involves a special classification—indeed, the statistical problem at every stage is a question of adequate classification and adequate sampling of each class, as will be pointed out in the study of inductive logic. The four groups suggested and the two groups settled on, experimental and control (paragraph 16), are classifications crucial to the design of the experiment if it was to yield findings of any scientific value at all. Wallis and Roberts very properly point this out (paragraph 14).

These points have only just begun to touch on the elements of classification involved in this experiment. The reader can pursue the examination at length. Enough has been indicated to stress the fact that this scientific report at least uses much classification. And, of course, all numbers and quantification are classes of classes, as modern logic has made clear. Therefore, each of these types of assertion can be scientific. There can be, therefore, scientific narration, scientific description, scientific classification, and scientific evaluation.

The Basic Nature
of Scientific Discourse

So far, we have seen that scientific discourse consists in a consideration of one facet of an object and the making of certain kinds of assertions (descriptive, narrative, classificatory, and evaluative) about this facet. These two characteristics, however, are certainly not enough to isolate scientific discourse from other discourse. First, the assertions must be referential. This means that the main concern of the discourse must be the reality under consideration. Therefore, the personal feelings and emotions of the writer are excluded (except as they intrude unconsciously or accidentally). Therefore, also, the reader as a target of persuasion, emotional or otherwise, intrudes only indirectly and implicitly. And finally, the discourse is not meant to call attention to itself as an object of delight; literary effect, therefore, is incidental and not usual in scientific discourse.

A discourse which becomes noticeably expressive or directly persuasive or literarily preoccupied is a discourse which is in danger of becoming nonscientific. It is sacrificing the subject matter to some other concern. The primary concern with subject matter is, consequently, the continuing province of referential discourse. Consequently, the descriptive, the narrative, the classificatory, and the evaluative statements of science must be continuously oriented to the reality under consideration. Science, for this reason, is often called "objective." It is "thing"-oriented, not person-oriented. Aristotle defined it as language directed to things, not to hearers (*Rhetoric,* 1358 a). However, all reference discourse is "reality"-oriented. How does scientific discourse differ from the other two types of reference discourse, informative and exploratory?

One distinction seems to be that science is more "thing"-oriented than information and exploration. Science is more impersonal and objective than either of these two. This is true at two separate levels: communication framework and style. In these kinds of discourse both encoder and decoder intrude more frequently and noticeably than in science. This is reflected in the history of objectivity in science as contrasted to the history of objectivity in newspapers, which are typical media of mere information. The newspaper has always reflected, sometimes too strongly, both the influence and policies of the writer (or editor) and those of the readers. Because of these forces, mere information often leans much closer to persuasion than does science. Exploration, likewise, reflects much more the impress of expressor and reactor. Thus, in typical exploratory media such as the Platonic dialogues, the personalities engaged in the exploration or dialectic emerge much more forcefully than they would in comparable scientific media. The same author, writing science at one time and exploration at another time, appears almost as two distinct authors. The impersonal Russell of the *Principia* is not at all the distinct personality of the exploratory essays in, say, *Unpopular Essays* or *Marriage and Morals*. The stylistic characteristics of the three types will be differentiated below.

A second fundamental principle of division among these three is the matter of probability. Exploratory discourse fundamentally asks a question. Informative discourse answers it. Scientific discourse proves it. Presumably, in the sphere of reference discourse, one raises a question or erects a hypothesis because there is some initial probability that it might be possible to prove it is true. This is the province of exploratory discourse. And information is actually the answer to a set of implicit questions or expectancies; but there is only assertion, not accompanying proof, in simple informative discourse. It is stated as certain, but the certainty is not verified. In scientific discourse there are accompanying proofs of certainty or high probability. The presence in the discourse of proof is, therefore, one distinguishing attribute of scientific discourse. This component of scientific discourse is examined under the section on logic, pp. 106 ff.

The General Characteristics of Informative Discourse

As with most of the other types of discourse, we implicitly trust our intuitions about informative discourse; most of us feel we know what is meant by an informative statement. Possibly because of such strong intuitions, the analysis of the exact nature of informative discourse is still in the beginning stages. As we have seen, few distinguish it clearly from either scientific or exploratory discourse. "Information theory" of any type is distinctly a twentieth-century phenomenon, though there are materials from the past which can be made relevant in retrospect. The beginning of information theory is usually credited to Claude E. Shannon, a scientist who worked on the problem of efficiency of signal trasmission in a given channel for the Bell Telephone Laboratories. His classic monograph, "The Mathematical Theory of Communication," was published in the *Bell System Technical Journal* in 1948. Since then, information theory has practically become a separate science, requiring a fairly sophisticated mathematical and physical background.

Shannon himself stressed the fact that information theory really had nothing to do with the meaning of discourse as such. Shannon's basic consideration was the engineering problem of discovering the optimum signal transmission load for an electric channel, regardless of whether the signals actually meant anything or not. Despite the warnings of Shannon and Weaver and many others (cf. Weaver in Shannon, m, 8; Mackay, o, 182; Bar-Hillel, 1, 222 f.; Cherry, h, 383) however, premature and over-enthusiastic applications to semantics and discourse problems were almost immediately made (e.g., Rapaport, w, 8). Actually Shannon's theory constituted only a syntactic theory of information. Later a semantic theory of information was added, and at present there are some beginning attempts at a pragmatic theory of information—these divisions are usually recognized by information theorists (see Wells, m, 237; Bar-Hillel, 1, 305; Shannon, m, 4 ff.). Even the pragmatic can be further subdivided: there is information conveyed by the mere structure of the components of the discourse; there is information conveyed about reality by the referring components of the discourse, and there is information conveyed which will differ according to the subjective background of individual decoders. It is these *discourse* facets of information theory which will concern us here. Much of the treatment will extend the present linguistic theory to the discourse level.

Syntactic Information
in Discourse

The usual criteria for distinguishing syntactic, semantic, and subjective (pragmatic) are followed here: "syntactic information" means the components of information; "semantic information" means their relevance to reality; and "pragmatic information" means their relevance to the users.

The people who have most concerned themselves with the mere components of information are those who have been searching for a mechanical method of information retrieval by indexing, extracting, or abstracting from discourse. Automatic indexing consists of scanning the discourse by some mechanical procedure and drawing out of it words or word-strings that "fulfill certain formal conditions such as occurring more than five times, occurring with a relative frequency at least double the relative frequency in English in general...etc." (Bar-Hillel, 1, 338). Determining exactly whether a given occurrence is really a desired instance of the word (e.g., differ, differentiate, differently, difference, differential), synonyms, negations, deviations, etc., have presented difficulties in automatic indexing (Bar-Hillel, 1, 338–39). The same can be said, often for similar reasons, of automatic extraction and automatic abstracting (Bar-Hillel, 1, 338–42). Nonetheless, some suggestions can be transferred to the composition and analysis of discourse.

All three of these techniques have in common the problem of finding out what and how much information is contained in a document and making this information available to a user in a research process. Most of the time the retrieval is achieved by deriving a set of topics from the documents. The number of headings which can be derived from a document is a matter of how detailed an index one wants for reference purposes. Some university presses which are more particular about indexes than commercial publishers can afford to be will occasionally allow fifteen pages of index for a 300-page book; fifteen pages of index can list 900 or more terms. This would mean that each page, on the average, yields three items of indexed information. This ratio is much more generous than the ratio used in most of the automatic indexing techniques (except Mayer). Automatic indexers have varied from three to thirty terms per document (usually a scholarly article). An experiment with three was found to be inadequate for reference purposes (see Word Correlation w, 3). *Chemical Abstracts* used seven per document in its automatic abstracting experiments (w, 11). And others have used eight or nine (w, 4).

The most obvious illustration of information derived strictly from the components of the discourse and their structuring can be seen in the typical news story in journalism. Here the order of occurrence is determined by the inverted-triangle principle of organization, as it is usually called in books on journalism. The most important components of the story come first, then those of secondary and tertiary importance, and so on. Knowing this convention, the reader derives information about the components of information from the mere placement order of the items. This is a fairly clear example of pure syntactic discourse information.

One of the more promising approaches in information retrieval is the methodology suggested by S. N. Jacobson (m). He distinguishes text-dependent sentences like "However, this is merely a psychological theory" from text-independent sentences like "Gestalt theory is a psychological theory" by the presence in the former of text-tied words like "However," "this," and "merely." By following up the clues established by such words, he erects a set of sentence relationships in a discourse and a hierarchy of importance of sentences. A principal path of information sentences is established and these constitute a kind of information basis for the discourse.

However, Jacobson's work is only seminal and needs further development for extended discourse use. Some other theories also seem relevant to syntactic information in discourse. Thus, Francis Christensen has a "rhetoric" of the sentence, of the paragraph, and of the composition which contains some items relevant to our present concern. He maintains, following John Erskine, that most of the important information in modern English is carried in subordinate, not main clauses (Christensen, n, 24 ff.). Despite the lack of an operational norm for determining the exact nature of "important information," Christensen's intuition may possess some validity. In paragraph 1 of "Vitamins and Endurance," the omission of the subordinate clauses immediately removes two of the most important ideas of the paragraph. This does not happen in paragraph 2, unless one reduces prepositional phrases to subordinate clauses. Nor in paragraph 3. But it is partly true of paragraph 4. In general, in twelve of thirty-three paragraphs Christensen's thesis seems to hold; in five of the thirty-three, the thesis holds partially; in the remaining sixteen, the thesis does not seem to be valid. However, of the remaining sixteen paragraphs, seven are short transition paragraphs, three are summary or conclusion paragraphs. In line count, if one attempts to weigh proportionately the paragraphs in which the thesis only partially holds, about seventy-eight per cent of the paragraphs present this structure. The transition, summary, and concluding paragraphs, of course, are not engaged in presenting new information.

Zelig Harris has also applied his "Discourse Analysis" to the problem of information (Harris, d), but so far the attempts have been only very tentative (cf. Bar-Hillel, f, 342 f.). If successful, this would also be a component of a theory of syntactic information for discourse. In conclusion it can only be said that we still don't know what the rules of occurrence and structure of the components of information are in any depth.

SEMANTIC INFORMATION
IN DISCOURSE

Given the components of information in a discourse and given a possible pattern in their occurrence and structure, the second question is: how relevant to reality are they? This is the semantic information issue. What and how much information about reality does the discourse give us? These questions have been subjected to a more systematic analysis than have the questions of syntactic information, but only for artificial miniature systems. This is a customary procedure in much logical analysis. A fictional and very simplified little universe of discourse is posited and the problem at issue is examined. Then the extrapolation to the more complicated real world is attempted.

Carnap and Bar-Hillel have made such a miniature analysis in order to establish the foundations for their semantic theory of information, and a brief summary of their analysis is presented below, under "Logic" of informative discourse. At this stage, three important facets of their theory can be of some use to us in establishing the nature of information.

In the first place, a statement that carries semantic "informativeness" is shown to be a factual statement, that is, a statement capable of being subjected to empirical verification. It is not a statement that could be verified by merely logical norms. A merely logical tautology carries zero information. If I say that I either shaved or did not shave this morning, my statement carries no information (in this technical semantic sense), though it is a logical statement. This position will be somewhat modified when we move on to pragmatic information.

Given this factual basis of informativeness, Carnap and Bar-Hillel go on to two further characteristics of informative statements. The next characteristic is what they call the "content" of an informative statement. To be informative, a statement must enable us to relate the factual basis to some explicit or implicit system about which information is desired. The content of the statement then comes to be equivalent to the logical implications about this system which may be inferred from the statement. In effect, the content of a statement consists in how much about a system is implied by the given statement (Bar-Hillel, 1, 232).

By extrapolation the "content" of a discourse comes to be equivalent to the completeness or comprehensiveness of the discourse vis-à-vis the reality being talked about. A discourse has more content if it has covered the reality being talked about in a more thorough way than say another discourse attempting to cover the same reality. If a substantial segment of the reality under consideration has not been covered, the content of a discourse is seriously deficient. For this reason, Carnap considers "content" to be roughly equivalent to the "substantial aspect" of a statement (Bar-Hillel, 1, 307). In this text, the term used is "comprehensiveness."

To be comprehensive, therefore, a statement must have a context, must exist within a discernible system. Within such a system it has more or less comprehensiveness if it tells us more or less about the system. The bald statement: "The colleges and universities of the state of Texas produced only eighteen secondary teachers in physics in 1966" is almost noninformative. Given a context, it could be a fairly informative statement.

The "information" in a statement, in contrast to its "content," consists in the degree of predictability of the statement. A statement which is completely predictable carries no information. If I inform my wife that I shaved this morning, she really learns nothing from this statement. Since she knows that I shave every morning, she could predict with almost 100 per cent certainty that I would do so this morning. But if I tell her this morning (November 9, 1966) that incumbent Texas Republican Senator Tower had definitively defeated the Democratic challenger for his office in the elections yesterday, she feels she has been informed, since this was considered rather unpredictable, even unlikely.

In other words, the "information" in a statement consists in the degree of improbability of a statement. "Information" is news, and news is the unpredictable, the unforeseen, the improbable. Many important conclusions follow from this characteristic of information. This attribute of information is common to nearly all theories of information which have been erected: mathematical (Weaver in Shannon, m, 100 ff.), semantic (Bar-Hillel, 1, 247 ff.; Van Dantzig, 141 f.), and pragmatic or subjective (Wells, m, 240 f.).

In this sense, "Vitamins and Endurance" is significantly informational, even though it was a negative conclusion, because it was rather improbable. What was known about vitamins (paragraph 10) and especially the position taken on their use by the Canadian Army, made the opposite prediction more likely. Subsidiary statements in the account also are informational by this norm: (1) the control group which had no vitamin supplementation improved in endurance throughout the experiment (paragraph 27)—notice the terms used to describe this finding ("striking," "unanticipated"); (2) "a caloric deficit of 1200 calories per day for 22 days did not lead to detectable impairment of physical performance" (paragraph 38)— this also would initially have seemed improbable. In fact, the four conclusions are significant information precisely *because* they were initially fairly unpredictable. A more detailed analysis of informative discourse is given on pp. 138–41. It might be pointed out, in passing, that this attribute of surprisingness and *seeming* improbability is also shared by literary discourse, in an analogical way, as we shall see.

PRAGMATIC INFORMATION
IN DISCOURSE

Pragmatic or subjective information consists in information viewed in relation to actual, not ideal, receivers. Of the three kinds of information conveyed by discourse, this last has received least attention from information theorists. Martin (t) and Wells are the only two, as far as the author is aware, who have given it any serious consideration.

Once one says that information is to be gauged, not objectively but subjectively, by different decoders, important things happen to some of the concepts of semantic information. In the first place, not only factual, but many logical statements become informative. Indeed, any logical inference which is not obvious to the receiver becomes informative.

Secondly, the "content" or "comprehensiveness" of a statement becomes a workable, not just a theoretical, concept. For, in a practical way, no one, not even encyclopedia makers, are interested in everything that can be predicated of a given system. Practically speaking, the range of interests of the reader of an informative piece is usually quite severely, if implicitly, restricted. The reader of the report on "Vitamins and Endurance," for example, is usually willing to ignore many really relevant predications that could be made about the system. For example, "soldiers" are some of the individuals in the system, and "health" is one of the attributes. But no mention is made of the past history of any of the soldiers' health, for instance, though really these predications could be relevant. What was said about concerns which are abstracted from is again pertinent here.

In practice, an informative report, in view of certain assumed interests, arbitrarily rules out many possible considerations. A thorough report might advert to some of these arbitrary exclusions (see Paragraphs 4, 7, 9, 10, 12), thus safeguarding the reader. But the reader himself must judge of the validity of these exclusions. Thus, in an article in *The Saturday Evening Post* (April, 1965), entitled "The Meaning of the Dead [in Vietnam]," by Stewart Alsop, one of the arbitrary exclusions was the meaning to the average American reader. The meaning to the Vietnamese and Americans who had relatives in the fighting was considered, but the meaning to the vast majority of those to whom the article was addressed was not considered. This seems to be a crucial and delinquent exclusion. In fact, it practically invalidated the basic importance of the information contained in the article. The information was too incomplete, the system was not large enough, the discourse was not "substantial" enough. This point is established below.

The determinations of the limitations to be given to an informative system are not always easy to specify in a satisfactory manner. They are partly a matter of cultural context, largely a matter of situational context, and significantly a matter of textual context. The cultural context dictates certain limitations: the kinds of expectations generated by a title like "The Meaning of the Dead in Vietnam" in a periodical like *The Saturday Evening Post* in 1965 are certainly different from those that would have been generated a century or so earlier in *The North British Review* by a title like "The Meaning of the Dead in the Boer War" addressed to the English public or, *a fortiori*, by a speech to the Carthaginians by Hannibal on "The Meaning of the Dead at Cannae." But cultural contexts, usually, though not always nor necessarily, operate unconsciously.

More immediately important are the restrictions placed by the situational context. The fact that Alsop's article appeared at a time when many components of the American public were indeed questioning whether the war in Vietnam had a meaning important enough to justify its continuance was a crucial determinant of the expectancies generated by the title. Indeed, for *informative* discourse, situational contexts of time and place are probably more critical than for any other kind of discourse. The cliché that nothing is more worthless than yesterday's newspapers has some validity.

Part of the situational context—and a crucial part—is the audience to whom the text is addressed. Informative discourse, generally, is much less exclusive than scientific discourse. Scientific discourse is usually addressed to one's peers in a discipline. One can, consequently make assumptions about the background, vocabulary, logical sophistication, and acquaintance with current content. But an article in a popular journal like *The Saturday Evening Post* cannot make such assumptions. Alsop's audience was the general American public and he had the duty of addressing himself to their fair expectancies. Because he didn't, the article failed.

Informative essays like Alsop's are usually written down to a generally less-informed audience; scientific essays are written to peers. Tests and quizzes are written up—to teachers. And sometimes classroom compositions are similarly teacher-directed. But tests and quizzes are artificial academic discourse situations. Compositions, of course, are also artificial; but at least one facet of the artificiality can be stripped from them by writing them for peers—one's fellow students. The universe of discourse, then, for an ordinary classroom situation is determined by the expectancies of one's fellow students. This is part of the situational context of a classroom theme.

In addition to the kind of assertion (factual), and the concept of comprehensiveness, a third notion which undergoes some radical interpretation in subjective information theory is the concept of information as improbability or unpredictability. Improbability here becomes a matter of subjective rather than objective predictability (Bar-Hillel, 1, 307). What might objectively be quite predictable (if all of the facts were known) could still be quite unpredictable to the average receptor, and therefore quite informative. At this level, information becomes a matter of what the receptor knows. And what is very informative to a high school student might seem fairly uninformative to a graduate student. Textbooks are informative from this standpoint—they inform students, not teachers. Writing informative discourse for an audience, then, involves estimating how informed the average reader will be and attempting to surmise what would be surprising or novel to this hypothetical reader.

No rigid norms exist in making these suppositions. In college classroom compositions, one operative norm is to suggest that material from a general encyclopedia is considered average information and is not, therefore, informative for a college composition (and, in consequence, does not have to be footnoted). Similarly, general textbook materials of lower levels are also looked upon as average information. But encyclopedia and textbook norms are only suggestive at best, and there are many exceptions to this standard. In practice, a writer of informative material should know the usual market for his work, judge its informational level, and write at approximately this level. The typical writer for *College English* knows the average presumptions of the run-of-the-mill articles in *College English* and *writes* at this level. Sometimes he hopefully tries to raise it, suspecting it is not really exploiting the actual background of its readers.

Exploratory Discourse

INTRODUCTORY REMARKS

The explicit distinction of exploratory discourse from scientific discourse is hardly ever made in textbooks on composition or in anthologies of essays. Several reasons for this can be adduced. The disappearance of "dialectic" or the disputation as a norm for examination and advancement in university study may have been a contributing factor. The gradual realization that science itself could not be rigidly defined in terms of certainty and exploration in terms of probability may also have contributed to the blurring of the distinction. At the present time, also, there are several groups which, for sometimes opposite reasons, deny the distinction. The school of philosophers of science and language whose organ is the periodical *Dialectica* would subsume all science into the area of the tentative or exploratory (Gonseth, i, 32). On the other hand, there is a very disputed issue in the philosophy of science which attempts to answer the question, "Is there a specific logic of discovery as opposed to a logic of scientific proof?" Some weighty names answer "No," and consequently tend to subsume exploration into science (cf. Smith, p, 227 f). Both groups, therefore, would also promote the blurring of the distinction. The educational influence of Dewey's view of logic as inquiry and the current unpopularity of "dialectic" with all of its residual medieval, Hegelian, and Marxian connotations certainly may also be influential in this regard.

Whatever the reason, the fact remains: exploration as distinct from science and exploratory discourse as distinct from scientific discourse are not fashionable discriminations. Yet there seem to be compelling linguistic and philosophic reasons for making the distinctions. Exploratory discourse does differ radically from scientific in style, organizational patterns, and logic. Each of these will be discussed below. Such differences would seem to point to a fundamental distinction in the nature of the discourse. The distinction, as usual, is reflected in the long history of a terminology which sought to distinguish the two. And the referents of the terminology give some suggestions as to the underlying differences in nature.

Terminology

Undoubtedly the very best term which history offers for the text of a discourse that was merely exploratory, not conclusive, in aim is the term "essay." Unfortunately the term, which had a fairly clear discourse meaning in Montaigne, soon took on literary, and later expressive, connotations, and despite a vogue of several centuries seems currently almost obsolescent. At any rate the later connotations and ambiguities make it presently inacceptable in any precise context. In addition, it is almost exclusively reserved for written compositions, and exploratory discourse is often oral.

Most of the terms which have referred to exploratory discourse have differentiated from the scientifically proven, the demonstrated, the certain, and the verifiable. A suggestive catalogue of distinctions having some kind of a common denominator like this is drawn up in Figure III, 1. No pretense is made here that all of the terms listed under "exploration" or

"scientific proof" have equivalent or even closely similar referents sometimes; for purposes of clarity, grammatical parallelism has been disregarded.
The references attempt to be a summary of significant ones.

Figure III, 1: Distinctions Between Exploration and Science

Exploration	Scientific Proof	User
opinion	knowledge by dialectic	Plato (see Taylor, p, 291–92) Peter of Spain (see Ong, r, 60)
dialectic	science	Aristotle (101b 4; 159a 25; see Ong, r, 61) Aquinas (S. T., II-II, 48, c)
way of invention	way of judgment	Cicero, Albert the Great, Aquinas, Hugh of St. Victor (see Ong, r,113)
discovery	demonstration	Bacon, Galileo, Newton Descartes (see Carmichael, 2, 15 ff.)
dialectic (by Reason)	analytic (by Understanding) and aesthetic (by Sensibility)	Kant (c, 37; 119 ff.)
analytic (by Understanding)	dialectic (by Reason)	Hegel (e, 72–77)[2]
proposing	testing	Peirce (c, I, 29; II, 381–88)
inquiry	judgment	Dewey (l, 101ff.; 120ff.)
heuristic	probative, demonstrative	Day (i, 7); Beth (m,86ff.)
context of discovery	context of justification	Kuhn (s, 8 f.)
discovery	hypothetico-deductive method	Hanson (see Smith in Hutchins, g, 1965, 227–28)
exploration	dialectics (derogatory)	Belth (e, 80 ff.)

The "users" are intentionally drawn from Antiquity, the Middle
Ages, the Renaissance, and the modern and contemporary periods in order
to show the persistence of the tradition. Undoubtedly, the most persistent
term has been "dialectic." But in Plato, dialectic arrives at certainty. In
Aristotle, in addition to being the principle of all inquiries (*Topics*, 101b

2 The reference is to Mueller's translation of the *Encyclopedia of Philosophy,* but the terms used here are the traditional ones, not Mueller's (who
uses Reason for what is here called Understanding and Comprehension for
what is here called Reason).

4), it is also "indifferent to truth, and aims only at proving its point, and thereby refuting an adversary, whose existence is always assumed in every dialectical discussion, even when it is carried on in a man's own brain and in his study" (Cope, i, 88). In Kant, it must ever remain illusion (c, 109). In Hegel, it alone can attain to certainty (e, 72). And in Hegel and Marx it becomes the active agent of historical progress by war and class struggle, not just a mode of the thinking mind (Hegel, e, 254 ff.; Marx, c, 11; and m, 419 ff.).

The term has obviously had its vagaries. If one were to add to it the various meanings in Cicero, Peter of Spain, Ramus, Emerson, Kierkegaard and some moderns, it is no wonder the very word frightens a prospective user in search of some univocity.

The term "invention" is really much more used in a rhetorical context and is best reserved for that. The term "discovery" would be good, but it is rarely used for the kind of discourse which embodies the findings or the process of finding. The same can be said of Peirce's "proposing," and of Dewey's "inquiry," and Day's "heuristic." Other terms have been suggested for this kind of discourse. Whatmough, curiously, calls discourse which stimulates to thought "dynamic" (Whatmough, 1, 87); but this term has been used by others to refer to emotive and persuasive discourse. Russell calls it "questioning."

"Exploratory" seems surrounded by fewer misleading connotations than most of the others and is also applicable to discourse. It has been objected to by Kuhn, who feels that it carries connotations of the explorer's haphazard, random, and nonstructured meandering without a goal; he objects to this since nearly all modern research is not of this type (Kuhn, f, 363). But "exploratory," even in research, need not carry these connotations; it doesn't, for example, in medicine. The term is used by several writers in contexts similar to the present (e.g., Belth, e, 80 ff.), although its juxtaposition to "dialectics" by Belth and some others hardly seems historically justified; and "dialectics" will not be used here at all.

Basic Characteristics
of the Exploratory Process

Nearly all of the authorities listed in Figure III, 1 (and many others) have tried to outline their own procedures of discovery. It is not surprising that there are features common to many. The most frequent application of such procedures to discourse has been made by the writers on speech in their treatments of discussion and debate. In the Renaissance and later, "dialectic" even came generally to be defined in terms of discourse. Ramus' definition is typical, "the art of dialectic is the teaching of how to discourse" (quoted in Ong, r, 176). In modern times, speech writers often bodily transfer Dewey's inquiry procedures into a framework for discussion. Keltner, for instance, reviews previous writers on this subject, and after a summary presentation of Wagner and Arnold, Utterback, Elliott, Sattler, and Miller, concludes that the logic of problem solving is the specific logic of discussion (Keltner, g, 32–34).[3] To these, Fansler and many subsequent writers might be added (Fansler, c, 148–62). Following the precedent of these earlier writers Keltner then presents the Dewey logic of problem solving.

But the oral media are not the only channels. Throughout history, exploratory discourse has often taken the very typical channel of the dialogue. Plato's dialogues, Aristotle's lost exoteric dialogues (as opposed to his scientific esoteric writings), Cicero's *disputationes,* medieval "debates" ("The Debate Between the Body and the Soul"), and the many Renaissance dialogues are all representative samples of exploratory discourse in written form, as are some "essays" (Montaigne, Matthew Arnold, Emerson, Thoreau). By keeping in mind such examples, and analyzing the similarities among the various discovery procedures, it should be possible to arrive at some general features of exploratory discourse.

The various discovery procedures actually involve *change* in intellectual views. Consequently, it is not surprising that several of the analyses can be examined in a framework of the nature of change (described in the chapter on narration, in *The Modes of Discourse,* the forthcoming sequel to the present volume).

Some rough parallelisms in several dialectical procedures are indicated below. In order to forestall an accusation of a Procrustean forcing, let it be remarked immediately that many violent dissimilarities have been abstracted from in order to focus, for the moment, on similarities. And even some of the similarities are uneasy in the indicated categories. Yet the synthesis seems worthwhile, as a tentative formulation (my own discourse is distinctly exploratory here). The formulation actually pictures only the exploration half of a full cycle of what is usually called the "scientific method." Exploration leads to a testable hypothesis which scientific proof then demonstrates as tenable or not. This continuum is represented in Figure III, 2.

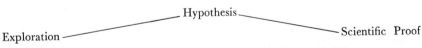

Figure III, 2: The Continuum of Exploration and Science

The steps leading up to the hypothesis are indicated in Figure III, 3 below.

3 This is a conclusion which I do not agree with; discussion is often exploratory in aim, but sometimes it is persuasive, and sometimes informative, and sometimes even entertaining in aim.

Person	Preliminary Knowledge of Field	Cognitive Dissonance	Focus of Problem	Search for New Model	Imposition of New Model	Hypothesis: Tentative Explanation
Plato	Myth: choice of antagonist	Wonder	Division	In Rumor, then Thought; Definition, Elenctic testing by Induction, Doubt	Conjecture, then Hypothesis, Deduction, Doubt	then
Aristotle	Historical Survey	Wonder	Thesis	In Topics	Choice of Relevant Topic	Dialectical enthymeme
Aquinas	Historical Survey of Arguments for and against the Article	"Disputed Question"	Article	By Arguments Against Article and Arguments for Article	Corpus: Arguments for his position	Reply to Objections
Hegel	Analytic Thesis	Instability	Dialectical Thesis	By Antithesis	Thesis *vs.* Antithesis	Synthesis
Dewey	Matrix of Inquiry	Indeterminacy and Discomfort	Statement of Problem	Selections of Facts Relevant to Problem Solution by Affirmation and Negation	"Suggestions"	"Reasoning" from Suggestions to "Hypothesis"
Kuhn	Initial Acceptance of Current Dogma	Anomalies	Crisis	Search for New Paradigm		
Hanson		Anomalies		Search for New Model outside current ones	Imposition of Form or Model	

Figure III, 3: Some Similarities in Designs of Exploration

The headings are derived, in the main, from Hanson, whose theory of the logic of discovery has been given considerable attention in recent years (Hanson, c, p, i; Smith, p, 227 f.). In the first stage, possibly the most categoric position is taken by Kuhn who designates the current theories by the term "dogma," for the process of becoming aware of them is almost like an indoctrination (Kuhn, f, 350 ff.). This acceptance of current paradigms serves several purposes: it helps a discipline move forward and prevents recurrent starts from bald rudiments each time, and it frames the field of the discipline; and thus serves as an idea source for the routine research of the discipline; but especially it serves as the norm from which deviations are observable. Without a norm, there are no abnormalities (Kuhn, f, 365 f.).

The corollary in discourse is that for an exploratory composition, there must first be a grounding in fact and accepted notions. No great exploration can normally be expected from a vacuum. Exploration is not creation from a prior nothing. This point has long been acknowledged by writers on discussion techniques. Chenoweth remarks that discussions engaged in without preliminary background preparation often result in only the "pooling of ignorance" and solve nothing (d, 215) and Popper makes the same point. Speaking of an awareness of what has preceded, Popper says:

> This seems to me important because it is part of the general method of rational discussion. If we ignore what other people are thinking, or have thought in the past, then rational discussion must come to an end, though each of us may go on happily talking to himself (Popper, 1, 16–17).

Once the current dogma is known, it establishes a framework of consistency. Inferences from it should prove valid and observed facts relevant to it should be consonant with the dogma. The establishment of these inferences and congruent sets of observed facts constitutes the normal process of research (Kuhn, f, 360). They do not challenge the dogma; they extend, apply, and confirm it.

But it may happen that certain inferences deduced from the dogmatic system seem inconsistent with prior axioms or inferences in another part of the system. Or certain observed facts do not seem consistent with what the system would have predicted they should be. A dissonance between the dogma and these inferences or observations is created. This disagreement creates wonder, instability, or discomfort. This is the stage of cognitive dissonance (cf. Festinger, t, 17 ff.). If enough of these anomalies exist, they may converge into a crisis which calls into question some features of the dogma itself (Kuhn, f, 367). The problem now has crystallized and demands some solution. This stage in the process is called the focus of the problem, for the issue has emerged from indeterminacy and can be stated as an alternate thesis to the dogma.

Since the dogma no longer provides a framework for the solution, a new framework must be sought elsewhere. It is here that imagination has its highest moment in the scientific process. And some scientists and philosophers have been almost lyrical in their expressions about this creative stage of the process (cf. Kierkegaard in Diem, k, 13; Black, m, 242 f.). There is no formula or inferential set of mechanical directions for producing a theory from a set of observations (Toulmin, p, 106 ff.). Certainly negation of previous dogma is one of the components; and such variant philosophers as Aquinas, Hegel (Hegel, l, I, 66; McTaggart, st, 10), and Dewey (l, 166 ff.) insist on this at length in theory and practice. Dewey, indeed, says "Nothing is more important in inquiry than institution of contradictory propositions" (l, 197). Though this may be residual Hegelianism in Dewey, it is continually stressed in most discovery procedures (Cohen, r, 165 ff.). Indeed, the exclusion of opposition and "controversy" and "polarity" from a classroom or a society results inevitably in the exclusion of exploration for truth (Cohen, r, 165–68).

But mere negation is often not enough. The positive aspect of the exploratory process, once the issue has become clear, consists in the search for a new theory, model or paradigm. The new model or paradigm, coming from without the confines of the dogmatic camp, almost inevitably strikes an instrusive and nonconformist note. Toynbee has stressed the necessity of a culture to be fertilized from without if it is to stay alive (sa, 62 ff., 307 ff.), and much the same can be said of an intellectual discipline.

Since the current concepts about the given reality are unsatisfactory and may be unclear, the tendency is to search for a somewhat similar issue which is presently clear and satisfactory and see if the pattern of the familiar can be imposed on the unsatisfactory and unclear. This familiar and clear pattern imparted from elsewhere is the new model. It can be defined as a similarly structured pattern of design which helps to explain, describe, or even predict a given reality (Chao, m, 558)—though the term has other somewhat variant meanings (cf. Chao, m, 563 f.; Toulmin, p, 39; Braithwaite, m, 235 ff.; *Synthese,* XII, Nos. 2, 3 (1960), whole issue; Black, m, 219 ff.). The model, imported from the already familiar, clear, explained, better organized, and proven in the secondary domain, carries with it the possibility of transferring its own clarities, explanations, structures, and proofs into the primary domain of the given reality to be explained (Black, m, 230 f.; Braithwaite, m, 224 f.). This projection of the known to explain the unknown gives rise to the fertility of the model (cf. Black, m, 226 f., 231; Toulmin, p, 39; Chao, m, 564 f.).

Hanson's classic example of the whole exploration process vividly illustrates the use of the model. He uses Kepler's discovery of the ellipitical orbit of Mars, for "Kepler typifies all reasoning in physical science" (Hanson, p, 84). The dogma current from Aristotle to Galileo was that planetary orbits were necessarily circular (cf. Hanson, p, 195, for references). He says, "Before Kepler, circular motion was to the concept of planet as 'tangibility' is to our concept of 'physical object'" (Hanson, p, 74).

But the circular model did not account for the anomalies in measurements of Mars's varied distances from the sun and of Mars's varied velocities at different points in its orbit. Even inaccuracies in measuring procedures should not have led to such notable departures from what the theory dictated (Hanson, p, 75). To explain these anomalies Kepler then repudiated the circular orbit model and cast about for another model (Hanson, p, 74). He first tried an oval and then an ellipse as models, settling eventually on the ellipse (Hanson, p, 76–84). The ellipse offered a plausible explanation of all of the anomalies which had been bothering him and suggested other testable hypotheses. These he followed through and the results confirmed the validity of the new model. This constitutes the "scientific," rather than the "exploratory" aspect of Kepler's method.

The new model, therefore, was mathematical, as was the old, but it was a different mathematical model. Mathematics here, as in many instances in the physical sciences (e.g., Maxwell, Einstein), logic (Boole, Russell), linguistics (Chomsky), and sociology (Lewin), is a fertile hunting place for new models. Other kinds of models exist, of course. Braithwaite and Black both detail the following: scale models—spatial or temporal reproductions larger or smaller than the original; analogues—reproductions of only one or several significant aspects of the original; mathematical—abstractions of relevant variables in a manner to make them amenable to mathematical manipulations; theoretical models or theories—general structures or systems capable of several interpretations each of which would constitute a specific model (Braithwaite, m, 225 ff.; Black, m, 220 f.). In the last sense, the communication triangle in this text could be said to constitute the communication theory, and the many interpretations at various levels would be specific models. Chao goes further than these four basic kinds of models and lists 30 meanings of model (Chao, m, 563 f.).

BRIEF ANALYSIS
OF THE EXPLORATORY COMPONENTS
OF THE ANTHOLOGIZED SELECTION

There are exploratory components both in Wallis' and Roberts' total chapter on "The Effective Use of Statistics" and in the report on the vitamin experiments. In the introduction to the chapter, "Common Sense and Statistics," the issue is the introduction of the student to the use of statistics.

It is interesting, that, given this problem, Wallis and Roberts immediately advert to a very obvious model for a handling of the problem, and the model neatly structures the first part of the chapter. The model could be called Hegelian, in that a thesis is established, then the opposite antithesis is entertained, and the final position is a compromise synthesis of the two positions. The thesis is that statistics are to be accepted indiscriminately, that they are the fundamental procedure for proving anything. The antithesis is that, since statistics can be so clearly manipulated to prove almost anything, they really "can prove nothing" (paragraph 2). This polarity of indiscriminate acceptance and indiscriminate rejection actually serves as the structural principle for four of the five paragraphs of this section of the chapter. As a matter of fact, it has structured this whole chapter and the ensuing chapter of the book: Chapter Two considers "The Effective Use of Statistics" and Chapter Three considers the "Misuse of Statistics." Indeed, the message of both Chapter Two and Chapter Three is that the truth of this matter is at the meridian, in between both extremes.

The model used by the people who made the experiment on vitamins which they report is quite different. Yet it also is a very common model. The report of the experiment indicates briefly some of the classic stages in the exploratory process. The accepted dogma was that vitamin supplements would be helpful to animals and men operating in a cold environment. Several studies and the Canadian Army practice supported this dogma. But there were anomalies: the evidence that existed for rats might not be immediately applicable to humans, and the *cost* of mass vitamin supplementation would be expensive. Consequently the problem took on a more careful focus: how effective would vitamin supplementation be to soldiers in combat conditions in a cold environment? Eventually the problem was even more carefully focused.

The solution of the problem here was somewhat mechanical. Given the problem, no original thought was given to the model which could point to the solution. In effect, the problem immediately became the hypothesis, and the model which was turned to for the testing of the hypothesis was a very common testing model, the contrast of control and experimental groups. This particular model for a proof procedure is so common that some disciplines tend to look upon it as almost the only method of proof, a fairly naive assumption, it might be pointed out in passing. The method is a refinement of one of Mill's five canons of inquiry, and these had their roots in Bacon's methods of discovery by presence or absence, outlined in his *Novum Organum.*[4]

4 A careful analysis of Mill's canons and a consideration of part of the historical development of which they were a part can be seen in Stebbing, m, 326–55.

Once the model of proof has been settled on, the exploratory process proper has been culminated and the matter of scientific proof is now in the forefront. Consequently, and properly, the *Problem* gives way to *Statistical Planning*. The details of this section will be examined under "Scientific Logic" which follows shortly.

The Logic of Reference Discourse

Introduction

It seems obvious enough that a theory of discourse has some connections with logical theory and practice. It might be well to recall, at the outset, that "logic" and the Greek work for discourse (*logos*) both have the same root, as do "discourse" and "discursive" (one important meaning of which is "logical") in Latin. But it seems equally obvious that it is not the proper province of a theory of discourse to give an exhaustive treatment of all of the various fields of logic. Further, since in each discipline of the academic world there are particular techniques and methodologies of proof, it is all the more impractical and impossible to sketch all of these variant methodologies of logical demonstration. A practictioner of discourse in any given area must be initiated into his unique scientific methods and employ them in discourse in that area.

What seems useful and desirable here is to distinguish the specific areas of logic which are relevant to specific areas of discourse. Sometimes the important correlations between areas of logic and areas of discourse have not yet been made. And occasionally some have been made and then forgotten or ignored in discourse theory.

The specific desideratum of this rapprochement of logic to discourse is to enable the student of discourse to recognize at least the major tools of effective demonstration, discovery, persuasion, and the like, when they are employed in discourse and to be able to use them himself in his own original attempts at discourse.

As in many of his other skills, man is frequently intuitively logical long before he can consciously analyze his own logical processes. Some of our most common logical inferences have still to be subjected to systematic analysis. DeMorgan, for example, once remarked that all of Aristotle's logic could not prove the following inference: "If horses are animals, then heads of horses are heads of animals" (cf. Whitehead, pm, 291). Yet in any high school composition, we should expect a student to make such an inference and others immeasureably more subtle.

But an awareness of some of the basic logical processes which have been analyzed does seem highly desirable, even mandatory. For the rest, one can only hope that a mind trained to perceive logical efficiency or deficiency in basic areas will at least be more cautious of his own and others' intuitions in frontier areas.

It has already been pointed out the term "logic" has here been given an extension which some would object to (see above, pp. 63–64). In this large sense, logic is conceived as the rules that determine successful sequences of statements in discoure. In this sense, there are different logics for each of the various aims of discourse, and there are different logics for each of the various modes of discourse. Within the aims, reference discourse has its various logical procedures, and they are quite distinct from the so-called "rhetorical proofs" which constitute the logic of persuasion. All of these are quite unlike the logic governing esthetic form. Similarly, within the modes, the construction of a narrative is governed by the logical principle of causality which orders the sequences of the incidents of a narrative. And evaluative discourse is governed by the logical principle of teleology (achievement of purpose). The various modes, like the various aims, have their own logics. Even within reference discourse, there are logical procedures of scientific proof which differ from logical procedures of exploration, and both of these are to be distinguished from the logical procedures of information.

Most of these various logics have come to be recognized as distinct fields of logic by some professional logicians. Of course, scientific logic is recognized by everyone. And there is a large group of philosophers who argue for a distinct logic of discovery, or exploration; these include Aristotle, Bacon, Newton, Galileo, Peirce, Hanson, Kuhn, Harrah, Medvedev, Stahl, Hamblin, and others—though there are respectable opponents to this position. Most professional logicians now recognize the existence of a logic of persuasion, usually called imperative or deontic logic and closely related to a logic of obligation or commitment (cf. Prior, f, 220 ff.; Von Wright, m, 36–42 ff.; Day, i, 113 f.). Traditionally the problem of obligation was covered in the field of ethics, which was not, however, classified as an area of logic, although some now so classify it (e.g., Day, i, 113). The same is true of the problems of literary discourse; they are a part of the general philosophic field of esthetics. But few logicians today consider esthetics to be a division of logic although some do (e.g., Day, i, 113) and speak of a specific logic of esthetic form (Cassirer, lo, 159–81; Northrop 1, 169–90; 328–98). As for expressive logic, Langer, a professional logician, says that no one has yet discovered a logic for this kind of discourse (Werner, e, 9).

The recognition of different logics for the modes of discourse is possibly more widespread among professional logicians—although they are usually concerned with these modes in a scientific framework. Of course, everyone recognizes the logic of classes, governing classification. And, since Frege and Whitehead and Russell, most symbolic logicians concern themselves with a logic of descriptions (Whitehead, pm, 231 ff., 279 ff., 296 ff.).

And some professional logicians have tackled the problem of a logic of evaluations (cf. Prior, f, 216 ff.). No one, as far as I know, has related the principle of causality to the problem of narration; this is done in the second volume of this work.

The place of logic with regard to a theory of discourse is quite important. Logic itself, in the history of philosophy, has been looked upon as a tool of philosophy by Aristotle and his followers, as a separate branch of philosophy by the Stoics, as an art of language in the liberal arts tradition, as equivalent to mathematics or arithmetic (Frege and Russell), and as equivalent to the true philosophy (some logical positivists).[5] From the time of the Greeks until the early twentieth century, logic was generally considered to be an integral part of the study of language or discourse. From 1900 till 1950, roughly, logic as such was not generally viewed as an integral part of discourse study. Now it seems to be making a return. Consequently, its exile must be looked upon as only a short and unfortunate interim in a long tradition. Actually, it is the logic of a discourse, almost as much as any other single factor, which establishes a discourse as being of a given aim or mode. Consequently, logic is one of the fundamental determinants of the nature of a discourse. And one can no more separate logic from discourse than one could separate gasoline from a working automobile with a gas engine.

The Logic
of Scientific Discourse

The purpose of scientific logic is to demonstrate the truth or validity of a referential assertion with as much certainty as the techniques of the given logic can achieve. The nature of these assertions has been analyzed above. For a long time, it was claimed that science arrived at a certainty which could be considered absolute. This was so true that the traditional definition of science was in terms of certainty. Aristotle so defined science: "Consequently the proper object of unqualified scientific knowledge is something which cannot be other than it is" (*Poster. Anal,* 71b 14 ff.). He was only echoing Plato on this (e.g., *Rep.* 371b, 373c). And from Plato to Aquinas, sciences were classified in a hierarchy of descending certitude (Aquinas, *Summa,* Part I, Question I, Response to 5; Q 1, Ad 5, i; Plato, *Rep.,* 371c–373c). Descartes took a similar stand (cf. Hutchins, g, II, 687). And Bain, in the nineteenth century, follows this tradition (Bain, e, 185).

Today, for several reasons, we are not so certain about the certainties of science. Adler, more aware than many of this tradition of cer-

---

5 In a general theory of language, logic would seem to be a part of semantics, not grammar or pragmatics (see Carnap, lo, 199), though it is very relevant to scientific discourse.

tainty, finds it necessary to qualify (Adler, c, 29). Others are even more reticent to claim absolute certainty; for example, the Swiss group of thinkers whose vehicle is *Dialectica* chose this term because it carries the connotation that nothing is irrevocably definitive, everything is subject to revision. As Gonseth says, in what might be regarded as the manifesto of the movement:

> Real scientific progress is not a step from certitude to certitude, from reality to reality, it is a step from provisional and cumulative evidence to further provisional and cumulative evidence (Gonseth, i, 32).

In part, this caution has emerged from a more careful analysis by logicians of the kind of certainties which are embodied in deduction and induction. The "problem of deduction," as it is usually called is that in reality no deduction is ever a real advance in knowledge. What is inferred was already implicit in the premises. From Mill to Wittgenstein, this is usually recognized. Wittgenstein epigrammatically, if dramatically, says, "But it is no less remarkable that the infinite number of propositions of logic (mathematics) follow from half a dozen 'primitive propositions.' But in fact all the propositions of logic say the same thing, to wit nothing" (t, 89). Of course, an inference to something of which one was previously not aware is, in practice, if not in theory, an advance in knowledge.

The "problem of induction" is the problem of attempting to justify the jump from particulars to a generalization, a jump involved in any induction. Some earlier theories of induction attempted to prove that given the right conditions, such generalizations could indeed be certain (e.g., Hume, Mill—cf. Day, i, 182–94). Nearly all modern logicians, however, view them as only probable, at best (Russell, Williams, Keynes, Black, Day—see Day, i, 194–225). And since inductions supply many of the premises of deduction, such deductions also are only probable.

Because of the caution engendered both by the problem of deduction and by that of induction, absolute certainty is an ideal which has been largely relinquished by logic. Nevertheless, certainty as something to be approximated is still the ideal of scientific logic.

The means by which such high degrees of probability are demonstrated are usually considered to be deduction and induction. It is not difficult to demonstrate that deduction is a syntactic proof and that induction is a semantic proof. The question naturally arises, then, is there a pragmatic proof coordinate to these two? The answer will be given in the third section below, on "ethnologic."

INDUCTIVE LOGIC

Induction is usually given as one kind of proof for scientific discourse. Unlike deduction, the systematic consideration of induction is a fairly modern phenomenon. It is true that Aristotle, Epicurus, and Philodemus in Antiquity pay a little attention to it (Day, i, 14), but the systematic treatment of induction began with Bacon and Hume, was given some development by Kant and Mill, and in modern times has been extended by such names as Keynes, Braithwaite, Carnap, Day, Reichenbach, Kneale, and others.

Unlike deduction, which has more or less accepted Whitehead and Russell's *Principia Mathematica* as a classical treatment and point of departure, induction has no such dominating paradigm or symbolic notation. The ensuing treatment will consider the following points: definition of induction, kinds of induction, and general rules governing induction.

Definition of Induction

The usual definition of induction is that it is a generalization drawn from particulars (cf., Day, i, 1–8). Thus, if I observe five female redheads in one of my classes, three in another, and six in another, from these particulars I may infer that "The University of Texas has a disproportionate number of redheads." This is an induction. The particulars I have considered constitute the "sample" and the generalization is to the "population," the females of the University of Texas.

The example illustrates a connection often established by writers on induction today. The relation between my evidence (my sample) and my generalization is a matter of probability, that is, the evidence only confirms my generalization within a limited range of probability. It is obviously not certain, from my sample, that my inference is valid. I may, in fact, be very wrong. Induction, therefore, is closely related to probability theory. Day (i), Carnap (lo, e), and Reichenbach (t) are some of the modern theorists who practically equate induction with part or all of probability theory. There are, of course, deductions which are only probable in science (and in rhetoric, see below, p. 250 ff.).

The so-called "inductive leap" from the evidence to the generalization constitutes an advance in knowledge in the sense that the generalization is not really contained in the particulars. But the relation between the evidence and the generalization is a matter of logical analysis. The issue in inductive analysis is always the confrontation of the generalization with the evidence and the determination of the degree of probability which the evidence actually offers for the generalization (Carnap, lo, 181, 200–202, and *passim*).

The production of the inference, the generalization, is not a matter of analysis in induction, no more than the production of a specific inference is a matter of deduction. These are both the concern of the logic of discovery or exploration (see Carnap, lo, 194). Deduction and induction examine the inference vis-à-vis the evidence and pronounce upon validity (Carnap, lo, 196–99). In the case of deduction no further information is needed than the rules of the deductive system within which the deduction is being made. No additional factual knowledge can change the validity of the inference (Carnap, lo, 202).

In the case of induction, the rules of "degree of confirmation" are needed (Carnap, lo, 202). These rules must take into account further factual knowledge, and the degree of confirmation may change radically in the light of further information. A brief summary of some of the important rules is presented below.

The rules actually are attempts to clarify the relationship between the sample and the population. To put it somewhat differently, the rules attempt to show what part of the total structure is given by the sample. The probability of a statement, then, depends on the universe of discourse within which the statement exists as an alternative. Just as the "information" or "content" of a statement depends on the structure within which it is placed, so does the probability of a statement. Indeed, as we have already mentioned, the "information" and the "probability" of a statement are inversely related, the more improbable a statement is, the more informative it is.

Since scientific discourse attempts to arrive at high probability, even to approximate certainty, it follows that scientific discourse which is attempting to be informative always has the paradoxical assignment of attempting to prove as highly probable some statements which initially seem highly improbable. Scientists are of necessity nonconformists—in this sense.

To illustrate the issue of the necessity of a context, take the case of the probability of throwing an ace with one throw of one die; the probability is 1/6. But the probability of turning up an ace out of a deck of 52 cards is 1/13. To turn this into a case in literary criticism, the probability that five instances of a "gold" image constitute a significant structural pattern is considerably higher in a sonnet than in a novel—unless the occurrences are critical for some reason or other (title, chapter heading, or climax of plot).

Kinds of Induction

Normally four kinds of induction are mentioned in an introductory treatment of the subject: perfect induction, intuitive induction, mathematical induction, and probability induction.

Summary or complete or perfect induction consists in the rather unusual case in which the sample equals the population: all of the elements about which the generalization is made are examined. If I contact every foreign student from Iran on the campus and then say, in a general statement, "All of the Iranian foreign students are in need of financial help," the generalization is a summary induction. The number of people contacted (the sample) is equal to the generalization. Some logicians refuse to call this induction; Stebbing calls it a disguised syllogism, and Day calls it a description (Stebbing, m, 244; Day, i, 4). But Aristotle, Mace (p, 245 f.), and many others consider it induction, and it will be so called here.

One particular case of this is the class of one member. If I consider it and then state about it, I have some typical direct observation statements. Actually these are the most fundamental of our kinds of scientific proof. To consider one individual as an instance of generalization is in accord with much modern logical practice (cf. Quine, m, 80).

The second kind of induction is the intuitive or philosophic induction. This consists in the case of generalizing to the universal from the *nature* of the particular. Because the particular has to be this way, *owing to its very nature,* I do not have to examine many cases to substantiate my generalization. Though some consider this to be a disguised deduction, for practical purposes in discourse analysis it seems best to follow many respectable authors who do consider it a kind of induction (Mace, p, 248 ff.; Aristotle 71a, 81b).

Actually, many explanations in scientific discourse use this kind of induction; even those who do not consider it a valid kind of induction use it. Three paragraphs above, I gave one example of perfect induction; from this example one could draw the nature of perfect induction because it illustrates the nature of the case. Such an inference would be an intuitive induction. No one feels that it is necessary to collect a representative, random, and unbiased sample of such concepts before generalizing to the definition.

A particularly sensational example of such an induction in the history of physics is illustrated by the case of the density of argon. "In 1894, Rayleigh and Ramsey discovered a new element argon, determined the density of a single specimen of it, and concluded that this was certainly the density of all argon," (Day, i, 165, Mace, p, 252 f.). This was "considered to be perfectly in order" because argon is an inert element, and all elements are constant in respect of density. In other words, the *nature* of argon allowed this generalization. Of course, for an intuitive induction to be valid, the scientist must be certain the nature of the class is validly established.

A third kind of induction is mathematical induction. Here, given a series, such as $1, 1/2, 1/4, 1/8, \ldots$, it is possible to generalize to the series as a whole and indeed, to specify any particular member of the series $(1/2^{n-1})$. In general mathematical induction says that if a property belongs to the first member of a series and to its successor, then it belongs to all of the members of a series (cf. Day, i, 5 f.). Some say it is actually a form of deduction. For purposes of discourse analysis, mathematical induction is not an ordinary issue for the English major. It is only mentioned here for complete coverage. Actually, it is one kind of intuitive induction.

At times in the history of logic, analogy has been mentioned as a kind of induction. But it seems that this concept of analogy as seen in Mill and Keynes can be handled by the rule of variety, which will be treated below (cf. Day, i, 162–64). And, of course, analogy as an equivalence of common relationships is actually a part of the logic of relations. In any case, analogy is not here treated as a special kind of induction nor as a distinct kind of logic, different from either deduction or induction.

The last and most important kind of induction is called by various terms, the most common of which is "probability induction."[6] Like all the previous types, it is a generalization from particulars. But the generalization is now made without benefit of complete enumeration or the nature of the thing under consideration or the nature of a series. Consequently the generalization is only probable at best—whence the name probability induction.

Probability induction is what is usually referred to when "induction" without qualification is used. And it is the most frequent kind of induction in matters of discourse analysis. There are several types of probability inductions. A distinction is first made between an attribute and a variable induction. An attribute is a quality or property which does not vary in degree (e.g., "being a ruminant" or "being American"). A variable is a quality which varies in degree (e.g., "being hot," or "being tall").

Attribute inductions include one-place attributes and two or more-place attributes; the latter are sometimes called associative inductions. A one-place attribute induction would be: "All men are mortal" ("mortality" is predicated). A two-place variable induction would be: "Sixty per cent of all drinkers are both dangerous and immoral" ("dangerous" and "immoral" are predicated). Sometimes the distinction is also made between universal ("*All* men are mortal") and proportional ("*Most* [or *some*] drinkers are dangerous") inductions.

Rules of Induction

RULE OF VARIETY   There are differences of opinion as to what rules of inductive evidence are more important than others. Not too long ago even some sophisticated analyists could still insist that the more numbers, the better, was the prime consideration (cf. Day, i, 95). In other words, numerosity would be first norm of inductive validity. But with the popular disseminations of information about such techniques as the NBC, CBS, and ABC voter-analysis methods in the last few major elections, it is clear to many that something more than mere numbers is used when the whole election is predicted with less than one per cent of the vote in. Similarly,

---

6 Ampliative and problematic are others sometimes used (Peirce, Kneale and Johnson, Mace).

three "experts" several years ago testified before a Congressional committee that a sample of only 400 homes would be adequate for a national television poll (if the sample were ideal). This means that 400 homes serve as an adequate sample for a population of 55,000,000 homes. This is actually not one per cent (1/100) but 1/137,500, or not even 1/1000 of one per cent.

What made the voting profiles accurate in many cases and would make the television ratings reliable is actually the principle of variety. The votes are carefully classified as to probable economic status, geographic placement, religion, ethnic group, and political affiliation. Similarly, the television homes would have to be carefully selected on the bases of geographic location, economic status, age, education, and vocation.

These factors constitute the "variety" of the sample. A sample is varied when properties judged to be probably relevant to the predicate property at issue are considered, and, if possible, eliminated. Thus, in a consideration of smoking and its relationship to cancer, if subclasses separating urban dwellers from nonurban dwellers are established and no appreciable difference between the smoking–cancer relationship is noticed, then urban-dwelling can be eliminated as irrelevant. But if the groups are not stratified as to urban-dwelling, then the relevance of urban air pollution and other urban factors can not be ignored.

Variety by stratification, therefore, makes it possible to eliminate or not eliminate what seem to be issues relevant to the main induction (on eliminations, see Day, i, 92 ff.). Most logicians maintain that variety is impossible to determine with strict scientific adequacy (e.g. Nagel, p, 69 ff. but Carnap disagrees, lo, 575). Day, typically, says that variety is a matter of the antecedent probabilities (Day, i, 96,246). Thus previous research, past experience, common sense, even hunches, may help to determine the stratified groups. For a practical application of the principle of variety in discourse, see below, pp. 154 ff.

Errors due to lack of proper stratification are very common in inductive probabilities and are called errors of bias. Thus, in the first Kinsey report, several fairly important issues that would seem to have deserved consideration were not stratified. The survey, for example, did not provide an adequate control sampling of farm dwellers or Catholics. And one could "presume" that these issues would be relevant to sexual habits of males (see Wallis, st).

Once a subclass has been chosen, then the sampling should be done on the basis of the ratio of that subclass to the total population (Day, i, 174). Thus, the sample of Catholics chosen for sexual-habit analysis should constitute about one-fifth of the final sample, since Catholics constitute one-fifth of the total population in this country.

RULE OF RANDOMNESS Once the sample space is properly stratified, in order to be able to discern relevance and irrelevance, the next step is to secure a "random" sample. The sample is random when the selection of the sample occurs in such a manner that each member of the class or subclass has an equal chance of being chosen. Randomness, paradoxically, is difficult to secure in a random fashion (Wallis, s, 337 f.). Several methods are used. Choice by lottery is a simple method. More reliable is the method of a set of random tables or numbers. The Rand Corporation has a large series of such tables that are used for statistical analysis; and other such tables exist.

Random selection prevents many common faults in sampling, especially the danger of limiting observations to a particular range of time or space and then extrapolating. A recent example of many people failing to extend the range of observations over a long enough time occurred in the case of the so-called Air Force Diet, supposedly allowing a person to lose weight and yet eat the meat he wanted and drink the alcohol he usually consumed. Many people lost sensationally the first several weeks and immediately jumped to enthusiastic conclusions. A few weeks later, however, their weight went up again (on the Air Force diet) and then leveled off. And of course, there were dangers of vitamin and even starch deficiencies. A farmer, again, who wants to test his wheat plants and passes through his fields grabbing those he can reach from a standing position, has eliminated the chance of the smaller plants being chosen for the sample.The error is a random error.

RULE OF NUMEROSITY   The general rule of numerosity is very simple—the larger the numbers, the better the sample (assuming variety and randomness). However, the error of bias, due to lack of variety, may merely be reenforced by more numbers. Thus, if I am studying the relation of I.Q. to race in an investigation of Negro versus white secondary students and choose my samples of Negroes from a slum area in Washington, D.C., and my whites from a middle class suburb in the same city, the bias error will only be confirmed by more numbers.

If large numbers can be obtained, of course, the random error tends to diminish. Unfortunately, large numbers are sometimes difficult to obtain or even may be undesirable—for various reasons: research costs make them prohibitive, sampling sometimes involves the destruction of the sample (e.g., in weapon testing), large samples are simply unavailable, or the sampling has already taken place in a historical situation which cannot be duplicated. In these cases, the smaller sample must suffice. And some sort of check must be made to see if the sample is *probably* representative of the population. In statistics, there are some relatively simple procedures by which some important characteristics of the sample can be checked against the probable nature of these characteristics in the population.

It is difficult to summarize these procedures without assuming a background in statistics. Indeed, anyone seriously interested in a career in scientific discourse involving this kind of analysis can hardly get along without a grounding in statistical procedures. For the general reader it may mean something to say that numbers of many kinds of things tend to group themselves around a mean, a midpoint, in what is usually presented in graphic form as the normal distribution curve, that pride of statisticians and refuge of teachers in grading. If the numbers in a particular study do not follow this pattern of distribution with some fidelity, then it is probable that the numbers are not large enough to permit valid generalization, or the kind of things under investigation does not follow normal distribution patterns. If the report of the induction does not contain some assurance on the part of the investigator that these patterns have shown up in his studies, or some reasons why they have not, there must be some doubt as to the adequacy of the numbers selected for the sample.

With these general cautions, our survey of induction must conclude. Enough has been said, it is hoped, to alert the student to the danger of illicit generalizations. In the field of English studies (except in linguistics), negligence is almost the rule rather than the exception in generalizations made in such varied areas as: imagery patterns, symbolic structures of all sorts, character analyses, setting, dialect analyses in novels, and thematic motifs.

DEDUCTIVE LOGIC

In deductive logic, the following main points are to be covered: the definition of deduction, the nature of a deductive system, and some remarks on the kinds of deduction.

Definition of Deduction

Deduction is probably best defined in simple language as the process of inferring conclusions from premises (Whitehead, pm, 90, 94; cf. Stebbing, m, 192; Langer, i, 76). A premise is a "given" statement, that is, one adopted as a starting point and assumed to be valid, at least for the time being, for some reason. The definition "an inferential movement from the general to the particular," is true of only a limited number of deductions and is not comprehensive enough to encompass many common deductions which all of us make every day. Suppose I am going to a university book store with a friend of mine and inform him, "If Chomsky's book costs more than $10.00, I won't buy it." We get to the store and he wanders off among the literary criticism shelves. I find the book, notice its price, and call over to him, "It costs $12.95." From these two given statements, he can infer, "Kinneavy won't buy the book." This is a valid *deduction* from the two statements. But it is not a movement from the general to the particular. It is, in fact, an inference in the logic of statements, and is not concerned with general classes and their members. Many of the instances of deduction found in normal discourse will be instances of this kind of deduction, rather than deductions made in the logic of classes. And there are other deductive patterns which are not covered by the "general to particular" or "general to less general" definition.

Nature of a Deductive System

The process of inferring conclusion from given propositions presupposes certain postulates. It presupposes first that there are meaningful statements about things. Secondly, it presupposes that there are rules of inference which allow one to draw conclusions from given statements. These suppositions constitute the basis of any deductive system.

The first presupposition posits a set of rules of grammar and semantics. There must be assumed or explicit oral or written symbols that are put together according to the syntax rules of some grammar. And the words which are used refer, by convention, to some kind of reality. These agreements constitute the semantic rules of the system. Together, the grammatical and semantic rules constitute the *rules of formation* of the system. In ordinary scientific discourse, the grammar rules are assumed to be the grammar rules of everyday English. And the meanings of ordinary words are assumed to be their usual dictionary definitions. But these normal semantic rules of meaning are often supplemented in science by technical and restricted meanings of ordinary terms. And frequently, of course, new terms are added to the vocabulary.

After these rules of formation, a deductive system must have either implicit or explicit *rules of inference,* or rules of transformation, as they are sometimes called. These rules permit conclusions to be elicited from given statements by means of substitutions of equivalences or similar operations. In ordinary scientific discourse the rules of inference are assumed to be imported from ordinary logic. In very formalized deductive systems, the rules of inference are spelled out in precise detail and no inference can be made without explicitly naming the rule of inference which is being invoked. But the amateur who is analyzing or producing a deductive system must rely on his own intuitions or training to perceive these rules in operation. Luckily we all have a fairly sophisticated set of inferential rules which we can normally rely on. But it is certainly helpful to supplement our own amateur sense of logic by special training. Indeed a course or two of elementary logic is a great sharpener of our own rather primitive logical tools. A person who intends to engage in scientific discourse as a career can hardly get along without a general training in scientific inferences and special applications of these to his own discipline. Unfortunately, entire disciplines sometimes treat this concern rather casually. English, for instance, often turns out Ph.D.'s, trained to "research," who frequently have only their own crude, primitive tools of inference to work with.

The student, at this stage, might profitably take up one or several of the many excellent introductions to symbolic logic currently available in cheap editions in an attempt to improve his own logical acumen.[7]

The third component of a given deductive system consists of the "given" statements, or axioms of the system. In carefully formalized systems, these axioms are explicitly stated and no new axioms are introduced. And in carefully formalized systems these axioms must be *consistent* with each other; must be *complete,* that is, allow for the derivation of all of the inferences of the system; and must be *independent,* that is, not derivable from other axioms of the system. But in ordinary scientific discourse some axioms are often only implicit. And they may be explicitly or implicitly introduced anywhere in the progress of the discourse. Nor is there a systematic attempt to make the axioms complete or independent, although *consistency* is still a requirement.

Given these casual, almost haphazard procedures in ordinary deductive inference, it is easy to see why the analysis or production of a deductive system is a hazardous undertaking. Yet the ordinary student of discourse operates under precisely these hazards. He must often detect for himself the special semantic variations from ordinary language. He must rely on his own inferential rules. And he must, above all, ferret out implicit or explicit axioms, distinguish them from internal inferences within the system, and assess their consistency with other axioms being used. Finally, in ordinary scientific discourse, there is no neat separation of deductive from inductive inference.

Kinds of Deduction

In treating the definition of deduction, it was necessary to call attention to the fact that there were at least two different kinds of deductions. The usual concept of deduction, involving a movement from the general class to a member of the class or a part of the class, is an aspect of the deductive logic of classes or sets. The second, instanced by the statement about the purchase of the Chomsky book, is an example of the logic of statements or propositions. A third type, involving a logic of relations, is usually juxtaposed to these two. A statement like "if horses are animals, then heads of horses are heads of animals" cannot be proved either by a simple logic of statement or an ordinary logic of classes. Yet we all make such deductions every day. Our logical intuitions enable us to see the validity of such deductions, yet the strict logical proof of such a deduction had to wait

---

[7] In earlier manuscript versions of this book, a thirty-page summary of the logic of propositions, the logic of classes, and the logic of relations was included. Regretfully, this summary had to be deleted.

till the modern theory of a logic of relations. And the strict logical proof is a very intricate procedure which no mere amateur can ordinarily hope to master. But we do encounter such reasoning in much ordinary discourse.

A second very intricate and quite modern sophistication enables logicians to handle simple cases of another kind of deductive issue which we encounter in much everyday discourse. Ordinary college texts on deductive logic deal only in a two-valued logic. This means that a statement must be either true or false—and there are no other possibilities. Nevertheless, it is quite obvious that many assertions cannot be so categorized. If I say now "I shall give my wife a Christmas present" and then ask you to categorize this as either true or false, you should justifiably refuse to do so. You might say, "It depends. . ." This statement might be said to have a *conditional* truth value. So that statements might be categorized in a three-valued logical system: True–Conditional–False. Although Aristotle was aware of this problem, such systems were carefully analyzed only in 1920 by the Polish logician Lukasiewicz and in 1921 by Post.

The same statement might be categorized as "more–likely–true–than–false" in a five-valued system providing for these truth values: True—More likely true than false—Equally true or false—More likely false than true—False. Indeed, six-valued logics and even infinite-valued logical systems have been analyzed by logicians. And, although many-valued logics can be systematically analyzed only by quite complex symbolic procedures, they occur frequently in everyday discourse (see Kneale, d, 568 ff.). Ordinary language is a very subtle instrument.

Sample Analysis
of a Deductive Argument
from Camus, The Rebel

1. There are crimes of passion and crimes of logic. The line that divides them is not clear. But the Penal Code distinguishes between them by the useful concept of premeditation. We are living in the era of premeditation and perfect crimes. Our criminals are no longer those helpless children who pleaded love as their excuse. On the contrary, they are adults, and they have a perfect alibi: philosophy, which can be used for anything, even for transforming murderers into judges.

2. Heathcliff, in *Wuthering Heights,* would kill everybody on earth in order to gain Cathie, but he would never think of saying that murder is reasonable or theoretically defensible. He would commit it; there his theory comes to a halt. This implies powerful love and it implies character. Since intense love is rare, such murders are uncommon, and they retain an air of waywardness. But as soon as a man, through lack of

character, takes refuge in a doctrine, as soon as he makes his crime *reasonable,* it multiplies like Reason herself and assumes all the figures of the syllogism. It was unique like a cry; now it is universal like science. Yesterday, it was put on trial; today it is the law.

3. This is not the place for indignation. The purpose of this essay is once more to accept the reality of to-day, which is logical crime, and to examine meticulously the arguments by which it is sustained; it is an attempt to understand the time I live in. One might think that a period which, within fifty years, uproots, enslaves or kills seventy million human beings, should only, and forthwith, be condemned. But also its guilt must be understood. In more ingenuous times, when the tyrant razed cities for his own greater glory, when the slave chained to the conqueror's chariot was dragged through the rejoicing streets, when enemies were thrown to wild animals in front of the assembled people, before such naked crimes consciousness could be steady and judgment unclouded. But slave camps under the flag of freedom, massacres justified by philanthropy or the taste for the superhuman, cripple judgment. On the day when crime puts on the apparel of innocence, through a curious reversal peculiar to our age, it is innocence that is called on to justify itself. The purpose of this essay is to accept and study that strange challenge.

4. It is a question of finding out whether innocence, the moment it begins to act, can avoid committing murder. We can act only in our own time, among the people who surround us. We shall be capable of nothing until we know whether we have the right to kill our fellow-men, or the right to let them be killed. Since all contemporary action leads to murder, direct or indirect, we cannot act until we know whether, and why, we have the right to kill.

5. What matters here is not to follow things back to their origins, but, the world being what it is, to know how to live in it. In the age of negation, it was of some avail to examine one's position concerning suicide. In the age of ideologies, we must make up our minds about murder. If murder has rational foundations, then our period and we ourselves have significance. If it has no such foundations, then we are plunged in madness and there is no way out except to find some significance or to desist. We must in any case give a clear answer to the question put to us by the blood and strife of our century. For we are being interrogated. Thirty years ago, before making the decision to kill, it was the custom to repudiate many things, to the point of repudiating oneself by suicide. God is a cheat; the whole world (including myself) is a cheat; therefore I choose to die: suicide was the question then. But Ideology, a contemporary phenomenon, limits itself to repudiating other people; they alone are the cheats. This leads to murder. Every dawn masked assassins slip into some cell; murder is the question to-day.

6. The two ideas cling together. Or rather they cling to us, and so pressingly that we ourselves are no longer able to choose our problems. They choose us, one after the other. Let us consent to being chosen. This

essay proposes to follow, into the realm of murder and revolt, a mode of thinking that began with suicide and the idea of the absurd.

7. But this mode of thinking, for the moment, yields only one concept, that of the absurd. And the concept of the absurd, in its turn, only yields a contradiction where the problem of murder is concerned. The sense of the absurd, when one first undertakes to deduce a rule of action from it, makes murder seem a matter of indifference, hence, permissible. If one believes in nothing, if nothing makes sense, if we can assert no value whatsoever, everything is permissible and nothing is important. There is no pro or con; the murderer is neither right nor wrong. One is free to stoke the crematory fires, or to give one's life to the care of lepers. Wickedness and virtue are just accident or whim.

8. We may then decide not to act at all, which comes down to condoning other people's murder, plus a little fastidious sorrow over human imperfection. Or we may hit upon tragic dilettantism as a substitute for action; in this case, human lives become counters in a game. Finally, we may resolve to undertake some action that is not wholly arbitrary. In this case, since we have no higher value to direct our action, we shall aim at *efficiency*. Since nothing is true or false, good or bad, our principle will become that of showing ourselves to be the most effective, in other words the most powerful. And then the world will no longer be divided into the just and the unjust, but into masters and slaves. Thus, whatever way we turn in the depths of negation and nihilism, murder has its privileged position.

9. Hence, if we profess the absurdist position, we should be ready to kill, thus giving logic more weight than scruples we consider illusory. Certainly, some compromises will be necessary. But, on the whole, fewer than one might suppose—to judge from experience. Besides, it is always possible, as we see every day, to have the killing done for one. Thus everything would be settled in accordance with logic, if logic were really satisfied.

10. But logic cannot find satisfaction in an attitude which indicates first that murder is permissible and then that it is impermissible. For the absurdist analysis, after having shown that killing is a matter of indifference, eventually, in its most important deduction, condemns killing. The final conclusion of the absurdist process is, in fact, the rejection of suicide and persistence in that hopeless encounter between human questioning and the silence of the universe. Suicide would mean the end of this encounter, and the absurdist position realizes that it could not endorse suicide without abolishing its own foundations. It would consider such an outcome running away or being rescued. But it is plain that absurdist reasoning thereby recognizes human life as the single necessary good, because it makes possible that confrontation, and because without life the absurdist wager could not go on. To say that life is absurd, one must be alive. How can one, without indulging one's desire for comfort, keep for oneself the exclusive benefits of this argument? The moment life is

recognized as a necessary good, it becomes so for all men. One cannot find logical consistency in murder, if one denies it in suicide. A mind that is imbued with the idea of the absurd will doubtless accept murder that is fated; it could not accept murder that proceeds from reasoning. In view of that confrontation which they both render impossible, murder and suicide are the same thing; one must accept them both or reject them (Camus, r, 3–6).

As soon as one steps out of the logic book into real discourse, the differences between the ideal deductive system and the operating actuality become immediately evident. Camus' first six pages of *The Rebel* are a good illustration of the difference.

It is clear, almost immediately, that Camus is writing a serious essay, that he is engaging in rational discourse. He could be emotional about these issues, but he chooses to make a meticulous logical examination in this essay (paragraphs 3, 5, 6, and 10). Camus is like Sartre who can write about a philosophical issue as a philosopher in scientific discourse or embody the same issue in a novel as a theme. Thus the notions of the absurd, of individual isolations, and of suicide are treated philosophically in *The Myth of Sisyphus* and literarily in *The Stranger*. And the problem of communal cooperation is treated philosophically in *The Rebel* and literarily in *The Plague*.

Camus' rational technique is largely deductive in that part of the essay which we shall examine, though there are some uses of induction and at least one crucial instance. Yet Camus' deductive technique does not have any superficial resemblance to the neat deductive systems of a symbolic logic text. There is no careful formulary of syntax or semantic rules of formation. Rules of inference are assumed, but only rarely stated (an exception is the first sentence of paragraph 10). There is no initial parading of a set of four or five axioms from which conclusions will be drawn. Consequently, much of the system is implicit. As a result, part of our analysis must attempt to make explicit these underlying aspects. In the analysis, the rules of formation, then the rules of inference, then the axioms of the system, and finally the conclusions will be presented. The analysis will generally be descriptive, but occasionally evaluative comments will be made.

Rules of Formation—Syntax

The syntax rules originally adopted by Camus were obviously those of contemporary French. We are using a translation, so we accept the rules of contemporary English, although there are some vestiges of French syntax in the present translation. The one characteristic of French syntax which does affect the deductive validity of Camus' essay is his strong tendency to a paradoxical style, expressed grammatically in the short clausal oppositions so frequent in Camus (and other French writers) and that strike the American reader as being more recurrent than one would expect in normal American philosophical writing.

The following passage is typical:

> There is no pro or con: the murderer is neither right nor wrong. We are free to stoke the crematory fires or to devote ourselves to the care of lepers. Evil and virtue are mere chance or caprice (paragraph 7).

What this does to the deductive argument will be pointed out in the next section on the semantic rules of formation.

Rules of Formation—Semantic

There are some crucial variations from the ordinary dictionary rules of contemporary English in this short passage. Indeed, these semantic variations are central to the validity of Camus' whole argument. And, I believe, their lack of precision is also responsible for some of the weaknesses of his argument. Four terms (or clusters of terms) have meanings very peculiar to Camus, constituting a scientific idiolect. The first cluster is built around the terms: rebel, revolt, and revolution. Other important terms are: absurd, innocence, and efficiency. *Absurd* and *efficiency* are particularly crucial to his inferences.

Revolt has connotations peculiar to Camus. The French title of *The Rebel* is *L'Homme Révolté*, not *Le Rebelle*. For Camus, *revolt* has two important and individual dimensions of meaning. In the first place *révolte* (often translated "rebellion") is opposed to *revolution*. The first preserves the principle of respect for human life; *revolution* postpones this respect to a distant future. The distinction runs through the whole book, and there is a whole chapter devoted to it (r, 246–52; see also 106, 108, 163–4, 173–5, 179–87; and especially 250). Secondly, the period in Camus' work emphasizing *revolt* is a development from and crucially different from the period emphasizing the *absurd*. The *absurd* period stressed individualism, and existential isolation; the main problem for this period was the individual problem of suicide. The *revolt* period stressed the human solidarity of the group being oppressed; and the main problem became murder, the killing of the other. As Camus carefully remarks, "In the absurd experiences, suffering is individual. From the first moment of revolt, it is the adventure of all. . . . The malady which until then was suffered by one sole individual becomes collective plague," (from Camus, *Remarques sur la Révolte,* quoted by Maquet, a, 74).

The second crucial term in Camus' argument is *absurd;* and whole chapters of books have been written on its variegated meanings in Malraux, Camus, Sartre, the writers in the theater movement by that name, and others. The entire logic of Camus becomes unintelligible if one simply reads the word with its ordinary denotation and connotations. For Camus the word meant the emotional feelings and intellectual attitude that arise from the confrontation between man's demand for rationality and the ultimate irrationality of the universe. Emotionally, the absurd is a sentiment of disillusionment with the meaningless routine of life, the implacable march of time, the recognition that we are strangers to even our closest associates, and especially the inevitability of death (see Camus, m, 10–12). Intellectually, the absurd arises from the recognition of the radical incapacity of science and reason to explain the universe (see Camus, m, 12–16; Maquet, a, 38–42; Cruickshank, c, 45–58). Because of its weaknesses, reason cannot supply man with any absolute values or prove any transcendent, i.e., religious values. It is this notion that is the premise for the first major set of inferences which we shall examine below.

But, *and this must be remembered,* the absurd man must retain his demand for reason and use it to the best of his abilities. That is why, throughout both *The Myth of Sisyphus* and *The Rebel,* reason is used as the norm of judgment. To abdicate from reason, despite its weaknesses, would be philosophical suicide, as bad in its own way as physical suicide (see Camus, m, 7–8, especially 21–38).

For that reason, Camus' term *innocence* takes on an idiolectal character also. It really is, for Camus, more of an intellectual than a moral term. It means man innocent of the absolute or transcendent values. The sin opposed to this innocence is mystical faith. But innocence of absolute values does not mean absolute license; though there can be no religious reasons there may be human and rational reasons for ethical choice.

Finally, in this essay, *efficiency* and *efficacy* take on quite restricted meanings. Deprived of absolute norms for action, says Camus, man must act by a principle of immediate efficiency (paragraph 8). And efficacy immediately is paraphrased as "strength." This is a curious semantic rule, but it also is necessary in the evaluation of Camus' logic. With these semantic rules, we are now in a position to move on to Camus' rules of inference in this system.

Rules of Inference

Camus continuously stresses the fact that this essay (and *The Myth of Sisyphus*) is logically based. There are other situations that could justify getting emotional about these matters, but he chooses here to be rational (see paragraphs 3, 5, 6, 7, 10). And the rational principles to which he appeals are rarely explicitly invoked. At one critical point, the beginning of paragraph 10, he does acknowledge the principle of noncontradiction. Otherwise, the rules of inference of the trained thinker, though not the trained logician, are merely used but not verbalized.

Axioms of the System

The semantic rules have already indicated some of the axioms which Camus assumes in this demonstration. Generally, Camus assumes as "given" those positions which he had established in *The Myth of Sisyphus.* He has, therefore, a more solid foundation for his "given" than most arbitrary assumptions. For the moment, let us limit our analysis to the succinct logical development in paragraphs 7 through 10 and attempt to establish a set of axioms which could serve as bases from which this development starts. Other formulations might be made, but the following have been found workable in class analyses with upper-division undergraduates:

Axiom 1—The absurd man must recognize the rationality of man, his desire for total rationality, and the irrationality of the world (particularly explicit, paragraphs 3 and 10).

Axiom 2—The absurd confrontation between rational man and the irrational world must be sustained (paragraph 10).

Axiom 3—Philosophical suicide, repudiation of rationality in favor of faith or any absolute or transcendent value system, must be rejected (only vaguely implicit).

Axiom 4—Physical suicide must be rejected (paragraph 10).

Axiom 5—Murder is common in the world (paragraph 2).

Actually Axioms 3 and 4 were conclusions from Axiom 2 in *The Myth,* but they can here be regarded as given axioms.

The Development of the System

The general purpose of the argument is to establish the dilemma that the absurd man must both accept and reject murder (paragraphs 7 and 10). To establish this, each half of the dilemma must be proven. These can be called lemma 1 and lemma 2, a lemma being a basic step in the production of the main argument.

To establish lemma 1, the following deductions are made from the axioms:

Conclusion 1—The absurd leads to complete indifference in morality (paragraph 7; from Axiom 1).

Lemma 1—Whether the absurd man does not act or acts arbitrarily or nonarbitrarily, he must accept murder (paragraph 8; from Axiom 5, Conclusion 1, and the inevitability of the alternatives proposed; the non-arbitrary acting presupposes another axiom he inserts: we must have a predisposition to murder).

To establish lemma 2, absurd man must reject murder, the following steps are taken:

> *Conclusion 2*—Since suicide must be rejected, human life is a value (Axiom 2, 4, and an implicit semantic rule about the nature of value).
> *Conclusion 3*—Therefore every human life is a value (an intuitive induction, based on the *necessary* nature of the case, paragraph 10).
> *Lemma 2*—Therefore the absurd man must reject murder (from Axioms 2, 4, and Conclusion 3).

Because each lemma of the dilemma is established, the dilemma follows (stated explicitly in paragraphs 7 and 10). It can, therefore, be concluded that the absurd is a contradiction (last sentence). This brief description of Camus' logic in the last five paragraphs tries to abstract the main lines of his arguments. But description is, of course, only a necessary step to evaluation.

Evaluations of the System

A few brief comments on the validity and truth of the logic must therefore be made. And again the crucial foci must be the semantic rules and the axioms of the system. The first problem in the semantic rules has to do with the notion of the absurd. From the *partial* irrationality of man's confrontation with the world, Camus easily slips over to the *complete* meaninglessness of life (see especially m, 5, 7). This is an extension that must be questioned, and it is an important extension, for from it is derived the operating position that "we believe in nothing" (paragraph 7), which is behind part of Axiom 1. Others have criticized the variations on the meaning of *absurd,* though not quite in the same connection (cf. Cruickshank, a, 63). Secondly, one must severely question the opposite movement with *efficiency,* the restriction to the strength involved in murder. And this argument is crucial to lemma 1. Thirdly, the restriction of arbitrary action to gamesmanship in the same lemma is questionable. This vagueness must then call into question the validity of the exhaustiveness of the alternatives in lemma 1. Finally, the vagueness of the concept of a value in lemma 2 must be noted.

Once the semantic rules have been questioned, some doubt must be cast upon the validity of the axioms which incorporate these terms. But, Axiom 2, even granting the semantic rules, must be further called into question. For this reader (and others), Axiom 2 does not emerge as a valid conclusion from *The Myth*. And Axiom 2 is the basis for Axioms 3 and 4. Consequently, the truth of both lemmas and of the consequent dilemma must be questioned. All of this illustrates the hazardous process of the production of a deductive system in matters such as this. Yet Camus' logic is more careful than many similar attempts in these areas.

ETHNOLOGIC

As has been indicated above, deduction can be construed as a syntactics of proof and induction as a semantics of proof. The question naturally arises: Is there a pragmatics of proof?

A pragmatics of proof would be the use to which writers or readers put deduction or induction in order to achieve proof. In other words, it comes to mean the "subjective" or personal aspect of proof. This comes very close to the concept of belief. A pragmatics of proof, therefore, has to ask the question: Will the deductive and inductive techniques used to demonstrate the issues at hand actually be accepted by the reader as demonstrative? The author is not aware of any comprehensive treatment of the problems of a pragmatics of proof.[8] Nevertheless a few points ought to be made in this regard.

Since the time of Aristotle at least, it has been argued that there is a unity of logic, common to all cultures. This sometimes takes the position of merely assuming a fundamental human rationalism; sometimes it has gone much further and postulated a common logic that will be revealed in quite similar linguistic structures. For many centuries it was often assumed that such linguistic structures would necessarily have to incorporate the supposed "logical" character of Greek or Latin grammar. With modern advances in comparative linguistics, this latter position has been almost universally discarded. The modern linguistic counterpart to this notion, the concept of grammatical and semantic innate universals which are realized in different ways in different languages, is currently used by some linguists who are attempting to formulate a universal theory of grammar (cf. Chomsky, a, 27–30; Greenberg, u, xv–xxvii). The theory of universals has, at some levels, become embroiled in some rather vitriolic controversy; especially is this true in attempts to arrive at a "basic" human vocabulary by means of statistical analyses of various languages (cf. Dyen, v, Hymes, l and c, and Lunt, c). But the controversy does not seem to have been extended into the pragmatics of language as yet—or more specifically, into scientific proof.

Rather, scientists often speak in enthusiastic terms of the international character of the language of science. Einstein gives the following

---

8 Martin has a brief and very theoretical treatment of some aspects of the problem in t, 33–60.

reason for this: "The super-national character of scientific concepts and scientific language is due to the fact that they have been set up by the best brains of all countries and all times" (c, 325).

This may be an ideal towards which all science strives, but the hard facts of history sometimes tell a different story. Individuals and even whole groups have sometimes failed to understand or accept what have appeared to be, in retrospect, quite conclusive and irreproachable demonstrations of scientists in pioneer situations. Sometimes whole cultures are guilty of this. As Pike has remarked,

> People of one nation sometimes appear to be "illogical" or "stupid" or incomprehensible simply because the observer is over a long period of time taking an alien standpoint from which to view their activity, instead of seeking to learn their emic [internal to the culture] patterns of overt and covert behavior (Pike, 1, I, 17).

The orientation in some cases may have to be only slight. Thus, despite the lack of contact, Hindu logic as developed by Dinna and diffused even to China and Japan, nonetheless has striking similarities to Aristotelean logic. It was predicational, it presupposed the so-called three laws of thought (noncontradiction, excluded middle, and identity), it focused on a three-proposition syllogism and concerned itself with the distribution of the middle term (Sujiura, h, 22–23, 35).

On the other hand, Whorf has shown that the logic behind Shawnee, Noatka, Hopi, and Apache is not predicational and had the potential of developing into a very different sophisticated logic (Whorf, 1, 233–45). Similarly a Hopi or an Algonkian physics offer possibilities of interpreting reality in quite different modes from our Western European views of the importance of time (and consequent speed and velocity) in physics (Whorf, 1, 217, 267). Even within the matrix of Western civilization, the German view of "science" can tolerate a brand of metaphysics and a *Literaturwissenschaft* which much Anglo-Saxon thought would term speculation, at best.

Indeed one does not have to go beyond the province of a single major university. Many physicists, sociologists, even educators would not label much dissertation work by literary critics "scientific" at all. Similarily, many English professors consider the endless survey and statistical techniques of educators trivial and inconsequential. Even within the individual English departments, the time is not too removed when historical critics would not speak to "new critics" or "descriptive" to "prescriptive" linguists.

Science may have a unity, but, as Russell once remarked, no one has proven it to be unified. And if science is an international language, many people still speak their own provincial patois. In practice, the writer of scientific discourse must recognize that there is as yet no universal or even university-wide concept of "research." He must prove by the ethnologic of his peers of the group for which he writes, while striving to move his own discipline towards a more cosmopolitan view of research.[9]

The Logic of Informative Discourse

At the outset of the discussion of scientific discourse, it was pointed out that in many of our reasonings whereby we attempt to prove something, intuitive techniques have to be relied on. The systematic analysis of quite simple relational concepts, for instance, is a very complex undertaking. *A fortiori,* the logic behind informative discourse must also be intuitive to a large extent. In fact the logical sophistication of information theory, as worked out by Carnap and Bar-Hillel (1), is far beyond the normal logical ability of an average upper-class or even graduate English student. Nevertheless, an awareness of the general framework of such a logic is not beyond the average capabilities of such students—and it is such a framework only that will be briefly sketched here.

The framework involves the logical issues related to the three components of informative discourse treated in the nature of information: factuality, content comprehensiveness, and informative surprise value.

FACTUALITY

The notion of factuality is usually regarded as intuitively simple. It is not usually subjected to analysis. Some would probably maintain that the student ought not to be confused by this sort of analysis. Indeed, some would probably argue that with regard to such basic notions as narrative, logic, information, and class, the student generally ought to be left to his intuitions. No Hume should thus disturb the dogmatic slumbers of a Kant in these matters.

Obviously the author does not concur with this optimistic naïveté. No discipline can be said to be mature if it has not analyzed its own fundamental concepts (La Drière, r, 123). By now the student will suspect that the ostensible simplicity of the concept of factuality is probably about to be dissolved into complexity. And his suspicions are well grounded.

The definition of "fact" in high school or college texts is usually done in a context of differentiating fact from something generally called

---

9 In addition to an ethnologic in science, there is clearly an ethnologic in exploration, possibly in information, certainly in persuasion, and in literature.

"opinion" or even "value judgment" (cf. Pollock, m, 130; Martin, 1, 52–56).[10] And usually a fact is established as something which can be verified and an opinion as something which eludes strict verification (Pollock, m, 130; Martin, 1, 53).

More technical treatments allow us to make some important distinctions which these formats ignore, namely, the distinction between logical and empirical verification and the distinction between absolute verification and verification with only a measure of inductive probability. If we use the division of propositions, given above (p. 76), into factually true, factually false, logically true, logically false, and unverifiable, we have a concept of factuality which is more serviceable.

The first four kinds of propositions are scientifically verifiable and are opposed to statements which are not scientifically verifiable. Verifiable statements are then divided into those which are factually verifiable as either true or false and those which are logically verifiable as true or false.[11] Factual verifiability is established by examining the universe, or by what is usually called empirical verification. Empirical verification is verification by means of sense data or observable data or measurable data. A statement of fact is a statement which is amenable to verification by observation of the universe. "My pen is red," "Heavy smoking is related to incidence of lung cancer," "Carnap wrote a major portion of 'An Outline of a Theory of Semantic Information,'" "The American flag is green" are factual statements. They can be verified as true or false, totally or in some measure by observable data.

Logical statements are verified by analyzing "given" statements on the basis of their deductive validity vis-à-vis themselves or other statements of a given deductive or inductive system, "If p implies q, and p is true, then q is true," and "The statistical evidence, e, allows us to conclude h with 95 percent probability" are statements which are amenable to logical verification, deductive and inductive respectively. These latter, in this framework, are not called factual statements. "He was near Odette, in contact with Odette, but blind and dead, the train was carrying his ears and eyes to Marseille" is a scientifically unverifiable statement from Sartre's *The Reprieve* (242).

There are problems, even with such distinctions. Some philosophers today question the strict dichotomy of empirical versus logical. This problem has become quite an issue in modern semantics. In Linsky's anthology of essays on semantics, half of the essays are devoted, in large part, to this issue

---

10 In the high school series referred to here, edited by Pollock, "fact" is further distinguished from "inference" (137), and the definitions for opinion and inference are equivalent almost word for word (130 and 137).

11 Some writers reserve "verified" for empirical verification and use "demonstrated" for logical proof (Hartnack, w, 48).

(see especially Quine and White in Linsky, l, 120 ff. and 272–86). Other authors repeatedly insist that all facts are theory-laden. Cassirer aptly quotes Goethe, "The highest wisdom would be to realize that all fact is already theory" (quoted in Cassirer, e, 174). And Northrop says even more strongly,

> The only way to get pure facts independent of all concepts and theory, is merely to look for them and forthwith to remain perpetually dumb (l, 317).

These cautions are well taken and are sometimes very relevant to a serious discourse analysis at a deep philosophical level. Nonetheless, the logical-empirical distinction still seems to be a serviceable classification in ordinary analysis.[12] Certainly, in the anthologized essay of Wallis and Roberts, as well as in the other selections that have been used in this chapter (Alsop's article on Vietnam, and the piece from Camus), the distinction is easy enough to make.

Of course, once it has been established that a given statement was or is susceptible to empirical verification, the matter of the informative validity of the fact is not thereby closed. Indeed, it may only be opened. For the process of evaluating the facts may still be a crucial one. The evaluation in this case is usually a matter or determining whether the observed or observable data are what they actually profess to be. Some useful general cautions can be made in this regard.[13]

If one is himself the observer, he should attempt to discount his own preconceptions and make a selection from the available materials which will be appropriate for amassing facts in the first place. This selection, obviously, will be related to the comprehensiveness of the informative system, a point to be covered in the next section. One safeguards oneself from one's own preconceptions by following the rules of variety, randomness, and numerosity discussed above under scientific induction.

Secondly, if one has to rely on one's own past observations and experience, proper safeguards should be erected insofar as possible: consulting records, diaries, contemporary newspapers, and other accounts. If one has to rely on others for observations, even more safeguards are needed. Is the source a primary source, i.e., an immediate observer of the data? If so, is the primary source well qualified to make intelligent observations? Is the primary source likely to have a known bias in selection of data?

On the other hand, is the data from a secondary or tertiary, or

---

12 For variant views on the nature of fact, cf. Scheffler, a, 58 ff.; Coles, f, 180 ff.; Wittgenstein, t, 7 ff., 15 ff., 39 ff. and *passim;* Peirce, c, I, 427 ff.; Cope, i, 20 ff. (on Aristotle); Carnap, lo, 85 ff.; Carnap, m, 28 ff.

13 In the following paragraphs I have found Graves, f, 20 ff., and Cooper, a, 245 ff., quite useful.

quaternary source? If so, the original events may well have been "leveled" by later sources leaving out data undesirable to them, or "sharpened" by exaggeration, or "assimilated" into later sources' stereotypes and prejudices (the terms are Allport's and Postman's, *The Nature of Prejudice,* as paraphrased by Graves, f, 29). If so, allowance must be made for this.

Having evaluated the credibility of the source, the data itself must be examined. Is it internally consistent? Is it consistent with other data from other sources? Is it presently still verifiable? (cf. Graves, f, 31 ff. and Cooper, a, 248 ff.). Was the sample a representative sample to begin with?

In addition to the data, the medium in which they are given can be very relevant. Material written for a newspaper account may well reflect the policy of the newspaper or the general "sensational" character of all journalistic media. The same may be true of television or radio reports. The data from a neutral scientific set of observations might be more sober. The "information" about Van Gogh in Irving Stone's "biography," *Lust for Life,* may not be as verifiable as that in the *Encyclopedia Britannica,* in fact may even be intentionally "fictional" (e.g., the episode with the fictional girl Maya)—even if this sort of "fictionality" is in accord with Stone's sensitive perception of the tone and atmosphere of the situation.

Different sciences often have to set up their own criteria for data credibility. Legal science, possibly the most thorough, has its own precise norms for admissible evidence, hearsay, expert evidence, opinion, confessions, legislative rights to prescribe rules of evidence and methods of proof, and circumstantial evidence (cf., for a typical popular survey, Marshall, p, 269 ff.).

Unfortunately, the field of English lacks a systematic survey of rules of scientific or scholarly evidence. Literary history and textual criticism (study of valid editions, manuscripts, etc.) usually import bodily the canons of historical study itself (cf. Wellek, t, 31, 51, and especially 263–4). But literary criticism and literary analysis are still in the folklore period as far as scientific evidence is concerned. Even linguistics, which has much closer affinities to typical physical or social science approaches, is still attempting to establish its own canons of scientific data. Should the scholar trust his own intuition of grammaticality, or should he use a corpus or several typical corpora for his samples? Should the data be quantitative or not? And even more fundamental questions are still controversial issues in modern linguistic science (cf. Katz, p).

THE LOGIC OF CONTENT
(COMPREHENSIVENESS)

In order to explain the logic of the content or comprehensiveness of an informative statement, it seems simplest to follow a typical stratagem of logicians—erect a miniature system and explain the concept within that system, then later extrapolate to more complex systems.

The miniature system used here is that given by Carnap and Bar-Hillel in their analysis of the concepts of semantic information (Bar-Hillel, 1, 226). They analyze "content" and "information" in statements made within an artificial language system, $L_{a,b,c}^{M,Y}$. Statements in this system are about the inhabitants of a little town which has three inhabitants: a, b, and c. In this artificial language, it can be predicated of an inhabitant that it is male or female and that it is young or old. These are the only possible predicates in the language and a, b, and c are the only possible subjects. So the language system is symbolized by $L_{a,b,c}^{M,Y}$.

To get a complete picture of this universe of discourse, one would have to know of each inhabitant whether it is male (or not) and young (or not). "Young" is defined as under thirty-five.

Even in a simple universe like this there are sixty-four possible combinations; "a is male and young, b is male and young, and c is male and young" would be only one of the sixty-four possibilities. By taking a single or composite statement (e.g., "a is male," and "a is male and old"), it can easily be ascertained how many of the sixty-four possibilities are ruled out if this statement holds. So the "content" of a statement can be measured by ascertaining how much one learns about the whole framework of possibilities of the system. Merely logical statements, like "a is either male or female," rule out no possibilities and so have zero content. By pursuing this direction, Carnap and Bar-Hillel can establish a whole series of theorems about the "content" of a statement (Bar-Hillel, 1, 237 ff.).

The translation of such a theory into actual discourse can be partially effected in the following manner. A topic about which information is desired can be considered to have a context of possible factual expectancies —the average reader interested in such a topic would presumably want certain implicit questions about the topic satisfactorily answered. These expectancies constitute the "universe of discourse" about the topic. When they have been adequately covered, information about the topic can be considered to be comprehensive. The nature of this comprehensiveness has been considered in the section on the nature of information. A strict logical analysis of total comprehensiveness for an actual discourse could only be made by a very complicated computer analysis, but the practical implementation of the concept is amenable to common-sense analysis.

The important consideration is the erection of the system implied by the given universe of discourse and the consequent erection of the various alternative possibilities (state-descriptions). If this large framework is envisaged, then content can be evaluated with some security. The erection of the system is a matter of the reader's expectancies of the topic, as was pointed out in the consideration of the nature of content (see p. 94). Sometimes the reader can rely on the system erected by the writer. But sometimes, the reader must begin content evaluation by rejecting or enlarging or restricting the universe of discourse of the writer.

THE LOGIC OF SURPRISE VALUE

The third component of informative discourse is the surprise value of the discourse. The nature of this has been briefly adverted to above (see pp. 93–94, 95–96). Since the surprise value of a statement is directly proportional to its unpredictability or improbability, the logic of information as improbable involves the logic of probability (better still, the logic of improbability).

It is possible to work out, for a miniature system, the surprise value of a given statement, just as the content value of a given statement was worked out above (cf. Bar-Hillel, 1, 241–48). Surprise value does not behave in the same manner as content value. In practice, whereas a few cogent statements early in an essay may contain most of the content, the surprise value of statements may well continue unabated throughout the scientific essay. In some kinds of informative discourse, such as journalism and ordinary conversation, the surprise statements are often clustered in the beginning of the discourse.

To revert to the artificial language $L_{a,b,c}^{M,Y}$, suppose that the census taker comes to the town and first finds out that "a is male." The only probability induction he can make is that there is more of a probability for males than females in the town. Suppose he next finds out that "b is male." His induction about a heavy male population is confirmed. Then, suppose that he encounters c and finds out that "c is female." This is of great surprise value, for the opposite was inductively (statistically) more predictable.

In practice, such merely internal (or semantic) surprise value does not seem, as yet, to have useful translation potential as far as analysis of actual *informative* discourse is concerned. For narration, especially literary narration, internal surprise value is very significant and can be closely tied to the classical concepts of discovery and peripety (cf. Volume II, Chapter II, "Narrative Discourse").

In most informative discourse, the probability is not internal to the discourse, but concerns the relation of the statements of the discourse to the situational context, i.e., to the "current" probabilities of a group audience or an individual receptor. Measurement of the sort of surprise value in any kind of quantified or objective logical norms still seems quite unattainable. As was stated earlier, "subjective" or pragmatic" information is still an infant discipline. Some tentative conclusions about the interrelationships of the three logical components of informative writing seem to suggest themselves. To be adequately informative, a piece of discourse would seem to require the presence of all three components. If factuality is present along with surprise value, but comprehensiveness is missing, the piece may actually be misleading or misinforming because the proper perspective of the facts and their surprise value is not displayed. Such is the case of the "Vietnam: The Meaning of the Dead" referred to above. The article is sensational and actually misleading.

If, on the other hand, the items are factual and comprehensive, but have no surprise value, the piece is commonplace, routine, dull, hackneyed. Such are the myriad high school themes which dismiss the history of the Civil War in two brief paragraphs. For informational value, such are many typical noncommittal but safe, political speeches.

Finally, and obviously, if surprise value and comprehensiveness are adequately present but factuality is absent, the result is fiction, possibly even good fiction.

SAMPLE ANALYSIS:
"VIETNAM: THE MEANING OF THE DEAD"

On April 24, 1965, Stewart Alsop published his regular column for *The Saturday Evening Post,* which was titled "The Meaning of the Dead." A magazine or newspaper column, can, in our present cultural context, be either reference, or persuasive, or even occasionally paraliterary or expressive discourse. And obviously it is often an overlap of several of these. Sometimes it can use entertaining devices for persuasive purposes. And, even more frequently, it can use a facade of information or explanation or logical proof for the real purpose of achieving persuasion. Such seems to be the case with Alsop's column in this instance. And just as it is possible to see what happens to logic in a persuasive text, so is it also possible to see what happens to information in a predominantly persuasive text (for a lengthy consideration of both of these issues, cf. below, pp. 245–63). The short analysis here must be understood to exist within this framework and will actually be concerned as much with the nature of informative discourse as with the logic of informative discourse. For purposes of analysis the full text of Alsop's column, "The Meaning of the Dead," is reprinted here.

> In 1962, when Secretary of Defense Robert McNamara made his first trip to Vietnam, he complained forcefully that the war was insufficiently "quantified"—a horrible verb which is one of McNamara's favorites. He would ask questions, he complained, and nobody would have the answers. As a result, the Vietnamese war is now the most quantified in history.
> You helicopter into some little village in a heavily Communist-infested

area, and you are immediately led into a "briefing room." The local Vietnamese army commander, with his American adviser proudly looking on, then proceeds to quantify the war in his area, in terms of killed, wounded, prisoners, weapons captured or lost, numbers of actions, and a half dozen other categories.

The first category is always K. I. A.—Killed in Action. Every time a Viet Cong Communist is killed, or a South Vietnamese soldier, or an American, he becomes part of the statistics which are gathered from every little hamlet and sent back to Saigon and Washington. The official K. I. A. statistics for last year are as follows: Americans: 141; South Vietnamese Forces: 7,000; Viet Cong: 17,000.

This grim tabulation of the dead tells a lot about the nature of the strange struggle in Vietnam. In the first place, the K. I. A. totals mean that, on our side at least, the Vietnamese war is notably unlethal in comparison with a conventional infantry war. For purposes of comparison, in the limited Korean war the total fatal casualties on both sides came to over a million. And the comparatively undeadly nature of the Vietnamese war has its meaning for all the participants.

Take the Americans first. No sensitive man could have anything but admiration for the Americans who have given their lives in Vietnam and sympathy for their families. But no sensible man could suppose that 141 fatal casualties put any very terrible strain on a nation of 190,000,000.

Moreover, those who weep crocodile tears about "American boys" dying in the jungle overlook the fact that the American soldiers in Vietnam are not boys but men. Almost without exception the few thousand Americans who have the really dangerous jobs out in the boondocks are professional soldiers. A man does not become a professional soldier, after all, in order to avoid all risk.

After chatting with some of the American soldiers in the field in Vietnam, I scribbled in my notebook: "These guys seem so damn happy." That may sound fatuous, but it is true. Living on rice and noodles and chasing hardcore Communists may not be the average American's idea of happiness. But these men are not average Americans—they are regular soldiers by choice. They are "so damn happy" in part, I suspect, because they have at last escaped the elephantine Army bureaucracy and are on their own. But they are also happy because they are doing a job that needs doing, and they are doing it well, which is a pretty good recipe for happiness.

It is just plain silly, in short, to maintain that the American commitment in Vietnam places an intolerable strain on the United States, or even on the few thousand soldiers who are in the dangerous jobs there. These soldiers would be infuriated, to a man, by any official decision to withdraw the American commitment, and let South Vietnam go down the drain.

The K. I. A. tabulation also has its meaning for the loyal South Vietnamese forces. There are about half a million men in the South

Vietnamese army, divided about equally between regular army and local militiamen. According to Americans who have been with them in action, these men are still, after all these years, fighting their war surprisingly well. How long will they continue to fight?

That is the key question in Vietnam—not which one of Saigon's squabbling generals and politicians eventually emerges as No. 1. No one knows the answer to the question. But the K. I. A. tabulation at least suggests a fairly hopeful answer.

No army can take very heavy casualties year after year and fight on indefinitely. But a fatal casualty rate of less than 2 percent is a tolerable percentage for any reasonably disciplined army. Thus it is certainly possible that the Vietnamese forces will be able to carry on the fight for a long time—provided that they have what any army must have, hope of victory.

Hope of victory is precisely what the third K. I. A. tabulation—17,000 dead Viet Cong—*ought* to provide. American officers in the field swear that the figures of killed Communists are accurate. They are based largely, they say, on a count of dead bodies, and the bodies do not include killed South Vietnamese civilians. And if the figures are accurate, the Viet Cong *ought* to be running out of live bodies.

There are roughly 100,000 Viet Cong guerrillas in South Vietnam today, according to intelligence estimates. Even given the Viet Cong's ruthless system of draft-by-kidnapping, that figure represents about the maximum manpower available to the Viet Cong, *in South Vietnam*. A 17 per cent lethal casualty rate is a nasty business, especially for guerrillas. If the war were really a civil war within South Vietnam, it would be possible to foresee a time when the Viet Cong would be whittled down to manageable proportions. Then the little country could get around to the business of organizing a rational political and economic life. It would be possible to foresee, in short, what would for all practical purposes be a victory for our side.

In fact, the Viet Cong would already have been whittled down to size, if the North Vietnamese Communists had not replaced the Viet Cong's losses. According to the intelligence, some 40,000 trained men were infiltrated from North Vietnam into South Vietnam in the last three years. In the first few months of this year, the "kill rate" of Viet Cong has been ever higher than previously, thanks to improved techniques and total air supremacy. Thus if the war were confined to South Vietnam, our side would certainly be winning it.

But as long as the Viet Cong can draw on a virtually unlimited reserve of trained men from the North, the Viet Cong cannot be whittled down to size. In such circumstances, the war cannot be won, and must in the end be lost. That in turn is why President Johnson really had no choice but to order air strikes against the North, to force the North Vietnamese to pay a price for their oblique aggression. If the price is high enough, they may halt the aggression. In that case, as the K. I. A.

tabulations suggest, the supposedly unwinnable war in Vietnam might be won, for all practical purposes, in rather short order. That is the clear meaning of the counting of the dead.

It is clear from a reading of this column that some information is conveyed, regardless of what other purposes of discourse the column accomplishes. Let us take a brief look at the factuality of the information, at the surprise value of the information, and at the comprehensiveness of the information.

The factuality of the information contained in Alsop's column can be examined under the light of several different types of considerations. In the first place, there are considerations of factuality relevant to the cultural context within which columns like this take place. In our American culture, journalists get their information from sources which oftentimes they cannot divulge because to do so would dry up these sources in the future. Consequently the factuality of much journalistic material is often incapable of verification at the source. In the case of news stories, even the journalist's name disappears, so that writer and source become impersonal and are absorbed into a news agency like the Associated Press or *Time* magazine. Such anonymity has both desirable and undesirable effects as far as factuality is concerned. In the present case, the primary sources are stated in general terms: "the local Vietnamese army commander with his American adviser proudly looking on," "American soldiers in the field in Vietnam." Alsop follows customary journalistic conventions by not identifying the sources precisely.

At the level of situational context, the factuality of these primary sources can also be examined, even questioned. At this early stage of American involvement in the war, it might be assumed that the local Vietnamese and American commanders were giving accurate facts to a respected American journalist. But the selective rhetoric of the divulging of military statistics in any war and in this war in particular must give the information analyst some pause. And the selective filtering by the journalist of what he is allowed to divulge or chooses to divulge must also be considered before the analyst accepts this kind of information as "factual." And, in this particular situation, some advertence must be made to the actual validity of filed reports on "dead" Viet Cong or South Vietnamese or Americans.

Further, some assessments of the "factuality" value of the medium is possible in this, as in many cases. How reliable, in general, are the facts of *The Saturday Evening Post?* The magazine had a very respectable history of responsibility in American journalism for almost two hundred years. But for several years in the period during which this issue appeared, the *Post* had been having subscription problems and had, on occasion, published some rather sensational material, some of which had been questioned on factual bases. In one instance, Wally Butts, football coach at Georgia, had been accused of controlling the point spread in some games. The case eventually reached the U. S. Supreme Court. And this body had rapped the fingers of *The Saturday Evening Post* for delinquency in factual matters. This is almost certainly irrelevant to the Alsop column, but a thorough analysis of the factuality of a given medium must take such considerations in its purview.

Finally, the responsibility of the individual writer is relevant to a consideration of factuality. In this case, Alsop's reputation would give heavy support to the validity of the facts in his column. Generally, therefore, although there are some negative considerations at the level of cultural and situational context, the majority of the considerations seem to lend support to the basic reliability of the facts in Alsop's column. There is no assessment implied here of the inferences he draws from these facts—that would be another analysis.

The second component of information has to do with surprise value. Since the author has used this text with over 250 college students for analytical purposes, it might be presumed that their verdict about the surprise value of some of the information in Alsop's column would have some validity. They have, by a heavy percentage over a three-year period, indicated that a fair amount of the information supplied by Alsop was "surprising" to them. Generally, the figures for the South Vietnamese and the Viet Cong, the curiously quantified and economic interpretation of "nondrain" on America, the idea that most professional soldiers were happy doing this job, the concept that casualties for an army could be estimated in terms of a margin of safety loss, etc., were items that were surprising to the majority of the audience (though not to a few isolated veterans). After several years, some of the information in Alsop's column has become common knowledge. But at the time, it had a fairly high percentage of news for the college students who read it, and, even more, for the average reader of *The Saturday Evening Post*. Its grading for surprise value might even be higher than its rating for factuality.

The third component of information is comprehensiveness. This consists, as has been shown, in the implications about the full system which can be drawn from the facts presented. Crucial to such a set of implications is the system or context about which implications can be drawn. It is evident that Alsop can not pretend to give an encyclopedic completeness to his system in a brief one-page column in a bimonthly magazine. In practice, as was pointed out, the writer must fulfill the basic reasonable expectancies of his average audience. It is only fair to point out that a writer may, especially in a short piece, arbitrarily delimit these expectancies in order to give some depth to his treatment. The criterion of comprehensiveness then might be said to be gauged by establishing a proper perspective with regard to the whole or partial system. It is also clear that the reader, especially at first, might not approach the text with the same context as the author, and the author may properly erect a better or novel context.

In order to assess the comprehensiveness of the system which Alsop has provided to serve as context for his surprising facts, I have again resorted to the expediency of using my classes over a period of three years as an index of context expectancies. It may be objected, with some fairness, that college students are not the average audience of *The Saturday Evening Post*. Nonetheless they are not too removed from such an audience, and their expectancies should not be too atypical.

Sometimes I asked the students to write down their context expectancies after they had read only the title of the column, sometimes after they had read two or three paragraphs, sometimes after they had read the entire column. In all cases, with over ten different classes, I have found that the expectancies of the students were vastly different from Alsop's actual context. Usually most of the students expected a "meaning of the dead" in terms of a moral or ethical meaning, or a political meaning, or a strategic military meaning for Asia, or a democratic meaning in terms of the worth of individuals' lives.

It seems clear that Alsop has obviously provided a rather novel context here: the importance of bombing North Vietnam if the resources of America and South Vietnam are not to be strained, while those of the Viet Cong are to be strained. For nearly all of the students this context itself had surprise value—a commendable contribution as far as that goes. But the vital question is: Did this restricted context preserve a proper perspective for the whole system? Almost unanimously the students felt it did not. The erected context did violence to the implication for the whole system. In fact, the implications for the whole system became distortions. Perspective was lost. Not only are the implications which Alsop draws about the system questionable, they are misleading. Alsop, of course, could have indicated that he was arbitrarily limiting the "meaning of the dead" to something like a statistical economic meaning, but he didn't. Counting the title, Alsop repeats the phrase the "meaning of the dead" (or its equivalent) six times in the column. He concludes categorically: "That is the clear meaning of the counting of the dead." What he said was clear, but what wasn't clear to the majority of the students was the real and important meaning(s) of the dead.

Given the nature of the genre and the medium, I postulated that possibly Alsop had considered these other issues in other columns of the period. A check on all of his columns over a half-year before and a half-year after this particular one revealed no consideration of these other issues which the college readers thought relevant at the time. For Alsop, this really was the meaning of the dead. The meaning of the dead to the families of the killed, the existential meaning of the death of any one individual, the meaning of the dead in terms of the strategic importance of Vietnam in the Southeast Asian general picture, the meaning of the dead in Vietnam to Europe, Africa, South America, Red China, Japan—those meanings had no meaning to Alsop.

In consequence, it has to be said that the information value of Alsop's column fails significantly at the level of comprehensiveness. It is misleading, and it distorts the total picture. What does this rating do to the total information value of the column? Given a high factuality and a high surprise value, but a low comprehensive value, what is the final assessment of such a piece. Actually these two other ratings make the distortions even more dangerous and sensational. The piece is misinforming, and this is a more grievous sin than dullness or even than lapses in factuality.

The Logic
of Exploratory Discourse

It is currently a contested point that there is a specific logic of exploratory discourse as distinct from the logic of proof in scientific discourse. Traditionally, Aristotle, Bacon, Kant, Hegel, and Marx had taken the position that there is a specific logic of the discovery procedure. Bacon, on the one hand, and Kant, Hegel, and Marx on the other, even repudiated traditional Aristotelian logic as a logic of discovery and substituted a new organum and a dialectical procedure respectively for traditional logic. Newton, Galileo, and Descartes even suggested that induction was a logic of discovery and deduction a logic of proof or demonstration—a dubious position at best.

In the modern period, the adherents of a distinction between the two logics have been challenged by several important people who maintain that the "hypothetico-deductive" method used in scientific method is reducible to the logic of science which was surveyed above. Popper (1, 31–32), Reichenbach (e, 382), Harré (i, 114), Braithwaite (s, 21–22) and Alexander (s, 219–32), are some who deny a specific logic to discovery procedures. Popper quotes Einstein, in a statement typical of this group:

> There is no logical path leading to these...[universal scientific] laws. They can only be reached by intuition, based on something like an interested love ("Einfühling") of the object of experience. (Quoted in Popper, 1, 32.)

As has already been pointed out, however, many modern writers disagree with this (cf. pp. 98–99), and agree with Toulmin, who says that one cannot simply say that science consists in making deductions and inductions—much of the stuff of science is quite different from either (p, 39; cf. 42, 64.)

Kurt Lewin, describing Cassirer's work in philosophy, even goes further:

> He discloses the basic character of science as the eternal attempt to go beyond what is regarded scientifically accessible at any specific time. To proceed beyond the limitations of a given level of knowledge the researcher, as a rule, has to break down the methodological taboos which condemn as "unscientific" or "illogical" the very methods or concepts which later on prove to be basic for the next major progress (Lewin, c, 275).

The "illogical" character of some aspects of the exploratory process is brought out by several professional logicians; Peirce, Day, and Harrah all distinguish what they call "abduction" or "retroduction" from induction and deduction; and by abduction they mean the hypothetical type of inference involved in exploration.

It might be profitable to examine the logical processes involved in the various stages of the exploratory process as they were outlined above. In the "dogma" state, the problem is simply acquainting oneself with what has been said on the subject before. There is nothing peculiar to the logic of discovery in this stage. It involves ideally an acquaintanceship with the history of the problem, a comparison and classification of the various solutions proposed, and, of course, an evaluation of these solutions. There are specific logical processes involved here, of course, the logic of information and the logic peculiar to narration, classification, and evaluation—the last three of which will be considered in Volume II of this work, *The Modes of Discourse*.

The logical processes involved in the stage of "cognitive dissonance" and "crisis" are those of perceiving inconsistencies between the inferences which should follow logically from the axioms and theorems of the dogma and the observed facts or inferences known from other sources. These inconsistencies can generally be characterized as logical incompatibilities, "not both p and q." And, of course, if enough of these occur, the axioms and theorems dictating the supposed inferences will have to be questioned, and this is the stage of crisis. But, again, these inferences prescribed by the system and the disturbing incompatible facts or intruder inferences are given by normal "scientific" logic. There is no peculiar logic of discovery in the anomaly or crisis stages of exploration.[14]

---

[14] Hegel, however, would maintain that the instability of the analytic thesis (the dogma) and of the new dialectical thesis is dictated by the necessary incompleteness of any finite category. Any concept is necessarily incomplete, requiring completion by its opposite (1, I, 66; McTaggart, st, 5).

It is in the next stage, the search for a new model, that the logic peculiar to the disovery procedure is to be found. Hanson makes the distinction quite clear:

> Imagine yourself in a logic classroom (i.e., in a classroom in which logic is being taught). There are notoriously, two different kinds of questions the teacher can pose. He can say: 'Here are some premises P^1, P^2, and P^3—generate from them some theorem.' But he can also say: 'Here is a theorem; find three premises from which it can be generated.' The latter undertaking is vastly more difficult, as every mathematician and scientist knows. Being presented with an anomalous phenomenon and then being charged to discover an H [hypothesis] from which E [evidence] follows is a different conceptual task from being given premises, *If H, then E, and E* and concluding that H is (insofar) confirmed. The process of actual discovery in science involves passing from the conclusion (some state of affairs to be explained) to a sought-for premise (hypothesis) that renders the phenomena intelligible, whereas the deductive process requires the reasoner to move from premises to conclusion when he is actually proving a theorem for the first time (Smith, quoting Hanson in Hutchins g, 1965, 227–228).

This working backwards from evidence to hypothesis is called by several logicians "abduction" or "retroduction" (Day l, 66 ff.; Peirce c, V, pp. 146, 171; Bochénski m, 92 ff.) Bochénski, in a lucid diagram, contrasts the two processes, which he calls methodologies. Figure 111, 4, is an adaptation of Bochénski's diagram. In the process of abductive discovery, two separate pieces of data, d_1 and d_2, could both be explained by a hypothesis H_1; if this hypothesis were true, further data should exist which would corroborate the existence of H_1; this corroborative data is cd_3. Similarly d_4 and d_5 could be explained by H_2 and its existence could be corroborated by the finding of cd_6. Supposing the corroborative data to have been found, H_1 and H_2 both suggest a common explanation E. If E were true, then it would suggest another hypothesis H_3, which could be corroborated by cd_7. The finding of cd_7 further strengthens the likelihood of H_3, E, and H_1 and H_2. This back and forth movement of suggestion and checking is typical of the process of abduction.

Deduction and induction, on the other hand, work in a different fashion. Given an axiom assumed to be true (T_1), it can be deduced from this that intermediate theorems T_2, T_3, and T_4 will follow. These, in turn, imply the further conclusions, c_1 through c_7.

Thus, in deduction, if the axiom implies the theorems and the axiom is true, the theorems logically follow. The movement is from the asserted antecedent to its consequent.This is the typical modus ponendo ponens: If A implies T and A is true, then T is true, a common deductive pattern. But in abduction the movement is different: d_1 and d_2 suggest H_1 as an explanation. But H_1 then implies cd_3. The existence of cd_3 is used to confirm the truth of H_1. The movement is: H_1 implies cd_3, but cd_3 is true, therefore H_1 is (probably) true. This is not a valid operation in deductive logic, but it is the basis of much discovery logic. In deductive logic it is called the fallacy of affirming the consequent. Yet Lukasiewicz, Bochénski, Day, and many serious logicians consider it the basis of abduction or retroduction (see Bochénski m, 68–69—along with several historical examples; also Day i, 66).

The question still remains, what suggested H_1 to explain d_1 and E to explain H_1 and H_2, etc.?

Since the process of explaining d_1 and d_2 is achieved by erecting a deductive antecedent for d_1 and d_2, and since H_1 and H_2 are explained by erecting a deductive antecedent for them, it would seem that the discovery procedure consists in the creation of a deductive system (cf. Bochénski m, 99).

Because this is the nature of the discovery procedure, the creative process is sometimes immeasurably facilitated by borrowing suggestions, as it were, from another deductive or inductive system which seems to have similarities to the one under construction. Such a borrowed deductive system is a "model."

This is the usual definition of a model (cf. Braithwaite m, 225; Suppes c, 163 ff.; Apostel f, 36), though the definition varies considerably in meaning.

The value in importing a model lies in the fact that the borrowed system represents an area which has already been analyzed and is thus more familiar, more secure, and more complete than the system under investigation. We are thus able to transfer what we know about one domain into another domain (Black m, 230–232; Braithwaite m, 226).

This transfer can be in several directions. The model can help to structure a relatively unstructured domain, or simplify a domain, or complete a domain, or explain a domain, or concretise a too abstract domain, or abstract a too concrete domain, or enable a domain to get a complete picture of its own framework; or allow for experimentation where the domain does not permit it (these functions are adapted from Apostel f, 1 ff.). It is clear that the model of the communications triangle has served several of these purposes in the present text.

To be useful, the model must, in addition to being more familiar and already analyzed, be similar in logical structure to the domain being investigated. It is the danger of nonsimilarity, though there may be facile resemblances, which has caused some authors to warn against the injudicious use of models (especially Duhem, a, 70; even Braithwaithe, s, 92–93).

It is certainly true that there has sometimes been an injudicious

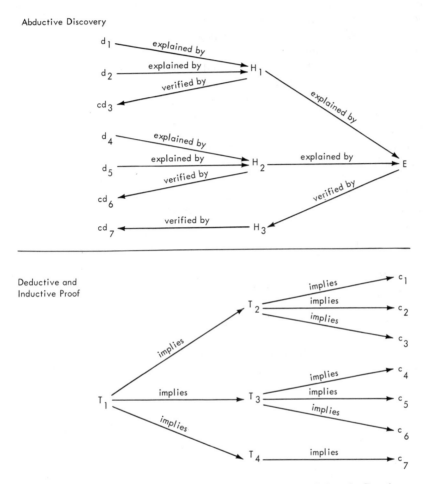

Figure III, 4: Procedures of Logic in Discovery and Scientific Proof

importation of models into literary criticism and the area of English general-ly. Thus, the Freudian model used by Murray to explain *Moby Dick* is an import of very questionable value. It is not convincing (to the author, at least) that Ahab–Moby Dick–Ishmael have the same structure as the id–ego–super ego (Murray, i, 25–34). Nor, similarly, has Korzybski's model of his concept of meaning as being analogous in semantics to non-Euclidean geometry or non-Newtonian physics been a useful concept—in the author's opinion. Similarly, Rapaport's hurried importation of the mathematical theory of information into discourse analysis seemed to some more misleading than useful (Rapaport, w; cf. Bar-Hillel, l, 222 f. and Mackay, o, 182).

On the other hand, Abrams' use of the communications triangle (Abrams, m) was a very rewarding importation into literary theory and criticism. And Chomsky's importation of the mathematical models of axiomatic systems, recursive definitions, and transformations has made of grammar an almost entirely new discipline. However, English has generally suffered much more from a dearth of such models than from an over-abundance or the injudicious uses of models. Oddly enough, writers in composition theory, grammar, and literary theory and criticism have not been very imaginative in their discovery procedures at all.

In addition to being isomorphic (having fitness or similarity of structure), the model must obviously be fertile (cf. Chao, m, 564–65; Toulmin, p, 39; Black, m, 230–32). That, of course, is the whole point of using a model. For instance the model of the archetype in literary criticism, coming from Jungian psychology, must be acknowledged to have been a highly fertile importation—regardless of what one thinks of the progeny. But the use of models does not absolve the explorer from the exercise of imagination. Black, concluding his treatment of models, makes this point very strongly:

> All intellectual pursuits, however different their aims and methods, rely firmly upon such exercises of the imagination as I have been recalling. Similar archetypes may play their parts in different disciplines; a soci-ologist's pattern of thought may also be the key to understanding a novel. So perhaps those interested in excavating the presuppositions and latent archetypes of scientists may have something to learn from the industry of literary critics. When the understanding of scientific models and arche-types comes to be regarded as a reputable part of scientific culture, the gap between the sciences and the humanities will have been partly filled. For exercise of the imagination, with all its promises and dangers, provides a common ground. If I have so much emphasized the importance of scientific models and archetypes, it is because of a conviction that the imaginative aspects of scientific thought have in the past been too much neglected. For science, like the humanities, like literature, is an exercise of the imagination (Black, m, 242–43).

Sample Analysis
of Some Logical Procedures
in an Exploratory Essay

A careful look at some of the more important logical processes employed in the anthologized essay can serve as a practical illustration of some of the theory given above. The first and most notable characteristic of the logic employed is that the logic of Wallis and Roberts, in their original material, the introductions to the detailed example on vitamins, is quite different from the logical procedures used by the people who carried out the experiment reported in the chapter.

The logic of Wallis and Roberts is consistently exploratory, and, curiously enough, might best be labeled "Hegelian," because this is distinctly the dialectic of investigation which is employed in the macrostructure of the chapter. The technique is disarmingly simple: a radical thesis is set up, it is opposed by an equally radical antithesis, and the workable truth is presented as a synthesis somewhere between the two. This might derisively be called "happy medium" logic, but it has its precedents from the Aristotelian concept of virtue as a mean between two extremes, through Hegel, to Camus "Thought at the Meridian" (Camus, r, 279 ff., esp. 300 ff.). Regardless of its precedents, it is clear that Wallis and Roberts repeatedly found the basic arguments of their chapter on the validity of the mean. The argumentative structure is posed four times in the two pages of introduction. First of all, it is the structure upon which the superstructure of Chapters 2 and 3 is based: the "Effective Use of Statistics" (Chapter 2) and the "Misuses of Statistics" (Chapter 3). The reader is told in the first sentence that most people pass through two stages in their "attitudes toward statistical conclusions," first an uncritical admiration of its uses and then a repudiation of statistics for its abuses. The truth is midway: "A main objective of the book is to show that there is an accessible alternative between blind gullibility and blind distrust" (paragraph 2). Thus, the structure of the two chapters is advocated as one of the main themes of the book—as, indeed, it is.

Third, the antithetical views that statistics is a relatively unsophisticated discipline and that statistics is the esoteric concern of only the initiated are both repudiated for a workable middle ground; clear and careful thinking can accomplish a great deal on its own. "This book represents an attempt to illustrate the fact that many important ideas of technical statistics can be conveyed to the nonstatistician without distortion or dilution" (paragraph 2).

In slightly different dress, this same argument is given as the reasons for the three detailed studies which are presented: (1) and (2) show the beginners they can glimpse the inner "works" of statistical investigators; but (3) and (4) warn the beginner that care and caution are needed, as the studies demonstrate. Thus, the editorial apparatus of introduction to the basic parts of the chapter is, in about three pages of material, constructed on four fundamental arguments, all of which are essentially Hegelian in format.[15]

Within these larger structures, inductions, of a rather informal and common-sense validity, provide support for generalizations. With a nonchalant indifference for statistical evidence (especially for professional statisticians), Wallis and Roberts begin their opening sentence with an unverified generalization: "Most of us pass through two stages in our attitudes toward statistical conclusions" (paragraph 1). And the easy inductions quickly become benevolently paternal in a series of epigrammatic aphorisms: "He who accepts statistics indiscriminately will often be duped unnecessarily," "A receptive yet critical mind is essential," etc. (paragraphs 2 and 4). These sound more like rhetorical maxims than anything else, but, as Aristotle pointed out, the line between dialectic and rhetoric is sometimes very thin (*Rhet.,* 1355 a). These inductions support the theses, antitheses, and the syntheses.

More careful than these hortatory admonitions, however, is the inductive evidence built up for the main purpose of the chapter, to convince the student of the usefulness of statistics. After the brief page and a half of introduction, Wallis and Roberts give some examples of the use of statistics in various areas. (This part of the essay was not excerpted.) In this section six sample research studies using statistical techniques in the military are summarized, eight in business, five in social studies, three in biological sciences, two in physical sciences, and two in the humanities (one in linguistic dating and one in literary style). There is a distinct attempt to achieve two of the basic norms of inductive validity: variety (by choosing different areas and *successful* applications) and numerosity (to a limited extent).

It is obvious that certain areas have been excluded: philosophy, religion, mathematics, and so on. The reader gets no impression of randomness within the varied classes. But of course the survey is not intended to be either comprehensive or numerically valid or random. It is not an attempt at scientific proof—it is an exploration. And the "examples," as they are called, fulfill their stated purposes, especially because they disturb both of the dogmatic extremes which they were selected to disturb.

The logic of the report on "Vitamins and Endurance" differs

---

[15] The same pattern of Hegelian opposites and compromise resolution is evident in the summary of Wallis' analysis of the first Kinsey report: enthusiasm—severe distrust—some limited use (Wallis, s, in quoting Wallis, st, 466).

markedly from the introductory material. In this report of a typical "scientific experiment," we can see some normal operations of the exploratory and the verificational logics. And both the exploratory and the scientific logical procedures are a good deal more careful than was the logic of the introduction.

In the first paragraph of *The Problem,* the current dogma, the disturbing anomalies, and the crisis are clearly presented. These are the usual first three stages of the exploratory process. The dogma is that "extremely large doses of certain vitamins might enable animals and possibly humans better to withstand severe physical and psychological stresses that exist under conditions of extreme cold" (paragraph 9). Two items of evidence for this are given. The only anomaly reported is that there was "less conclusive" evidence for humans than for rats. The crisis is clearly a financial one—the cost of massive vitamin supplementation.

There is no time wasted in searching for a new model in this case. The solution to the problem can very easily be reduced to a simple hypothesis: If vitamin supplementation was useful in improving physical performance in extreme cold (H), its effects should be measureable in a high-activity program (E). It was hoped that E would prove factual. From this, H could be established as tenable. The argument follows the typical retroduction schema outlined in the logic of discovery above: If H, then E; but E is true; therefore H is true.

Notice that this is a typical retroduction argument, not a valid deduction. The general structure of the logic in the experiment, is, therefore, retroductive. The implication, H implies E, is actually based upon an application of deductive class logic. Since the kinds of activities to be measured in the high-activity program certainly belong to the general class of measureable activities which should be improved by vitamin supplementation, if one could assert H, one should be able to assert E (as a class included in H).

However, the establishing of the validity of E, the evidence, is typically inductive. In other words, just as in the case of Wallis' and Roberts' own exploratory logic, induction is a smaller structure within the larger discovery procedure. The inductive procedure is very interesting and illustrates vividly each of the basic concerns of the norms of inductive validity: numerosity, variety, and randomness.

Numerosity is one of the basic issues and is given much attention. Since only 100 soldiers were available for the experiment, the question is raised as to whether this number would permit a generalization valid enough to extend to the armed forces operating in cold climates (paragraph 18). This problem is solved, in both cases, by the application of an equivalence of relationships. Here, therefore, deductive relational logic is used. The first instance of this application came in the determination of the score which could be viewed as a significant improvement. Since the pre- and post-test being used was the Army Physical Fitness Test (APFT), and since "it was known that an average improvement of 20 points on the test might be expected during six weeks of the basic training period," this improvement score was to be viewed as significant enough to justify vitamin supplementation. The argument might be logically represented as follows:

$$20 \; R_1 \; APFT \equiv 20 \; R_2 \; APFT,$$

where $R_1 =$ the improvement relation in basic training, and where $R_2 =$ the improvement relation in E, the evidence of the experiment. That is, the first relation of 20 to the APFT is viewed as equivalent (in significance) to the second relation of 20 to the APFT. The justification for this equivalence is an induction (such an improvement seems like a valid-enough general norm).

A similar procedure is followed in the problem of variations. About 100 men were needed to rise above chance variations in taking the test at basic training. It is assumed the same number would be necessary to do so in the vitamin experiment. From both of these equivalences the inference is drawn that 100 men will be sufficient.

Randomness also bothered the experimenters. First, they were concerned that the soldiers were not randomly drawn from the Army at large (paragraph 12). But at least the control and the experimental groups were randomly selected once the four platoons were selected (paragraph 23). But the major concern of the experimenters was variety of class differentiations in order to eliminate as many factors as could be eliminated. This is the basic idea behind the control versus the experimental groups. Only if the experimental group, assuming equal conditions, registered a significantly different score from the control group could the inference to H be made. Variety is also the principle behind the pre- versus the post-test scores. And variety is the reason for all of the careful records in temperature, altitude, isolation, clothing, diet, time, activities, and blood glucose counts. Given adequate numerosity and "adequate" randomness, the principle of variety allows the inductive conclusions to be drawn.

Although both groups doubled their scores on the APFT, the differences between the two groups were not large enough to be ascribable to the vitamin supplementation (paragraph 35). Evidence E did not factually exist—the hypothesis H cannot be asserted. Basically, the experiment's logic ends up this way: H implies E, and E is not true; therefore H is not true. This, incidentally, is a valid deduction.

The remaining four conclusions are positive, but secondary. And they are all justified only because of the variety in the control and experimental groups. Of course all of the E is a matter of inductive generalizations. In this case, unlike the inductions of Wallis and Roberts in the first part of the chapter, the inductions have a high degree of probability.

The Organization of Reference Discourse

Introduction

One of the most obvious characteristics of science is the system which it imposes on the manifold of reality. Indeed, "system" is almost as frequent a component of the definition of science traditionally as is "certainty" or "proof." Yet the systematizing techniques of science, as such, have not been subjected to analysis with anything remotely resembling the care accorded to the logical techniques of science. One can parallel reference discourse to persuasion and see the similarity between logic in reference discourse and "invention" in rhetorical persuasion; there is a long analytical tradition for both. But there is not a corresponding analytical tradition for the organization of scientific and informative discourse paralleling the "arrangement" (*dispositio*) tradition in rhetoric. This is undoubtedly regrettable.

The immediate consequence of this, for the purposes of the present chapter, is that the following generalities must be viewed as tentative and subject to revision in the light of future inductive verifications. Precisely because of their hypothetical nature, however, it is necessary to accompany them with more illustrative examples than have heretofore been employed.

The organization of reference discourse is subject to at least three variables. In the first place, the structure of any piece of discourse is severely conditioned by the medium in which it occurs. Medium here means the channel of publication, using the term "publication" broadly, in which the discourse is delivered. Reference discourse, whether scientific or informative or exploratory, is more at home in certain media than in others—television, for example, has not yet proved a viable medium for much scientific discourse. Some of the problems of the media of reference discourse are considered in Section V on style, for medium is a facet of the "signal" component of the communications triangle.

Second, and more important, the organization of a piece of reference discourse can be determined as much by the subject matter of the discourse as by the purpose of the discourse. This position, of course, is at variance with McLuhan's contention that the medium is the message; and it is at variance with an earlier *a priori* view of the present author that purpose or aim should be the dominant structuring principle of a discourse. But a good deal of analysis of scientific discourse has convinced the author that modal principles of organization are very frequent in much of scientific discourse.

In consequence, it seems that the actual principle behind the sequential ordering of material in a discourse is more frequently a function of the subject matter than the aims of the discourse. What this means, in effect, is that the logic of subject matter rather than the logic of proof frequently provides the matrix of organization. Scientific history, for instance, is chronologically structured, rather than deductively or inductively structured; and the deductions and inductions in history are *organizationally* subordinate to the progress of the narrative.

It might be recalled that, since the modes are actually discourses about different facets of a given reality, it is possible to have scientific discourse in all four modes. Scientific narratives (history), scientific classifications (some theories and taxonomies), scientific descriptions (analysis), and scientific evaluations (criticism) often follow narrative, classificatory, structural-descriptive, and evaluative principles of organization rather than logical procedures of scientific proof. But, given these two organizational variables of medium and mode, there are still some scientific discourses which are structurally determined by the order of proof and some informative discourses which are "informationally" ordered and some exploratory discourses which are "dialectically" ordered. It is to these ordering principles that we now turn.

The Organization of Scientific Discourse

Conceivably, therefore, there could be deductive and inductive principles of organization for the body of the material. The title, introduction, conclusion, and mechanics of scientific discourse are heavily conventional—and these conventions will be treated later. But it is the main body of matter which is under consideration here.

DEDUCTIVE ORGANIZATION

There are, of course, some examples of scientific discourse which follow a rather rigid and straightforward deductive pattern. Most modern books on symbolic logic and some generative grammars are illustrations of this. But these are hardly typical discourses for the student of composition. More representative types of deductive organizational patterns are those which initially set up some theorem of propositional logic and then draw some inferences from it. In the process, assertion or negation of the premises may be needed. This is often provided by induction. Thus, deductive logic provides the macrostructure and inductive the microstructure. The excerpt from Camus' *The Rebel,* analyzed above, is an example of this.

INDUCTIVE ORGANIZATION

Inductively ordered patterns of organization also exist in some scientific discourses. For example, some legal evidence in court is presented in this fashion: particulars, particulars...concluding generalizations. Frequently, however, instead of presenting the particulars first and following up with the generalization, the generalization is presented first and the particulars which are its evidence follow. This very common pattern of what might be called inverted induction is used in many disciplines. The excerpt below is an instance from a historian or better, a philosopher of history, Toynbee.

First the summary of the chapter is presented, as it is given in the "Argument," and outlined in the Appendix to the one-volume abridgement of volumes I-VI. It is an abstract of the logical argument and it also faithfully reproduces the overall structure of the chapter in the abridgement and the chapter in the original.[16]

From the "Argument":

THE VIRTUES OF ADVERSITY

The explanation of the geneses of civilizations given in the last chapter rests on the hypothesis that it is difficult rather than easy conditions that produce these achievements. This hypothesis is now brought nearer to proof by illustrations taken from localities where civilization once flourished but subsequently failed and where the land has reverted to its original conditions.

What was once the scene of the Mayan Civilization is now again tropical forest.

The Indic Civilization in Ceylon flourished in the rainless half of the island. This is now entirely barren, though the ruins of the Indic irrigation system remain as evidence of the civilization that once flourished there.

The ruins of Petra and Palmyra stand on small oases in the Arabian Desert.

Easter Island, one of the remotest spots in the Pacific, is proved by its statues to have been once a centre of the Polynesian Civilization.

16 The abridgement (including the "Argument") was approved by Toynbee, who wrote, "I have now made it fully my own by here and there recasting the language..." (Toynbee, sa, ix). The abridgement was done by D. C. Somerwell.

New England, whose European colonists have played a predominant part in the history of North America, is one of the bleakest and most barren parts of that continent.

The Latin townships of the Roman Campagna, till recently a malarial wilderness, made a great contribution to the rise of the Roman Power. Contrast the favourable situation and poor performance of Capua. Illustrations are also drawn from Herodotus, the Odyssey, and the Book of Exodus.

The natives of Nyasaland, where life is easy, remained primitive savages down to the advent of invaders from a distant and inclement Europe. (Toynbee, sa, 570–71)

Several remarks ought to be made about the organization of Toynbee's chapter in the "Argument" (and therefore the organization of the original). The organizations of the three (original, abridgement, and "Argument") are completely parallel. First the inductive generalization is announced. Then the sections of the chapter provide the inductive particulars from which the generalization was induced. It is clear that "proof" is intended. "This hypothesis is brought nearer to proof," says the "Argument" (sa, 571). "And in the present chapter we propose to drive our point home," says the abridgement (sa, 80). And in the original, it is said that the previous chapter had probably convinced the "scientific student" to the point of moral certainty; but the layman may need direct observations (s, 2–3), consequently: "We will therefore try to clinch our arguments by passing a few instances of such reversions under review" (s, 3). At the end of the first set of instances, the idea of proof is strongly reiterated; and, once all of the instances have been examined, the next section can confidently begin, "We have now perhaps established decisively the truth that ease is inimical to civilization" (s, 31).

The last statement is actually the negative statement of the hypothesis for which evidence is being offered. The positive statement is: "man achieves civilization...as a response to a challenge in a situation of special difficulty" (sa, 570). Egypt, and the conquering of the Nile Valley, was the first and major argument for this hypothesis, though the Sumeric, the Sinic, the Mayan, and the Minoan civilizations are also brought in as evidence (sa, 570). But since the Egyptian and the Sumeric and the Sinic and the Minoan civilizations do not currently present us with the picture of the environment which was to be conquered—the Nile Valley is still a "going concern"—the argument can be reenforced by two additional ways of looking at the same problem. (These others were considered in his previous chapter.)

The first is to consider cases where a conquered civilization has reverted, through lack of continual vigor, to its earlier inhospitable nature and the civilization has disappeared. This is one side of the argument. The other side is the reverse side of the coin: civilizations do not arise in conditions of ease.

The basic consideration for the necessity of the whole chapter is the matter of inductive *variety*. The chapter is needed after the preceding chapter, for the examples given there have an element which makes the generalization appear weak: once an environment has been conquered, possibly vigilance can be relaxed and ease may not be inimical. This is answered in IIA of the outline of Figure III, 4. Even more crucial: it is true that challenge has given rise to civilizations, yet may not civilizations be maintained if challenge is no longer required by movement to a new environment, and may not civilizations rise when no challenge is required at all? These are answered in II.

It is true that I and IIA, IIB, and IIC consider four basic alternatives.[17] If inductive evidence can be given for the hypothesis in these four circumstances, the generalization is valid. We are not concerned with IA, except as a necessary complement to the logic structure of IIA, B, and C.

IIA has a further substructure again dominated by the principle of variety: determining possible relevant issues and establishing various categories. In the original essay, though not in the abridgement, the rationale for this is given at the conclusion of this section; Toynbee writes:

> We have now passed in review a number of sites—in the American and Asiatic Tropics, in the Afrasian Steppe, in the Pacific Archipelago, in North America, in the Mediterranean—which have reverted to their pristine state of Nature after having been the scene of signal human achievements that are now commemorated by desert ruins. *In this array, there is the utmost diversity* [my italics] both in the character of the local physical environment and in the shape of the yoke which Man has once laid upon it; yet all these sites agree in bearing unanimous witness to one essential condition of successful human activity: "Nur der verdient sich Freiheit wie das Leben/Der taglich sie erobern muss." (s, 17).[18]

It is clear that, as the outline shows, various climates, geographies, and techniques of conquest are all considered. To some extent, the principle of variety is distinctly at work.

The next section, referring to situations of nonchallenge, does not betray any suborganizational patterns dictated by logic. The only differentiating pattern in the choice of particulars is that the first and last are factual and the remainder are fictional (except, possibly, the example from the

---

17 A fifth, handled in Chapter VIII, is that too much challenge might be inimical.

18 Of freedom and of life he only is deserving who every day must conquer them anew.—Goethe, *Faust*, ll. 11575–6, tr. George Madison Priest. Great Books, XLVII. Ed. R. M. Hutchins. Chicago: Encyclopedia Britannica, 1952.

Bible). Toynbee also adverts to this kind of a distinction in his evidence (cf. s, 30 and 21, fn. 2); he deliberately uses myth and history.

GENERALIZATION: " Man achieves civilization . . . as a response to a challenge in a situation of special dfficulty."

I. *Positive View:* Challenge is beneficial (Considered in Toynbee's previous chapter).
    A. Egyptian
    B. Sumeric
    C. Sinic
    D. Mayan and Andean
    E. Minoan

II. *Negative View:* Ease is inimical.
    A. *In a Situation of Challenge:* Civilizations deteriorate when challenge is not maintained though the danger still exists.
        1. Mayan—Forest
        2. Ceylon—Plain
        3. North Aealinan—Desert
        4. Easter Island—Water
        5. New England—
        6. Roman Campagna—Wilderness

    B. *In Situations of Nonchallenge:* Civilizations deteriorate when challenge is no longer required, after having been required.
        1. Capua
        2. Herodotus' Fable
        3. Odyssey
        4. Exodus
        5. Doasyoulikes

    C. *In Situations of Nonchallenge:* Civilization never arises if no challenge is required.

        1. Nyasaland

Figure III, 4: Outline of an Inductive Organization

Basically, therefore, the large structure of the "Argument" and the original chapter is dictated by an inverted inductive pattern of organization. And the various subdivisions are organized by a conscious application of what logicians call the principle of inductive variety.

The major concern here has been organization. But a few brief remarks might be made on the logical validity of the inductions. It is clear that variety is observed, to some extent in IIA. But in IIB variety is weak, and factual versus fictional evidence is a strange principle for scientific evidence, as far as variety is concerned. In IIC there is no variety at all in the abridgement (though supporting instances are given in the original, with time and space operating as variety principles, cf. s, 27–28).

Of course randomness does not seem to be crucially operative at all —there are, after all, only a limited number of civilizations—Toynbee usually distinguishes twenty-one (cf. sa, 568). This naturally limits the principle of numerosity in this use of inductive probability.

Further, though Toynbee claims that this kind of evidence is "empirical" (cf. the first sentence in the section on Capua in the original), the empirical character of some of his evidence must be questioned. First, the "empirical" evidence of instances from myth and fiction is certainly of dubious value. There are six major uses of fiction and myth as evidence in the chapter.

Again, some of the particular cases are highly speculative in nature. In the absence of historic fact, Toynbee hypothesizes on the failures of these civilizations to meet the challenge. Indeed in all but the last case (the Roman Compagna), there is reference to the speculative nature of the evidence (cf. s, 4, 8–9, 10, 13–14). These references are considerably weakened or altogether lacking in the abridgement and the "Argument."

In addition, there is one noticeable difference between the instances chosen to illustrate the positive view that challenge is beneficial and those chosen to prove the negative view that ease is inimical. The positive instances are all major civilizations in the basic list of twenty-one civilizations. Of the instances chosen to illustrate the negative side, only one of the twelve is a major civilization. All the others are either subcultures or individual cities or islands or even fictions. Indeed, New England is hardly one of the most bleak and barren parts of the continent; and Town Hill is hardly a representative sample of New England. For all of these reasons, the inductive probability of Toynbee's generalizations can hardly be of a very high degree. Given Toynbee's transition sentence to the next section, "we have perhaps established decisively the truth that ease is inimical to civilization," one must underscore the word "perhaps" much more than "decisively."

In addition to the basic logical patterns of deduction and induction that serve as the organizational matrix for a piece of scientific discourse, there are certain conventional matters of organization to which scientific material generally adheres today. These concern the title, the introduction, the conclusion, and the mechanics of footnoting and bibliography.

The title of scientific discourse should indicate the topic of the essay in as concise and accurate a formulation as possible. Imaginative titles are totally out of place in scientific discourse. Titles should be as comprehensive as possible, attempting an exhaustive inclusion of the areas under discussion in the discourse to follow. The novice at scientific discourse will often find that the choice of a succinct title to crystalize his topic initially can do much to give unity to the paper which follows; conversely a bad title is only too frequently symptomatic of a bad topic—one either too large or too narrow or too nebulous. Nothing is possibly more indicative of the poor thinking of beginning writers than the frightening titles which they append to their initial productions. The title may end up sounding pedantic when the student has clearly focused the topic and its formulation in a title, but there should be no hesitation in choosing between seeming pedantry and vague or formless thinking.

The introduction to a scientific paper should announce very clearly the topic under consideration, should indicate the self-appointed limitations of the analysis, and should outline the general method of procedure. These may seem arbitrary and stilted to the average undergraduate, but no Ph.D. researcher sends in the results of his findings to a learned journal without such an introduction. A quick check into such a journal as *The Journal of the American Chemical Society* and comparable vehicles in other fields will convince even the most skeptical of this. *A fortiori* the beginner in science should not feel that such a degree of clarity is below him, though experience has taught the present author that many a sophisticated student thinks it is.

The introduction often includes a quick survey of the literature on the subject previous to the present study. Ideally much scientific analysis is made against the background of an acquaintance with the entire corpus of writings on the subject. Often this is impractical, and the beginning scientist must sometimes limit his acquaintance with past scholarship on the subject to several articles or books arbitrarily but carefully selected. Even the beginner must realize, however, that this procedure is only a practical compromise. Of course, a rigorous background acquaintance with a topic is potentially infinite. Consequently only the abstraction of the writer can establish a responsible limit to his background.

The body of the scientific paper follows the introduction. This body should betray the structure demanded by the material, as has been discussed above. After the body of the essay, a conclusion is in order. Again this is not just a contrivance designed to please small-minded professors who correct college compositions. The introduction and body of a theme have been established for a purpose, and the conclusion summarizes this purpose. The conclusion, then, is organically related to the rest of the discourse. It should logically follow from the structure of the introduction and body. Many undergraduates here sin egregiously. Accustomed to the nonchalant non-sequitur conclusions which abound in the nonscientific discourses of such periodicals as *Reader's Digest* and *The Saturday Evening Post,* the undergraduate often appends such an artistic or rhetorical conclusion to a paper which has laboriously, to this point, followed the procedures of scientific methodology. These artistic or rhetorical codas may often bring a delightful, if abortive, end to other types of discourse, but they are out of place in scientific writing. As a matter of fact, they are often only rationalizations to bring to a conclusion something that has not yet really arrived at a conclusion at all.

This brings up a last remark about the conclusion—it should only be made when the essay has rounded itself out, and logically led up to the inevitable conclusion. The rounding out process is determined by the initial arbitrary limitations established by the introduction. When these have been realized, the conclusion is in order. In reality the invariable question after each assignment has been announced, "How long should it be?" is one that only the writer can answer. If the teacher replies, "About 500 words," he really intends that the student so limit his topic that an adequate treatment can be given in roughly 500 words. This means that a problem should be selected of such a narrow scope that it is amenable to a conscientious treatment in the limits of two or three pages of evidence. Really, very few problems are so narrow. Consequently the writer must either specialize to a very narrow focus, or be dilettantish and superficial (therefore reprehensible and scholastically criminal). In exploratory discourse, which will be examined below, the student may be permitted to indulge in generalizations which may temporarily be rash and impulsive, but such indiscretions are not desirable in science. And, of course, such imaginative and even irresponsible conclusions are also permissible, even becoming, in rhetorical and belletristic writing. Indeed, rhetoric usually ends up in a burst of emotional appeal which almost invariably oversteps the limits of its strictly allowable logical foundations.

This concludes our discussion of the introduction, body, and conclusion of scientific discourse. As Plato has remarked, any composition requires a beginning, a middle, and an end, and possibly this statement may now seem to the student to be more than an obvious truism.

The presentation of the evidence in a scientific paper is accomplished in part by referring the reader to the sources for quoted or paraphrased material. This is given in footnotes and bibiliographies. Since this text is not a handbook and not a freshman textbook, it is not felt necessary to go into the mechanics of footnoting or presentation of bibliographical material. Various systems are, of course, in use, each having some advantages for reader or writer in its favor. The writer of scientific material must, if he wishes to publish, meet the standards of his editor. If there is a choice, he must explain his system early and consistently adhere to it.

The Organization of Informative Discourse

ORGANIZATION BY FACTUALITY AND SURPRISE VALUE

Given the three basic determinants of informative discourse discussed under "Nature" and "Logic" above, it is possible to make some general considerations about the organization of informative discourse. The three basic constituents of informative discourse are, it will be recalled: factuality, surprise value, and comprehensiveness.

Factuality does not in itself provide any organizational principles. Facts, as such, are mere brute statements about events (see above, pp. 83 f, 129 ff.), and have no inherent organizing principle. Facts, it might be said, are not factitious. Consequently, any ordering of facts must come from a nonfactual source. Such nonfactual sources can be of several kinds. If facts about change are ordered to a chronological sequence of cause and effect, a narrative results. If facts are placed in a structural relationship of part to part and part to whole, description results. If facts about something are considered as being possessed or not possessed in common with other beings, and categories are established on the basis of such possessions, then classification results. Similarly facts can be marshalled to an evaluation. Consequently, facts can be organized by a *modal* principle, and many informative discourses are so ordered. But the ordering principle, it must be noted, is not based on the nature of information.

Second, facts may be ordered to prove a point by some kind of logic. This ordering may be included in an informative discourse. This is a frequent occurrence and happens in the "Vitamins and Endurance" selection being analyzed in this chapter. But here the ordering principle is scientific and is simply subsumed into an information context.

Facts can also be ordered by persuasive principles, or literary principles, or expressive principles, or by the nature of media or different arts, or even by principles deriving from the informative principles of surprise value or comprehensiveness—as we shall see in a moment. But facts never organize themselves. As F.S.C. Northrop has said, the only thing one can do in presence of a pure fact is to face it and remain perpetually dumb (1, 317).

More important in the organization of informative discourse is the organizational principle based on surprise value. This principle is partially used in journalism in headlines and news stories. The principle is to state the most important facts first and then the facts of secondary importance, then those of tertiary importance. Presumably the least important facts come last, and may even be deleted if the editor has space limitations. "Importance," in journalism, is determined partially by surprise value and partially by a need for comprehensiveness. The need for comprehensiveness in journalism is covered by considering the five W's, who, what, where, when, why (or how)—this will be considered in the next section. But importance is also a matter of surprise value; and headlines, subheads, and parts of the story are also ordered by this principle. Journalists call this the organizing principle of the inverted triangle.

This journalistic news structure is also characteristic of other media of discourses. Generally speaking, the organization of much ordinary conversation follows this pattern. Upon my return from school every evening I first tell my wife the most surprising events of the day and slowly work down to the least surprising. She intersperses my recital with her own headlines in a parallel descending order of sensationalism. The term "sensationalism" used here is not intended to carry any derogatory connotations with it. One should not have to apologize for such a structure in either journalism or conversation or any other medium. An illustration of such a structure can be seen in any news story in any respectable journalistic vehicle. It hardly needs illustration. Any respectable textbook on journalism will provide a discussion of the structure.

ORGANIZATION BY COMPREHENSIVENESS

Although it is not a journalistic cliché, like the inverted triangle of importance, "comprehensiveness" also can act as an organizing principle in informative discourse (and sometimes scientific discourse). In news stories, comprehensiveness is supposedly achieved by including the five W's in the lead sentence: who, what, where, when, why (or how). The lead, then, is both comprehensive and surprising. But after that, importance (judged by surprise value) becomes the structuring principle.

However, in much informative discourse comprehensiveness is the basic structuring principle. Sometimes, to achieve comprehensive coverage, mechanical ordering principles are used. Thus encyclopedias of all sorts include, as they often advertise, everything from a to z; this is a boast founded upon comprehensiveness *as a structuring principle*. Alphabetical and numerical listings, for instance, are mechanical principles intended to assure comprehensiveness in encyclopedias and dictionaries of all sorts, catalogues, directories, thesauruses (sometimes), cookbooks (sometimes), funeral notices, etc. These listing techniques sacrifice the hierarchy of importance principle to comprehensiveness. Again, the principle is so ubiquitous it does not need exemplification.

As in the case of the logical ordering principles of deduction and induction, the principle of comprehensiveness may provide only the macrostructure with some other organizing principle(s) serving in the substructures. This is often true of articles in an encyclopedia. However, even at the substructure levels, principles of comprehensiveness may be operating *as such*. In the case of the Toynbee chapter analyzed above, the divisions of "The Virtues of Adversity" also prove to be comprehensive, and their comprehensiveness is established logically by the principle of variety.

Complete comprehensiveness coincides quite closely with the present connotations of the "encyclopedic." And this kind of comprehensiveness is often achieved by principles that achieve comprehensiveness by indirection. Thus, encyclopedia entries like "Costume," "English Literature," and the like are comprehensively covered by following a chronological sequence. Other modal ordering principles are frequently used. Thus "Engineering" considers the *classes* of engineering, and these are alphabetically covered. In *Consumer Reports* a frequent ordering principle is evaluative (the best first, then on down through acceptable to unacceptable). And, of course, descriptive principles operate—cf. treatments of "motor," "engine," "atom," in a typical encyclopedia. Here, as the reader can verify, there are narrative, classificatory, evaluative, and descriptive principles operating to give comprehensiveness.

Comprehensiveness, from a systematic point of view, has been analyzed in connection with deductive systems, which are analyzed for "completeness" along with independence and consistency. The "completeness" of some deductive systems and the necessary incompleteness of others has been a matter of much concern in *modern* logical theory. But neither these approaches nor the handling of comprehensiveness in semantic information theory have been translated into practical and usable norms in discourse theory. As with other aspects of information theory, this remains an unexplored area.

The Organization
of Exploratory Discourse

If it is difficult to be doctrinaire about the organizational patterns of scientific and informative discourse it is all the more hazardous to be so in the area of exploratory discourse. Precisely because of the uncertain nature of the inquiry, exploratory discourses often do not display the precise formulations that scientific and informative discourses exhibit, even when the formulations vary.

As will be pointed out below, some of the organizational concerns in exploratory discourse are a matter of the art and medium in which the discourse is presented. Actual exploratory discourse is much more apt to occur in speech than in writing, for example. The written reconstruction of an exploratory discourse is usually a factitious enterprise. Plato's dialogues are really somewhat artificial since Plato actually knew just where he was going at the outset. A transcription of a recorded discussion would be a more real instance of actual exploratory discourse. Plato himself preferred the oral to the written form.

Second, real exploratory discourse is, as often as not, plural rather than monologual in form. This is why the panel discussion in the seminar is at least as congenial to exploration as is the straight lecture. And in written form, the dialogue is a comfortable medium for exploratory discourse.

Oral exploratory discourse is, undoubtedly, a good deal more haphazard than is written discourse. The general dialectical procedure can be interrupted by a flashback, for the discussion of the moment may clarify something earlier left indeterminate. Similarly, the present issue may suddenly establish relations which at the moment seem irrelevant to the current topic and again the logical sequence may be interrupted by intuitions into the future. Such irregularities make the final pattern of dialectic appear crude and unordered in comparison with the rigid organization of science. Yet, this is desirably so, for the flashbacks and intuitive jumps are as necessary to dialectic as its orderly deductive or inductive progress. If the student wonders at this, let him try to chart the course of a panel discussion or a seminar.

However, even oral discourse has its patterns. Treatments of interviewing techniques and discussions of all kinds stress certain desirable formats. In the case of discussion, such writers usually begin by assuming that the purpose of discussion is always the exploration for truth (an assumption the present writer does not accept). With such a view of purpose, it is not surprising that these writers—almost to a man—go on to conclude that the logic behind discussion is something like a Dewey problem-solving methodology. Keltner, for instance, reviews previous writers on the subject before beginning his own treatment, and after a summary presentation of Wagner, Arnold, Utterback, Elliott, Sattler, and Miller, concludes that the logic of problem solving is the specific logic of discussion (Keltner, g, 32–34). These writers then translate this logic into a desirable organizational format for discussion. Chenoweth is typical:

> The well-organized discussion outline consists of the properly interrelated materials in the solution of a problem: the statement of the question, the definition of terms, the history of the question, the analysis of the problem, the statement of probable solutions, the evaluation and comparison of the solutions, and the inauguration of the most practicable solution or solutions (Chenoweth, d, 153).

Similar treatments are given debates. Here the formats are even more conventionally crystallized.

In both of these situations, discussion and debate, recommended organizational patterns can sometimes be too rigidly formalized. Thus, although Dewey's problem-solving methods have large parallels to other logics of inquiry (see above, p. 101), it does not seem desirable to reduce formats of discussion to only Dewey's structure. Similarly, in the case of debates, for example, the sterility of the medieval disputation certainly stemmed in part from the ossification of the format into syllogistic formulae.

In written media, the factitious reconstruction of exploratory discourse can sometimes be a simple chronicle of the steps taken; and in this case the structure may very well mirror the exploratory logic. Many instances of this exist. Newman's *Apologia pro Vita Sua,* which began, of course, as a retaliatory justification of his personal and intellectual honesty in response to a remark by Charles Kingsley, ends up by being a history of Newman's intellectual explorations for religious truth. And the exploratory cycle is complete: initial and naïve acceptance of dogma (literally), disturbing anomalies, crises, searches for new models, their disconcerting discovery, and their verification. Many intellectual biographies are so organized.

Plato's early dialogues reveal a similar structure. The *Laches,* for example, follows the typical stages of the early Platonic dialectic (Gauss, h, 9 ff.). Among the Platonic dialogues, it was traditionally classified in the genus "zetetic" (exploratory), rather than scientific ("hyphegetic"), and the species "gymnastic," rather than "controversial," and the subspecies "maieutic," rather than "probing" (see Alline, h, 52 ff.). In addition it is early Plato and characteristic of his aporetic (often called "inconclusive") dialogues, the kind of Platonic dialogues admired by Kierkegaard (on the aporetic dialogues, see Goldschmidt, d, 34 ff.).

The *Laches'* structure embodies the basic Platonic exploratory process outlined in Figure III, 3 on p. 101. In fact Plato discusses the specific matter of dialectical organization in the *Phaedrus.* A dialectical composition, Socrates tells Phaedrus, must be like an organism—it must have a beginning, a middle, and an end (264bf.). There must be adequate definitions, classifications, and divisions at the outset (263c, 265b, 265d). There must be careful distinctions made between the mere opinions of the populace (rumor) and the careful truths of the philosopher (263b); there must be a concern for the one and the many (266c–d). A writer who follows these structural principles is a dialectician, not a mere rhetorician: "And those who have this art, I have hitherto been in the habit of calling dialecticians; but God knows whether the name is right or not" (266b).

Plato might be describing his actual practice here for these are the sequential steps of the *Laches* and the other early dialogues. The introductory section establishes the myth, the narrative component, in which two [real] generals of Athens, Laches and Nicias, are discussing the problems of educating their children. The spirit of intelligent curiosity and *wonder* is established among the participants. They agree to talk this over with Socrates (by *discussing* to arrive at truth). False wonder directed to mere means (the art of fencing) is corrected and oriented to the real object of wonder, the end, namely education to virtue (185d–e). The principle of evidence is established, not mere majority opinion, but opinion based on real authority (184e). Then the *division* of the topic is made. Not all virtue will be discussed, but only courage, in this instance (190b).

The second section of the dialogue moves into the hypothesis on the nature of courage proposed first by Laches and then by Nicias. Laches suggests that courage consists in not running away from danger (190e); Socrates sets this up as a hypothesis, which, if true, carries with it certain implications: all cases of running away in battle would be cowardice. In the cross-examination (elenchus) which follows, Socrates gets Laches to see the fallacy of this hypothesis (191a ff.). Laches tries to improve on his definition: courage consists in endurance of the soul (192b). Socrates again sets this up as a hypothesis which would entail further consequences. These consequences he also gets Laches to repudiate in the second elenchus which follows. At the end of this cross-examination, Laches' self-confidence has deserted him—he is a man of doubt (193e). Socrates exhorts him to continue in the investigation (194a).

Socrates pursues a similar policy with Nicias. But, just as Laches' second definition was an improvement on his first, so is Nicias' definition a more scientific one than Laches'. Courage, says Nicias, is a kind of wisdom (194a). The hypothesis and elenchus again follow (194e ff.). In the conclusion of the dialogue, all admit their frustration and doubt, and all agree to persevere in the investigation tomorrow (199a ff.).

The structure, briefly, has been from myth and wonder to rumor, to division of topic, to belief, to conjecture, and finally to serious thought. In the latter cases, the rumor, conjecture, belief, and thought have been set up as hypotheses and inductively tested in a cross-examination and successively rejected. The sequence of the dialogue is a brilliant exemplification of the Socratic dialectic. The process of the dialectic has served as the principle of order in the discourse (on the structure of the Platonic dialogue, cf. Goldschmidt, d, 11 ff.; on this interpretation of the structure of the *Laches,* cf. Kohák, r, 123).

Platonic dialectic, of course, is not the only dialectical or exploratory procedure that can be used as a structuring principle. Aquinas, for example, uses a dialectical structuring principle for his scientific discourse. The various topics, called questions, are divided into articles, each of which is posed as a hypothetical question itself. Thus in the article, "Whether Moral Virtue Differs from Intellectual Virtue?" the first section of the treatment marshalls all the arguments which seem to imply that moral virtues are not different from intellectual virtues—this section is the "Objections" (to his position). He here gives arguments from Augustine (twice), Aristotle (three times), Andronicus of Rhodes, Diogenes Laertius, Stobeus, and Clement of Alexandria. Then, he opposes these arguments in the *sed contra* with an argument from Aristotle which clearly says that the two kinds of virtues are different. The body (*corpus*) of the article follows. In this Aquinas states his own position and attempts to prove that moral virtues and intellectual virtues do differ; in the process he buttresses his own arguments with three references to Aristotle, two quotations from Socrates, and a principle adopted from Augustine. The last part of the treatment is the systematic reply to each of the four objections to this position which had been raised at the outset (cf. st, I-II, Q. 58, Art 2).

It is clear throughout that Aquinas uses the exploratory procedure as the structuring principle for his organization. And, of course the whole *Summa* is so organized. Given the times and library facilities, it is, incidentally a remarkable methodology for research, synthesis, and original thought—whatever one may think of the individual positions or Thomistic theology in general.

The Style of Reference Discourse

Possibly the most important remark to make at the outset of a discussion of the style of reference discourse is that there is no systematic coverage of the topic, either historically, critically, descriptively or comparatively—as far as the author is aware. This is true of scientific discourse, of informative discourse, of exploratory discourse, and, of course, of all three considered together. When comprehensive treatments of such discourses are made, there is invariably much more attention paid to content than to style. This is true, for instance, of the treatment of the "Literature of Science" of the eighteenth and nineteenth centuries in the *Cambridge History of English Literature,* Volume 14, where practically nothing is said about the styles of the authors under consideration. When stylistic treatments are made, there is usually a tendency to apply "general rules of good style" to the discourse under investigation—whether scientific or technical or journalistic.

Some writers do distinguish characteristics of scientific from informative style (e.g., Morris, p, 55–56). Racker, especially, makes careful distinctions among five levels of scientific and technical writing and establishes rules for each (Racker, t, 12, and 4–67, *passim*).

Some philosophers indirectly consider the stylistic problem of reference discourse when they discuss the general possibility of language adequately referring to reality at all, and when they discuss the pros and cons of the Sapir-Whorf hypothesis of the relativity of views of the universe as being a function of the language of a given culture. But these considerations are only stylistic in a peripheral way.

Part of the problem of style consists in the fact that there is no generally accepted framework of stylistic concepts. As in discourse study generally, there is no currently accepted "model" or "dogma" which can serve as a point of departure. Sometimes, indeed, "style" has only belletristic or rhetorical connotations. Thus Aristotle's oft-quoted remark that nobody uses style in teaching geometry would seem to imply that there is no such thing as a scientific style (or even a pedagogical one).

Yet "style" can be positively talked about in reference discourse. And the communications triangle can provide a convenient framework for the discussion of various styles—referential, persuasive, literary, and expressive. Nor will this necessitate a departure from the usual assertions made about styles. Indeed, it seems to provide a remarkably consistent matrix for categorizing some hitherto seemingly unrelated factors of style.

The detailing of the various components of structure will be given in the chapter on literary discourse, and the student is especially referred to Chart V, 2.[19] This chart is merely an expansion of suggestive components of structure at all levels of the language spectrum—discourse (aims, modes, arts), semantic (psycholinguistic, reference, and meaning), and grammatical (syntax, morphemic, and phonographemic, cf. Figure I, 4, p. 31). Starting with the components of discourse (the right end of Figure I, 4) and moving through aim, mode, etc., it can be shown that intelligent assertions about style have been made at all points of the spectrum.

Thus it is often said that a person has a logical style, a prolix or compact style, or a persuasive style. Such assertions about style are assertions about qualities of style having to do with aim: logic has to do with science; compactness or prolixity has to do with quantity of information; persuasiveness has to do with rhetoric. Modes seem to have less to do with ordinary assertions about style than the rest of the continuum; but the choice of viewpoint in narration (Olympian, Jamesian, stream-of-consciousness) is a stylistic choice and has stylistic corollaries, and the same holds true of point of view (stationary, moving) in description. Components of the arts must be separated into those deriving from the medium or channel and those deriving from the kind of signal used. Thus, from medium we speak of a telegraphic style, a journalistic style, a dramatic style, a pedantic style, or a bookish style.

The semantic components are possibly even more determinative of style than are the discourse components. The psycholinguistic components of meaning derive from individual language peculiarities (idiolect) and group peculiarities (dialect). Here distinctions like "formal," "informal," "masculine," "academic," "sociologese," "substandard," "slangish," and others are encountered.

The middle section of semantics—reference—gives crucial stylistic distinctions having to do with the kind of things referred to (referents), the kind of referring words (referends), and the process of setting up correspondences between things and words (referral). In the area of referents we speak of an "abstract" or an "imagistic," or an "objective" and neutral or a "personal" and "connotative" and "warm" style. With regard to referends, a style can be heavily "literal" or nonliteral (i.e., "metaphorical," "symbolic," "paradoxical," "ironic," "given to overstatement or understatement").

---

[19] The last section of Chapter V contains a more systematic attempt at defining style.

In the area of referral, styles are often characterized as "obscure," "clear," "ambiguous," "given to coinages" [e.g., Carlyle]. This is one of the most significant factors of style.

Finally, of course, grammatical choices *as such* also heavily determine style. With regard to syntax, we can speak of an "embedded or complex," a "simple," a "heavily loaded prenominal" style. Morphemic stylistic differences arise when there is a heavy "affix" or "compound word" style. And phonemic and graphemic stylistic characteristics can be seen in such stylistic terms as "symbol-laden" [in mathematics], "monotonous" [in inflection]. This quick sampling illustrates the fact that stylistic characteristics are drawn from the whole spectrum of the components of language. They even extend into metalanguage. Situational context supplies such norms as "given to gestures," "reserved" in delivery," and so on. From the cultural context such concepts as "conventional," "epic," "lyric," have often been applied to characterize styles.

Let us now attempt to make some generalizations about scientific, informative, and exploratory styles within this framework.

The Style
of Scientific Discourse

It would be foolhardy to pretend that there is a rigid unity of scientific style or even that there ought to be. Nevertheless, there are significant tendencies which do serve to differentiate scientific style from other aims of discourse. Unfortunately, relatively little systematic study has been made of the characteristics of scientific style either historically, theoretically, analytically, or critically. This remark is not intended to disparage some fine work in restricted areas, such as Andrews' *The History of Scientific English,* which is an excellent history of the introduction of medical terminology in English, or the work of Croll, Jones, and Williamson in the complicated strands of seventeenth- and eighteenth-century Attic, Ciceronian, and euphuistic prose, but a comprehensive consideration of scientific style remains yet to be written.

Historically, some good work has been done on the creation of a scientific terminology from ordinary language in Greece, expecially by Plato and Aristotle, a problem never encountered in such magnitude in the later history of scientific discourse, since science drew heavily from the Greek tradition (Snell, f, 50). What Euclid did for mathematics, Aristotle did for biology, physics, methaphysics, rhetoric, literary criticism, ethics, politics, and government. Aristotle's stylistic innovations and departures from Plato are so obvious that their importance is sometimes overlooked (on all of this cf. Ruch, p, 38). Aristotle could speak with what Cicero called his "golden flame of oratory" in his dialogues, unfortunately lost, but this phrase hardly applies to his extant treatises on physics, ethics, or even poetics (see Ruch, p, 47, n. 1).

This distinction of a philosophical from a persuasive style became part of the rhetorical tradition (Williamson, s, 128). Cicero pointed out that the style of the philosopher is designed for instruction rather than persuasion, "and some think they exceed due bounds in aiming to give a little pleasure with their style," (Cicero, quoted in Williamson, s, 128). Seneca is said to be responsible for the doctrine of preference of things to words in style, although Seneca himself, even in philosophy could be heavily ornamental (cf. Williamson, s, 79, 131), and for this Bacon attacked him (Williamson, s, 112 ff.).

The medieval writers in various scientific fields followed this tradition. Aquinas, for instance, in beginning his *Summa Theologica,* devotes the last two articles of his first question to the stylistic problems of his undertaking (st, I, Q 1, Art. 9 and 10). His style was typical of the period in many respects. Erasmus, Bacon, Sprat, and other Renaissance writers generically speak of the scholastic style as a unit and, as a variety of the philosophical style, oppose it to a Ciceronian style (Williamson, s, 150–51; 276; 287). Bacon himself, repudiating both Cicero and Seneca, has much to say on the distinction between a "magistral" and a "probationary" style. Roughly, Bacon meant a style which delivered a finished product of knowledge and a style which delivered knowledge still in progress or under investigation. In one sense this corresponds to the distinction between scientific and exploratory styles; but, in another sense, this parallelism does not hold, for Bacon also included persuasion in the "magistral" kind of discourse (see Williamson, s, 152 ff.).

Bacon and others were responsible for the directions taken by the Royal Society in its stand on scientific style. Sprat, the historian of the Royal Society, in a familiar passage, speaks of this stand:

> There is one more thing about which the *Society* has been most solicitous; and that is the manner of their *Discourse*: which unless they had been only watchful to keep in due temper, the whole spirit and vigour of their *Design* had been soon eaten out by the luxury and redundancy of speech. . . . And, in few words, I dare say that of all the Studies of men, nothing may be sooner obtained than this vicious abundance of *Phrase,* this trick of *metaphors,* this volubility of *Tongue,* which makes so great a noise in the *World.* . . . It will suffice my present purpose to point out what has been done by the *Royal Society* towards the correcting of excesses in Natural Philosophy to which it is of all others, a most profest enemy. They have therefore been most vigorous in putting into execution the only Remedy that can be found for this *extravagance,* and that has

been a consistent Resolution to reject all amplification, digressions, and swellings of style, to return back to the primitive purity and shortness, when men delivered so many *things* almost in an equal number of *words*. They have exacted from all their members a clear, naked, natural way of speaking, positive expressions, clear senses, a native easiness, bringing all things as near the mathematical plainness as they can, and preferring the language of Artizans, Countrymen, and Merchants, before that of Wits and Scholars (Sprat, quoted in Tillen, e, 368–69).

Some historians maintain that the advent of the new science was the main force in the formation of the new scientific style. It is probably true that the main prescriptions of a scientific style in English had been consciously written by the mid-seventeenth century. There have been refinements since but only rare dissension. Kierkegaard, one of the rare dissenters, opposed a philosophy which took an objective view of reality:

> For it is regarded as a settled thing that the objective tendency toward intellectual contemplation is, in the newer linguistic usage, the *ethical* answer to the question of what I ethically have to do (c, 210; his italics).

For Kierkegaard, who professed himself to be always a "religious" author, bent on making true Christians out of his readers, the impersonal objectivity of science could induce no *real* acceptance of a scientist's message. Nor could *direct* persuasion in strictly religious or ethical works. Therefore, the *indirect* method of persuasion in aesthetic works which enticed the reader to accept the bait of the religious or ethical message was the medium of persuasions he adopted. Thus he eschews both the strictly scientific and the strictly aesthetic. The rejection of science is really the burden of the *Concluding Unscientific Postscript,* and the rejection of the aesthetic is the theme of *The Point of View of My Work as an Author*. Both science and esthetics are viewed as ultimately unethical (cf. c, 202–203; 107, 210–214, 220 f. 228 ff; p, 26, 29, 33).

Some modern existentialists take a somewhat similar position. But not all latter-day existentialists have followed Kierkegaard in this respect. Sartre, for example, while decrying the inhumanity of science which removes man as an outsider and puts him with the rest of nature in an inhuman universe (c, 123–24; cf. Kierkegaard c, 210), still writes in a cold and objective style in his philosophical works. He saves his emotions for his rhetorical and literary pieces. Much the same is true of Camus.

Let us turn to the characteristics of the scientific style. In turn, the discourse components, the semantic components and the grammatical components will be treated.

Discourse Components
of the Scientific Style

The discourse components of scientific style are tendencies of the discourse viewed as a whole. They concern the media, the writer, the reader, the topic, and the speed with which this topic is communicated to the reader.

The media of scientific discourse have varied considerably throughout history. Early Greek philosophers and even Lucretius used verse as a medium, the dialogue was a popular form in Antiquity both in Greek and Latin, and aphorisms were used. But with Hippocrates, Galen, Euclid, Herodotus, Archimedes, and especially Aristotle, the sustained written prose, monologual exposition or narration became established as the most consistent medium of scientific discourse. These exhaustive (for the time) and dull (to the layman) papers have remained the traditional media of scientific discourse.

In the Middle Ages this attempt at thoroughness often took the form of a so-called "introduction" (or *summa*) or encyclopedia (as in Vincent of Beauvais' *Mirror*), but most of the other forms persisted.

In the Renaissance, the dialogue again became a popular form for nearly every topic (cf. Giovannini, d). Most of the other forms also survived: the aphorism, verse, the summa, and the encyclopedia. But the major scientific productions of the Renaissance were in the sustained monologual expository form. Other forms also began to emerge and came into increasing prominence in the seventeenth and eighteenth centuries.

The letter, for instance, which had been used in Antiquity by Seneca and Epictetus, again became a convenient form for exchange of scientific information—and the letter, even the systematic letter exchange, is still used today (see La Drière, 1). The dialogue declined but some great writers continued to use it (Hume, Berkeley). The aphorism continued to be used (Pascal). But again the greatest scientific productions were in lengthy monologual discourse (Newton, Huygens).

In modern times, because of the availability of quick dissemination, several noticeable changes are taking place. The long book or monograph is much less frequent. The more frequent medium is the journal article in nearly every area. And today, the journal article is often only for "recording" purposes. Because of scientific conventions, symposia, and the like, the scientist who wants to keep up with the recent advances in his field cannot trust the published journal articles; he must often be aware of quite recent speeches and even unpublished research discoveries anywhere in the world. In linguistics, for example, by the time findings get into print they are often already outmoded. And the same is true of physics, chemistry, medicine, and nearly every scientific field.

It is these small and compact articles and reports which make up the large majority of scientific writing today. To the layman who thinks of science in terms of brilliant new discoveries, these little journal articles may seem trivial. As Andrews has said,

> Prediction of the discovery of unseen planets and satellites, prediction of the behavior of light in magnetic and gravitational fields are striking examples of the abstractions of science. On the other hand, these spectacular flights are all based on discoveries in the first category: accumulations of facts, facts bizarre, laughable at times, subjects of scholarly papers whose contents seem so utterly unworthy of record in their strangeness that the scholar has become the butt of a thousand jokes. Nevertheless, most of our overwhelming scientific literature is made up of just that and nothing more (h, 2).

Of course the comprehensive, even encyclopedic monograph still has some viability. Such, in this century, have been Whitehead and Russell's *Principia Mathematica* and Toynbee's *A Study of History*.

All of these media obviously exert important influences on style and are, indeed, part of the style of scientific discourse. Some modern popular media have not as yet proven very adaptable as vehicles of scientific thought: radio, television, and the daily and weekly news journals. Undoubtedly, it is the audiences of these media rather than anything endemic to the media themselves which have prevented this sort of adaptation.

This leads naturally to the next characteristic of scientific discourse: its audience. The readers of a given scientific journal are inevitably a very restricted group within the larger group of scholars. It is a special and intelligent group, generally capable of the same mental calculations and possessed of the same logical sophistications as the writer, but uninformed of the particular topic at issue (cf. Mills, t, 17). This is all the more true when the science has developed for some time and gotten considerably beyond the reach of common information and common sense (cf. Maritain, i, 133–43; Kinneavy, s, 38 ff.). This is so true that Tannenbaum, writing in *Science* some years ago could say:

> J. Robert Oppenheimer stated the dilemma of science communication succinctly when he said some years ago that science is defined in words and phrases which are "almost impossible to translate" into conventional lay language (c, 581).

There are still a few disciplines some of whose votaries tenaciously cling to the notion of an amateur audience of the generally educated public. Until twenty years ago, grammar was still in this stage. And some literary critics especially continue to argue for this as a sort of ideal. Leslie Fiedler in America and Julien Benda in France fight the encroachments of the restricted audience (Fiedler, t, 561 ff.; on Benda, see Kinneavy, s, 135).

The opposite tendency, the desire to popularize and thus to reach a larger audience usually entails a consequent watering down of the material. This sort of "clarity" is unscientific, it distorts reality to enlarge the audience. Many a writer has had to make this compromise, frequently suggested by the monetary considerations of publishers. Viktor Frankl recently referred to this in speaking of his own publishing efforts:

> The publishers want to popularize and oversimplify everything. I feel as Einstein did, "Either we write understandably or we write correctly" (quoted from a speech given at Austin, and reported in *The Daily Texan*, Nov. 10, 1964, Vol. 64, No. 67, p. 1).

Some experts on technical writing establish a hierarchy of kinds of audiences. Racker, for example, has five levels of technical writing addressed to the operator (nontechnician), field technician, advanced technician, engineer, and scientist. Only in writing intended for the last, for example, does Racker recommend including all of the proofs and mathematical formulae (Racker, t, 12). Racker's distinctions illustrate the fact that science can gradually shade off into mere information (Racker, t, 4–67; see especially his summaries for each level).

Once the audience has been determined, however, it remains unobtrusive. For this reason it is assumed but hardly ever addressed as such. Some authorities on technical writing are currently attempting to relax the long-time standards of editors prohibiting "the indefinite you" (e.g. Morris, p, 58–60). The conventions concerning the use of "you" are similar to those relating to the use of "I" or "we." The reason usually alleged to justify these conventions is that the subject matter should not be distorted by the intrusion of either the writer or reader (cf. Mills, t, 18), a valid general principle. However, it does entail some awkward circumlocutions. Morris says it introduces a whole cast of fictitious characters: the author, the reader, the experimenter, the engineer (Morris, p, 58). He and others suggest the use of "I" and "we" when opinion or speculation are validly involved (p, 60). Mills and others recommend "we" when a research organization is involved.

The taboo against the first person leads to the use of the third person and this "encourages impersonal pronouns and passive verbs; and the passive creates dangling participles, multiple modifiers, and cryptic statements" as well as indirect statements (Menzel, w, 74, 75). Here, it seems the writer should weigh the advantage of objectivity against the loss of clarity in the individual situation. In much technical writing there is no real "I" anymore. The experimenter may be supplanted by a ghost technical writer plus two or three editors who edit for different reasons such as style, company policy, and technical accuracy (Morris, p, 11).

The nonintrusion of writer and reader both are advocated in order to allow the control to come from the subject matter. Hopefully, an "objective" style results. And "objectivity" is the great virtue of scientific style. Granted that complete objectivity is theoretically unattainable, it still remains an ideal to be approximated. Modern physicists remind us, in this connection, of the principle of indeterminacy—the measuring instrument always distorts the reality being measured; and medieval philosophers had a similar scholastic axiom, "Whatever is received is received according to the mode of the receiver." These kinds of instrumental and human subjectivity are unavoidable, but other kinds of distortions can be shunned.

Max Planck, in fact, once described the whole process of scientific thought as the attempt to eliminate all "anthropological" elements (Cassirer, e, 191). Sometimes this reaches heroic proportions. Heinrich von Treitschke once complained of the historian von Ranke's bloodless objectivity "which does not say which side the narrator's heart is on" (Cassirer, e, 188). And though some existentialists and rhetoricians may inveigh against this neutrality, it seems to be a necessary virtue of scientific discourse. It does not imply that the scientist is not emotionally involved with the object of his analysis; it may only mean that for the sake of the truth he is willing to abstract temporarily from his feelings in the hope that the truth which he finally achieves is purer and richer and consequently worthy of more ultimate committment and involvement.

Most of the semantic and grammatical characteristics of style stem from the objectivity of science, the attempt to reproduce reality as accurately as possible. Before turning to this however, one additional discourse element must be considered. This has to do with the speed with which the topic is unraveled to the reader, the "pace."

Since the size of most scientific articles is fairly closely controlled by editorial policy and the length of scientific reports by considerations of time, and since all publishing is a matter of money, much scientific writing is under several pressures calling for compression and condensation. Consequently, scientific reports often tend to pack much, sometimes too much, information into a short space and to avoid any repetition whatsoever. As a result, even necessary redundancy may be sacrificed. Information theorists maintain that for any code to be intelligible, as a mere sequence of signals, some redundancy is necessary (Shannon, m, 13). This law has its parallel at the level of discourse. Mills and Walter, for example, give five basic rules for technical writing at the beginning of their excellent book. One of these reads as follows:

At the beginning and end of every section of your report, check your writing according to this principle: "First you tell the reader what you're going to tell him, then you tell him, then you tell him what you've told him (Mills, t, 13–14, 23; Rapaport, w, 166–67).

SEMANTIC COMPONENTS
OF SCIENTIFIC STYLE

For the structure which is being adhered to in this analysis of style, the reader is again referred to Chart V, 2, which outlines some fundamental components of style in a literary framework. In Chapter I, the areas of semantics were established as being the linguistic components of significance arising from psycholinguistics, from reference, and from "meaning" (see Figure I, 4, p. 31). In the area of psycholinguistics, meanings arising from special personal or group usages (idiolect or dialect), a few major issues arise in connection with scientific discourse.

Scientific writers often are forced to establish their own new words or to give new meanings to old words because of the nature of their activity.

A scientist, by the nature of his work, is a philologist. He comes upon a new discovery or invention and almost automatically gives it a name which soon may become another apt term in the vocabulary of science. This was done in the case of iconoscope, kinescope, orthican, ultrafax, and others (Racker, t, 68).

This is a quotation from an RCA pamphlet on style. Toulmin, a respected philosopher of science, goes even further, maintaining that scientific language nearly always consists in giving new meanings to old terms. He instances the new meanings given to both "light" and "travel" when physicists began to treat of light in geometric contexts like "Light travels in straight lines" (Toulmin, p, 20–21). Gilman devotes an interesting chapter to coinages, called "New Words to Conquer," in *The Language of Science* (1, 49 ff.).

American writers are sometimes too callous in their coinages or new meanings. German writers, in the author's experience, often devote several pages of historical review before inflicting new terms on the reader. This may be because in the past, particularly in German philosophy and literary theory, German writers have sometimes been accused of each speaking a new language. In any case, while recognizing the occasional need for coinages or peculiar meanings, most authorities on technical writing discourage coinages except when absolutely necessary to establish important new distinctions. They then advise a paced introduction of the new terms (Gilman, 1, 73, 77).

Once a group has accepted the new or at least unfamiliar terms, we no longer have an idiolect, but a dialect. And the dialects of various academic disciplines are usually called jargon, and sometimes may be referred to as argot, cant, gibberish, gobbledegook, or more specifically as educationese or sociologese, nearly all of which have derogatory connotations. Jargon, however, nearly always has good intentions—it seeks to establish accuracy and precision of reference. Jargon is often necessary in an age of increasing specialization in esoteric subject fields. And some of the decriers of jargon are dilettantes who are simply intellectually indolent or who naïvely imagine that all science can and should be digested and watered down to their own levels of ignorance. This is a version of the democratic heresy of mediocrity operating in the linguistics of science, as it also operates in music, in modern art, and in many other cultural areas.

In any case, the scholar engaged in scientific discourse should strive as assiduously as his literary colleague for *le mot juste* to express his concept with precision, and if this means engaging in jargon or neologisms, so much the worse for the lay and amateur reader.

But when jargon is not necessary for accuracy, it only results in obscurity, a frequent vice in scientific style.[20] And every treatment of technical writing denounces this kind of obscurity. Thomas O. Richards and Ralph A. Richardson, both of General Motors Research Laboratories, make this point:

> We have never had a report submitted by an engineer in our organization in which the explanations and terms were too simple. We avoid highly technical words and phrases and try to make the work understandable, because we know that even the best engineer is not an expert in all lines. ...Most reports err in being too technical and formal (quoted in Mills, t, 24).

Many texts on technical writing give long lists of jargon which is unnecessary and can be eliminated by using simpler expressions (cf. Gilman, 1, 82–93). Such simpler expressions belong not to a special dialect but to the general language. This brings us to some semantic issues in the area of reference proper. These can be conveniently divided into problems having to do with the kind of object referred to (referent), the kind of referring term (referend), and the process of relating term to object (referral).

---

[20] Obscurity can also be a characteristic of literary style, as anyone who has read some modern poetry knows. Savory, in a text on technical writing, has an interesting example of literary jargon caused by allusions in a passage from Milton (Savory, 1, 103).

From high school texts to books on technical writing, there is usually a consistent refrain: "Use language that is simple, concrete, and familiar." This is another of Mills' and Walter's five basic principles of technical writing (t, 13). This recommendation is usually accompanied by the corresponding negative: avoid abstract terms (this really means terms referring to abstract, not concrete, realities and is therefore a matter of the referent). Of course, if the reality being referred to *is* abstract, attempting to make it concrete may only obscure the meaning. This was Duhem's basic objection to the use of models. And science, of course, does deal with abstract realities. Consequently, a universal rule to use always concrete language must be guarded against. However, abstractions can often be exemplified by concrete instances and this is what these texts are advocating (Mills, t, 22).

Another kind of reference generally eschewed in science is the humorous. "The sparkle of a report should be derived from its clarity and not from adornment by occasional gems of wit or wording," says Rhodes (t, 37). This is an echo of Cicero, who remarks that the style of the philosophers is designed for instruction rather than persuasion "and some think they exceed due bounds in aiming to give even a little pleasure by their style" (*Orator*, 63, quoted in Williamson, s, 128). Cicero, the man of measure, notice, only reports the tendency.

Finally, scientific style prefers the simple denotative to the connotative term which carries emotional associations with it (e.g., Savory, l, 107 ff.).

In the matter of referend (the kind of referring term), several issues are usually discussed. The texts continually advocate the shorter rather than the longer term (Gilman, l, 82 ff.). Secondly, science usually prefers the literal to the nonliteral term—that is, figures of speech are often out of place in science. Of course, models and analogies are nonliteral terms and are necessary in science, so again the injunction cannot be absolute, as several writers are at pains to point out (Rathbone, w, 197 ff.; Menzel, w, 96–97). Even euphemisms are sometimes quite conventional in scientific reports in reporting failures or in hedging (cf. Rathbone, w, 145).

The process of referral, finally, provides several categories very relevant to scientific discourse. If term and object have a one-to-one correspondence, we have a univocal term. If there is one term and several objects, we have an ambiguous or equivocal term. If we have several terms and one object, we have a synonymous term. If we have a term and no object, we have an anomalous term. And, desirably, science tries to use univocal and synonymous terms as much as possible, for anomaly and ambiguity contribute to obscurity. Gilman, typically, refers to ambiguity as "the real enemy" of the language of science (Gilman, l, 34 ff.). It can be a virtue of style in exploratory, or persuasive or literary discourse, but it is a vice in scientific discourse.

GRAMMATICAL COMPONENTS OF SCIENTIFIC STYLE

There remain certain grammatical features of scientific discourse to be pointed out. As with the discourse and semantic features, they have been only haphazardly studied. Most of the grammatical features are corollaries of the discourse and semantic features. And some have already been considered: the avoidance of first-person pronouns and the resulting heavy use of third-person pronouns.

Also related to the avoidance of the first person is the tendency to use the passive since the active form would entail the use of a first person. Yet some good authorities frown on the excessive use of the passive. Menzel, for instance, writes,

> A well-known literary axiom states that the passive voice is the false mistress of every bad writer. Passive verbs increase the probability of mistakes in grammar; they start long trains of prepositional phrases; they foster circumlocution; and they encourage vagueness (Menzel, w, 79).

For these reasons Menzel and others advocate the active voice whenever possible (Menzel, w, 51; Gilman, l, 122). Nonetheless, the passive voice is a strong characteristic of much modern scientific prose.

Historically, one of the syntax differentiations of plain style from Ciceronian style in the seventeenth century was the recommendation of the plain stylists to avoid the periodic and the inverted sentence and to use the loose and normal orders. This seems to have become a characteristic of modern prose generally and certainly of most scientific prose (cf. Williamson, s, 27). It almost goes without saying that another characteristic of the syntax of scientific prose is the usual abstention from the exclamatory and the imperative sentences.

Syntactically also, the modern scientific style, in its attempts to make precise distinctions, is often characterized by the presence of multiple modifiers. Menzel illustrates this with an actual example the like of which all of us have too often seen: "the upward-migrating intensity front hypothesis" (the hypothesis that an intensity front migrates upwards; Menzel, w, 106). There is also a concomitant tendency to make adjectives out of nouns. This would seem to be in direct opposition to the cliché often found in books on technical writing that, "Good nouns and good verbs need no modifiers. Adjectives and adverbs usually weaken and complicate the meaning," a rule which Gilman points out is often passed on from one textbook to another without critical examination (Gilman, 1, 101). Nonetheless, Gilman does recommend avoiding the adjective and adverb when possible.

Just as nouns tend to be turned into adjectives so do they also tend to be turned into adverbs in some disciplines by the encroaching use of the "-wise" suffix. Similarly, nouns and adjectives can be turned into verbs by the "-ize" suffix. Rathbone gives an extreme example from a social worker's report:

> The court at first considered that prisonization was the appropriate mentalism but eventually decided that domiciliarization was more suited to the prisoner, who was duly probationalized (Rathbone, w, 148).

This is hardly an example of good scientific writing. One cannot help but wonder how prison can be a 'mentalism," appropriate or not, and why "domiciliarization" is more meaningful than "sent home" is beyond me.

In addition to these morphemic features, scientific prose is also characterized by some very obvious graphemic features. Abbreviations, dialectal symbols, special fonts, even a pure numeric outline form rather than the combined Roman and alphabetic system, are all characteristic of much modern scientific prose. Likewise because of its level of formality, scientific prose also tends to avoid the usual contractions of informal and colloquial prose.

The Style of Informative Discourse

There is no general history of informative discourse, just as there is no general history of scientific discourse—as far as the author is aware. There are, of course, histories of science and histories of some kinds of informative writing, such as journalism, but style is ancillary in such treatments—as indeed it should be. In fact in some modern books on journalism, style is relegated to an appendix handbook. Much more important are: getting the news, areas of reporting, kinds of stories, and news photography.

If informative discourse has a history it is probably bound up with the history of the plain style as opposed to the grand style and the middle style. This story will be discussed in the next chapter, for the three styles are really more bound up with the history of rhetoric. But, in an important sense, the struggle between the plain style and the other styles is partly the story of the attempt of informative and scientific discourse to separate themselves from persuasive discourse.

Of course, informative discourse has some features in common with scientific discourse and with exploratory discourse. All are "reality"-dominated, rather than person- or signal-dominated, and certain basic features of style follow from this fundamental orientation. "Res, non verba," (the thing, not the word), the slogan of the Royal Academy, is appropriate for reference discourse generally. Yet there are some significant differences among the three kinds of reference discourse. The considerations on informative and exploratory discourse will often stress these differences rather than report some of the characteristics of scientific discourse which also apply in informative and exploratory discourse. For this reason, these two following treatments will also be shorter. This is also due to the fact that the styles of these two latter kinds of discourse have not received the attention which scientific discourse has.

Following the format established for scientific discourse, discourse, then semantic, and finally grammatical components of style will be treated.

Discourse Components
of Informative Style

Some of the discourse features of informative style concern the media, some the voice, some the addressee, and some the topic or reality.

The media of information are often markedly different from the media of science. There are overlaps; some kinds of technical writing could be classed as either scientific or informative, for example. And some journals modulate from one kind of discourse to the other in a given issue, or even within the same article. *Science,* for example, carries both kinds of articles and hybrid articles also. But there are some fairly clear-cut distinctions in the media. Most of the mass media (daily newspapers and weekly magazines, radio, television) are not normal vehicles of science. Their "scientific" columns and sections are informative, not scientific. There has been a heavy emphasis on journalistic media so far in the treatment, but journalistic media are not at all the only media of information. In business, many letters and reports are basically informative in nature. Most encyclopedias are fundamentally informative in nature. Much technical writing, it has already been remarked, is informative. Many textbooks are simply informative, especially at lower levels (elementary, high school, and undergraduate in college). Most of the current nonfiction best-sellers are informative (though some are also persuasive and a few are even basically expressive). Many current magazines are basically informative in such varied areas as drag racing, hobbies, gardening, and sports. Thus informative discourse makes up a good deal of the contemporary printed and oral-aural output.

The concerns of nonintrusion of encoder that were considered under scientific discourse are generally applicable to informative discourse, though less rigidly. In one sense, informative discourse has become even more impersonal than has science. Whereas the individual scientist (or an unnamed ghost technical writer) is usually personally responsible for his work and signs it, much informative discourse is unsigned and is attributable to the newspaper or magazine (e.g., *Newsweek, Business Week, The New York Times*) or even to a larger impersonality (e.g., the Associated Press, the United Press International). In a sense this is regrettable, for anonymity can absolve from personal responsibility. In another sense, there is distinct gain from the multiple source stories put together under a central subeditorial hand. Thus a story on election returns with sources reporting from all over the country can be given unity and intelligent centralization in an editorial office in Washington or New York with immense information gain.

Most of the concern with informative style, however, comes with the decoder. Three issues are usually given attention: readability, avoiding dullness, and pacing.

Readability actually has to do with ease of reading. It is a concern of many of the books in journalism and some in writing for business and government. Several formulae for readability have been evolved. Gray and Leary in 1935 are some of the earliest to have worked out readability formulas. Flesch, in 1944, worked out the first version of the readability formula which has received the most attention or notoriety. His formula was used in writing leads for the Associated Press (MacDougall, i, 99), and Flesch was even hired by the Internal Revenue Service to simplify tax forms and notices (he was not pointedly successful, it might be added). Gunning's formula had influence on some United Press writing (MacDougall, i, 99). Dale and Chall's formula has been used in some educational circles.

Flesch's formula originally recommended short sentences, few affixes, and as many references to persons in the content as possible. Later it was revised to consider: number of syllables per word, number of words per sentence, number of words with person reference, number of sentences with person reference. Still later, recognizing that some short words are quite technical and esoteric and some long words quite common, he revised his first norm again (cf. Campbell, h, 126 ff.). In terms of the second formula given above, he rated as standard readability a piece of discourse which would have an average syllable-to-word ratio of less than 1.5, an average sentence length of less than nineteen words per sentence, a six per cent use of person reference words and a twelve per cent use of person or human interest sentences. Very poor prose, at the other end of his scale, would have an average syllable-to-word ratio of 1.86, an average sentence length of forty-seven or more words to the sentence, no word or sentence person references (cf. Campbell, h, 127, for a more complete chart). Under Flesch's influence, "the Associated Press reduced its average lead sentence from 27 to 23 words and its average lead word length from 1.75 to 1.55 syllables" (MacDougall, i, 99). Flesch rated various media according to his formulas as follows: comics, a 90-to-100 reading ease rating, pulp fiction, 80-to-90; quality magazines, 50-to-60; academic prose, 30-to-50; scientific journals, 2-to-30 (cf. Hohenberger, p, 79).

Gunning's formulas were similar. They considered sentence-pattern "fog index," and human interest. "Fog index" is a matter of sentence length and word length (cf. Hohenberger, p, 79). Basically, Gunning's formula is based on criteria similar to Flesch's, and so are Dale and Chall's. Hohenberger summarizes them as follows:

> The base for the Flesch, Gunning and similar notions for improving communication in newspaper work is a sentence of 15 to 20 words, the use of familiar words, a low percentage of words with more than three syllables, and a highly personal flavor to the style (Hohenberger, p. 77).

Such formulas, even when interpreted intelligently and not just mechanically applied, are still open to severe criticisms. They are hard to reconcile with the inverted pyramid and the five W formulas of the regular journalism news story and lead, as Westley and others have pointed out. The human interest component of both Flesch's and Gunning's formulas are sometimes difficult to reconcile with journalistic impersonality. Of course, it seems plain distortion to attempt to humanize by person references much informative material which is fundamentally nonhuman—though humans may be interested in it (cf. further, MacDougall, i, 102–103). Further, both Flesch and Gunning were really attempting to lower the reading maturity level of the audience. Gunning's formula is said to have reduced the reading level of the UPI materials from 16.7 to 11.7 years of age (MacDougall, i, 99). To attempt to reduce all informative writing to a least common denominator, somewhere between the comics and the popular digests, would seem to be fatuous on the face of it.

Nonetheless, given an audience of a certain level, readability *at that level* should be a concern of a writer of informative discourse. And although there are factors other than word length and sentence length, these are certainly factors to consider.

Part of the problem of readability in journalism particularly stems from the increasing shortness of news articles on the front page. Today a newspaper may have as many as 15 to 40 articles on a front page, some quite short, of course. And in some, even paragraph unity and completeness of thought are sacrificed to brevity and front-page placement (Campbell, h, 11). This causes problems in pacing, an issue considered in scientific writing also.

The "human interest" factor is related to another issue, avoidance of dullness. Indeed, Campbell makes this equivalent to readability.

Effectiveness is the common denominator of journalistic writing. An axiom of such writing is that the only sin to fear is dullness. Timing, length, vocabulary, and emphasis may vary between media, but readability (in printed news) and listenability (in broadcast news) are of greater importance (Campbell, h, 108).

Hohenberger also speaks of "the daily battle against dullness" (p, 33). Actually, this really seems only to be a translation into style of what the nature of information requires: information must be surprising (see above, pp. 93, 96, 134 ff.). Certainly "factuality" has stylistic ramifications. The "surprise" element in information naturally lends a sense of sensationalism, and this implies a degree of emotion. There is excitement involved in being surprised. The reporter who has an exclusive scoop is justifiably excited about it, and the reader also takes justifiable pleasure in reading about it. One shouldn't have to apologize for the pleasure in the acquisition of knowledge. But the drama of headlines can be carried too far. McLuhan complains that often "the headline is a primitive shout of rage, triumph or warning" (b, 7); he points out the exploitation of this emotion:

> And the press used as a means of thrill and excitement produces a general emotional situation which leads to a crescendo, and crescendo calls for a catharsis—a blood bath. The actual outbreak of the Second World War was a visible relief to many after years of tense waiting (m, 7).

This may be an exaggeration. Nonetheless, behind the argument lies the suspicion, voiced by others also, that present-day sensational journalism may often precipitate crises as well as report them. One cannot but recall Hearst's response to the photographer who wanted to return from Cuba just before the Spanish American War, complaining that there was really nothing happening. Said Hearst, "You furnish the pictures and I'll furnish the war" (Swanberg, c, 108).

Other aspects of informative discourse style are peculiar to some media. Thus page placement and headlining are journalistic concerns; accompanying photography and art work are common concerns of newspapers and magazines; telegraphy has its peculiar stylistic problems; so does telephony; so do radio and television.

Semantic Components
of Informative Discourse

Informative discourse has many of the semantic characteristics of scientific discourse—with adaptations made for the level of audience. Jargon, for example, which is quite justifiable in much scientific writing, becomes considerably less justifiable in informative writing precisely because it may tend to prevent communication of information. Particularly when informative discourse is aimed at a general audience, jargon becomes a major vice. For this reason texts on journalistic writing have little patience with jargon of any sort (cf. Hohenberger, p, 73 f.). Nor, *a fortiori*, are coinages of much importance in informative discourse, though some brilliant exceptions occur.

With regard to the kind of object referred to, informative discourses, like scientific discourse, normally avoid connotative words, i.e., words with emotional associations (Bernstein, w, 195; MacDougall, i, 124 ff.). However, a few journalistic theorists, arguing that on-the-spot reactions are a part of "the whole truth" of the news, do allow some emotional involvement in a news story (MacDougall, i, 128). This, of course, is contrary to the *fact* bias of traditional newspaper reporting. On somewhat similar grounds, Theodore M. Bernstein, long-time managing editor of *The New York Times,* approves of the direction in which the following lead is moving:

> The quixotic Mr. Quill, who holds the undisputed national championship for threatening strikes and other pressure moves that never come to pass, announced that the union was scuttling its 'Operation Santa Claus' before it saved riders on eight privately owned bus lines their first dime. (Quoted in Bernstein, w, 88).

But he generally disapproves of emotion in objective news reporting (w, 196).

Abstract terms are another kind of referent usually proscribed in both lower-level technical writing and journalism. Westley, following something like Flesch's and Gunning's formula, even suggests "translating" abstract terms into "people" or "person" terms (Westley, n, 93). This seems to be an indefensible position, however, subject to the same criticism raised against Flesch's and Gunning's "human interest" distortions.

Bernstein, reflecting a common journalistic prudery, even rubs out certain referents in news stories (Bernstein, w, 189). But this sort of taboo can hardly be made a general rule for informative discourse. Some informative discourse must be about "filth, stench, gore, and the purely animal functions" even if "they meet with little hospitality in the news columns," as he remarks (Bernstein, w, 189). Humor, however, is a kind of reference which is generally given more hospitality in informative discourse than in scientific discourse——although its use is also restricted.

Only a few topics normally arise in discussions of style in informative discourse having to do with kinds of referring terms. Most of these have to do with the use of nonliteral terms, and their discussion is usually considered under "metaphor." There does not seem to be the usual fear of metaphor which writers on scientific language often evince. Bernstein, for example, simply cautions against inappropriate metaphors. He comments on a lead someone had used in the *Times*:

> "While Moscow is thus stoking up the 'cold war,' however, Peiping is playing it pianissimo." Depends on whether you like your "cold war" hot or sweet (Bernstein, w, 131).

Problems of referral of term to object—anomaly, univocity, ambiguity, synonymy—are also relevant to informative discourse. Journalists, with aspirations to fine writing, are possibly more worried about repetition of the same word again and again and consequently sometimes overindulge in synonyms. The disease Bernstein calls "synonymomania," and he defines it as a "compulsion to distract and, if possible, puzzle the reader by calling a spade successively a garden implement and an earth-turning tool" (Bernstein, w, 132). Sports writers, condemned to reporting much the same sort of event day after day, often suffer from the disease:

> Sugar Ray flattened Bobo in twelve *rounds* in 1950, outpointed him in fifteen *sessions* in 1952 and knocked him out in two *heats* last Dec. 9 (quoted in Bernstein, w, 132; his italics).

The opposite disease is the repetition of the same word or root in an awkward and close sequence: "Mr. Gomulka's *decision* to join with the Polish 'liberals' could be *decisive* in *deciding* the fierce factional struggle" (quoted in Bernstein, w, 132; his italics).

Grammatical Components of Informative Style

Some of the discourse and semantic components discussed above have had grammatical corollaries which need not be repeated here. Such are the avoidance of "I" and "we" and the sentence and word length involved in readability formulas.

In general, in perusing texts in journalism, business English, and technical writing, the author was surprised to find a very conservative approach to both semantic and grammatical problems rather the rule than the exception. Not too long ago, of course, journalism pioneered in simplified punctuation, especially in the use of the comma and semicolon. Business English, likewise, seemed somewhat unconventional in orientation a short time ago, rebelling openly against the fussiness of English teachers. Now, however, the English teachers seem the more liberal. This is no doubt due to the influence of modern descriptive linguistics in English. But the influence has not reached most other fields yet (e.g., Westley, n, 66 ff., on transitiveness; MacDougall, i, 115 ff., on usage).

Just as with scientific discourse, there are a few traditional recommendations which are passed on from text to text. With regard to adjectives and adverbs, for instance, Campbell says, "For more than half a century, adjectives have been unpopular in United States journalism" (h, 115). They lead to "opinion" rather than "fact," he maintains (h, 115–16). Hohenberger relates an incident from the life of Clémenceau having to do with this same proscription:

> When Georges Clémenceau was editor of the newspaper *La Justice,*
> he told a reporter, "Young man, when you write a sentence, you are to
> use a noun, a verb, and a complement. If you use an adjective, you must
> ask my permission" (Hohenberger, p, 50).

The qualifications made on this same topic in scientific style also apply here.

Since conjunctions encourage long sentences, several writers discourage their consistent use (Campbell, h, 116). Such remarks hardly constitute an adequate coverage of the grammar of informative discourse. Most treatments in journalism texts are quite perfunctory, though there may be long lists of cautions with regard to individual words (cf. Bernstein, w, 10–73). A more adequate grammar, structural or transformational, and a more adequate dialectology, both social and regional, could be profitably applied to journalism, business letters and reports, textbook writing, and the like.

The Style
of Exploratory Discourse

There is even less systematic coverage of the styles of exploratory discourse than of the scientific and informative styles. Since many authors do not even recognize exploratory discourse as a distinct genre, it would logically follow that the styles would not be differentiated. Yet the styles are as distinct as Plato's is from Aristotle's. The following comments are only, therefore, suggestive of what might be a fertile field for future analysis.

DISCOURSE COMPONENTS
OF EXPLORATORY STYLE

Possibly the most important discourse features of exploratory discourse have to do with the media in which exploratory discourse appears. Exploratory discourse is much more likely to be oral than written, and consequently not recorded. Real search for truth is often found in serious bull sessions in chemistry and physics laboratories, informal conferences in front of a recalcitrant computer, discussions of a seminar paper, or in angry disagreements at conferences and conventions. Even television and radio have proved valuable media for exploratory discourse (*Meet the Press* and *Face the Nation*). Such discourse is characteristically oral and dialogual, not written and monologual, as most science and information is. Plato recognized both attributes. He was loath to commit his discourse to writing and he felt that truth was found in dialogue, and therefore in the busy city where men congregate, not in the country, he said, where men are isolated (*Phaedrus*, 230c).

Regardless of Plato, and partially because of our more visual than oral-aural culture since the advent of printing, much modern research is carried on in isolation—even in the midst of cities and academic communities. In such cases, a man's dialogue may often be with himself. He must sometimes even furnish his own opposition. Not that this is a new dialectical phenomenon. Plato, Aquinas, Hume and many others are often their own best opponents.

Written exploratory discourse can exist, however. Transcripts of real dialogues exist (*The Dialogues of Alfred North Whitehead*), artificial reconstructions of exploratory processes (Platonic dialogues), interim and progress reports of research going on, speculative essays, and anthologies that explore a given but unresolved issue are some of the common written media of exploratory discourse.

Another frequent medium of exploration in the past has been the aphorism or epigram. Bacon held that the aphorism was the proper stylistic vehicle for probation, for progress in learning, whereas the magistral style was the proper vehicle for dispensing finished systems in the use of learning. Bacon, Pascal, Wittgenstein, and other eminent writers have successfully used this medium.

The communication framework of exploratory discourse often differs markedly from that of scientific discourse. The first notable distinction is that in dialectical discourse both voice and addresses can intrude noticeably. The control is still from the reality under research, but because the minds are still actively investigating the object, rigid objective control is neither possible nor totally desirable. And since the inquiring mind is open to any path leading to truth, he must be aware of other minds canvassing the same area.

Because of this awareness of other personalities and of the personally different attitudes they may take vis-à-vis reality, there are "character" intrusions into dialectical writing which are rarely seen in scientific writing. Socrates, as a personality, aside from his views of reality, emerges very clearly delineated in the various dialogues of Plato. Ion, Parmenides, and Crites are real people with personal idiosyncrasies. Dialectic is much closer to drama for this and for other reasons. Immediately consequent on this is the possibility of various idiolects in language. The image patterns of Laches are not those of Nicias nor those of Socrates.

In true dialectic, the opposition elements are not necessarily committed to be "good guys" and the others to be "bad guys." There is a continual shifting of positions as the dialectic proceeds, and the hero of one stage of the discussion may well be the goat of the next. Unfortunately this is not conducive to good *literature,* as such, and consequently even the best dialectical writing in our paraliterary tradition does not maintain this fluidity. Socrates in the Platonic dialogues is more often the victor than the vanquished—only in the *Parmenides* is this departed from.[21] And most of the dialogue writers in history have not even approached the Platonic level. This is not true of some other dialogues. In Hume's *Dialogues Concerning Natural Religion,* it is a point of contention among scholars whether Cleanthes represents the position of Hume or that of his opponents (cf. Hurlbutt, h, 137). Usually the antagonist is a straw man who is easily and repeatedly routed by the protagonist. The successive withdrawals of Ion before Socrates eventually make Ion appear very much in the role of a simpleton, as a result of which even Socrates' stature is lessened for it takes no great genius to outmaneuver an imbecile.

Despite the character intrusions and the closer proximity to drama, exploratory discourse is still discourse fundamentally focused on reality, albeit a partially unknown reality. It is still an "objective" discourse. Plato's characters and his "style" are less important than what they say. A technique quite contrary to intrusion, much used in psychological interviewing, is the so-called nondirective technique. In this technique, the psychologist operates on the principle that distortion from the intrusion of the psychologist frequently may spoil the final resolution of the problem.

SEMANTIC COMPONENTS
OF EXPLORATORY STYLE

Some semantic components of exploratory style are different enough from scientific and informative style to merit a little passing notice. It is clear that, since at least certain aspects of the object under investigation are unknown, some tentativeness in the language is to be expected. This is different from the fairly categoric references of science and the factual references of information. Further, as pointed out above, personality traits enter into exploratory discourse, and with them some emotion. This is not totally undesirable in a process of inquiry (cf. Dewey, 1, 44) and is related to Kierkegaard's stress on the subjective in dialectic. Humor is also an in-

---

[21] This might be related to the fact that Speiser, for example, following Hegel, considers the *Parmenides* the greatest dialectical effort of antiquity (cf. Speiser, as quoted in MacDonald, p, viii).

gredient, sometimes an important one, in exploratory discourse. It may remove in a flash entire commitments which are hindering true exploration. This is another differentiation from science, and even ordinary information. Finally, where science is abstract, exploration often makes use of concrete images. Imagery structures similar to those used in lyric and drama are characteristic of many Platonic dialogues.

In addition to referents (objects), the referends (referring terms) of exploratory discourse are sometimes different from scientific discourse. There are generally many more nonliteral terms, where science tends to adhere to literal terms (for the structure of this distinction, see Figure V, 2). These nonliteral terms are often referred to as figures of speech, and though their use is more restricted here than in rhetoric or literature, they have their importance in exploratory discourse. Thus metaphor, analogy, and model are almost *de rigueur* in exploration—as the analysis of the nature of exploration has shown. Irony is another important semantic tool quite frequently employed in dialectic, but out of place in science and most information—Socrates' use of it is classic but not atypical. Paradox, similarly, is another normal feature of much exploratory discourse. The inconsistencies between the current dogma and other known facts are often best expressed in paradox. Galileo's "Nonetheless it moves" is classic here. And often the aphorism or epigram which is a common medium for exploratory discourse is paradoxical in nature. Even euphemism is not excluded from exploratory discourse.

Finally, at least one manner of referral of term to object radically differentiates exploratory from scientific discourse. This has to do with ambiguity. Ambiguity was called by at least one writer "the real enemy" of scientific discourse. But it is frequently a necessary virtue in exploratory discourse. The reason for this is that the nature of the reference may still be in question and to impose a one-to-one relationship of language to reality might be to close the door to the possible real meaning(s) the word may have.

Hobbes, following the Cartesian lead, argues for a careful definition of words at the outset of any science. As he says, "In the right definition of names lies the first use of speech, which is the acquisition of science; and in the wrong, or no definitions, lies the first abuse, from which proceed all false or senseless tenets" (quoted in Hutchins, g, II, 685).

Freud expresses the opposite view, which is generally more characteristic of the attitude of the modern scientist, especially the experimentalist or empiricist in method. The view is often defended, he writes, "that sciences should be built on clear and sharply defined basic concepts." But " in actual fact, no science, even the most exact, begins with such definitions." The true beginning of scientific activity, Freud holds,

...consists rather in describing phenomena and then proceeding to group, classify and correlate them. Even at the stage of description, it is not possible to avoid applying certain abstract ideas to the material in hand, ideas derived from various sources and certainly not the fruit of new experience only.... They must at first necessarily possess some measure of uncertainty; there can be no question of any clear limitation of their content. So long as they remain in this condition, we come to an understanding about their meaning by repeated references to the material of observation, from which we seem to have deduced our abstract ideas, but which is in point of fact subject to them (quoted in Hutchins, g, II, 685).

The basic concepts of definitions of a science are, according to Freud, "in the nature of conventions: although," he adds,

...everything depends on their being chosen in no arbitrary manner, but determined by the important relations they have to the empirical material.... It is only after more searching investigation of the field in question that we are able to formulate with increasing clarity the scientific concepts underlying it.... Then, indeed, it may be time to immerse them in definitions. The progress of science, however, demands a certain elasticity even in these definitions (quoted in Hutchins, g, II, 685–86).

Of course it might be pointed out by some that the nature of Freud's science, depth psychology, and the fact that it was then in its infancy, might have motivated these statements. Freud, however, pointed out that even physics is continually altering its definitions, and today Freud could speak with even more vigor on this.

One thing which Freud mentioned in passing in the above quotation might be abstracted for a slightly more lengthy consideration. The arbitrary limitations of the meaning—i.e., the range of possible ambiguities—is not infinite, for only a certain number are possible within the probabilities being analyzed in the essay. Thus "courage" in the *Laches* means the virtue of not running away, or the virtue of endurance, or the virtue of knowledge, but "courage" is not limitlessly indeterminate.

Hegel, going even further than Freud, delighted in the ambiguity of words in dialectical inquiry. In the preface to the second edition of his *Logic,* he expresses deep satisfaction in the fact that many German words have not only various, but even opposite meanings:

...indeed, many of its [German's] words have the further peculiarity that they have not only various, but even opposed, meanings...it is a joy to stumble on such words, and to meet with the union of opposites...in the naive shape of one word with opposite meanings registered in a dictionary (1, Vol. II, 40).

I. A. Richards has reiterated the importance for the reader of holding ambiguous meanings in suspension in attempting to understand one's readings (h, 24; p, 72–73). And, of course, ambiguity will be referred to again in literary discourse. It is not maintained that uninhibited ambiguity, irresponsible emotionalism, paradox for its own sake, or pointless irony are the staples of exploratory discourse. But they do occur occasionally.

GRAMMATICAL COMPONENTS
OF EXPLORATORY STYLE

So little examination has been done in this area that it almost seems pretentious to devote a subsection to it. This category is mentioned only for comprehensiveness. Russell does point out, as was seen above in Chapter II, that interrogative discourse is one basic use of language. In effect, every exploratory dicourse should terminate with a big question mark. Indeed, the interrogative does figure heavily in the early Platonic dialogues, particularly in the elenchus (cross-examination by Socrates, cf. *Laches,* 190–96).

One might speculate that the conditional and the if-then, either-or kinds of clauses would be more abundant in exploratory discourse than in science. Again, in oral discourse, certainly, there are more sentence fragments and unfinished linguistic components in real exploration than in the polished certainties of science. All of this is yet to be examined.

This concludes the discussion of the style of reference discourse. It is hoped that by now it is clear that there are certain stylistic features of reference discourse that rather incisively distinguish it from the other aims of discourse. If, as Newman remarks, style is a thinking out into language, different kinds of thinking should emerge quite differently. They do.

The Style
of the Anthologized Essay

The word "style," ordinarily reserved for literary or paraliterary productions, would not usually be predicated of a piece like the chapter from Wallis and Roberts. Yet it does have a style in the sense of characteristic discourse and linguistic choices that enable the language to fulfill its various overlapping aims. Indeed, the anthologized essay has not one, but two rather distinct styles, as I shall attempt to show.

Actually, the section prior to the "Vitamins and Endurance" report achieves one kind of aim, primarily, and the report itself achieves another kind of aim. These aims were discussed above. The chapter has informative and exploratory elements, and some scientific components residual in the report on the scientific experiment. Basically, however, the sections prior to the report on vitamins are exploratory (with some strands of pedagogical rhetoric woven in), and the report itself is an informative report at a fairly low level of technicality. There are, in fact, two styles, one for the first part of the chapter and one for the report. It seems that Wallis and Roberts are writing in their own style at this early point in their book, and then become impersonal ghost writers abstracting the quite technical report of the Staff of the Army Medical Nutrition Laboratory. At any rate there are quite surprising shifts in style.

Since the report is considerably larger than the preliminary section, only a sample of the report was analyzed. The first paragraph and every fifth paragraph after it were selected for analysis. This gave a sample of 849 words in 7 paragraphs to be compared with 911 words in 7 paragraphs in the preliminary section.

The discourse components of the two selections differ radically in some respects. The preliminary section is actually a part of a college text-book intended for students at the sophomore and junior levels (Wallis, s, ix). The report section is an abstract of a long technical report made for the Office of the Surgeon General of the United States Army. The original media are, therefore, quite distinct, and the influences of both media are quite evident. The original report had 99 pages of actual text, including 7 and 1/2 pages of bibliography (96 items), 90 pages of tables, 17 pages of charts and graphs, 18 pages on statistical methodology, 52 pages of further tables, and 22 pages of photograph or document reproductions. All told, the original report was a massive 298 pages. In addition there was further material kept in files, but not published.

The first and possibly most notable difference is in the number of encoder and decoder intrusions. In the preliminary section there are twenty-one uses of the first- or second-person pronouns (I, we, you, us, your). In the report section there are only four such uses. In the preliminary section, for example, in paragraph 1, "we" is the logical subject of each main clause in the paragraph and of several of the subordinate clauses. The same is true of paragraph 4. To a slightly less degree this is also true of paragraph 3. In the long quotation in paragraph 5, out of 14 clauses, 10 have as grammatical (or logical) subject "I," "we," or "my—." In the second paragraph which has only one personal (first or second) pronoun, it is clear that the seemingly impersonal axioms are almost moral admonitions to the student reader: "He who accepts statistics indiscriminately will often be duped unnecessarily. But he who distrusts statistics indiscriminately will often be ignorant unnecessarily." They really mean: "If you accept. . ." and "if you distrust . . . ."

In fact, the whole preliminary section is grammatically dominated by the first- and second-person intrusions. In no sense is this even faintly true of the report section. The "we" of the preliminary section is an exploratory "we:" together let us explore the attitudes towards statistics. And, as we have seen, the logic is almost totally exploratory—Hegelian, to be specific. Thus the preliminary section is highly personal and exploratory, whereas the report section is almost totally objective and informative. Even the concerns of the preliminary section are somewhat emotional. The first section begins with a statement about attitudes and ends with purposes which include imparting a "feel" for caution and dispelling an "aura of magic."

In readability and pacing the two sections seem fairly comparable. The average sentence length of the preliminary section is twenty-six words; the average sentence length of the report section is twenty-one words. Using Gunning's Fog Index as a partial measure of readability, the Fog Index of the preliminary section was found to be 14.8, that of the report section 14.48—that is, the reading level of both sections is that of juniors in college (and indeed, this is the intended level).

There are, however, some radically different semantic features. There are only two instances of jargon in the preliminary section ("error factor" and "seeding" of clouds). There are twelve instances of jargon in the report (some might be debatable). Five of those, it might be noted, occur in a direct quotation from the original.

Further, semantically, the preliminary report makes use of a goodly number of nonliteral terms: metaphor, paradox, irony. Some of the metaphors are dormant ("main stream," "immune to attitudes"), but some are live ("we wilt the first time somebody quotes statistics," "blemishes on the monument" [of the Kinsey report]). Paradox is also used throughout the entire section: statistics which can prove anything, that is, nothing; a receptive yet critical mind; statistics is not a difficult discipline, but not an easy one. In fact the recurrent aphorisms all tend to the paradoxical. The antithetical nature of the logic lends itself to paradoxical expression. Even irony is used on one or two occasions: "writers who deceive us with correct facts."

By contrast, metaphor, paradox, irony—figures of speech generally —are almost totally absent in the report on vitamins. Even though some of the conclusions were contrary to expectations and other facts, and would have lent themselves to paradoxical expression, the authors resisted the temptation to use this nonliteral language (remember that the conclusions were taken verbatim from the original report).

With regard to referral, the third component of reference, ambiguity is also an important characteristic of the style of the preliminary report. The problem really stems from the ambiguities of the phrase "statistical conclusions." Are they valid or not, are they hard to come by or not, are they only used or only abused? These ambiguities provide the framework which permits the application of a Hegelian logic. There is, of course, an ambiguity involved in the use of "vitamins" in the report also. But it is not stylistically exploited.

Finally, there are some grammatical stylistic features of the style(s) of the essay which call for brief comments. Attention has already been called to the length of the sentences, the length of the words (involved in the Fog Index), and the use of personal pronouns. Two other grammatical features of the selection are quite distinctive in the two styles. The use of the adversative conjunctions "but" and "yet" seems very characteristic of the style of the preliminary report. In the first page and a half, there are twelve instances of a syntactic eyement being balanced by a following syntactic element beginning with an adversative conjunction. This produces an antithetical, balanced and highly parallel style: "At first we tend....But then we are misled...;" "In the next chapter...but in this one;" etc. This is consonant with the other features of the exploratory style of the preliminary section. It is also somewhat characteristic of the report (seven instances, including "however" and "rather than"), but not as pronounced.

One final positive feature seems to differentiate the two styles. In the preliminary report there are thirteen uses of the passive verb whereas in the report there are twenty-nine uses. Again, in the report this is probably a residue from the original report (I did not make a sample count).

Finally, by negation, there are certain stylistic features common to both sections. There is, of course, little attention paid to prose rhythm, although some (probably unconscious) rhythm obtains in the balanced features of the preliminary section. But alliteration, assonance, conscious rhythm, and sound structures generally are not at all conspicuous as they would be in a literary style or even a rhetorical style.

EXERCISES

I. *The Nature of Reference Discourse*

A. *Scientific*

1. Examine a piece of discourse from a scientific journal for:
   a. probability level;
   b. referential or emotional statements;
   c. focus on subject matter rather than on the writer, the reader, or the stylistic cleverness;
   d. kinds of sentences used (declarative, interrogative, imperative, exclamatory);

     e. indications of sociopsychological motives for communication (see. *supra,* 53, for the source of this component);

     f. faculty addressed (see. *supra,* 65, for this component);

2. Contrast a scientific piece of writing with a persuasive piece on one or several of the points outlined in exercise 1.

3. Contrast a scientific piece of writing with a literary piece on one or several of the points outlined in question 1.

4. Compare a scientific discourse of Antiquity with one from the Middle Ages or with one from the Renaissance or with one from the contemporary period, considering one or several of the points outlined in exercise 1.

5. Compare Aquinas' concept of scientific style with Bacon's (cf. p. 169 for references to start).

6. Discuss Kierkegaard's rejection of scientific objectivity (cf. p. 170 for references to start).

7. Take a piece of scientific discourse and isolate:

     a. the evaluative components;

     b. the narrative components;

     c. the descriptive components;

     d. the classificatory components.

     Make some considerations about the nature of scientific discourse with regard to the kinds of statements found in the sample you analyzed.

8. Discuss the rejection of evaluation by a linguist or an ethical theorist (e.g., Alfred Ayer's rejection of any but descriptive judgments in "On the Analysis of Moral Judgments," *Philosophical Essays*). Is Ayer's rejection itself an evaluation; if so, what are its "scientific" bases?

B. *Informative*

1. Take a piece of informative discourse (news story, low-level encyclopedia, etc.) and analyze it for:

     a. factuality;

     b. comprehensiveness;

     c. surprise value.

2. Compare the assumptions of factuality in a piece of informative discourse with the proofs of factuality in a piece of scientific discourse (cf. Ch. I, Exercise 1, for some similar topics).

3. Contrast the treatment of a common "content" informative piece in *The New Republic* and *The National Review*. Consider factuality, comprehensiveness, and surprise value. Don't forget the usual assumed audience.

4. Take a sports event as reported in two competitive or town newspapers and analyze the respective treatments for factuality, comprehensiveness, and surprise value. If possible, get a third neutral treatment.

5. Analyze a piece of informative discourse for one or several of the points outlined in Exercise 1. under *Scientific.*

6. Compare and contrast news stories from the early nineteenth, late nineteenth, and mid-twentieth centuries.

C. *Exploratory*

1. Analyze Plato's *Ion* as a piece of exploratory discourse (or *Charmides* or *Lysis*).

2. Analyze the general exploratory structure of Newman's *Apologia pro Vita Sua* (or a similar development story).

3. Contrast a dialogue of Plato with one of Berkeley's *Three Dialogues of Hylas and Philonous* as examples of exploratory discourse.

4. Discuss a piece of exploratory discourse for one or several of the points outlined in Exercise 1, under *Scientific.*

5. Get a transcript of "Meet the Press' or a similar television format and analyze the nature of the questions and of the answers as to aim.

6. Secure a questionnaire on some social topic and analyze the content and structure of the questions. Is there a dialectical or rhetorical progression in the sequence of questions? Can you discern questions which "check" on each other?

7. If you are in a seminar or group meeting of some sort, transcribe the discussion for one session and try to analyze the exploratory structure of the proceedings.

8. Analyze the teaching techniques of one of your professor's lessons in terms of use of exploratory procedures. Is there a heavy overlap of informative, scientific, persuasive, entertaining, or expressive aims also?

9. Analyze one of the discourses mentioned in the preceding questions for one or several of these specific points:
   a. intrusions of encoders and decoders;
   b. use of reference vs. emotional statements;
   c. percentages of narrative, descriptive, classificatory, or evaluative statements;
   d. faculty-addressed;
   e. focus on components of the communications triangle;
   f. levels of probability;
   g. percentages of grammatical sentences used (declarative, interrogative, imperative, exclamatory).

II. *Logics of Reference Discourse.*

A. *Scientific.*

1. Analyze the use of deductive arguments in any piece of discourse in which you see the operation of drawing inferences from premises in reference discourse. Inductive material is often

mingled with the deductive to establish the truth of the generalizations. Separate the two. Some suggestions:
   a. Mill's arguments in "On the Liberty of Thought and Dis-
      cussion," Chapter II of *On Liberty.*
   b. One of the traditional arguments for the existence of God,
      (see Hutchins, *The Great Ideas,* 564, for references).
   c. Arguments against the proofs for God's existence (see
      Hutchins, *The Great Ideas,* 564–65, for references).
2. Take a current article from one of the journals: *Publications
   of the Modern Language Association, Modern Fiction Studies,
   Philological Quarterly, Modern Philology, College English,* or
   a similar periodical, and attempt to describe and evaluate its
   assumed or explicit norms of scientific evidence in terms of
   deductive and inductive logic.
3. Contrast a current article in one of the periodicals mentioned
   in the previous exercise with an article in a journal from another field (history, science, mathematics, sociology, or education) for assumed or explicit norms of scientific evidence and
   for evidences of ethnologic.
4. Take a section of a careful generative grammar sequence and
   analyze it as a deductive system. Attempt to isolate primitive
   rules of formation and rules of transformation.
5. Take two or three assumptions with which you would not
   ordinarily agree (in religion or politics or education) and write
   a theme showing how your life would be rearranged by them.
6. Analyze and evaluate the norms of scientific evidence assumed
   or explicit in this text to establish a certain point, for example:
   a. the aims of discourse;
   b. the nature of scientific explanation.
7. Analyze and evaluate any of your current texts with regard
   to the assumed or explicit norms of evidence used in an important section.
8. Analyze and evaluate any of your current professors with regard
   to his assumed or explicit norms of evidence when he is establishing an important issue or position in the course you are
   following.

B. *Informative*

1. Take a typical piece of informative writing (news article, nontechnical encyclopedia, textbook) and analyze it for the assumed or stated bases for the factuality of its statements. If
   the writer is not given (as in many news stories in dailies and
   weeklies), what assurance does the reader have for factuality?
2. Analyze a section from a textbook or an article from an encyclopedia for its assumptions about the surprise value of its
   contents.

3. Analyze a section from a textbook or an article from an encyclopedia for its treatment of comprehensiveness. How does it achieve comprehensiveness?

4. Constrast two articles from different encyclopedias or two sections on the same topic from different textbooks. Consider how each has achieved comprehensiveness. Evaluate the comprehensiveness of each.

5. Take an article from a college-level encyclopedia (*Americana, Britannica*) and extract the sections in it which are *new* or *surprising* to you. Contrast this with an article on the same topic from a technical encyclopedia (*Encyclopaedia of Poetry, Encyclopaedia of Educational Research*) or with an article on the same topic from an elementary or high school-level encyclopedia. What norms of surprise value seem to be operating, if any?

6. Contrast a news story on a current topic from *The New York Times* with one of the same topics from some other newspaper. Consider either or both for comprehensiveness or surprise value.

C. *Exploratory.*

1. Analyze in more detail than the text does the exploratory logic of a section from Plato's *Laches*. What logical pattern does Socrates use to arrive at the hypothesis which the elenchus destroys? What logical pattern is used to destroy the hypothesis?

2. Discuss the case for and against a logic of discovery (cf. Hanson, the various references in the footnotes, p. 205 versus the references given for the opposite position, p. 141).

3. Analyze the logical steps used by the scientist in some great discovery. For example, Harvey, in his studies of the quantity of blood in the heart (*On the Motion of the Heart and Blood in Animals,* Great Books of the Western World, pp. 268 ff.).

4. Analyze the logic of the exploratory process in sections of Conant's discussions of discovery (*On Understanding Science: An Historical Approach,* pp. 65 ff.).

5. Isolate the logical reasons as Newman presents them for his religious conversion (in *Apologia Pro Vita Sua*).

6. Analyze the logic behind sections of Bertrand Russell's *Why I am Not a Christian*.

7. Isolate the logical reasons for Crane's repudiation of the historical approach in favor of a critical approach to literature (see Bibliography, Chapter I, for the reference).

III. *ORGANIZATION OF REFERENCE DISCOURSE*

A. *Scientific*

1. Analyze the structure of the pieces of scientific discourse men-

tioned in the first exercise under the "Logics of Reference Discourse."

2. Analyze the organizational patterns of two articles on the same topic from *Modern Fiction Studies, Sewanee Review,* or similar periodicals.

3. Contrast the organization of a piece of scientific history with a piece of scientific theory.

4. Contrast Aristotle's organization of his treatment of anger in the *Ethics,* IV, Ch. 5 (1125b 26 f.) with his treatment of the same topic in the *Rhetoric,* II, (1378a 23 f.). How do you account for the differences in structure? (See Chapter IV, p. 242.)

5. Analyze the organization of Chapter I of this text. Would you consider this predominantly scientific or informative discourse? What logic, if any, is displayed in Chapter I? Does the organization of the historical section differ markedly from that of the theoretical section?

B. *Informative*

1. Analyze a typical piece of news writing about a basically narrative event. What effect have the conventions of the lead embodying the five W's and the inverted triangle of diminishing importance had upon the chronological structure of the presentation?

2. Contrast two informative presentations of the same event, one from an encyclopedia or textbook and one from a newspaper (e.g., one of the major battles of World War II). Account for the differences in organization.

3. Analyze the structure of a report in *Consumer Reports.* What principle of organization determines the sequence of facts?

4. Contrast the organization of the presentation of the battle of Waterloo in Thackeray's *Vanity Fair* with a report of the battle from an encyclopedia.

C. *Exploratory*

1. Relate the logic of the *Laches* to its organization. Does the logic of exploration determine the organization?

2. Record the steps of a discussion in one of your classes and attempt to determine what principles impose the organization.

3. Analyze the pattern of organization of Harvey's study of the quantity of blood in the heart (see p. 198 for the references).

4. Contrast the organization of one of Plato's early dialogues with that of one of his latest (e.g., the *Laches* with the *Laws*). What has happened to the aim of discourse in the two sets of dialogues?

5. Obtain or make a recording of or obtain a transcript of *Meet*

the Press, Face the Nation or a similar interview program. Then analyze the organization of the topics discussed. Relate these to the interviewers involved. Is there a correlation?

6. Analyze the Hegelian macrostructure of the speeches at the Congress of the Peloponnesian Confederacy at Lacedaemon in Thucydides, Book I, Chapter III. Analyze the rhetorical structure of the individual speeches.

7. Analyze the organizational pattern of one of Aquinas' articles in the *Summa Theologica*.

IV. *STYLE OF REFERENCE DISCOURSE*

A. *Scientific*

1. Compare and contrast two pieces of scientific discourse from several periods, e.g., Aristotle's treatment of the purpose of the state (*Politics*, 1252a ff.) and Aquinas (*Summa Theologica*, Part I-II, 2. 90, Article 2); or Plato (*Laws*, Book IV) with Hobbes (*Leviathan*, Introduction); or Locke (*Civil Government*, Chapter VII) with *The Federalist* (Number 29). Take several features of style at different levels and analyze their occurrence.

2. Write a paper on the various media of scientific discourse from Antiquity to the present. Try to account for the near disappearance of some of these media, e.g., the written dialogue, so popular in the Renaissance.

3. Take several features of style and contrast their occurrence in a piece of literature and a piece of science. For example, take ambiguity or univocity, strict denotation or connotation, rhythm, etc.

4. Compare and contrast the styles of two scientific writers in similar or different disciplines. For example, contrast the styles of Newton and Aristotle in writing about physics, or of Toynbee and Carnap, writing respectively of history and logic. Are there different scientific styles?

5. Take a scientific piece of discourse and attempt a comprehensive categorization of its stylistic features. Include grammatical, semantic, discourse, and metalanguage features of all types.

6. Make an in-depth analysis of a scientific style at one level. Thus, a careful study of ambiguity or univocity in one piece of writing might be made; or a careful study of graphemic features of style might be made (in a logician, a chemist, a physicist, or a mathematician).

B. *Exploratory*

1. Contrast Plato's style in an early dialogue with Aristotle's writing on the same topic (e.g., temperance in *Charmides* and

Ethics, BK. II, Chapters 3 and 7). Does Plato write as a dialectician and Aristotle as a scientist?

2. Contrast Plato's style in an early dialogue with his style in a later one, dealing in part with the same topic (e.g., *Charmides* with *Laws,* BK. I). Has the basic aim of the discourse altered as evidenced by the style?

3. Analyze the style of one of Hume's dialogues on religion. Compare or contrast its features to some of Hume's monologual prose.

4. Analyze Newman's style in a part of *Apologia Pro Vita Sua* or one of the essays in *The Idea of a University.* Are the stylistic characteristics exploratory or scientific or persuasive? Contrast this with Newman's style in one of his university sermons.

5. Get a copy of an *oral* exploratory discourse (a seminar, a transcript of *Meet the Press, Face the Nation,* or a similar program). Analyze its style. Contrast it to a *written* exploratory dialogue.

C. *Informative*

1. Contrast a college-level encyclopedia to a high school-level encyclopedia article on the same topic, in several stylistic features. Is the difference in the direction of more information or does it tend to move to the inclusion of proof, and therefore to an overlap with science?

2. Check a newspaper article and accompanying headlines for emotional reference or connotations in words. To what degree does the emphasis on surprisingness and sensationalism reveal itself stylistically? Do the emotional words tend to occur more at the beginning of the article or are they consistent throughout?

3. Contrast a newspaper article and an encyclopedia article for stylistic evidences of comprehensiveness.

4. Contrast two articles in different newspapers or periodicals for stylistic evidences of bias or partiality. Take the report of an election in *The New Republic* and *The National Review* or the report on a sports event from two home newspapers.

5. Contrast the style of one of your English textbooks to that of one from another course.

6. Record a national or local radio or television news broadcast. Analyze it for several levels of stylistic features. What differences seem to inhere in the medium?

BIBLIOGRAPHY AND FOOTNOTE REFERENCES

Abrams, M. H. *The Mirror and the Lamp.* New York: Oxford University Press, 1953 (m).

Adler, Mortimer J. *The Conditions of Philosophy.* New York: Atheneum, 1965 (c).

Alexander, Peter. *Sensationalism and Scientific Explanation.* London: Routledge & Kegan Paul Ltd., 1963 (s).

Alline, Henri. *Histoire du texte de Platon.* Paris: Champion, 1915 (h).

Alsop, Stewart. "The Meaning of the Dead." *Saturday Evening Post* (April 24, 1965), 16 (v).

Andrews, Edmund. *The History of Scientific English.* New York: R. Smith, 1947 (h).

Apostel, Leo. "Formal Study of Models." In *The Concept and the Role of the Model in Mathematics and Natural and Social Sciences,* ed. Hans Freudenthal. Dordrecht, Holland: D. Reidel Publishing Company, 1961. Pp. 1–37 (f).

Aquinas, Saint Thomas. *Summa Theologica.* Tr. Fathers of the English Dominican Province; ed. Rev. Daniel J. Sullivan. Vols. XIX and XX of *Great Books of the Western World,* eds., Robert M. Hutchins and Mortimer J. Adler. Chicago: Encyclopaedia Britannica, Inc., 1952 (st).

Aristotle. *The Works of Aristotle.* Tr. under the editorship of W. D. Ross. *Metaphysics,* tr. W. D. Ross, IX, 1908. *Poetics,* tr. I. Bywater, 1924. *Rhetoric,* tr. W. R. Roberts, 1924. *Topics,* tr. W. A. Pickard-Cambridge. Oxford: Clarendon Press, 1908–52.

Bacon, Francis. "Novum Organum," *Bacon.* Vol. XXX of *Great Books of the Western World,* eds. Robert M. Hutchins and Mortimer J. Adler. Chicago: Encyclopaedia Britannica, Inc., 1952.

Bain, Alexander. *English Composition and Rhetoric.* New York: Appleton and Company, 1867 (e).

Bar-Hillel, Yehoshua. *Language and Information.* Reading, Mass.: Addison-Wesley, Inc., 1964 (l).

Basson, A. H., and D. J. O'Connor. *Introduction to Symbolic Logic.* London: University Tutorial Press, 1959 (i).

Belth, Marc. *Education as a Discipline.* Boston: Allyn and Bacon, 1965 (e).

Bernstein, Theodore M. *Watch Your Language.* Great Neck, N. Y.: Channel Press, 1958 (w).

Beth, Evert W., and Jean Piaget. *Mathematical Epistemology and Psychology.* Tr. W. Mays. Dordrecht, Holland: D. Reidel Publishing Company, 1966 (m).

Black, Max. *Models and Metaphors.* Ithaca, N. Y.: Cornell University Press, 1962 (m).

Bocheński, I. M. *The Methods of Contemporary Thought.* Dordrecht, Holland: D. Reidel Publishing Company, 1965 (m).

————. *A Précis of Mathematical Logic.* Tr. Otto Bird. New York: Gordon and Breach, 1959 (p).

Braithwaite, Richard B. "Models in the Empirical Sciences." In *Logic, Methodology and Philosophy of Science,* Ernest Nagel, Patrick Suppes, and Alfred Tarski, eds. Stanford, Calif.: Stanford University Press, 1962. Pp. 224–31 (m).

————. *Scientific Explanation.* Cambridge, England: Cambridge University Press, 1953 (s).

Campbell, Lawrence R., and Roland E. Wolseley. *How to Report and Write the News.* Englewood Cliffs, N. J.: Prentice-Hall, Inc., 1961 (h).

Camus, Albert. *The Myth of Sisyphus.* Tr. Justin O'Brien. New York: Vintage Books, 1960 (m).

Camus, Albert. *The Rebel: An Essay on Man in Revolt.* Tr. Anthony Bower. New York: Vintage Books, 1959 (r).

Carmichael, R. D. *The Logic of Discovery.* Chicago: The Open Court Publishing Co., 1930 (l).

Carnap, Rudolf. "Empiricism, Semantics, and Ontology." In *Semantics and the Philosophy of Language,* ed. Leonard Linsky. Urbana, Ill.: University of Illinois Press, 1952 (e).

————. "Intellectual Autobiography." In *The Philosophy of Rudolf Carnap,* ed. Paul Schilpp. LaSalle, Ill.: Open Court Publishing Co., 1963 (i).

————. *Logical Foundations of Probability.* 2nd Edition. Chicago, Ill.: University of Chicago Press, 1962 (lo).

————. "On Some Concepts of Pragmatics." *Meaning and Necessity.* Chicago: University of Chicago Press, 1956. Pp. 248–51 (m).

Cassirer, Ernst. *An Essay on Man.* New Haven, Conn.: Yale University Press, 1944 (e).

————.*The Logic of the Humanities.* Tr. Clarence Smith Howe. New Haven: Yale University Press, 1961 (lo).

Chao, Yuen Ren. "Models in Linguistics and Models in General." In *Logic, Methodology and the Philosophy of Science,* Ernest Nagel, Patrick Suppes, and Alfred Tarski, eds. Stanford, Calif.: Stanford University Press, 1962. Pp. 558–60 (m).

Chenoweth, Eugene C. *Discussion and Debate.* Dubuque, Iowa: Wm. C. Brown Company, 1951 (d).

Cherry, E. C. "A History of Information Theory." *Proceedings of the Institute of Electrical Engineers,* XCVIII (1951), 383–93 (h).

Cherry, Colin. *On Human Communication.* New York: Technology Press of M.I.T. and John Wiley & Sons, Inc., 1952 (o).

Chittick, Roger D., and Robert D. Stevick. *Rhetoric for Exposition.* New York: Appleton-Century-Crofts, 1961 (r).

Chomsky, Noam. *Aspects of the Theory of Syntax.* Cambridge.: Mass.: M.I.T. Press, 1965 (a).

Christensen, Francis. *Notes Toward a New Rhetoric: Six Essays for Teachers.* New York: Harper & Row, Publishers, 1967 (n).

Cicero. *Orator.* Tr. H. M. Hubbell. London: William Heinemann Ltd., 1942 (o).

Cohen, Morris R. *Reason and Nature.* New York: Harcourt and Brace, 1931 (r).

Coles, Norman. "Facts." *Ratio,* VII (December, 1965), 180–89 (f).

Cooper, Joseph D. *The Art of Decision Making.* Garden City, N. Y.: Doubleday & Company, Inc., 1961 (a).

Cope, Edward Meredith. *An Introduction to Aristotle's Rhetoric.* London: Macmillan & Co., Ltd., 1867 (i).

Cruickshank, John. *Albert Camus and the Literature of Revolt.* Oxford: Oxford University Press, 1959 (a).

Day, John Patrick. *Inductive Probability.* New York: Humanities Press, 1961 (i).

Dewey, John. *Logic: The Theory of Inquiry.* New York: Henry Holt and Company, 1938, Pp. 101–119 (l).

Diem, H. *Kierkegaard's Dialectic of Existence.* London: Oliver and Boyd, 1959 (k).

Duhem, Pierre. *The Aim and Structure of Physical Theory.* Tr. Philip Wiener. Princeton, N. J.: Princeton University Press, 1954 (a).

Dyen, Isidore. "On the Validity of Comparative Lexicostatistics." In *Proceedings of the Ninth International Congress of Linguistics, Cambridge, Massachusetts, August 27–31, 1962,* ed. Horace Lunt. The Hague: Mouton & Co., 1964. Pp. 238–47 (v).

Einstein, Albert. "The Common Language of Science." In *Classics in Semantics,* Donald E. Hayden and E. Paul Alworth, eds. New York: Philosophical Library, 1965. Pp. 323–26 (c).

Fansler, Thomas. *Creative Power Through Discussion.* New York: Harper & Brothers, 1950 (c).

Festinger, Leon. "The Theory of Cognitive Dissonance." In *The Science of Human Communication,* ed. Wilbur Schramm. New York: Basic Books, Inc., 1963. Pp. 17–27 (t).

Fiedler, Leslie A. "My Credo: I, Toward an Amateur Criticism." *Kenyon Review,* XII (1950), 561–74 (t).

Gauss, Hermann. *Handkommentar zu den Dialogen Platos.* Bern: Herbert Lang, 1954 (h).

Gilman, William. *The Language of Science: A Guide to Effective Writing.* New York: Harcourt, Brace & World, Inc., 1961 (l).

Giovannini, Giovanni. "Dialogue." In *Dictionary of World Literature,* ed. Joseph T. Shipley. New York: Philosophical Library, 1943 (d).

Goldschmidt, Victor. *Les dialogues de Platon.* Paris: Presses Universitaires de France, 1947 (d).

Gonseth, Frédéric. "L'idée de dialectique aux entretiens de Zurich." *Dialectica,* I (1947), 21–37 (i).

Graves, Harold F. and Bernard S. Oldsey. *From Fact to Judgment.* New York: The Macmillan Company, 1963 (f).

Greenberg, Joseph H. *Universals of Language.* 2nd Edition. Cambridge, Mass.: M.I.T. Press, 1966 (v).

Grünbaum, Adolf. "The Falsifiability of Theories: Total or Partial? A Contemporary Evaluation of the Duhem-Quine Thesis." In *Boston Studies in the Philosophy of Science,* ed. Marx W. Wartofsky. Dordrecht, Holland: D. Reidel Publishing Company, 1963 (f).

Hanson, N. R. "Commentaries [on Gerd Buchdahl's "Descartes's Anticipation of a 'Logic of Scientific Discovery' "]." In *Scientific Change,* ed. A. C. Crombie. New York: Basic Books, Inc., 1965 Pp. 458–66 (c).

———. "Is there a Logic of Discovery?" In *Current Issues in the Philosophy of Science,* Herbert Feigl and Grover Maxwell, eds. New York: Holt, Rinehart & Winston, Inc., 1959. Pp. 20–47 (i).

———. *Patterns of Discovery.* Cambridge, England: At the University Press, 1961 (p).

Harré, Romono. *An Introduction to the Logic of the Sciences.* London: Macmillan and Co., Ltd., 1960 (i).

Harris, Zelig. "Discourse Analysis." In *The Structure of Language,* J. Fodor, J. Katz, eds. Englewood Cliffs, N. J.: Prentice-Hall, Inc. 1964 (d).

———. "Linguistic Transformation for Information Retrieval." In *Proceedings of the International Conference on Scientific Information.* Washington, D. C., November 16–21, 1958. National Academy of Sciences—National Research Council, Washington, D. C., 1959. Pp. 937–50 (1).

Hartnack, Justus. *Wittgenstein and Modern Philosophy.* Tr. Maurice Cranston. Garden City, N. Y.: Doubleday & Company, Inc., 1965 (w).

Hegel, Georg. *Encyclopedia of Philosophy.* Tr. Gustav Emil Mueller. New York: Philosophical Library, Inc., 1959 (e).

———. *Hegel's Science of Logic.* 2 vols. Tr. W. H. Johnston and L. G. Strutars. New York: The Macmillan Company, 1929 (l).

Hempel, Carl G. *Philosophy of Natural Science.* Englewood Cliffs, N. J.: Prentice-Hall, Inc., 1966 (p).

Hohenberger, John. *The Professional Journalist.* New York: Henry Holt and Company, 1960 (p).

Hurlbutt, Robert H. *Hume, Newton, and the Design Argument.* Lincoln, Neb.: University of Nebraska Press, 1965 (h).

Hutchins, Robert M., and Mortimer J. Adler. *The Great Ideas Today, 1965.* Chicago: Encyclopaedia Britannica, Inc., 1965 (Hutchins, g, 1965).

———. *The Great Ideas: A Syntopicon of the Great Books of the Western World.* Vols. II and III of *Great Books of the Western World.* Chicago: Encyclopaedia Britannica, 1952 (g, II or III).

Hymes, D. A. "Lexicostatistics: A Critique." *Language,* XXXII (1956), 53–58 (c).

———. "Lexicostatistics So Far." *Current Anthropology,* I (1960), 3–44 (l).

Jacobson, S. N. "A Modifiable Routine for Connecting Related Sentences of English Text." *Computation in Linguistics: A Case Book,* Paul Garvin and Bernard Spolsky, eds. Bloomington, Ind.: Indiana University Press, 1966. Pp. 284–311 (m).

Kant, Immanuel. *The Critique of Pure Reason.* Tr. J. M. D. Meiklejohn. Vol. XLII of *Great Books of the Western World,* R. M. Hutchins and M. J. Adler, eds. Chicago: Encyclopaedia Britannica, Inc., 1952 (c).

Katz, Jerrold J. *The Philosophy of Language.* New York: Harper and Row, Publishers, 1966 (p).

Keltner, J. W. *Group Discussion Processes.* New York: Longmans, Green and Co., 1957 (g).

Kierkegaard, Søren. "Concluding Unscientific Postscript." *A Kierkegaard Anthology,* tr. Walter Lowrie; ed. R. Bretall. New York: Modern Library, Inc., 1959 (c).

————. *The Point of View for My Work as an Author: A Report to History and Related Writings,* tr. Walter Lowrie; ed. Benjamin Nelson. New York: Harper & Row, Publishers, 1962 (p).

Kinneavy, James L. *A Study of Three Contemporary Theories of the Lyric.* Washington, D. C.: Catholic University Press, 1956 (s).

Kneale, W., and Martha Kneale. *The Development of Logic.* Oxford: Clarendon Press, 1962 (d).

Kohák, Erazim V. "The Road to Wisdom: Lessons on Education from Plato's *Laches.*" *Classical Journal,* LVI (1960), 123–32 (r).

Kuhn, Thomas S. "The Function of Dogma in Scientific Research." In *Scientific Change,* ed., A. C. Crombie. New York: Basic Books, Inc., 1963. Pp. 347–69 (f).

————. *The Structure of Scientific Revolutions.* Chicago: University of Chicago Press, 1962 (s).

La Drière, James Craig. "Letter." In *Dictionary of World Literature,* ed. Joseph T. Shipley. New York: Philosophical Library, 1943 (1).

————. "Rhetoric and 'Merely Verbal Art.'" In *English Institute Essays, 1948,* ed. D. A. Robertson, Jr. New York: Columbia University Press, 1949. Pp. 123–52 (r).

Langer, Susanne. *An Introduction to Symbolic Logic.* New York: Dover Publications, Inc., 1953 (i).

Lewin, Kurt. "Cassirer's Philosophy of Science and the Social Sciences." In *The Philosophy of Ernst Cassirer,* ed. Paul Arthur Schilpp. Evanston, Ill.: Library of Living Philosophies, 1958. Pp. 269–88 (c).

Linsky, Leonard, ed. *Semantics and the Philosophy of Language.* Urbana: The University of Illinois Press, 1952 (s).

Lunt, Horace. "Critique of Isidore Dyen 'On the Validity of Lexicostatistics.'" In *Proceedings of the Ninth International Congress of Linguistics, Cambridge, Massachusetts, August 27–31, 1962,* ed. Horace Lunt. The Hague: Mouton & Co., 1964. Pp. 247 ff. (c).

MacDonald, Francis. *Plato and Parmenides.* New York: Liberal Arts Press, 1957 (p).

MacDougall, Curtis D. *Interpretative Reporting.* New York: The Macmillan Company, 1963 (i).

Mace, C. A. *The Principles of Logic.* New York: Longmans, Green and Co., 1933 (p).

Mackay, D. M. "Operational Aspects of Some Fundamental Concepts of Human Communication." *Synthèse,* IX (1953), 182–98 (o).

Malinowski, Branislaw. *Coral Gardens and their Magic.* 2 Vols. New York: American Book Company, 1935 (c).

Mallett, Charles E. *A History of the University of Oxford.* London: Methuen & Co. Ltd., 1924 (h).

Maquet, Albert. *Albert Camus: The Invincible Summer.* Tr. Herma Briffault, New York: George Braziller, 1958 (a).

Maritain, Jacques. *An Introduction to Philosophy.* New York: Sheed and Ward, 1930 (i).

Marshall, Francis W. *Popular Guide to Modern Legal Principles.* New York: Wm. H. Wise & Co., Inc., 1949 (p).

Martin, Harold C., and Richard M. Ohmann. *The Logic and Rhetoric of Exposition.* New York: Holt, Rinehart and Winston, Inc., 1963 (l).

Martin, Richard W. *Toward a Systematic Pragmatics.* In *Studies in Logic,* L. E. J. Brouwer, E. W. Beth, and A. Heyting, eds. Amsterdam: North-Holland Publishing Company, 1959 (t).

Marx, Karl. "Capital." In *Marx,* tr. Samuel Moore, Edward Aveling, Maria Sachey and Herbert Lamm. Vol. L of *Great Books of the Western World,* R. M. Hutchins and M. J. Adler, eds. Chicago: Encyclopaedia Britannica, Inc., 1952 (c).

————, and F. Engels. "Manifesto of the Communist Party." *Marx,* tr. Samuel Moore. Vol. L of *Great Books of the Western World,* R. M. Hutchins and M. J. Adler, eds. Chicago: Encyclopaedia Britannica, Inc., 1952 (m).

McLuhan, Marshall. *Understanding Media: The Extensions of Man.* New York: McGraw-Hill Book Company, 1965 (u).

————. *The Mechanical Bride: Folklore of Industrial Man.* New York: Vanguard Press, 1951 (m).

McTaggart, John M. E. *Studies in the Hegelian Dialectic.* Cambridge, England: University Press, 1896 (st).

Menzel, Donald H., Howard Mumford Jones, and Lyle G. Boyd. *Writing a Technical Paper.* New York: McGraw-Hill Book Company, 1961 (w).

Miller, George A. *Language and Communication.* New York: McGraw-Hill Book Company, 1951 (l).

Mills, Gordon H., and John A. Walter. *Technical Writing.* New York: Holt, Rinehart, and Winston, 1962 (t).

Morris, C. W. *Signs, Language, and Behavior.* Englewood Cliffs, N. J.: Prentice-Hall, Inc., 1964 (s).

Morris, Jackson E. *Principles of Scientific and Technical Writing.* New York: McGraw-Hill Book Company, 1966 (p).

Murray, Henry A. "In Nomine Diaboli." In *Discussions of Moby Dick,* ed. Milton R. Stern. Boston: D. C. Heath and Company, 1960. Pp. 25–34 (i).

Nagel, Ernest. *Principles of the Theory of Probability. International Encyclopedia of Unified Science.* Vol. I, No. 6. Chicago: University of Chicago Press, 1939 (p).

————.*The Structure of Science. Problems in the Logic of Scientific Explanation.* New York: Harcourt, Brace & World, Inc., 1960 (s).

Northrop, F. S. C. *The Logic of the Sciences and the Humanities.* New York: The Macmillan Company, 1948 (l).

Olson, Elder. "An Outline of Poetic Theory." *Critics and Criticism: Ancient and Modern,* ed. R. S. Crane. Chicago: University of Chicago Press, 1952 (c).

Ong, Walter J. *Ramus: Method and the Decay of Dialogue.* Cambridge, Mass.: Harvard University Press, 1958 (r).

Oppenheim, Paul. "Studies in the Logic of Explanation." *Philosophy of Science,* X (1948), 137–38, 146–52 (s).

Pearson, Karl. *The Grammar of Science.* 3rd Edition. London: Adam and Charles Black, 1911 (g).

Peirce, Charles Sanders. *Collected Papers.* Vols. I and II. Charles Hartshorne and Paul Weiss, eds. Cambridge, Mass.: Harvard University Press, 1960 (c).

Pike, Kenneth. *Language in Relation to a Unified Theory of the Structure of Human Behavior.* 3 Vols. Glendale, Calif.: Summer Institute of Linguistics, 1960 (l).

Plato. "Laches." In *Plato,* tr. Benjamin Jowett. Vol. VII of *Great Books of the Western World,* R. M. Hutchins and M. J. Adler, eds. Chicago: Encyclopaedia Britannica, Inc., 1952 (l).

————. "Phaedrus." In *Plato,* tr. Benjamin Jowett. Vol. VII of *Great Books of the Western World,* R. M. Hutchins and M. J. Adler, eds. Chicago: Encyclopaedia Britannica, Inc., 1952 (p).

————. "The Republic." In *Plato,* tr. Benjamin Jowett. Vol. VII of *Great Books of the Western World,* R. M. Hutchins and M. J. Adler, eds. Chicago: Encyclopaedia Britannica, Inc., 1952 (r).

Pollock, Thomas C., ed. *The Macmillan English Series, 10th grade.* New York: The Macmillan Company, 1964 (m).

Popper, Karl R. *The Logic of Scientific Discovery.* Tr. Julius and Lan V. Fried. London: Hutchinson & Co. (Publishers) Limited, 1959 (l).

Prior, A. N. *Formal Logic.* Oxford: Clarendon Press, 1962 (f).

Quine, W. V. *From a Logical Point of View.* Cambridge, Mass.: Harvard University Press, 1961; 2nd ed., 1953 (f).

————. *Mathematical Logic.* Revised Edition. Cambridge, Mass.: Harvard University Press, 1958 (m).

Racker, Joseph. *Technical Writing: Techniques for Engineers.* Englewood Cliffs, N. J.: Prentice-Hall, Inc., 1960 (t).

Rapaport, Anatol. "What is Information?" *Synthèse,* IX (1953), 16–17 (w).

Rathbone, Robert R., and James B. Stone. *A Writer's Guide for Engineers and Scientists.* Englewood Cliffs, N. J.: Prentice-Hall, Inc., 1962 (w).

Reichenbach, Hans. *Experience of Prediction. An Analysis of the Foundations and Structure of Knowledge.* Chicago, Ill.: University of Chicago Press, 1938 (e).

————. *The Theory of Probability.* Tr. Ernest H. Hutten and Maria Reichenbach. Berkeley, Calif.: University of California Press, 1949 (t).

Richards, I. A. *How to Read a Page.* London: K. Paul, Trench, Trubner and Company, 1943 (h).

————. *Principles of Literary Criticism.* London: K. Paul, Trench, Trubner and Company, 1925 (p).

Rhodes, Fred H. *Technical Report Writing.* New York: McGraw-Hill Book Company, 1961 (t).

Ruch, Michel. *Le préambule dans les oeuvres philosophiques de Cicéron.* Paris: Les Belles Lettres, 1958 (p).

Russell, Bertrand. *Human Knowledge: Its Scope and Limits.* New York: Simon and Schuster, Inc., 1948 (h).

————. *An Inquiry into Meaning and Truth.* London: George Allen and Unwin, Ltd., 1956 (m).

Ryle, Gilbert. *The Concept of Mind.* New York: Barnes & Noble, Inc., 1949 (c).

Sartre, Jean Paul. *La critique de la raison dialectique, précédé de question de méthode.* Paris: Librairie Gallimard, 1960 (c).

————. *The Reprieve.* Tr. Eric Sutton. New York: Bantam Books, Inc., 1947 (r).

Savory, Theodore H. *The Language of Science: Its Growth, Character and Usage.* London: Andre Deutsch, 1958 (l).

Scheffler, Israel. *The Anatomy of Inquiry: Philosophical Studies in the Theory of Science.* New York: Alfred A. Knopf, Inc., 1963 (a).

Shannon, Claude E., and Warren Weaver. *The Mathematical Theory of Communication.* Urbana, Ill.: University of Illinois Press, 1964 (Shannon, m).

Smith, John E. "Philosophy and Religion." In *The Great Ideas Today,* 1965, R. M. Hutchins and M. J. Adler, eds. Chicago: Encyclopaedia Britannica, Inc., 1966 (p).

Snell, Bruno. "The Forging of a Language of Science in Ancient Greece." *Classical Journal,* LVI, No. 2 (1960), 50–60 (f).

Stebbing, Lizzie S. *A Modern Introduction to Logic.* New York: Harper and Row, Publishers, 1950 (m).

Sturtevant, William C. "Studies in Ethnoscience." *American Anthropologist,* LVI (1964), 99–132 (s).

Sujiura, Sadajiro. *Hindu Logic as Preserved in China and Japan.* No. 4 in "Series in Philosophy," University of Pennsylvania. Ed. Edgar A. Singer. Boston, Mass.: Ginn and Company, 1900 (h).

Suppes, Patrick. "A Comparison of the Meaning and Use of Models in Mathematics and the Empirical Sciences." In *The Concept and the Role of the Model in Mathematics and Natural and Social Science,* ed. Hans Frierdenthal. Dordrecht-Holland: D. Reidel Publishing Company, 1961 (c).

Swanberg, W. A. *Citizen Hearst: A Biography of William Randolph Hearst.* New York: Charles Scribner's Sons, 1961 (c).

Tannenbaum, Percy H. "Communication of Scientific Information." *Science,* CLX (May 10, 1963), 579–84 (c).

Taylor, A. E. *The Mind of Plato*. Ann Arbor: University of Michigan Press, 1966 (originally published as *Plato*) (p.)

Thorpe, James. *The Aims and Methods of Scholarship in Modern Languages and Literature*. New York: Modern Language Association of America, 1963 (a).

Tillen, A. A. "The Essay and the Beginning of English Prose." In *The Cambridge History of English Literature,* eds. A. W. Ward and A. R. Waller. Vol. IX. Cambridge, Eng.: The University Press, 1912. Pp. 368–90 (e).

Toulmin, Stephen E. *The Philosophy of Science*. New York: Hutchinson's University Library, 1953 (p).

Toynbee, Arnold J. *A Study of History*. Vol. II. Oxford: Oxford University Press, 1934 (s).

──────. *A Study of History*. Abridgement of Vols. I to VI, by D. C. Somerwell. New York: Oxford University Press, 1947 (sa).

Urban, W. M. *Language and Reality*. New York: The Macmillan Company, 1939 (l).

Von Wright, Georg H. *An Essay in Modal Logic*. Amsterdam: North-Holland Publishing Company, 1951 (m).

Wallis, Wilson Allen, and Harry V. Roberts. *Statistics: A New Approach*. Glencoe, Ill.: The Free Press, 1956 (s).

──────. "Statistics of the Kinsey Report." *Journal of the American Statistical Association,* XLIV (1949), 463–83 (st).

Wellek, René, and A. Warren. *Theory of Literature*. New York: Harcourt, Brace and Company, 1949 (t).

Wells, Rulon S. "A Measure of Subjective Information." In *Twelfth Symposium in Applied Mathematics,* ed. Roman Jakobson. Providence, R. I.: American Mathematical Society, 1961 (m).

Werner, Heinz, ed. *On Expressive Language*. Worcester, Mass.: Clark University Press, 1955 (e).

Westley, Bruce. *News Editing*. New York: Houghton Mifflin Company, 1953 (n).

Whatmough, Joshua. *Language: A Modern Synthesis*. New York: New American Library of World Literature, Inc., 1956 (l).

Whitehead, A. N., and Bertrand Russell. *Principia Mathematica.* Reprinted to *56. Cambridge: At the University Press, 1962, (pm).

Whorf, Benjamin. "Language and Logic." In *Language, Thought and Reality,* ed. John B. Carroll. New York: John Wiley & Sons, Inc., 1959. Pp. 233–45 (l).

Williamson, George. *The Senecan Amble: English Prose from Bacon to Collier*. London: Faber & Faber Ltd., 1951 (s).

Wittgenstein, Ludwig. *Tractatus Logico-Philosophicus*. Tr. D. F. Fears and B. F. McGuinness. New York: Humanities Press, 1911 (t).

Word Correlation and Automatic Indexing. Phase II: A Final Report c82-2VI, (January, 1962). Canoga Park, Calif.: Thompson Ramo Wooldridge, Inc., R. W. Division (w).

4

Persuasive Discourse

Mere knowledge of the truth will not give you the art of persuasion.
Socrates, in *Phaedrus* (260D)

Introduction and Terminology

Introduction

This chapter deals with that kind of discourse which is primarily
focused on the decoder and attempts to elicit from him a specific action or
emotion or conviction. Such discourse is called "persuasive." It has been
treated briefly in Chapter I (p. 39) and Chapter II (59–60); there, in
outline form, it was distinguished from discourse which is referential,
literary, and expressive. Here the details of its nature as a particular kind
of discourse, the logic peculiar to it, its patterns of organization, and its
characteristic styles will be considered.

Persuasion, as such, especially when it involves emotional appeals,
is not usually held to be the province of a course in English or composition.
It is usually disregarded in high school and especially in college courses in
English. There are several reasons which might be adduced for this neglect.
Historically, the departure of speech from English departments since 1914
usually entailed the allocating of rhetoric viewed as persuasion to the new
departments of speech. Persuasion, as a course (or several courses), is now
usually the province of speech. Of course, many of the more obvious forms
of persuasion are spoken, rather than written (ads, political propaganda,
preaching). Further, the continued study of literature as an art form seems
to often produce among its votaries an aversion to the blatant forms of
persuasion. Literature is the main focus of interest in English departments.
This attitude may be related to the problem of the ethics of rhetoric, to be
considered below.

Yet serious reasons militate for the inclusion of the study of persuasion in a full theory of discourse, and even in the regular offerings of
English departments. In the first place, if an important use of discourse is

211

neglected in a systematic study of discourse, there is a serious danger of a lack of perspective in the study of the other aims. This danger can, in fact, be documented in the history of both the study of literature in English departments and the study of persuasion in speech departments. In the former, there are all too many teachers who advocate the study of literature for its lessons, its themes, its universal truths. As will be seen in the next chapter, this is one important view of the nature of literature. In this view, literature often becomes a subtler form of persuasion. On the contrary, in departments of speech, persuasion has come to include for many the entire range of reference discourse, whether scientific, exploratory, or informative. Under the subdivision of persuasion called "argumentation," courses are offered in many universities which approximate courses in logic. This confusion of persuasion with reference discourse is as dangerous as the confusion of literature with persuasion by many in English departments. The fault, in both cases, seems to lie partly in the failure to study the aims of discourse in conjunction with each other. Indeed, the nature of literature often emerges most clearly when contrasted with other aims of discourse. It is thus to the advantage of a literature department to study persuasion.

Secondly, of course, a full theory of discourse has to consider one of the most pervasive uses of discourse. Private conversation, books, newspapers, radio, television, periodicals (in fact any medium), all serve as instruments of persuasive discourse. Where there is language there is the possibility and likelihood of persuasion. Neither the scholar, nor the cloistered nun, nor the poet in Bohemia is untouched by the persuasive use of language. Indeed, of all the uses of language, persuasion may be the most frequent.[1] Finally, the reasons adduced by Aristotle for the study of rhetoric (persuasion) are even more valid today than they were in the time of the Greeks. In fact, it can be said that English, as a discipline, ignores persuasion at its own peril.

Terminology

Throughout history, several terms have been used for the kinds of discourse to be studied in this chapter: rhetoric, oratory, persuasion, eloquence, elocution, and propaganda. A brief review of each and the reasons why "persuasion" was adopted may prove of some assistance to the student confronted here, as in reference discourse, with a serious problem of terminology. The issue is not merely an arbitrary choice of terms, for in this area a choice of terms may unconsciously involve a whole theory of discourse.

[1] For several years, the author has had some of his classes make a catalogue of the uses to which these students put language, and persuasion always figures prominently.

The term most consistently used throughout history to refer to a study of persuasion or a piece of persuasion was "rhetoric." Etymologically, "rhetoric" was the adjective coming from *rhetor*, a speaker. Rhetoric, as an art, is often said to have started in Sicily with Corax and to have spread to Greece with his disciples. Corax defined rhetoric as the art of persuasion. However, this quickly took on at least three quite different meanings, and rhetoric today still has these three basic meanings. In fact, it has several others, but some of the others do not raise serious issues in interpretation. But, unless the student of persuasion is able to discriminate precisely among these three basic meanings of rhetoric, he is in danger of completely misunderstanding whole schools of writers on rhetoric.

The three main views of rhetoric might be called the stylistic, the Aristotelian, and the communication approaches. All three have hardy traditions through western civilization. In a sense the first is a quite narrow view of rhetoric, the second wider but limited, and the third a very broad view embracing nearly all discourse.

The stylistic view sees rhetoric as a group of linguistic techniques by which one can ornament thought. Throughout history the list of these techniques for ornamentation became longer and longer. Because these techniques were early classified as either figures of sound or figures of meaning, this view of rhetoric is sometimes called "figurist" (cf. Corbett, c, 549). These figures include such techniques as hyperbole, synecdoche, simile, antithesis, insinuation, rime (initial and end), repetition, and so forth. Because many of the early sophists held this position, it has also been called the "sophistic" view of rhetoric. As Baldwin says, speaking of the second sophistic period, "Sophistic practically reduces rhetoric to style" (Baldwin, a, 7).

Gorgias, an early sophist, was one of the first to catalogue some of these figures, and he also seems to have practiced a stylistic view of rhetoric (Kennedy, a, 62, 65). Thrasymachus was one of the first to stress the rhythmic patterns in prose style. These early sophists constitute the First Sophistic period of rhetoric (fifth and fourth centuries B.C.). Sophistic oratory, especially after the decline of democracy in Greece and the taking over of legal pleading by specialists, tended to stress not political or legal oratory, but ceremonial orations at funerals and festivities (Baldwin, a, 5–6). This increased the emphasis on mere style in sophistic rhetoric and contributed to the confusion of rhetoric with poetic (Baldwin, a, 39–41) — a confusion which has persisted down to our time.

The stylistic conception of rhetoric was continued by the Second Sophistic in the second, third, and fourth centuries of the Christian era. Many of the fathers of the Church were trained in such a conception—and this was true from Athens to Carthage to Gaul, in Greek and in Latin (Baldwin, m, 8–11). The tradition can be seen in Ausonius and Sidonius

Appolinaris in Gaul in the fifth and sixth centuries (Baldwin, m, 75 ff., 78 ff.).

With the crystallization of the tradition of the seven liberal arts in the early Middle Ages, the stylistic tradition was carried by the major transmitters of the liberal arts tradition. Thus Martianus Capella, Bede, Brunetto Latini, and John of Salisbury so interpret rhetoric (Baldwin, m, 93f., 129, 153, 178). And manuals of poetics often apply rules of composition indiscriminately to poetry or letter writing; John of Garlandia's *Poetria* is a clear example of this confusion (Baldwin, m, 191).

The many manuals of tropes and figures in the Renaissance also continue a stylistic conception of rhetoric (Peacham's *The Garden of Eloquence,* in 1577, distinguished 184 rhetorical figures; Sherry's *A Treatise on Schemes and Tropes,* in 1550, distinguished 120). In addition such authorities as Erasmus and Minturno maintained the stress on rhetoric as ornamentation and style, and most writers on rhetoric in the Renaissance "long accepted tacitly the medieval confusion of poetic with rhetoric" (Baldwin, r, 15).

The stylistic view of rhetoric received further support from several other influential sources, a few of which were attempting to be anything but traditional. Ramus relegates rhetoric to style and delivery, and Bacon's view of rhetoric is also fundamentally a matter of style. In the eighteenth century John Stirling's very popular *A System of Rhetoric* (1733) preserved the figurist position. In our day, many articles in the scholarly journals still consider a rhetorical analysis to be a matter of checking on stylistic techniques, particularly figures of speech and sound. Thus one very live view of rhetoric in the field of English is the stylistic conception which goes back to the early sophists.

A second and persistent view of rhetoric is the Aristotelian. For Aristotle, rhetoric is not simply a matter of style. It involves, in fact, a special kind of thinking with a distinctly limited range of applicability. It must never be forgotten, in discussing Aristotle's view of rhetoric, that for Aristotle, rhetorical discourse is not scientific discourse, it is not dialectical discourse, it is not poetic discourse, and it is not mere sophistic discourse. Aristotle wrote separate treatises or parts of treatises on all five of these kinds of discourse and carefully distinguished them from one another in nature, in logic, and in style. Though persuasion of some general sort is involved in all of these forms of discourse, Aristotle restricts persuasion, as a kind of discourse, to what he calls rhetoric. Aristotle's view of rhetoric will be explained in detail later on in this chapter. For the present, it can be remarked that Aristotle restricted rhetoric to the kind of persuasion which he saw exemplified in the political speeches, the informal legal pleadings, and the ceremonial speeches of praise or blame in festival or funeral oratory. This kind of persuasion made heavy use of personal appeal; its logic reduced deduction to incomplete patterns of reasoning from dubious premises and reduced induction to isolated or even fictional examples; and it made extensive use of emotional biases and appeal. In particular, rhetoric focused on the hearer, not reality. Rhetoric also had its own organizational patterns and characteristic virtues of style. Clearly, then, in Aristotle's view rhetoric was more than mere stylistic technique; but just as clearly it did not embrace all communication, not even all prose communication.

This "limited persuasion" concept of rhetoric can also be seen in Plato, although Aristotle and Plato differed radically in their moral appraisals of such persuasive techniques. In late Antiquity, Augustine adhered to a modified Aristotelian view of rhetoric. He carefully rejected the concept of rhetoric represented in the second sophistic (Baldwin, a, 218).

In the high Middle Ages, the Aristotelian view can be seen in the Arabian philosophers Averroës and Avicenna, and especially in Aquinas. La Drière has carefully documented this tradition down to the Renaissance (r, 134–52). The tradition also was maintained in the medieval art of letter writing (Baldwin, m, 2, 4), and to some extent in the art of preaching, though this often tended to the sophistic. In the Renaissance, although the sophistic view dominated, the Aristotelian concept can be seen in Lawson (cf. Corbett, c, 561). A pure Aristotelianism can also be seen in the nineteenth century in a classical critic like Cope in his commentary and edition of Aristotle's *Rhetoric*. In the twentieth century, some writers in the speech field continue the "limited persuasion" notion of rhetoric. Black even maintains that it has been the dominant view in the field of speech since 1925, and he lists Wichelns, Hochmuth, Parrish, and others as hewing to this line (Black, r, 11–12, 28–32, 61 ff.). Like the stylistic view, the "limited persuasion" view of rhetoric also has a hardy tradition.

Thirdly, there has also persisted a "communication" view of rhetoric. This concept of rhetoric certainly has its main fount in Isocrates. Isocrates continually distinguished himself from the other sophists, and even wrote a major discourse opposing them (*Against the Sophists,* and cf. *Antidosis,* a, 42 ff., 148). Though he does not ignore style, with him content becomes all-important (Wagner, r, 175). He usually calls his art "the art of discourse" (a, 180, 185, 253, and *passim*). Though he does not claim all prose as his province, he seems to claim all serious prose (a, 46). He calls himself a teacher of philosophy and directs himself to training in "all the forms of discourse in which the mind expresses itself" (a, 183). Some train the body, he trains the mind to discourse (a, 180, 185). Wagner describes his sphere as "literary taste and study—culture generally" (r, 176). For Isocrates, as for Cicero later, political science and rhetoric are almost one and the same (Wagner, r, 171–72). And for Isocrates, as for Quintilian, the orator is also the moral and good man (a, 276 ff.).

Cicero is actually the disciple of Isocrates (rather than of Aristotle) in his concept of rhetoric (Wagner, r, 170–71). As he says:

> The art of eloquence is something greater, and collected from more sciences and studies than people imagine. . . . In my opinion, indeed, no man can be an orator possessed of every praiseworthy accomplishment, unless he has attained the knowledge of everything important, and of all the liberal arts (Cicero, d, I, 4, 16 and I, 6, 19–20, as summarized in Wise, n, 43).

In both the *Brutus* and the *De Oratore,* Cicero maintains that oratory is above law and philosophy and includes the virtues of both (b, 40, 150; b, 41, 151; d, III, 35, 143). For Cicero, as for Isocrates, rhetoric is "culture generally." Cicero sometimes distinguishes rhetoric from philosophy, history, and poetry, but he often conflates them, as we have seen.

Quintilian continued this concept. After reviewing other definitions (cf. i, Bk. II, Ch. XV), Quintilian defined the orator as "the good man speaking well." Thus Cope observes of this definition, "This is brief and concise in expression. . . but very comprehensive in meaning since it includes the possession of all virtues and accomplishments" (Cope, i, 35).

This comprehensive notion of rhetoric has had its adherents all through history. For our purposes, however, the most notable rendition of it can be seen in Campbell, in the eighteenth century. Campbell defines rhetoric or "eloquence" as "that art or talent by which discourse is adapted to its end." He adduces Cicero and Quintilian as the main sources of his view (cf. p, 23 ff.) And Cope remarks, "It is identical with Quintilian's. . . . It exactly corresponds to Tully's [Cicero's] idea of a perfect orator" (i, 35). This definition has been accepted by many in our times. I. A. Richards so defines rhetoric; indeed, Richards speaks very favorably of Campbell (p, 51). And Richards comments that pure exposition (reference discourse) is "of relatively rare occurrence outside the routine of train services and the tamer, more settled parts of the sciences" (p, 41).

Some of the leaders in the field of speech follow this position. A. Craig Baird, for example, includes in the area of rhetoric the following purposes, which he indicates are "usually listed in treatises of today": information, ceremony, conviction, persuasion, discussion, criticism, entertainment, some combination of these purposes (Baird, r, 10–11; cf. also Thonssen, s, vi). Bryant, another acknowledged leader, takes the same stand (Bryant r, 404 ff.).

Black and others in speech oppose this comprehensive view of rhetoric (Black, r, 11 ff.)—as does the author. The reason is not just an arbitrary matter of definition, as some would call it. The reason for a prescriptive semantic position is that most of those who adopt this comprehensive communication view of rhetoric have still derived their main categories of analysis from Aristotle and consequently extend Aristotle's limited rhetorical proofs to all types of composition—including the ethical and emotional proofs, as well as Aristotle's watered-down notions of scientific proof (enthymeme and example). This implies that the same sort of conviction is achieved in science and information and exploration as in strictly persuasive work. Bacon, Campbell, Baird, Crocker, and many others make these illicit extensions of Aristotle's *Rhetoric*. A typical popular example of this is Walter's *Speaking to Inform and Persuade* (Walter, s).

Yet persuasive discourse is generically different from reference discourse (and literary and expressive discourse as well). Otherwise everything is rhetoric; even Plato's dialogues and Aristotle's treatises and Baudelaire's poems are rhetoric—a thought which would cause all three of these gentlemen to turn over in their graves. Similarly, it seems equally inadvisable to restrict rhetoric to a matter of stylistic gimmicks and figures. This view conceives style as a mere ornament added to thought and denies the various kinds of logic which differentiate the scientist from the propagandist, and both from the poet and the novelist. Both the stylistic and the communication view of "rhetoric," therefore, seem inadvisable. However, since these two other meanings have consistently been connotations of the term, I have decided not to use "rhetoric" as a term consistently at all, except in a historical context.

A few other terms used at various times throughout history must be given brief consideration. "Propaganda," originally not a derogatory term in the religious rhetoric of the Catholic Church, has, particularly since World War II, increasingly taken on sinister associations (Brown, t, 10–11). For this reason it is not used here, because persuasion need not be sinister.

"Oratory" was preferred by Cicero and Quintilian to "rhetoric" because "rhetoric" did not carry the associations of a man of genius or officialdom (Jebb, as cited in Sandys, o, 70). In addition, Cicero refers to "the mechanical workshops of rhetoric" (o, III, 12); and Quintilian does not see in the "rhetorician" the connotations of his "good man" (i, II, XIV, 1–5; cf. Wise, n, 58). Yet "oratory" seems too pretentious a term to be applied to a half-minute toothpaste commercial or a billboard advertisement —both persuasive discourses. "Elocution" and "eloquence" now seem obsolescent or too restricted to cover such general kinds of rhetoric as political propaganda and advertising. "Persuasion," finally, has its drawbacks too. In many departments of speech it includes argumentation, an inclusion which sometimes carries with it the scent of medieval dialectic (on "argumentation," cf. Black, r, 148 ff.).

Another kind of objection is brought against the term "persuasion" by both Richards and Burke. Richards is aware that traditional rhetoric had been defined in terms of "persuasion," and he is also aware of the mechanical routines into which traditional rhetoric often degenerated.

Quite justifiably, he feels that persuasion was a much more important matter than the treatment given it in some of the formulary rhetorics. Of course, Richards also belongs to the communication school of rhetoric which would include in rhetoric all but poetry and the rarest discourses of pure science (pr, 261; h, 100). Burke, as will be seen later, changed the notion of "persuasion" in rhetoric to that of "identification." Burke's motivation seems basically to be a valid one: he realizes that rhetoric always operates in a determined situational context and he feels that this situation is better described in terms of an attempt at identification of encoder and decoder than merely in terms of the encoder's trying to "persuade" the decoder (cf. Burke, r, 442, 482). Despite the validity of both concerns, the alternatives suggested by Richards and Burke have had only very limited acceptance. Consequently, "persuasion" is here retained, despite the fact that there will be some undesirable connotations attached to it.

In addition, persuasion has been predicated of all discourse (see above, p. 59 ff.). Nonetheless, since the Aristotelian school of rhetoric has used it to define their notion, and since many psychologists separate persuasion from reference discourse in the way envisaged here (e.g., Brown, t, 20 f.), as do many writers on speech (cf. Black, r, 11 ff.), and many classical Latin and Greek scholars (e.g., Cope), there seem to be fewer objections to this term than to others.

The Nature of
Persuasive Discourse

Possibly the easiest way to define persuasive discourse is to point to obvious examples of it. Thus, it has been pointed out several times that political propaganda, religious preaching, and advertising are clear examples of persuasive discourse. From Aristotle to modern propaganda analysts like Harold Lasswell, legal pleadings have been classed as one of the main categories of rhetorical discourse (Lasswell, 1, 22–23). This is true, despite the legal assumption that two persuasive pleas on opposite sides of a question establish a procedure of exploration for truth. Similarly, funeral orations and speeches of praise or blame have also been classed as "rhetoric" throughout the tradition.

But, of course, there are many other instances of persuasive discourse in ordinary life: safety warnings, education to citizenship or honesty, attempts to cajole a board of trustees to adopt a new manufacturing technique, and so on. Indeed, it is doubtful if any area of discourse is immune to persuasion. And some examples of persuasion are considerably more subtle than these. Is it possible to extract characteristics common to most of these examples and define persuasion by a set of distinguishing characteristics? Despite the fact that there is little scientific empirical evidence on the nature of persuasion (Hovland, c, v), common sense and a long tradition have settled on some convincing attributes of such discourse.

In Chapters I and II persuasion was defined as discourse primarily focused on the decoder (see above, pp. 39, 59 f.). This is one of Aristotle's defining characteristics (*Rhet.*, 1358a 39). Modern speech writers insist on this too. Kenneth Burke also stresses the importance of the addressee (even if it is oneself) in rhetoric (r, 38 f.) ; the decoder is, presumably, divided in attitude from the encoder; otherwise there is no point to persuasion (cf. r, 22). Thus, the purpose of persuasion is to achieve identification of speaker and hearer, according to Burke (r, 22). This persuasion of the hearer may be to some new intellectual conviction, or to a new emotional attitude, or it may be a direct inducement to physical action. Sometimes writers in speech distinguish these effects by such terms as conviction, stimulation, and actuation; and such distinctions are no doubt valid, but I shall include all of them under the general category of persuasion.

Of course, all of the above may be achieved by scientific proof, or information, or an exploratory process, or even by literature. But, as was pointed out, persuasion of the decoder is indirect and secondary in these latter aims of discourse (see above, p. 59 f.). It is in this sense that persuasion is decoder-oriented discourse. And, because of its direct inducement to some kind of action (intellectual, emotional, or physical), it therefore differs from science and literature. Both of these latter have been called neutral or objective by various theorists. Weaver, Kierkegaard, and Burke make statements to this effect (Weaver, e, 7 ff., 21 ff.; Burke, r, 42; for Kierkegaard references, see above, pp. 170–71).

Another common method of distinguishing reference discourse from persuasion has been to establish persuasion at a lower level of probability than science or exploration. Plato accuses Tisias, one of the founders of rhetoric, of valuing probabilities more than truths (*Phaedrus*, 267). Both Plato and Aristotle make this concept of probability clearer by calling the probability of rhetoric a "seeming" probability. Hunt remarks that Plato views the rhetorician as "presenting to the audience something which at least resembles the truth" (Hunt, s, 37).

Aristotle, of course, considers rhetoric as dealing with the "approximately true" (*Rhetoric*, 1355a 14,), with "proof" or "apparent proof" (1356a 3, 1356b 1; 1356a 20), with the "apparent enthymeme" (1356b 4), with "what seems probable" (1356b 35). The duty of rhetoric, he says, "is to deal with such matters as we deliberate upon without arts or systems to guide us, in the hearing of persons who cannot take in at a glance a complicated argument or follow a long chain of reasoning" (1357a 1–3). Again, "The more we try to make dialectic or rhetoric not what they really are, practical faculties, but sciences, the more we shall inadvertently be destroying their true nature" (1359b 12 ff.).

Aristotle's topics were, says Hunt,

> ...a sort of rhetorician's first aid. They were to assist him in producing immediately, and perhaps without any special knowledge of the subject, a plausible argument upon either side of a debatable proposition (Hunt, s, 50).

Aristotle's two "logical" proofs are not really logical in a scientific sense: they only seem so. Example and enthymeme are not really conclusive, as are real induction and deduction. Many in modern times reiterate this. Hovland and Brown, psychological analysts of the nature of persuasion, distinguish it as operating in the areas of attitude and opinion, not fact and science (Hovland, c, 7–8; Brown, t, 20 ff.). Even the argument from personality in persuasion, as will be seen, is not real personality, but personality projected as what Madison Avenue calls "image." And many virtues of style are really only apparent virtues.

In view of all this, it seems fairly clear that persuasion has to do with the "plausible," with apparent proof and seeming logic, and with image personality and the simulated virtues of style. Persuasion, as such, is averidical, neither true nor false (cf. Cope, i, 9, 78–79). This does not mean, of course, that the subject matter may not be true (or false). If the speaker does know the truth and finds it expedient to use, he may be all the more convincing. As Brentlinger says, in "The Aristotelian Concept of Truth in Rhetorical Discourse,"

> Although not the primary concern of the speaker, the higher truths of scientific knowledge will be sought when it is possible to attain them without loss of the more practical objectives of rhetoric. . . . The level of truth which governs the selection and construction of the rhetorical argument is usually that of opinion or probability (a, in *Dissertation Abstracts,* XX, 3426 and 3429.)

A further specific differentia of persuasion from reference discourse is the usual presence in persuasive discourse of emotional terms and references. Plato insisted that love must be added to truth in true rhetoric— if one accepts Weaver's interpretation of the *Phaedrus.* Aristotle devotes sixteen chapters of his *Rhetoric* to the emotional appeal, more than to any other single aspect of his system. Some traditional rhetoricians, it is true, have slighted the emotional component in their treatments, though none as far as I know, has ever denied it. Campbell insists strongly on the "passions" as a vital element in persuasion (p, 99–117). Black, attempting to formulate a majority position in the field of speech, insists on this element (12 ff.). I. A. Richards makes emotional components the essence of poetry and the mixture of referential and emotional the essence of rhetoric (pr, 261; h, 100). Brown, approaching persuasion from the viewpoint of a psychologist, likewise insists on the presence of the emotional (t, 25), as does Hovland, working in a similar context (c, 7–8). Sometimes, indeed, the hearer is not even aware of the emotional appeal (Burke, r, 28 ff.; McLuhan, u, 93).

Many rhetoricians, likewise, stress the fact that rhetoric always involves a choice in the realm of the practical. Weaver sees this component in Plato's notion of rhetoric: "That is why rhetoric, with its passion for the actual, is more complete than mere dialectic with its dry understanding" (Weaver, e, 21; the whole book treats this topic from various points of view and with different kinds of examples). Aristotle insisted that all rhetoric is directed to a decision (*Rhet.*, 1391b, 18). Burke, in modern times, puts this idea in a slightly different manner. By emphasizing that all rhetoric exists in a situational context of nonagreement which the rhetorician is attempting to bring to a state of identification, he stresses the "scene" or background of the rhetorical situation. As he says, "Words are aspects of a much wider communicative context, most of which is not verbal at all" (r, 482, quoting from his own *Philosophy of Literary Form;* and cf. r, 442). Rhetoric relates more to the immediate life situation in which the discourse occurs. Literature and science are less immediately bound to a given time and place.

One final point about the nature of persuasion must be given some attention. Is it moral to persuade people by means of the techniques of rhetoric? Various answers have been given to this question. It might be useful to pass in review three basic answers to the question of the ethics of rhetoric. The classical loci of these answers are to be found in Plato, Isocrates, and Aristotle, but there are just as articulate modern defenders of each position.

Plato, in the *Gorgias* and elsewhere crystallizes one polar position. Rhetoric is "ignoble" and "bad" (g, 463 ff.); it is a deceit of the soul, an appearance of justice, it is the ghost and counterfeit of a part of politics (g, 464); it ministers to the pleasure of the soul, not its good (g, 502 ff.); it induces "belief without knowledge" (g, 454). Socrates admits to Gorgias and Callicles that a good rhetoric could exist, but no one has ever practiced it (g, 503). It is only flattery, not really an art at all (g, *passim*). The English teacher often sides with Plato on this matter. One might even enlarge this statement. Minds which continually are exposed to the neutral kinds of language represented by literature and science often take on, possibly unconsciously, a distrust and distaste of persuasion. This may be another reason why English departments have neglected it—both at the college and the high school level.

Some other approaches to persuasion also question its morality. Doob, for instance, includes "insincerity," or attempting to fool the audience, as an essential ingredient in all propaganda (cf. Brown, t, 22, who disagrees, 23). Lasswell, in a consideration of political propaganda, concludes that actual propaganda, wherever it has been studied, has a large element of the fake in it, and says that using only true statements in political propaganda would be an impractical policy (p, 206, 208). In a survey of commercial advertising agencies several years ago, ninety-two per cent felt that the competing agencies were dishonest. And of course, some have questioned the honesty of instilling religious faith in someone before he is able to understand what he is being asked to believe. By the same token, one could question raising a child to believe in any value system—political, religious, economic, moral, esthetic—before he can rationally appraise it. If pushed to the extreme, this position could result in not educating the child at all.

The opposite position from the Platonic takes several variations. For Isocrates, as for Quintilian, the orator was the *good* man (Isocrates, a, 276 ff.; cf. Wagner, r, 177). Although Cicero recognizes the good and evil uses of rhetoric (i, I, i–I, v; o, I, 32 ff.; n, II, 148; t, V, 5), yet he considers the orator as the summation of the virtues of a civilized society. Campbell and others follow Cicero in this view—the orator embraces all of the lower capabilities of intellectual appeal, emotional appeal, and influencing the will (p, 26).

From a very different standpoint, Kierkegaard enthrones persuasion as the only moral use of language. In an objective use of language, truth is not personally applied; and therefore it is wasted, there is no subjective acceptance of truth. He prefers a falsehood accepted subjectively to a truth accepted only objectively (see above, p.170 for references). Weaver does not condemn as immoral the scientific and the literary. Rather, these "neuter" uses of language are incomplete. The rhetorician is the complete man, he is the lover added to the scientist (e, 21). This is a position similar to Campbell's.

In specific areas of persuasion there have been defenses which can sometimes be generalized and made applicable to the total field of persuasion. Commercial advertising, in particular, has attempted some systematic justifications which have some relevance to the field of persuasion. Some of the defenses of advertising have been provoked by frontal attacks. Vance Packard claims, for instance, that "Americans have become the most manipulated people outside the Iron Curtain" (quoted in Harris, a, 179).

Other critics of advertising maintain that the primary purpose of advertising is to inform, and since it does not do this efficiently, it should be abolished or radically transformed. Nicholas Kaldor, for instance, takes this view of the primacy of the informative purpose in advertising and maintains that an independent or government information service could perform this duty much more efficiently and economically (cf. Harris, a, 71–72). A. C. Pijou favors informative over competitive advertising because the latter tends to encourage trade monopolies (cf. Harris, a, 68, 82); Henry C. Simons says that persuasive advertising tends to move people to buy what is produced, not what is needed, leads to great waste of money on advertising, and leads to the necessity of middlemen in the economy (Harris, a, 69–70); Bob R. Holdren says that advertising leads to a multiplicity of brands to get shelf space and free advertising; it tends to favor the large firms who can advertise nationally, and may lead to bribing the retailer (cf. Harris, a, 70–71). Most of these critics of advertising, Harris points out, are believers in a free economy.

These claims are countered by the defenders of advertising. Advertising increases the scale of production, stimulates demand, creates new products, is open to far fewer and less serious objections than political propaganda, is a helpful guarantee of quality, and sharpens incentive (Harris, a, 88 ff.). As Sir Dennis Robertson has said,

> There is...real spiritual comfort in buying a packet of a known and trusted brand of cocoa rather than a shovelful of brown powder of uncertain origin (quoted in Harris, a, 102).

Others have maintained that the advent of commercial advertising "played a major part in making newspapers honest and moderately respectable" (cf. Brown, t, 19).

The most comprehensive defense of advertising, however, is that it is an inherent feature of a free society and that the abuses it entails are the corollaries of freedom. Where freedom exists, evil and abuse are possibilities (cf. Harris, a, 88). Harris concludes one section of his discussion of this issue with the following paragraph,

> A final judgment [of the ethics and legality of advertising] must also take into account that advertising in the general sense of advocating the merits of competing products, services, opinions, ideas and policies looms very much larger than commercial salesmanship. It is an all-pervasive and unavoidable feature of every society where the means of communication are highly developed and where economic and political institutions are based on consent so that citizens, both as consumers and electors, must be persuaded rather than coerced into accepting a product or a policy (a, 161).

It is tempting to say that there is a third and intermediary position between these two and to cite Aristotle as the proponent of this position. Aristotle occasionally takes an amoral view of persuasion (cf. Gomperz, g, 458.) The techniques of persuasions are neither good nor bad in themselves —the existential context of the purposes to which they are oriented determines their goodness or badness. These techniques are instruments; like knives which can cut either bread or throats, the instruments of persuasion can operate in good or evil situations.

Aristotle adduces four main reasons for the necessity of rhetoric: (1) it assists in the general triumph of good over evil; (2) it is necessary to influence those incapable of real instruction; (3) examining both sides of a topic helps to find out the truth [this is, in large measure, the foundation of our legal system]; (4) it is necessary as a means of self-defense against the rhetoric of others (r, 1355a 21 ff.). These justifications for persuasion seem even more urgent today than in the Athenian democracy after Pericles. To a world which has seen the virtual enslavement of a third of the world since World War II by effective propaganda and the rhetorical magic of Roosevelt, Hitler, and Mussolini in one generation, it hardly seems necessary to justify the study of rhetoric. Finally, if the world's events have not penetrated the consciousness of some provincial American minds, the ubiquitous advertisers' chants certainly have. Who can ignore, in our age, the omnipresence of the rhetoric of advertising on the road by signs and radio signals, in the parlor by television and radio?

Rhetoric, finally, is necessary because man is not a creature with just an intellect. Because he is a discerning man who discriminates among his fellows and listens to one more than another, he is subject to the ethical argument, the argument from personality. Because he is a perceptive being who is sensitive to emotion, he is influenced by the pathetic argument. Nor is either of these an acknowledgment of weakness in man. It is commendable in man to discriminate among his fellows, and it is also commendable for man to be subject to emotions. Few people have persuaded their sweethearts to marriage by mere lists of information or pure demonstrative reasoning.

Rhetoric, therefore, is necessary as long as man is a being with a body, with emotions, and with persistent character judgments. It would, indeed, be a cold and forbidding cosmos in which rhetoric did not exist. Literature and love, among other things, would not find entrance therein, for rhetorical structures are among the most important tools of the dramatist, the poet, the novelist, and the lover. For the ordinary person who rarely breathes the pure atmosphere of science or dialectic, the air of this universe has a heavy dose of rhetoric in it.

It may seem that the general orientation of this chapter is preponderantly Aristotelian in its positions and frameworks. To some extent this is so—though there are large reservations to be made about Aristotle's *Rhetoric* throughout the remainder of the chapter. The decision to adhere to an Aristotelian structure in analyzing persuasion was made because of the nature of the structure of Aristotle's *Rhetoric*.

This structure is consistently modeled on the communications triangle—to a much larger extent than is commonly recognized even by good commentators on the *Rhetoric*. One of Aristotle's defining characteristics of rhetoric is that it is language directed to the hearer, not to things (1358a 39). This parallels the basic view of persuasion taken in this book. Secondly, Aristotle's three basic techniques of inducing persuasion, the so-called rhetorical proofs, are based on the three points of the triangle, as will be shown shortly. And his subdivisions of both the ethical proof, the pathetic proof, and the logical proof are also based on the triangle. These frameworks provide a convenient structure for incorporating much of what is known about the process of persuasion. Finally, Aristotle's four virtues of style are also drawn immediately from the four basic components of the communications triangle, as will also be shown. The communications triangle offers a very convenient framework for analyzing persuasive style, as well as referential style. Thus, the triangle is the basic structural principle of Aristotle's rhetoric. Figure IV, 1 attempts to portray this in graphic form.

Other past and current approaches to the consideration of persuasion have also adopted this basic structure. Since nearly all of the major rhetorics of Western civilization since the time of the Greeks have drawn heavily on Aristotle's framework, consciously or subconsciously, the major rhetoricians of our culture have used this scaffolding for their constructs. It thus has the advantages (and some of the disadvantages) of a long historical tradition. Corbett, attempting to summarize *Classical Rhetoric for the Modern Student,* uses this structure.

At the present time, it is still the model serving the majority of writers in departments of speech (cf. Black, r, 11 ff., for references on this). In fact, Wayne Thompson, in a comprehensive survey of empirical research in seven major speech periodicals in this century, uses this structure as his basic framework (Thompson, q). The research in persuasion of Hovland and his associates has also been reported within the same general framework (Hovland, c). The massive research of Lasswell and his associates into political propaganda has also been recorded—in the main bibliographic compilation—within this same framework(Smith, pr). Kenneth Burke feels that his rhetoric is strongly within the Aristotelian tradition, though the structural similarities are drawn as much from aspects of Aristotle's physics, metaphysics, and poetics as from his *Rhetoric*. I. A. Richards uses a communication triangle in his rhetoric also—though there are also serious

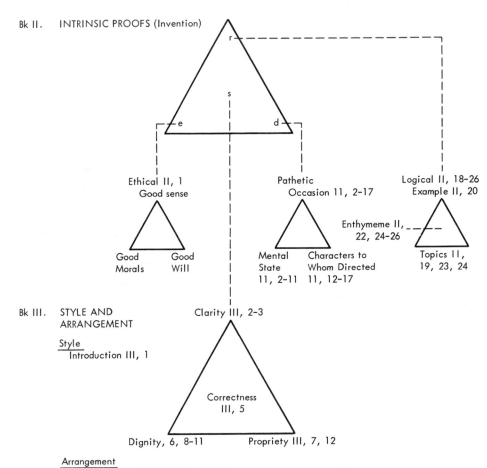

Bk 1.   DEFINITION AND KINDS
        Introduction and Justification 1, 1*
        Definition 1, 2
        Kinds 1, 3
              Political 1, 4-8
              Ceremonial 1, 9
              Legal 1, 10-14

    Extrinsic Proofs 1, 15

Bk II.   INTRINSIC PROOFS (Invention)

r

s

e   d

Ethical II, 1   Pathetic   Logical II, 18-26
Good sense   Occasion 11, 2-17   Example II, 20

                                             Enthymeme II,
                                                22, 24-26

Good   Good   Mental   Characters to   Topics 11,
Morals   Will   State   Whom Directed   19, 23, 24
                       11, 2-11 11, 12-17

Bk III.   STYLE AND   Clarity III, 2-3
          ARRANGEMENT

    Style
        Introduction III, 1

                               Correctness
                                  III, 5

        Dignity, 6, 8-11   Propriety III, 7, 12

    Arrangement
        Introduction and Justification III, 13
              Prooemium III, 14-15
              Narration III, 16
              Arguments III, 17-18
              Epilogue III, 19

*Roman numbers refer to Book, Arabic Numbers refer to chapters within that Book.

Figure IV, 1: A Representation of the Structure of Aristotle's *Rhetoric*

226

divergences from Aristotelian rhetoric in Richards. Some writers in the field of freshman composition still view the classical rhetorical tradition as a major font of inspiration (Ohmann, i; Corbett, c; Hughes and Duhamel, r).

Thus there is good precedent for using Aristotle's rhetorical structure in approaching the study of persuasion. However, the author has found, by practical experience, that simply telling students to go read the *Rhetoric* can have disastrous effects. Certain cautions have been found helpful in warding off these effects. A few words, then, on the text of the *Rhetoric,* some of its pitfalls, some of its strengths, and some of its weaknesses may be in order, though both strengths and inadequacies will be detailed in the sections which follow.

First, Aristotle wrote his *Rhetoric* in the context of a situation that had its immediate circumstances, which are not crucially relevant to our age (Ross a, 276). Therefore some of Aristotle's emphases must be put into their historical context before being bodily imposed upon the rhetorical situation today. Thus, Aristotle's division of the kinds of rhetoric into judiciary, political, and ceremonial may have been a valid and important division for his time. But today other kinds such as commercial advertising, religious oratory, and others must be added to these, and the importance of ceremonial oratory has certainly diminished. Therefore, the student reading the *Rhetoric* for the first time might well be advised to read Book I, Chapters 1, 2, and 3, to get Aristotle's justification, nature, and kinds of rhetoric straight and then move on to Book II, postponing for a time the eleven long chapters on the kinds of rhetoric. Similarly, although the sixteen chapters of Book II on the emotional proof are interesting, the student might at first reading sample one or two of them to grasp the methodology (say II, 2 and II, 12 and II, 16), and then move on to the logical proof of Chapters 18 to 26. Many students get bogged down in these two sections and fail to see the overall structure of the *Rhetoric* and its relevance to present-day persuasion.

A second caution relates to the ideas and style of the *Rhetoric*. It must never be forgotten, in reading the *Rhetoric,* that Aristotle intended definitions and other ideas in the *Rhetoric* to be applicable to the immediate business of writing speeches for the populace. Thus the definitions of virtues and vices, of governments, and the like are not intended to be technically correct but rather "folksy," superficial, and acceptable to the popular mind. In at least one case Aristotle gives pleasure a useful "rhetorical" definition which he goes to some pains to argue against and destroy in his careful "scientific" treatment of the same topic in the *Ethics* (contrast *Rhetoric,* 1369b 33 with *Ethics,* 1173a 32; for other instances cf. Cope, i, 13–14).

More specific cautions concerning special parts of the *Rhetoric* will be made in treating the topics and the logical proof generally, the cultural relativism of Aristotle's handling of the emotional proof, and the doctrine of style and correctness. It has already been pointed out that Aristotle's three kinds of speeches were locally and temporally conditioned. In addition, the view of rhetoric as a kind of "eloquence" with rather lengthy, fully developed speeches has to be adjusted to our own different media and circumstances.

Again, any reading of Aristotle in translation must recognize the dangers inherent in reading a person who was himself trying to create a new scientific terminology from "popular vocabulary." Words such as "art," "action," "enthymeme," and many others are often very ambiguous in the *Rhetoric*. Finally, in the past and at the present, too many read only the *Rhetoric* of Aristotle and fail to appreciate the fact that this is only a portion of Aristotle's complete theory of discourse. The full *Organon* and the *Poetics* are just as relevant to a comprehensive theory of discourse.

ANALYSIS OF THE NATURE OF PERSUASIVE DISCOURSE AS ILLUSTRATED IN FRANKLIN D. ROOSEVELT'S "FIRST INAUGURAL ADDRESS" OF MARCH 4, 1933

1. I am certain that my fellow Americans expect that on my induction into the Presidency I will address them with a candor and a decision which the present situation of our Nation impels. This is preeminently the time to speak the truth, the whole truth, frankly and boldly. Nor need we shrink from honestly facing conditions in our country today. This great Nation will endure as it has endured, will revive and will prosper. So, first of all, let me assert my firm belief that the only thing we have to fear is fear itself—nameless, unreasoning, unjustified terror which paralyzes needed efforts to convert retreat into advance. In every dark hour of our national life a leadership of frankness and vigor has met with the understanding and support of the people themselves which is essential to victory. I am convinced that you will again give that support to leadership in these critical days.

2. In such a spirit on my part and on yours we face our common difficulties. They concern, thank God, only material things. Values have shrunken to fantastic levels; taxes have risen; our ability to pay has fallen; government of all kinds is faced by serious curtailment of income; the means of exchange are frozen in the currents of trade; the withered leaves of industrial enterprise lie on every side; farmers find no markets for their produce; the savings of many years in thousands of families are gone.

3. More important, a host of unemployed citizens face the grim problem of existence, and an equally great number toil with little return. Only a foolish optimist can deny the dark realities of the moment.

4. Yet our distress comes from no failure of substance. We are stricken by no plague of locusts. Compared with the perils which our forefathers

conquered because they believed and were not afraid, we have still much to be thankful for. Nature still offers her bounty and human efforts have multiplied it. Plenty is at our doorstep, but a generous use of it languishes in the very sight of the supply. Primarily this is because rulers of the exchange of mankind's goods have failed through their own stubbornness and their own incompetence, have admitted their failure, and have abdicated. Practices of the unscrupulous money changers stand indicted in the court of public opinion, rejected by the hearts and minds of men.

5. True they have tried, but their efforts have been cast in the pattern of an outworn tradition. Faced by failure of credit they have proposed only the lending of more money. Stripped of the lure of profit by which to induce our people to follow their false leadership, they have resorted to exhortations, pleading tearfully for restored confidence. They know only the rules of a generation of self-seekers. They have no vision, and when there is no vision the people perish.

6. The money changers have fled from their high seats in the temple of our civilization. We may now restore that temple to the ancient truths. The measure of the restoration lies in the extent to which we apply social values more noble than mere monetary profit.

7. Happiness lies not in the mere possession of money; it lies in the joy of achievement, in the thrill of creative effort. The joy and moral stimulation of work no longer must be forgotten in the mad chase of evanescent profits. These dark days will be worth all they cost us if they teach us that our true destiny is not to be ministered unto but to minister to ourselves and to our fellow men.

8. Recognition of the falsity of material wealth as the standard of success goes hand in hand with the abandonment of the false belief that public office and high political position are to be valued only by the standards of pride of place and personal profit; and there must be an end to a conduct in banking and in business which too often has given to a sacred trust the likeness of callous and selfish wrongdoing. Small wonder that confidence languishes, for it thrives only on honesty, on honor, on the sacredness of obligations, on faithful protection, on unselfish performance; without them it cannot live.

9. Restoration calls, however, not for changes in ethics alone. This Nation asks for action, and action now.

10. Our greatest primary task is to put people to work. This is no unsolvable problem if we face it wisely and courageously. It can be accomplished in part by direct recruiting by the Government itself, treating the task as we would treat the emergency of a war, but at the same time, through this employment, accomplishing greatly needed projects to stimulate and reorganize the use of our natural resources.

11. Hand in hand with this we must frankly recognize the overbalance of population in our industrial centers and, by engaging on a national scale in a redistribution, endeavor to provide a better use of the land for those best fitted for the land. The task can be helped by definite efforts

to raise the values of agricultural products and with this the power to purchase the output of our cities. It can be helped by preventing realistically the tragedy of the growing loss through foreclosure of our small homes and our farms. It can be helped by insistence that the Federal, State, and local governments act forthwith on the demand that their cost be drastically reduced. It can be helped by the unifying of relief activities which today are often scattered, uneconomical, and unequal. It can be helped by national planning for and supervision of all forms of transportation and of communications and other utilities which have a definitely public character. There are many ways in which it can be helped, but it can never be helped merely by talking about it. We must act and act quickly.

12. Finally, in our progress toward a resumption of work we require two safeguards against a return of the evils of the old order; there must be a strict supervision of all banking and credits and investments, so that there will be an end to speculation with other people's money; and there must be provision for an adequate but sound currency.

13. These are the lines of attack. I shall presently urge upon a new Congress, in special session, detailed measures for their fulfillment, and I shall seek the immediate assistance of the several States.

14. Through this program of action we address ourselves to putting our own national house in order and making income balance outgo. Our international trade relations, though vastly important, are in point of time and necessity secondary to the establishment of a sound national economy. I favor as a practical policy the putting of first things first. I shall spare no effort to restore world trade by international economic readjustment, but the emergency at home cannot wait on that accomplishment.

15. The basic thought that guides these specific means of national recovery is not narrowly nationalistic. It is the insistence, as a first consideration, upon the interdependence of the various elements in and parts of the United States—a recognition of the old and permanently important manifestation of the American spirit of the pioneer. It is the way to recovery. It is the immediate way. It is the strongest assurance that the recovery will endure.

16. In the field of world policy I would dedicate this Nation to the policy of the good neighbor—the neighbor who resolutely respects himself and, because he does so, respects the rights of others—the neighbor who respects his obligations and respects the sanctity of his agreements in and with a world of neighbors.

17. If I read the temper of our people correctly, we now realize as we have never realized before our interdependence on each other; that we cannot merely take but we must give as well; that if we are to go forward, we must move as a trained and loyal army willing to sacrifice for the good of a common discipline, because without such discipline no progress is made, no leadership becomes effective. We are, I know, ready

and willing to submit our lives and property to such discipline, because it makes possible a leadership which aims at a larger good. This I propose to offer, pledging that the larger purposes will bind upon us all as a sacred obligation with a unity of duty hitherto evoked only in time of armed strife.

18. With this pledge taken, I assume unhesitatingly the leadership of this great army of our people dedicated to a disciplined attack upon our common problems.

19. Action in this image and to this end is feasible under the form of government which we have inherited from our ancestors. Our Constitution is so simple and practical that it is possible always to meet extraordinary needs by changes in emphasis and arrangement without loss of essential form. That is why our constitutional system has proved itself the most superbly enduring political mechanism the modern world has produced. It has met every stress of vast expansion of territory, of foreign wars, of bitter internal strife, of world relations.

20. It is to be hoped that the normal balance of Executive and legislative authority may be wholly adequate to meet the unprecedented task before us. But it may be that an unprecedented demand and need for undelayed action may call for temporary departure from that normal balance of public procedure.

21. I am prepared under my constitutional duty to recommend the measures that a stricken Nation in the midst of a stricken world may require. These measures, or such other measures as the Congress may build out of its experience and wisdom, I shall seek, within my constitutional authority, to bring to speedy adoption.

22. But in the event that the Congress shall fail to take one of these two courses, and in the event that the national emergency is still critical, I shall not evade the clear course of duty that will then confront me. I shall ask the Congress for the one remaining instrument to meet the crisis—broad Executive power to wage a war against the emergency, as great as the power that would be given to me if we were in fact invaded by a foreign foe.

23. For the trust reposed in me I will return the courage and the devotion that befit the time. I can do no less.

24. We face the arduous days that lie before us in the warm courage of national unity; with the clear consciousness of seeking old and precious moral values; with the clean satisfaction that comes from the stern performance of duty by old and young alike. We aim at the assurance of a rounded and permanent national life.

25. We do not distrust the future of essential democracy. The people of the United States have not failed. In their need they have registered a mandate that they want direct, vigorous action. They have asked for discipline and direction under leadership. They have made me the present instrument of their wishes. In the spirit of the gift I take it.

26. In this dedication of a Nation we humbly ask the blessing of God.

May He protect each and every one of us. May He guide me in the days to come (from Roosevelt, p).

To illustrate the nature of persuasive discourse, a fairly obvious example of such discourse has been chosen, Franklin D. Roosevelt's "First Inaugural Address." The major constitutive components outlined above had to do with the following points: (1) focus on the decoder—an attempt to dissolve an opposition existing in the circumstances of the times into an identification of decoder and encoder in making a distinct choice (or several) among practical alternatives; (2) a seeming "probability"—the encoder's attempt to make what may be only questionable or even false appear as highly probable, even certain; (3) emotional appeal. Each of these components will be analyzed in Roosevelt's speech.

The emphasis on the decoder is fairly obvious. It is not accomplished, however, by explicit references to the addressees as such; indeed, there are only two direct uses of second person reference ("you" in paragraph 1 and "yours" in paragraph 2). The audience is, on the contrary, treated in two very distinct manners, both continuing throughout the speech. On the one hand, the speaker continuously unites the audience with him in a comradely "we," "us," or "our." There are some fifty such uses of the first person plural in this brief speech. Thus the decoder is referred to, but is identified with the encoder in resolves, in decisions, in attitudes, in likes and dislikes, in emotional positions, indeed, in practically everything. This assumption of identity with the audience is clearly related to one aspect of the character proof to be analyzed below—sympathy with the hearers.

The margin of Roosevelt's victory in the 1932 election to some extent allowed him to make such an assumption of identity with hearers. But he obviously pushes the identity into the future to prepare for the plans he is to present Congress shortly. Such an extrapolation can be seen typically in a sort of summary paragraph occurring at about the two-thirds point of the speech:

If I read the temper of our people correctly, we now realize as we have never realized before our interdependence on each other; that we cannot merely take but we must give as well; that if we are to go forward, we must move as a trained and loyal army willing to sacrifice for the good of a common discipline, because without such discipline no progress is made, no leadership becomes effective. We are, I know, ready and willing to submit our lives and property to such discipline, because it makes possible a leadership which aims at a larger good. This I propose to offer, pledging that the larger purposes will bind upon us all as a sacred obligation with a unity of duty hitherto evoked only in time of armed strife (paragraph 17).

The second manner in which Roosevelt refers to the audience is by referring to them as "my fellow Americans," "this Nation," "the people of the United States." This third-person reference does not come across impersonally, however. Rather the general effect lends a clear dignity to the audience. There are about twenty-two such references throughout the speech, and they often come at crucial places in his talk: "my fellow Americans" (paragraph 1); "The Nation asks for action, and action now" (paragraph 9); "I am prepared under my constitutional duties to recommend the measures that a stricken Nation in the midst of a stricken world may require" (paragraph 21); "The people of the United States have not failed" (paragraph 25). It might be remarked that in print Roosevelt consistently capitalizes "Nation." Occasionally these references are to a subgroup: "the Congress," "a host of unemployed citizens," "thousands of families." This dignity is certainly consonant with the circumstances: a presidential inaugural address (other components of dignity are analyzed in "Style," below). The three manners of referring to the audience, therefore, make up seventy-four references to the audience or segments of it in five brief pages of text—certainly enough to justify calling this decoder-centered discourse. It might be useful to contrast this speech to the several samples of reference discourse analyzed in Chapter III.

There are other indirect means of focusing on the audience. Instead of using direct imperatives, Roosevelt often makes implicit imperatives of maxim or policy: "there must be a strict supervision of all banking and credits and investments," "there must be provision for an adequate but sound currency" (paragraph 12), "the joy and moral stimulation of work no longer must be forgotten in the mad chase of evanescent profits" (paragraph 7), "It is the way to recovery. It is the immediate way" (paragraph 15). The Congress and the people are obviously the targets of these indirect imperatives.

All of these addressee references, direct or indirect, are unified towards a central emotional thesis and a central legislative choice; both are immediate matters of the situational context. In this respect, Roosevelt's speech typifies the immediate practicality of persuasion. To understand this, one must place the speech in its situational context, that is, the circumstances of time and place motivating it. The urgencies of this context may well be lost on the average student of the present time, some thirty-seven years removed from the critical events of 1933. It is significant that Roosevelt, publishing the speech in his public papers in 1938, already felt it necessary to reconstruct the situational context for the reader (p, 16), as do many of the subsequent editors (e.g., Zevin, an editor, in Roosevelt m, 12–13).

Roosevelt's own description of the situational context is admirably suited to our present purposes. In his explanatory note to the speech he wrote:

Those who lived through the months immediately preceding March, 1933, do not require a description of the desperate condition into which the American economy had fallen since the crash of 1929. . . .

By Inauguration Day, 1933, the banks of the United States were all closed, financial transactions had ceased, business and industry had sunk to their lowest levels. The widespread unemployment which accompanied the collapse had created a general feeling of utter helplessness. I sought principally in the foregoing Inaugural Address to banish, as far as possible, the fear of the present and of the future which held the American people and the American spirit in its grasp.

For many months the people had looked to Government for help, but Government had looked away, I promised a program of action; first, to put people to work; and second, to correct the abuses in many fields of human endeavor which had in great measure contributed to the crisis. I promised action immediately, stating that if necessary I would ask for and would use all the war powers of the Executive to wage war against the emergency (Roosevelt, p, 16).

There is undoubtedly some rhetoric even in this description, but generally, it outlines the situation and the two choices to which the audience is oriented: abandoning of fear and embracing of the program of action which he as leader was to propose to Congress. It is clear from internal evidence in the text, I believe, that these aims can be read independently of Roosevelt's saying he intended them. The danger of being trapped by the intentional fallacy is thus averted. Thus the "fear" motif is struck immediately in paragraph 1. Its causes are outlined in the next two paragraphs; hope is offered in paragraphs 4, 5, 6, 7, and 8 by Roosevelt's showing that the resources exist to correct the situation and that mismanagement and ineffective leadership have hitherto prevented the use of these resources. The next several paragraphs outline the course of action which an effective leadership should take to confront these problems (paragraphs 9 to 18). The concluding paragraphs (19 to 26) stress the importance of the leadership being endowed with the broad executive powers in order to accomplish the stated reforms.

Each paragraph and sentence of the speech has a direct bearing on the two immediate decisions that he is asking the people and their representatives to make. In point of fact, these two decisions were forthcoming, as history attests. Despite the deemphasis on international problems (paragraphs 14, 15, 16), *The London Observer* reacted typically:

America has found a man. In him...the world must find a leader. Undaunted by the magnitude of his stupendous task and cool in the face of its urgency, Mr. Roosevelt has made a splendid beginning. . . . Calmly and fearlessly he must aim at the highest in international as in domestic affairs. There is no mediocre way for him. His name must be one of the greater names in history or nothing. In accent and action his beginnings suggest success (quoted in Roosevelt, m, 13).

And Harry L. Hopkins later wrote, "For myself I think his first inaugural address was the best speech he ever made" (in the preface to Roosevelt, m, viii). Statements of confidence came from the Governor's Conference two days later (see Roosevelt, p, 21–23), from a very selective Committee of Citizens (Roosevelt, p, 22–23), even from an adverse press (Roosevelt, p, 40). History chronicles the success of his legislative program in the first hundred days of his presidency. Finally, the legislature has probably never recovered some of the extraordinary powers given to Roosevelt at this time. The speech obviously achieved its purposes.

The second major factor of persuasive discourse is its probability level. Unlike focus on the decoder, the real probability level of a persuasive discourse is not immediately evident in the text itself. What is evident is the *seeming* probability or plausibility of the choices outlined. Reading the text, one has to derive the impression that all is categoric, the villains and heroes are clearly differentiated, the basic moral and economic issues can be analyzed under the glare of a very bright white light. The speech begins "I am certain..." and this self-confident certainty exudes from every sentence in the text. Such self-confidence is a basic component of the ethical argument, as will be shown very soon.

Yet the certainty was really not nearly so positive as it was made to appear. Indeed, it is highly questionable that "the only thing we have to fear is fear itself," that "in every dark hour of our national life a leadership of frankness and vigor has met with the understanding and support of the people themselves which is essential to victory" (paragraph 1), that the primary cause of the depression was the incompetence and selfishness of the Republican leaders (paragraph 4), or that the Republican leaders were a generation of self-seekers (paragraph 5). One can go on and on in the speech and question the many categoric maxims and generalizations; but the questioning usually came later (as a child of twelve at that time, I do not recall questioning anything).

The art of Roosevelt, then, has consisted in making something *appear* very plausible when in fact, its probability is really, by objective standards, much lower. This is the problem of the rhetorician when his choices are not *really* highly probable. Of course, if they are already highly probable, his job is that much easier, if his audience can be made to understand the reasons for the probability.

The third crucial component of persuasion, emotional reference, is also evident throughout the speech. The full analysis of this component will be given when the pathetic argument is analyzed below. For our purposes here, however, it hardly needs documentation. This is not at all pure expository prose, as I. A. Richards calls that species. The gamut of emotions appealed to is impressive: fear, hope, religion, patriotism, survival, moral righteousness. By the classificatory norms of persuasive writing, Roosevelt's speech therefore, certainly belongs to the category. Since it is political oratory, it belongs to one of the divisions of rhetoric recognized in the classical tradition and in nearly any modern grouping of the areas of persuasion.

The Logic of Persuasive Discourse

In this century there has been a good deal of analysis, mainly from three special quarters, of the nature of persuasion. They would seem at first to be quite relevant to discourse analysis of persuasion. Psychologists with varied approaches have elaborated interesting theories of the nature of persuasion as a psychological process (see DeFleur, t, 119 ff.). To date, however, as far as the author is aware, there has not been a systematic application of these models to the concerns of discourse analysis. It is to be hoped that a rapprochement of the two disciplines can be brought about in the near future. When this happens, we may be forced to restructure our traditional notions of how one brings about a change of view or attitude in actual discourse. For the present, however, I shall not draw on psychological theories, though I felt they should be pointed out.

Similarly, in anthropology and sociology a matter of considerable moment in recent years has been the analysis of innovation acceptance in different kinds of society. Some of this material will be drawn on in the treatment of change in the chapter on narration in Volume II, *The Modes of Discourse*. In the present chapter, however, this approach to persuasion will not be related to discourse analysis. Again, it is hoped that such studies will be related to composition studies in the future (for a survey of the nature of persuasion from this point of view, cf. Rogers, d, 208–47).

Finally, the logic of persuasion has also been the subject of analysis by some symbolic and traditional logicians in what is sometimes called the logic of imperatives or deontic logic. This is a relatively new field in logic and its applications to discourse analysis have not yet been made. Most of the studies are short and tentative periodical articles, but there have been a few full-length studies (Hare, 1; Hintikka, q; cf. also Prior, f, 220–29; Von Wright, m, 36–41). In the future this may also prove a fruitful source for applications to discourse analysis, but in the treatment in this chapter, these materials will not be tapped. These psychological, anthropological, and logical studies of persuasion have, in the main, been theoretical approaches to the nature of persuasion, not empirically based researches. In fact, there has not been much empirical work on the nature of persuasion (Hovland, c, v).

The traditional framework for the study of the techniques of persuasion is provided by Aristotle's second and third books of the *Rhetoric,* the second having to do with what is usually called invention and the third with style and organization. This is also the framework adopted by some modern approaches to persuasion, as was pointed out above in the study of the nature of persuasive discourse. Aristotle begins his section on methods of inducing belief by distinguishing between methods which are actually extraneous to the use of the art of speech as a means of persuasion. Among these extraneous (extrinsic, inartistic, nontechnical) means of persuasion Aristotle lists torture, oaths, laws, witnesses, and contracts (Bk I, Ch. 15). Modern brainwashing techniques list many more, such as rhythmic stimulation by percussion, flashing electric lights, some kinds of dancing and chanting, drugs (cf. Brown, t, 235 ff.). These methods are not the concern of the student of discourse, however interesting they may be in themselves. Some of them, such as rhythm and chant, can be made relevant to discourse and are studied under style.

Among the methods of persuasion intrinsic to the art of rhetoric, Aristotle distinguishes four: those deriving from the influence of the speaker, those deriving from the subject matter under consideration, those deriving from the appeals to the emotions of the audience, and those based upon the stylistic techniques of the speaker or writer. To each of these Aristotle devotes one or several chapters of his *Rhetoric.* It is clear that these are founded upon the basic elements of the process of communication; they might well be called encoder proof, reality proof, decoder proof, and signal proof. Traditionally they are called the ethical, the logical, and the pathetic proofs; the fourth is simply referred to as rhetorical style. The first three together comprise the rhetorical "proofs" or "arguments," and are considered under that part of rhetoric called "invention." They are considered here under "The Logic of Persuasive Discourse."

The Aristotelian structure may not be perfect, but it has several advantages. First, it is based on the nature of the discipline involved. Second, it has the merit of a long historical tradition. Third, as a framework it seems capable of absorbing most of what has been learned up to now about the techniques of persuasion deriving from discourse. Thus the Institute for Propaganda Analysis, in a pedagogical attempt to teach Americans of the late thirties and early forties the techniques of persuasion, used a list which has been frequently reproduced in high school and college textbooks. An early number of the first volume established this list:

> We can more easily recognize propaganda when we see it if we are familiar with the seven common propaganda devices. These are:
> 1. The Name Calling Device
> 2. The Glittering Generalities Device
> 3. The Transfer Device
> 4. The Testimonial Device

5. The Plain Folks Device
6. The Card Stacking Device
7. The Band Wagon Device (Institute, h, 5).

These devices can easily be assimilated into the Aristotelian framework. Name Calling, Plain Folks, and Band Wagon are aspects of the emotional argument. Glittering Generalities and Card Stacking are techniques of the logical argument. Transfer and Testimonial are components of the ethical argument. As with the Aristotelian techniques, there is considerable overlap; thus, Card Stacking, though a logical technique, has heavy overtones of emotionalism (cf. Institute, h, 6).

The Ethical Argument

Of the arguments intrinsic to the speech itself, Aristotle first considers the ethical argument. In his analysis of the *Rhetoric,* Cope defines this as the argument

> ...which consists in conveying to the audience a favorable impression of *your own* character..., in making them believe *by the speech itself* that you are an honest man and incapable of misrepresenting the facts of the case, intelligent enough thoroughly to understand them, and well disposed to your hearers and their interests. In this way you represent *your own character* in the speech (Cope, i, 109, his italics).

The term "ethical" must not obviously be taken as completely equivalent to its ordinary English sense of moral. Other terms which have been used in the tradition and in modern times make this clear. Quintilian uses the term authority (*auctoritas,* cf. III, 8, 12); "the argument from authority" has become a familiar term. Clevenger and Andersen, in a careful analysis of its components, tend to call it the argument from "character." Others in speech often call it the "personal" argument. Madison Avenue calls it the "image" that the person projects. This, properly, calls attention to the appearance, rather than to the reality of the projection. When the authority of someone else's character is adduced, the result is a "testimonial" or "transfer," terms used in the Institute for Propaganda Analysis.

Aristotle listed three factors of the ethical argument, and Cope included them in the definition quoted above. The speaker must appear to have a practical knowledge about the *reality* at issue, he must seem to have the good of the *audience* at heart, and he must portray *himself* as a person who would not deceive the audience in the matter at hand. In the previous sentence, I have underlined the three words *reality, audience,* and *himself* to show that Aristotle again derives his components of the ethical proof from the communication triangle. The three components have occasionally been translated as good sense, good will, and good moral character—Rhys Roberts so translates them in the Oxford translation (1378a 8–9).

Good sense (*phronesis*) means a manifest ability to make practical decisions, to choose the proper means to achieve an end. It derives from the self-assurance and knowledgeableness of the speaker. He must come across as a person who knows the issue and is confident in his grasp of it. It will, consequently, be bolstered indirectly by the logical arguments that he uses in his speech as well as by the categoric certainties of the style. It must be subtle to keep from sounding like snobbery or condescension. But the speaker must have a reason for not being a listener himself.

Good will, the second component of the ethical argument, consists in the speaker's making clear to the members of an audience that he has good intentions toward them. To show his good will with the audience, he must identify with them somehow. He must share some of their basic aspirations, he must speak their language in some respects, he must share their biases and prejudices, if necessary. Just as good sense is built up by the logical argument, so good will is supported by the pathetic argument.

The third factor of the ethical argument, good moral character, is established by the speaker's giving evidence in his speech that he is being sincere and trustworthy in his statements. The audience must be convinced that the speaker would not deceive them. It is the most nearly "ethical" part of the ethical argument. Assuming frankness and candor will often help in this matter.

Aristotle seems to have derived these factors of the ethical argument from Thucydides. They are also mentioned by Aristotle as the characteristics of the statesman in the *Politics* (cf. Cope, r, II, 5n.). Some modern analyses of the ethical argument structure the components very similarly to Aristotle. Thus Hovland, discussing communicator credibility, states:

> In summary, the research indicates that the reactions to a communication are significantly affected by cues as to the communicator's intentions, expertness, and trustworthiness (c, 35).

These patently correspond to good will, good sense, and good moral character. McCroskey, attempting a statistical reduction of the independent factors of the ethical argument, concluded that "authoritativeness and character are the only important constituents of ethos" (cf. Thompson, q, 57). Concerning sincerity, McCroskey indicates that what is important is audience acceptance of a speech as sincere, not necessarily real sincerity; but research indicates that audiences find it difficult to evaluate sincerity (cf. Thompson, q, 58). Andersen and Clevenger, in a survey of experimental research on character proof, arrive at somewhat different conclusions. In their summary they give the following factors as relevant to ethos: the status

of the speaker, his dress, his voice and delivery, his manner, and his perceived sincerity. Factors, in their opinion, which do not appear to affect
ethos are: giving both sides of a question, citing sources as evidence, conciliatory remarks, and self-praise (cf. Thompson, q, 54). Some of these
factors are extrinsic to the discourse itself, but those that are can be related
to the Aristotelian framework, although they tend to discount the importance of some of the traditional components.

Indeed, Aristotle's emphasis on the effectiveness of the ethical argument is sometimes disputed by modern research. Modern practice, however,
in advertising and in politics, betrays considerable stress on the ethical
argument. As everyone must realize, certain character types dominate
much advertising. Sports heroes sell us razor blades, cigarettes, foot powder,
hair oil, and a host of other items often not even remotely connected with
athletics. And the beautiful actress or the young starlet sells cosmetics, soaps,
detergents, automobiles, drugs, and many other effects having little or
nothing to do with either beauty or acting ability. Indeed, if one were to
judge by the ads, the character heroes of our nation, *the kind of people
whom we find credible,* are the Achilles and Helen types. Ours is an age of
the *Iliad,* not the *Odyssey;* we are a Spartan not an Athenian civilization.

In politics, the ethical argument is also extremely important. Two
months before the presidential election between Johnson and Goldwater,
Time magazine, whose editors do have some obvious rhetorical insights—
witness their sales appeal—made the following analysis of the political
rhetoric at that time:

> Many political theorists nurse the notion that upper-case *Issues* are the
> only things that count; they tend to treat political personality as an inter
> esting but unimportant sidelight to any presidential campaign. But per
> sonality and issues are inextricably intertwined.
>
> It is the first order of business for any national candidate to establish
> a personal image that gives credibility to his stand on issues. He must
> also try to convince the American voter that his opponent is so wrong-
> minded, ignorant, incompetent, mendacious or just plain wishy-washy as
> to be disbelieved in any statement about the issues. In 1964, the election
> outcome could depend upon whether Johnson or Goldwater best projects
> his intended image. In short, personality may be the biggest issue of all
> (*Time,* c, 20).

In the view of many, the prediction of the last sentence was fulfilled
in the 1964 election. Issues were often very subordinate to personalities.
In 1968, Nixon's image problem was crucial, and *The Making of a President*
by Joe Maginnis is a fascinating treatment of how Madison Avenue went
about handling it. So important has "image" become in the advertising
world that many companies are investing heavily in "institutional advertis-

ing," advertising not designed to promote a special product but merely to establish the company's image favorably in the public mind.

Despite the practical exploitation of the ethical argument, some modern research tends to question Aristotle's statement that the speaker's character as revealed in his speech "may almost be called the most effective means of persuasion he possesses" (1356a 12). Brown, Hovland, Andersen, Clevenger, and Thompson all agree that communicator credibility tends to exert its strongest influences immediately and to diminish considerably with the passage of time (Brown, t, 50–51; Thompson, q, 39, 54, 58 ff.). In the rhetoric of the teaching situation particularly, some experimental evidence indicates that the ethical argument does not affect learning significantly, despite the long-standing notion that it does (Thompson, q, 58).

The disparity between research and practice and between traditional views and modern attitudes towards the ethical argument as well as the still rather sparse experimental evidence on the effectiveness of the ethical argument must lead today's analyst of discourse to keep an open mind on this point. It certainly is true, whatever theory and research may say about its effect, that the ethical argument is a notable constituent of much persuasive discourse. In the analysis of the persuasive logic of Roosevelt's "Inaugural Address," which follows this presentation of theory, the strong presence of the ethical argument is obvious.

The Pathetic Argument

The second fundamental technique of persuasion analyzed by Aristotle in the *Rhetoric* is the emotional or pathetic argument. The term "pathetic" comes from the Greek word *pathetike,* which is the adjectival form for *pathos,* the basic meaning of which here is "emotion" (cf. Cope, i, 116 ff.). Persuasion is achieved by arousing emotions in the audience, and these emotions precipitate action.

Aristotle devotes sixteen chapters to the emotional argument, more than to any other aspect of the rhetorical process. Chapters 2 through 11 are devoted to the treatment of the individual emotions which Aristotle believes important in the process of persuasion: anger (Ch. 2), calmness (3), friendship and enmity (4), fear and confidence (5), shame and shamelessness (6), kindness and unkindness (7), pity (8), indignation (9), envy (10), and emulation (11). Chapters 12 through 17 are concerned with general types of social groups or characters: the young (12), the elderly (13), men in their prime (14), the aristocrats (15), the wealthy (16), the powerful (17).

Aristotle's treatment of the specific emotions differs considerably from his handling of much of the same material in the *Ethics,* Books III and IV (1115a-1129a). It must be remembered, as was pointed out earlier, that his treatment embodies a popular view of the emotions, one that could be used by a practitioner of persuasion. It does not necessarily represent Aristotle's "scientific" view on these problems. Indeed, the internal structure of the various chapters is very different. In the *Ethics,* the structure is generally the presentation of the two extremes as vices and of the mean between these two as a virtue. Thus the emotion of anger, treated in *Ethics,* IV, Ch. 5 (1125b 26 ff.), first speaks of the mean "good temper," then of the deficiency of anger, "inirascibility," and finally of the excess of anger, "irascibility." This structure is determined by Aristotle's concept of virtue as a mean between the extremes of deficiency and excess of emotion.

On the other hand, the treatment of anger in the *Rhetoric* (and of all the other emotions) is structured by the components of the communications process. To arouse anger in someone, says Aristotle at the outset of the section on the pathetic argument, we must always know three things: the state of mind of angry people, the people with whom they get angry, and the grounds on which they get angry. It is palpably apparent that these three considerations derive from the angry person viewed in the light of the communications triangle—the angry person himself, the audience for his anger, and the occasions in reality which arouse anger. This structure is repeated again and again in the treatment of emotions in the *Rhetoric.* In the case of anger, the specific structure is adverted to explicitly at the outset of the treatment of anger (1378a 23 f.), in the middle of the chapter (1379a 8 f.), and at the end of the chapter (1379b 38 f.); in addition it actually structures the definition of anger itself.[2] In other words, the treatment of the emotions in the *Rhetoric* is a treatment dictated by the nature of the process of communication and persuasion, whereas the treatment in the *Ethics* is dictated by the nature of virtue.

Aristotle's treatment of the various emotions was undoubtedly a useful analysis at the time. Today, although some reservations must be made concerning Aristotle's analysis, the general validity of the importance of the emotional appeal is still accepted, indeed even reinforced. Yet this aspect of the logic of persuasion has also been subjected to relatively little experi-

---

2 This structure is also at the base of different sections in the first book of the *Rhetoric.* Thus, in treating accusation and defense at the beginning of the chapters devoted to judicial or court oratory, Aristotle says,

> There are three things we must ascertain—first, the nature and number of the incentives to wrong-doing; second, the state of mind of wrong-doers; third, the kind of persons who are wronged, and their condition (1368b 2–5).

This structure directly parallels the treatment of emotions in Book II. It dictates the organization of Chapters 10 through 13, and at the end of Chapter 12 Aristotle reminds the reader of what he has been doing (1372b 37).

mental testing. Hovland summarizes the present status of our knowledge as follows:

> Political scientists and sociologists as well as social psychologists frequently emphasize the importance of motive in relation to public opinion formation and social change. But despite widespread agreement on this point, social science research has provided little precise information on the conditions under which motivational [emotional] factors facilitate or interfere with opinion change (c, 56).

In a sense, therefore, analysis of the emotional appeal is still at a common-sense stage. Modern motivational research in advertising, Freudian psychology and its offshoots, and many other current analyses of groups and individuals have yet to be applied to discourse analysis in a systematic fashion.

It is unmistakably plain, in any case, that emotional appeals account for a goodly portion of past and current persuasive techniques. Clearly the history of successful propaganda, religious rhetoric, and commercial advertising underscores the importance of the pathetic argument. The reader has only to contemplate the billboards along the highway, the full-page spreads in newspapers and magazines, the television ad spots, or listen to the door-to-door salesman and the local or national politician or preacher to realize the extent to which emotions are exploited in modern persuasion. The almost insidious exploitation of mother love in some ads for baby food, the sex appeal in many cosmetic, automobile, cigarette ads, the chauvinism in local and national political propaganda are only a few of the myriad appeals to our emotions which we encounter practically every day.

A few reservations might be made concerning Aristotle's coverage of the pathetic argument. In the first place, Aristotle's list of emotions to be exploited in rhetorical circumstances is a Hellenic list of available emotions. In other civilizations, the rhetorical effectiveness of some of these emotions would perhaps not have been nearly as powerful as Aristotle imagined. Emotions have different rhetorical leverage in different cultures. Anthropologists point out that assertiveness, boastfulness, and anger shock the Arapesh of New Guinea, while these same emotions are prized as ideals by the nearby Mundugumor (Brown, t, 40). Other contrasting sets of emotional ideals in different cultures are given by several anthropologists (cf. Brown, t, 40–41).

Some of Aristotle's provincialism can be seen in his almost complete neglect of religious emotions and his failure to give much consideration to love of woman. In the chapter on love (*philia,* significantly usually translated "friendship") the whole concern of the chapter is with love among men, although in the chapter on happiness in Book I, some consideration was paid to women. He concludes: "where, as among the Lacedaemonians, the state of woman is bad, almost half of human life is spoilt" (1361a 11). With regard to religion Randall has said of Aristotle, "The one thing the mature Aristotle did not understand, and apparently had no interest in investigating, was religion" (a, 137). Today, after twenty centuries of Christianity's undeniably vigorous rhetorical exploitation of religious emotions, Aristotle would at least have to record their use in a treatise on persuasion.

Second, and possibly because of cultural relativism, some of Aristotle's trust in the effectiveness of fear and threats has been questioned by some modern research. Occasionally, threats can backfire; and although the immediate effect of a frightening presentation may appear much stronger than a simple factual presentation, the long-term effects may be quite the reverse (cf. Brown, t, 79–81; Hovland, c, 73 ff.).

Third, modern depth psychology has warned us not to be taken in by the surface appearance of many emotions. Yet Aristotle's analysis of the emotions is designedly a surface analysis. Sometimes the real emotional appeals are actually the opposite of what they appear to a surface diagnosis, and the rhetorician can profitably be aware of this (cf. Brown, t, 70 ff., for interesting examples of this).

Fourth, modern sociological and psychological analyses have brought considerable refinement to Aristotle's character groups. The concept of "persuasibility" has been given a good deal of analysis. The existence of various kinds of social groups as different targets of persuasion is the basis of one important modern theory of persuasion, that of social categories (cf. DeFleur, t, 129 ff.).

Women generally seem to be more persuadable than men, although some maintain they tend to retain the persuasion less (cf. Thompson, q, 46, 48 ff.). People of high I.Q. are more persuadable by intellectual arguments than people of low I.Q.; people of lower I.Q. seem more persuaded by mere slogans and images (Hovland, c, 183, 187–90). People of low self-esteem, overtly aggressive people, the socially withdrawn, and people with acute psychoneurotic complaints are groups of low persuadability (Hovland, c, 192 ff.).

People seem to be much more amenable to persuasion when they are in small groups, rather than when they are addressed as single individuals (Brown, t, 294). Some psychoanalysts, indeed, have analyzed groups by Freudian norms into conservative (father-submissive) and radical (father-rebellious) classes, into persecutory or oppressive, depending on their infant-mother relationships. They suggest that the persecutory are amenable to fear of punishment and threats, the oppressive to love (Brown, t, 45 ff., 59–60). Other studies suggest that the older are more persuadable (Hovland, c, 49), despite the rather obvious everyday evidence of the young rebel. From Aristotle to Hovland, in any case, it must still be conceded that the study of emotions in the techniques of persuasion is still in a near-folklore state as far as scientific evidence is concerned.

The Logical Argument

The third fundamental technique of inducing belief is usually called the "logical" argument. The term is unfortunate because it suggests that rational logic is here in question, whereas, as has been demonstrated above (see above, p. 220), the logic of rhetoric is only *seemingly* rational. Aristotle never pretended that any of his three main kinds of rhetorical logic (topics, enthymemes, or examples) were really logical. Indeed, all of the chapters on the "logical" argument (Chapters 18 through 26) are a scathing denunciation of the *seeming* rationality, but ultimate irrationality of man as a persuadable being. In the discussion of topics, for example, Aristotle almost invariably points out that a given topic can prove a point *or its opposite* (1397a 7 ff.; cf. Cope, i, 129; Cope, r, II, 238). The reader is reminded again and again of the differences among the scientific, the dialectical, and the rhetorical syllogisms (enthymemes). It is difficult to see how anyone who reads Chapters 18 through 26, even casually, can ever emerge with the notion that Aristotle viewed persuadable man, the populace (*idiotai*), as really rational. The point of the whole section is that man only thinks he is rational. He is persuaded by the appearance of rationality.

It is ironic, in view of all of this, that Aristotle should be attacked for having too rational a view of man as the object of persuasion. Yet this is one of Black's main objections to the Aristotelian rhetoric (Black, r, 118, 125 ff.). This is partly due to the historical fact that too many rhetoricians, especially since the time of Whately, have interpreted the "logical" argument as meaning real logic. Some speech courses in modern universities, in fact, actually give miniature treatments of the scientific syllogism in courses labeled "Persuasion: Argumentation." Such an interpretation of the "logical" argument is one of the real dangers of adopting the large "communication" view of rhetoric outlined above (p. 215 f).

Aristotle divided these seemingly logical arguments into three types: topics, examples, and enthymemes. He devotes Chapter 19 to the common topics, Chapter 20 to examples, and Chapters 21–25 to enthymemes.

The Topics

By "topics," Aristotle understood what might best be described in contemporary terms as stereotyped arguments. A persuader should be ready, in any situation, to draw from a set of arguments that seem plausible to the populace. The term "topic" comes from the Greek *topos,* meaning a "place." A topic is therefore a place where arguments can be found. Cope, in explaining Aristotle at this juncture, paraphrases a passage from Cicero that aptly summarizes the concept of "topic":

> As in writing, we ought to have the letters that we require to use ready at hand, and not to be obliged to hunt about for them whenever we want them, so when a case is to be argued we should have a stock of arguments all ready classified, arranged in "places" where we can make sure of finding them, and ticketed and labelled as it were in their repository, or like bottles in the bins of a cellar, so that they offer themselves to us at once as soon as they are required (Cope, i, 126, paraphrasing Cicero, *de Oratore,* II, 30, 130).

The Greek term *topoi* (plural) was literally translated into Latin, and the topics were called the *loci*. In Renaissance England they came to be called the "commonplaces." But the Renaissance meaning was subtly shifted from a kind of argument to a subject on which one could discourse. This is the usual meaning of the word "topic" today; consequently, we do not usually employ the term with the connotations of "a way to convince or prove." And indeed, some modern writers on the rhetorical topics simply construe them as subject matters of themes, not as ways of proving something. This really misses the point of the topics as a part of the logical argument.

Aristotle distinguished three kinds of topics: *special* topics peculiar to a special science, such as politics or ethics; *common* topics, universal enough to be applied to any subject matter; and *enthymeme* topics, those especially useful in serving as elements of rhetorical enthymemes (cf. Cope, i, 126–29).

The special topics are those arguments which derive from propositions about good and evil, justice and injustice, nobility and baseness, concerns of ethics and politics, or from propositions having to do with types of characters and emotions. Actually, Aristotle had treated these in Book I, Chapters 4 through 14, in which he had discussed the different kinds of rhetorical speeches, and in Book II, Chapters 11 through 17, in which he had handled the kinds of characters.

The common topics Aristotle considers in Chapter 19. They are arguments deriving from the possible and impossible, from past fact, from future fact, and from degrees of greatness or smallness. Thus, if one can argue that a man can be cured, one can also argue that he can fall ill (1392a 10); if one of two similar things is possible, so is the other (1392a 12).

The enthymeme topics are treated in Chapter 23. Twenty-eight enthymeme topics are illustrated. These include arguing from opposites, from correlative ideas, from *a fortiori,* from time, from various meanings of words, from cause and effect, among others. Aristotle illustrates the argument from *a fortiori*: "Thus it may be argued that even if the gods are not omniscient, certainly human beings are not" (1397b 12); and he similarly illustrates all of his enthymeme topics.

It may be significant that, comparatively speaking, there is relatively little scholarship on the topics in modern commentators—compared, for example, to the scholarship on the *Poetics,* the *Ethics,* or even the *Rhetoric.* This might be interpreted as negative evidence that the topics, whether of the *Topics* or of the *Rhetoric,* are not fertile frameworks for exploration or persuasion in modern times. One might be led to suspect that these frameworks are not grounded in any valid philosophical or rhetorical foundation. It is true that the topics as outlined in the *Organon* (*Topics*), are structured by the various relationships of predicate to its subject—a predicate expresses the essence of a subject, or a property of a subject, of a genus or differentia of a subject, or an accident of a subject (cf. Ross a, 57; Grote, a, 276–77, 284). And the list of enthymeme topics in the *Rhetoric,* Book II, Chapter 23, is a selection from those in the *Organon* (Ross, a, 273). It seems more difficult to establish a rationale for the common topics of Chapter 19, or to distinguish them carefully from the enthymeme topics. Ross even hypothesizes that these two sets of topics represent notes for more than one course of lectures (Ross, a, 273).

In any case, Cicero and Quintilian shifted the basic frameworks for the topics somewhat and introduced the interpretations that view topics as subjects for discourse as well as lines of argument (though some authorities find Aristotelian precedent for this). Some modern writers, attempting to teach the rhetorical topics, revert to a structure more reminiscent of the *Organon* than the *Rhetoric* (cf. Corbett, c, 97 ff,; Hughes and Duhamel, r, 255 ff.). Dudley Bailey, in "A Plea for a Modern Set of Topoi," interprets the topics as devices for organization and suggests time, space, detail and illustration, definition, logical analysis, comparison and contrast, hypothesis, and impressionism for a possible framework (Bailey, p, 115). Bailey's interpretation is an innovation in the tradition of the topics. In reality it enlarges the topics to the structural principle for an entire theory of composition or discourse.

Innovation in some sense does seem needed if something like the topics is to be retained as a device of persuasion. Very little use is made of the topics in many modern treatments of persuasion in departments of English (Corbett, c, 97 ff., and Hughes, r, 255 ff., are exceptions); in speech departments more consideration is sometimes given them (cf. Dick, t; Bitzer, a; and McBurney, p). Yet the basic notion of the topics seems very valid. Fundamentally, the topics represent an attempt to formulate the kinds of arguments which *seem plausible* to a given audience. There is, therefore, a necessary relativism in such a formulation. In discussing the *Topics*, Grote calls attention to this relativism:

> In every society there are various floating opinions and beliefs, each carrying with it a certain measure of authority, often inconsistent with each other, not the same in different societies, nor always the same even in the same society. Each youthful citizen, as he grows to manhood, imbibes these opinions and beliefs insensibly and without special or professional teaching. The stock of opinions thus transmitted would not be identical even at Athens and Sparta: the difference would still be greater, if we compared Athens with Rome, Alexandria, or Jerusalem. Such opinions all carry with them more or less of authority, and it is from them the reasonings of common life, among unscientific men, are supplied. The practice of dialectical discussion, prevalent in Athens during and before the time of Aristotle, was only a more elaborate, improved, and ingenious exhibition of this common talk, proceeding on the same premisses, but bringing them together from a greater variety of sources, handling them more clearly, and having for its purpose to convict an opponent of inconsistency. The dialecticians dwelt exclusively in the region of these received opinions; and the purpose of their debates was to prove inconsistency, or to repel the proof of inconsistency, between one opinion and another (Grote, a, 267).

It is true that Grote is speaking here of dialectic, not rhetoric. But it must not be forgotten that Aristotelian dialect was really more rhetoric than exploration—in fact, a curious hybrid of the two. Of Aristotle's three aims of dialectic, the discovery of truth is only the third and least important of the purposes of dialectic (101a 34). As Grote says very clearly: It is plain that neither the direct purpose of the debaters, nor the usual result of the debate, is to prove truth or to disprove falsehood" (Grote, a, 271). In this respect, truth is also a byproduct of rhetoric sometimes (*Rhetoric*, 1355a, 28 ff.).

Actually, Aristotle bequeathed two treatises on persuasion to western culture, the *Rhetoric* and the *Topics*. The first is persuasion by monologue and the second is persuasion by dialogue or debate. The Middle Ages understood this very clearly. Readings and lectures in the *Topics* were consistently a part of the arts program in rhetoric, not in logic. At Paris, Oxford, and Bologna, for instance, the *Topics* of Aristotle or Boëthius' commentary on it were regular alternatives to Aristotle's *Rhetoric* (Rashdall, u, I, 36; II, 457).

The practical usefulness as techniques of persuasion of the lines of argument represented by the various topics of Aristotle is a matter of some conjecture. Some of them, for instance, do not seem terribly convincing to me in our present culture. And, it is a matter of historical evidence that some of the dialectical techniques of the medieval Schoolmen, for example, were very distasteful to many Renaissance, as well as later, minds. This would seem to indicate that each age and culture must reformulate its own topics; this has not been systematically done by anyone for any culture since the time of Aristotle. Even Aristotle's framework was theoretical and intuitive, not empirically tested in the field, as it were. In other words, a speaker engaged in the business of persuading a current audience who would indiscriminately adopt Aristotle's topics in toto might run the risk of appearing to his audience as a cultural anachronism.

But the concept of the topics is a valid one. In reality, just as scientific logic has its syntactic, semantic, and pragmatic logics represented respectively in deduction, induction, and ethnologic (see above, p. 127 ff.), so persuasion has three parallel logics represented in enthymeme, example, and topics. The topics in persuasion correspond to ethnologic in science. Just as a scientist must choose methods of demonstration acceptable to the members of his culture (see above, pp. 127–28), so must the persuader exploit the kinds of rhetorical proof which his own audience will accept as plausible.

EXAMPLES

After considering the common topics in Chapter 19, Aristotle then treats examples in Chapter 20 of the second book of the *Rhetoric*. The rest of the second book is devoted to enthymemes. Example is the watered-down form which induction takes in persuasion; and enthymeme is the popularized form of deduction (Cope, i, 105). These constitute the two forms of arriving at truth and knowledge, according to Aristotle. Aristotle's treatment of example here accords with the treatment given the same topic in the *Prior Analytics*, II, Chapter 24. In the *Prior Analytics,* Aristotle restricted induction to perfect induction, and considers any generalization not from all of the particulars to be example. But Aristotle did not always so carefully distinguish example from induction (cf. Ross, a, 39–41). In any case, rhetorical example consists in using inductive forms in persuasion. "Example" here should not be interpreted to mean that the inductive generalization is always from a single instance, as our use of the term might imply.

Aristotle divided examples into historical or fictitious. The fictitious he divided into parables and fables; by parables he meant parallels taken from what could happen in real life. Fable he further subdivided into literary allusions and fables properly so-called, such as those of Æsop or Stesichorus (for these distinctions, see Cope, i, 254–55).

Aristotle concludes the chapter on example with some admonitions on when to use this method of persuasion. Although fictitious examples are easier to invent, he says, historical examples are more persuasive in political oratory (1349a 3 ff.). In addition, he favors the use of example only as a supplement to enthymeme and after the evidence of the ethymeme has been given. If examples must come first, there should be a large number of them. These admonitions are not in total accord with some other remarks of Aristotle on the same general topic. In at least five other specific instances he states that induction seems clearer, more persuasive, and more general in appeal than forms of deduction (cf. Ross, a, 38, and Cope, i, 108, for references). However, Aristotle does give prominence throughout the *Rhetoric* to the enthymeme, which he considers the heart of his rhetoric.

There is not much empirical evidence on the relative superiority of one or the other form of argument. A medieval Schoolman might well be more convinced by a neat syllogism, whereas the typical nineteenth-century positivist would probably prefer the probability of a few empirical examples. If modern advertising is any indication, example would seem to be more congenial than the regular enthymeme to the American populace today (cf. Bailey, p, 116). The advertisers use this device hundreds of times a day in the many case reports of Mrs. Weber, who found that her laundry was much whiter once she used Oxtide, or of the lumberjack who was forced to borrow a stray Cameluck. And it does not seem to make much difference if the example is fictitious or real. In the case of a much-publicized tooth-paste series of ads with factual bases reported in scientific journals, it seemed preferable to the advertisers to fictionalize the case reports.

In the rhetoric of family and neighbor life, the immediate example is probably much more compelling than would be systematic inductive statistical evidence. How many of us know whole families who will never buy a Ford because a favorite uncle two generations ago complained that he had bought a lemon. And one spoiled T-bone from a local supermarket can practically cause a meat boycott from every housewife on the same block when the word gets over the back fences. Whatever the form, historical fact, fictitious case report, fable, or literary allusion, the example is certainly one of the most potent devices of persuasion.

Enthymemes and Maxims

In the remainder of Book II, Chapter 21 through 26, Aristotle considers the enthymeme. He first treats the maxim in Chapter 21. But since the maxim is a form of the enthymeme, it will here be treated after the enthymeme proper. Though he upbraids his predecessors with lack of clarity in their discussions, Aristotle himself has left room for several interpretations of what he meant by the enthymeme (cf. Cope, i, 99 ff.; Black, r, 125, 130, for some modern versions). Putting together statements from several of his works, most authors today distinguish the enthymeme from the strict deduction by two characteristics. First, the enthymeme is based on premises that are only probable, whereas the scientific syllogism has premises which are certain (cf. Cope, i, 101–2). Secondly, the rhetorical enthymeme leaves out one or several of the parts of the strict syllogism (premises or conclusion). Much of the controversy about the nature of the enthymeme centers on which of these two distinguishing characteristics is more important especially if one is to separate the dialectical from the rhetorical enthymeme (cf. Cope, i, 103; Cope, r, II, 220–21).

Although the matter of Aristotle's meaning has its own historical importance, the issue does not seem crucial to a current theory of rhetoric. In the first place, Aristotle's dialectic is basically rhetorically oriented anyway—a rhetoric of dialogue, not a monologue, as was pointed out above. In the second place, Aristotle's concept of deduction itself must be enlarged to accommodate the much larger scope of modern logic. Aristotle's syllogism includes only a part of the logic of classes and has no provision for the logic of sentences or the logic of relations (see above, p. 118 ff.). Yet, these also may be applied to persuasive purposes to produce enthymemes. And there is no necessity for a premise in the logic of sentences to be universal at all, as Aristotle's syllogistic premises had to be. Finally, "certainty" of the absolute sort which Aristotle required of his syllogistic premises we no longer feel we have a right to expect even of the premises in scientific deductions; this also was discussed above when the issue of the "certainty" of scientific knowledge was considered.

It seems, therefore, that if the concept of the enthymeme is to be maintained, some modifications will have to be made of the traditional notion. Keeping in mind the qualifications of the preceding paragraph, it might be best to define an enthymeme as a deductive form of argument used in persuasion. This definition merely supplies the purpose, persuasion, for the kind of argument. If this definition be adopted, the level of probability and the incompleteness of the deductive form become irrelevant. In actual practice, most if not all persuasive enthymemes will operate at fairly low levels of probability. And, in actual practice, the complete deductive pattern of the argument will rarely, if ever, be entirely presented. Consequently, in practice, Aristotle's two norms are retained.

The reasons for these practical manners of presenting persuasive deductions are not difficult to divine. Presentation of a formal pattern of logic would call attention to the logic of the deduction and cause it to be scrutinized more carefully than would be desirable. Most persuasive deductions will not stand up under scrutiny. Second, by allowing the audience to fill in the missing components of a deduction, the power of suggestion is enlisted in the cause of persuasion. Examples of enthymeme used in a modern political speech will be given in the analysis of the persuasive logic of Roosevelt's "First Inaugural Address," which follows the next section.

One particular kind of enthymeme to which Aristotle devotes a full chapter is the maxim. He defines a maxim as "a statement about questions of practical conduct, courses of conduct to be chosen or avoided" (1394a 24–25). A maxim is really an enthymeme dealing with practical subjects. It is usually either a premise or a conclusion of an enthymeme. Aristotle gives this example from Euripides, "There is no man in all things free." This is a maxim, but is becomes an enthymeme, if what follows it is added: "For all are slaves of money or chance" (1394b 5 ff.).

A good deal of attention is given to the consideration of when to give the reason why a maxim is true and when not to. Proof of the maxim should normally be given if the statement appears paradoxical or if an effect of strong emotion can be conveyed by contradicting a well-known proverb, or if contradicting an accepted maxim can serve to raise the opinion of the speaker's character in the eyes of the audience. Aristotle illustrates this last point with a very apt example:

> It will raise people's opinion of our character to say, for instance, "We ought not to follow the saying that bids us treat our friends as future enemies: much better to treat our enemies as future friends (1395a 25 ff.).

Here Aristotle is again exemplifying that aspect of dialectical and rhetorical reasoning which enables it to adopt either side of an argument. Proverbs and maxims indeed often are half-truths and can be countered by other half-truths. Thus, "Early to bed, early to rise/Makes a man healthy, wealthy, and wise" might be considered in the light of the adage that talks about burning the midnight oil; and "A penny saved is a penny earned" might be contrasted with "Nothing ventured, nothing gained."

With one enlargement, Aristotle's doctrine of maxims seems very viable in this age. The maxim is very like the slogan in many respects; and the slogan is one of the most used of modern persuasive techniques; it is properly called the "rallying cry," and often has been emblazoned on banners and shields. "Delenda est Carthago," "Remember the Alamo," "54–40 or fight," "We shall overcome," "Hell no, we won't go" are examples that come to mind immediately from political history of the past and the present. Religious groups have had their slogans throughout history (Brown, t, 231). Nowhere, possibly, do we find more effective use of the slogan than in modern commercial advertising. Most firms hire brilliant young men or women to coin slogans with which their product can become identified: "Winston tastes good like a cigarette should," "I'd walk a mile for a Camel," "The pause that refreshes," "Men of distinction switch to Calvert" and so on.

The slogan, in any case, is like the maxim in that it is usually an abbreviated deductive argument. At the risk of appearing ridiculous, I might reconstruct the deduction:

You should smoke a cigarette that tastes good, as a cigarette should.
Winston tastes good like a cigarette should.
Therefore you should smoke a Winston.

The conclusion is invalid, even given the two premises; it would be difficult to give conclusive evidence for either premise; the argument is certainly in the realm of mere probability; and, of course, the complete deduction is never, never presented (except by people like me).

Some of Aristotle's final admonitions on the use of maxims are obviously not applicable to slogans. Maxims are appropriate coming from older men, he says. And he seems to restrict the range of emotions to which slogans are applicable; they are "most appropriate when working up feelings of horror and indignation in our hearers" (1395a 7). Both cautions would not seem universally applicable, especially when the concept of maxim is enlarged to that of slogan.

Information and Explanation in Persuasion

Because Aristotle lacked a theory of information to parallel his theory of science, his treatment of the informative components of persuasive discourse is only haphazard and suggestive. He completely incorporates his theory of science and of dialectic into the "logical" proofs of enthymemes, example, and topics; but he had no systematic body of information theory to incorporate into his invention, or thought elements of rhetoric. Consequently the deficiency must be noted and at least partially atoned for by a few suggestions coming from what we now possess in information theory. In other words, what happens to information when it is incorporated into a persuasive document? More specifically, what happens to the three components of information discussed in the preceding chapter: factuality, comprehensiveness, and surprise value?

To ask these questions is to suggest some obvious answers to them. Actually, the brief analysis of Alsop's column, "The Meaning of the Dead," given in the preceding chapter, is a good illustration of what happens to information in persuasion.

"Facts" in persuasion are put to work to prove a specific thesis. The facts which could do a disservice to the cause must be either concealed or minimized, and facts which tend to support the cause must be magnified. If no facts exist to support a cause which could use some facts, the speaker may fabricate them—Aristotle cynically suggests doing this only if the opponent can not check on the fabrication. The handling of "fact" in persuasion is treated in traditional rhetoric under the status "matters of facts."

When facts have been minimized or concealed or fabricated or magnified out of proportion, the result is a lack of comprehensiveness, the second component of ideal information. The omission of some facts very relevant to a discussion of the "Meaning of the Dead" in Vietnam allowed Alsop to draw his distorted conclusion. Macaulay's history, really a persuasive history, uses the same techniques. In the essay on Lord Clive's subjugation of India, the concealing of some facts, the minimizing of others, and the magnification of still others allows Macaulay to justify England's taking over of India as an act of benevolence on the part of a civilized and competent nation. No doubt some oriental despots have been incompetent and immoral, but Macaulay's generalizations can only be described as irresponsible:

> The race by whom this rich tract was peopled, enervated by a soft climate and accustomed to peaceful employments, bore the same relation to other Asiatics which the Asiatics bear to the bold and energetic children of Europe. . . . Whatever the Bengalee does, he does languidly. His favorite pursuits are sedentary. . . . There never, perhaps, existed a people so thoroughly fitted by nature and by habit for a foreign yoke.
>
> . . .Oriental despots are perhaps the worst clan of human beings; and this unhappy boy [Surajah Dowlah] was one of the worst specimens of his race.
>
> . . .[Clive] knew that he had to deal with men destitute of what in Europe is called honor. . . .
>
> The Nabob behaved with all the faithlessness of an Indian statesman. (Macaulay, 1, 47–50)

Checking on facts and checking on comprehensiveness nearly always involves going out of the text into other texts or into other aspects of the situational context. Digging up the concealed or ignored facts that would be necessary to put the history of Lord Clive into a proper perspective entails writing another history of that event or of a whole series of events. It often involves using different sources from those used by the persuader, in this case, Macaulay.

Modern propaganda analysts give great emphasis to the extratextual procedure in the detection of propaganda. Harold Lasswell and his research associates suggest eight important methods of detecting propaganda. Five of the eight have to do with viewing information embedded in a persuasive document from the proper perspective. The other three are semantic checks and will be considered in the section on "Style" below. The five methods relevant to our present discussion are defined by Lasswell as follows:

2. The Parallel Test. The content of a given channel is compared with the content of a known propaganda channel. Content is classified according to themes.

3. The Consistency Test. The consistency of a stream of propaganda with the declared propaganda aims of a party to a controversy. The aims may be official declarations or propaganda instructions.

5. The Source Test. Relatively heavy reliance upon one party to a controversy for material.

6. The Concealed Source Test. The use of one party to a controversy as a source, without disclosure.

8. The Distortion Test. Persistent modification of statements on a common topic in a direction favorable to one side of a controversy. Statements may be added, or over- or underemphasized (for example). (Lasswell 1, 177–78).

Lasswell gives examples of each of these techniques at some length and the interested reader is referred to his treatment (Lasswell, 1, 178 ff.).

Finally, of course, the effective persuader exploits the surprise value of his information to its fullest potential. This is the equivalent in journalism of the screaming headline. He may do this as journalists do by effecting a stunning beginning with its announcement or he may slowly lead up to it as the climax to a drama.

One final word upon the use of exploratory techniques in persuasion. The very existence of the examination and cross-examination in our legal system is ample evidence of the usefulness of exploratory techniques in persuasion. The structure of the legal "protections" that determine the procedures reveals the exploratory orientation of persuasive discourse. The questions are all from *one source,* the interrogating attorney; the witness is allowed only as much of an answer as the attorney allows him, sometimes a simple "yes" or "no"; the opposing attorney can intervene only to protest on parliamentary grounds, and so forth. The apparent dialogue is really a disguised monologue. Fortunately for the legal system, the opposing attorney has his rhetorical chance later. One can certainly speculate on the feasibility of two pieces of rhetoric adding up to science or real discovery.

This concludes the presentation of the logical proofs of persuasion. An analysis of a modern piece of political persuasion may help to exemplify the theoretical concepts which have been presented above.

ANALYSIS OF THE LOGIC
OF PERSUASION AS EXEMPLIFIED
IN ROOSEVELT'S "FIRST INAUGURAL ADDRESS"

The structure of this analysis will follow the structure of the theory presented above. Therefore, first the techniques of the ethical, then of the emotional, and finally of the "logical" arguments will be presented.

The Ethical Argument of Roosevelt's First Inaugural Address

Certainly if one wanted to pick a superb example of the ethical argument, one might well choose this particular speech. To understand the necessity of an efficient ethical argument in this speech, one must recall the situational context. The young president was making his first official appearance as the leader of the nation. His relative youth, his obvious handicap, the distressing circumstances of the time—all militated against an immediate acceptance of his personality as an acknowledged leader. Yet he did not have time to wait for a gradual acceptance by the people or the Congress. In effect the people and Congress had to buy the package in the week of March 4.

He met this challenge admirably and immediately. In the first several paragraphs the ethical argument is solidly established. His good character, his good sense, and his good will—the three components of the ethical argument—are each given careful attention.

To insure his credibility as a "good character" he stresses the fact that he will be "frank" and address the nation with "candor," he will tell "the truth the whole truth, frankly and boldly," he will face conditions "honestly" (all references from paragraph 1). Paragraph 3 reiterates the honesty; paragraphs 4 and 5 suggest that the preceding administration has not been either frank or bold; it has been, in fact, "unscrupulous;" paragraph 6 suggests a return to the "ancient truth;" paragraph 8 also stresses a return to reliance on "honesty, on honor, on the sacredness of obligations;" a change in "ethics" is needed (paragraph 9). The notes of frankness and honesty continue throughout the speech (paragraph 11, paragraph 13, paragraphs 16, 17). He also supports his "good character" by his consistent use of the religious Messiah image. The Republicans have been the "money changers" in the temple, but they have fled, "we may now restore that temple to the ancient truths" (paragraph 6). The religious motif recurs frequently throughout the speech and is frequently associated with the dark-light image. The "good character" is also supported by the emphasis on the "moral" nature of his pleas, especially his pleas for a return to work (the "moral stimulation of work"), his repudiation of the unscrupulous and "false" "selfishness" of the preceding administration. In fact the audience is hardly ever permitted to forget that the speaker is a very credible person, with a high sense of honesty, frankness, morality, and religion.

Second, the audience is clearly advised that the speaker is a man of practical and good sense. He must obviously be knowledgeable about the present situation and make the correct decisions as to means to achieve the end. The whole of Roosevelt's speech is a vivid exemplification of this component of the ethical argument. Above all, he establishes himself as a man of decision—and persuasion is directed to decision. The first sentence uses the word decision and the entire speech *bespeaks* a man of decision. His means are clearly foreseen: putting people to work (paragraph 10), encouraging agricultural groups and organizing relief activities (paragraph 11), controlling banking and providing for a sound currency (paragraph 12), living as good neighbors with other groups (paragraphs 14 to 16). To accomplish these he asserts the necessity of a leadership vested with near-wartime powers, and he spends nine paragraphs on this issue (paragraphs 17 to 25). It had been announced in the last two sentences of paragraph 1. It is, in fact, the largest single thesis of the speech. It is likewise strengthened by the recurrent war and army-leader image (paragraphs 10, 17, 18, 19, 20, 22).

Reinforcing this concept of a resolute leader is the categoric certainty that rings in many of his statements. We have examined this already in showing how a persuasive speech presents as certain positions that are probable and questionable. The terms used to describe his positions carry this connotation of self-confidence: "I am *certain*," "my *firm* belief," "this is no unsolvable problem." There are twenty-nine direct first-person singular pronoun references, clustered strongly at the beginning and end, and in the section on leadership. There are also fifty direct first-person plural pronoun references fairly evenly distributed throughout the speech.

Many other motifs support the "good sense" component of the ethical argument. One reiterated message is the sense of urgency which he attributes to his decisions: "the dark realities of the *moment*" (paragraph 3); "the Nation asks for action, and action *now*" (paragraph 9); "I shall seek the *immediate* assistance of the several states" (paragraph 13); "we must act and act *quickly*" (paragraph 11); "*speedy* adoption" (paragraph 21). Of course, the entire "logical" argument—maxims, enthymemes, and examples—support the "good sense" of the speaker. Some of the characteristics of his style also support this aspect of his personality. These will be examined below.

The third factor of the ethical argument is the "good will" which the speaker must project towards the audience. Roosevelt emerges as very sympathetic to the people at large by many obvious devices. His many uses of "we" clearly bridge into a camaraderie with the audience. His appeals to the emotional biases of his audience account for a goodly percentage of his good-will appeal. For, if the speaker has properly sounded the emotional sensitivities of his audience, he certainly should be able to appeal to the group.

Roosevelt seemed particularly apt at convincing Americans that he had their good at heart. The mere fact that he was elected four times would seem compelling evidence of this hypothesis. But, though his legislative and executive actions accounted for this in part, there is no doubt that much of Roosevelt's political power lay in his verbal prowess. In this particular speech, it is not difficult to extract some of this charm. Since this is heavily dependent on the emotional argument, it may be useful to consider the two together.

The Pathetic Argument of Roosevelt's First Inaugural Address

The broad emotional appeal of Roosevelt to the common man of America, an appeal which probably contributed heavily to the fixed idea in this century that the Democratic party is the party of the common man, is made up of several fairly easily discernible components.

First of all, Roosevelt appealed to his audience's nationalistic feelings as Americans. The early Roosevelt was a president with a domestic orientation. In speaking of international problems he clearly subordinates them to the domestic issues: "I favor as a practical policy the putting of first things first" (paragraph 15). This note of almost provincial chauvinism, for which he almost apologizes (paragraph 15), is established in the first paragraph and is reiterated in practically every paragraph of the speech. The concern with "my fellow Americans," "the Nation," "the temper of our people," "a stricken Nation," "our national house," the high moral sense of America nationally and internationally is certainly one of the dominant emotional motifs of the speech. And it was a concern that had to be attended to immediately. The sense of urgency discussed above was an obvious component of this appeal.

Second, the audience was as broadly American as it could be. It did not exclude the Republicans as a party. It did exclude the villains of that party, the unscrupulous leaders and moneyed bankers behind the policies responsible for the depression and the unsuccessful attempts to improve. These exclusions were not a large group. Particular segments of the American audience are singled out for early attention: people with low incomes, the "withered leaves of industrial enterprise," farmers, people who have lost their savings (paragraph 2), the unemployed and the poorly paid (paragraph 3). The unemployed are his primary concern (paragraph 10); the overtaxed population centers and the understaffed agricultural areas are his second target (paragraph 11); and finally the victims of the evils of unscrupulous banking and credit practices are his third main audience segment (paragraph 12). These three groups determine his legislative proposals.

There is a development in the emotional argument—and it is closely related to the general organization of the speech. At the outset there is considerable emphasis on what might be called the negative sides of his emotional spectrum. In the first three paragraphs attention is focused on fear, the discouraging reactions of the people out of work, of the industrialists whose factories are idle, and of the poorly paid. In the next six paragraphs (4 through 9), these passive emotions are shifted to active resentments against the engineers of the present plight, and this emotion is given strong moral justifications: these people are self-seekers, they lack vision, they are unscrupulous. Together with this moral appeal, there is also the accompanying moral appeal to the dignity of work. These moral sentiments are expressed in interesting biblical imagery. These moral sentiments, political resentments, and religious appeals are all given a feeling of immediacy.

The next three paragraphs, the three main legislative proposals, are closely related to the emotive appeals which have preceded them. After the early concern over unemployment and the sermon on the dignity and happiness resulting from work, the first proposal to put everyone back to work follows as a direct effect (paragraph 10), and after the moral resentment aroused against the villains, their punishment and corrective measures also follow directly (paragraph 12). The proposals to help farmers and to coordinate relief are also directly related to previous emotional appeals. The sense of urgency is reiterated in paragraphs 11 and 12.

The next three paragraphs relate to the international relations of America. And it is here that restricted nationalism is appealed to. Two other emotions enter in here. Just as the domestic issues have been made a matter of ethics and religion, so also are the international. America is a "good neighbor," "the neighbor who respects his obligations and respects the sanctity of his agreements in and with a world of neighbors" (paragraph 16). Along with this orientation, domestic and international behaviors will require neighborly cooperation and interdependence (paragraphs 15 and 17).

This interdependence is compared to the movement of a disciplined army and leads at once to the main concern of the next eight paragraphs: the acceptance of Roosevelt's leadership. Several crucial transitional sentences summarize all of these emotions and direct them to this major preoccupation of the last part of the speech:

> We are, I know, ready and willing to submit our lives and property to such discipline, because it makes possible a leadership which aims at a larger good. This I propose to offer, pledging that the larger purposes will bind upon us all as a sacred obligation with a unity of duty hitherto evoked only in time of armed strife (paragraph 17).

These two sentences embody many of the major emotional appeals of the speech (hope, religion, morality, nationalism, and urgency).

The eight following paragraphs are not as overtly emotional as the preceding sections. But to prepare the audience for his request for extraordinary executive powers, Roosevelt again appeals to their national pride in history and stresses the adaptability of the Constitution (paragraph 19). He underscores the unprecedented nature of the tasks facing him and then uses the near threat of executive war power (paragraph 22). In the meantime he emphasizes the moral nature of the reasons that motivate him in these requests:

> I am prepared under my constitutional duty to recommend the measures that a stricken Nation in the midst of a stricken world may require....
> ...I shall not evade the clear course of duty that will then confront me....
> For the trust reposed in me I will return the courage and the devotion that befit the time. I can do no less. (paragraphs 21 to 23)

The moral, patriotic, and religious sentiments of his audience he here demands of himself. The same emotions occur in the next paragraph. The speech ends in a sense of humility with a prayer (paragraphs 25 to 26).

Summarily, it can be seen that each section of the speech has its own emotional chords, with certain basic recurrences. A more thorough analysis would reveal many other subtle ploys of emotional appeal. Those analyzed here serve our present purpose: Roosevelt was a sensitive practitioner of the pathetic argument.

The "Logical" Argument

A comprehensive analysis of Roosevelt's quasi-rational appeals in this speech would require a large chapter in a dissertation. But some highlights may help to concretize the theoretical points made above. I shall give some instances of his use of topics, of examples, of enthymemes, and of maxims. Of these four, possibly the most striking is Roosevelt's use of maxims and slogans. Again, paragraph 1 is a rich source: "This is preeminently the time to speak the truth, the whole truth, frankly and boldly." An interesting technique of Roosevelt is exemplified here. He avoids the effect of mere hackneyed expression by a personal adaptation and slight rephrasing of the traditional maxim. He does this elsewhere: "I favor as a practical policy the putting of first things first" (paragraph 14); "They have no vision, and when there is no vision the people perish" (paragraph 5); "Nature still offers her bounty and human efforts have multiplied it" (paragraph 4); "Our true destiny is not to be ministered unto but to minister to ourselves and to our fellow men" (paragraph 8). Occasionally, the homely maxim is balanced by an unfolklike, even sophisticated diction: "Plenty is at our doorstep, but a generous use of it languishes in the very sight of the supply" (paragraph 4). When the traditional maxim is not existent, Roosevelt coins one that sounds every bit as genuine as the historical article: "the only thing we have to fear is fear itself" (paragraph 1); "happiness lies not in the mere possession of money" (paragraph 7).

The analysis of topics, examples, and enthymemes is possibly better handled as a unit since in the speech the three are very closely linked. To illustrate these I shall take a careful look at some of the arguments in the early paragraphs. Paragraph 1 draws three similar logical inferences:

1. a. Americans expect candor of me;
   b. therefore I shall speak the truth.
2. a. America has always endured and prospered and will endure and prosper.
   b. Therefore we need not shrink from facing conditions today.
3. a. In every dark hour, Americans have supported frank and vigorous leaders;
   b. therefore, I know you will support me in these critical days.

The pattern of argument is similar in each instance. First, an inductive generalization is made, and then an inference is deduced from the generalization. The generalizations concern Americans' attitude to him, America's continued prosperity, and America's support of leadership in critical times. All of these are inductions from historical evidence which he does not bother to adduce (and which would almost be impossible to adduce). The generalizations are, therefore, only probable, at best. Next from the stated inductive generalization, another inductive leap must be made before the conclusions can be related to the premises. In the first case there must be something like the following premise understood: "I give Americans what they expect," so that the conclusion can follow at all. In the second and third cases, once the generalizations about America's past endurance and leadership attitudes have been made, there must also be inductive extrapolations to the present and future; in the second case this generalization is expressed "this...Nation will endure...will revive and will prosper." In the third case, the extrapolation to the present and future is not expressed; it might have been, "Americans will always support vigorous leadership in critical times." From these premises, some implied, some expressed, all dubious, the deductive inferences are then drawn: therefore I shall speak the truth, therefore we need not shrink, therefore you will support the present leadership.

The convincing power of the second and third arguments depends upon using the evidence of the past to prove the possibility and probability of the future. This is one of Aristotle's common topics, "future fact" (1393a 1 ff.). It is a common argument of Roosevelt in this speech (paragraph 6, paragraph 15, esp. paragraph 19). It is also significant and typical of persuasive logic that, when expedient, the opposite argument can be used. And Roosevelt employs the opposite topic in paragraph 5. There, instead of arguing that the past policies of the nation should be maintained in order to bring about prosperity, he argues that efforts "cast in the pattern of an outworn tradition" should not be pursued—vision and new approaches are needed. This is one of Aristotle's enthymeme topics: sometimes, because of different circumstances, men must reverse previous choices (1399b 13 ff.).

One other deductive inference of considerable importance is drawn in paragraph 1. Since he has already demonstrated by implicit historical evidence and inductive generalization that the country will revive and prosper and that we need not be afraid of facing conditions today, therefore the only thing we have to fear is fear itself. Here the logic might be reconstructed somewhat as follows: Fear in the face of conditions is either really justified or only an imaginary, unjustified fear. Since it is not really justified, we must only worry about an imaginary, unjustified fear. In this form, the argument is a rhetorical example of the "modus tollendo ponens," considered in the logic of sentences: Either p or q is true; p is not true, therefore q is true. Of course its truth validity depends upon the reasons for asserting that the fear is not really justified; and these reasons are at best probable. The same pattern of argument from "modus tollendo ponens" is also employed in paragraphs 20 and 22, where the leadership powers are under discussion: Either normal or temporary abnormal or executive war powers will be needed for the present situation. And he considers each in turn. There are other logical subtleties of paragraph 1, but these are some of the major inferences in it. Their analysis indicates the typical operation of persuasive logic.

Compared to paragraph 1, the logic of paragraph 2 is relatively simple. Basically, it consists of a series of inductive generalizations. The first sentence is transitional. The second sentence states a generalization about the difficulties: they are only material problems. The evidence for this generalization comes in the following long sentence, which itself is a series of low-level generalizations about values, taxes, payability, government income shortage, money freezings, industrial inactivity, lack of farm markets, and losses of savings. The structure of the paragraph is, therefore, that of an inverted induction, the kind analyzed in Toynbee's chapter. The real logical validity of the generalization that the problems of the country are only material would depend upon the comprehensiveness of the list of problems and the actual mere materiality of all of them. Both issues could be contested. Roosevelt himself, after attacking in several paragraphs the immorality of the bankers and money lenders, concludes in paragraph 9 that the problem is a matter of ethics—though not totally. It might be irreverently asked if matters of ethics are merely material matters. In paragraph 3, further inductive generalizations are made; paragraph 4 is quite similar, though there are complications which I shall not go into. Paragraph 5 has already been referred to above, and there are also some large generalizations about the generation of self-seekers with no vision.

The next paragraph is particularly interesting, for its basis is several arguments from analogy, and the analogies are both alluded to only implicitly. One analogy compares the money changers to the money lenders whom Christ chased from the temple, and by implication compares Roosevelt to Christ the savior and restorer:

$$\frac{Christ}{Jewish\ money\ lenders} = \frac{Roosevelt}{bankers\ and\ creditors}$$

Like most of the deductive premises in the speech, this relationship would be very difficult to prove. But it has its plausible aspects: Roosevelt had just defeated the "money" party at the polls, and, in a sense, was beginning his public ministry in a much more important role than his earlier ones, just as Jesus began his public ministry by the chasing of the money changers from the temple. From the moral and religious connotations of this equivalent relationship, Roosevelt then draws an inference: his restoration will be successful in the measure of its spirituality, just as Jesus' restoration was. Again the reasoning is based on an analogy, along with a probability prediction based on a variable induction (degree, not attribute).

The Organization of Persuasive Discourse

Some General Considerations

The term "organization" of persuasive discourse can be ambiguous. It can mean: what are the processes which the mind of the speaker must go through in the preparation, composition, and delivery of his speech? Or it can also mean: what are the parts of the speech itself as it finally appears as the text of an oral or a written discourse? Organization can therefore mean organization of the whole process of persuading or only organization of the actual text. Giving "organization" the former meaning, the stages of the process of persuading were traditionally considered to be five: invention, disposition or arrangement, style, memory, and delivery—the Latin terms were: *inventio, dispositio, elocutio, memoria,* and *pronuntiatio* (on these cf. Irwin, c). After discussing the nature and kinds of rhetoric, Aristotle devotes some attention to all of these except memory, although his treatment of delivery is very slight. Actually Aristotle's treatment of arrangement follows his chapters on style, but the usual framework is followed here.

By "invention," traditional rhetoricians understood the thought processes of the techniques of rhetorical proof (Aristotle's term *dianoia* means "by means of thought"). The other four terms hardly need explanation. These divisions are, in fact, the structuring principle of each chapter of the present work; for each chapter is divided into considerations of the nature of the kind of discourse, its "logical" processes of thought (corresponding to invention), its organization or arrangement, and its style. Memory and delivery are not considered here—though a full theory of persuasive discourse and literary discourse, at least, would devote some attention to delivery especially. However, in the overall theory of this work, these are more properly the concerns of the arts and media of discourse than of the particular aims in question.

Under the present heading of this chapter, "organization" has the second meaning mentioned above: the structure of the parts of the actual text. The rhetorical tradition was also quite explicit on this topic. Any respectable rhetorical speech was supposed to incorporate the following parts: entrance, narration, proposition, division, confirmation, confutation, and conclusion (cf. Cicero, d, 11, 19, 80; o, 35, 122). Most of these terms seem self-explanatory: entrance meant introducing the topic; narration meant a recital of the circumstances that are required to understand the points at issue; proposition meant specifically stating the speaker's stand on the issue; division meant outlining the points the speaker is going to prove; confirmation meant the body of the proofs for the speaker's thesis; confutation meant the destruction of the opponent's arguments; and conclusion meant the review and emotional exhortation (cf. Cope, i, 332 ff.).

Isocrates and pre-Aristotelian rhetoricians usually had only four divisions: introduction, narration, proofs, and epilogue (cf. Cope, i, 331). Aristotle argues that there are actually only two really necessary: "A speech has two parts. You must state your case, and you must prove it" (1414a 30). Even the proof may sometimes be omitted, he remarks, for there can be no "epilogue to an argument" in ceremonial oratory if there has been no argument (1414b 1). All other divisions of a speech are dependent upon the nature of a given kind of topic or audience. Modern advertising would probably concur with Aristotle; certainly terms like "narration," "confirmation," and "confutation" are not always, at least superficially, a part of a thirty-second television ad or a political billboard. In Austin, in 1968 before Johnson had withdrawn from the presidential race, on my way to school I drove by three immense black billboards in different parts of the city, and each billboard had only three words in large white letters, "Bring Lyndon Home." In this case there seems to be only a statement of thesis in the actual text. Despite this reduction to essentials, Aristotle does give consideration to most of the traditional divisions of organization and accepts them as useful notions in some circumstances.

Later treatments of organization or "arrangement" differ somewhat from Aristotle's. Latin rhetoricians generally placed arrangement before style in the rhetorical process. The eighteenth- and nineteenth-century rhetoricians often fused arrangement with invention. Campbell, Blair, and

Whately followed this procedure—Blair, for example, calls this fusion "management" (cf. Ehninger, c, 366).

Modern propaganda and advertising do not at first glance seem to correlate very closely with Aristotle's framework. Brown, attempting to summarize the structure of the Chinese brainwashing process, includes the following steps: stripping of identity, establishment of guilt, self-betrayal, period of lenience and opportunity, confession, channelling of guilt to a repudiation of former ideology, reeducation to the people's viewpoint (Brown, t, 278 ff.). The concerns of advertising texts often seem quite removed from the concerns of traditional rhetoric. Generally there is a chapter or so on buying motives and stimulation of desire, on copy-writing, on slogans and labels, on layout, and on media choice and problems. Admittedly, the brainwashing process does not represent the structure of a single text—supposedly a good many. And the advertising concerns overlap in part with "organization" viewed as the whole rhetorical process of invention, arrangement, style, and delivery. Yet upon closer analysis, such formulations as these and others can be shown to be not as divergent from traditional rhetoric as they seem at first. Thus Brown's summary of the structure of Russian brainwashing includes these five steps: the disorientation and disillusion, the interrogation, the rationalization, and the exploitation (Brown, t, 286). These can, not unfairly, be paralleled to: narration and confutation, interrogation, confirmation, and peroration (or conclusion) —Aristotle included a chapter on interrogation (Book III, Ch. 18). Brown's sequence is different, but the components are decidedly similar. Further, Brown's sequence for Russian brainwashing is not too dissimilar from that for the Chinese. By way of further illustration, take these four steps of the advertising process outlined by Sandage: arouse attention, intensify desire, inspire belief, motivate buying action. Again, not unfairly, these can easily be translated: narration, pathetic argument, logical argument, peroration. The equivalence of entrance and narration with arousing attention will be justified below.

In consequence, it might be concluded that, with some adaptation of the traditional notions and with some reservations about their sequence, much can be retained from classical arrangement patterns in persuasion. The ultimate danger, the Achilles heel of classical rhetoric, is to insist on a rigid formula which must be adhered to. Rhetoric, more even than literature or science, has too often attempted to codify its useful conventions into hard and fast rules. The treatment of letters in the late Middle Ages and after the Renaissance is a good example. From an intelligent set of notions, the persuasive letter descended to a code of rules, and the production of treatises on letterwriting, once a common employment of the chief humanists (e.g., Erasmus), has descended to hands incapable of speculation (La Drière l, 353).

Persuasion, in practice, is not committed to any order. Just as exploratory discourse is subject to the intuitive jumps, flashbacks, and revisions of the associative mind, so persuasion must inevitably be subject to the patterns contingent upon the speaker's on the spot analysis of the auditors' reactions. In the stage of delivery a prepared pattern may have to dissolve under the exigencies of the moment, and a seeming but successful chaos may result, as far as organization is concerned. It may defy analysis only because the human beings which condition it also defy analysis at times. Some brief considerations on each of the parts of the organization may show how a more liberal interpretation of some traditional concepts can remove them from the historical freezer, defrost them, and make them palatable to the modern persuader.

The Entrance and Narration

Terms other than "entrance" have been used for this part of a speech: exordium, proem or proemium, or prologue. Aristotle compares the entrances to prologues in poetry or preludes in music. He then devotes much of his attention in the early and later parts of the chapter (III, 14) to the kinds of entrances advisable in his three main types of rhetoric—ceremonial, judicial, and political.

The middle section of the chapter is possibly most relevant to our present purposes. Here he dwells on two main points. The first is the distinctive function of the entrance: to introduce the subject and make clear the end and object of the speech (1415a). When not necessary, it should be dispensed with. The second topic is the matter of securing or distracting the attention of the audience. Although he considers this secondary to the main function of the entrance, he devotes considerably more space to it (1415a ff.). Later writers made subdivisions of the qualities of the hearer: he should be kindly disposed, docile, and attentive (cf. Cope, r, 171). To get this attention Aristotle says, in Cope's paraphrase:

> The things to which the audience is most *inclined* to listen are things great (momentous, important), things of special interest (to the hearers themselves), things wonderful (surprising), and things pleasant (to hear; either in themselves, or their associations); and therefore the speaker should always try to produce the impression (...in his hearers' minds) that things of such kind are his subject (Cope, r, III, 172, paraphrasing 1415b ff.).

"Great, personally interesting, wonderful, surprising, pleasant" could certainly serve as recipes for the attention-arousing gimmicks of modern advertising and propaganda. Of course, arousing attention is much more an issue for the makers of modern billboards or newspaper ads than for a speaker who already has the microphone or is standing on an elevated platform addressing a captive audience. Edwin W. Ebel, then marketing director for General Foods Corporation, once calculated that the members of a typical New York family in an average day were exposed to 1518 ads from newspapers, magazines, bus and subway posters, and radio and television commercials (cf. Sandage, a, 242). To detach itself from this continual stream, an ad must have some device to attract attention to itself.

Sometimes, in modern media, the attention gimmicks are outside the text. Thus, the sponsors of Gillette use sports to get the attention of their audience, and try to hold this attention between innings or in time-outs. Liquor advertisers in the Austin paper also prefer the sports section. Indeed, a good deal of thought goes into the time of day or evening, the kind of program, the previous and following ads as attention arousers or sustainers. Similarly, the situational context, the circumstances of time and place, are crucial to many a political announcement or religious exhortation. In any case, it is clear that there is no great divergence from the thinking of Aristotle and that of modern advertising concerning the importance of arousing attention early in the persuasive process.

The treatment of narration in Chapter 16 of the *Rhetoric* is almost totally devoted to narration in ceremonial and judicial oratory. "Narration" here means the recital of the background facts necessary to understand the issue. Given the kinds of considerations which can enter into the narrations of the three types of speeches, Aristotle makes two other interesting points: the use of narrative to build up the ethical argument and to introduce the emotional appeal. The use of the narrative to embody the ethical argument is returned to in three separate paragraphs of the chapter (1417a 2 ff., 1417a 16 ff., and 1417b 6 ff.). It is the point to which most space is devoted in the chapter. Secondly, the narration is the place to work in the emotional appeal (1417a 36 ff.).

The different emphases in the treatment of narration among the Latin writers came about because of the almost exclusive orientation to legal oratory. Both Cicero and Quintilian here treat the question of the rhetorical status—the kind of question at issue before the court. It might be a matter of fact: Did such a thing happen or not? It might be a matter of definition: What class of crime is this action? It might be a matter of quality or value: Is this act desirable or unjust or useful or preferable to some other act? These three kinds of issues were accepted by both Cicero and Quintilian as exhaustive, though both considered and eventually rejected other divisions (cf. Cicero, *Orator*, XXXIV, 121; *de Oratore*, III, 29; Quintilian, *Inst. Orat.*, III, 6). These three divisions have a close parallel to the modes of discourse of this book, as briefly presented in Chapter 1, pp. 35–37 (they form the subject of the forthcoming Volume II of *A Theory of Discourse*).

For if "fact" be subdivided into narrative and descriptive statements, and matters of definition be regarded as problems of classification, and matters of quality be regarded as issues of value judgments, then there is an exact parallel to the modes of discourse as developed in my theory of modes. And, these classifications do seem to exhaust the kinds of rhetorical and scientific issues that can be raised. That these classifications are the kinds of scientific assertions that can be made was shown in the section on scientific propositions (see p. 80 ff.).

At any rate, the purpose of the narration, as seen by Cicero and Quintilian, was basically to call careful attention to the specific issue at hand. They also included the ethical argument and the beginning of the emotional appeal. All three of these concerns are essentially questions of arousing attention: to the specific issue at hand, to the speaker as a man of credibility on this issue, and to the interest which the audience has at stake in the matter in question. It is in this sense that the narration of classical rhetoric can be regarded as equivalent to the attention-arousing and stimulation-of-desire stages in the advertising process.

Once the issue has been settled, the speaker traditionally was supposed to announce his stand on the matter at hand, to enunciate clearly what he intended to prove in the ensuing speech; this was called the "thesis." And he might find it helpful to outline to his audience the various steps of his proof: this was called the "division." The thesis therefore meant the proposition which was to be proved. In rhetoric, dialectic, and logic it was distinguished from the "hypothesis," a proposition or principle which was assumed or taken for granted as not needing proof and from which inferences could be drawn.[3]

The classical thesis has much in common with what advertisers call the "headline." It is the focal statement of the advertisement and should occupy a very prominent place in the layout (cf. Dirksen, a, 106–9). In discourse, however, there are circumstances in which taking a stand on the issue may profitably be postponed until after the evidence has been given. This, in effect, gives the persuasion the appearance of an honest exploration. Many lawyers, of course, use this stratagem in their interrogations. The discussion of whether thesis should precede or follow the evidence is closely related to the next topic, the presentation of arguments.

The Proofs:
Confirmation and Confutation

After the narration, classical rhetoric followed up by the presentation of the body of the speech, the arguments for and against the thesis.

---

[3] Aristotle in the *Rhetoric* uses the term prothesis at this point. It is roughly equivalent to the *problema* in dialectic (cf. Cope, i, 333).

In advertising, an intermediate step usually intervenes: the problem of "layout." This involves the total design to be given to the advertising material, the placement of headline, illustrations, and pictures, the color, the balance of the parts, and so on.

Most of these considerations are the business of artists or printers, not writers of discourse, and are not properly the concern of this book, which has chosen to abstract the issues peculiar to the aims of discourse. Such matters as print size and font, the most effective magazines or radio programs, and placement in the magazine are the province of the arts and media of discourse. But they are also clearly in the province of the persuader, though they will not be considered here.[4] This abstraction from the concerns of arts and media is an apt illustration of the fallacious concept that discourse is autonomous and can be effectively analyzed apart from its situational context. Persuasive discourse, more than referential and literary discourse, is intimately an organic part of its situational context—and this context is presented by the entire layout, by the position in the magazine or time slot on the radio program.

The important point in all layout concerns is that the design of the entire advertisement be functionally related to the sales motif. There is a real danger of the art becoming an end in itself and providing not persuasion but entertainment. A prominent commercial artist, Fred Ludekens, makes this point in an interesting article appropriately entitled "A Plague on Art for Art's Sake" (*Advertising Age,* Nov. 11, 1957, pp. 109–11).

However, let us return to the main charge of this section, the organization of the proofs. Insofar as the proofs are actually logical or seemingly so, the organizational patterns which are available to the persuader, if he wishes a logical or seemingly logical sequence, will be those already handled in the section of the preceding chapter devoted to the organization of logical discourse. These were the deductive, the inverted deductive, the inductive, and the inverted inductive patterns. Of course there are also available to him the informative and exploratory organization patterns, both readily subsumed into persuasion. But logical sequences are not the only kinds of sequences available. There are also sequences based on the *modes,* not the aims. These narrative, classificatory, descriptive, and evaluative kinds of organization are to be treated in Volume II, *The Modes of Discourse.* And as far as organization is concerned, these modal patterns are at least as important as the logical patterns.

Given these preliminary reservations, several specifically "persuasive" concerns still remain. The first of these has to do with the order of presentation of the thesis. Should the thesis be led up to by preparatory

---

[4] The reader who is interested can refer to any textbook on advertising or journalism. For some fascinating analyses relating picture and illustration to copy, the student is referred to McLuhan, m, 70, 72, 81. For a psychological analysis of the visual process of ad perception, cf. Dirksen, a, 177.

presentation of the evidence? Or should the thesis be announced first and then established? The first is called the climax, the second the anticlimax order. A variation of this issue is to interpret "climax" as the presentation of the weakest arguments first and the strongest arguments last, and to interpret "anticlimax" in the opposite fashion. What little experimental evidence that does exist on this matter seems inconclusive, sometimes even contradictory (Thompson, q, 68 ff.; Hovland, c, 112 ff.). Certainly there seems to be a gain in dramatic effect and seeming objectivity by using a climax order. But the anticlimax order does let the listener know exactly what the evidence is adding up to. Hovland concludes his discussion of this topic with the tentative propositions: "that climax order will be favored on issues with which the audience is familiar and where deep concern is felt, but that anticlimax order will be favored on unfamiliar topics and with uninterested audiences" (Hovland, c, 120).

A second concern given much attention in both traditional and modern treatments has to do with the placement and relative importance of arguments that prove one's own position and arguments that destroy the opponent's position. The first were usually called the "confirmation" and the second the "refutation" or "confutation." Aristotle does not consider the refutation a necessary part of the organization, although it may be important in special situations. Quintilian disagrees with Aristotle on this matter (cf. Cope, i, 334, n. 2). Certainly, at least implicitly, there must be some refutation of the opponent's position, for the fact that persuasion is necessary at all must mean that there was an initial disagreement on the issue, as Kenneth Burke properly maintains. But whether or not specific attention should be given to them is a disputed matter. Some rhetoricians say that if the opponent's arguments are strong, they might be best ignored. Quintilian highly disapproves of this tactic, "Nothing could be more easy, except perhaps to throw up the case altogether," and "It is surely the worst art to admit the badness of the case by keeping silence" (i, IV, ii, 66).

Some studies in modern propaganda analysis, however, disagree with Quintilian. Brown maintains, for example, that one of the significant failures in German propaganda in World War I was the overemphasis on the negative:

> ...its [German propaganda] worst failing was that it allowed itself to be constantly on the defensive, expending most of its energies in announcing that Allied propaganda was both untrue and unfair and making laboured attempts to correct what were regarded as false impressions. *This broke one of the first rules of the propagandist, which is that the message must always be positive, never negative* (Brown, t, 89, my italics; cf. also 96).

It is one thing to make the message negative, quite another to devote some time to considering the arguments of one's opponents. Traditional rhetoric and modern political propaganda often tend to this second alternative. Modern advertising, on the other hand, usually ignores the claims of specific competitors, and has even made an ethical issue of this during some periods of its brief history. "Knocking copy," as it is called, was much more common sixty years ago in newspapers than in the recent past. However, auto rentals, toothpaste, and automobile advertisements in the past few years have betrayed a tendency to return to the confutation and to mention by unmistakable signs or even by name specific competitors (Ford, Crest, and Hertz have been singled out by their competitors), and the tendency can also be seen in England (Harris, a, 172). Generally, however, "positive" ads predominate. In a study of *The 100 Greatest Advertisements,* J. L. Watkins includes only 29 "negative" approach ads (cited in Sandage, a 295). Though some kinds of political propaganda tend almost wholly to the positive, other forms admit the usefulness of the negative approach. The projection of guilt, the exploitation of weakness, and the undermining of previous commitments are recognized techniques in much modern revolutionary propaganda and brainwashing (see Lasswell, p, 322, 324; Brown, t, 278 ff., 286 ff.). Harold Lasswell, who devoted immense personal and group resources for many years to the analysis of war propaganda, puts first in the list of the major objectives of war propaganda the mobilization of hate for the enemy (pr, 190). Part of this mobilization must sometimes take the form of specific answers to enemy propaganda; merely ignoring it or flatly denying it is often harmful (Lasswell, pr, 204). Hovland summarizes the conclusions of some experimental evidence on the matter of presenting one or both sides of the question. If the audience seems generally opposed to the speaker's stand, then both sides ought to be presented. If the audience is of some sophistication, then both sides should be presented. If there is a likelihood of subsequent exposure to the opponent's position, then both sides should be presented (Hovland, o, 107 ff.).

The organizational problem of when to present the positive and the negative proofs is a function of several important variables. Everything else being equal, the question can be raised: Is the listener more impressed by the arguments he hears first or by the arguments he hears last? F. H. Lund, on the basis of some experimental evidence, proposed his "law of primacy" in persuasion; and some further research seems to support his law (cf. Hovland, c, 121). Other research seems to support a "law of recency": the hearer is most impressed with the final arguments (cf. Hovland, c, 121 f., Thompson, q, 70). The inconclusive nature of the evidence should at least bring other variables into consideration.

Aristotle argues that in general the first speaker should put his own arguments first. But if the opponent has preceded you, then you should first attack his points in order to prepare the audience for your own (1418b 9 ff.). Hovland considers several other factors. Thus women and less-educated people seem more impressed by primacy. Men, especially educated men, seem not to be materially affected by either primacy or recency in the order of presentation (Hovland, o, 33–62).

The Conclusion

The last chapter of Aristotle's *Rhetoric* is devoted to the conclusion, or epilogue, recapitulation, peroration, as it has been variously called. Aristotle advises that it should do four things: reassert the ethical argument, emphasize the importance of the logical proofs established, appeal to the emotions of the audience, and finally, pass in review the main issues that have been discussed. The components of the conclusion are obviously derived from the components of the communications process. With minor variations, these are the same components considered by later rhetoricians (cf. Cope, i, 367). Cicero and Quintilian stress the emotional appeal more than Aristotle.

A few reservations about the doctrine of classical rhetoric are made by some modern authors. It is probably true that, especially for less intelligent readers, the conclusion must be hammered home, lest they miss the point of the speech (Hovland, c, 100–101). And when the issue is not particularly personal, driving home the conclusion in an explicit manner may be helpful (Hovland, c, 104). But if the readers or listeners are more intelligent, or if the audience has been suspicious and fearful of being trapped, or if the issue is a very personal one, there are occasions when an indirect and toned-down conclusion can be more effective (Hovland, c, 100 ff.).

Analysis of the Organization of Roosevelt's First Inaugural Address

In many respects, Roosevelt's *First Inaugural Address* can almost be said to exemplify the patterns of organization which a textbook on persuasion might recommend, and the writer of the text could well have been Aristotle, Cicero, or Quintilian. It is not at all Procrustean to see four basic divisions in the speech: the exordium or introduction (paragraph 1), the narration (paragraphs 2 to 3), the confutation (paragraphs 4 to 6), the confirmation (paragraphs 7 to 22), and the peroration (paragraphs 23 to 26). The details of this organization can be seen in the following outline, in which the Arabic numbers represent the actual numeration of the paragraphs as given in the text as it was reproduced above.

I INTRODUCTION
1. Time for candor and truth; no need to fear: America's leaders have always met crises.

II NARRATION
2. Material problems: shrunken values, rising taxes; falling ability to pay; less government income; frozen finance, industry and farming; lost savings.
3. More problems: starvation and inadequate salaries.

III CONFUTATION
4. Failure due not to lack of resources but to incompetent and stubborn management.
5. Outworn traditions no longer successful.
6. Time for repudiation of these values and restoration based on moral principles.

IV CONFIRMATION

A *Moral and Economic Bases of the Proposed Program*
7. Reassertion of moral value of work and altruism.
8. Reassertion of confidence in leadership based on honesty, honor, and unselfish performance.
9. Not ethics alone, but action.

B *Domestic Aspects of the Program*
10. Putting people to work.
11. Redistribution of urban and agrarian populations; relief, transportation, and communication measures.
12. Financial and banking reforms.
13. Urgency of these measures.

C *International Aspects of the Program*
14. Secondary nature of these concerns.
15. Not a selfish nationalism.
16. "Good neighbor" policy.

D *Leadership Demanded by the Program*
17. The discipline and sacrifice of the program require a leadership similar to that of an army.
18. His willingness to accept this leadership.
19. Such leadership not unconstitutional.
20. Normal or temporary deviations from normal executive authority should suffice.
21. Recommendations under constitutional authority.
22. If not enough, request for war-like executive authority will be made.

V CONCLUSION
23. Promise of return in courage and devotion.
24. Recapitulation of unity, moral values.

25. Recapitulation of trust in democracy and mandate for leadership.
26. Prayer for blessing of God.

It seems clear that the main functions of the introduction were to establish the ethical argument and to lay the grounds for the emotional appeal. Both of these facets of the introduction have been referred to already in the examination of the ethical and pathetic arguments. The ethical argument is particularly important in this speech, for one of the main issues of the speech is the appeal to the country to trust the leadership of the speaker in the months ahead. In this sense, the ethical argument becomes one of the basic constituents of the thesis itself.

The thesis, as a specific formula, is not a part of the introduction. The leadership component is implicitly expressed at the end of paragraph 1: "I am convinced that you will again give that support to leadership in these critical days." But this is not an explicit statement of the thesis; nor is the second component of the thesis any more explicit at the outset. References to temple restoration, immediate action, and the like are quite indeterminate. Actually both components of the thesis are led up to by a climax, rather than an anticlimax, order. The real statement of the program part of the thesis occurs only after the details of the domestic program have been sketched:

> These are the lines of attack. I shall presently urge upon a new Congress, in special session, detailed measures for their fulfillment, and I shall seek the immediate assistance of the several States (paragraph 13).

Similarly, the possible necessity of a departure from the conventions of normal executive leadership is announced only after careful preparation, and the probability is minimized. Yet the thesis comes through clearly; if necessary:

> . . .I shall ask the Congress for the one remaining instrument to meet the crisis—broad executive power, as great as the power that would be given to me if we were in fact invaded by a foreign foe (paragraph 22).

In both cases the approach to the thesis has been climactic, even dramatic. Other aspects of the organization might profitably be examined: the restraint and conciseness of the narration, the fact that the confutation precedes the confirmation, the overlap in pagaraphs 7 and 8 of the confutation with the ground principles of the confirmation, the heavy emphasis in the confirmation on the leadership component (six paragraphs) as compared to the actual details of the domestic program (three paragraphs), the insertion of three paragraphs minimizing international problems between the two major components of the development of his thesis, and the seeming (though not real) irrelevance of the religious conclusion. Enough has been said, it is hoped, to show the relevance of the organizational techniques of persuasion to a brilliant example of political rhetoric.

The Style of Persuasive Discourse

Introduction
and Historical Survey

The complaints about a lack of reference material which were expressed at the beginning of the sections on scientific, informative, and exploratory discourse can certainly not be made about persuasive discourse. If anything, the writer on persuasive style is inundated by a mass of past and current discussions of rhetorical style. As we have seen, rhetoric is so obviously a matter of style that a whole school of rhetoricians has reduced rhetoric to style. But if the preceding sections of this chapter have denied the reduction of rhetoric to style, they have not, it is hoped, given the impression that style is not an important concern of rhetoric. Nor must this separation of treatment of style from invention and organization give the impression that style is an artificial imposition of form upon matter. It must be granted that some traditional treatments of style do give that impression. Speaking of this tendency among some traditional rhetoricians, W. K. Wimsatt has noted that if one arbitrarily separates form from matter, there will remain "an irreducible something that is superficial, a kind of scum—which they call style" (quoted in Lasswell, 1, 39). On the contrary, style in persuasion is an immediate corollary of the nature, logic, and organizational components of persuasive discourse. And to speak of certain general characteristics of a persuasive style is as valid as to speak of the characteristics of scientific or literary styles. Walker Gibson has recently attempted this distinction in very much the same framework as the author. His book *Tough, Sweet and Stuffy,* is, he says, a book about I–talk, you–talk, and it–talk. He equates these to literary, advertising, and scientific discourse, and his entire book is a description of these styles.

Yet, despite the abundance of material on something like "the characteristics of persuasive discourse," it remains true that much of what is said about rhetorical style is intuitive and speculative (Lasswell, 1, 44 ff.). This is particularly true of the treatment of style in classical rhetoric. This treatment usually referred the problems of style under the four virtues of style, as they were called. These four are found in Aristotle and are often translated: clarity, dignity, propriety, and correctness. Although Aristotle considers the four virtues, he does not carefully structure his treatment of style by them and often considers several in the same chapter. Later writers in the tradition used the four virtues as the main heads for their discussions. Clarity obviously has to do with the reality or subject—the matter being talked about. Propriety has to do with adaptation to the style of a particular audience involved. Dignity is concerned with the author's ability to produce a good impression by his style (Roberts translates this virtue as "impressiveness"). Correctness is a matter of following the rules of the language involved. It seems clear, therefore, that the four virtues of style are drawn from the components of the triangle.

Each of these four virtues spawned important doctrines in the history of style. Under clarity, Aristotle considered such notions as the use of natural language and the use of metaphors. Clarity has always been given a high place in the rhetorical tradition. In fact, at some time in the tradition, clarity almost preempted all other considerations in style, not only for persuasion but for all kinds of discourse. This is probably most true in the period dominated by Ramus and in modern speech textbooks.[5] In Descartes, clarity became not only a stylistic but a philosophic norm, on which he erects his *Discourse on Methods;* and Wittgenstein takes a similar stand in the beginning of his *Tractatus:*

> The whole sense of this book might be summed up in the following words: what can be said at all can be said *clearly,* and what we cannot talk about we must pass over in silence (t, 3, my italics, cf. also 51).

In Tolstoy, clarity becomes a matter of ethics, so that for him "the unintelligibility of Baudelaire was almost the same thing as his immorality" (Wimsatt, e, 10).

The virtue of dignity or impressiveness was a complement to the virtue of clarity. But whereas clarity stressed the use of ordinary and natural language, impressiveness stressed the use of the extraordinary to call attention to one's style. The main devices to achieve this came to be called the figures of speech. These figures gave ornamentation to a speech—and this virtue was often called "ornamentation." Indeed, the "figurist" or "ornamentation" component of rhetoric often assumed such importance that it became synonymous with rhetoric itself and now constitutes one of the three basic meanings of the term, as we have seen. Figures of sound and figures of meaning were analyzed at great length throughout the entire rhetorical tradition.

The virtue of propriety was the locus for another important rhetorical tradition, the levels of style. Although the beginnings of the notion of the three styles can be traced in Greek thought, Cicero seems to be the one who crystallized the doctrine. In the *Brutus,* he treats of two

---

[5] On the clarification of "clarity" by Ramus, see Ong, r, 251.

styles: the grand, connected with moving the audience by emotion, and the plain, connected with teaching the audience by intellectual persuasion. Later, however, in the *Orator,* Cicero distinguished the Asian or grand, from the Rhodian or middle, and both from the Attic or plain. The middle style was oriented to delighting (Cicero, o, v, 20 ff.).

Despite the many interpretations given this doctrine, it has persevered through twenty centuries of rhetorical tradition. It is, in fact, amazing how many different variations are made on the theme of the three styles. What is considered Attic in one culture is often viewed as Asian by another culture, so that the three levels are continually being given new interpretations by different civilizations. Augustine bodily adopts the three styles, but gives them a solely religious orientation. He instances examples of each from the Scriptures and the fathers of the Church (*De Doctrina Christiana,* IV, Chapters 17–27). Literary historians and evaluationists have used the concepts to classify works of single authors or whole periods of a civilization. Thus Homer's epics can be viewed as in the grand style, Hesiod's middle-style effusions can be interpreted as the expression of a feudal period, and Callimachus' plain style poetry can be seen as appropriate to a modern period. There have been genre interpretations with tragedy linked to the grand style and comedy to the low style. Even single authors have been characterized as writing at various levels: Virgil's *Æneid* is in high style, his *Georgics* are middle, and his *Eclogues* are low. Asianism in its early Greek period was said to favor individuality while Atticism represented uniformity of rule (Campbell, i, 10–11); in contrast to this concept, Lasswell, in the *Language of Politics,* contrasts a democratic plain style and a despotic ornamental style (Lasswell, 1, 24–29). Sound structures have also been used to differentiate the styles. In modern times, Northrop Frye, in a very perceptive essay, distinguishes between the expressive rhythms of ordinary speech, the sentence rhythms of prose, and the recurrent rhythms of poetry (Frye, w, 24 f.). He interprets the doctrine of the styles in terms of these basic concepts. There can be a high style of prose; and for the mob, high style may be epitomized by advertising or even propaganda (w, 85). Some of Frye's distinctions will be returned to in this and later chapters.

In any case the fertility of the doctrine of the three styles is evident in the different constructions put on the notion since its rise in late Greek thought. Like the virtue of clarity, the concept of propriety or fitness or decorum often took on more than rhetorical importance. As will be shown in the next chapter, it is one of the most prevalent and pervasive concepts in the history of literary criticism. In addition to making it central to their stylistic doctrines, Cicero and other Stoics made it one of the cornerstones of their ethical structures (cf. *De Officiis,* 93–99). In the Middle Ages, it made its way into theology; thus Aquinas devotes a long section to the "fitness of the Incarnation" (st, III, q. 1), makes it one of the three components of his notion of the good (st, I, q. 5, art. 6), and makes it the most important element in his aesthetic (st, II, ii, q. 48).

The last of the four virtues is often called purity or correctness of language. In fact, it has usually been given a nationalistic terminology. Aristotle says that the language must be "Hellenic," and that is his term for this virtue; the corresponding vices are barbarisms and ungrammaticality (cf. Cope, r, III, 55). Cicero, repeating Aristotle, says in the *Brutus:* "The ground...or so to speak the foundation, on which oratory rests, is, you see, a faultless and pure Latin diction" (b, lxxiv, 258). And when Campbell formulated the doctrine of good usage which dominated English language teaching for almost two centuries, he stressed "Correct English" (p, 168–70). His concept of correctness, which has been seriously challenged only in our times by modern descriptive grammarians thus derives from a long tradition extending back to Aristotle (cf. Cope, i, 279, note 3). Being "correct," of course, like being clear, appropriate, and impressive, has had other than linguistic extrapolations.

Despite the long tradition of the four virtues of style and the peculiar attractiveness of the doctrine that is grounded in the communications triangle, there are some serious objections to using this framework as the basic structure for a discussion of rhetorical style. In the first place, it can easily be seen that these are not virtues of style peculiarly proper to persuasive discourse. It is easy to see that clarity, propriety, correctness, and dignity of some sort are also characteristic of scientific prose. And it is obvious that, with the proper modifications, they also apply to literary or journalistic writing. Are they not, then, the virtues of style in general? So that if they are to be used in a context of persuasion, there must be special distinctions made distinguishing scientific from informative from persuasive clarity, for example. In the history of rhetoric such distinctions have never been made.

Second, some important features of persuasive style do not seem to be provided for within the framework suggested by the four virtues. For example, some of the issues concerning the media of persuasion are relevant to propriety, but other media issues must be forced to fit into this category. Many other features of persuasive style are similarly difficult to fit into this framework: the nondialogue character of persuasion and the necessity of persuasive discourse to participate in the current myths. A third reason for not adopting the framework of the four virtues of style lies in the unfortunate associations which are made with these virtues and some of the doctrines which they have engendered throughout history. Thus the virtue of correctness is almost irrevocably tied to the tradition of "good usage," and such an association is highly undesirable. Similarly, the virtue of dignity is almost irretrievably associated with notions of ornateness and the figures of speech—also an objectionable alliance.

On the other hand, it is relatively easy to incorporate what is usable from the traditional virtues into a framework for handling style which is based on the grammatical, semantic, discourse, and metalanguage characteristics of the piece in question. The adaptation of the four virtues to this framework is not difficult because the two structures have the same metastructure. Indeed, most of the issues of traditional correctness or purity are grammatical issues. Many, though not all, of the concerns of propriety and impressiveness are discourse issues. And most of the problems of clarity are semantic problems. But some rearrangements must be made and notions liberalized. Except accidentally, traditional rhetoric did not place the rhetorical piece within the cultural and situational context. This framework of stylistic analysis, therefore, is the same as that used to analyze the three kinds of reference discourse. Lasswell, in his analysis of propaganda, seems to have been the first to suggest that persuasive style could be analyzed in terms of syntactic, semantic, and pragmatic features (Lasswell, 1, 57).

Metalanguage and Discourse Characteristics

The stylistic characteristics of persuasive speech or writing can be considered at different levels, for analytical purposes. In the following theoretical presentation I shall first consider the components of the discourse which are grounded in and assume crucial aspects of the cultural context; then the relevance of elements in the situational context that must often be considered; then the actual discourse components that involve aim, mode, art, and media. It must be emphasized that the following treatment suggests a framework for analyzing persuasive discourse, but it is not complete in its coverage; many gaps in the structure must yet be filled in, and many of the present inclusions are highly tentative. But they are typical of the kind of stylistic postulate which fits into that portion of the framework of analysis.

PERSUASIVE STYLE
AND THE CULTURAL
AND SITUATIONAL CONTEXT

The relevance of persuasive style to the cultural and the situational context is easy to ascertain. Science and literature, and to some extent, exploration have an element of the timeless to them, but rhetoric is eminently involved in the here and now. Much of the brilliant rhetoric of the past can now be appreciated only by a technician who is equipped with a historical perspective. Today the rhetoric of Macaulay's history rings hollow to the twentieth-century American college student. Yet how full did it ring to the English reader of a century ago. Hitler's flaming addresses of the thirties now have lost most of their fire for the Germany of 1968; even F.D.R.'s fireside chats now burn like dying embers. The sermons of St. Bernard or Peter the Hermit would sound quaint, even slightly heretical, to the modern ecumenical Catholic. The successful rhetor, precisely because he is so much of the times, must be willing to face eventual discountenancing. By the same token, the sober and timeless scientist or dialectician is not usually the successful swayer of the multitudes. Plato's philosopher-king may or may not be a desirable entity, but he is a rather unreal and improbable figure from the viewpoint of the pragmatics of language.

The most important quality of persuasive discourse, if it is to be successful, is that it must participate in the current political "myth," says Lasswell, in his analysis of the language of politics. By the political myth he understands the current underlying assumptions or explicit formulations of political theory, laws, and the popular manner in which these are realized in a state. There are, therefore, three basic elements to the myth: the doctrine, the formula, and the miranda, which might be translated as things believed, things legislated, and things admired. "The chosen province of the political philosopher is the doctrine; lawyers concentrate on the formula; ritualists and artists embellish the miranda" (Lasswell, 1, 12). "The miranda are the symbols of sentiment and identification in the political myth. . . . Flags and anthems, ceremonials and demonstrations, group heroes and the legends surrounding them—these exemplify the importance of miranda in the political process" (Lasswell, 1, 11).

Common denominators to doctrine, formula, and miranda are the key symbols of the culture. In Communism, for example, "bourgeoisie," "capitalism," "imperialism," "God," and "anarchism" are all negative key symbols; whereas "world revolution," "dialectical materialism," "classless society," and "class struggle" are positive key symbols (Laswell, 1, 14–15). Actually these symbols become semantic features of style and will be referred to below.

The effective persuader is sensitive to the current myth, particularly if it is changing. Lenin, Hitler, and Roosevelt all had a vivid vision of the contemporary myths in their respective countries in this century. Nor is the myth restricted to politics. The religious myths of history are equally important for preachers, pontiffs, and hierophants of all persuasions. The commerical propagandists must likewise have a firm, if intuitive grasp of the familial and social myths of the buying populace.

The perception of the acute relevance of the cultural myths to the needs and desires of a particular audience at a precise moment in history is the sign of the genius of the persuader. The geniuses of Madison Avenue are the people who can tell that the large and ornate automobiles of Detroit are no longer appealing to significant segments of the consumer populace —are no longer a part of their "miranda"—and must be replaced with Volkswagens or Fiats or Falcons. Finally, the importance of placing the persuasion in the proper situational context can be seen in the care with which advertisers fight and compete for the high-priority times and programs in television. It can also be seen in the scrupulous attention given by political candidates to the time and place at which they make their announcements of candidacy and elaborations of programs.

Also relevant to the actual process of persuasion are the "para-linguistic" facets of the situational context. The efficient use of cultural conventions such as space distances between speaker and hearer, bodily contacts, gesture, and posture are all parts of the situational context directly relevant to the effective persuasion. Research in speech is almost unanimous in emphasizing the importance of delivery in persuasion for instance (cf. Thompson, q, 82–83).

DISCOURSE COMPONENTS
OF PERSUASIVE STYLE

The discourse components can be classified according to media, art, mode, and aim. As far as I can discern, writers on advertising seem to have been the first to consider what effect the medium has on the persuasive efficacy of a given advertisement. Long before McLuhan, advertising textbooks devoted considerable space to the choice of media for different products and consumer groups. Today, of course, advertising textbooks give even more space to the topic: Sandage and Fryburger's text, a long-lived example in the field, has over one hundred pages on media in

FIGURE IV, 2: U. S. Advertising in 1961—by Media*

Medium	% of Total
Newspapers	30.6
Direct mail	15.8
Television	13.6
Magazines	7.8
Radio	5.9
Business papers	4.9
Outdoor	1.5
Miscellaneous	19.6
(Dealer displays, match covers, calendars, telephone directories, films, etc.).	

* Adapted from Sandage, a, 398, whose source was "Guide to Marketing for 1963," *Printers' Ink* (August 31, 1962), 383–85.

the sixth edition of their book (a, 397–507). Media selection is one of the three or four major topics of such texts, along with creativity, research, getting and handling accounts, and the structure of the advertising agency (cf. McMahan, w, 70–72, for a very current view).

Studies are constantly being made to assess the use of various media for advertising. One such study in 1962 came up with the following percentages of advertising appearing in the various media. Thus 30.6 per cent for newspapers means that advertising in newspapers accounted for almost one third of all advertisements in the United States in 1961 (see Figure IV, 2). Of course, other kinds of persuasion take different media—for instance, religious persuasion is heavily oral. When Lasswell made his early studies of the language of politics, he and his associates chose the newspaper as their medium for analysis, and in the newspapers they focused on the editorials (Lasswell, c, 17). Today political propaganda is steadily shifting to television as a competing medium, though radio, direct speech, billboards, direct mail, and other media are still being used. The use of television as a political medium is rapidly making the cost of political persuasion astronomical. Before President Johnson announced he would not run for reelection in March, 1968, *Advertising Age* had already announced that he was expected to select Mary Wells Lawrence of the advertising agency of Wells, Rich and Greene to handle his publicity for the 1968 campaign at an estimated budget of $20,000,000 (*Advertising Age,* February 19, 1968, p. 1).

Television is undoubtedly an effective medium, with some 55,000,000 sets in the U.S. at this time, but other media are also far-reaching. *Life* magazine, for example, was estimated in 1962 to have a weekly audience of 31,140,000 since there were estimated to be 4.55 readers per copy, and the circulation was 6,845,000 copies per week (Sandage, a, 410).

More important than mere numbers, however, is the psychological effect of a given medium. Marshal McLuhan is undoubtedly the theoretician who has given more consideration to this point than has any other writer. McLuhan contends that media are really extensions of our senses (u, 105, 114ff., 141f., 233). The sensitivities of various cultures to the kinds of media differ greatly; consequently the effects of different media on different cultures vary considerably. For McLuhan, these various media exert their effects more subliminally than consciously (u, 34). The "content" of a particular message therefore is of much less importance than the medium in which it occurs (u, 32, 34, 99, 274, 277). McLuhan, in fact, almost rewrites history solely in terms of the effects of media upon cultures. Not Roman rhetoric and law, but the wheel, Roman roads, and the phonetic alphabet fashioned the Roman empire (u, 99). In some seemingly wild causal relationships he makes Gutenberg responsible for the concepts of zero and infinity, the differential calculus, and Newtonian physics (u, 112–14). "Print," he says, "created individualism and nationalism in the sixteenth century" (u, 34). He remarks that, "If the 'Voice of America' suddenly switched to jazz, the Kremlin would have reason to crumble" (u, 152). In a very real sense, these notions constitute a revolutionary theory of persuasion. Persuasion is not achieved primarily by ideas or emotions but by the sense extensions of man we call media. One may cautiously discount some of McLuhan's positions and historical interpretations as overenthusiastic, but one cannot but be impressed with the validity of his emphasis on the persuasive effect of medium as such. If any of this is true, an analysis of persuasive discourse should certainly take into account the medium in which it occurs.

Somewhat parallel concepts in the areas of speech and group dynamics offer a different kind of confirmation of the importance of medium in persuasion. Traditional rhetoric dealt with the continuous speech, not the interrupted dialogue, which was more characteristic of the exploratory aspect of dialectic (Cope, r, 1, note 3). In fact, persuasion is not a process of reciprocal give and take. Real propaganda ends when dialogue begins, as Jean Cellule has remarked (quoted by McLuhan in a speech).[6] This, on the face of it, seems inconsistent with the tentative conclusions of some discussion theorists who claim that group discussions, especially small group discussions, produce more opinion change than monologual effects (cf. Thompson, q, 104, 107). The inconsistency might be resolved if it could be shown that the monologual tendency is true in persuasion, but the group dynamic holds for valid exploration.

A few comments on the art of discourse used will supplement these remarks on the media of discourse. Judged by the mass of written persuasion in all of the various media, it seems clear that persuasion is obviously adapted to oral or visual vehicles. Although rhetoric had the original connotation of "speaking," it did not always preserve that restriction. In fact, for some authors in the nineteenth and twentieth century, "rhetoric" came to be almost exclusively restricted to written discourse. There seems to be no valid reason to restrict either "rhetoric" or "persuasion" or "propaganda" to either vehicle.

Some attributes of the piece of writing or speaking call for additional comment. Much has been made of the length of the text at various times in history. Brevity was considered so important by the Stoics that they made of it a fifth virtue of style coordinate to the other four of the tradition, and it persisted and was given more or less attention in different cycles of rhetorical style (cf. Williamson s, 128 ff.). Advertising, for financial and perceptual reasons (e.g., length of time a billboard can be scanned from a passing automobile), certainly tends to brevity. Dirksen, in a textbook on advertising, lists these qualities of style: Be Brief, Be Apt, Be Interesting,

6 July 23, 1963, on national television.

Be Personal, Be Sincere and Convincing (a, 82–89); and concerning advertising headlines, he says, "There are four major characteristics in most good headlines: (1) brevity, (2) clarity, (3) aptness, and (4) interest (a, 107). Dirksen can almost be placed bodily in the Stoic rhetorical tradition of the virtues of style. Certainly, the demands of the advertising media dictate a brevity in advertising generally. But television and some other media are perfectly capable of giving an amplified treatment to some kinds of persuasion, such as political speeches and religious rhetoric.

What advertising media lack in length they make up in repetition. "Reiterate, reiterate, reiterate. That is the basis of advertising," said Sir William Crawford (quoted in Harris, a, 175). McLuhan refers to the modern advertising technique of wearing the consumer down "by the drip-drip-drip or Chinese water-torture method of endless repetition" (m, quoting from *Fortune,* November, 1947). Political propaganda, advertising practice, and the religious formulas of the centuries all underscore the necessity of repetition. Research insists that without repetition, regression to the original attitude may occur, often in a very short time (cf. Thompson, q, 42 ff.; for some reservations, cf. Harris, a, 175–76). Information theory pointed out early that all style is necessarily redundant (Shannon, m, 13), but persuasion is far more redundant than science or information or exploration.

Redundance in persuasion is related to the problem of pace, an issue also considered in scientific and informative styles. In a summary of oral persuasive speech, Petrie comes up with a formula for listenability very reminiscent of the Flesch and Gunning formulas for readability: concrete and specific words, personal pronouns, personification, imagery, "and other stylistic devices designed to personalize the composition and to make it more interesting and instantly intelligible" (reported in Thompson, q, 73–74). Students in speech concern themselves with the pace of delivery. "The normal speaking rate is between 125 and 190 words per minute, with a reduction in listenability beginning somewhere above 200 w.p.m." (Thompson, q, 88). This will vary from medium to medium, of course (Thompson, q, 88–89).

The application of the norms of readability and listenability to reference discourse was criticized in the previous chapter. The qualifications there suggested are not nearly so tenable in persuasive style. Readability and listenability are necessary virtues of persuasive style, much more than of reference style. In reference discourse, for example, there was an objection to the emphasis on "personalizing" intrusions; in persuasion, this is a virtue. Actually, the formulas of Flesch and Gunning should really be looked upon as techniques of persuasion, not information. With this understanding, one can refer back to the notions of readability and make effective use of them in rhetoric.

One last point can be made about the style of persuasive discourse.

This is the aim of the discourse. It is obvious that persuasive discourse must emerge as being an intent on the part of the speaker or writer. Traditional rhetoric suggested that the speaker carefully take his stand and explicitly state his thesis at the beginning of his speech. But much modern rhetorical practice and some interesting research suggests that an obvious intent has less chance of persuasion than a hidden intent. Soldiers in World War II seemed more persuadable when material was presented to them as "objective information" than as overt persuasion (Hovland, c, 24). Media here often exert unconscious effects. News columns seem more persuasive than ads or editorials (Hovland, c, 23). Thus, persuasion is often most successful when it parades under the guise of information or exploration or even literature. Thus, the *appearance* character of persuasive discourse which has continually been adverted to in this chapter, is true even of the aim of the discourse. Persuasion must often not appear to be persuasion; true art hides the art.

Semantic Characteristics
of Persuasive Discourse

Most of the traditional and modern attempts to characterize persuasive discourse focus on the semantic attributes of style. Without attempting a full semantic characterization of persuasive style, I shall nonetheless try to give typical features of that style as presented by some authors, necessarily selective and limited. The treatment will follow the same structure that was followed in the analysis of the style of the three kinds of references. First some concerns having to do with semantic differential will be looked at, then some of the basic issues in the theory of reference of semantics.

In the field of semantic differential, two issues have persistently been raised since the time of Aristotle and are paradoxically related. On the one hand there is the stress on using language that will appear "natural" to hearers in order to establish a linguistic bond between speaker and hearer. On the other hand there is the stress on having a quality of language, a style, that will be "extraordinary" enough to call some attention to the speaker's language and separate it from the commonplace and routine. Aristotle wrestles with this problem in the second chapter of Book III of the *Rhetoric*. Regarding the "extraordinary" in language he says,

> People do not feel towards strangers as they do towards their own countrymen, and the same is true of their feeling for language. It is therefore well to give to everyday speech an unfamiliar air: people like what strikes them, and are struck by what is out of the way (1404b 9–12).

Yet a few lines later he is saying,

> We can now see that a writer must disguise his art and give the impres-
> sion of speaking naturally and not artificially. Naturalness is persuasive,
> artificiality is the contrary; for our hearers are prejudicial and think we
> have some design against them, as if we were mixing their wines for
> them (1404b 18–21).

These issues of "obscurity" and "obviousness" are returned to in Chapter V.

The extraordinary character of the language of the speaker is related by Aristotle and the tradition to the virtue of impressiveness (or dignity): "Such variation from what is usual makes the language appear more stately" (1404b 9). These unusual words or combinations of words may be individual to the speaker himself or may be importations from other dialects (cf. Cope, i, 282–83, notes). In modern linguistic terminology the speaker may have an idiolect of his own and may import a foreign dialect to give unusualness to his speech. The unusual character of style is much more characteristic of the poetic than the persuasive style and will be considered in the next chapter.

At the same time, however, the persuasive style must generally be in the dialect of the audience. This is the supreme demand of propriety as a virtue of rhetorical style. The necessary tension between the ordinary and the extraordinary constitutes one of the basic features of persuasive style. If the extraordinary asserts itself too much, the style becomes literary, an object of delight in itself, and persuasion may be forgotten. If the style becomes too ordinary, the listener may lose interest and, for a different reason, persuasion is not achieved.

It is clear that modern propagandistic techniques recognize both poles of this spectrum in their practice, if not in their theory. Modern advertising will do almost anything with language to call attention to itself; but then it must channel this attention away from itself to the product. A glance at any set of good advertisements will betray this dual movement and will be illustrated in the analysis of the style of Roosevelt's speech which follows this theory.

In the semantic area of reference, some important points must be made about persuasive style. The most obvious concern here has been the issue of clarity. Yet the concept of "persuasive clarity" itself could stand some clarification. It is true that the issue, *as the speaker wants it presented to the audience,* must be clear to the audience. Often the presentation of the issue in the light the speaker desires will necessitate a distortion of the real issue or a withholding of facts or a screened view of the reality. The clarity of persuasion is then a filtered clarity. It is not the complete objective clarity of science or information, but the hearer must think he has a clear picture of reality.

Despite the lip service paid to clarity, it is often difficult to abstract the issues of clarity from other issues in traditional rhetoric. Aristotle remarks that clarity is achieved by using terms that are current and ordinary (1404b 5). Often metaphors can clarify meaning (1405a 7), and he devotes a good deal of attention to metaphor in several parts of the third book (Chapters 2, 4, 10, 11). Metaphor receives more attention than any other aspect of style. But the purpose of metaphor in Aristotle is much more for vividness and vivacity of style than for clarity. Cicero is likewise very perfunctory in his treatment of clarity. Speaking of correctness and clarity, he says,

> Of the two which I mentioned first, purity and clearness of language, I do not suppose that any account is expected from me.... Let us therefore omit these matters, which are easy of attainment, though necessary in practice; for the one [correctness or purity] is taught in school-learning and the rudiments of children; the other is cultivated for this reason, that what every person says may be understood,—a qualification which we perceive indeed to be necessary, yet that none can be held in less estimation (d, III, x).

Watson, Cicero's translator, remarks "this seems to be speaking rather too lightly of the merit of perspicuity, which Quintilian pronounces the chief virtue of language" (Watson, in Cicero, d, III, x, 342, n, 2). As we have already observed, later writers like Descartes and Tolstoy were to elevate clarity even higher.

Two of Lasswell's methods of detecting propaganda are related to this. By "presentation" he means the balance of favorable or unfavorable treatment given to each symbol in a given controversy. The key symbols of the myth must come through. This means, equivalently, that the *myth emerges clearly*. Similarly, the "distinctiveness" test of Lasswell consists in detecting the heavy use of vocabulary peculiar to one side of a controversy (cf. Lasswell, l, 177 ff.). This is clearly a semantic feature of style too, and, as with "presentation," the heavy use of a slanted vocabulary also clarifies the myth to the audience. The vocabulary of the myth and the preference of one set of symbols to another is partly accomplished by the emotional connotations of the symbols. Everyone agrees that the vocabulary of persuasion has more than a cold denotative referential function: the words also "refer" to emotional associations, attitudes, affective and conative elements. This is another important distinguishing characteristic of all non-reference discourse (cf. Stevenson, e, 13 and *passim*). The words can usually be classed into "purr" and "snarl" words, as Hayakawa has so felicitously named them. Somewhat allied to this feature is the stronger presence of humor, wit, and satire in persuasive than in reference discourse. Most rhetoricians since Aristotle have devoted some time to this aspect of rhetoric; and nearly all practicing persuaders know of the effectiveness of humor. Many modern ads make this the dominant feature.

Nearly everyone in persuasion theory also makes the point that persuasive speakers should avoid the abstract and use the concrete term. This may be a cliché in the tradition which, because it has a half-truth in its favor, can be overemphasized. The other side of the coin must be the obvious fact that persuasive speakers continually use such abstract terms as good, love, patriotism, God, happiness, freedom, and the like. Possibly these abstract terms are given a concrete, if vague, referent by being absorbed into the culture's myth; and some abstractions are rendered concrete by imagery. Preachers have proven very adept at concretizing the fundamental abstractions of Christianity. In modern times, with the aid of the visual images in photography and television, the power of the imposed image rather than the suggested image is seen in advertising and propaganda. The superiority of television ads over radio ads is evidence of the additive power of another dimension of imagery. Even in television the persuasive superiority of color over black-and-white ads is compounded evidence of the power of the image.

It is in the kinds of referring terms that traditional rhetoric has made its greatest contribution to the semantics of persuasive discourse. Since Aristotle's time, it has been recognized that persuasion makes a heavy use of nonliteral terms. The figures of speech of traditional rhetoric are so patently a component of rhetorical style that rhetoric has often been reduced to them. Simile, symbol, paradox, metaphor, euphemism, synedoche, metonymy, hyperbole—the list became longer and longer up to the Renaissance, at which time some authors could detail 150 kinds of such figures. Though not peculiar to persuasion, the figures are certainly a characteristic of persuasive discourse.

The functions of nonliteral language have traditionally been said to be "ornamental" in order to achieve impressiveness and clarification. Marvin Herrick, a notable historian of rhetoric and poetic, also points out that some modern writers see in the figure another and possibly more important function:

> When Milton speaks of Chaos as "the womb of Nature and perhaps her grave" he offers his reader more than illustration and clarification. His figure not only advances the indescribable toward the particular and comprehensible, but evokes a harmonious and coherent perception of similitudes in apparent dissimilitudes, evoking thought beyond thought in an aesthetic frame (f, 240).

This aesthetic effect can certainly, like most aesthetic techniques, be subsumed into a rhetorical purpose. Perhaps this subtle psychological effect goes further to explain the vast importance of figures of speech in persuasion than do the two traditional functions.

Modern literary and propaganda analysis has given more emphasis to the symbol than to any other of all of the long list of figures. In literature, some critics have almost reduced poetics to symbol hunting. Lasswell, in a careful propaganda analysis, uses the symbols of the culture as his main analytical instrument. His analysis of the amount, distribution, and prominence of key symbols in the May Day slogans of the U.S.S.R. for a twenty-five-year period is a brilliant example of how a semantic feature of style can be used. Similarly, his study of the leading newspapers in five countries for sixty years, 1890–1950, is another brilliant exposition of this technique. For this second analysis he used 416 key symbols (cf. Lasswell, c, 43, for examples; cf. Lasswell, l, 34 ff. for some details of the analysis).

Another semantic feature of persuasive discourse, to which some attention in modern times has been paid, will cast further light on the paradoxical character of rhetorical clarity. This has to do with the relation between referring term and object referred to. I. A. Richards, Lasswell, and Stevenson (analyzing rhetorical, propagandistic, and ethical language, respectively) all point out the essential ambiguity of many of the terms in these areas. Richards speaks of the continual shifts of meanings of which speaker or hearer may be unaware (p, 71–74). Stevenson says that "ethical terms are more than ambiguous; they are *vague*" (e, 34, his italics). This means that they may not have only plural referents (ambiguity), they may move in the direction of no referent (anomaly). Lasswell, Stevenson, and Brown pose some interesting reasons for this ambiguity and vagueness.

Lasswell maintains that when the persuaders are affecting a revolutionary change in the populace, the language is undergoing a change in meaning:

> We postulate the consequences of revolutionary change—in whatever society it occurs and from whatever sequence of events it results—in rapid and extensive change in the composition and the vocabulary of the ruling few (c, 28).

The vocabulary of persuasion, in other words, is either a new vocabulary or is in the process of taking on new meanings. Stevenson explains how this may occur. The denotative meaning of a term may remain the same, but its emotional connotations may be rapidly being replaced; or the emotional aura of a word may remain constant while the actual descriptive meaning of the term changes (cf. Stevenson, e, 72). When a myth is changing, as was the case of the Marxist myth as it moved away from a Stalinist interpretation, key emotive symbols may remain a part of the myth while taking on radically different actual referents. This explains the necessity of the Soviet Encyclopedia to rewrite Russian history whenever current heroes topple, as Brown has shown in his analysis of the psychological aspects of ambiguity in persuasion (t, 121–23). This dynamism of the semantics of persuasive discourse is one of the most interesting and best-explored aspects of rhetoric. Yet the ambiguous terms of rhetoric are not usually presented as ambiguous, anomalous, or dynamic. The vocabulary of the persuader has a categoric ring of certainty which reassures the hearer of the confidence and stability of the position being advocated. Like much else in the persuasive discourse, the categoric and stable vocabulary is only an appearance.

Grammatical Characteristics of Persuasive Discourse

The term "grammar," when predicated of persuasive discourse, must not be taken in a formal or standard sense, for the grammar of persuasion may often strike the purist as highly ungrammatical by the norms of his prestige dialect. The traditional notion of correctness or good usage is particularly vulnerable since it tends to connote a specifically aristocratic notion of grammar. It may well be true that some subcultures are not persuaded by substandard grammar in formal situations, but to generalize from these restricted cultures and situations to persuasion generally is extremely hazardous. Since the analyst of persuasion will usually be a member of an educated aristocratic minority, such a danger is ever present. The analyst is often in a subculture with different grammatical norms, the kind of norms he might frequently call "ungrammatical." Sometimes for attention effects or for purposes of showing preference for the dialect of a given proletarian audience over that of another bourgeois or aristocratic one, a speaker may even be consciously "antigrammatical," to use the term of Northrop Frye (w, 31). Certainly the writer of "Winston tastes good like a cigarette should" had been exposed to the good usage admonition which would recommend "as" for such conjunctive adverbial uses. But, even to the professor of grammar, "as a cigarette should" must sound inappropriate for this level of formality—*a fortiori* to the great unwashed of America who buy most of the Winstons. Similarly, the politician, who can speak prestige grammar when he wants to in Baton Rouge, chooses to speak the hybrid Cajun-American dialect of southwestern Louisiana when he speaks in Maurice in an election campaign. These are simple demands of propriety; and there should have been, though there often was not, a considerable tension between the demands of propriety and those of correctness in traditional rhetoric.

Aside from a too pure notion of purity or correctness in traditional rhetoric, possibly the most exploited concept in the grammar of persuasion had to do with the sound structures of persuasive discourse. Cicero, possibly more than many others, seemed particulary impressed with the persuasive power of rhythm. About half of the *Orator* is devoted to sound structures, especially rhythm. It is to his achievements in this that he owes his success in oratory, he hints (o, xl, 140). He spends an inordinate amount of time convincing some who might not feel it is important. Some of his lyrical statements about prose rhythm he himself qualifies in other parts of the same book or other books of his corpus. Thus:

> For what purpose is it used? To give pleasure. When? Always. In what place? Throughout the whole period (o, lx, 203).

After analyzing several successive rhythmic patterns used by the tribune Gaius Garbo in a speech before the assembly, and noticing the recurrent and final ditrochee ($\acute{\smile}$ $\acute{\smile}$) at the end of the clauses, Cicero enthusiastically concludes:

> ...it was marvellous what a shout arose from the crowd at this ditrochee. Was it not, I ask, the rhythm which produced this? (o, lxiii, 214)

Hubbell, whose translation I have used here, discounts Cicero's unction in this instance; but others have also spoken vehemently on the subject of rhythm in Antiquity. Campbell, a modern ecclesiastic, analyzing the stylistic character of the second sophistic, refers to the "lascivious" ditrochee of the Asian style and says that in these writers the "position of the words is completely at the mercy of the rhythm" (i, 7–8).

Ditrochees, somehow, do not seem so rousing or stimulating to me as they did to Cicero or Campbell. Nonetheless, it would be rash to discount the persuasive influence of structures of sound, especially rhythms. Even today, Frye makes rhythmic distinctions the bases for his kinds of style, as we have seen. And Aldous Huxley sounds deterministic when speaking of the effects of some kinds of rhythm:

> No man, however highly civilized, can listen for very long to African drumming, or Indian chanting, or Welsh hymn singing, and retain intact his critical and self-conscious personality. It would be interesting to take a group of the most eminent philosophers from the best universities, shut them up in a hot room with Moroccan dervishes or Haitian Voodooists and measure, with a stop watch, the strength of their psychological resistance to the effects of rhythmic sound...all we can safely predict is that if exposed long enough to the tom-toms and the singing, every one of our philosophers would end by capering and howling with the savages (quoted in Brown, t, 237, who tends to temper Huxley's enthusiasm, cf. 305).

Nor in this regard, can one ignore the almost necessarily rhythmic character of political and religious slogans and maxims (cf. Brown, t, 120), as well as the omnipresent rhythm accompanying most modern advertising slogans.

Prose rhythms were carefully legislated in Greek and in classical and medieval Latin. The basic units of sound structure were the period, the colon, and the comma. The period was a sentence "so arranged that the thought is held suspended to the end." A colon was an "integral part of the sentence, making complete sense, but not revealing the whole thought of the period." A comma was a smaller segment, not making complete sense in itself" (Finch, p, 428). Roughly, one can say they were respectively equivalent to the sentence, the clause, and the phrase of traditional grammar. The end-pattern of these units was called a *cursus;* and most of the concerns of ancient and medieval prose rhythm were with these end-patterns (for a summary treatment, cf. La Drière pr, 454–55).

The transfer of these patterns to modern languages is a matter of debate. As La Drière has remarked,

> The influence of the L. [atin] *cursus* in the production of similar rhythmic patterns in modern vernacular prose, and the actual characters of native vernacular prose rhythms, have not been sufficiently studied (pr, 455; see his bibliography).

Even today, with the advances of modern linguistics, the study of modern prose rhythm is still an infant discipline.

In addition to rhythm, of course, rhyme, alliteration, and other sound patterns can also be used in persuasion. The figures of sound in traditional rhetoric were quite numerous also. Traditional rhetoric stressed the phonemic devices which could be used in persuasion. But modern typography has given us many sophisticated graphemic devices for written persuasive discourse. Varied fonts in different sizes, italics, headlines, divisions, indentations, and marks of punctuation and capitalization can be put to effective persuasive use. Carlyle, with the relatively limited resources of his day, was a past master with these devices. Today, McLuhan, aware more than most people of the potential of even the written medium, is an excellent example of the use of more modern techniques.

A few sporadic remarks have been made about the morphemic features of persuasive discourse. The tendency of some modern political myths to promote a jargon of -isms in their vocabulary has been noted by Brown and others (Brown, t, 120). The New Deal and many subsequent American subcultures have gone heavily alphabetical in their jargons. Even our own discipline cannot resist this tendency: MLA, NCTE, CCCC, AAUP.

Lasswell, with a somewhat different emphasis, felt that nouns seem to be much more indicative of revolutionary change than verbs, for instance. In his analyses, he limited his key symbols to nouns (cf. c, 58 f.). But the superlative adjectival form also is a characteristic persuasive morpheme. Macaulay's prose is typical:

> Oriental despots are perhaps the worst class of human beings; and this unhappy boy was one of the worst specimens of his class. His education

had been such as would have enervated even a vigorous intellect, and perverted even a generous disposition (1, 47).

At the syntax level, there have been elaborate attempts, such as in the Renaissance, to categorize styles or parts of a discourse by certain kinds of sentences or lengths of sentences (cf. Williamson, s). There is undoubtedly much descriptive and normative worth in such attempts; but before they can be adopted in a systematic theory of discourse, more research, historical and structural, must be done to substantiate such suggestions.

The work of some value theorists is more precise in analyzing the various grammatical realizations which ethical and persuasive statements take. The sum total of a persuasive discourse is an imperative sentence in aim and a narrative sentence in mode: Vote for Wintergreen, Marry me, Enroll Now in the Trim and Swim Health Spa, Stop Drinking. This does explain the frequent occurrence of the addressee in the persuasive style; and the ethical arguments explain the necessary presence of the first-person nouns and pronouns. But the persuasive sentence can take many forms: That's naughty!—I'm warning you, "All hippies are godless."—You did *that*?—I wish you would stop using my cigars.—That gear is out of place here.—Would that you were free. Persuasive sentences can be declarative, interrogative, exclamatory, imperative in form; indicative or subjunctive in mood; classificatory, narrative, descriptive, evaluative in mode. Stevenson has a good discussion on these kinds of distinctions in ethical discourse (cf. e, 21 ff.).

This concludes the analysis of the style of persuasive discourse. It is hoped that the broad framework which has been drawn is adequate to a placement of the elements of a persuasive style. What is valid, it is hoped, is the basic structure of analysis. It only remains to apply some of the aspects of this theory to a brief analysis of Roosevelt's style in his "First Inaugural Address."

Selected Aspects
of Persuasive Style
in Roosevelt's "First Inaugual Address"

In analyzing the nature, logic, and organization of Roosevelt's address in the preceding sections, some aspects of style have already been given some attention. There the intrusions of speaker and audience, the categoric nature of the assertions, the use of emotionally loaded terms, in addition to constituting the speech as basically persuasive in nature also emerge as stylistic features of the piece. This merely illustrates the general principle that style is a thinking out into language, as Newman observed. These features will not be reiterated here. Nor, for that matter, does the following analysis intend to be complete. It only intends to illustrate some of the many features of persuasive style which are exemplified in Roosevelt's speech. The features arbitrarily chosen for analysis here seem pertinent for reasons of dominance or because they are sometimes neglected in routine speech analysis. Consequently, Roosevelt's superb delivery techniques, his close awareness of the situational context, his exploitation of the radio medium, the length of the speech in comparison to other inaugural addresses, and many similar topics will be bypassed, not because they are not relevant, but because it is easy enough to find a comparable analysis in many other places.

Here I shall stress his use of the current political myth by the use of symbol and imagery techniques, his use of metaphor, and the ambiguity of his language; and I shall also briefly look at his rhythms and his use of repetition.

A close look reveals that Roosevelt's speech incorporates and exploits the current political myth; it seems clear that by an almost endless repetition of key symbols and images three rather distinct components of the American myth of 1933 emerge. They might be called, at the risk of simplification, the idea of the unity of the body politic, the idea of religion and morality, and the idea of progress.

The recurrent symbols which establish the political components of the myth are terms like the following: nation (used 18 times, counting adjective but not pronoun forms); President, leadership, authority, power (13); people and public (11), Congress, Constitution, government (12), America, U.S., our country (6); endure, prosper, restore, revive (11); farms and lands (4), homes and houses (3); nature, bounty, plenty (4). If pronoun forms were counted, the figures would be much higher. Other symbols of the myth which occur but do not recur as frequently are: forefathers and ancestors, pioneer spirit, and destiny. By actual count, the symbols of the religious and moral components of the myth are much more frequent, although more scattered. They include the following: obligations, tasks, duties, right (12); truth, candor, honesty (10); moral, ethical, evil, wrong, selfish, selfless, spiritual (13); sanctity, sacred (4); God, He (4); belief, faith (4). Many others occur, sometimes in crucial imagery patterns or metaphors, though they are not as recurrent: host, plague of locusts, temple, money changers, vision, temple, minister, good neighbor, dedication, devotion, blessing, hearts and minds. In all, excluding pronoun references to symbols, some sixty-nine religious symbols are used throughout the speech.

Finally, the idea of progress by means of disciplined martial movements under leadership is a third important dimension of the basic composite myth. As is to be expected, some of the symbols of the political myth are also elements of the progress through leadership myth, such as: leadership (14); endure, etc. (11), task (12). Other relevant symbols are war, army, foe, invader, attack, discipline (24); perils, difficulties, crisis, emergency, problems (13); progress, forward, accomplish, help, act (21). In all, some ninety-five symbols are registered that contribute to the progress component and other tangential symbols reenforce them.

Not counting symbols twice that contribute to several components, some 209 key symbols frame the composite myth which rises from the constant positioning of the components. The myth may be crudely paraphrased: We are a strong and determined body politic, organized under law and governmental forces, held together by moral and religious ties, firmly decided to progress forward to the attainment of our material and spiritual goals under the generalship of a fearless leader. The myth would sound much more accurate if recited in the form of a political or religious credo. It has its doctrines, its laws, and its miranda, the ingredients of myth according to Lasswell.

Stylistically, the myth engenders much of the basic imagery, some of the crucial metaphors, and many of the slogans and clichés of the piece. Of course the three dimensions of the myth themselves constitute three powerful imagery clusters. It might be noted—and I did not perceive this consciously until after analysis—that by far the most dominant single image cluster of the speech is the war image. Yet the speech does not strike one as warlike at all. The strongest of the three dimensions of the myth is the progress component. This seems consonant with Roosevelt's own statement that his major objective was to instill hope and confidence.

Some as yet unanalyzed image and metaphor patterns are closely linked to the myth. Overshadowing all three dimensions, politics, religion, and progress, is the metaphor likening Roosevelt to Jesus and Moses, the people of America to the faithful Jews and Christians marching to a restored temple in a promised land, and the Republicans to the Egyptians and "publicans" (the money changers and tax collectors in Jesus' time). But most of this elaborate metaphor is accomplished by indirection and does not emerge in a count of obvious key symbols. The Moses image comes out of such hints as: the plague of locusts, the forefathers, the "host," the dark-light image that suggests the pillar of fire and the pillar of cloud by which God guided the Israelites (paragraph 26). The Jesus image is much more explicit: the money changers fleeing the temple, the restoration of the temple to ancient truths, the ministering to ourselves and our fellow men, the good neighbor analogy. The metaphor is a good deal more than ornamentation. As Herrick suggests, it links the various elements of the myth together into an almost aesthetic whole. It places the many elements into an amazing analogical unity: the perils and difficulties, as problems in a transitory desert, Roosevelt's program as a promised land, the Republican leaders as villains, the money and profit motif as evil, the common people as Jewish and Christian pilgrims, and Roosevelt as a happy amalgam of Jesus, Moses, and Joshua. The metaphor, of course, fulfills many other functions. It clarifies the myth; it provides a religious dignity to the style; it tremendously enhances the ethical argument and provides the basis for the logical argument; it leads directly to the basic theme of the speech: accept my leadership and program.

A word on the semantic ambiguity of the style may help to explain the theoretical position established. Roosevelt is well aware that he is giving new meanings to some traditional elements of the myth, yet he wants to hold onto the emotive links that attach to these changing elements. He is using the technique described by Stevenson: change the denotative, but preserve the connotative aspect of the meaning. This is true of two important facets of his argument; his New Deal program and his concept of leadership as similar to that of wartime emergency.

He reassures the people frequently on both counts. Though he upbraids the Republicans for casting their efforts in the "pattern of an outworn tradition," he contends strongly and frequently that his program is of a piece with the "ancient truth;" it is the same nation which has endured and will endure, the temple is being restored; this action is "feasible under the form of government which we have inherited from our ancestors;" there is no loss of "essential form; "we do not distrust the future of essential democracy."

Buttressed by the emotional links he has established, he can then insist that the present task is "unprecedented," as is the demand: it is a critical situation. Though the "form of government," the "essential form," the "essential democracy" is not menaced, there may be a partial and "temporary departure from that normal balance of public procedure." Actually, the American notion of democracy was severely altered in this one speech and in the subsequent career of Roosevelt. The executive took away from the legislative and the judicial powers which it has never subsequently relinquished. The American notion of democracy in the program of this speech moved radically closer to the concept of parasocialism, a proximity it has not budged from since. Yet these shifting ambiguities of the speech are not posed as tentative or groping. The categoric ring of certainty, referred to in the analysis of the ethical argument above, exudes a confidence, a security, and a stability that was obviously contagious even to an unfriendly press, as we pointed out above.

Finally, a brief look at some of Roosevelt's sound structures may give us another insight into his style. To the average American, the most conspicuous peculiarity of Roosevelt's style was his New York-New England "accent." This immediately gave Roosevelt's delivery an extraordinary quality and, because this was valued as the prestige dialect, a dignity and impressiveness. In more recent times, Kennedy had this same dialect advantage. On the contrary, Johnson never completely surmounted the deprecatory connotations that many average Americans attach to a Texan accent. Modern linguistics has asserted the theoretical equality of all dialects, but even today only the very linguistically sophisticated can overcome a long tradition of inequality.

Another, more unconscious effect was undoubtedly wrought by Roosevelt's rhythms. In the next chapter a distinction will be drawn between rhythm, groupings, and intonation, structures composed respectively of stress, juncture, and pitch. Here, the three will be loosely considered together and referred to as rhythm. Roosevelt's rhythm seems to derive, in many instances, from his paralleling of phrasal, clausal, or sentence units in simple series. These parallel structures give much the same effect as the parallel units in Whitman's verse. Then the parallelism is broken by a more prosaic, usually longer and not so rhythmically ordered unit. These parallelisms often go in units of three: *the truth, the whole truth, frankly and boldly; will endure as it has endured, will revive and will prosper; nameless, unreasoning, unjustified* terror. All of these occur in the first paragraph, and are verbal or phrasal repetitions; the verbal or phrasal repetitions often occur in clausal repetitions, and the verbal or phrasal repetitions occur in clauses of varying lengths. The following arrangement of segments of paragraphs 1, 2, 4, 5, 6, 10, 11, 15, and 26 shows some of these parallel devices, often, though not always, in units of three.

Paragraph 1 I am certain. . .
    This is preeminently the time to speak
      the truth,
      the whole truth,
      frankly and boldly.
    This great nation *will endure* as it has endured,
      will revive and
      will prosper.
    So, first of all, let me assert my firm belief that
    the only thing we have to fear is fear itself—
      nameless,
      unreasoning,
      unjustified
    terror. . . .

Paragraph 2 In such a spirit on my part. . .
    Values *have shrunken* to fantastic levels
    taxes *have risen;*
      our ability to pay *has fallen;*
    government of all kinds *is faced* with serious. . .

the means of exchange *are frozen.* . . ;
the withered leaves of industrial enterprise lie
on every side. . .
farmers find no market for their. . .
the savings of many years. . .*are gone.*

Paragraph 4 Yet our distress comes from *no failure of substance*
We are stricken by *no plague of locusts.* . . .
Primarily this is because rulers of exchange. . .
have failed through their stubborness. . .
have admitted their failure, and
have abdicated.

Paragraph 5 True *they have tried,* but their efforts. . . .
Faced by. . .*they have proposed* only the lending of more money.
Stripped of. . .*they have resorted* to exhortations, . . .
They have no vision, and when there is no
vision. . . .

Paragraph 10 Our greatest primary task. . . .
It can be accomplished in part
by direct *recruiting* by the Government itself,
treating the task as we would. . . .
accomplishing greatly needed projects. . . .

Paragraph 11 Hand in hand with this. . . .
The *task can be helped* by definite efforts. . . .
It can be helped by preventing realistically. . .
It can be helped by insistence that. . . .
It can be helped by the unifying of relief. . . .
It can be helped by national planning. . . . in
which
it can be helped, but
it can never be helped merely by talking
about it.

Paragraph 15 The basic thought that guides these specific. . . .
It is the insistence, as. . . .
It is the way to recovery.
It is the immediate way.
It is the strongest assurance that the recovery
will endure.

The rhythmic effect achieved by repetitions of similar or the same elements
in these paragraphs is overwhelming. It is no wonder that Roosevelt's

speeches held the audience with the spell of poetry. The prose rhythm is almost obtrusive. But variety is given by the juxtaposition of these rhythmic effects to longer and structured clausal or sentence units.

Much more could be said about Roosevelt's sound structures and about his style in general. The preceding account has been only an attempt to outline suggested areas for analysis. In sound structure, as in all style, our present knowledge is in little more than the folk stage. But modern linguistics does seem to be preparing the way to a more careful and systematic analysis of the prosody of prose than has ever been possible in the history of the discipline.

EXERCISES

I *Nature of Persuasive Discourse*

1. Take three or four newspaper or magazine advertisements and analyze them for: evidence of focus on decoder, emotional use of language (and pictures), situational choice indicated.

2. Analyze a section of a high school or elementary school textbook on civics for persuasive components. Does it emerge as predominantly informative or persuasive? In your paper speculate on the desirability of persuasive components in such texts.

3. Write a paper contrasting Aristotle's view of persuasion with Plato's (cf. *Rhetoric*, Ch. I, and *Gorgias*).

4. Compare Kierkegaard's views on the ethics of rhetoric to those of Weaver.

5. Contrast a piece of scientific discourse with an example of persuasive discourse for: decoder evidence, emotional components, evidence of a choice being indicated.

6. Analyze Macaulay's *Lord Clive* as a piece of persuasive history.

7. Analyze a piece of science, literature, or expression for its subordinate persuasive components.

8. Write a few advertisements for current products, designing them for different media: television, magazines, newspapers, billboards.

9. As a speech writer for one of your political choices, write a speech for him designed for a specific audience.

II *Logic of Persuasive Discourse*

1. Analyze Macaulay's *Lord Clive* for ethical or pathetic or "logical" proof.

2. Analyze the use of information in Macaulay's *Lord Clive*. Contrast this to an American encyclopedia report of the subjugation of India.

3. Analyze the use of persuasive logic in one of the speeches of the assembly of fallen angels in Book II of *Paradise Lost;* or analyze the logic of Anthony's speech in *Julius Caesar.* In these or similar instances of persuasion used within a literary framework, attempt to ascertain what influence the general structure of the play or epic had on the persuasive components embodied.

4. Analyze one or several advertisements for ethical, pathetic, and "logical" proof.

5. Take any one of the longer paragraphs from Roosevelt's "Inaugural Address" and point out any inference, implicit or explicit, used in the paragraph. Attempt to discern a possible pattern in such uses.

6. Analyze the article by Stewart Alsop referred to in Chapter III for its persuasive elements. Is it predominantly persuasive or informative in its logic?

7. Contrast William Jennings Bryan's "Cross of Gold, Crown of Thorns" speech with a modern political speech for persuasive logic.

8. Contrast Newman's rhetorical logic in his university sermon on "The Use of Emotions in Everyday Life" with his exploratory logic in "Knowledge Its Own End" in *The Idea of a University.*

9. Compare Aristotle's treatment of emotional proof with Alexander Bain's "Oratory of the Feelings" in *English Composition and Rhetoric.*

III *Organization of Persuasive Discourse*

1. Analyze the structure of a visual advertisement in a magazine. Does it have any relation to the traditional rhetorical arrangement (see above, p. 266 ff.)?

2. Analyze the sequences of a minute or half-minute advertisement on television. Do they have any relation to classical rhetorical arrangement (see above, p. 266 ff.)?

3. Analyze the organization of the speeches of one of the fallen angels in Book II of *Paradise Lost* or of Antony's speech in *Julius Caesar.* Indicate the relevance of the literary framework to these structures.

4. Analyze the structure of the sermon on the last ends in Joyce's *A Portrait of the Artist As a Young Man.* Indicate the relevance, if any, of its structure to the literary framework in which it occurs.

5. Analyze the relationships between the narrative structure of Macaulay's *Lord Clive* and the narrative interruptions. Does persuasion occur equally in both sections?

6. Analyze the organizational patterns of a sermon and of an editorial. Try to discern the influence of the media on the organization.

IV *Style of Persuasive Discourse*

1. Analyze Macaulay's *Lord Clive* for his use of superlative forms.

2. Compare and contrast a radio, a television, and a magazine advertisement of the same product. Try to account for the stylistic differences that derive from the media.

3. Try to find evidence and/or counter-evidence for Lasswell's terseness-prolixity rule: "when the collective outlook is optimistic, the style becomes more prolix and diversified; when the outlook is pessimistic, style grows terse and repetitious" (see Lasswell, 1, 28). Possibly take speeches from the early and late periods of the presidency of Lyndon Johnson to test the hypothesis.

4. Try to find evidence and/or counter-evidence for Lasswell's generalization about the language of despotism and the language of democracy (see Lasswell, 1, 28). Choose examples from similar levels of the same culture in order to control the variables in such an analysis, as much as possible.

5. Analyze the deviations from "normal" prose that might be considered attention gimmicks in several advertisements. What is the "normal language" against which these departures can be considered deviations?

6. Discuss at some length the concept of persuasive clarity (see above, p. 286 ff., for some priming notions).

7. Attempt to isolate the components of the American "myth," as Lasswell understands the term, in Lincoln's "Gettysburg Address." You might compare or contrast it to the myth found in the "Declaration of Independence" or Roosevelt's "Inaugural Address."

8. Analyze the use of ambiguity, imagery, symbolism, connotation, abstract terms, synecdoche, etc., in several modern advertisements or in a political speech or religious sermon.

9. Analyze so-called substandard usage practices in advertisements.

10. Analyze the use of sound structures in some modern advertisements.

11. What use do advertisements make of modern graphemic devices in printing? Analyze their occurrence in several advertisements.

BIBLIOGRAPHY AND FOOTNOTE REFERENCES

Aristotle. *The Works of Aristotle.* Tr. under the direction of W. D. Ross. Vols. VIII and IX of *Great Books of the Western World,* ed. Robert M. Hutchins and Mortimer J. Adler. Chicago: Encyclopaedia Britannica,

Inc., 1952 (*Ethics,* e; *Politics,* p; *Rhetoric,* r; *Poetics,* po; *Metaphysics,* m; *Topics,* t).

———. *The Rhetoric of Aristotle.* Ed. Lane Cooper. New York: D. Appleton and Co., 1932 (r).

Bailey, Dudley, ed. *Essays on Rhetoric.* New York: New York University Press, 1965 (e).

———. "A Plea for a Modern Set of Topoi." *College English,* XXVI (November, 1964), 111–16 (p).

Baird, A. Craig. *Rhetoric: A Philosophical Inquiry.* New York: The Ronald Press Company, 1965 (r).

Baldwin, Charles Sears. *Ancient Rhetoric and Poetic.* Gloucester, Mass.: Peter Smith, 1924 (a).

———. *Medieval Rhetoric and Poetic.* Gloucester, Mass.: Peter Smith, 1950 (m).

———. *Renaissance Literary Theory and Practice.* Ed. Donald L. Clark Gloucester, Mass.: Peter Smith, 1959 (r).

Bitzer, Lloyd. "Aristotle's Enthymeme Revisited." *Quarterly Journal of Speech,* XLV (1959), 399–408.

Black, Edwin. *Rhetorical Criticism: A Study In Method.* New York: The Macmillan Company, 1965 (r).

Bormann, G. *Theory and Research in the Communicative Arts.* New York: Holt, Rinehart and Winston, Inc., 1968 (t).

Brentlinger, W. B. "The Aristotelian Conception of Truth in Rhetorical Discourse." *Dissertation Abstracts,* XX (1960), 3425–26 (a).

Brown, J. A. C. *Techniques of Persuasion, From Propaganda to Brainwashing.* Baltimore, Md.: Penguin Books, 1963 (t).

Bryant, Donald. "Rhetoric: Its Function and Its Scope." *Quarterly Journal of Speech,* XXXIX (December, 1953), 401–4 (r).

Burke, Kenneth. *A Rhetoric of Motives.* Englewood Cliffs, N. J.: Prentice-Hall, Inc., 1950 (r).

Campbell, George. *The Philosophy of Rhetoric.* New York: Harper & Brothers, 1885 (p).

Campbell, James M. *The Influence of the Second Sophistic on the Style of the Sermons of St. Basil the Great.* Washington, D. C.: Catholic University of America Press, 1922 (i).

Chaignet, A., ed. *La rhétorique et son histoire.* Paris: E. Bouillon and E. Verweg, 1888 (r).

Cicero, Marcus Tullius. *Brutus,* tr. G. L. Hendrickson (b); *De Oratore,* tr. E. W. Sutton (d), *Orator,* tr. H. M. Hubbell (o); *De Natura Deorum,* tr. H. Rackham (n); *De Officiis,* tr. W. Miller (of); *Tusculan Disputations,* tr. J. E. King (t); *de Inventione,* tr. H. M. Hubbell (i). Loeb Classical Library Editions. Cambridge, Mass.: Harvard University press, 1952, 1959–60, 1952, 1956, 1956, 1950, 1960, respectively.

———. *On Oratory and Orators, with His Letters to Quintus and Brutus.* Tr. and ed. J. S. Watson. London: Henry G. Bohn, 1855 (d, for *de Oratore*).

Cope, Edward M. *An Introduction to Aristotle's Rhetoric with Analysis, Notes, and Appendices.* London: Macmillan and Co., 1867 (by Wm. C. Brown of Dubuque, Ia., reprint) (i).

———. *The Rhetoric of Aristotle, with a Commentary.* Rev. and ed. John Edwin Sandys. 3 Vols. Cambridge, England: At the University Press, 1877 (r).

Corbett, Edward P. J. *Classical Rhetoric for the Modern Student.* New York: Oxford University Press, 1965 (c).

De Fleur, Mervin L. *Theories of Mass Communications.* New York: David McKay Company, Inc., 1966 (t).

Dick, Robert C. "Topoi: An Approach to Inventing Arguments." *Speech Teacher,* XIII (November, 1964), 313–19.

Dirksen, Charles J., and Arthur Kroeger. *Advertising Principles and Problems.* Homewood, Ill.: Richard D. Irwin, Inc., 1960 (a).

Ehninger, Douglas. "Campbell, Blair, and Whately Revisited." In Lionel Crocker and Paul A. Carmack, eds., *Readings in Rhetoric.* Springfield, Ill.: Charles K. Thomas, Publisher, 1965. Pp. 359–73 (c).

Finch, Chauncey E. "Period." *Dictionary of World Literature.* Ed. Joseph T. Shipley. New York: The Philosophical Library, 1943. P. 428 (p).

Fogarty, Daniel J., S. J. *Roots for a New Rhetoric.* New York: Columbia University Press, 1959 (r).

Frye, Northrop. *The Well-Tempered Critic.* Bloomington, Ind.: Indiana University Press, 1963 (w).

Gibson, Walker. *Tough, Sweet and Stuffy.* Bloomington, Ind.: Indiana University Press, 1966 (t).

Gilman, William. *The Language of Science: A Guide to Effective Writing.* New York: Harcourt, Brace & World, Inc., 1961 (l).

Gomperz, Theodor. *Greek Thinkers.* Vol. IV. Tr. L. Magnus and G. G. Berry. London: John Murray, 1912 (g).

Grote, George. *Aristotle.* Ed. A. Bain, G. G. Robertson. London: J. Murray, 1883 (a).

Hare, R. M. *The Language of Morals.* Oxford: Clarendon Press, 1952 (l).

Harris, Ralph, and Arthur Seldon. *Advertising and the Public.* London: A. Deutsch, 1962 (a).

Herrick, Marvin T. "Figure." *The Dictionary of World Literature.* Ed. Joseph T. Shipley. New York: The Philosophical Library, 1943. Pp. 239–40 (f).

———. *The Poetics of Aristotle in England.* New Haven, Conn.: Yale University Press, 1930 (p).

Hintikka, Kaarlo J. J. *Quantifiers in Deontic Logic.* Helsingfors: Societas Scientiarum Fennica, 1957 (q).

Hovland, Carl I., Janis, Irving R., and Harold H. Kelley. *Communications and Persuasion.* New Haven, Conn.: Yale University Press, 1953 (c).

———, et al. *The Order of Presentation in Persuasion.* New Haven, Conn.: Yale University Press, 1957 (o).

Howes, Raymond J. *Historical Studies of Rhetoric and Rhetoricians.* Ithaca, N. Y.: Cornell University Press, 1961 (h).

Hughes, Richard E., and P. Albert Duhamel. *Rhetoric, Principles and Usage.* Englewood Cliffs, N. J.: Prentice-Hall, Inc., 1962 (r).

Hunt, Everett Lee. "Plato and Aristotle on Rhetoric and Rhetoricians." In *Studies in Rhetoric and Public Speaking,* ed. A. M. Drummond. New York: Century Co., 1925. Pp. 1–60 (s).

Institute for Propaganda Analysis. "How to Detect Propaganda." *Propaganda Analysis,* I, No. 2 (November, 1937), 5–8 (h).

Irwin, Ramon L. "The Classical Speech Divisions." *Quarterly Journal of Speech,* XXV (April, 1939), 212–13 (c).

Isocrates. "Antidosis." *Isocrates.* Tr. George Norlin. 3 Vols. Cambridge, Mass.: Harvard University Press, 1954 (a).

Kennedy, George. *The Art of Persuasion in Greece.* Princeton, N. J.: Princeton University Press, 1963 (a).

La Drière, J. Craig. "Letter." *Dictionary of World Literature.* Ed. Joseph T. Shipley. New York: The Philosophical Library, 1943. Pp. 352–54 (1).

———. "Prose Rhythm." *Dictionary of World Literature.* Ed. Joseph T. Shipley. New York: The Philosophical Library, 1945. 454–55 (p).

———. "Rhetoric and 'Merely Verbal Art.'" *English Institute Essays, 1948.* Ed. D. A. Robertson, Jr. New York: Columbia University Press, 1949. Pp. 134–52 (r).

Lasswell, Harold D., Leites, Nathan, *et al. Language of Politics.* Cambridge, Mass.: M.I.T. Press, 1965. (First ed., 1949) (1).

———, Lerner, Daniel, and I. de Sola Pool. *The Comparative Study of Symbols. An Introduction.* Stanford, Calif.: Stanford University Press, 1952 (c).

———. *Politics: Who Gets What, When, How.* New York: McGraw-Hill Book Company, 1936 (p).

———. *Propaganda Technique in the World War.* New York: Alfred A. Knopf, Inc., 1927 (pr).

Lausberg, Heinrich. *Handbuch der Literarischen Rhetorik: Eine Grundlegung der Literaturwissenschaft.* München, Germany: Max Hueber Verlag, 1960 (h).

Lodge, Rupert C. *The Philosophy of Plato.* New York: Humanities Press, Inc., 1956 (p).

Ludekens, Fred. "A Plague on Art for Art's Sake." *Advertising Age,* XXVIII, No. 45 (Nov. 11, 1957), 109–11 (p).

Macaulay, T. B. "Lord Clive." In *The Victorian Age,* ed. John Wilson Bowyer and John Lee Brooks. New York: F. S. Crofts and Co., 1941. Pp. 47–54 (1).

McBurney, James. "The Place of the Enthymeme in Rhetorical Theory." *Speech Monographs,* III (1936), 49–74.

McLuhan, Marshall. *The Mechanical Bride: Folklore of Industrial Man.* New York: The Vanguard Press, Inc., 1951 (m).

————. *Understanding Media: The Extensions of Man.* New York: McGraw-Hill Book Company, 1965 (u).

McMahan, Harry Wayne. "What's Behind New 'Creative Presidents.'" *Advertising Age* (February 9, 1968), 70–72 (w).

Murphy, James J. "Saint Augustine and the Debate about a Christian Rhetoric." In Lionel Crocker and Paul A. Carmack, eds., *Readings in Rhetoric.* Princeton, N. J. and Springfield, Ill.: Charles C. Thomas, Publisher, 1965. Pp. 204–19 (a).

Ohmann, Richard M. "In Lieu of a New Rhetoric." *College English,* XXVI, No. 1 (October, 1964), 17–22, (i).

Ong, Walter J. *Ramus: Method and the Decay of Dialogue.* Cambridge, Mass.: Harvard University Press, 1958 (r).

Parrish, Wayland Maxfield. "Whately and His Rhetoric." In Lionel Crocker and Paul A. Carmack, eds., *Readings in Rhetoric.* Springfield, Ill.: Charles C. Thomas, Publisher 1965. Pp. 374–96 (w).

Plato. *Plato.* Tr. Benjamin Jowett. Vol. VII of *Great Books of the Western World,* eds. R. M. Hutchins and M. J. Adler. Chicago, Ill.: Encyclopaedia Britannica, 1952. (*Gorgias,* g; *Phaedrus,* p).

Prior, A. N. *Formal Logic.* Oxford: The Clarendon Press, 1962 (f).

Quintilian, M. F. *The Institutio Oratoria.* Tr. H. E. Butler. 4 Vols. Cambridge: Mass.: Harvard University Press, 1953–56 (i).

Randall, John Herman. *Aristotle.* New York: Columbia University Press, 1960 (a).

Rashdall, Hastings. *The Universities of Europe in the Middle Ages.* Eds. F. M. Powicke and A. B. Emden. 3 Vols. Oxford: Clarendon Press, 1936 (u).

Richards, I. A. *How to Read a Page.* London: K. Paul, Trench, Trubner and Company, 1943 (h).

————. *The Philosophy of Rhetoric.* New York: Oxford University Press, 1965 (p).

————. *Principles of Literary Criticism.* New York: Harcourt, Brace and Company, 1929 (pr).

Rogers, Everett M. *Diffusion of Innovations.* New York: The Free Press, 1962 (d).

Roosevelt, F. D. *Masking the Fear: The Selected Addresses of Franklin Delano Roosevelt, 1932–1945.* Ed. B. D. Zevin. Cambridge, Mass.: Houghton Mifflin Company, 1946 (m).

————. *The Public Papers and Addresses of Franklin D. Roosevelt, With a Special Introduction and Explanatory Notes by President Roosevelt.* Vol. II: *The Year of Crisis, 1933.* New York: Random House, Inc., 1938 (p).

Ross, W. D. *Aristotle.* 2nd Edition. London: Methuen & Co., Ltd., 1930 (a).

Sandage, Charles H., and Vernon Fryburger. *Advertising Theory and Practice.* Homewood, Ill.: Richard D. Irwin, Inc., 1960 (a).

Sandys, John Edwin. *A Short History of Classical Scholarship.* Cambridge: The University Press, 1915 (s).

———. *M. Tulli Ciceronis ad M. Brutum Orator.* Cambridge: Cambridge University Press, 1885 (o).

Shannon, Claude M., and Warren Weaver. *The Mathematical Theory of Communication.* Urbana, Ill.: University of Illinois Press, 1964 (m).

Sherif, Muzafer, and Carl I. Hovland. *Social Judgment: Assimilation and Contrast Effects in Communication and Attitude Change.* New Haven, Conn.: Yale University Press, 1961 (s).

Smith, Bruce Lannes, Harold D. Lasswell, and Ralph D. Casey. *Propaganda, Communication and Public Opinion.* Princeton, N. J.: Princeton University Press, 1946 (pr).

Stearn, Gerald, ed. *McLuhan, Hot and Cool.* New York: The Dial Press, Inc., 1967 (m).

Stevenson, Charles L. *Ethics and Language.* New Haven, Conn.: Yale University Press, 1944 (e).

Thompson, Wayne N. *Quantitative Research in Public Address and Communication.* New York: Random House, Inc., 1967 (q).

Thonssen, Lester, and A. Craig Baird. *Speech Criticism.* New York: The Ronald Press Company, 1948 (s).

Time. "The Campaign," LXXXVIII, No. 11 (September 11, 1963), 20 (c).

Toulmin, Stephen. *The Uses of Argument.* Cambridge, England: The University Press, 1958 (u).

Von Wright, Georg H. *An Essay in Modal Logic.* Amsterdam: North-Holland Publishing Company, 1951 (m).

Wagner, Russel H. "The Rhetorical Theory of Isocrates." In Lionel Crocker and Paul A. Carmack, eds., *Readings in Rhetoric.* Springfield, Ill.: Charles C. Thomas, Publisher 1965, pp. 169–83 (r).

Walter, Otis M. *Speaking to Inform and to Persuade.* New York: The Macmillan Company, 1966 (s).

Weaver, Richard M. *Composition: A Course in Writing and Rhetoric.* New York: Holt, Rinehart and Winston, Inc., 1957 (c).

———. *The Ethics of Rhetoric.* Chicago: Henry Regnery, Co., 1965 (e).

Whately, Richard. *Elements of Rhetoric.* Ed. Douglas Ehninger. Bloomington, Ill.: University of Illinois Press, 1963 (e).

Williamson, George. *The Senecan Amble: A Study in Prose from Bacon to Collier.* Chicago: University of Chicago Press, 1966 (s).

Wimsatt, W. K., Jr. "Explication as Criticism, 1951." In *Explication as Criticism, 1951,* ed. W. K. Wimsatt, Jr. New York: Columbia University Press, 1963 (e).

Wise, John E. *The Nature of the Liberal Arts.* Milwaukee: The Bruce Publishing Co., 1946 (n).

Wittgenstein, Ludwig. *Tractatus Logico-Philosophicus.* Tr. D. F. Fears and B. F. McGuinness. New York: Humanities Press, Inc., 1961 (t).

5

Literary Discourse

Introduction

The present chapter deals with a third basic aim of discourse, the literary. Of all the aims of discourse, the literary is the one with which the college student in English is most acquainted. In fact, many in the discipline would like to restrict the field of English to the study of literature and to exile grammar to a department of linguistics, semantics to philosophy or linguistics, speech to its own department, reading and listening to education, information and media to communications, persuasion to speech, science and exploration to philosophy, and expression to psychiatry. This restriction of English to the study of literature has even been advocated for high school departments of English (cf. Lynch, h, 419 f). At any rate, one does not have to apologize for the study of literature in departments of English. The reasons for including literature in a course of study will be considered when the nature of literature has been examined in some detail.

The problem of terminology which was fairly acute in the two preceding chapters is not nearly so critical for this aim of discourse. There have been, however, a few other terms which have been used for this kind of discourse throughout history, and a look at them might forestall some confusions later on.

In Antiquity, the general term used most frequently for literary discourse was "poetry." The term comes from the Greek word for "to make," *poiein*. Thus, the Greek word stresses a concept of craftsmanship, a connotation which the word has, unfortunately, largely lost in most modern languages. In modern times, "poetry" is not entirely equivalent to what is called "literary discourse." Poetry is usually taken to be the opposite of prose, and the criterion of differentia is a matter of elaborateness of sound structures. Poetry, in this sense, is characterized by recurrent rhythmic or rhymic structures, whereas prose is not characterized by such conspicuous sound structures. In this sense, poetry is almost equivalent to verse. But the opposition of verse to prose is not the same as that between literary and nonliterary uses of language. For, on the one hand, especially in modern times, much that is in prose is generally included under the term literary—the novel, the short story, the informal essay, the character sketch, even Baudelaire's *Petits Poèmes en Prose*. And, conversely, many verse compositions are not necessarily literary: church hymns, patriotic songs, advertising jingles, sentimental love lyrics; one might question whether some verse material, occasionally anthologized in literary textbooks, is really literary: Lucretius' *De rerum natura,* Virgil's *Georgics,* Dryden's *Religio Laici,* Pope's *An Essay on Man.* Certainly Horace carefully distinguished his satires in verse from his odes, insofar as his purposes were concerned (cf. La Drière, s, 131 ff.; on the basic distinction of poetry from prose, cf. La Drière, p, 441–45).

From Antiquity up until at least the seventeenth century, the word "grammar" was used not for literature itself, but for the study of literature. The trilogy of liberal arts could well have been called literature, rhetoric, and logic. In Antiquity grammar meant more the study of literature than the study of language. In the early Middle Ages, in Martianus Capella, Isidore, and Bede, grammar still included the study of poetry, to a large extent (Baldwin, m, 92, 96, 131). In the Middle Ages, grammar came to mean the systematic study of what we would now call grammarians, usually Priscian, though it still included some reading assignments in rather unsophisticated "literature."

The term "artistic" would be acceptable were it not for the fact that it implies a lack of "art" in referential and persuasive composition, as well as in making shoes, pies, or bridges; yet, there is certainly a craftsmanship involved in making these objects. They involve arts, though not fine arts. It seems advisable to keep this general meaning for the term "artistic," a comprehension it had both in Antiquity and the Middle Ages (cf. Maritain, a, 20–22). The term "belles lettres" attempts to do for literary productions what "fine arts" does for the arts in general. The distinction is a useful one, but "belles lettres" would not include, for the average reader, much of the folk art and popular art which I intend to include in the extension of the term "literary." In addition, "belles lettres" has seen only very limited acceptance. Some of the same difficulties attach to the term "esthetic." It has the broad sense of "fine arts," but is rarely applied to literature as a species.

Despite its humble origin, the term "literary" is probably the best for our purposes. It is true that a secondary meaning of literature is that of scholarship on a given topic ("Look up the literature on the subject"), and occasionally literature can mean all written materials, but these ambiguities rarely cause trouble. There is a body of literary works which most people in

English would accept as the referent for the term, though individuals might make particular inclusions or exclusions.

In one sense, my particular inclusion of folk literature and popular literature will undoubtedly disturb some purists who would reserve the term for the "classics." This last term "classical" had precisely this high-brow sense at its origin. Aulus Gellius, in the second century A.D., used the word "scriptor classicus" in contrast to a "scriptor proletarius," following a metaphor of Servius Tullius, who divided Roman people into "classici" (of the first class), "infra classem" (middle class), and "proletarii." "It is from this rare use of *classicus* that the modern term 'classical' is derived" (Sandys, s, 63). "Literature" in this book will therefore include folk, pop, and classical literature. A pun or a dirty joke is literature, "Gunsmoke" on TV is literature, and "Measure for Measure" is literature. But some of the materials often anthologized in high school and college textbooks are not literature in the sense adopted here. Bradford's *History of the Plymouth Plantation*, Edwards' "Sinners in the Hands of an Angry God," Mather's theological tracts, Hume's philosophical treatises, and Bertrand Russell's essays on marriage are not literature in the present sense—not that they are not culturally valuable for other equally valid reasons.

The Nature of Literature

The theoretical nature of literary discourse is more difficult to establish than any of the other aims of discourse. As has been shown, the nature of science, of information, and of persuasion is a subject of much controversy. Yet, in the history of Western civilization, the nature of the literary has been more debated than any of these three. Theories about the nature of the artistic or the esthetic are almost as numerous as philosophies of life.

The first problem facing the analyst of such diversity is classification. It would simply be unmanageable to attempt to handle fifteen or thirty variant approaches to the nature of literature. Can these varied theories be reduced to some fundamental clusters that can be treated together while acknowledging minor differences? A survey of some modern books and articles on various critical approaches to literature does reveal some attempts at classification. *Kenyon Review,* in 1950 and 1951, ran a series of articles on the humanist, the formalist, the historical, the amateur, the verbal, the political, the emotional, and the archetypal critics with an outstanding representative of each school doing separate articles (Autumn, 1950, and Winter and Spring, 1951). Robert W. Stallman, in an influential anthology in the late forties, included criticism of the kinds represented by

Taine and Sainte-Beuve, those represented by Baudelaire and Remy de Gourmont, the historical, the "Americanism" of Van Wyck Brooks, I. A. Richards, and the new critics (Stallman, c, 412–508). Wellek and Warren, in what was undoubtedly the most influential American book on literary theory in this century, distinguished the historical and biographical, the formalist, the psychological, the Marxist, and the sociological (Wellek, t). Guerin et al., in *A Handbook to Critical Approaches,* currently enjoying some favor, has chapters treating the traditional, the formalistic, the psychological, the mythological and archetypal, the exponential, and a miscellany chapter. The traditional includes the textual, the historical-biographical, the moral, and the genre and paraphrase. The miscellany chapter includes the sociological, the linguistic, the appreciative, the Aristotelian, the generic, and the genetic. In all, Guerin has seventeen groups. Stanley Hyman, in *The Armed Vision: A Study in the Methods of Modern Literary Criticism,* considers examples of biographical, folk, psychological, Marxist, categorical, and symbolic action criticisms, as well as the use of translation, tradition, evaluation, interpretation, scholarship, and painstaking research in criticism (Hyman, a). Lemon, a modern British writer, distinguishes only two basic approaches to literature, the mimetic and the formalistic. As he says,

> The basic division of this study needs little explanation. Poems are said to have value either as imitations of something else or as achieved forms. The difficult fact is that either source of value, considered simply, excludes the other, yet any respectable theory must in some way manage to include both. *Mimetic* theories are those that value the poem as imitation; all other theories are *formalistic* (Lemon, p, 15; cf. Stallman, c, 17 for a similar division).

In his book, Lemon does give several subdivisions of each of his two main approaches and several subdivisions of each of the subdivisions. Lemon's approach consistently has the logical advantage of operating principles of division that separate his various species. In that respect his system is rationally preferable to the ad hoc classification of Wellek, Guerin, Hyman, Stallman, the *Kenyon Review* series, and others.

Another writer also operates with clearly indicated principles of division. M. H. Abrams, in the succinct introductory chapter of *The Mirror and the Lamp,* uses the components of the communication triangle, and distinguishes expressionistic, pragmatic, mimetic, and objective approaches to literature, according to whether the approach views literature as the vehicle of expression of the *artist,* or as a means of giving the *audience* a useful lesson, or as a medium whereby the *universe* is adequately mirrored, or as a focus on the structure of the art *object*.[1] Abrams uses the following diagram to illustrate the structure that he is working with (Figure V, 1).

Figure V, 1

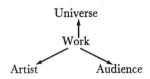

In the terms of this book these elements would translate more generally as ✓ reality, signal, encoder, and decoder. Here, however, the communication model is being interpreted in a context of literary theory. Most theories, he maintains, do not eclectically stress all four elements equally. As he says,

> Although any reasonably adequate theory takes some account of all four elements, almost all theories, as we shall see, exhibit a discernible orientation toward one only. That is, a critic tends to derive from one of these terms his principal categories for defining, classifying, and analyzing a work of art, as well as the major criteria by which he judges its value. Application of this analytic scheme, therefore, will sort attempts to explain the nature and worth of a work of art into four broad classes. Three will explain the work of art principally by relating it to another thing: the universe, the audience, or the artist. The fourth will explain the work by considering it in isolation, as an autonomous whole, whose significance and value are determined without any reference beyond itself (Abrams, m, 6–7).

It is no accident that Abrams discovered in his historical research that almost all theories "exhibit a discernible orientation toward one only" of the basic elements. As we shall see, a serious commitment to imitation, for example, as the fundamental constituting principle of art will not always allow the radical distortions of reality which the pragmatist will sometimes have to effect to establish his thesis, or the idealization of reality which the structuralist will achieve to produce pleasure by form, or the personalized misapprehensions of reality which a necessarily emotional subject has of reality. Similarly, a primary commitment to pleasure through form will not usually permit the intrusions of the other three preoccupations. There is a strong tendency to a hierarchy of importance. If one uses e for

---

1 For a somewhat similar grouping of theories, cf. Richard McKeon, *Thought, Action, and Passion* (t).

encoder, s for signal, r for reality, and d for decoder, in any given system one of the components is capitalized and the others are distinctly lower case, and in an order which may vary: Serd, Sedr, Erds, Desr, Reds, etc.

This primacy of one component suggests strongly that it is not really possible to have a pluralistic notion of literature or of criticism, that is, a view of literature or criticism which accepts the coexistence of a plurality of valid, even if contradictory approaches. Such a pluralism was proposed by the Chicago Neo-Aristotelians, Crane, Olson, Maclean, and others (cf. Olson, o, 547, 551, 553; Crane, i, 10 ff.) Their hypotheses will be carefully entertained after the various theories have been outlined and evaluated.

As prolegomena to the consideration of these four theories of art, I would like to examine why it is necessary to consider them at all (cf. Lemon, p, 9 ff.). Is it necessary to have thought out one's philosophy of art to be a student or a teacher or a practitioner or reader of literature? Can't one simply appreciate or write poetry and forget all the theory and analysis? At one level, of course one can; many do, many have both written and read well, as it were by intuition, for centuries. But such readers and writers were the conscious or unconscious recipients of a heritage of reading and writing that they accepted and operated on, and which was, fortunately, an intelligent heritage. It is difficult to instance a single major writer in Western culture who was not very aware of his culture. The writers who were not recipients, analytically or not, of an intelligent heritage have been forgotten or never were remembered. Others, recipients of unintelligent theoretical systems, have been rescued by their own genius, their own intuitions, and the continual exposure to good art.

In an earlier age this intuitive escape was more possible than in our times. As in politics, religion, ethics, and economics, so also in the fine arts, today with almost universal education there has been a serious questioning of basic axioms in nearly every sphere of human activity. As a result, the axioms of opposing systems have been pursued to their radical conclusions. It is much easier today, as a result of many minds exploring the issues, to detect the real nature of what is meant by a commitment to Christianity or to Communism, or to other ideologies. Similarly, in the fine arts, certain axioms of esthetics have also been heroically pursued to their conclusions. The other day, on educational television, I saw a man groan for five minutes in front of a curtain; this was labeled poetry. Actually it is poetry, if one accepts one definition of poetry. And random hoofprints of a mule on canvas are sold as "paintings."

In the face of such absurdities, it becomes more critical for the student of literature to rationalize his position. It might also become clear to him that what some mistook for art in the past was really sentimentality or edification or psychotherapy. In an age where anything can be called art and peddled as such, intuition and exposure are not the guides they once were. And in an age in which not the upper five per cent, but the entire populace is to be cultured, genius cannot be counted on so regularly. As far as teachers are concerned, the author has encountered only too many teachers of high school and even college English whose views of art could well stand some soul-searching. Some are simply disguised preachers, didactic or pornographic, to use Joyce's terms. These various positions will be analyzed in the "Critique" sections in each theory. The issue of the rationality of art will be returned to at several places in the following pages.

The Mimetic Theory of Art

The task of describing and evaluating the basic approaches to art has been much simplified because of the excellent work of writers like Abrams, Lemon, McKeon, Crane, and others. Abrams's *The Mirror and the Lamp* is a very carefully documented presentation of many aspects of the four theories as they can be seen in Romantic theories of literature. In addition, many of the precedents of these positions in Antiquity and the subsequent appearances in our time are indicated in Abrams. If, in addition to Abrams, the work of Lemon is considered, the student should emerge with a fairly adequate historical survey of the four positions. In this presentation, only a summary of each of the four positions can be given. Lemon consistently evaluates the positions besides describing them. Abrams did not systematically include evaluation, since his was basically a historical and descriptive work. However, when the writers whom he is describing and placing historically include evaluations of their previously held tenets, Abrams records such evaluations.

A DEFINITION OF
THE MIMETIC THEORY

Theories that emphasize the incorporation of the universe into art make the art object an imitation of reality. The core of this theory is that, whatever else may be in the art object, what makes it art as such is the careful reproduction of some aspects of reality or nature. For this reason, such theories usually are called by some term that derives from imitation or reality or nature. Abrams calls this cluster of theories "mimetic," from the Greek word for imitation. Particularly in the area of the novel, terms such as "realism" and "naturalism" have been used.

The idea that an adequate incorporation of reality into the art object is what makes a work artistic is one of the most popular concepts of art, even today. The man on the street usually judges a landscape painting by such a phrase as, "My, that's good. It's just like the real view." The same criterion is applied to portraits, "What a wonderful portrait! It looks just like Aunt Susan." And to movies: "Great movie! Things were just like that on Saipan." So also are novels, short stories, and television plays judged. And negative evaluations are made by the same norm. Take the man on the street into a gallery of modern abstract or surrealistic painting and he will often condemn it because he does not know what it "represents." The man on the street is often a mimeticist, as far as art theory is concerned.

He has a respectable number of philosophers and practitioners of art to support his common-sense position. Estheticians from Plato to Zola are often held up as exemplifying the view that the primary function of art is to imitate reality, and as a corollary, the view that any work of art which manages to incorporate a fair percentage of the characteristics of reality into itself is said to be a work of art of a high level. Imitation for such theories is the essence of art. Such theories do not deny the necessity of the artist's expressing his own individual emotions, or the necessity of pleasing structures in the work, or the communication of some conviction to a receptor; but these three other elements in the artistic process or product are viewed only as necessary accompaniments to art, not as constituting elements that determine whether the work is *artistic*. They may, to use Aristotle's terminology, be properties, but they are not essence.

Plato and Aristotle are often instanced as theorists who hold an imitation theory of art. It is easy to adduce passages from Plato's works which show that all artists are imitators (cf. McKeon, l, 149–59, for a lengthy consideration of "imitation" in Plato). But it is more difficult to prove that imitation, as such, made them artists. Lodge, who devoted two chapters of his work on *The Philosophy of Plato* to esthetics, pays little attention to the mimetic aspect of Plato's theory of art, though he does not totally ignore it (cf. p, 20–25). And the very respected editor of the great German encyclopedia on classical antiquity, the *Real-Enzyklopädie*, maintains that Plato's view of art is a compromise between the two main Greek notions of art as pleasure and art as a teaching vehicle (cf. Barwick, g, 56). Aristotle, likewise, maintains that all art involves imitation, but few today would maintain that Aristotle conceived imitation to be the constituting principle of art. In any case, however, many theorists in the history of esthetics have understood Plato and Aristotle to be mimeticists.

Abrams also instances the English Bishop Richard Hurd, the French writer Charles Batteux, and the German philosopher G. E. Lessing as examples of mimeticists in the eighteenth century (m, 11–13). The neoclassic proponents of imitation, aware that art did not really reproduce reality as it was, adapted the concept in various ways. Art was said to imitate an improved nature "la belle nature," or to amalgamate the best of several parts of nature, or to represent an average or general nature (cf. Abrams, m, 37–42). In the nineteenth century the view that art is imitative was taken over mainly by novelists and short story writers. The realists, the local colorists, the regionalists, and sometimes the naturalists felt that novels must imitate reality.

Although imitation as a theory for critics and practitioners is not so widely held today as formerly, there are several current modern versions of this view of art. Among novelists the mimetic view remains strong. In the review of the novel in 1966, Susan Sontag could still write:

> According to the "tradition," the novel is understood not so much as a work of art but as a mirror of reality. For most people the interest in novels consists in what they are "about." There are political novels...there are academic novels; there is the Southern novel, the advertising agency novel, the art world novel. And since most people sort out novels by their subjects, the segments of the world they depict, the principal standard applied to novels is how well, how accurately, how pungently they give us news about unfamiliar social milieus. As far as literature... has a serious purpose (something other than mere diversion, entertainment, escape), it is this: the responsible and intelligent dramatizing of psychological and social and ethical issues, and the supplying of information.
>
> In other words, most critically respectable novels written in England and America these days are—however sophisticated the intelligence behind them—journalistic in conception. I include the work of the American writers who are most admired today: for example, Saul Bellow, Norman Mailer, James Baldwin William Styron, Philip Roth, Bernard Malamud (Sontag, 1, 154–55).

In this sense, the mimetic theory of art is far from dead.[2] Among some new critics and at least one quite respected philosopher of art the mimetic theory is still a vital issue. The philosopher of art is Susanne Langer. In *Philosophy in a New Key,* Langer makes it clear that she conceives music to be imitative. Music, in the history of the mimetic approach, was usually the first to be severed from a view of art as imitation (cf. McKeon, 1, 147, note 2). Insisting that music *is* imitative, she maintains that it

> ...is not self-expression, but *formulation and representation* of emotions, moods, mental tensions and resolutions—a "logical picture" of sentiment, responsive life, a source of insight, not a plea for sympathy (p, 180).

Though she is paraphrasing Richard Wagner, she is establishing this as her own view. Music, she says, has the power of imitating the structure or form

---

[2] For a French version of the novel as a mimetic genre and the poem as an expressive genre, cf. Kinneavy, s, 124–41.

of emotions. She quotes Wolfgang Köhler, the pioneer of Gestalt psychology, to show the usefulness of "musical" dynamics to describe the forms of mental life.

> Quite generally the inner processes, whether emotional or intellectual, show types of development which may be given names, usually applied to musical events, such as: *crescendo* and *diminuendo, accelerando* and *ritardando* (*Gestalt Psychology*, 248–49, quoted in Langer, p, 183).

It is the general, not the specific, forms of emotional dynamics that are imitated in music, Langer asserts. "For *what music can actually reflect is only a morphology of feeling*; and it is quite plausible that some sad and some happy conditions may have a very similar morphology (Langer, p, 193, her italics). Music actually can reveal the forms of feelings even better than language can (p, 191), although all esthetic pleasure gives us this satisfaction of discovering truth (p, 211). In the case of verbal art forms such as poetry, the truth arises from the form, not the meanings of the words (p, 211–13).[3]

A third and somewhat popular modern version of mimeticism can be seen in some of the new critics, especially Ransom and his disciples. Ransom continually opposes poetry to science and maintains that each represents the world in a different way. Science generalizes and represents the world to us by means of "ideas," but necessarily loses the individuality of the "things" of the world in so doing (Ransom, w, 116, 206, *passim*). "What we cannot know constitutionally as scientists is the world which is made up of whole and indefeasible objects, and this the world of poetry recovers for us," (w, x–xi). Because the individual "things" of the world are perceived as images, the job of poetry is to represent this particularity by means of images:

> The poetic impulse is not free, yet it holds out stubbornly against science for the enjoyment of its images. It means to reconstitute the world of perceptions (w, 130).

Imagination is the "organ of knowledge whose technique is images," and it works in a different mode from reason whose technique is universals (w, 156). In a poem, "every detail in it is accurate detail, or it should be" (w, 158). Images are the habitual means we have to the understanding of the "things" of reality (w, 161).

Ransom's doctrine of poetry is clearly mimetic, therefore. It can be seen in some of his disciples also. Thus William Handy often sounds like

---

[3] In another work I have given some attention to Langer's later presentation of her theory in *Feeling and Form* (cf. Kinneavy, s, 151 ff.).

a mimeticist (cf. Handy, k, 51, 72), though Handy also seems to be a pragmatist (k, 34–35). Wimsatt, a prominent literary theorist, has written a celebrated essay in which he attempts to preserve both the universal and the concrete in poetry (v, 69–84). He objects to an inordinate use of either universals or particulars:

> Neither of the extremes gives a good account of art and each leads out of art. The theory of particularity leads to individuality and originality ...then to the idiosyncratic and the unintelligible and to the psychology of the author, which is not the work of art and is not a standard for judgment. The theory of universality as it appears in Johnson and Reynolds leads to platitude and to a standard of material objectivity, the average tulip, the average human form, some sort of average (v, 74).

However, after presenting the issue as a problem of what is imitated in a work of art, Wimsatt spends most of the time in his solution stressing the importance of structuring the elements, and really pays little attention to the question of whether or not the universals or particulars actually mirror the world at all.

There are, obviously, more than mere residues of mimeticism present in our culture today in the populace, in the practitioners of some genres of literature, in the philosophers of art, and in literary critics and theorists. Let us now take a quick look at some of the objections raised against an imitative theory of art.

A Critique of the Mimetic Theory of Art

I can outline only briefly some of the objections that have been raised against this theory. It is hoped that the reader who feels that his own art theory is being challenged will follow up the indicated references and seriously question (and maybe answer) his own assumptions. There are much more lengthy evaluations of each position. Lemon, for example, in *The Partial Critics*, deals extensively with most of these positions. William Rooney, in *The Problem of Poetry and Belief in Contemporary Criticism* devotes a whole chapter to Ransom (p, 50–67). Abrams, in *The Mirror and The Lamp,* records many of the objections raised against the mimetic and other positions. Other lengthy critiques abound; these three are singled out because they operate in a context which will be intelligible to the reader who has followed the sequence of this text.

Traditionally, the frontal challenges to imitation as a comprehensive theory of art began in the neoclassic period when people like Beattie pointed out the serious difficulties involved in predicating imitation in music (cf. Abrams, m, 92). Indeed, we have the right to ask, "What is imitated in a Bach fugue?" Hobbes, Sprat, Samuel Johnson, and others rightfully objected to the use in literature of such manifestly unreal beings as fairies, gnomes, false gods and goddesses, and the like, if poetry is seriously imitative (cf. Abrams m, 266). The usual justification of the "supernatural" or "marvelous" on grounds of pleasure seemed to evade the issue of imitation (cf. Abrams, m, 219). Indeed it seems difficult to reconcile Ransom's advocacy of fiction and the miraculous with his admonition to make the "thing" as accurate in all details as it can be.

In the nineteenth century and even earlier, Bain and others extended the assault to other arts, "Music, dancing, architecture, and fanciful decoration can hardly be said to imitate anything, or to refer the mind to any natural objects" (Bain, e, 269). In this century, the visual arts and music again followed suit. In his memoirs, Wassily Kandinsky anguishes over this problem. He concludes that representation of objects is "injurious" to his painting. And he asks, "What should replace the object?" Roy McMullen, who is quoting Kandinsky, shows that for a time "form" replaced imitation in modern art. He then concludes:

> The up-to-date answer, that is, to Kandinsky's anguished question is that his represented object should be replaced by a cool refusal to imagine *any* kind of referent in a work of visual art. This answer, in various degrees of explicitness, has been common for some time among far-out sculptors and neo-Dadaist or Pop practitioners of solid collage, but finding it in a realm where one used to come and go talking of Plato seems a little odd (McMullen, m, 126–27, his italics; the whole section is very relevant).

Literature has always seemed less vulnerable to these assaults precisely because literature uses words as its medium, and words obviously *do* refer to reality. Yet unless the literary art is not art in the same general sense as the other arts, it can also be questioned that imitation is what constitutes even literary art as art and as literature. Susanne Langer herself has discussed the impossibility of language to reproduce reality with any pretense to immediate individuality (Langer, f, 13). The assumption of Ransom and others that poetry can present individuals better than can science has never, it seems to me, been seriously proved. In fact, the botanist in his descriptions, the geologist in his, the psychologist in his case studies, the architect in his specifications seem to reconstruct individuality as well as or better than the poet. And images are not forbidden to them; nor are they to the persuader. The pictures of hell drawn by Johathan Edwards in his sermons and St.

Ignatius Loyola in his *Spiritual Exercises* draw on imagery as continually as Dante; and all three pictures have yet, thank God, to be verified as accurate. The artistic substitute for reality is a poor substitute indeed. And, of course, one has the right to ask why there should be a substitute at all. If I really want daffodils, I can find them in a nursery; I do not have to ask Wordsworth about them. As Lemon has remarked, reading "'Tintern Abbey" is not quite like seeing it (p, 33) ; in fact, if one of the two would have to be destroyed, I should shed fewer tears over seeing the abbey demolished. Rebecca West's caustic remark is more than facetiously relevant, "A copy of the universe is not what is required of art; one of the damned thing is ample" (quoted in Abrams, m, 100).

Mimeticism has always had problems with the distortions which art and literary art wreak on reality. For it is quite true that some of the most important periods in art history have been characterized by deliberate attempts to deviate from the real into the impressionistic, the abstract, the expressionistic, the surrealistic, the nonobjective. Ortega y Gasset continually points out that much modern art is a distortion of reality, and he maintains this is of the essence of art. "Art is appreciated precisely because it is recognized as a farce" (Ortega y Gasset, d, 44; cf. also 20–23).

Occasionally artistic distortions of reality, because some do take them seriously, irritate the respecters of reality into retaliation: "In November 1956 the American Group for the Advancement of Psychiatry held a conference 'to clarify the differences between Orwell's fantastic account and the real processes actually used in authentic cases' [of brainwashing]" (Brown, t, 268).

Another and more vitriolic retaliation is provided by Bernard DeVoto's *The Literary Fallacy*. In this series of lectures, DeVoto, a very respectable historian of American culture, juxtaposes the picture of America presented by the "realistic" novelists of the 1920's with the picture presented by sober history. He poses his analysis in these terms:

> Let us ask a question, briefly answer it, and set the answer aside as a bench mark to return to later. Select a number of writers who any informed critic will agree were leading and characteristic writers of the period. Select, say, H. L. Mencken, Sinclair Lewis, Ernest Hemingway, John Dos Passos, William Faulkner, and Thomas Wolfe. If someone who was ignorant of American life during the 1920's were to consult the books of these men in an effort to understand it, could he use their work as a trustworthy guide? Does the picture which their work contains correspond to American experience and could our stranger rely on it when he came to appraise our culture? Is it trustworthy data for historians who may hope to inform future generations about our past?
> The answer is no (DeVoto, 1, 22).

In lecture after lecture he examines the America of Sinclair Lewis, of Hemingway, of Van Wyck Brooks, of Faulkner, of John Dos Passos, and others. He concludes that these separate portraits and the conglomerate picture they present are "almost entirely myth" (1, 23). Towards the end of the book he reiterates his thesis:

> We have thus come back to a familiar fact: the repudiation of American life by American literature during the 1920's signified that writers were isolated or insulated from the common culture. There is something intrinsically absurd in the image of a literary man informing a hundred and twenty million people that their ideas are base, their beliefs unworthy, their ideas vulgar, their institutions corrupt, and, in sum, their civilization too trivial to engage that literary man's respect. That absurdity is arrogant but also it is naive and most of all it is ignorant(1, 150).

And he concludes,

> Never in any country or any age had writers so misrepresented their culture, never had they been so unanimously wrong. Never had writers been so completely separated from the experiences that alone give life and validity to literature (1, 167).

The Expressive Theory of Art

A DEFINITION

A second element which has been stressed in esthetic theories as determining the nature of art is the artist himself. The form which this theory usually takes is in an emphasis upon the expression in the work of art of the unique individuality of the artist. Because art is viewed as "self-expression," Abrams calls this theory the expressionistic theory. Other writers refer to this cluster of approaches as "personality," "psychological," or "experience" theories. Some even make the catharsis of the moments of the process of composition more important than the resulting art product; and for this reason several writers call this the "process" or the "ordealist" view of poetry. Because the self-expression is almost inevitably an emotional expression, these theories have also been called "emotional" views of poetry or literature. Abrams defines the expressive theory of art at follows:

> Poetry is the overflow, utterance, or projection of the thought or feelings of the poet; or else (in the chief variant formulation) poetry is defined in terms of the imaginative process which modifies and synthesizes the images, thoughts, and feelings of the poet. This way of thinking, in which the artist himself becomes the major element generating both the artistic product and the criteria by which it is to be judged, I shall call the expressive theory of art (Abrams, m, 22).

Given these characteristics as determining the work *as art*, certain cardinal doctrines followed as immediate corollaries in most of the traditional formulations of this theory. Abrams lists them as follows: poetry is the expression of feeling; poetry is opposed to science; the origin of poetry is in passion and it is naturally expressed in rhythmic and figurative language; poetry is spontaneous and genuine; the poet is more emotional and sensitive than other men; the most "important function of poetry is, by its pleasurable resources, to foster and subtilize the sensibility, emotions, and sympathies of the reader" (Abrams, m, 101–3).

Some other characteristic emphases of this approach can be viewed as secondary corollaries. The lyric, always a secondary genre, has become the type of "pure poetry" or literature and has remained so for more than a century and a half. In some modern French theorists, for example, only the lyric is poetic; other forms of literature are artistic, i.e., appeal to the intellect and imitate reality, which the lyric does not (cf. the theories of Bonnet, Hytier, and Benda, as outlined in Kinneavy, s, 129 ff.). There is a heavy stress on intuition as opposed to reason, especially in the many theories that stem from German expressionism or from Croce's very influential brand of expressionism (cf. La Drière, e, 226–27). Closely related to this is an accentuation of the native inspiration of the poet and the relative denigration of the craft and rational control of the poet (cf. Abrams, m, 188 ff. and 203 ff.). As with many aspects of expressionism, this loss of rational control is also transferred from poet to reader. Joseph Watson says characteristically, "No man of a true poetical spirit, is master of himself while he reads them [Homer and Milton]" (quoted in Abrams, m, 133); and Hazlitt generalizes, "In art, in taste, in life, in speech, you decide from feeling, and not from reason" (quoted in Abrams, m, 135). Further, if emotion constitutes poetry, since emotional effusions cannot be sustained for any great length of time, the shorter forms of literature, such as the lyric and the short story, become the most typical literary products. Parallel to this emphasis was the isolation of great single lines or short passages from context and the presentation of these passages as embodying passion and therefore being richly poetic (cf. Abrams, m, 134). Keble even went so far as to use the many kinds of emotion to differentiate the genres of poetry (cf. Abrams, m, 145 f.).

The structure of the communication triangle is radically affected by such a theory. Usually there is a denial or at least a decline of the importance of the audience. Goethe, Mill, Shelley, and others exhibit this facet of expressionism strongly. As Goethe remarked,

> For the one thing that matters is the artist.... As for the gaping public, and whether when it has finished gaping it can justify why it has gaped, what difference does that make? (quoted in Abrams, m, 90)

Reality too is, especially in twentieth-century versions of expressionism, equally denigrated. As Henri Bonnet, a modern French critic says,

One could say that the poetic value of a descriptive poem can be measured by the deviation that exists between the object described and that which the poet makes us see in it.... [The poet] is not interested in reality for itself (quoted in Kinneavy, s, 131–32).

In these modern French theorists even the art object and its structures are depreciated; the real poem is the train of reveries and emotions which are evoked in the mind. In Croce, the poem need never leave the poet's mind—the art object has lost its objectivity. The verse is only the springboard. An interest in the structures of the poem is an "esthetic" rational interest, not a poetic emotional interest, says another modern French critic in this school, Jean Hytier. Hytier even says that such an esthetic interest is an obstacle to true poetry:

> The only relation that poetic pleasure has to the beautiful [the object of *esthetic* pleasure in his system] is negative; as when, in the cultivated amateur reader, esthetic exigencies prevent the poetic emotion from being constructed" (quoted in Kinneavy, s, 149).

Even Abrams has not chronicled such radical conclusions which the heroic logic of the French mind pursues in the dialectic of expressionism. Wordsworth with his manifesto of expressionism might have been frightened by these modern conclusions. As Abrams remarks,

> The extreme consequences latent in the central analogue to which Wordsworth gave impetus in England—the elimination, for all practical purposes, of the conditions of the given world, the requirements of the audience, and the control by conscious purpose and art as important determinants of a poem—did not appear in that country until three decades later in such critics as Keble, Carlyle, and John Stuart Mill (Abrams, m, 48).

These nineteenth-century critics seem pale and timid alongside their twentieth-century avatars, Hytier, Benda, and Bonnet (cf. Kinneavy, s, 148 ff.).

In the delineation of the axioms and corollaries of the expressive theory, many adherents have already been indicated. Most of the names associated with this theory are names from the eighteenth, nineteenth, and twentieth centuries. In Antiquity, there is no full-fledged theory of expressionsim. Longinus is usually instanced as foreshadowing many of its doctrines, however (cf. Abrams, m, 72–74). In another work I have shown that there are other important antecedents to this doctrine in Aristotle, Horace, the Epicureans, Proclus, and the general Greek theory of music (cf. Kinneavy, s, 117 ff., 56 ff.). The Renaissance also had its adherents, especially in lyric theory (cf. Kinneavy, s, 119–20). But the greatest exponents of the theory were the pre-Romantics and Romantics of the eighteenth and nineteenth centuries. Abrams has chronicled the many facets of this theory in the nineteenth century, and the list of the authors whom he quotes makes an interesting inventory of the Romantic period in England and Germany. Even people like Coleridge and Goethe who incorporate strong orientations to the objective approach in their work were not unaffected by the expressive currents.

By the end of the nineteenth century, the expressive doctrine of art had become widely accepted on the continent, in England, and in America, not only in literature but in other art fields as well. Writing as late as 1942, Susanne Langer could still say:

> In this form the doctrine has come down to our day, and is widely accepted by musicians and philosophers alike. From Rousseau to Kierkegaard and Croce among philosophers, from Marpurg to Hausegger and Riemann among music critics, but above all among musicians themselves —composers, conductors, and performers—we find the belief very widely disseminated that music is an emotional catharsis, that its essence is self-expression (Langer, p, 174).

A year later, writing in the *Dictionary of World Literature,* Craig La Drière could say, concerning expressionism,

> This conception of fine art prevailed throughout Europe during the nineteenth century, and though it has been subjected to much criticism in the twentieth it remains the commonest unconscious aesthetic prejudice of our time (e, 227).

The allies of expressionism as a theory of fine arts were undoubtedly the expressionistic psychology of psychoanalysis and the educational theories of Dewey and his followers which stressed the self-expression of the child.

One interesting variant of this theory was a kind of social expressionism that viewed art more as the expression of a society than of an individual. Ruskin's theory that great art was the expression of a free society and mediocre art the expression of a slave society was an interesting version of social expressionism. Some Marxist theories can also be classed here, when their emphasis is on the social expression in literature of a given class (cf. Lunacharsky, in Lemon, r, 78).

The educational effect of a social expressive theory is to stress the history and social background of a period, just as an educational corollary of individual expressionism emphasizes the biographical and psychological background of the writer. Both orientations were rampant in English departments for many years, nor have they totally lost their force even today.

THE EXPRESSIVE THEORY OF ART:
A CRITIQUE

As La Drière indicated in the passage quoted above, the expressive theory was severely assaulted in this century. T. E. Hulme, T. S. Eliot with other literary critics, Susanne Langer and Ortega y Gasset with other philosophers of art, literary theorists like Lemon, music theorists like Hanslick, and many others attacked nearly every dogma of the expressive credo as it was outlined above. For a full critique of expressionism, the student is referred to these authors. A few of their common attacks will be recorded here.

Nearly all agree that to make literature coterminous with emotional expression is to lose any distinctive meaning for literature as art at all. How, they ask, if emotional expression is literature can we distinguish art from many everyday expressions of emotion which no one pretends are art? It is true that Hazlitt was willing, given his premises, to recognize oaths and nicknames as "only a more vulgar sort of poetry" (quoted in Abrams, m, 151); and it is also true that some modern French expressive theorists would maintain that some of our emotional recollections or objects which stimulate these recollections, such as the faded flower from a high school prom dance, are poems despite the fact that they possess no esthetic value; Bonnet and Hytier both assert this (cf. Kinneavy, s, 148–50). Most critics and writers of literature, however, would admit that this destroys the meaning of literature. As Christopher North, in Wordsworth's time, pointed out, given Wordsworth's definition,

> Thus all men, women, and children, birds, beasts, and fishes, are poets, except versifiers. Oysters are poets. Nobody will deny that, whoever in the neighborhood of Prestonpons beheld them passionately gaping, on their native bed, for the flow of tide.... Not less so the snails.... The beetle, against the traveller borne in heedless hum, if we knew all his feelings in that soliloquy, might safely be pronounced a Wordsworth (quoted in Abrams, m, 155).

And almost eighty years later Susanne Langer reiterates the same argument:

> *Sheer self-expression requires no artistic form.* A lynching party howling round the gallows tree, a woman wringing her hands over a sick child, a lover who has just rescued his sweetheart in an accident and stands trembling, sweating, and perhaps laughing or crying is giving vent to intense feelings; but such scenes are not occasions for music, least of all for composing (Langer, p, 175, her italics).

In a similar vein, Ortega y Gasset has contrasted the emotional distances that separate a wife, a doctor, a reporter, and a painter assisting at the deathbed of a great man. He finds the least emotional intervention in the case of the painter (cf. Ortega y Gasset, d, 9–16). As Lemon rightly observes, "And, if emotion is the basis of poetry, how do we distinguish the poet from the neurotic? And finally, why should a reader prefer canned emotion to fresh?" (Lemon, p, 39–40)

Second, expressive theories of poetry give no evaluative criteria of art. As Langer says, they make "no distinction between good and bad art" (p, 168). She quotes a passage from Wilhelm Stekel, "one of the leading Freudian psychologists interested in artistic productions as a field of analysis," which vividly illustrates her point (p, 168). She then adds, "An analysis to which the artistic merit of a work is irrelevant can hardly be regarded as a promising technique of art criticism" (p, 168). The reason for this is the utter disregard of such theories for form. Indeed they cannot account for form, say both Lemon and Langer (cf. Lemon, p, 95); nor do such theories account for the long-standing existence of dramatic projection by the poet into different personalities. Is Shakespeare *sincerely* all of his villains and heroes? The theory, on psychological grounds, would make multiple schizophrenics of many dramatists or novelists.

Since the expressive theory does not account for form, it does not account for a specific esthetic emotion different from the emotions expressed or referred to in the poem. Ortega y Gasset distinguishes carefully the esthetic emotions from the emotions of ordinary life.

> Not that this [esthetic] life lacks sentiments and passions, but those sentiments and passions evidently belong to a flora other than that which covers the hills and dales of primary and human life. What those ultra-objects [art objects] evoke in our inner artist are secondary passions, specifically aesthetic sentiments (Ortega y Gasset, d, 20).

The primary and ordinary emotions of human life are, in fact, specifically not the emotions of art, says Ortega y Gasset: "Tears and laughter are, aesthetically, frauds" (d, 25). Speaking of Debussy, he says, "That was the deed of Debussy. Owing to him, it has become possible to listen to music serenely, without swoons and tears" (d, 27). For Ortega y Gasset, the esthetic is a conscious mental perception of form, and this precipitates a pleasurable emotion, the esthetic emotion. If specific emotions of love or fear or terror are aroused by art, one has the right to ask, as Langer does, "If music really grieves or frightens us, why do we listen to it?" (p, 173) Expressionism cannot answer this question either.

A theory of art which cannot distinguish art from grunts or howls, which is not interested in discriminating good from bad art, which is really more interested in the artist than the art object, which cannot account for form or the esthetic emotion is certainly a theory which has some serious drawbacks as a full-fledged theory of literature. It is not really surprising, therefore, that Ortega y Gasset can say of the nineteenth-century theory of expressive art:

> The nineteenth century was remarkably cross-eyed. That is why its products, far from representing a normal type of art, may be said to mark a maximum aberration in the history of taste (d, 23).

Without going so far, one can still question the art and art theory of expressionism.

The Pragmatic Theory of Art

A DEFINITION

Just as the mimetic theory of art emphasizes reality, and the expressive the artist, so the pragmatic theory of art focuses on the receptor. The receptor is said to determine the work of art in the following manner. If a work of art can achieve an emotional conviction or intellectual persuasion in the receptor, it is viewed by these theories as successful. Because some pragmatic or useful effect is thus achieved in the receptors, Abrams calls this cluster of theories "pragmatic." The usual connotations of this term preclude the consideration of the purely esthetic pleasure effect in the receiver. Pleasure, in these theories, is nearly always instrumental to teaching.

Other terms have also been used for the cluster of theories included here. Commonly such theories are called didactic theories of poetry; Joyce even distinguishes between the "didactic" and the "pornographical" arts, the ones advocating good, the others evil; both are improper arts, because they are dynamic; the esthetic arts are static: "the mind is arrested and raised above desire and loathing" (Joyce, p, 205). Lemon, somewhat disrespectfully, uses the term "edification theories" as the subtitle for his second chapter (p, 42–75). And, of course, these theories have been called the "moral" theories of literature. In Antiquity, the usual alternatives to pleasure as an aim of art were profit or usefulness (cf. Barwick, g, 56–58, for the terms used in Greek and Latin). From *utile,* Horace's term, "utilitarian" could be derived, and it would be an accurate term for this view of literature. Literature as "communications," as "teaching," and as "knowledge" are other terms sometimes used for this cluster of theories.

The characteristic emphasis is on the decoder, with the other three components of the artistic process taking on secondary importance. Normally the function of literature is viewed as communicating to the reader or hearer an intellectual truth, usually one viewed as having universal application and appeal. However, it can stress communication of an emotional response, though this is usually more characteristic of expressive theories. When the evocation of the emotional response becomes a matter of persuasion, however, the theory tends more to the pragmatic. Puttenham, the Elizabethan critic, portrays the poet as a physician who cures the reader (cf. Abrams, m, 138). A modern critic, Stanley Kauffmann, reviewing Lawrence's *Lady Chatterley's Lover,* takes an explicit stand on the emotional, even glandular effect of literature:

> The erotic passages in *Lady Chatterley* are most certainly intended to evoke erotic responses. Not something mistily lovely but distinctly sexual. The artist has as much right —*even necessity*—to evoke that response in a reader as he has to evoke appreciation of a landscape. If Lawrence doesn't make you feel in your very glands what it meant to Connie and Mellors to find at last a satisfactory sexual partner, then he has failed *as an artist* (Kauffmann, 1, 14, my italics).

Kaufmann's position here is very close to that of the Epicureans, who, according to Sextus Empiricus, read the love poems of Alcaeus, the wine poetry of Anacreon, and the satires of Archilochus to arouse themselves to love, drunkenness, or anger (see "Adversus Mathematicus" in Sextus Empiricus s, I, 298).

Sheer, unmitigated didacticism has rarely been promulgated by anyone in the literary tradition. There are those outside the tradition who condemn literature as the sometimes harmful residue of an infantile and primitive culture in which unenlightened man did not know any better. Locke, Newton, and especially Bentham take this view (cf. Abrams, m, 300 ff.). For such writers only pure science is a teaching vehicle, but even outside the literary tradition these are rare postures. Within the literary tradition, the pragmatic view of literature, though it gives primacy to the teaching function, usually makes some compromise with the pleasurable function. Horace is usually considered the grandfather of this position. In a famous passage in the *Ars Poetica* he remarked:

> The poet's aim is either to teach or to please, or to blend in one the delightful and the useful. Whatever the lesson you would convey, be brief, that your hearers may catch quickly what is said and faithfully retain it (a, ll. 333 ff.).

Horace's compromise was a typical one in Antiquity, as Kroll and Barwick have shown (cf. Barwick, g, 56–57), as well as in the Middle Ages. Horace's formula was, as Spingarn remarks, "the starting point of all discussions on

this subject [the function of poetry] in the Renaissance" (Spingarn, 1, 47).
Scaliger, in a curious perversion of Horace, says:

> Imitation, however, is not the end of poetry, but is intermediate to the
> end. The end is the giving of instruction in pleasurable form, for poetry
> teaches, and does not simply amuse, as some used to think (anthologized
> in Smith, g, 15).

Castelvetro, in the Renaissance, was one of those who did believe
in the pleasure aim of poetry. But Sidney, Varchi, and other Renaissance
writers used phrases similar to Scaliger's: "to teach delightfully," "to teach
by delighting," "to teach with delight" (cf. Gilbert, 1, 414, note 18).

A modern restatement of this doctrine can be seen in William
Handy, a disciple of Ransom. Handy maintains that literature is a form of
knowledge and that the knowledge is transmitted by means of the structures
of the poem (Handy, k, 10, 13, 17). Here the agent of pleasure, structure,
is stressed, whereas the Renaissance formulation stressed the psychological
effect of the apprehension of the structures. Such a transfer is one that would
be expected in the era of the new criticism. But the structure (and consequent pleasure) is still subordinate to the aim of teaching.

It does not seem necessary to make a comprehensive survey of the
adherents of the pragmatic position throughout history. It is clear from what
has been mentioned above that it was the basic position of many of the
Stoics in Antiquity, that Plato partly espoused it, that it was a hardy tradition coming down through the Middle Ages, that it was strong in the
Renaissance, and that there are some modern versions of it. Abrams has
chronicled some of the traditional pragmatists (m, 14 ff.). Lemon considers
many twentieth-century critics in his chapter on edification theories, among
others T. S. Eliot, Allen Tate, E. M. Tillyard, and Yvor Winters (cf. p,
52–70). William Rooney has carefully analyzed Tate's and Winters's theories
of poetry and belief and concludes that both are essentially "communicative"
views of poetry (p, 48 f., 87); and by "communicative" he means what
Abrams calls "pragmatic" and Lemon calls "edifying." Some important
philosophers, especially among the existentialists, view literature as a
pragmatic vehicle. Marcel, for example, contends that poetry may be a
better medium for philosophy than systematic treatises (h, 214–15). And
Heidegger continually approaches philosophic problems in their poetic
formulations by poets like Hölderlin. Kierkegaard's conception of the esthetic
as an enticement to lure men to the religious message, which is primary, has
already been adverted to (see above p, 170; and Kierkegaard, p, 26, 29, 33).

In addition to the theorists, many poets, novelists, dramatists, and
epic writers can be cited who view theirs as a teaching function. Milton says
he wrote his great poem "to justify the ways of God to man," Spenser's

Fairie Queene is supposed "to fashion a gentleman or noble person in virtuous and gentle discipline," as he himself tells us. Shelley considered the poets the unacknowledged legislators of the world. De Quincey, in a phrase reminiscent of Renaissance Horationism, speaks of appealing to the "higher understanding or reason through affections of pleasure and sympathy." Tolstoy is unabashedly moralistic in his *What is Art?* The twentieth century has seen many variations of the pragmatic theory of art among practitioners of the arts. Cézanne once remarked to Emile Bernard, "The painter ought to consecrate himself entirely to the study of nature and try to produce a picture which will be a teaching" (Loran, c, 15). Novelists like Upton Sinclair have used the medium to bring about reform. His novel about the stockyards of Chicago, *The Jungle,* was largely responsible for the passage of the Pure Food and Drug Act in the early 1900's. And, if we believe Susan Sontag, such sociological novels make up the vast majority of the novels written today (Sontag, 1, 155).

THE PRAGMATIC THEORY
OF LITERATURE:
A CRITIQUE

The pragmatic theory of poetry has also been subjected to some very severe criticisms in the present and in other centuries. Again in this section, I shall present only a brief survey of a few of the trenchant points made by these critics. For a fuller treatment, the student is referred to Lemon, "Edification Theories" (p, 42–76), to Rooney (p, 14–33, on Richards; 37–49, on Winters; 78–87, on Tate), and to Sontag (1 and a, *passim*).

It is, of course, undeniably true that literary art does communicate meaning. This is necessarily so because literature uses words as its artistic material, just as painting uses color and lines; and words refer to reality, they have meaning. Further, many of these meanings are usually marshalled by a unified ordering into what is normally called "theme." This thought element has from the beginning of Western civilization been considered an important component of literature and literary analysis. But many have questioned the assumption of pragmatism that the communication of theme is the determining constituent of literary art, even if it is an almost invariable concomitant of literature; for the communication of meaning is the essence of reference discourse, and the communication of theme or thesis, whether cognitive or emotive, is the essence of persuasion. Certainly there are many scientific treatises and informative news stories that have very successfully communicated cognitive meanings and have never been called literary. From Euclid to Einstein there have been many such productions. Yet, as Lemon quite properly remarks, edification theories provide no way of differentiating mathematics from poetry (p, 50, 65). Similarly, many successful persuasive discourses have existed which would never be called literary. Salesmen, lawyers, preachers, and politicians have all effectively been purveyors of cognitive and emotional meanings, often more so than their acknowledged literary competitors, and yet they have not been placed in literary halls of fame or buried in Westminster Abbey. Neither Clarence Darrow, nor Billy Graham, nor Mary Wells Lawrence (in Madison Avenue advertising) have been granted literary laurel wreaths. I. A. Richards, does, it is true, in one passage come perilously close to equating literature and better advertising, however:

> The Critic and the Sales Manager are not ordinarily regarded as of the same craft, nor are the poet and the advertising agent. . . . But the written appeals which have the soundest financial prospects as estimated by the most able American advertisers are such that no critic can safely ignore them. *For they do undoubtedly represent the literary ideals present and future of the people to whom they are addressed* (*Practical Criticism*, 5–6; quoted in Rooney, p, 21; my italics).

As Thomas Clark Pollock points out, this kind of dangerous conclusion follows from the facile division of all language use into emotive and scientific (cf. Rooney, p, 21, note 55).

Yet the reduction of literature to a sugar-coated informative pill or a more subtle and surreptitious rhetoric is exactly what pragmatism would do. It is undoubtedly true that we derive some information from novels and literature generally. It may even be true that some people derive information important for their lives from literary rather than from ordinary scientific or informative sources. Lemon does not think so, for he says, "Very few persons go to poems for advice about anything that matters" (m, 181). And Somerset Maugham once wrote, in the same vein:

> Only the very ingenuous can suppose that a work of fiction can give us reliable information on the topics which it is important to us for the conduct of our lives to be apprised of. By the very nature of his creative gifts the novelist is incompetent to deal with such matters; his is not to reason why, but to feel, to imagine, and to invent (c, 112).

Maugham here is having one of his most candid and best moments in literary theory. I. A. Richards makes a similar comment "The bulk of poetry consists of statements which only the very foolish would think of attempting to verify" (quoted in Rooney, p, 10).

However, because some dilettante minds never do go to original scientific or informative sources, and because literary writers are often transmitters of avant-garde and important ideas, it is no doubt true that literary writers for some are pragmatic source books for the conduct of their lives. But these writers are usually transmitters of existing systems of thought created by some contemporary scholarly genius. The system becomes, in the literary texts, a structure of thought that exists among other structures. If one really wants Scholastic theology, one should go to Aquinas, rather than to Dante; and if one wants real revolutionism, Paine will do rather than Shelley, Stokely Carmichael rather than James Baldwin. The works of Freud are a better place to study psychoanalysis than D. H. Lawrence's or Thomas Mann's. As a writer in the *London Sunday Times* has pointed out, André Malraux is the only first-class creative literary artist who has made a success of a political career at the present time (Forster, a, 43). In English or American politics one almost has to go back to Macaulay, maybe even Chaucer. In a candid comment, W. H. Auden referred to this typical political naïveté of literary writers:

> Why writers should be canvassed for their opinions on controversial issues I cannot imagine. Their views have not more authority than those of any reasonably well-educated person. Indeed, when read in bulk, the statements made by writers, including the greatest, would seem to indicate that literary talent and political common sense are rarely found together (quoted in *Time,* Sept. 8, 1967, 45).

Many other writers, in the same issue of *Encounter* from which Auden is cited (by the author in *Time*) use even stronger language to condemn some of their colleagues who believe that expertise in literature qualifies them as experts in everything.

In the light of all this, Shelley's enthusiastic statement that poets are the unacknowledged legislators of the world and that Homer was the teacher of all Greece must be looked upon with grave suspicion. Closer to Homer by some 2100 years, Socrates addresses Homer, "Friend Homer...tell us what State was ever better governed by your help?" And Glaucon must reply, "Not even the Homerids themselves pretend that he was a legislator" (*Republic,* 599). Socrates then considers the specific issue of Homer's being an unacknowledged legislator and, in a long passage, denies that he was (600). Shelley knew his Plato well, but he needed the protected removal of twenty-one centuries to contradict this claim of Socrates and Glaucon.

Of course, the mere communication of such themes or convictions is rarely unalloyed. As we have seen, most pragmatic theories compound emotion and pleasure with the thematic presentation and make pleasure a means to the end. But pleasure and emotion as means of communicating conviction are the stock-in-trade of traditional rhetoric and modern advertising and propaganda. Delight has been one of the traditional aims of rhetoric since the time of Cicero. The entertaining component of many modern advertisements hardly has to be pointed out.

Many modern critics and theorists in several art forms have considered the problem of the message in their art forms and the dangers it entails. In literature Cleanth Brooks says that message-hunting leads to the heresy of paraphrase, the false notion that a theme can be neatly abstracted from a poem and formulated in a handy maxim. Of course that is precisely what many secondary and college textbooks advocate in their editorial apparatus with such questions as this following a poem: "What lesson does this poem teach?" or "What is the central thematic concern of this novel?" Such a response to the content of a literary work is considered by Northrop Frye to be the essence of the stock response, a reaction to literature that can completely derail the reader from the esthetic response (w, 123 ff.). Valéry's view on the danger of paraphrase seems a proper parting commentary: "Résumer une thèse, c'est en retenir l'essentiel. Résumer une œuvre d'art, c'est en perdre l'essentiel" (v, 158).

In other arts, the message problem is not so crucial as it is in literature because other art media are not so palpably referential. Nevertheless, pragmatism has had to be combated in them also. Roy McMullen, in a review of the positions current in music, painting, and sculpture in 1967, feels that the pragmatic excursions of these arts into meanings have about spent their forces today (m, 85). He quotes some typical strong maxims of the American abstractionist Ad Reinhardt on this score:

Messages in art are not messages.
Explanation in art is no explanation.
Knowledge in art is not knowledge.
Learning in art is not learning (quoted in McMullen, m, 84).

Susanne Langer herself tends to deprecate the power of music in terms which almost deny any significant persuasive power to music at all. "Its somatic effects are transient, and its moral hangovers or uplifts seem to be negligible" (p, 172). She is talking of classical music in general, not, I would suspect, of martial music or rock or any other persuasive mode of music. In film, Samuel Goldwyn's irreverent remark might be relevant, "If you have a message, call Western Union" (quoted by Joan Bennet, cf. *TV Guide,* August 20–27, 1967).

A serious issue which creates more problems for pragmatism than for any other view of literature is what is usually called "the question of poetry and belief." If poetry is supposed to engender convictions or beliefs, what happens when the beliefs advocated by the poem seriously conflict with the beliefs of the reader? Allen Tate, classified by both Lemon and Rooney as a pragmatist, is naturally concerned with the problem. In a discussion of David Daiches, Tate poses the issue:

> Mr. Daiches is properly overwhelmed by Yeats's genius and power; he cannot dismiss him; yet he is puzzled because the great poetry cannot be distinguished from ideas that he finds nonsensical, even "crazy."
> There is Yeats with his "fantastic philosophy" and his great poetry. There is Day Lewis with his—to Mr. Daiches—sound philosophy and his—to me—bad poetry. This is our common predicament as readers of poetry, and it indicates, I believe, the direction one must take to find the chief problem of poetic criticism (quoted in Rooney, p, 1).

Rooney's book is a careful analysis of four attempts on the part of important contemporary pragmatists to solve this problem. His treatment is all the evidence one needs to see that they eventuate in inconsistency and disaster. Any theory of literature committed to mimeticism or pragmatism cannot come up with a satisfactory answer to this ticklish problem.

Finally, like expressionism, pragmatism cannot account for forms which are specifically literary, nor for a specific esthetic emotion. It can only account primarily for the rhetorical structures of persuasion, many of which literature subsumes into its own forms, but propaganda is not literature.

In summary, one must seriously question a theory of art that ultimately cannot differentiate literary texts from information or propaganda, that has to invest literature with a philosophic dignity which the history of thought refuses to accord to literature, that leads to cheap paraphrases and stock responses, that must carve out for literature an aim generically distinct from other fine arts, that has no serious answer to the problem of poetry and belief, and that cannot account for literary form or esthetic emotions.

The Objective
Theory of Literature

A DEFINITION

The final cluster of theories which Abrams considers is the "objective." Other terms have been used for this same group of approaches and it might be worthwhile to mention them so that the student can orient his readings. In Antiquity and the Middle Ages, art was essentially viewed as the intellectual virtue of the practical, as opposed to the speculative order. The two virtues of the practical order were prudence, which resulted in *doing* an act, and art, which resulted in *making* a product. Thus the theory of art that stressed the product or the object was the theory that viewed art as *making* (Greek *poieton,* Latin *factibile*). Classical scholars who write of this theory as it is found in Antiquity call it the "pleasure" theory as opposed to the "profit" or "use" theory of literature. Modern terms for this approach include "structural," "formalist," "art for art's sake," and sometimes "organic" and "esthetic." In literary theory, "new criticism" is often considered to be equivalent to a structural approach. But as we have already seen, despite considerable stress on structure, some new critics are really expressionistic, or mimetic, or pragmatic. I. A. Richards, John Crowe Ransom, Allen Tate, and Yvor Winters have already been referred to in these categories.

The intrinsic emphases of an objective approach to literature are easily discerned. First, there is an affirmation of the importance of the art object or product. This emphasis was a built-in feature of the general theory of art of both Antiquity and the Middle Ages, as we shall see. Its immediate corollary is the stress on the characteristics of the object that establish it as artistic. These characteristics are described in formal or structural terms —consequently, the use of the terms "formalist" or "structuralist" to categorize this group. When the artist is referred to in this theory, his craftsmanship and technical capacities to produce forms and structures are accentuated. When the reader or audience is referred to, the pleasure which he derives from the contemplation of the art object is emphasized. The prominent traits of the theory are therefore: a stress on the object or product, an emphasis on structures and form, a consideration of the artist as craftsman, and an affirmation of the pleasure in the receptor. These will do for a working definition of the theory. Further clarification will come from an outlining of some of the main adherents' views and a consideration of some of the objections to the view.

Beginning his treatment of this theory, Abrams remarks, "This point of view has been comparatively rare in literary criticism" (m, 26), and "As an all-inclusive approach to poetry, the objective orientation was just beginning to emerge in the late eighteenth and early nineteenth century" (m, 27). These two statements are somewhat misleading for there lurks behind them the suspicion that, if in fact this is the valid theory of art, most of the art of Western civilization was produced without an articulated theory or under the auspices of an invalid theory of art. Both alternatives are, of course, possible. But it is also true that, all through Antiquity, the Middle Ages, and the Renaissance, enough of this theory was articulated to provide a matrix for artistic production. The articulations occur much more fully in general theories of art, however, than in literary criticism. Even in the literary criticism prior to the nineteenth century, however, I am inclined to see more evidence of this position than is Abrams. A brief survey of these articulations may help to establish the existence of a distinct continuity of this approach in Western civilization and bring further clarification to the brief sketch of the axioms of the position outlined above.

The general theory of art (*techne*) in Greek thought that held from the pre-Socratic to the Hellenistic writers is intimately related to the general Greek cosmology. *Chaos,* which is made up of indefinite, indeterminate, and infinite matter (*to apeiron*), is made into a *cosmos* by the operations of a demiurge or prime mover of some kind who, precisely, puts order and imposes form on this pristine unordered matter. Matter which has been formalized is nature (*physis*), and ordered natures are the basis of the cosmos. A second creator, the *poieta* or artist, then imposes further order on nature by the process of art (*techne*), and the art product results. Such a concept of art can be seen in both Aristotle and Plato (cf. Aristotle 199a 15 ff., 204a ff., 984b 15, 985b 15, 1071b 3 ff.; cf. Plato 28A ff., 889A ff.; for secondary sources cf. Randall, a, 174, 192–94; Butcher, a, 156 ff., Joachim, a, 203; Lodge, p, 113–16). Because art draws its forms from nature, it always involves imitation, but because it imposes further form on nature, more than reproduction is involved. The products of art, therefore, are differentiated from those of nature by the imposition of additional forms on nature. Aristotle and Plato differed radically on the degree of rationality involved in this structuring process and on the desirability of further altering nature, but they agreed on the concept of the process. The stress on the object and its structures was, therefore, inherent in a general theory of art. The second crucial component of the objective theory, the pleasure in the receiver, was given primacy by Aristotle and by the Peripatetic school in general, as we have seen; and Plato wavers continually between a pleasure and a profit view of poetry, as the German classics scholar, Barwick, has shown by careful documentation (Barwick, g, 56–58). This conflict between pleasure and profit remained one of the consistent conflicts in esthetic theory in Antiquity (cf. Kroll, s, 76, 78–79). In Hellenistic times, Eratosthenes advocated the pure pleasure theory, as Strabo tells us:

> As I was saying, Eratosthenes contends that the aim of every poet is to entertain, not to instruct.... Eratosthenes, then, should have said that "every poet writes partly for purposes of mere entertainment and partly for instruction," but his words were "mere entertainment and not instruction" (Strabo, g, 16, 1, 2, 3).

Eratosthenes had just as little truck with the mimeticists: "The scenes of the wanderings of Odysseus will be found when you find the cobbler who sewed up the bag of winds" (quoted in Sandys, h, 1, 37). Longinus also stressed the "enthrallment" derived from poetry; and, of course, Horace was the transmitter of the Platonic compromise between pleasure and profit.

The early Christian fathers aided this theory of stress on pleasure and structure. Jaeger even claims that they invented it (though the evidence given above contradicts this allegation):

> ...it is the Christians who finally taught men to appraise poetry by a purely aesthetic standard—a standard which enabled them to reject most of the moral and religious teaching of the classical poets as false and ungodly, while accepting the formal elements in their work as instructive and aesthetically beautiful (Jaeger, p, 1, 3).

The main ingredients of the objective theory of art are, therefore, basic to the general Greek theory of art. They are even more pronounced in the general Scholastic theory of art in the Middle Ages, as Maritain has so conclusively shown in *Art and Scholasticism*.[4] There is probably no better introduction to the medieval theory of art. In his treatment Maritain reiterates the medieval emphasis on the fundamental components of the objective theory. Art is an intellectual virtue which always culminates in the making of a *product,* and the perfection of the artifact determines the success of the artistic process (a, 15). Art is, therefore, "entirely amoral" (a, 16). The perfection of the object is a result of the operation of the rational intellect— art is defined as *recta ratio factibilium,* right reason in making things (18– 21). Aquinas, Albert Magnus, Augustine, and the Schoolmen generally stress both the pleasure effect arising from the contemplation of the art object and the characteristics of the object which give rise to this pleasure. Aquinas says that the beautiful is "id quod visum placet," that which pleases upon being perceived by the senses (a, 23 f.). This pleasure is something enjoyable, not useful; *frui,* to enjoy, is opposed to *uti,* to use, in medieval philosophy (Maritain, a, 6). As Maritain says, speaking of fine arts,

> They are disinterested, desired for themselves, truly noble because their work taken in itself is not made in order that one may use it as a means, but in order that one may enjoy it as an end, being a true *fruit, aliquid ultimum et delectabile* (A true "object of enjoyment, something ultimate and delightful," Maritain, a, 33–34, his italics).

"The beautiful is essentially delightful," paraphrases Maritain (a, 24); and the delight arises from the characteristics of the object (a, 24). Aquinas therefore assigns three conditions to the beautiful object: unity or integrity, proportion, but above all a splendor of form (cf. Maritain, a, 24 ff.). Augustine speaks of the splendor of order, and Albertus Magnus and Aquinas use the terms the radiance and splendor of form (cf. Maritain,

---

[4] For a treatment of the Scholastic theory of art, Maritain's little book is invaluable. I have found by experience that some students are irritated by Maritain's theology. But the esthetic is self-sustaining and can be easily abstracted from the theology.

a, 24–29). These concepts will be expanded below. For the time being, however, it is clear that there was a precisely articulated objective theory of fine art in the Middle Ages, and it runs from Augustine in the fourth century to the late Renaissance Scholastics of the seventeenth century.

As Abrams indicates, it is especially in modern times that one can see the full articulation of the formalist or objective theory. Kant is instanced by Abrams as a proponent of this theory (m, 27), as are the neo-Aristotelians of Chicago, and several new critics. One could add many others. Schiller's concept of art as play, which will be talked about below, is such a theory and was formulated at the end of the eighteenth century. Coleridge is a Romantic, but he is basically an objectivist. His concluding definition of poetry could be taken as a formula for that theory:

> The final definition then, so deduced, may be thus worded. A poem is that species of composition, which is opposed to works of science, by proposing for its *immediate* object pleasure, not truth; and from all other species (having *this* object in common with it) it is discriminated by proposing to itself such delight from the *whole,* as is compatible with a distinct gratification from each component *part* (b, II, 10, his italics).

Poe and the French symbolists who so admired him are of this school. Alexander Bain, the rhetorician and psychologist, takes a similar stand in the nineteenth century (e, 258, 260–67). Philosophers like George Santayana, Samuel Alexander, Jacques Maritain, and Etienne Gilson; literary critics like Susan Sontag, Cleanth Brooks, and many new critics; art critics like Irwin Panofsky and many others use this approach to art. To list the writers, painters, sculptors, and musicians who have consciously practiced within the matrix of this theory in this and the last century would be to make an inventory of many great modern artists. Susan Sontag in her consideration of current novelists writing in the "Joycean" or formalist tradition, examines several of these (1, 170–75), as well as several moderns who both theorize and practice with such theories (180–90). For the record, one should probably list at least José Ortega y Gasset, James Joyce, Henry James, Poe, Vladimir Nabokov, Paul Valéry, Charles Baudelaire, Susan Sontag, the early Truman Capote, to give only a few major proponents. Nor has the structuralist viewpoint been an emphasis in only Western Europe and Anglo-Saxon literatures. One of the most vociferous of the structuralist groups in this century was the school of Russian formalists. Beginning around 1915 as a reaction against the historical and psychological study of literature, two separate groups from Petersburg and Moscow quickly coalesced into a coherent body of critics and writers, led by Roman Jakobson, Boris Eichenbaum, and Viktor Shklovsky. Unfortunately the Marxist attacks on the school caused its disintegration in Russia in the thirties, but its legacy to Russian criticism and its satellite schools in Czech and Polish circles assured some permanency to the movement in Slavic countries. Jakobson and others carried the movement to Western Europe and this country (on the movement, cf. Erlich, r, and Lemon, r).

It thus seems clear that there is a persistent objective theory of literature that emphasizes the art object, the structured characteristics of the art object, the craft required of the artist to produce these structures, and the terminal pleasure of the receptor in contemplating these structures. Like the other theories, however, this position has had its assailants. Let us turn to their objections.

THE OBJECTIVE THEORY:
A CRITIQUE

As with the previous critiques, I do not plan here a thorough presentation or refutation of the objections made to an objective theory of art. Such surveys have been made elsewhere, by such eminent critics and philosophers as Lemon (p, 107–80), Ortega y Gasset (d, *passim*), Maritain (a, 39 ff., 70 ff., 85 ff.), Sontag (1 and a, *passim*), and many others. I shall only briefly review some of the main allegations. Summarily, this view of art has been attacked as being immoral and irresponsible, snobbish, trivial, inhuman, and partial.

If one adopts a pragmatic theory of art and views literature as seriously competing for souls by propagating alternatives in political, religious, or economic arenas, then censorship of heterodoxy follows as a corollary, unless one is a pluralist or tolerant of pluralism. The objective theory generally does not take such a serious view of theme in literature, however, as we have seen in the critique of the pragmatic view of literature. Consequently the objective theory is really much less vulnerable to the charge of immorality than other views of art. As Maritain says, art is "entirely amoral" (a, 16). And, despite the assertions of some of the art-for-art's sake movement, an objective theory of art, which maintains that the product *as art product* or the artist *as artist* are to be judged simply and solely on artistic grounds, does not at all entail the social irresponsibility of the artist as a man, or the ignoring of the possible good or bad social effects of the art object in the stream of culture—as many have pointed out. At any rate, in a democratic pluralistic society, this does not seem to be the issue it has been in other times and other places.

Second, it has been maintained that this view of art is snobbish, that by stressing the intellectual aspect of art, there is the tendency to create art forms which only an elite can appreciate, and therefore an aristocracy of art is established. Formerly, it is maintained, the great poets had universal appeal—Homer and Shakespeare were the property of everyone. But the new poets and novelists of the present time are the property of only a private coterie. Such a view is supported by statements from both practitioners and theorists today. T. S. Eliot, it is true, maintains that every poet would like to be a popular entertainer (u, 154) ; but Joyce, possibly more typically, once remarked that a popular novel was almost necessarily a bad novel (and cf. Ortega y Gasset, d, 6–7; Langer, p, 166). On the other hand, there seems to be some truth to the position that there were elements in Shakespearean drama that even the groundlings could appreciate, though the full apprecia-tion of the play was still reserved for an aristocracy. These "universal" elements are now denied the audience in the poetry of Pound or the drama of Pirandello. In this sense, art has become snobbish. An objective theory of art, in conjunction with modern anthropological study, is quite willing to grant that there are levels of art, that there are at least a folk art, a popular art, and a classical art (the term "classical" literature had, as we have seen, precisely this etymology). There seems nothing inherently un-democratic in recognizing that a group of art works exists which only an aristocracy of art can appreciate, just as there exists a mass of scientific work which can only be understood by a scientific elite. Conversely, an objective theory of art must also recognize degrees of structural excellence and must be willing to grant that a simple folk song or a good joke or a popular television drama is also "literature" in a very real way, though it may not be on a classical level. In this sense, an objective theory of art is not snobbish, indeed may be more tolerant and comprehensive in its notion of literature than other views have been.

Third, it has been maintained that a formalist view of art makes art a trivial thing. If art is didactic or mimetic, it can claim a dignity which mere pleasure in form cannot. If poets are the "unacknowledged legislators of the world," they are important people, but if they are only entertainers, their social role seems trivial. Gide uses a different metaphor, "The artist is expected to appear after dinner. His function is not to provide food, but intoxication" (quoted in Maritain, a, 91). Locke attacks literature from this viewpoint, "Poetry and gaming...seldom give any advantage but to those who have nothing else to live on" (quoted in Abrams, m, 300). Such a view of art as luxury may indeed seem trivial to some who view pleasure and happiness as almost unnecessary adjuncts to human life. Hedonism in any form has always appeared suspect to certain religious, moral, and political biases. The decision to allow man to indulge in plea-sures can be made only by a philosophy which has determined that man's fundamental aim is happiness and that in achieving this he is realizing his humanity at its fullest. Other uses of language are tools and man is a tool in using them; literature gives man his humanity and he is a real man in enjoying it. Philosophers like Aristotle, Aquinas, Schiller, and many others see in the contemplation and enjoyment of the true, the beautiful, and the good the fulfillment of man's purpose and essence. In this sense, art (and other terminal activities of man) is not adventitious to human life, but crucial to its essence. Otherwise man is just a more efficient beast of burden. Schiller's lengthy argument on this issue culminates in these statements:

> For, to speak out once for all, man only plays when in the full sense of the word he is a man and *he is only completely a man when he plays.*
>
> *　　*　　*
>
> By beauty the sensuous man is led to form; by beauty the spiritual man is brought back to matter and restored to the world of sense (Schiller, w, IVb, 7, 9, 85; all of the letters in that section are relevant).

Lemon's accusation against complete objective theories, that "poetry becomes chess played with emotions and ideas—it toys with, rather than tests ideas" (p, 170), carries with it the distinct impression that in his grim universe there is not much place for either chess or toys. Yet there ought to be room in a big universe for intellectual play. Sartre, following Marx, maintains that the serious man who refuses to play has dismissed human reality in favor of the world; for him there are not people, only things; not subjects, only objects (b, 711).

Another charge leveled at the objective theory of art is that it makes art inhuman, that it "dehumanizes" art, to use Ortega y Gasset's term. By stressing the intellectual apprehension of the structures of the art object, art is said to lose its "human content" and its emotional components. There are several directions this charge can take. Sometimes the loss of humanity is said to arise from the downgrading of the importance of the civilizing and teaching influence of art and the stress on form and pleasure. Sometimes the depreciation of the emotional component of art is viewed as dehumanizing. The first argument is actually almost a restatement of the triviality of art, and can be met with the same responses. However, it might also be added that an objective theory of art does not deny a teaching value in some art products, or, for that matter, a mimetic or an expressionistic value. It only asserts that they are of secondary or tertiary value. No objectivist wants to demean the fact that themes are important in literature. He only wants to assert their subordination to other values. If literature has, as byproducts, certain utilitarian effects, no one wants to pass them by; and that an esthetic sensitivity in itself will have certain civilizing influences is certainly not to be denied. By educating man's esthetic feelings, perceptions, and apprehensions, literature and art certainly have civilizing and cultural value beyond the moments of enjoyment they bring.

The second argument, the deemphasis of the emotional, has to be handled somewhat differently. It is true that some modern artists in various media have moved so far in their adulation of structure that they seem to approach a mathematical or geometric conception of art. Hans Werner Henze, whom McMullen calls "unquestionably the most lavishly gifted composer of the postwar Germain renaissance" (m, 89), began his career under the influence of Hindemith, Stravinsky, and later Schoenberg, then moved on to an extreme avant-garde music.

> But then, in 1953, he suddenly committed what many of the more extreme modernists still feel was an act of desertion: he moved to the island of Ischia (eventually to Naples) and fell in love with Italian melody. He began to fear that the more strict kinds of serialism would, in his own words, *"lead music into the grayness of dry algebra and destroy the ability to represent the most simple of authentic musical events"* (McMullen, m, 89, my italics).

His current music is now much more emotionally intense and dramatically pointed than any he has hitherto written (McMullen, m, 90). Henze's case is not at all unique. I personally have a good painter friend in Santa Fe who has refused to paint for ten years, since he reached his abstractionist position where, as he said, "painting was becoming geometry. I no longer felt my work emotionally." These assertions from the artificers could be paralleled with many from the receptors who complain that emotion has been drained out of modern poetry.

It is true that asserting the importance of structure can move one very close to modern mathematics, which in the words of one of the most prominent modern mathematicians is actually best defined as the study of structure (Bourbaki, a, 221). There is a crucial difference in the way art and mathematics approach structure, however, as will be seen when we examine the notion of literary structure. It is certainly also true that, deprived of emotional reference and content, art seems to move, as Henze claims, into the "grayness of dry algebra." In fact, the necessity of art to incorporate the emotional, and the resulting relationships between feeling and form, to use Susanne Langer's terms, have yet, in the author's opinion, to be comprehensively investigated. It seems undeniable, despite Ortega y Gasset, that something like laughter and tears are a component of most great art; to deny this would be to deny the difference between tragedy and comedy. There does seem to be an emotional empathy of some sort which is a component of the esthetic emotion and at least theoretically distinguishable from the intellectual act of apprehending form and the sensuous components of color or rhythm perception. To apprehend a structure of emotion, one must first apprehend the emotion. Finally, however, any discussion of emotion in an objective theory of art must always allow for the presence of the esthetic reaction, which is usually called an emotion; in fact, it is usually dubbed "pleasure," as we have seen in most objective theories. If the objective theory deprecates the importance of the emotions referred to in the art construct, it always elevates the status of the esthetic emotion.

The final volley fired at the objective theory is that it is an incomplete and partial approach to art or life. Lemon, Kierkegaard, Weaver, and the Chicago neo-Aristotelians mount this assault from various directions. Kierkegaard and Weaver both charge literature (and science) with being neutral uses of language, one not involving commitments. We have already analyzed this position in connection with science and persuasion. In a sense this is true, but there does not seem to be any overpowering reason compelling us to be everlastingly "committed" to some cause or other. We really ought to be allowed to relax from our commitments every now and then. Language should not always have to be put to work, it should be allowed its holidays and sabbaticals.

Lemon's accusation that the objective theory, at least in its "closed form" varieties, leads to a "partial" criticism is actually another version of the same objection. In his chapter on the "closed form" varieties of formalism he says that in Allen Tate, "tension has become the sole standard of evaluation" (p, 130); that Cleanth Brooks does very much the same with the concept of "irony" (139 ff.); and that Empson has made a similar reductionism with "ambiguity" (130 ff.). He finds that such reductionisms do not account for all poetry, and for this reason he labels these approaches "partial." The Chicago critics have also attacked some "new critics" on similar grounds: Crane criticizes the critical monism of Brooks in his use of irony as if that were all that mattered (c, 84 ff.); W. R. Keast has accused Robert B. Heilman of reducing structure in drama to recurrent image patterns (n, 108 ff.); and Elder Olson has challenged Empson's omnipresent ambiguities (e, 46 ff.). I am inclined to agree with Lemon and the Chicago critics in their criticisms of such reductionisms. As I shall point out later, nearly every aspect of structure has been deified by some critic or other to the point where it becomes the essence of literature, and very little else really matters. Such reductionisms are nearly always the result of overenthusiasms for a new analytical tool. After the initial excitement is over, the tool usually becomes just one among many other tools of analysis, and literary criticism is the better for it. One easily forgives the early fixation and is grateful for the addition; and possibly such infatuations are the necessary companions of genius. Gilson, at least, thinks they are in philosophy, where similar reductionisms have occurred (u, 315). Nor is this phenomenon restricted to philosophy or literary criticism. In consequence, it seems unfair to accuse an objective theory of art of such reductionisms simply because some of its votaries have been too enamored of their own discoveries. Nowhere, in fact, has Lemon shown that such "partial" approaches are inherent in an objective theory of art. Nor, I believe, can this be demonstrated.

What can be demonstrated is what the Chicago critics have shown: that any one approach to literature cannot give an exhaustive account of a given art object. In this sense, their advocacy of a "pluralism" of valid criticisms seems right. As was pointed out above in Chapter III, when the abstractions necessary to science were considered, no one science has all of the tools and media of analysis to investigate all aspects of a given reality (see above, p. 80 ff.). There is nothing so sacred about an art object that cannot be investigated by people with nonliterary interests. An art object is obviously a product of an intense creative process, and such a process and the results of such a process are valid objects of analysis by a psychologist only marginally and accidentally interested in the work as an "art" object. The same is true of a sociologist, an historian, a linguist, a theologian, or an anthropologist. Their findings will be not literary, but psychological, sociological, historical, linguistic, or anthropological. The tolerance of pluralism does not extend, however, to a theologian who uses a moral criterion to arrive at a literary evaluation or to an economist who uses Keynesian norms to judge the symbolic structures of a novel. Nor does the tolerance of pluralism, so understood, allow the reductionisms of structuralism to symbolism or imagery, or plot, or any single structure. Nor, finally, does pluralism in this sense, imply that it is a matter of indifference which basic approach one takes to art: whether expressive, pragmatic, mimetic, or objective. In essence the first three respectively approach art from a psychological, a rhetorical, or a scientific point of view. Now there is nothing wrong in doing this, as long as one realizes that one does not then come up with findings relevant to art *as art*. One comes up with views of art objects as formal objects of analysis by psychologists, propagandists, or historians.

It is clear from the conclusion of the last paragraph, which in itself is the conclusion of all that has preceded in this chapter, that the view taken of the nature of literature in this book belongs to the cluster of theories which Abrams calls "objective" theories of art. The practical application of this theory to individual art objects will be made in the following sections in which a poem of Hopkins will be examined as embodying various levels of patterns or structures. This analysis will, it is hoped, exemplify the affirmative position arrived at on the nature of literature in this section. It would undoubtedly be advantageous to attempt analyses of art objects with the axioms of expressionism, pragmatism, and mimeticism in order to demonstrate the practical inability of such approaches and their ultimate prostitution of art. Lemon and Rooney have done some excellent work in this regard and the reader is referred to their treatments.

The Logic of Literature:
The Primacy of Structure

The extensions given to the term "logic" in this book may seem to many either offensive or so unconventional as to constitute a personal jargon when the term "logic" is taken to include rules of systematizing or serializing structures. Yet, as we have already seen, "logic" has been given this and similar meanings by writers both in the past and at the present time. If successful scientific proof is achieved by rules of deductive or inductive inference, if successful exploration is achieved by following a logic of discovery, if successful persuasion is achieved by stylistic, ethical, pathetic, and seemingly "logical" arguments, it is also true that literary pleasure is achieved by techniques of structuring a special way. In this important sense, the logic of literature consists in structural devices.

Of course not just any structure produces the peculiar esthetic pleasure. Everything that exists has structure of some sort, yet not every existent provides esthetic pleasure when it is contemplated. There is, therefore, in an objective theory of art, the necessity of distinguishing esthetic structures from nonesthetic structures. Actually, the remainder of this chapter is an attempt to do this, but particularly in the next section, devoted to "organization" in literary discourse this problem will be given lengthy consideration. The fundamental notion of structure, as such, will be examined in the chapter on "Description," in Volume II, *The Modes of Discourse.* Many of us operate with fairly intuitive notions of structure.

Partly because these intuitive meanings are in the air in academic and nonacademic circles, students often have very different ideas of the concept "structure." It may be well initially to point out some meanings from other areas which the term does not have in this chapter. A common meaning of "structured" in social psychology and educational disciplines is in contrast to "unstructured" or "creative," the former signifying a restricted or outwardly imposed set of norms as opposed to a free set of responses or actions in tests or in play situations (cf. Pagès, in Bastide, s, 92–93). This connotation of structure is not intended here. In fact, what especially constitutes the creative act will be the invention of new structures or the adaptation of old structures. Again, in architecture, form is sometimes distinguished from structure, form being a general idea which is embodied in particular structures (cf. Francastel in Bastide, s, 48–49). No such distinction is implied here. In medicine, economics, and law, structure is often distinguished from function. Thus anatomy is a study of structure, but physiology is a study of function (cf. Charbonnier in Bastide, s, 74–75). This is akin to the distinction in linguistics and anthropology, where structure is viewed as static or descriptive, and is opposed to process or event (cf. Lévi-Strauss in Bastide, s, 41). It is true that in this textbook, literary analysis is distinguished from literary history and descriptive linguistics from historical linguistics, and descriptive semantics from historical semantics, as we have seen. But in the context of literary analysis, a narrative, loosely defined as a causal sequence of events, is still viewed as a structure, even though in other contexts, it is useful to distinguish the static from the dynamic (process or event). In fact, Kenneth Rothwell faces this problem specifically in a discussion of literary structure (s, 604). Finally, and most important of all, literary structures are not here limited to a few traditional sound structures, such as alliteration, meter, rhythm, and a few stanzaic forms. Such a restricted view of structure can atrophy at the outset any attempt to arrive at a useful notion of structure. Nor do such reductionist notions as tension, irony, symbolism, and imagery exhaust the concept of structure, as has already been pointed out.

There are, in the literary tradition, a few very usable and sometimes very similar notions that seem general enough to embrace the full range of structures in literature. A definition of structure in terms of combination of identities and differences has come down to us from Antiquity and has been useful to some in determining a general notion of structure in literature and linguistics (cf. La Drière, pr, 670; Whatmough, p, 9–10). One of the dominating metaphors used to indicate structural relations within a unity has been the view of the literary work as an organism. Plato, Aristotle, Goethe, Kant, but especially Coleridge, and in our times, Cleanth Brooks, have used this concept of structure (cf. Abrams, m, 171 ff., 206 ff.). The organic notion of structure is very closely related to the potency-act and matter-form concepts of structure that can be seen in the Aristotelian tradition. For Aristotle, form consisted in any determination given to matter by an agent for a specific purpose. The matter is the material cause, the specific determination the formal cause, the agent who imposes the form the efficient cause, and his purpose in so doing the final cause. Form and matter are thus causes intrinsic to the object, whereas agency and finality are extrinsic causes. Since an already formalized matter may be looked upon as matter which can receive further form, the process can go on indefinitely. Consequently, there can be an indefinite hierarchy of forms. Thus a sentence may be looked upon as a group of words which have been *formed* into a sentence and is therefore a structure. However, it may be combined with other sentences to *form* a paragraph. This concept of structure is exceptionally flexible and yet specific enough to use—as long as one determines the particular level of "matter" and imposition of "form" that is operating in any instance. Bertrand Russell and many others take a similar view of structure. For Russell, the structure of anything is the sum total of all the relationships that exist among the parts and between the parts and the whole. The level at which one chooses to identify "part" is arbitrary, for one could always view the part as itself subdivided and made up of smaller parts and their interrelationships. As Russell says,

> The analysis of structure usually proceeds by successive stages. . . . What are taken as unanalysed units in one stage are themselves exhibited as complex structures in the next stage. The skeleton is composed of bones, the bones of cells and cells of molecules, the molecules of atoms, the

atoms of electrons, positrons, and neutrons; further analysis is as yet conjectural. Bones, molecules, atoms, and electrons may each be treated, for certain purposes, as if they were unanalyzable units devoid of structure, but at no stage is there any positive reason to suppose that this is in fact the case. The ultimate units so far reached may at any moment turn out to be capable of analysis. Whether there must be units incapable of analysis because they are destitute of parts is a question which there seems no way of deciding. Nor is it important, since there is nothing erroneous in an account of structure which starts from units that are afterward found to be themselves complex. For example, points may be defined as classes of events, that does not falsify anything in traditional geometry, which treated points as simples. Every account of structure is relative to certain units which are, for the time being, treated as if they were devoid of structure, but it must never be assumed that these units will not, in another context, have a structure which it is important to recognize (h, 271–72).

This concept of structure as the sum total of the relationships of parts to parts and parts to whole may well be the most common definition of structure today. It can be found in linguists like Hjelmslev and Pike, philosophers like Lalande, psychologists like Piaget (cf. Bastide, s, 34, 37–38; Pike, l, 1, 31, 41–43). Hjelmslev, discussing a linguistic structure says that one can

> ...describe it as being *essentially an autonomous entity of internal dependencies,* in a word, a structure.... The analysis of this entity permits one to detach constantly parts which are reciprocally conditioned, and each of which depends on the others and would not be conceivable or definable without these other parts. It reduces the object to a network of dependencies (quoted by Bénéviste in Bastide, s, 37–38, Bénéviste's italics).

Such a concept of structure is related to Aristotle's in several ways. First, the determination of parts or "matter" is arbitrary. Any relationship among parts gives further structure or formalities to these parts or matter. There are, in addition, some other fertile concepts in the Aristotelian notions of matter and form which are very relevant to structural analysis. In Aristotle matter is viewed as a potency which can be actualized by the imposition of form. The process of construction can therefore be viewed as the progressive actualization of a potency. This potency is not just indeterminately actualized. As the matter becomes progressively formalized, its potentialities lessen and it can only take on more limited number of forms. The potency thus becomes progressively more committed to certain necessary formalizations and its probabilities of taking on any forms whatsoever diminish. Paul Goodman, in *The Structure of Literature,* clearly shows the relation of the concept of potency to that of probability:

The relationship of being after parts already presented and leading to other parts we call "probability," as there is a probability that Macbeth will seek out the Witches again after the incidents, character speeches, and atmosphere presented in Acts I–III. *The formal analysis of a poem is largely the demonstration of a probability through all the parts.* Or better, in the light of the previous paragraphs, in *the beginning anything is possible; in the middle things become probable; in the ending everything is necessary* (Goodman, s, 14, my italics).

Thus, it is possible to state the logic of literary structures in terms of a logic of developing probability. Besides Aristotle and his modern disciple Goodman, others have used similar notions. Goethe defines the internal cosmos of an opera as developing by its own positive laws which he speaks of in terms of probabilities (cf. Abrams, m, 278–79). It is important to call attention to the self-contained nature of these probabilities, as Goethe, Hurd, Lessing, Shaftesbury Bradley, Olson, and others have done (cf. Abrams, m, 278–85). As Elder Olson says:

> In a sense, every poem is a micro-cosmos, a discrete and independent universe with its laws provided by the poet; his decision is absolute; he can make things good or bad, great or small, powerful or weak, just as he wills; he may make men taller than mountains or smaller than atoms, he may suspend whole cities in the air, he may destroy creation or reform it; within his universe, the impossible becomes the possible, the necessary the contingent—if he but says they do (quoted in Abrams, m, 284).

Nonetheless, given the laws of the poem's universe, they then operate just as logically as the laws of external probability that operate in scientific and informative discourse. This is what Aristotle means when he says that there must be nothing illogical in the plot structure (1454b; cf. 1460a 30 ff., and 1460b 13 ff.).

Such a notion of logical growth is quite analogous to the organic metaphor of developing from a seed. In this respect, the logic of literature which we have been discussing is readily translated into the terms of the organism metaphor. In fact, Aristotle uses both—as one would expect a biologist interested in poetry to do. Zola, in *The Experimental Novel,* has used a different metaphor. He compares the initial conditions as determined by the novelist to the axioms of a scientist. Given the kind of character, of environment, of initial incidents, the development of these follows as logically as the deductions of a scholar (Zola, e, 227). Such a notion of structural development was very congenial to a naturalistic determinism of the kind embraced by Zola. Even if it does not work in life, it is an admirable formula for art.

The Aristotelian notion of matter and form or its modern parallel, that of parts and interrelationships, then, gives us a general notion of structure which can be used in literature. It becomes more useful when we can distinguish the hierarchies of parts or matters. Such a delineation of parts and the structures at given levels will be given in the section on style—at which point these theories will be also illustrated. Before this comprehensive delineation of literary components and corresponding structures is presented, however, it is necessary to make a more careful distinction of the structures of other kinds of discourse from those of literary discourse, since the same language and discourse components can be used in all constructs of language. In effect, the next section will be an elaboration of the concept "the *primacy*" of structure.

The Organization of Literary Discourse

Actually, a study of the organization of literary discourse could well be a part of the preceding section on logic or a part of the following section on style. The reason for this is that in the case of literature the logic is the internal probability of its structures, the structures are patently the organization, and the style is achieved by the distinctive patterns of organization. Logic is not a matter of structure in other aims of discourse. However, it does seem proper, at this point, to specifically distinguish literary structures from other kinds of structures. This has already been partially achieved in the previous section when it was pointed out that literary probability is a matter of internally fictional laws created by the novelist, poet, or dramatist; but there are some other crucial distinctions.

In order to understand the specific nature of literary structures it is necessary to have some knowledge of what is being structured. The architect must know the potentialities of bricks, mortar, steel, and wood. This supposes that a writer knows something about the language, about meanings, about dialect, about his medium, about actions, about emotions, and about people, before he can structure them. This is only to say that a theory of structure viewed as form imposed upon matter cannot ignore the matter. The theory is not pure formalism, it is *hylemorphism* (*hyle*—Greek for matter, and *morphe*—Greek for form). The same principle applies to the reader—no one reacts to pure form because pure form is nonexistent. Forms only exist when imposed on matter. One cannot have relations between things without having things.

The matters or components that are structured in literature are not different from the other language and discourse components available to other kinds of discourse; literature only does something different with them. Consequently, a list of components available to literary writers will simply be a catalog of the materials which any writer has at his disposal (see Figure V, 2). Even the structures which can be made of these components are not the sole propriety of littérateurs. Take the first item on the list as an example: a writer has the consonants of the language available to him. He can structure these into alliterative or consonantal patterns. But it is clear that persuasive writers also use these same structures on occasion.

Figure V, 2: Language Components and Literary Structures

I. LINGUISTIC

  A. *Grammatical*

1. *Phonemic and Graphemic Components*	*Structures*
21 consonants	consonance, alliteration
3 glides (y, w, h)	assonance, consonance
9 vowels	assonance
(9 diphthongs)	assonance
(combinations of the above)	rhyme
4 junctures	groupings
4 stresses	rhythm
4 pitches	intonation

2. *Morphemic Components*	*Structures*
Free forms	⎫
Bound forms	⎬ Diction
Inflections	⎪
Compounds	⎭

3. *Syntax Components*	*Structures*
Phrases	⎫ Phrasal structures
Clauses	⎬ Clausal structures
Sentences	⎭ Sentence structures

  B. *Semantic Components*

1. *Meaning Components*	*Structures*
Predications	no particular
Nominalizations	name used for
Transformations	such structures
Parts of speech	
Sentence types (as meanings)	

2. *Reference Components*	*Structures*
a. *Referents* (Kinds of reality)	
{ Concrete (image)	⎫ Imagery
{ Abstract	⎪
{ Subjective, serious, humorous, . . .	⎬ no special
{ Objective	⎪ name
{ Singular, plural, empty class	⎪
{ Denotative	⎭
{ Connotative	

b. *Referends* (Kinds of referring
term)
Literal
Nonliteral   Figures of Speech
  Opposite   Irony
  Opposite and literal   Paradox
  More than   Hyperbole
  Less than   Understatement
  Thing for human   Personification
  Expressed similarity   Simile
  Implied similarity   Metaphor
  Second level of artificial meaning   Symbolism
  Part for whole   Synecdoche
  Better than   Euphemism
  Previous literary referent   Allusion
  Sound for object   Onomatopoeia
c. *Referral* (Relation of term to
reality)
Anomaly   no special name
Ambiguity
Synonymy
Univocity
Truth value

3. *Semantic Differentials*   *Structures*
Personal deviations (Idiolect)   no special name
  Private symbols
  Private connotations
  Private referends
Social deviations (Dialect)
  By time
  By place
  By class structure, economic, sex,
  education...

II. METALINGUISTIC

A. *Partial Components*   *Structures*
Part paragraphs
Paragraphs
Stanzas, couplets
Sections   } Organization
Chapters, cantos
Books
Volumes

B. *Discourse Components*   *Structures*
1. *Arts and Media*
Common to all
  Voice, assumed or real   Viewpoint, point of view,

Addressee
Peculiar to Speech-Listening
Gesture, Posture, etc.
Peculiar to Writing-Reading
Page placement,
Pictures
Peculiar to Various Media

tone, attitude, apostrophe
Delivery

2. *Modes*
Dynamic Reference
Emotions
Characters
Action
Static Reference
Description
Ideas, Valuations

Narrative
Emotive Structure
Characterization
Plot
Exposition
Setting, spectacle, costume
Theme

3. *Aims*
Scientific
Informative
Exploratory
Persuasive
Expressive

⎫
⎪
⎬ Usually emerge as
⎪ theme or setting
⎭

III. METALANGUAGE

A. *Situational Context*

Components and structures of the immediate historical or biographical situation which could be relevant to analysis

B. *Cultural Context*

Components and structures of conventions and traditions which could be relevant to analysis

Structures

Genre, stanzaic forms, types, etc.

N. B. This chart represents a simplification. All of the sections are only suggestive, and do not attempt to be complete. In addition to all of these horizontal structures, it is important for a literary work to interrelate (i.e., structure) these structures vertically. Thus setting will dictate a parallel diction and parallel characterization; and these may be symbolized in imagistic patterns, etc.

All of these components and their corresponding structures have been recognized in literary analysis throughout the history of Western culture. Only the ordering here is somewhat innovative.[5] Aristotle, for instance, calls all of the elements under phonemics *melos* or melody; those under mor-

---

[5] A similar grouping can be seen in Enkvist, o, 30–31.

phemics, syntax, and semantics he calls *lexis* or style; partial components he calls *taxis* or organization, a term he uses in the *Rhetoric,* though not continually in the *Poetics;* the emotive components are called *pathos* or emotive; character components he calls *ethos* or characterization; actions, *mythos* or plot; ideas and valuations, *dianoia* or theme; descriptive components, *opsis* or spectacle. He does not have a special name for cultural context, but he considers some of the problems involved. In other words, this catalog of components and structures fits very well into the framework of analysis of the *Poetics.* It is true that some of the structures have no special names, even though they are frequently used in poems, novels, and plays.

These components and structures will be examined in more detail in the following section. However, we now have the materials and terminology available to us for a discussion of the peculiar nature of literary structures.

Possibly the most obvious reaction that comes from a perusal of these component structures is that although all are available to all aims of discourse, some are more congenial to one aim than another. Poetry, for instance, tends to use the phonemic structures much more consistently than other aims of discourse or other genres of literature. The differentiation of genre is best effected by seeing what kinds of structures and components are stressed in a given work.

The second, and without doubt the most important difference between the structures of literature and the structures of other kinds of discourse is that in the other discourses, structure is an instrumental means to something more important in the discourse. In literature, structure is primary. This primacy of structure immediately differentiates literary from other discourses. It is the primacy of structure which beauty and ugliness have in common. Both call attention to themselves as conspicuous structures, conspicuous *because* of their structures. A college student in the hall, turning to look at a pretty girl who passes by, remarks to his companion: "Gads, what a shape." The expression is very apt: the girl has called attention to herself because she is shapely and well formed. These are synonyms of structure. On the contrary, an ugly building, a pock-marked face, a maimed body also call attention to themselves by their conspicuous structures. The beautiful is differentiated from the ugly by its unity or integrity and its harmony or fitness. Before we examine these two aspects, however, let us look more closely at the concept of primacy of structure.

The Middle Ages continually asserted the primacy of structure in interesting metaphors. Augustine used the terms "the splendor of order" (cf. Maritain, a, 24, 163), and Albertus Magnus and Aquinas used the term "the splendor of form" (cf. Maritain, a, 24, 25, 162). As Maritain observes, after cataloguing such expressions from Plotinus and the neo-Platonists through the high Middle Ages up to John of St. Thomas in the Renaissance,

"A certain splendor is, in fact, according to all the ancients, the essential characteristic of beauty" (a, 24). Instead of "splendor," radiance of form or clarity of form are terms often used (cf. Maritain a, 24, 28). Joyce, following Aquinas, also uses the word "radiance" (p, 211–13).[6]

The immediate corollary of a concept of structure as primary, as splendorous, as shining or radiating through matter, as conspicuous, is to suggest the question, "How can form be made to be primary, that is, to call attention to itself?" Since the ordinary does not call attention to itself, the form of art must, in some sense, be extraordinary, different, novel, original. This explains the continual stress in literary history on the necessity of the extraordinary in art. As Craig La Drière has said,

> In all distinctions between poetry and prose there is one common element implied or explicit: prose is ordinary language, poetry is speech which is somehow extraordinary. The problem of defining poetry is the problem of defining its extraordinariness (La Drière, p, 441).

Different attempts to define the extraordinariness of literature have, as a matter of fact, ranged through nearly all the components and literary structures outlined above. Whately distinguishes poetry from prose solely on the basis of the extraordinariness of its sound structures (cf. La Drière, p, 441–42). But poetry is not coextensive with literature. In modern times Northrop Frye distinguishes the rhythms of literature from the sentential rhythms of referential prose and both from the associative rhythms of expressive speech (w, 18 ff.). He examines very carefully the demotic (ordinary) and hieratic (extraordinary) tendencies in literature, all in terms of subtle combinations of rhythm (w, 94 ff.). Aristotle frequently refers to the morphemic and semantic extraordinariness of poetic language (1404b 11 ff.; 1410b 11; 1457b 1 ff.; Cope, r, III, 2, 14). Whatmough, Mukařovský, and many other modern writers insist on the syntactic deviations of literature from normal language. As Whatmough says,

> Language is a symbolism, a systematic and orderly symbolism; but again and again it is often anomalous, judged by the standards of grammarians and editors, as every piece of modern literature testifies (p, 98; cf. Mukařovský, f, 241 ff.).

A few, such as Max Eastman and Owen Barfield, have even carried this doctrine so far as to maintain that poetry has its own special language (cf. Lemon, 117–18), and Valéry regrets that poetry does not have a special language (Frye, w, 94).

---

[6] As Maritain points out, radiance or clarity (or conspicuousness) do not at all necessarily imply "obvious." In fact, initial obscurity of form may be the characteristic of new kinds of art works (a, 28).

In the discourse areas beyond the grammatical and syntactic, there are affirmations of other kinds of deviations from the ordinary. Henri Bonnet, a French critic, thinks that the specific function of the novel is to portray the settings, the lives, the characters of people who are different from us in some extraordinary way (cf. Bonnet, r, 8, 34, 39). Such an "escapist" view of the content of literature was quite common in the Romantic period, and it finds its parallel today in the stress on the extreme and extraordinary situations in modern novels. Susan Sontag generalizes on this trait in modern literature:

> One of the primary features of literature (as of much activity in the other arts) in our time is a chronic attachment to materials belonging to the realm of "extreme situations": madness, crime, taboo sexual longings, drug addiction, emotional degradation, violent death. The motive, or justification, for this loyalty to extreme situations is obscure. It is felt that such situations are somehow "more true" than others; that an art immersed in these situations is "more serious" than other art; and, finally, that only art that embraces the irrational and repellent, the violent and the outrageous, can make a valuable impact on the sluggish consciousness of the contemporary audience (1, 175, the whole section is relevant, 175–84).

Aristotle himself had, early in our critical traditions, stressed the necessity of the poet's using extraordinary persons and situations, and two important elements of plot to which he devotes considerable time, recognition and reversal, are elements that give plot extraordinariness. The themes, finally, of literature are rarely the routine commonplaces of the reading populace. To call attention to itself, a literary theme must be bizarre, avant-garde, reactionary, novel, or original. Literary writers must get their themes from the fringes of society; they cannot move in the mainstream. For this reason, littérateurs keep in touch with the politically radical or the extremely reactionary, with religious novelties, with sociological innovations. For this reason also they are often thought to be the map-makers of the future.

All of these movements to the extraordinary force the literary writers to be original. Originality is not a characteristic of certain periods of literature, it is essential to all literature. That is why literary writing is called "creative" writing, though littérateurs have no monopoly on creativity. Poe, Young, Novalis, and, in our day Eliseo Vivas, stressing the necessity of literary originality and creativity, are simply pointing out the direct corollary of literature being extraordinary discourse, and this is itself a corollary of the primacy of structure.

But merely being extraordinary is not the sole claim of literature. It is also the nature of the ugly and the informative to be conspicuous and surprising. It is true, some modern art occasionally gives the impression that mere sensationalism and notoriety are enough to achieve recognition. But this would reduce art to cheap journalism or, in the end, to monstrosities.

The two accompanying qualities which the conspicuous structures of art must have are usually said to be unity and fitness. Both are long-lived components of the artistic tradition, and both are difficult to define in strictly literary terms. Unity, of course, has been given some extremely narrow interpretations historically, especially the unities of time, place, and plot in drama. Despite abuses, however, unity is preached by practically all literary theorists: "Unity is the most fundamental and comprehensive aesthetic criterion, upon which all others depend," says Fogle, beginning an article on "Unity" in the *Encyclopedia of Poetry and Poetics* (w, 880). Is there, however, a useful concept of literary unity which can be broad enough to take in the various kinds of literary unities and narrow enough to separate literature from other kinds of discourse? For it is clear that a scientific work has unity, and a successful piece of persuasion has rhetorical unity. It has often been said that literary discourse is more tightly unified than are other kinds of discourse. This does seem to be true in one very important sense. If we glance back at the components and levels of literary structure outlined in Figure V, 2, we see the various "separated" structures of the literary work represented *horizontally*: alliteration, assonance, rhyme, rhythm, imagery, symbolism, organization, setting, plot, and theme. The important thing about a literary work is that all or as many as possible of these horizontal structures must also be *vertically* interrelated. This means that a setting dictates characters of a certain type who speak dialects of the sort that are unified with the setting and personalities; these characters perform actions in plots and these actions must flow from the characters. The actions and thoughts of these characters illustrate themes which fit the rest of these components, and the symbolic devices must be unified with the imagery. There is, in other words, a rigid vertical unity of structure that unites the separate levels of structure. Such a rigid unity is not called for in other aims of discourse. It really does not spoil the informative nature of a criminal confession procedure if there are inconsistencies and inelegant deficiencies of unity among the various components of the process. In this sense, literary unity is a more rigid kind of unity than the unity of other kinds of discourse. It has, in fact, a necessary added dimension which makes appropriate the organic metaphor of the tradition: everything in a literary work is related to every other part. When it is not, the art suffers. Nothing can really be left out of an art object without significant diminution. Newspaper articles can be cut off to accommodate space problems and still remain informative; scientific articles can be abstracted and be of considerable value, exploratory procedures can be abbreviated and summarized and still be of worth; prayers can be shortened and the deities may be placated; but the mutilated sonnet, the paraphrase of a lyric, the précis of a short story are not art at all.

This complex interrelationship of the various parts is one of the elements crucial to Lemon's analysis of structure, an analysis adapted from Whitehead. It represents one of the few serious attempts I know of to erect a theory of literary structure. For Lemon the poem must have internal congruence and external coherence. Its internal congruence makes it a form, its coherence to outside reality makes it a symbol. So Lemon calls his a theory of symbolic form. Congruence is achieved by complexity and integrity. Other synonyms of complexity are richness, multivalence, scope, width: of integrity, depth, intensity, narrowness, power (Lemon, p, 217–22). He concludes: "The best poem is one which has most complexity and integrity" (p, 223). Despite semantic overlaps, it seems clear that Lemon is advocating, in complexity and integrity, the concept of intense unity which I am speaking of.

Finally, the conspicuous and unified structures of literature must also have fitness. This feature has been a component, under some term or other, of literary theory since the early period of Greek literary theory. Harmony, proportion, propriety, decorum, and other terms have been synonyms of fitness throughout history, with different nuances of meaning. We have already seen this concept as a rhetorical virtue of style in Aristotle, Cicero, Quintilian, and others. But it is also a literary virtue. Literary fitness or harmony is even more difficult to define than literary unity. La Drière is not dismayed by this:

> Perhaps its repugnance to specification is evidence that the idea of fitness is specific enough without reduction to any more concrete formula, and directly applicable to experience without being made less abstract. Perhaps its very obdurate abstractness, its resistance to assimilation by any particular context and its consequent elasticity in application to all contexts, explain its hardy persistence, and its permanent value, as an ultimate principle for aesthetic judgment (f, 241).

General definitions can be given:

> Conformity of related things to each other; conformity in a relation to some recognized ideal for such relation; coincidence, in matters of relatedness, of what is with what ought to be (La Drière, f, 241).

Such definitions stress the congruence of forms and the implied or explicit presence of an evaluative norm. Consequently, the idea of fitness has usually been accompanied by norms of fitness. Things are fit because they are natural or because they conform to some current conventions (La Drière, f, 241). These norms seem equally applicable to shoes that fit, to proper manners in eating, to propriety in literary manners, in matters of fashion in dress, or in behavior at a cocktail party. Nature as a norm seems to be more intrinsic to the literary object, whereas convention seems more external and seems to be much more a matter of the relation of a literary object to literary traditions and customs. This latter norm of fitness will be returned to when the metalanguage structures of literature are examined in the last section under the style of literary discourse.

Nature, as a norm partly intrinsic to the literary object, can sometimes seem very close to unity. To say that the speech of a character must fit his personality and the setting of the novel is to say that there must be a unity between speech and character, and these must both be part of the unity of setting. But fitness viewed as harmony or balance does not seem reducible to unity. Until closer analysis of the concept is made, fitness seems destined to remain a useful, albeit partly intuitive tool in creation and analysis.

In conclusion, then, organization in literature must give primacy to structure by making it conspicuous, these conspicuous structures must have an intense horizontal and vertical unity, and they must be harmonious and fit. These are the specific characteristics of literary structures as opposed to other structures. If this position strikes some as being too traditional in its incorporation of Greek and medieval as well as of some modern components, I can only say that I do not apologize. Good literature and good art theory did not necessarily begin fifteen years ago. Art and art theory are of the ages.

The big task that remains is to see the practical exemplification of these doctrines. I have chosen to defer such analyses till the treatment of style since this treatment will itself be lengthy enough and since it will be done at several levels. But the analysis will, it is hoped, exemplify the basic doctrines of primacy of structure, intensity and unity of structure, and proportion among the parts.

The Style of
Literary Discourse

Literary Style
in General

The initial sentence in "Criteria for Style Analysis" by Michael Riffaterre must give pause to the reader of this text. Riffaterre warns:

> Subjective impressionism, normative rhetoric and premature aesthetic evaluation have long interfered with the development of stylistics as a science, especially as a science of literary styles (c, 412).

The author can only express the hope that his rhetoric, his esthetic, and his subjective expressionisms will not interfere with the treatment of style that follows; for he must concur with Riffaterre's statement. The statement implies that there has been considerable attention devoted to literary style in the past. Indeed the abundance of material on literary style is comparable to that on persuasive style and in sharp contrast to the paucity of material on reference, and even more, on expressive discourse. General treatments on style abound, from many points of view. In addition, thousands of treatments of individual poems, dramas, and novels appear every year and are duly recorded in massive bibliographies; many of these contain extremely helpful implications for a general theory of literary style. It is clear from these considerations that a treatment of literary style must involve a very selective process and make no pretense to comprehensiveness.

To begin with, as is usual in these matters, the word style has many meanings. There is first of all the meaning which allows predication of style about only certain kinds of discourse; this is opposed to a more general notion of style which can speak of style in any kind of utterance. Tenney finds the beginning of the narrow view of style in Plato and of the broad view in Aristotle (Tenney, s, 554). Traditionally many have restricted style to literary or rhetorical works and not predicated it of reference discourse. Such a concept of style is closely relatd to the view that style is a shell that is added to or imposed upon a content of thought. This "shell" view of style has a long tradition. Nils Enkvist, in an essay in which he attempts to define style, says that Plato, Stendhal, Burke, De Quincey, and the linguist Charles Bally would all fit into this tradition (o, 12–15). One could add to this the entire sophistic (or stylistic) group of rhetoricians. Just as persistent, however, has been the view that style is organic, that the style of a discourse is dictated by its nature, its purpose, its logic, even its organization. Aristotle, Longinus, Ben Jonson, John Middleton Murry, and most modern students of "stylistics," such as Leo Spitzer, take this view (cf. Lerner, s, 814). From the discussions of style in reference and persuasive discourse it is clear that this text takes the organic view of style.

Nonetheless, owing to the lively persistence of the sophistic view of rhetoric, much of the traditional treatment of style was in terms of the rhetorical figures of speech. Because of the equal perseverance of the communication view of rhetoric, the analysis of literary style was often indistinguishable from the analysis of rhetorical style.

Beginning with the Romantic movement, some new approaches to style were advocated, especially the determination of style in terms of the personality of the author. Such a concept of style is an immediate corollary of the expressive theory of literature. De Quincey, in this respect a thorough Romantic, finds in subjectivity the main basis of style. "All subjective branches of study favor the cultivation of style" (s, 225), and objective studies and cultures tend to be devoid of style (cf. s, 212). Schopenhauer takes a similar view: "style is the physiognomy of the mind" and a man writes in a language which is "the physiognomy of the nation" (o, 251–52). This view that style is predicated of an individual or of a nation or of a period has become one of the most dominant concerns of style analysis in the twentieth century (Wellek, t, 183; Lerner, s, 816).

The careful analysis of the individual or period styles emerged as a separate discipline in the latter part of the nineteenth century, mainly in the study of Romance and Germanic literature. Until very recently the movement has not had as much influence in the study of English and American literature. Helmut Hatzfeld, the bibliographer and historian of the movement, places the beginnings in the 1880's (p, 325 ff.). The general English term "stylistics," given to the movement, embraces both the French *stylistique* and the German *Stilforschung* (style research or analysis). "Stylistique" for a long time stressed an analysis of the language from a linguistic point of view, whereas *Stilforschung* was more oriented to the analysis of individual works of art (Eustis, s, 817). However, this distinction is not at all rigid, particularly at the present time.

It is from the investigations of the stylistics movement that some of the more fertile concepts of style analysis have come. But many of their notions have solid precedents in traditional and in Romantic theories of literature. In a book that anthologized several of the important "stylistics" essays, Dell Hymes typically says "Style may be investigated, both as deviations from a norm and as 'a system of coherent ways or patterns of doing things'" (p, 33). Twenty-five years earlier, Wellek and Warren, in *Theory of Literature,* used the same two notions to define style (t, 184). Indeed, these two notions, style as deviation or style as structure, are probably the dominant views of style in linguistics, stylistics, and literary theory in this century. Sometimes, as with several recent theorists in stylistics, the two concepts are merged: style consists of patterned deviations from a norm. The notion of structure we have already examined cursorily and will return to later. The notion of deviation from a norm we have already seen in the guise of the surprise element in information theory. Let us now look at it from a stylistic point of view.

To the literary student who has unconsciously imbibed some concepts of style from such figures as Pope, Wordsworth, and Eliot, all of whom advise a return to nature and all of whom are reacting against previous conventions, and to students schooled in the Romantic idea that poetry is the natural language of excited feelings (cf. Spencer, p, 301), the reverse concept that poetry or literature is a deviation from the norm of natural language must come as something of a shock. Yet this second is much more venerable and elderly in literary theory than the former. As we have seen in the study of persuasive style, Aristotle posits "extraordinariness" as a feature of style which rhetoric imports from literature. This feature never disappeared completely from the rhetorical tradition. Even the rebellious Romantic period stressed originality, as we have seen, and originality is a deviation of some sort. Lewes, a typical nineteenth-century thinker writing on style, posits originality as a basic ingredient of literary style (p, 317 ff.). Remy de Gourmont, early in this century, is more pointed:

> Having a style means that in the midst of the language shared with others one speaks a particular, unique, and inimitable dialect, which is at the same time everybody's language and the language of a single individual (quoted in Enkvist, o, 21).

John Middleton Murray, in his popular *The Problem of Style* (1922), stressed idiosyncrasy and structure as the two components of style (p, 6–9, 15). The Russian formalists in the late teens and early twenties were stressing "defamiliarization" and structural devices as the components of style (Shklovsky, a, 13–22; Eichenbaum, t, 114; Erlich, r, 177–80, 234).

With such precedents, it is not surprising that modern linguists could define style, and especially poetic style, in terms of a deviation from the norm. The "norm" in this definition is usually assumed to be prosaic, ordinary, casual. Poetry or literature becomes deviant, divergent, extraordinary, noncasual language, language with a *Differenzqualität,* the Germans called it. Charles Osgood, a psycholinguist, categorically announces at the beginning of his paper,

> For the purposes of this paper, then, style is defined as the individual's deviations from the norm for the situation in which he is encoding (s, 293).

Some completely equate literature with such noncasual utterances (e.g., Saporta, a, 82; cf. Sebeok, s, 64); though Wellek, Greenberg, and Voegelin refuse to make such an easy equivalence, pointing out that prayer, ritual, and didactic verse are noncasual but not literary, and some novels are literary but casual (cf. Sebeok, s, 98, 101, 103, 57, 60, 64). In all of these cases the concern of the theorists was with normal and deviant language, viewed almost exclusively in a grammatical or semantic light. At even these levels, it seems clear that mere deviation from norms is not at all restricted to literature. At discourse levels, to view deviations from norms as always literary would be to reduce literature to information.

Since literary language is at least partly a matter of deviations from a probable norm, modern formulas of style often sound like the formulas of information theory stated in terms of probabilities, or better, improbabilities or unpredictabilities. Michael Riffaterre, who has, in my opinion, the most thorough approach to style to date from this viewpoint, maintains that in literature, if the writer wants to make a structure conspicuous or inescapable, he must make the structure unpredictable, "for predictability may result in superficial reading; unpredictability will compel attention" (c, 416; cf. Enkvist, o, 28, 32–33). Such a theory of style corresponds neatly to the theory of conspicuous structure outlined above.

Implicit in all theories of style that view it as a deviation from a norm is the problem of determining the norm. In stylistics three solutions have been proposed. Despite several serious objections many modern linguists feel that an intuitive knowledge of the language and an education in the literature provide an adequate sense of the norm to allow the reader to discern pertinent deviations. Leo Spitzer, Jan Mukařovský, Paul Garvin, René Wellek, Austin Warren, Richard Sayce, Bernard Bloch, to choose examples from Eastern and Western Europe, England, and the United States— all work with this assumption. (cf. Riffaterre, c, 424, n. 19, for references). The objection raised against it is that it is vague and difficult to apply: it implies a knowledge of all of present usage, the author's customs and affiliations, the contemporary culture, etc. (cf. Riffaterre, c, 424–26). It gives us, says Enkvist, the "formidable and theoretically objectionable task of using the entire language as a norm" (i, 25). To use a more attainable and definable norm, several authors have proposed the use of a text or several comparative texts, drawn from similar cultures, situational contexts, genres, or purposes. Spencer and Enkvist propose this method of comparison:

> Style is concerned with frequencies of linguistic items in a given context, and thus with *contextual* probabilities. To measure the style of a passage the frequencies of its linguistic items of different levels must be compared with the corresponding features in another text or corpus which is regarded as a norm and which has a definite contextual relationship with this passage. For the stylistic analysis of one of Pope's poems, for instance, norms with varying contextual relationships include English eighteenth-century poetry, the corpus of Pope's work, all poems written in English in rhymed pentameter couplets, or, for greater contrast as well as comparison, the poetry of Wordsworth. Contextually distant norms would be, e.g., Gray's *Anatomy* or the London Telephone Directory of 1960 (Enkvist, o, 29).

The third, and even more restricted norm suggested is the stylistic text of the work itself. This norm has been proposed by Riffaterre (c, 426 ff.). He defines any stylistic device as an unpredictable unit that creates an opposition, and therefore a structure, with elements in the actual text which precede it (c, 427). This structure then can become a context which a future element in the poem can also oppose to create another stylistic device, and so on. It is clear that this notion of norm is more scientifically verifiable than is either educated intuition or comparison of texts. But it also has the effect of seemingly ruling out (or taking for granted)) many extra-textual components and structures that are relevant. Given such an absolute internal autonomy of text, how could one determine, for example, that Hopkins' codas to "That Nature is a Heraclitean Fire and of the Comfort of the Resurrection" are significant deviations from the sonnet tradition, that Shakespeare's sonnet 130, "My mistress' eyes are nothing like the sun," is a parody use of the courtly love conventions, that Pope's description of the toilet of Belinda in "The Rape of the Lock" is mock epic? More than internal unpredictables are needed for detecting these devices.

The second modern view of style, that style is structure, has already been implicit in some of the preceding discussion, and explicit, in the paraphrases from Riffaterre. Style as structure had also been emphasized in classic treatments of style. Buffon, always quoted for his famous "The style is the man himself," actually devoted half of his famous discourse on style to the concept of the organic whole and to organization (d, 170–75). Robert Louis Stevenson's essay on style makes this point again and again:

> ...and it may be said with sufficient justice that the motive and end of any art is to make a pattern; a pattern, it may be, of colors, or sounds, of changing attitudes, geometrical figures, or imitative lines; but still a pattern. This is the plane on which these sisters [the arts] meet; it is by this that they are arts.
>
> *   *   *
>
> *The web, then, or the pattern; a web at once sensuous and logical, an elegant and pregnant structure: that is style, that is the foundation of the art of literature* (s, 368, 370, my italics).

A. L. Kroeber, a modern anthropologist, says much the same thing when he asserts, in *Style and Civilizations,* that style is

> ...something concerned essentially with form, and possessing some consistency of the forms operated with; plus a coherence of these into a set of related larger patterns (s, 26; cf. 76 ff.).

The stress on structure in modern stylistics is, therefore, grounded in some of the important texts on style in the tradition. This emphasis on structure is seen most explicitly in Riffaterre, Guirand and Richard A. Sayce (cf. Hatzfeld, p, 339–40). Implicitly, however, it can be seen in many of the practical analysts among the new critics, whether they analyze structures of imagery, of symbolism, of tension, of paradox, of ambiguity, and so on.

These structured deviations constituting style are predicated by different critics at different levels. A few arbitrarily limit stylistic analysis to grammatical deviations. Saporta and Osgood even exclude lexical or semantic deviations from stylistic considerations (Saporta, 1, 91–92; Osgood, s,

296, and Sebeok, s, 334). Most writers include semantic components such as word clusters, dialect variations, symbols, and images as relevant to style analysis. At the discourse level, some include the performance (or execution or delivery) of a work as a component of style analysis (cf. Kroeber, s, 32); others exclude this. Many writers include medium characteristics in stylistics (cf. De Quincey, s, 232 ff.; Osgood in Sebeok, s, 333). Of course mode and aim are usually considered as relevant to style analysis. And beyond discourse, quite a few modern writers consider aspects of situational context as being relevant to style analysis (cf. Enkvist, o, 29–31; Spencer, a, 99 ff.). Possibly most attention today is focused on deviations from cultural conventions as being pertinent to style analysis. Spencer (a, 100), Kroeber (s, 9, 33, 58–61, 37), Wölfflin (Erlich, s, 59), and many others have analyzed style in terms of large periods or cultures. In fact this has been one of the most fertile areas of style analysis in this century.

It seems, therefore, that literary style, like other kinds of style, can be seen revealed at any level of the language process. Eustis, in his encyclopedia article on stylistics takes this point of view (s, 817). Hatzfeld's two bibliographies on stylistics devote chapters to lexicological, grammatical, rhetorical (including modes and genres), rhymic and melodic, metalinguistic (myth, time, space, life, death, nature), and epochal elements of style. Enkvist takes a similar comprehensive view, including situational contexts and cultural contexts (o, 17, 25–26, 28–29). The Russian formalists maintained that stylistic deviations from norms occurred at all levels of language, at the discourse level of the kind of reality being deformed in literary presentations, and at the cultural level of the modifications of preceding literary conventions (cf. Erlich, r, 252, 283). Such a comprehensive view is taken in this book; it has already been adopted for referential and persuasive styles and it will be used here for literary style.

For a comprehensive, though far from exhaustive, survey of literary style, therefore, I shall take a look at some grammatical, some semantic, some discourse, some situational context, and some cultural context features of literary style. In this section, therefore, I shall follow the general outline of literary components and structures presented in Figure V, 2. This structure has served as the matrix for the discussion of referential and persuasive styles too, since the same components are available to them also. They are available to anyone who uses language as a vehicle for discourse. But the literary writer uses some of the components more than do writers of science or propaganda and makes structures of these components worthy of contemplation in their own right, whereas the structures of other kinds of discourse are instruments to the demonstration of a thesis, the transmitting of information, the explorations of a hypothesis, the persuasion of an audience.

In the treatment of style, the systematic approach moving from discourse down through semantic and grammatical features, which was used in the treatments of reference and persuasive styles, will not be strictly adhered to. Instead, for purposes of analysis, Hopkins' sonnet "That Nature is a Heraclitean Fire and of the Comfort of the Resurrection" has been chosen to exemplify some stylistic features at each level of the components and structures outlined in Figure V, 2. No single work can exemplify all components and all structures, but Hopkins' sonnet is an admirable test case for many levels. His phonemic structures of assonance, alliteration, and rhyme are among the best in the language. With Joyce, he is possibly the best exemplum for morphemic structures. His syntax is also a very rewarding study. At the level of semantics, Hopkins' use of archaisms and coinages is also very interesting, as is his use of imagery. The imagery leads into a discussion of theme, an important discourse element. Finally, Hopkins' handling of the sonnet tradition in this poem poses some typical problems at the metalanguage level of cultural context.

It seems better to treat one poem in detail rather than to survey all aspects of literary style with fragmented examples of each, isolated from context. This approach respects the artistic unity of the work of art and the interrelationships of its various levels of structures. At the same time, it makes possible some reference to the nature, logic, and "literary" organization of the work, discussions that have been put off until now.

Hopkins' " That Nature is a Heraclitean Fire and of the Comfort of the Resurrection "

Hopkins is one practitioner who was a formalist in literary theory and practice. In addition, possibly more than other poets, he was very concerned with the *extraordinary* nature of poetic language. His two notions, that poetry is structured to a shape, and that is it extraordinary language, are certainly embodied in the sonnet under consideration, "That Nature is a Heraclitean Fire and of the Comfort of the Resurrection." The poem is here reprinted, with the addition of the primary stress markings in each half of the line. The justification for the markings will be given in the treatment of rhythm. On the opposite page is given the rhythm grouping analysis, placed there for purposes of comparison. This will be explained later.

No one who reads Hopkins can fail to be struck immediately by the conspicuousness of his sound structures. Possibly more than any other poet in English, Hopkins is concerned with sound structures of all sorts. His structures of assonance, of consonance, of alliteration, and of rhythm are among the richest in English poetry. It is for this reason that he was selected for analysis here.

Since the poem is somewhat difficult, it may be useful to give a working paraphrase of the meaning particularly since the thematic structures of the poem will not be given much attention in this analysis. Gardner paraphrases the poem as follows:

> Everything in nature is in a perpetual state of flux: air, earth, and water make a constant cycle of disintegration—a motion which creates the dynamic beauty of the visible world. In fact, the inexhaustible energy of being and becoming throughout all creation is like a huge self-fuelling, non-consumed bonfire. And even man, the most clearly individuated being, higher and apart from all others on earth—he too dies and is qiuckly forgotten, swallowed up in the general flux. This thought fills us with horror, until we remember that through Christ's promise the disintegration of the physical body is (or should be) the immediate beginning of a richer life for the immortal spirit. Strong in this faith, we take heart, we exult, etc. (Gardner, g, I, 161).

THAT NATURE IS A HERACLITEAN FIRE AND OF THE COMFORT OF THE RESURRECTION

Cloud-puffball, torn tufts, tossed pillows | flaunt forth, then chevy on an air- 1
built thoroughfare: heaven-roysterers, in gay-gangs | they throng; they glitter
  in marches, 2
Down roughcast, down dazzling whitewash, | wherever an elm arches, 3
Shivelights and shadowtackle in long | lashes lace, lance, and pair. 4
Delightfully the bright wind boisterous | ropes, wrestles, beats earth bare 5
Of yestertempest's creases; | in pool and rut peel parches 6
Squandering ooze to squeezed | dough, crust, dust; stanches, starches 7
Squadroned masks and manmarks | treadmire toil there 8
Footfretted in it. Million-fueled, | nature's bonfire burns on. 9
But quench her bonniest, dearest | to her, her clearest-selved spark 10
Man, how fast his firedint, | his mark on mind, is gone! 11
Both are in an unfathomable, | all is in an enormous dark 12
Drowned. O pity and indig | nation! Manshape, that shone 13
Sheer off, disséveral, a star, | death blots black out; nor mark 14
            Is any of him at all so stark 15
But vastness blurs and time | beats level. Enough! the Resurrection, 16
A heart's-clarion! Away grief's gasping, | joyless days, dejection. 17
            Across my foundering deck shone 18
A beacon, an eternal beam. | Flesh fade, and mortal trash 19
Fall to the residuary worm; | world's wildfire, leave but ash: 20
            In a flash, at a trumpet crash, 21
I am all at once what Christ is, | since he was what I am, and 22
This Jack, joke, poor potsherd, | patch, matchwood, immortal diamond, 23
            Is immortal diamond. 24

Figure V, 3: "Heraclitean Fire"—Juncture Groupings

1　ô ó ò//ô ó//ô ó ò/　　　　ô ó//ò ó o/o o o ó+

2　ô ó o ò♯ó o ô o o//o♯ô ó/　ò ó♯ò ó o/o ó o//

3　ô ó ò//ô ó o/ó ô//　　　　o ó o o/o ó/ó o//

4　ó ò/o ó o ô o o/o ó/　　　ô o ó/ó/o ó♯

5　o ó ò o/o ó ò/ó o ò/　　　ó//ó o//ô ô ó/

6　o ó o+ ó o/ó o♯　　　　　o ó/o ó ò/ó o/

7　ó o o o/ó/o ó/　　　　　ô ó ò♯ó o//ó o/

8　ó o/ó/o ó o/　　　　　　ó ô/ó/ó/

9　ó ô o ò o♯ó o+ ó o//　　　ó o/ó ò/ô ó♯

10　ò ó/ò ó o o//ó o/　　　　o ò o ó o+ ó o/ó/

11　ó//o ó/o ó ô//　　　　　o ó/o ó//o ó♯

12　ó/ò o o ó+ ó o ò o//　　　ó/o o o o ó o/ó/

13　ó♯ô ó o/o ó o+　　　　　ó o♯ó ô//o ó/

14　o ó//o ó o o//o ó/　　　　ô ó/ó ô♯ò ó/

15　　　　　　　　　　　　o ó o o o/o ó/o ó/

16　ò ó o/ó/o ó/　　　　　　ô ó o♯o ó♯o ô o ó o//

17　o ó ô o o♯o ó/ô ó o//　　ó o/ó//o ó o♯

18　　　　　　　　　　　　o ó/o ó o o/ó ò/

19　o ó o//o o ó o/ó♯　　　　ó/ ó//o ô o ó/

20　ó/o o o ó o ò o/ó♯　　　ó/ ô ó//ô o ó♯

21　　　　　　　　　　　　ò o ó//ò o ó o/ó//

22　ó/o ò o ó/ô ó o//　　　　o ó/ó/ô ó o o

23　ó o/ó/o ó ô//　　　　　ó//ó ô//o ô o ó o o//

24　　　　　　　　　　　　ó/o ó o/ó o o♯

Despite some possible inaccuracies, this does make clear some of the important meanings of the poem. It also should enable the student to understand better a more thorough "grammatical" paraphrase of the poem. Below I have attempted to rephrase the sentences of the poem in more or less ordinary syntax.

> Cloud-puff ball, torn tufts, tossed pillows flaunt forth, then chevy [scamper away] on air-built thoroughfare; these heaven-roysterers, in gay-gangs throng and glitter in marches. Shivelights and shadowtackle in long lashes lace, lance, and pair wherever an elm arches, down roughcast and dazzling whitewash. The bright, boisterous wind delightfully ropes, wrestles and beats earth bare of yestertempest's creases. The wind parches squandering ooze to squeezed dough, crust, and dust in pool and rutpeel. The wind stanches and starches squadroned masks and manmarks footfretted by the toil of treading in the mire. Nature's bonfire burns on, million-fueled. But if [nature] quenches man, her bonniest, her dearest, her clearest-selved spark, how fast man's firedint, his mark on mind, is gone. Both nature and man are drowned in an unfathomable, enormous dark. O pity and indignation. Death blots out in blackness manshape, a star

that shone sheer off, disseveral. Nor is there any mark of him at all so stark [strong], but that vastness blurs and time beats level. Enough! the Resurrection! A heart's-clarion! Away the gasping of grief, away joyless days and dejection. A beacon, an eternal beam, shone across my foundering deck. Flesh may fade, and mortal trash may fall to the residuary worm; the world's wildfire may leave but ash. I am all at once what Christ is, in a flash, at a trumpet crash, since he was once what I am; and this Jack, joke, poor potsherd, patch, matchwood, immortal diamond is immortal diamond.

Even in this grammatical rephrasing, some grammatical ambiguities have been ignored. It is clear how far even the rephrasing is from the language of ordinary prose; and it is evident that mere syntactic deviations from sequences of ordinary prose are not the only constituents of literary language and style. However, given the paraphrase and the grammatical rephrasing, it should now be possible to refer to some of the crucial issues of structure and style in the poem. The main concern here is with some of the grammatical features and some of the genre problems raised by the sonnet.

At the phonemic level, the most obvious structures to the writer are consonance, assonance, alliteration, rhyme, rhythm, phrasal groupings, and intonation (cf. Figure V, 2, p. 349). There are other structures not listed in the outline in Figure V, 2 which can also be used, however. Some analyses of structures based only upon distinctive features have been reported by Chatman (1, 453). Distinctive features here mean the basic features of the vowels or consonants of the language (voiced, grave, diffuse, strident, nasal, continuant, flat, compact.[7] It is possible to establish a structure, say, of a series of nasal sounds, or a series of continuants or plosives; we have no name for such structures, though they resemble consonance or assonance. For some of Hopkins' structures, also, as we shall see, there are no names, in English at least.

Consonance, alliteration, assonance, and rhyme were major concerns of Hopkins. Regarding alliteration, for instance, Hopkins maintains that it is almost a necessity in English verse, "one may indeed wonder whether a good ear is satisfied with our verse without it" (quoted in Gardner, g, 11, 138). Judging by his use of assonance, he probably felt similarly about it. Assonance is produced by a repetition of the same vowel sound or sounds, consonance by the repetition of the same consonant sounds. Alliteration consists in the repetition of the same consonant sound at the beginning of a word

---

[7] For definitions of these terms, cf. Roman Jakobson, *Fundamentals of Language*, 29 ff. The poem is marked with the author's own dialect readings. Most readers do not attempt a British dialect, especially one of Hopkins' time.

or syllable, though vowels also can alliterate. Hopkins believed that any vowel could alliterate with any other, as was the case in Old English and Germanic alliterative meter (cf. Ong for Hopkins' view and use of this technique, h, 135).

In "Heraclitean Fire," Hopkins makes several distinctive structural uses of assonance. Line one is typical of some of his assonantal richness: the / o / is repeated in torn, pillows, forth; the / ʌ / in puffball, tufts; the / e / in then, chevy, air. If one counts eye assonance, there are six "o's" in the first line. Line two has / ʌ r / in thoroughfare, roysterers, glitter; / ei /in gay, they, they. Line three has / æ / in roughcast, dazzling; / e / in wherever, elm, etc. The pattern seen in these three lines persists: there is often a triple assonance in one half of the line and a double or triple assonance in the other. Occasionally the vowel sounds of the first half of the line are repeated in the second. Line twenty-three has / aou /in each half:

> This Jack, Joke, poor potsherd patch,
> matchwood, immortal diamond.

At other times, instead of a repeated set of vowel sounds, the repeated vowel sound of the second half of the line is carried in the first half of the line and the full assonance is seen in the second half: / æ / is in shadowtackle and then in lashes, lance (l. 4); / æ / is in Jack, then in patch, matchwood (l. 23). This continuing or phasing out of a vowel motif, while beginning another, Hopkins calls vowelling on and vowelling off (cf. Gardner, g, 11, 125 ff., 132 ff., 138 ff.). Vowelling on occurs with / æ / in lines four and twenty-three, vowelling off with / ai / occurs in line twenty-two.

The vowelling on or off does not stop with the individual line. Assonance or even near or full rhyme also act as line links in a technique derived from one kind of Welsh cynghanedd. In the tone cynghanedd, given a line divided into three parts, one and two rhyme and two and four alliterate: "In grimy, ỵasty, ỵault." In "Heraclitean Fire," the last part of the preceding line and the two parts of the next line constitute the three parts. The rhyme of part one assonates with one or several stressed syllables of part two, and part two and three alliterate or consonate, usually in stressed syllables. Thus there is a vowelling on from line to line and an alliteration within the line; and the vowelling on constitutes a rhyme link. Lines one through twelve are all structured by this modified cynghanedd, as can be seen in Figure V, 4, where the dotted lines show the assonance links of parts one and two and the underlines show the alliterations. Lines 13 and 14, 15 and 16, 16 and 17, 17 and 18, 18 and19, 20 and 21, 21 and22, 22 and 23, and 23 and 24 are also so structured (in some cases / a / and / ə / are vowelled on). Actually only three cases occur where the pattern is not discernible and in one of them, 12 to 13, the linking is substituted by a

Figure V, 4: Hopkins' "Heraclitean Fire"—Line and Segment Links by Assonance, Rhyme, Alliteration, and Consonance (Assonance:—; Alliteration: . . . .)

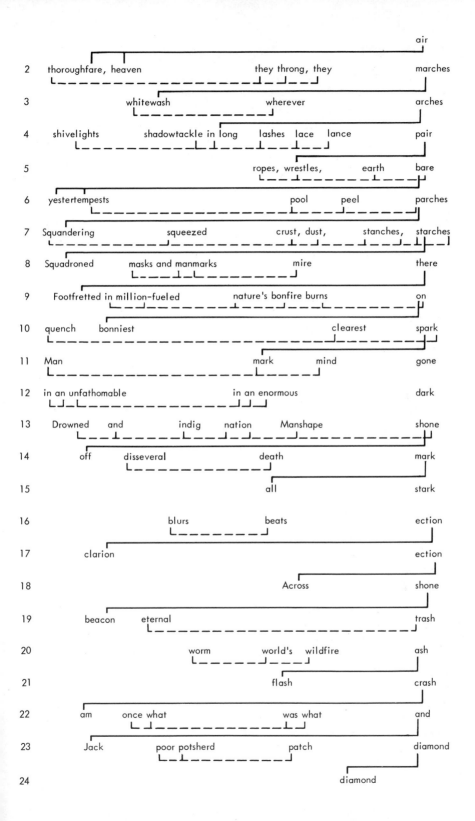

strong alliteration: dark / Drowned. To explain one instance: the end
rhyme of line one, "air," assonates with "thorough*fare*" and "h*e*aven" in the
first part of line two, and the "th" of "thoroughfare" alliterates with "throng"
in the second half of line two, and has all but the voicing feature in common with the two "they's." Thus the whole poem is tightly woven together
by assonance and alliteration.

     Another interesting assonantal line link can also be discerned at
the beginning of the lines. Line one begins with / aw –ʌ/ (cloud-puffball),
and so does line three (down-roughcast). The / ai / of "whitewash" in line
three is seen in the first word of line four, "shivelights," and the first and
third words of line five (Delightfully the bright). Line six has "creases" and
"pool," stressed syllables, echoed in "oozed" and "squeezed" in line seven.
The first word of line seven, "squandering," assonates with the first word of
line eight, "squadroned." And this initial assonantal linking carries on
throughout much of the poem. This initial linking of the lines by assonance
thus parallels terminal linking of the lines by rhyme—and of course, is
accompanied by the cynghanedd linkings. Both the initial assonance linkings
and the cynghanedd are slightly more pronounced in the first fourteen lines of
the sonnet than in the codas.

     We have already seen much alliteration and consonance in the dis-
cussions of the cynghanedd modified to accomodate to the English line. Both
Old English and Welsh influenced Hopkins in his use of alliteration. But
there are rich alliterative patterns in "Heraclitean Fire" that are not part
of the cynghanedd. Thus line three has the d's of "Down roughcast, down
dazzling whitewash" which are not part of the formal cynghanedd. Other
examples can be seen in the poem. Just as he has vowels phasing in and out,
so does he have consonances. Thus, in line three again, the d's of the first
half of the line lead up to the w's which take over in *w*hite*w*ash *w*herever.

     Rhyme is the last of the qualitative sound structures which will be
considered here. A perusal of the end rhymes of "Heraclitean Fire" shows
that Hopkins deviates from traditional rhymes in some unusual ways. The
breaking of "air-built" at the hyphen to rhyme with pair is a characteristic
Hopkins feat. Such a break, called synapheia, can also be seen in Sappho,
Ben Jonson, Campion, Lord Herbert of Cherbury, and, in modern times in
Ogden Nash, Marianne Moore, and others. However, the technique is rather
rare, especially in serious poetry.

     The technique of alternating masculine and feminine rhymes in
the first quatrain is carried on throughout the whole poem, as can be seen
in the rhyme scheme, shown in Figure V, 5. The masculine and feminine
rhymes are chiasmic in the two quatrains. There are no feminine rhymes
in the septet (nine through fifteen). The first coda is all feminine, the
second all masculine, and the third all feminine.

Figure V, 5: Hopkins' "Heraclitean Fire" Rhyme Scheme

1	a	air-
2	b	marches
3	b	arches
4	a	pair
5	a	bare
6	b	parches
7	b	starches
8	a	there
9	c	on
10	d	spark
11	c	gone
12	d	dark
13	c	shone
14	d	mark
15	d	stark
16	e–c	ection
17	e–c	ection
18	e–c	deck shone
19	f	trash
20	f	ash
21	f	crash
22	g	I am, and
23	g	diamond
24	g	diamond

Some other peculiarities are noticeable. "Shone" rhymes with gone (OED gives this as the only British pronunciation, IX, 700). But in the first coda "deck-shone" rhymes with "-ection," presumably giving "shone" the pronunciation / shʌn / a variant recognized in Webster's *Third,* along with / sh ə n /, and / shon / and / shan / (p. 2096). However, since "shone" is a carry-over from the septet, the -ion is more of a back vowel. That is why I have called an "-ection" an "ec" rhyme. Thus the first coda carries on the vowel of one of the rhymes of the septet, just as the "-ect" carries on the / e / of air, bare, there. The coda then is a carry-over of rhyme vowels from both quatrains and the septet. The "ash" of the second coda is a new end rhyme, though / æ / had been used internally for many assonantal patterns throughout the poem (ll. 4, 8, 11, 13). The / æ / of "crash" vowels off into "I am" of the next line and the final coda. This leads to the most arresting rhyme of the sonnet. "I am, and" rhymes with "diamond." This, in effect, distorts elements in both rhymes; the "am" must preserve enough of "am" to be recognizable and consequently it vowels off with crash and assonates with "am" at the beginning of the same line and "Jack" at the beginning of the next (to preserve the cynghanedd) link rhyme. Yet it must be toned downed to rhyme with the "-am" of diamond. This also forces "diamond" to be trisyllabic.

It is evident, with all of these departures from normal rhyming patterns, that Hopkins has established a set of peculiarities in his rhymes. He has a "rhyme" style of his own, just as he has a pattern of assonantal and consonantal structures that are unique and distinctive. Other structures based on inherent features of phonemes could be studied in the poem, but these certainly suffice to show the style of Hopkins at these levels of structure. We turn now to the prosodic features based on stress and juncture.

In English, structures made by some patterning of stressed and unstressed syllables are generally called rhythmic. Hopkins was as conscious of his rhythmic structures as of his assonantal and alliterative structures. Because he felt his rhythms were so distinctive, Hopkins used new terms to describe them, especially "counterpoint" and "sprung" rhythms, terms and realities which we shall return to shortly.

The first step in the discussion of rhythm must be the determination of the stressed and the unstressed syllables. This is not ordinarily a problem; normal accentuation of words and syntax conventions enable us to do this readily. If we accept the usual distinction among linguists of four levels of stress (primary, secondary, tertiary, and weak), our intuitive knowledge of the language would tell us that "torn tufts" (l. 1) probably has a ô ó sequence of stresses, as an adjective-noun sequence usually does. "Tossed pillows" is probably ô ó ò, though some might read it as ô ó o (where ó, ô, ò, o designate syllables with primary, secondary, tertiary, and weak stress, respectively). The normal linguistic rules of the language are certainly the starting point for prosodic analysis. But, precisely because poetry is a deviation from ordinary language and because an individual poet's *style* is a deviation from ordinary *and* other poetic norms, there must be some care exercised in simply imposing ordinary linguistic intuitions on poetic language. Thus, a poet may weaken or strengthen normal linguistic stresses in his rhythmic structure. The same principle applies to the syllables which group around a stressed syllable to form a juncture group. The juncture groups of poetry tend to be much smaller than those of prose (cf. La Drière, p, 457–58). As Riffaterre has remarked, the deviations from prose exist to force us to a more careful and slower reading (c, 416). In the case of Hopkins—and it is another significant aspect of his style—the reading is further slowed down by the many sequences of primary and secondary stresses and by the immediate juxtaposition of two primary stresses, a feature he felt was characteristic of sprung rhythm. However, even with all of these cautions, Gardner's remark about "Heraclitean Fire" still seems overly optimistic. He says that all of this

...need not worry the plain reader, since all he has to do is observe the caesural pause, make sure of the stressed syllables, and let his natural sense of rhythm do the rest (g, I, 107).

Hopkins himself, in his notebooks, give scansion indications for thirteen of the lines, Bridges has scanned two, and Gardner has scanned several lines. Though I have departed from two of Bridges' markings (l. 2), the indication of primary stresses in the copy on page 365 incorporates these various suggestions. The markings of other levels of stress and the juncture groupings, though based on the primary stresses, are my own (Figure V. 3). The little "o's" in Figure V, 3 represent syllables.

Let us first analyze the meter, defined here in La Drière's words simply as "a fixed schematization of the cyclically recurring identity in a rhythmic series" (pro, 670). The only basically recurring rhythmic identity in each line is the six-stress pattern, and this is invariable in each line. Such a meter is, of course, in several respects a radical divergence from the English sonnet tradition. First, there is no regard for an equal number of syllables in each line. Contrast this to Shakespeare's Sonnet 73, shown in Figure V, 6. Where Shakespeare typically has exactly ten syllables in each line, Hopkins' syllabic count varies from twenty in line two to six in line twenty-four. Hopkins is more reactionary than deviant. He says the English sonnet line is "trivial," and by lengthening it he is trying to recapture the dignity of the Italian sonnet line (cf. Gardner, g, I, 82–83.)

Second, Hopkins switches from an iambic pentameter to an Alexandrine, when only *six* stresses determine the lines, and syllables are of little account. He also uses the Alexandrine in two other sonnets. The determination of the line simply by stresses is the essence of sprung rhythm, though there are secondary embellishments. Sometimes, the restriction of only three stresses to each half-line results in some very forced readings. In line seven, for instance (a line he marks), dough and dust are reduced to secondary stresses, despite the commas. In line ten (another line marked by him), the "her" just before the comma is also reduced to a tertiary stress; and in line fourteen, "death" is reduced to a secondary stress. The language has obviously become idiosyncratic, almost an idiolect. Nevertheless the poem reads rather well despite all of these deviations. The Alexandrine allows Hopkins a caesural break in the middle of the line. Such consistent line breaks are also not in the English sonnet tradition, though they are in the Old English line. The line breaks allow Hopkins to use the cynghanedd we discussed above, and to use some Old English alliterative patterns.

Let us turn our attention briefly to the juncture groupings, indicated in Figure V, 4. In this chart I use the juncture markings of Bloch and Trager (+, /, //, # respectively for plus, single bar, double bar, and terminal juncture). I have recorded the plus junctures only when they are obviously used as the basis for a stress grouping (as in "air + built" and indig + nation where a new line and a caesura are indicated). Some critics do not think that intonation or juncture analysis is of much importance in English verse (cf. the remarks of Voegelin and Wells in Sebeok, s, 203–4). Others, however, feel that the tension between meter and groupings make for some of the most important aspects of rhythm. In a sense, meter is the bass, and groupings are the melody of poetry (cf. La Drière, pr, 458; Wimsatt, c, 112; Hrushovski, f, 178, n. 2).

Figure V, 6: Shakespeare's "Sonnet 73"—Meter and Juncture Groupings

That time of year thou may'st in me behold,
When yellow leaves, or none, or few do hang
Upon those boughs which shake against the cold,
Bare ruin'd choirs, where late the sweet birds sang.
In me thou seest the twilight of such day
As after sunset fadeth in the west,
Which by and by black night doth take away,
Death's second self that seals up all in rest.
In me thou seest the glowing of such fire,
That on the ashes of his youth doth lie,
As the death-bed whereon it must expire,
Consum'd with that which it was nourish'd by.
This thou perceiv'st, which makes thy love more strong,
To love that well, which thou must leave ere long.

Meter Analysis		*Juncture Analysis*
o ô o ó o ò o ò o ó		o ô o ó⁄ o ò o ò o ó⁄⁄
o ô o ó o ó o ó o ó		o ô o ó⁄⁄o ó⁄⁄o ó⁄⁄o ó⁄
o ò o ó o ó o ò o ó		o ò o ó⁄ o ó⁄ o ò o ó⁄⁄
ó ó o ó o ó o ó ó ó	4	ó⁄ ó o⁄ ó⁄ o ó⁄ o ó⁄ ó⁄ ó♯
o ò o ó o ó o o ô ó		o ò o ó⁄ o ó o⁄ o ô o ó⁄
o ò o ó o ó o o o ó		o ò o ó o⁄ ó o⁄ o o ó⁄⁄
o ò o ò ó ó o ó o ó		o ò o ò ó⁄ ó⁄ o ó⁄ o ó⁄⁄
ó ó o ó o ô ó ó o ó	8	ó⁄ ó o⁄ ó⁄ o ô ó⁄ ó⁄ o ó♯
o ò o ó o ó o o ô ó		o ò o ó⁄ o ó o⁄ o ô o ó⁄⁄
o o o ó o o o ó o ó		o o o ó o⁄ o o ó⁄ o ó⁄⁄
o o ó ô o ò o ò o ó		o o ó ô⁄ o ò o ò o ô⁄⁄
o ó o ò o o o ó o ó	12	o ó⁄ o ò o o o ó o⁄ ó♯
ó ò o ó o ó o ó ô ó		ó⁄ ò o o ó⁄ o ó⁄ o ó⁄ ô ó⁄⁄
o ó ô ó o ò o ó ò ó		o ó⁄ ô ó⁄ o ò o o ó⁄ ò ó♯

Some remarks on Hopkins' groupings may further help to distinguish his style. Possibly the most obvious characteristic of the juncture groups is the large number of groups, 135; but especially the large number of double bar (comma) groups, 31; and the large number of terminal juncture groups, 19. A contrast of this to Shakespeare's Sonnet 73 will be helpful, using only the first fourteen lines of Hopkins. Where Shakespeare has eleven double-bar junctures, Hopkins has eighteen; where Shakespeare has four terminal junctures, Hopkins has eleven; where Shakespeare has fifty-two juncture groups of all kinds, Hopkins has eighty-four. Shakespeare has different numbers of groups per line, varying from seven in line four to two in lines two and eleven. In fact Shakespeare uses this variety to underscore the rhetorical importance of certain lines (4, 8, 13, 14), a technique Hopkins can not avail himself of, given his equal-stress lines. Hopkins must have six primary stresses per line, whereas Shakespeare varies from two to seven (averaging 3.7). The speed of delivery of Shakespeare will naturally be quicker than that of Hopkins.

This point receives further confirmation when we look at the number of secondary stresses in Hopkins. There are forty-one secondary stresses in Hopkins (thirty-three up to line fourteen) and only eight in Shakespeare. Even allowing for an Alexandrine line, it can be seen that Hopkins uses almost four times as many secondary stresses in fourteen lines as does Shakespeare. By this time it begins to be clear how violently Hopkins' choice of an Alexandrine based on stress and not syllable deviates from the English sonnet. The poem has to sound radically different from the traditional sonnet.

Morphemic Elements
of Style

Hopkins' strange morphemic compounds are related to his elaborate sound structures. These are more common in Welsh poetry than in English, inevitably necessary in establishing some of the cynghanedd alliterations and rhyme sequences (Gardner, g, II, 155). Probably the reader first encountering Hopkins might label these the most striking of all Hopkins' deviations from the norms of language. "Shivelights, shadowtackle, heaven-roysterers, yestertempests, rutpeel, treadmire," and many others are novel combinations of morphemes that the reader encounters in other or simpler forms. In all, there are eighteen such combinations just in this poem. The reader lumps these together with the archaic and dialectal words, and what with the weird syntax inversions and shifts of function, and at first believes that this is almost a foreign language. It certainly is not normal prose, not even normal poetry. Only Joyce, possibly, rivals Hopkins in these morphemic novelties, although Shakespeare and Keats also perform this kind of magic with words.

In addition to sound structure, there are other motivations behind such formations. Hopkins' concept of an inner quintessence of a thing or an event, an "inscape" he calls it, is reflected in these attempts to capture it (Peters, g, 107 ff.). In addition, his tendency to accumulate images in rapid word clusters, also a Welsh technique, contributes to these compact coinages, along with his avowed intention to "heighten" natural language.

Most of the compounds in this poem are noun-noun joinings. In many, the first noun is a possessive (puffballs of cloud, tackle of shadow, marks of man, shape of man). Others are place or time referents (roysterers in heaven, tempests of yesterday or year). Others are instrumentals (by dint of fire, wood for matches). His verb-noun compounds are more striking, though rarer: lights that shiver (Peters, g, 186), peel made by rutting, mire in which one treads, made several by being dissevered. The participial forms are also novel: fretted or patterned into design by foot, most clearly achieving self-hood (clearest-selved), fueled by a million elements. Most of these compounds are formed by analogy with some normal form in the language, as several critics have pointed out. Manmark is analogous to watermark and hallmark; treadmire to treadmill; yestertempests to yesterday and year. In one case Hopkins has broken the morpheme away from its usual bound form to make it a free form. "Jack," though a good Shakespearean free form, is usually bound today: steeplejack, jack-of-all trades (to indicate, as Gardner remarks, an undistinguished but useful fellow, g, I, 119). And chevy, meaning "ride in chase" is usually joined, though not morphemically, in Chevy Chase. There is no doubt that these morphemic structures are one of the trademarks of Hopkins' style.

I can find no discernible macrostructure in their use. They are, of course, related to rhythmic structures, since all of them are stressed words. They do seem to predominate in the first fourteen lines of the poem, although there are some in the last part also. The unusual morphemic combinations exist alongside the ordinary compounds used in ordinary ways, such as thoroughfare, bonfire, wildfire. And there are several ordinary compounds made extraordinary by their syntactic functions: roughcast and whitewash.

These syntax shifts lead us to the few brief remarks on Hopkins deviant syntax. Again, some of these habits in Hopkins come from such usages in Greek, Latin, or Welsh poetry (cf. Gardner, g, II, 155–57). The omission of the subject before verbs where one would expect to see it repeated is typical of Hopkins. In lines six and seven one would expect "wind" to be repeated before "parches" and before "stanches" and "starches." The auxiliary "may" is left out in "flesh fade...trash fall, wildfire leave." The relative "that" (or preposition "by") is omitted in 'manmarks [that] treadmire toil there / Footfretted in it." The expletive "there" is left out in "nor mark / Is any of him at all so stark." His inversions are sometimes disconcerting. The inversions in the following four lines are examples:

> Manshape, that shone
> sheer off, disseveral, a star; death blots black out; nor mark
> Is any of him at all so stark
> But vastness blurs and time beats level. (ll. 13–16)

The inversion allows the poet to call attention to the items he wants rhetorically stressed, but the inversions also call attention to themselves as structures.

Possibly the most interesting grammatical structure in the poem has been noticed by Grennen. He calls attention to the very energetic verbs of movement in the first part of the poem as contrasted to the subjunctives and the final and crucial simple copulative "Is" to which the poem leads up as a climax in the last line (g, 208). The first quatrain is built on a set of energetic intransitive verbs, and the second quatrain is built around a series of transitive verbs. Line nine sums up all of this activity in the meaningless: "nature's bonfire burns on." Lines nine through sixteen are constructed on the results of the subjunctive "But quench...," and this thought is repeated in the conditionals of lines nineteen and twenty: "Flesh [may] fade, and mortal trash [may] fall...world's wildfire [may] leave but ash."

The reversal, the solution, is announced in two verbless exclamations:

> Enough! the Resurrection,
> A heart's-clarion! Away grief's gasping, joyless days, dejection.

This solution parallels the verbless summation of the problem, also presented earlier in an exclamation: O pity and indignation! (l. 14). The solution finally resolves into a meaningful assertion of eternal existence:

> This Jack...
> Is immortal diamond.

If Hopkins' grammar is fascinating, his semantic structures are no less so. Prominent among his semantic structures in this poem are his uses of archaic and dialectal terms, of coinages, and especially his imagery. Many of his terms are archaic or dialectal: flaunt, chevy, roysterers, Jack, patch, potsherd; his morphemic compounds are, of course, all coinages. We have already spoken of these above. The relation of the archaic and dialectal terms to the imagery is also interesting.

The images are built on the four elements of early Greek philosophy: water, air, earth, and fire. These represent nature, of which man is a part, even if a most important part. Hopkins wrote that the poem distilled a "great deal of early Greek philosophical thought" (quoted in Hopkins, p, 294). Thales held that the basic element was water, Anaximenes held it was air, Empedocles held they were earth, air, and water; but to Heraclitus the basic element was fire which was continually being transformed in an eternal flux into earth and water.

The first quatrain begins with water (clouds), which travels on air to produce shivers of light. The second quatrain speaks of the air (wind), which takes away the marks made in the earth by former storms and the toil of men. These changes are all a part of the vast Heraclitean bonfire, as line nine tells us. So the images have moved from water to air to earth to fire. Even man, nature's dearest spark, can be quenched and drowned in the enormous dark along with the rest of nature—the images of fire and water are continued when Hopkins talks about man (spark, firedint, quench, drowned).

The uncertain, half-shadow light images of the first eleven lines (glitter, shivelights, shadowtackle, fire, spark, firedint) give way to an enormous dark and blackness (ll. 12, 14). The imagery then changes radically. First of all, right after the exclamation about the Resurrection, there is the first solid sound image in the poem, with clarion and trumpet. Until this point the sonnet had been noiseless (though roysterers and boisterous might have some sound connotations). Second, the uncertain light and ensuing darkness give way to secure beacons and solid beams (l. 19). The elements are mentioned as unimportant—water in "foundering dark," earth in "residuary worm," fire in "world's wildfire" and ash (ll. 18–20). They are returned to in the second to last line where potsherd is earthen, patch and Jack are human, matchwood is fire, and the first immortal diamond maintains the shimmering light image. Man is, therefore, a summation of nature. But man, by the Resurrection becomes a real immortal diamond. Other subsidiary images also are operative. The motion of time versus the stability of eternity, the temporary patterns (frettings) and marks of man and nature versus the eternal beauty marks of the diamond, and the military images (marches, squadroned, clarion, trumpet).

Many of these image patterns occur in Hopkins' other poems, but it would be very difficult to say that they are unique to him. The images of air, water, earth, and fire as four elements occur in much Renaissance poetry and drama, along with the four humors, and the four seasons. As four elements, they obviously occur in Greek philosophy. Their use here, however, is specifically literary. They could, conceivably, be marshalled into a pagan versus Christian concept of cosmology in a treatise on nature and man, but it seems evident here that what is important is their reiterated appearance in a structure of language. To prove the comfort of the Resurrection a theologian would not and should not ordinarily use an outmoded cosmology, almost a mythical cosmology. What is important in the images and the ideas is not the images and ideas themselves, but their being shaped into a pattern which is contemplated, to use Hopkins' own words. Indeed, for many modern readers, the Christian idea of the comfort of the Resurrection may seem as at least as mythical as the outmoded Greek cosmology. That would not destroy the beauty of the poem. The imagery then, is given a specifically literary use. Hopkins really would not care whether the ordinary reader accepted or rejected a Heraclitean flux notion of cosmology. He sent the poem to Robert Bridges, a poet whose "pagan" philosophy, vague theism, and fondness for the Greek Pantheon often disturbed Hopkins (cf. Gardner, g, II, 218–19).

What is more individual in the imagery technique of this poem is the tendency to accumulate images to illuminate a central idea. This technique may also have been influenced by a similar Welsh technique (cf. Gardner, g, I, 110). The technique can be seen in all but three or four lines of the "Heraclitean Fire": "cloud-puffball, torn tufts, tossed pillows," "lace, lance, and pair," "ropes, wrestles, beats earth bare," "dough, crust, dust," etc. It climaxes in line twenty-three:

This Jack, joke, poor potsherd | patch, matchwood, immortal diamond,

the phonemic and image structures which have already been examined. This accumulation of images has several motivations. Like the morphemic compounds, the images are related to his desire to exhibit the inner essence, the inscape of an event. Since they occur in two's and three's usually, they also allow him to work on internal sound patterns, like a modified cynghanedd. They are admirable loci for summations of previously disparate image components—as in line twenty-three. These functions prevent the images from degenerating into mere listings, as they sometimes seem to be in Whitman. They have become an integral part of Hopkins' style, so that if the reader were confronted with these two lines he would probably say, "They sound like Hopkins":

> Earnest, earthless, equal, attuneable | vaulty,
> voluminous. . .stupendous
> Evening strains to be time's vast, | womb-of-all,
> home-of-all, hearse-of-all nights. (Spelt from Sybil's Leaves).

In the consideration of the imagery, I have also crossed over into the consideration of theme and setting, two discourse structures. I have said nothing of other interesting discourse components. In "Heraclitean Fire" we could also profitably analyze them, but this sonnet will serve as an illustration of one kind of structural deviation not really in the poem considered as an autonomous discourse. This last feature of Hopkins' style is an important one. For "Heraclitean Fire" is a sonnet, and part of its literary value is precisely what has been done to the sonnet form. Stylistic features that derive from metadiscourse features are classified in Figure V, 2 as metalanguage components and structures. Since belonging to a genre or subgenre is a matter beyond pure, isolated discourse, the "sonnetness" of this poem will enable us to examine a metalanguage component of style. Much of what I have to say here has already been said, at greater length and with excellent scholarly evidence, by Gardner in his chapter on "Sonnet Morphology" (g, I, 71–108), though I have made further attempts to indicate the structural relevance of some points.

As a preface to Hopkins' handling of the sonnet, one might quote his attitude to all great forms and masterpieces: "The effect of studying masterpieces is to make me admire and do otherwise" (quoted in Hopkins, p, 294). He certainly studied the sonnet tradition carefully, both in Italian and in English. He was very aware of other innovations, such as the Italian coda, the Miltonic line breaks and coda, the Shakespearean and Spenserian forms and their variants, and Bridges' innovations; though he did not know of Meredith's sixteen-line sonnets, he probably would have approved of them (Gardner, g, I, 128). In his studies of the sonnet he attempts to reduce the ratio of the line structures to mathematical formulas (Gardner, g, I, 80–81, 100), and he feels that he is preserving this formula in his departures.

He continually experimented with the sonnet form. Gardner lists ten different variations, and some of these could be subdivided. He composed Petrarchan sonnets, Miltonic sonnets with enjambment in standard rhythm, Miltonic sonnets with standard trochaic rhythm broken by counterpointing and sprung rhythm, Miltonic sonnets with extra syllables (outrides), curtal or shortened sonnets of ten lines in five-stress or Alexandrine rhythm, Miltonic sonnets with Alexandrines and strong caesuras, Petrarchan sonnets with Welsh sound structures added, an eight-stress line, and sonnets with one or several codas, of which "Heraclitean Fire" is an example (cf. Gardner, g, I, 97 ff.).

All of these innovations would be condemned by some purists who feel that the rules of the sonnet have been legislated by solid precedent and should not be deviated from. Precisely because these conventions had been so thoroughly exploited by the Renaissance and early nineteenth-century masters, Hopkins felt that innovations were needed. In other words, a pure Shakespearean or Miltonic form had a stale taste after the first bite. Freshness was needed. Notice that this concept of style must be partly extra-textual. Actually, what this means, in terms of literary theory, is that such a form no longer calls attention to itself, it has no surprise value. Let us examine some of Hopkins' surprises.

We have already called attention to some of them. His rhythm in "Heraclitean Fire" has already been examined. The myth of the necessity of iambic pentameter in a sonnet is assailed more vehemently in only one other sonnet, "Spelt from Sybil's Leaves," in an eight-stress line. We also discussed his line breaks in connection with juncture groups. One of the legislators of the sonnet, T. W. Crosland, writing a year before Hopkins' work was published (1918), said categorically:

> Full pauses should never be employed after the first word in a line, or at the end of the first, second, third, fifth, sixth or seventh line of the octet, or at the end of the first or fifth line of the sestet (quoted in Gardner, g, I, 78).

Hopkins probably broke all of these rules many times. The first rule forbidding a break after the first word in a line is broken three times in "Heraclitean Fire" (ll. 1, 11, 13). If one adds to the terminal and double-bar junctures, the single-bar junctures after the first word, twelve of the lines have such breaks after the first word. The three major breaks (Cloud-puffball, Man, and Drowned) actually summarize the first sixteen lines of the sonnet, telling us that nature (cloud-puffball) and man are drowned in unfathomable darkness—to be rescued by the Resurrection. Thus the breaks call attention to the major ideas of the first part of the sonnet. They announce, as in the beginning of a section of music, the major motif to be exploited in what follows. They are a kind of chordal commitment. The major line breaks, then, are an integral part of the sonnet structure.

Let us look more closely at the sonnet form, as it is used in "Heraclitean Fire." The octave, which roves over, is about the flux in nature's water, air, and earth. The rhyme scheme is abba, abba. Line nine finishes up the nature picture by adding fire, but it links with the next section of the poem by starting the septet rhyme scheme. After the first line, the remaining sestet is about man, whose destiny is no better than nature's. The rhyme scheme is cdcdcdd; by ordinary sonnet rules, this should be the end. Like nature and man, the sonnet should be finished, and in a non-Christian world, this would be true. But Hopkins' universe has not been totally heard from. Whereas in Italian, codas were used for satirical or humorous afterthoughts, Hopkins has some very serious afterthoughts. Christ has risen from the shades of death, so there is a first resurrection. And the sonnet likewise gets its first coda to celebrate its resurrection. Since Christ is also man and therefore part of nature, all men and nature have their resurrections, and this is the theme of the second coda. The speaker, finally, because of Christ's and the general resurrection, will also be rescued from eternal death, and this is the theme of the third coda. All of the resurrections are Christian additions to the dark story of mere man and nature. The Petrarchan sonnet form is therefore used thematically as a pagan symbol, and its three codas are its Christian baptismal immersions.

Some other minor deviations from traditional sonnet morphology can also be seen in "Heraclitean Fire." Crosland's seventeenth rule of the sonnet was:

> A sonnet should not be dramatic or exclamatory in its diction; it must not be overburdened with interrogative lines or sentences (quoted in Gardner, g, I, 79).

Hopkins is dramatic, exclamatory, and interrogative in many of his sonnets. In "Heraclitean Fire" he uses four exclamations. The first mourns the death of man (l. 11); the second, the death of man and nature (l. 13). The next announces the resurrection of Christ, and the last signals the meaning of Christ's resurrection to man (and nature). The exclamations, therefore, are the rhetorical and emotional climaxes of the drama. There is, therefore, a careful avoidance of the mere sentimentality Hopkins decried in the typical nineteenth-century sonnet and the assertion of the kind of real emotion which merits exclamation points.

Finally, of course, there are the Welsh sound patterns woven into this sonnet. These have already been discussed above. The effect of all of these innovations certainly produces a new sonnet style—and it is proper to so term it. The Hopkins sonnet is a more distinctive addition to the sonnet genre than possibly any since its inception.

EXERCISES

I *The Nature of Literary Discourse*

1. Take a short piece of literature and test it by several theories: what of the universe does it represent, what useful lesson does it convey, does the author or reader seriously achieve some measure of individuality in the work, what structures for pleasureful apprehension does it present?

2. Contrast a literary and nonliterary presentation of a similar topic. For example, contrast Kenneth Roberts' novel *Lydia Bailey* with his historical *Black Magic;* or *Arundel* with *March Against Quebec*.

3. Contrast the alleged source of a Shakespearean play and the play with an eye to contrasting aims of discourse.

4. Posit a theory of literature and then assess by it the inclusions in an anthology of American or English literature.

5. Devise a brief questionnaire to be handed to an audience assisting at a campus dramatic performance. By means of the questionnaire, try to ascertain their motives for attendance. Include all four basic theories in your questions. Also include motives largely extrinsic to any theory of literature, such as enforced class attendance, accompanying a date, etc.

6. Evaluate in detail the criticism of a particular theory of literature, e.g., Bernard de Voto's criticism of the mimetic theory in *The Literary Fallacy,* Lemon's evaluations of "edification" theories in *The Partial Critics,* Lemon's evaluation of purely formal theories in *The Partial Critics,* Jose Ortega y Gasset's criticisms of emotional theories in *The Dehumanization of Art and Other Essays,* or the author's critiques of the several theories in this text.

7. Write a short serious persuasive speech on a topic you sincerely believe in, then attempt to write a sonnet on the same topic. Attempt to see what has happened to your original conviction in each presentation.

8. Analyze a current ballad or love song for evidence of aim. Do persuasive, expressive, or literary evidences seem to predominate?

9. Attempt to differentiate between popular literature and classical literature by taking a great modern novel and contrasting it to a transient best seller. Are the differences you focus on matters of degree or kind? Contrast heroes or heroines (or antiheroes), themes, settings, etc.

10. Analyze and evaluate any current theory of myth (Cassirer, Malinowski, etc.).

11. Contrast Lévi-Strauss's view of the presence of literary discourse in primitive cultures with that of either Leonard Doob or Malinowski.

II *The Logic of Literary Discourse*

1. Take several of the alternative definitions of structure proposed in the chapter and analyze a brief literary piece from the several alternative points of view suggested by these definitions. Do the resulting analyses differ significantly? In other words, does a verbalized statement of the nature of structure offer a real alternative in actual analysis?

2. Analyze the plot of a short story by means of the notion of structure as a matter of internal probability. Does Goodman's notion of diminishing probability seem a useful technique in analysis?

3. Analyze the rhythm of several lines of a poem by means of structure viewed as a combination of unity and variety or sameness and difference. What is common and what is different from unit to unit (e.g., foot to foot)? Would Goodman's notion of structure as diminishing probability be useful in analyzing rhythmic structures?

4. Analyze several imagery structures in Yeats's "Sailing to Byzantium" by means of structure viewed as the actualizing of a potential. Would an alternative concept of structure offer a better handle to treat imagery structures? Try one.

5. Use Russell's notion of structure as relationship of part to part and part to whole at different layers of complexity to determine several levels of structure in a poem or short story or drama. Indicate how smaller structure layers are absorbed into larger layers (e.g., dialect into character determination, character into plot movement, etc.).

6. Write a small poem using a specific, verbalized concept of structure as opposed to an intuitive concept. For example, take Goodman's concept of structure as diminishing internal probability and attempt to write a poem by such an abstract norm. Comment on the poem and on the process of writing you have gone through.

III *The Organization of Literary Discourse*

1. Contrast the use of some sound structures in literary and persuasive samples of discourse. Can you suggest a generalization about the uses of alliteration, rhyme, rhythm, etc., in these two different kinds of constructs?

2. Contrast the use of plot structure in an advertisement and in a ballad or short story (cf. the preceding question).

3. Contrast the use of imagery structures in a poem and a piece of persuasive discourse. For example, contrast the use of the religious images in Roosevelt's "Inaugural Address" with the religious imagery patterns in Marvell's "To His Coy Mistress" or in Herrick's "Corinna's Going A-Maying."

4. Contrast specific aspects of Somerset Maugham's use of the theme of freedom in *Of Human Bondage* with the treatment of the freedom theme in specific sections of Sartre's *Being and Nothingness*.

5. Reconstruct the actual chronological series of events in the *Odyssey*. Contrast this to their occurrence in the plot and try to determine why the events were restructured in the order they occur.

6. Take any of the structural components of a work (as listed in

Figure V, 2) and consider the abstracted structure as *conspicuous,* by novelty (see pp. 352–55), as vertically unified (see pp. 355–56), and as a fit structure (see pp. 356–57). If the structure chosen is a large one (such as setting, in a novel) limit your treatment to one of these attributes.

IV *The Style of Literary Discourse*

1. Using a sample of expository or persuasive prose as a "norm," contrast it to the style of a poem written in the same period. For instance, contrast some of Keats's letters with his poems of the same period, or some of Aquinas' theology with his poetry, or one of Camus' philosophical with some of his literary work. Consider "style" as deviation (see p. 359 ff.).

2. Contrast two sonnets from different periods for stylistic differences (as was done in the text for the Shakespeare and Hopkins sonnets).

3. Contrast the styles of a writer who writes both scientific and literary discourse (e.g., Sartre, Russell, Allen Tate, Camus).

4. Take two or more different aims of discourse and draw up a distinctive feature table showing the general presence or absence of grammatical, semantic, media, art, mode, and metalanguage features in each style. To aid you in this, use the various sections on style in this book.

5. Take an Elizabethan elegy or lyric or narrative poem and contrast it to a similar nineteenth- or twentieth-century piece for stylistic features.

6. Analyze the departure from dramatic conventions in Euripides, Corneille, Victor Hugo, Shakespeare, Ibsen, Miller, Pirandello, Ionesco, or anyone else.

7. Analyze the graphemic deviations of E. E. Cummings. Attempt to determine their function in a given poem.

8. Discuss the symbolic idiosyncrasies in a poem by Yeats or Blake.

9. Discuss the use of the conventions of the elegy in "Lycidas" or "Thyrsis."

10. Take a current popular novel by Saul Bellow, Norman Mailer, James Baldwin, Henry Miller, or someone else and analyze its theme or its plot for sensationalism. What "norms" of theme or action are being deviated from? Do thematic or action deviations achieve significant literary structure or do they seem to be only journalistic, as Susan Sontag says some of them are (see Sontag, 1, 155, 175)?

11. Analyze any piece of literature for stylistic features at any level of Figure V, 2.

BIBLIOGRAPHY AND FOOTNOTE REFERENCES

Abrams, M. H. *The Mirror and the Lamp: Romantic Theory and the Critical Tradition.* New York: Oxford University Press, 1953 (m).

Aristotle. *The Works of Aristotle.* Translated under the direction of W. D. Ross. Vols. VIII and IX of *Great Books of the Western World,* ed. R. M. Hutchins and Mortimer J. Adler. Chicago: Encyclopaedia Britannica, 1952.

Bain, Alexander. *English Composition and Rhetoric.* 2nd American Edition. New York: D. Appleton and Company, 1867 (e).

Baldwin, Charles Sears. *Medieval Rhetoric and Poetic.* Gloucester, Mass.: Peter Smith, 1950 (m).

Barwick, K. "Die Gliederung der rhetorischen Techne und die Horazische Epistola ad Pisones." *Hermes,* LVII (1922), 1–60 (g).

Bastide, Roger, ed. *Sens et usages du terme "Structure."* No. 16 in *Janua Linguarum.* 'sGravenhage, Holland: Mouton & Co., 1962 (s).

Bonnet, Henri. *Roman et poésie: essai sur l'esthétique des genres.* Paris: Librairie Nizet, 1951 (r).

Booth, Wayne C. *The Rhetoric of Fiction.* Chicago, Ill.: University of Chicago Press, 1961 (r).

Bourbaki, Nicolas. "The Architecture of Mathematics." Tr. Arnold Dreden. *American Mathematical Monthly,* LVII (1950), 221–32. (a).

Brooks, Cleanth. *The Well-Wrought Urn.* Chapel Hill, N. C.: University of North Carolina Press, 1948 (w).

Brown, J. A. C. *Techniques of Persuasion, From Propaganda to Brainwashing.* Baltimore, Md.: Penguin Books, 1963 (t).

Buffon, Georges L. L. "Discours sur le style." In *Theories of Style,* ed. Lane Cooper. New York: The Macmillan Company, 1912. Pp. 170–79 (d).

Butcher, Samuel H. *Aristotle's Theory of Poetry and Fine Art.* 4th Edition. London: Macmillan and Co., 1932 (a).

Carrol, John B. "Vectors of Prose Style." In *Style and Language,* ed. Thomas A. Sebeok. New York: John Wiley & Sons Inc., and the Technology Press of Massachusetts Institute of Technology, 1960. Pp. 283–92 (v).

Chatman, Seymour, and Samuel R. Levin. "Linguistics and Poetics." In *Encyclopedia of Poetry and Poetics,* ed. Alex Preminger. Princeton, N. J.: Princeton University Press, 1965. Pp. 450–57 (l).

Coleridge, S. T. "On Style." In *Theories of Style,* ed. Lane Cooper. New York: The Macmillan Company, 1912. Pp. 199–208 (o).

———. *Biographic Literaria.* 2 Vols. Ed. J. Shawcross, Oxford: Oxford University Press, 1958 (b).

Cope, Edward M. *The Rhetoric of Aristotle, with a Commentary.* 3 Vols. Rev.

and ed., John Edwin Sandys. Cambridge, England: At the University Press, 1877 (r).

Crane, R. S. "The Critical Monism of Cleanth Brooks." In *Critics and Criticism, Ancient and Modern,* ed. R. S. Crane. Chicago: University of Chicago Press, 1952. Pp. 83–107 (c).

———. "Introduction." In *Critics and Criticism, Ancient and Modern,* ed. R. S. Crane. Chicago: University of Chicago Press, 1952. Pp. 1–24 (i).

Danz, Louis. *Dynamic Dissonance in Nature and the Arts.* New York: Farrar, Strauss and Young, 1952 (d).

DeQuincey, Thomas. "Style." In *Theories of Style,* ed. Lane Cooper. New York: The Macmillan Company, 1912. Pp. 209–44 (s).

De Voto, Bernard A. *The Literary Fallacy.* Boston: Little, Brown, 1944 (l).

Efron, Edith. "No Tears for Miss Bennett." *TV Guide* (August 26, 1967), 12–14 (n).

Eichenbaum, Boris. "The Theory of 'Formal Method.'" In *Russian Formalist Criticism: Four Essays,* ed. and tr. Lee T. Lemon and Marion J. Reis. Lincoln, Neb.: University of Nebraska Press, 1965. Pp. 99–140 (t).

Eliot, T. S. *The Use of Poetry and the Use of Criticism.* London: Faber & Faber Ltd., 1959 (u).

Enkvist, Nils Erik. "On Defining Style: An Essay in Applied Linguistics." In *Linguistics and Style,* ed. John Spencer. New York: Oxford University Press, 1964. Pp. 1–56 (o).

Erlich, Victor. *Russian Formalism: History-Doctrine.* London: Mouton & Co., 1965 (r).

Eustis, Alvin A. "Stylistics." In *Encyclopedia of Poetry and Poetics,* ed. Alex Preminger. Princeton, N. J.: Princeton University Press, 1965. Pp. 817–18 (s).

Fogle, Richard Harter. "Unity." In *Eycyclopedia of Poetry and Poetics,* ed. Alex Preminger. Princeton, N. J.: Princeton University Press, 1965. Pp. 880–81 (u).

Forster, Peter. "Column" from *The London Sunday Times.* Reprinted in *The Austin Statesman* (*October* 11, 1967), 43 (a).

Frye, Northrop. *The Well-Tempered Critic.* Bloomington, Ind.: Indiana University Press, 1963 (w).

Fussell, Paul. "Meter." In *Encyclopedia of Poetry and Poetics,* ed. Alex Preminger. Princeton, N. J.: Princeton University Press, 1965. Pp. 496–99 (m).

Gardner. W. H. *Gerard Manley Hopkins* (1844–1889). *A study of Poetic Idiosyncrasy in Relation to Poetic Tradition.* 2 Vols. London: Oxford University Press, 1949 (g).

Gilbert, Allan. *Literary Criticism: Plato to Dryden.* New York: American Book Company, 1940 (l).

Gilson, Etienne. *The Unity of Philosophical Experience.* New York: Charles Scribner's Sons, 1937 (u).

Goodman, Paul. *The Structure of Literature.* Chicago, Ill.: University of Chicago Press, 1954 (s).

Grennen, Joseph E. "Grammar as Thaumaturgy: Hopkins' "Heraclitean Fire.'" *Renascence,* XV, No. 4 (1963), 208–11 (g).

Guerin, Wilfred L., *et al. Handbook of Critical Approaches to Literature.* New York: Harper & Row, Publishers, 1966 (h).

Handy, William. *Kant and the Southern New Critics.* Austin, Texas: University of Texas Press, 1963 (k).

Hatzfeld, Helmut. "Points de repère dans l'évolution de la stylistique romane, 1886–1962." In *Mélanges de linguistique romane et de la philologie médiévale, offerts a M. Maurice Delbouille,* ed. Jean Renson. Gembloux, Belgium: J. Duculat, 1964. Pp. 325–40 (p).

Hopkins, Gerard Manley. *The Poems of Gerard Manley Hopkins.* 4th Edition. W. H. Gardner and N. A. Mackenzie, eds. New York: Oxford University Press, 1967 (p).

Horace. "Ars Poetica." In *Literary Criticism from Plato to Dryden,* tr. Edward Blakeney; ed. Allan H. Gilbert. New York: American Book Company, 1940. Pp. 128–43 (a).

Hrushovski, Benjamin. "On Free Rhythms in Modern Poetry." In *Style in Language,* ed. Thomas A Sebeok. New York: John Wiley & Sons, Inc., and the Technology Press of Massachusetts Institute of Technology, 1960. Pp. 173–90 (f).

Hyman, Stanley Edgar. *The Armed Vision: A Study in the Methods of Modern Literary Criticism.* New York: Alfred A. Knopf, Inc., 1948 (a).

Hymes, Dell H. "Phonological Aspects of Style: Some English Sonnets." In *Essays in the Language of Literature,* Seymour Chatman and Samuel R. Levin, eds. Boston, Mass.: Houghton Mifflin Company, 1967. Pp. 33–53 (p).

Jaeger, Werner. *Paideia.* 3 Vols. Tr. Gilbert Highet. New York: Oxford University Press, 1939 (p).

Jakobson, Roman, and Morris Halle. *Fundamentals of Language.* No. 1 of *Janua Linguarum.* 'sGravenhage, Holland: Mouton & Co., 1956 (f).

Joachim, H. H. *Aristotle: The Nicomachean Ethics.* Ed. D. A. Rees. Oxford: Clarendon Press, 1951 (a).

Joyce, James. *A Portrait of the Artist as a Young Man.* New York: The Viking Press, Inc., 1956 (p).

Juilland, Alphonse. *Structural Relations.* No. 15 of *Janua Linguarum.* 'sGravenhage, Holland: Mouton & Co., 1961 (s).

Kauffmann, Stanley. "'Lady Chatterley' at Last." *New Republic* (May 25, 1959), 13–16 (l).

Keast, W. R. "The 'New Criticism' and *King Lear."* In *Critics and Criticism, Ancient and Modern,* ed. R. S. Crane. Chicago, Ill.: University of Chicago Press, 1952. Pp. 108–137 (n).

Kierkegaard, Søren. "Concluding Unscientific Postscript." In *A Kierkegaard Anthology,* tr. Walter Lowrie; ed. R. Bretall. New York: Modern Library, Inc., 1959 (c).

———. *The Point of View for My Work as an Author: A Report to History and Related Writings.* Tr. Walter Lowrie. Ed. Benjamin Nelson. New York: Harper & Row, Publishers, 1962 (p).

Kinneavy, James L. *A Study of Three Contemporary Theories of the Lyric.* Washington, D. C.: Catholic University Press, 1956 (s).

Kroeber, Alfred L. *Style and Civilizations.* Ithaca, N. Y.: Cornell University Press, 1957 (s).

Kroll, Wilhelm. *Studien zum Verständnis der Romischen Literatur.* Stuttgart: J. B. Metzlersche Verlagsbuchhandlung, 1924 (s).

La Drière, J. Craig. "Expression." In *Dictionary of World Literature,* ed. Joseph T. Shipley. New York: The Philosophical Library, 1943. Pp. 225–27 (e).

———. "Fitness." In *Dictionary of World Literature,* ed. Joseph T. Shipley. New York: The Philosophical Library, 1943. Pp. 240–42 (f).

———. "Poetry and Prose." In *Dictionary of World Literature,* ed. Joseph T. Shipley. New York: The Philosophical Library, 1943. Pp. 441–45, (p).

———. "Prosody." In *Dictionary of World Literature,* ed. Joseph T. Shipley. New York: The Philosophical Library, 1943. Pp. 455–59 (pr).

———. "Prosody." In *Encyclopedia of Poetry and Poetics,* ed. Alex Preminger. Princeton, N. J.: Princeton University Press, 1965. Pp. 669–77 (pro).

———. "*Sermoni Propius:* A Study of the Horatian Theory of the Epistle, and of Dryden's Allusion to it in the Preface of *Religio Laici.*" Ann Arbor, Mich.: Unpublished dissertation, 1937 (s).

Langer, Susanne. *Feeling and Form.* New York: Charles Scribner's Sons, 1953 (f).

———. *Philosophy in a New Key.* New York: New American Library, Inc., 1942 (p).

Lawrence, D. H. *Pornography and Obscenity.* New York: Alfred A. Knopf, Inc., 1930 (p).

Lemon, Lee T. *The Partial Critics.* New York: Oxford University Press, 1965 (p).

———, and Marion J. Reis. *Russian Formalist Criticism: Four Essays.* Lincoln, Neb.: University of Nebraska Press, 1965 (r).

Lerner, Lawrence D. "Style." In *Encyclopedia of Poetry and Poetics,* ed. Alex Preminger. Princeton, N. J.: Princeton University Press, 1965. Pp. 814–17 (s).

Lewes, George Henry. "The Principle of Success in Literature." In *Theories of Style,* ed. Lane Cooper. New York: The Macmillan Company, 1912. Pp. 312–63 (p).

Lodge, Rupert C. *The Philosophy of Plato.* New York: Humanities Press, Inc., 1956 (p).

Loran, Erle. *Cézanne's Composition.* Berkeley, Calif.: University of California Press, 1946 (c).

Lynch, James J., and Bertrand Evans. *High School Textbooks: A Critical Examination.* Boston, Mass.: Little, Brown and Company, 1963 (h).

Marcel, Gabriel. *Homo Viator: Introduction to a Metaphysic of Hope.* Tr. Emma Craufurd. London: Victor Gollancz, Ltd., 1951 (h).

Maritain, Jacques. *Art and Scholasticism and the Frontiers of Poetry.* Tr J. Evans. New York: Charles Scribner's Sons, 1962 (a).

Maugham, Somerset. "Credo for a Story Teller." In *The Saturday Evening Post* (March 21, 1959), 38, 39, 108, 110, 112 (c).

McKeon, Richard. "Literary Criticism and the Concept of Imitation in Antiquity." In *Critics and Criticism, Ancient and Modern,* ed. R. S. Crane. Chicago, Ill.: University of Chicago Press, 1952. Pp. 147–75 (l).

———. *Thought, Action, and Passion.* Chicago, Ill.: University of Chicago Press, 1954 (t).

McMullen, Roy. "The Year's Development in the Arts and Sciences: Music, Painting, and Sculpture." In *The Great Ideas Today, 1967,* ed. Robert M. Hutchins and Mortimer J. Adler. Chicago, Ill.: Encyclopaedia Britannica, 1967. Pp. 82–157 (m).

Mukařovský, Jan. "From *Standard Language and Poetic Language.*" In *Essays on the Language of Literature,* Seymour Chatman and Samuel R. Levin, eds. Boston, Mass.: Houghton Mifflin Company, 1967. Pp. 241–49 (f).

Murphy, James J. "Saint Augustine and the Debate about a Christian Rhetoric." In *Readings in Rhetoric,* Lionel Crocker and Paul A. Carmack, eds. Spring field, Ill.: Charles C. Thomas, Publisher, 1965. Pp. 203–19 (a).

Murray, John Middleton. *The Problem of Style.* London: Oxford University Press, 1922 (p).

Olson, Elder. "An Outline of Poetic Theory." In *Critics and Criticism, Ancient and Modern,* ed. R. S. Crane. Chicago, Ill.: University of Chicago Press, 1952. Pp. 546–56 (o).

———. "William Empson, Contemporary Criticism, and Poetic Diction." In *Critics and Criticism, Ancient and Modern,* ed. R. S. Crane. Chicago, Ill.: University of Chicago Press, 1952. Pp. 45–82 (e).

Ong, Walter J., S. J. "Hopkins' Sprung Rhythm and the Life of English Poetry." In *Immortal Diamond,* ed. Norman Weyand, S. J. London: Sheed and Ward, 1949. Pp. 93–174 (h).

Oras, Ants. "Spenser and Milton: Some Parallels and Contrasts in the Handling of Sound." In *Essays on the Language of Literature,* Seymour Chatman and Samuel R. Levin, eds. Boston, Mass.: Houghton Mifflin Company, 1967. Pp. 19–32 (s).

Ortega y Gasset, José. *The Dehumanization of Art and Other Writings on Art.* Garden City, N. Y.: Doubleday & Company, Inc., 1956 (d).

Osgood, Charles E. "Some Effects of Motivation on Style of Decoding." In *Style in Language,* ed. Thomas A. Sebeok. New York: John Wiley & Sons Inc., and the Technology Press of Massachusetts Institute of Technology, 1960. Pp. 293–306 (s).

Peters, W. A. M. *Gerard Manley Hopkins.* London: Oxford University Press, 1948 (g).

Pike, Kenneth. *Language in Relation to a Unified Theory of the Structure of Human Behavior.* 3 Vols. Glendale, Calif.: Summer Institute of Linguistics, 1960 (l).

Plato. *Plato.* Tr. Benjamin Jowett. Vol. VII of *Great Books of the Western World,* R. M. Hutchins and M. J. Adler, eds. Chicago, Ill.: Encyclopaedia Britannica, 1952.

Randall, John Herman, Jr. *Aristotle.* New York: Columbia University Press, 1960 (a).

Ransom, John Crowe. *The World's Body.* New York: Charles Scribner's Sons, 1938 (w.)

Riffaterre, Michael. "Criteria for Style Analysis." In *Essays on the Language of Literature,* Seymour Chatman and Samuel R. Levin, eds. Boston, Mass.: Houghton Mifflin Company, 1967. Pp. 412–30 (c).

———. "L'Etude stylistique des formes littéraires conventionnelles." *French Review,* XXXVIII (1964), 3–14 (e).

———. "Stylistic Context." In *Essays on the Language of Literature,* Seymour Chatman and Samuel R. Levin. eds. Boston, Mass.: Houghton Mifflin Company, 1967. Pp. 431–41 (s).

———. "Vers la définition linguistique du style." *Word,* XVII (1961), 18–44 (v).

Rooney, W. J. *The Problem of Poetry and Belief in Contemporary Criticism.* Washington, D. C.: Catholic University of America Press, 1949 (p).

Rothwell, Kenneth. "Structure in Literature." *College English,* XXIV (1963), 602–7 (s).

Russell, Bertrand. *Human Knowledge: Its Scope and Limits.* New York: Simon and Schuster, Inc., 1948 (h).

Sandys, John Edwin. *A History of Classical Scholarship.* 3 Vols. Cambridge, England: At the University Press, 1908–1921 (h).

———. *A Short History of Classical Scholarship.* Cambridge, England: At the University Press, 1915 (s).

Saporta, Sol. "The Application of Linguistics to the Study of Poetic Language." In *Style in Language,* ed. Thomas A. Sebeok. New York: John Wiley & Sons, Inc., and the Technology Press of Massachusetts Institute of Technology, 1960. Pp. 82–93 (a).

Sartre, Jean-Paul. *Being and Nothingness.* Tr. H. E. Barnes. New York: Washington Square Press, 1966 (b).

Scaliger, Julius Caesar. "Poetics." In *The Great Critics,* tr. F. M. Padelford; James Harry Smith and E. W. Parks, eds. New York: W. W. Norton & Co., Inc., 1939 (p).

Schiller, Frederick. *Poems and Essays.* Vol. IV of *The Works of Frederick Schiller.* New York: Lovell Company, n. d. (w).

Schopenhauer, Arthur. "On Style." In *Theories of Style,* tr. T. Bailey Saunders; ed. Lane Cooper. New York: The Macmillan Company, 1912. Pp. 251–69 (o).

Sebeok, Thomas A. *Style in Language.* New York: John Wiley & Sons Inc., and the Technology Press of Massachusetts Institute of Technology, 1960 (s).

Sextus Empiricus. "Adversus Mathematicos." In *Sextus Empiricus,* tr. R. G. Bury. 3 Vols. London: William Heinemann, Ltd., 1933–36 (s).

Shklovsky, Victor. "Art as Technique." In *Russian Formalist Criticism: Four Essays,* ed. and tr. Lee T. Lemon and Marion J. Reis. Lincoln, Neb.: University of Nebraska Press, 1965. Pp. 3–24 (a).

Smith, James Harry, and Edd Winfield Parks, eds. *The Great Critics.* New York: W. W. Norton & Co., Inc., 1939 (g).

Sontag, Susan. *Against Interpretation and Other Essays.* New York: Dell Publishing Company, 1966 (a).

———. "The Year's Development in the Arts and Sciences: Literature." In *The Great Ideas Today, 1966,* R. M. Hutchins and M. J. Adler, eds. Chicago, Ill.: Encyclopaedia Britannica, 1966. Pp. 146–91 (1).

Spencer, Herbert. "The Philosophy of Style." In *Theories of Style,* ed. Lane Cooper. New York: The Macmillan Company, 1912. Pp. 270–311 (p).

Spencer, John, and Michael Gregory. "An Approach to the Study of Style." In *Linguistics and Style,* ed. John Spencer. London: Oxford University Press, 1964. Pp. 59–105 (a).

Spingarn, Joel E. *Literary Criticism in the Renaissance.* New York: Columbia University Press, 1925 (1).

Stallman, R. W. *The Critic's Notebook.* Minneapolis, Minn.: University of Minnesota Press, 1950 (n).

———. *Critiques and Essays in Criticism, 1920–1948.* The Ronald Press Company, 1949 (c).

Stankiewicz, Edward. "Linguistics and the Study of Poetry." In *Style in Language,* ed. Thomas A. Sebeok. New York: John Wiley & Sons, Inc., and the Technology Press of Massachusetts Institute of Technology, 1960. Pp. 69–81 (l).

Stevenson, R. L. "On Some Technical Elements of Style in Literature." In *Theories of Style,* ed. Lane Cooper. New York: Macmillan, 1912. Pp. 364–485 (s).

Strabo. *The Geography of Strabo.* Tr. Horace Leonard Jones. 8 Vols. London: William Heinemann, Ltd., 1917–1933 (g).

Tenney, Edward A. "Style." In *Dictionary of World Literature,* ed. Joseph T. Shipley. New York: The Philosophical Library, 1943. Pp. 554–56 (s).

Valéry, Paul *Variété, III.* Paris: Gallimard, 1936 (v).

Voegelin, C. F. "Casual and Noncasual Utterances within Unified Structures." In *Style in Language,* ed. Thomas A. Sebeok. New York: John Wiley & Sons, Inc., and the Technology Press of Massachusetts Institute of Technology, 1960. Pp. 57–68 (c).

Wellek, René, and Austin Warren. *Theory of Literature.* New York: Harcourt, Brace and Company, 1949 (t).

Whatmough, Joshua. *Poetic, Scientific and Other Forms of Discourse: A New Approach to Greek and Latin Literature.* Berkeley, Calif.: University of California Press, 1956 (p).

Wimsatt, W. K., Jr., and Monroe C. Beardsley. "The Concept of Meter: An Exercise in Abstraction." In *Essays in the Language of Literature,* Seymour Chatman and Samuel R. Levin, eds. Boston, Mass.: Houghton Mifflin Company, 1967 (c).

———. *The Verbal Icon.* Lexington, Ky.: University of Kentucky Press, 1954 (v).

Zola, Emile. *The Experimental Novel, and Other Essays.* Tr. Belle M. Sherman. New York: Cassell, 1893 (e).

6

Expressive Discourse

Introduction and Terminology

Since most college textbooks on writing or speaking devote no attention to expressive discourse, it might be good to provide, by examples, a working definition. Expressive components enter into all discourse, but in some discourse they become the dominating components. Such discourse is here called "expressive." Samples of discourse in which expressive components often dominate include the following: diaries, journals, much ordinary conversation, especially of the type labeled "I just had to get it off my mind," cathartic interviews in psychoanalysis ("blowing off steam"), spontaneous eulogies or condemnations of someone or something, cursing, a good deal of prayer, gripe sessions, suicide notes, some book reviews, some utopias, confessions, apologias, autobiographies. More sophisticated types of discourse are often preponderantly expressive of *social* personalities: cultural myths (viewed as embodiments of the aspirations of a culture), religious credos, manifestoes of minority groups, declarations of independence, constitutions of clubs or countries, and contracts.

Since the expressive component of a discourse is, in effect, the personal stake of the speaker in the discourse, there is naturally an expressive component in any discourse. Joe Adams has made brief studies of the "Expressive Aspects of Scientific Language" from four psychologists (in Werner, o, 47–52), and Hans Sperber has studied the "Expressive Aspects of Political Language" (Werner, o, 39–46). As we have seen in the preceding chapter, the expressive aspect is so obvious in most literature that it has been taken by some to be the constitutive factor of literature. In fact, any discourse will have some dosage of the expressive; and conversely, discourse that is preponderantly expressive will also have some informative or persuasive or literary or scientific aspects.

If this book had been written a number of years ago, there would

393

be no chapter on expressive discourse. Of course, some theorists had already established expression as one of the aims of discourse, and there was that era of post-Dewey progressive education in America in which "self-expression" had been the dominant aim in composition assignments in the elementary and secondary schools. *A fortiori,* the author felt the expressionistic theory of literature to be an unfortunate historical error of nineteenth-century Romanticism. But several reasons barred me from considering expression as a specific aim of discourse. In this respect, I sense that my position was all too typical. Consequently the enumeration of these reasons may aid the student of English to examine his own conscience. In the first place, the extremes of progressive education impelled many in the field to reject what was valid in the movement. In the second place, there was a violent reaction to Romantic expressionism. Third, and possibly more important, even if one admitted the existence of expressive discourse as a distinct kind, there did not seem to be much to say about it. Most of the theorists who provided for it treated it as equivalent to literature—Romantic expressionism was a literary phenomenon; even Dewey treated expression as equivalent to art (cf. Dewey, a, 38, 46, especially 80). Removed from a literary context, there did not seem to be much to say about emotional discourse. One cannot give a course in "Advanced Swearing 346." Fourth, as several philosophers have pointed out, it is easy to take the expressive component of language for granted precisely because it is so fundamental. Indeed, this has happened throughout the history of discourse education. As was pointed out in the brief survey in Chapter I, concern for the expressive function of language is a modern phenomenon. Unlike literary theory, or rhetoric, or dialectic, or science, there is no long tradition for expressive discourse with established disagreements or schools of consensus.

Cassirer, attempting to find historical antecedents to a concern for the emotional roots of language, points to Epicurus and Lucretius in Antiquity, then to Giambattista Vico in Italy in the seventeenth century, to Rousseau and J. A. von Herder in the eighteenth century, and to Wilhelm von Humboldt in the nineteenth century (cf. Cassirer, p, I, 148–56). By the end of the nineteenth century and especially in the twentieth century there were several converging streams of interest whose confluence created a philosophy of expressionism. With the increased criticism of emotional expression as the basis of literature (see pp. 324 ff. above), much emotional language was left unclassified, for it seemed clear that not all emotional language could be neatly parceled out into persuasion and literature. Also, the widespread study of myth in several disciplines brought forth some influential thinkers who tended to separate "mythical thinking" from knowledge, art, literature, and morality. Schelling made such a separation early, and Cassirer concurred with him (cf. Cassirer, p, II, 4). Freud likewise placed the essence of myth in unconscious emotion, especially the sexual emotion

(Cassirer, p, II, 30 ff.). And, of course, Jung went much further than Freud in his analysis of myth. Some of the phenomenologists, shortly to be considered, were also crucially interested in mythical thought, for example, Merleau-Ponty (cf. Langan, m, 51).

Some of the German writers in the field of psychology of speech also stressed the expressive function of speech. Thus Karl Bühler, in his "The Axiomatic of a Science of Speech" (a), devoted considerable attention to expression; he even used the communication triangle to differentiate three basic functions of speech, as we have seen. F. Kainz, in his *Psychologie der Sprache* (1941), gives three similar functions of speech. Most American treatments of a psychology of speech, however, tend to restrict their considerations of problems of expression to the abnormal and pathological person. As Eisenson says, typically, he is not concerned with the interrelationship of speech and the emergence of the ego in the child (cf. Eisenson, p, 336, 339).

Croce's influential philosophy of expressionism, brought to America by Joel E. Spingarn in the teens and early twenties, also represented a strong twentieth-century concern for expressionism, though in an esthetic context. And, of course, Dewey's educational concern for expression, also in an artistic context, reenforced the Crocean stream of influence in the thirties and forties, as I have already pointed out. But the most fertile investigations into expression in this century have been made by the phenomenologists and existentialists in Germany and France. Husserl, the founder of phenomenology, made "expression" an important concept in his system; and several of Husserl's disciples, notably Maurice Merleau-Ponty and Georges Gusdorf make it a central notion in their philosophies. Because of the many similarities of Merleau-Ponty's phenomenology to Sartre's, Sartre also can be closely related to the concern for expression—though there are important differences between Sartre and Merleau-Ponty, despite many years of co-editorial work for *Les Temps Modernes* and common causes they both fought for. In connection with the phenomenological school, it must be remembered that Cassirer viewed his work as part of a phenomenological movement (two of the three volumes of *The Philosophy of Symbolic Forms* use the term in their titles).

One of the tangential importations into English and American literary criticism and semantics of phenomenological thought was by Ogden and Richards in *The Meaning of Meaning*. Spiegelberg, one of the main historians of phenomenology, feels that their account of Husserl is misleading, however (cf. Spiegelberg, p, I, 104, n. 2). In any case, Richards' interests were not seriously oriented to expression as such, but more to the importance of emotional expression in literary works.

It can be seen by this brief survey that "expression" in some sense has been the concern of several important schools of thought in this century.

The consolidation of what they have to say about expression and its relationship to a theory of discourse will be the function of this chapter. Nonetheless, it still remains true that a thorough investigation into the nature and characteristics of expressive discourse has to be made. Yet such investigations have to be made. As I shall attempt to show, expressive discourse is, in a very important sense, psychologically prior to all the other uses of language. It is the expressive component which gives all discourse a personal significance to the speaker or listener. Indeed, the expressive component of discourse is what involves a man with the world and his fellows to give him his unique brand of humanity. The ignoring, by the disciplines of speech and English, of the very kind of discourse by which an individual or group can express his personal or its societal aspirations, is certainly a symptom, if not an effect, of the impersonality of the university machines of the present day. The high schools are probably even more culpable in this regard. If ignoring the study of persuasion begets a gullible populace, ignoring the study of expression begets rebellion, sometimes justified, sometimes irresponsible. A democracy which ignores expression has forgotten its own roots.

A word on terminology may be of some assistance. "Expression," of course, is sometimes coextensive with discourse itself. There is some justification for this conflation, as we shall see, but in this chapter, "expression" will be viewed as only one of the major aims of discourse. Here, "expression" is obviously not equated to literary expression, an equation many have made. Nor is it equated to "creativity," though expression has some features in common with creativity.

The Nature of Expressive Discourse

Without doubt, the concern common to all of the groups interested in expression was the reassertion of the importance of the individual, of subjectivity, of personal value in an academic, cultural, and social environment which tended to ignore the personal and the subjective. The original purpose of phenomenology, said Merleau-Ponty, was to

> ...restore to things their concrete physiognomy, to organisms their individual ways of dealing with the world, and to subjectivity its inherence in history (p, 57).

The phenomenologists felt that a crisis had been reached in European culture. On the one hand, empirical physical sciences treated everything as "objects" and seemed to be uninterested in problems of value or subject (cf. Spiegelberg, p, I, 79–80) ; the "scientific" way of looking at the universe deprived it of "human" meaning or sense as Merleau-Ponty maintained (p, 23–24). On the other hand, idealist philosophers kept on merrily spinning elaborate theoretical systems with little or no serious grounding in objective scientific reality. Neither empiricism nor idealism paid serious attention to the "other," to other persons as such. Culture, therefore, was seriously fragmented. Phenomenology represents a serious attempt to reintegrate culture, to give reality a meaning, and to integrate the "other" and the self into culture. The ideal of a "totality of culture" represented, therefore, a return to Hegel's ideal of such a unity, presented in his *The Phenomenology of Spirit,* an ideal, in this respect, referred to by Husserl, Sartre, Merleau-Ponty, Cassirer, and others. Both Cassirer and Merleau-Ponty maintained that this emphasis on the consideration of the subject and the consideration of the "other" through intersubjectivity is characteristic not only of philosophy (in phenomenology and existentialism), but has parallel movements in language, religion, sociology, and other disciplines (cf. Merleau-Ponty, s, 84–92).

This stress on the subjective and the consequent concern for expression makes some aspects of phenomenology relevant to the present chapter. There are many facets of the work of Merleau-Ponty, Husserl, Sartre, Cassirer, and Gusdorf that seem, at least on the surface, to be fairly far removed from the problem of this chapter. What I am attempting is a rapprochement of some of their ideas on the nature of the individual and his expressive acts with the specific issue of expressive discourse. Consequently, I shall short-circuit many of the basic epistemological and ontological foundations of their doctrines and present their psycholinguistic and discourse conclusions that are germane to our present concern. This may seem dogmatic, even doctrinaire, but the inquisitive and critical reader can always follow the footnotes back to the original sources and make his own judgments as to their validity.

There are undoubtedly other concepts of the self in competitive ontologies and psychologies. I have chosen the self-models of Sartre, Merleau-Ponty, and Gusdorf because these models are similar in structure to the general theory of language outlined in this book and because these models seem more fertile in the generation of a solution to the nature of self-expression than some of the other models of the self that I am acquainted with. As was pointed out above in the "Logic of Exploratory Discourse," similarity in logical structure and fertility are prime characteristics of an imported model. In addition, these philosophers have themselves related their theories of the self to the nature of expression—an extension others have not made.

*The Nature of
the Self that Expresses,
and the Act of Expression*

In the brief sketches of expressive discourse presented in Chapters
I and II, it was established that expressive discourse is that kind of discourse
which focuses on the encoder. Consequently, it is the speaking self which
dominates the discourse and it is by discourse that he expresses and partially
achieves his own individuality. It is natural, therefore, that a discussion of
expressive discourse should ask some fundamental questions about the nature
of the self that is being expressed and is achieving individuality.

The phenomenologists whose models of the self are to be incorporated into this analysis do not, it is true, agree in all points on the constitution of the self. In addition to some major differences in context, there are
some disturbing differences in terminology. For example, to some aspects
of Sartre's notion and term for the "For-Itself," Merleau-Ponty has crucial
objections. Nonetheless, Sartre, Merleau-Ponty, Gusdorf, and Cassirer have
enough common characteristics to allow of a composite model. For all of
them the self is constituted by combinations of different kinds of consciousnesses. There is a perceiving "For-Itself" which is constituted as consciousness by distinguishing itself from the world of which it is conscious
and to which it is present; this "For-Itself" is therefore in need of the world
to establish itself as consciousness. Further, to establish itself as a knowing
self-consciousness it must be aware of other knowing consiousnesses from
which it is also distinct—these other consciousnesses are the "Others." The
self, therefore, is a composite of a Being-for-Itself, a Being-for-Others, and
a Being-in-the-World. The term "For-Itself" is Sartre's (from Descartes and
Hegel) and the terms "Being-for-Others" and "Being-in-the-World" are
used by both Sartre and Merleau-Ponty. This trinity constitutes the self in
all four of the authors under consideration, as well as in Husserl and Hegel.

Sartre's concept of the For-Itself is made up of three dimensions.
As present, the For-Itself is constituted by its presence to the world; as
past, the For-Itself is constituted by what it has made of itself in its previous
actions and expressions; as future, the For-Itself is what it is working on to
make itself—it is its possibilities. In other words, we are what we are conscious of being in the face of reality; we are, whether we like it or not, what
we have made of ourselves in the past; finally, we are what we are striving
to be (Sartre, b, 152–72).

The Being-for-Others is agreed upon by all four of these writers,
as well as Husserl, Hegel, and others, as being partially constitutive of the
self. The consideration of the "Other" and the important position accorded
the "Other" in these philosophical systems is somewhat distinctive. Many

philosophical systems tend to reduce the other simply to another "I" or to another object in the manifold of reality (cf. Lasser in Kockelmans, p, 172 ff.; Sartre, b, 273). These four writers differ somewhat in the analysis of how the "Other" contributes to the self (cf. Sartre for a review of Husserl, Hegel, and Heidegger in b, 285 ff., and of classical positions b, 273 ff.; Merleau-Ponty, p, 346 ff.; Husserl, c, 90 ff.). Since I prefer Sartre's analysis for several reasons, I shall briefly summarize those aspects relevant to our present purposes.

In the ordinary unreflecting consciousness, I perceive that the "Other" views me as an object from the center of his universe of consciousness. I know that he looks at me but I am never fully aware of what view he takes of me, how he appraises me. In this respect, his view of me is conditioned by his own freedom, and this "me" as viewed by others is therefore his slave—he can view me any way he chooses (Sartre, b, 319–20, 322, 328). But at least I have gained what I could not give myself, I have gained "objectness" (b, 331). His viewing me constitutes me as "somebody" (b, 324). I have a nature (b, 322); further, I accept this "Other" me as being myself:

> When the other describes my character, I do not "recognize" myself and yet I know that "it is me." I accept the responsibility for this stranger who is presented to me but he does not cease to be a stranger (b, 336).

My Being-for-Others, thus, gives me an added dimension, although it involves a danger to my freedom. I cannot achieve this added dimension of myself, however, if I treat the Other as only another object in the world. I must respect him as another consciousness, another subject. If I treat the Other as only another object, I myself lose my nature, I am no longer "somebody," I have lost my own status as a real "object." The consequences of this necessary relationship to the Other will be examined below (for Cassirer, cf. p, II, 175 ff.; m, 141–43; Merleau-Ponty, p, 346 ff.; s, 68).

The third dimension of my being derives from my consciousness of the world, for my view of the world gives another view of myself. Since the For-Itself, as future, is the sum total of what I would like to be, the sum total of my "possibles," I need some instruments to help me to become this aspect of myself. These possibles are the *"something* which the For-Itself lacks *in order to be* itself" (b, 125, his italics). They are precisely, a lack of being, a negation (125). To achieve this being, I view the world as a set of instruments which can help me toward my goal. The conclusion to be drawn from this attitude to the world is clearly stated in Sartre's own words:

> It follows that if the infinite reference of instruments never refers to a for-itself which I *am*, then the totality of instruments is the exact cor-

relate of my possibilities; and as I *am* my possibilities, the order of instruments in the world is the image of my possibilities projected in the in-itself [the world], i.e., the image of what I am (b, 245, his italics).

We thus get another dimension of the self, that given by the world as a summation of possibilities. Thus the three dimensions of the self are the self viewed as Being-for-Itself, having a past and a future; the self viewed as Being-for-Others; and the self viewed as Being-in-the-World.

None of these three dimensions can be reduced to a pure intellectual consciousness. Even in the prereflective consciousness which the self has of each of these dimensions, there is a fundamental substratum of emotion or feeling or "attitude" involved, though there is also something more. For Sartre, the For-Itself is, both in its appraisal of its past and in its projections towards its future, fundamentally a value consciousness. As he says, "The for-itself cannot appear without being haunted by value and projected toward its own possibles" (b, 117). As Barnes says, explaining Sartre,

> In the first place, with Sartre, to destroy all desire would be to destroy the For-itself...absolutely. A satisfied For-itself would no longer be a For-itself. The For-itself is desire (in b, xxxiii–iv).

Similarly, the Being-for-Others is fundamentally realized in the affective order—by pride, shame, and fear (b, 353–55). And finally, the attitude of consciousness to reality, Being-in-the-World, is also an emotional matter. Indeed, says Barnes paraphrasing Sartre, "Emotion is simply a way by which consciousness chooses to live its relationship with the world" (in b, xvii). This is necessarily so, since the world is simply the potentialities I need to achieve my valued goal. Cassirer, Merleau-Ponty, and Gusdorf concur with this emotional basis of the self as consciousness. Cassirer has analyzed much of this in the context of mythical thought. Myth is rooted in emotion: "Here we grasp one of the most essential elements of myth. Myth does not arise solely from intellectual processes, it sprouts forth from deep human emotions" (m, 43), and "The real substratum of myth is not a substratum of thought, but of feeling" (e, 81). In his distinctions among the kinds of expression, he says, "Art gives us a unity of intention; science gives us a unity of thought; religion and myth give us a unity of feeling" (m, 37). Finally, in another work, but on the same topic, he concludes: "And this means that every *apprehension* of a particular empirical thing or specific empirical occurrence contains within it an act of evaluation" (p, II, 31). In consequence, the "I" in myth always sees things colored with a "specific life attitude and spiritual attitude" (p, II, 186). This is also true of our perception of nature as of other humans (p, II, 192), and even of such abstract notions as space and time (p, II, 85–97). Merleau-Ponty agrees with this, though he is not limiting these perceptions to mythical thought.

As Langan says, explaining Merleau-Ponty on this point, there is "an affectivity which structures my existential geography" (m, 48) ; and again "Most ordinary space is thus neither fully real nor fully imaginary; it is filled with affective content" (m, 48).

It is this emotional component, this value aspect, this drive which provides the basic impetus to the act of expression on the part of the self. For desire implies that the self is "involved" in its views of the world and the Other. As Sartre remarks,

> I never apprehend myself abstractly as the pure possibility of being myself, but I live my selfness in its concrete projection toward this or that particular end. I exist only as *engaged* and I am conscious (of being only as *engaged* (b, 357, his italics).

This notion of "engagement," originally outlined in this sense by another existentialist, Gabriel Marcel, is an important notion in both Sartre and Merleau-Ponty (cf. Spiegelberg, p, II, 439, 474, 490, 536). The self is therefore defined by its doing something to achieve its intentions. Merleau-Ponty very precisely says,

> If a being is consciousness, he must be nothing but a network of intentions. If he ceases to be definable in terms of the act of sense-giving [i.e. deriving meaning from intentions aimed at], he relapses into the condition of a thing, the thing being precisely what does not know, what slumbers in ignorance of itself and the world, what consequently is not a true "self" (p, 121).

To attain selfhood, therefore, the For-Itself must necessarily involve itself with the world and with others in the process of working towards specific goals (cf. Merleau-Ponty, s, 78–79). This carrying out of a project is the essence of the act of expression. Expression is therefore the structuring of a field of reality in order to realize a project, and this realization gives self-hood to the For-Itself. As Langan says, "only in expression does the new structuring of the field bring the latent possibilities towards actualization" (m, 84). Expression, therefore, involves some process of externalization or action dictated by the presence of a goal to be achieved. This notion of expression is not therefore a simple discharge of emotion or a relaying of impressions; the emotion must be directed to an aim. All theories of expression which I have analyzed agree on this aspect of expression, from Croce and Dewey to Sartre and Merleau-Ponty and Cassirer. As Sartre says, "Perception is naturally surpassed toward action; better yet, it can be revealed only in and through projects of action" (b, 394). Cassirer speaks of the necessity of taking into account both the inward and the outward aspects of expression,

...which provides the guiding lines for the understanding of all spiritual forms of expression, namely that the I finds and learns to know itself through its seeming externalization (p, II, 221).

Dewey continually refers to the necessity of the structuring towards a unifying end in the act of expression (a, 41 ff., 55–57, 58 ff.). The "I" therefore is the aim of the act—the "I" emerges as a result of the act. The "I" is as much the end of the myth as the beginning of myth, remarks Cassirer (p, II, 155).

If the self is constituted by its engaging in projects directed towards ends, and if this realization of projects is the nature of expression, then, as Langan observes in his treatment of Merleau-Ponty's concept of expression, it must be concluded that "expression, which is the act of taking up and extending a sens, is obviously the central phenomenon in human life" (m, 73; *sens* is Merleau-Ponty's term for sense-giving because of orientation to an end). It is this crucial function of expression in the derivation of the self that prompted my earlier remark about the primacy of expression as an aim of discourse.

Sartre expands the notion of the self as emerging from individual projects to postulate a governing "fundamental project" for each individual in terms of which the particular projects are only parts of a vast master plan, as it were. He defines "character" in terms of this "original choice" or "global project" of the individual, for it is this project which unifies him as a totality (b, 686–88), for a man is "a totality not just a collection" (b, 696). The global project is not a blind and slavish predetermination. It is conscious, and it may be abandoned in favor of another global project at certain "instants" of life (b, 702).

This ability of the For-Itself to choose its own projects and to freely abandon them in favor of others leads to another critical aspect of the self and of the act of expression. The self is a free agent and the act of expression is a free choice of ends and of means. Freedom is, therefore, essential to the nature of self and to the nature of expression. Sartre and Merleau-Ponty disagree on the degree of freedom involved in the pursuit of self, but both agree that to be a self is to be free. Both use similar terms to express this necessity. We are condemned to be free, says Sartre; we are condemned to meaning, says Merleau-Ponty. "Freedom" is, in fact, as important a word in existentialism as is "engagement." For Sartre freedom is involved in every determination of the various dimensions of the self. For our purposes here, it is important to point out the operation of freedom in the rejection of the past self in order to change oneself in the future, the choice of the projects for the future, the choice of the instruments of the world for the realization of the self's projects, and the reciprocal freedom between the self and the

Other. In other words, Being-for-Itself, Being-for-Others, and Being-in-the-World are all conditioned by freedom—in fact, are freedom. As Sartre says, "For human reality to be is to *choose oneself*" (b, 538, his italics). As we shall see, the use of language is also a matter of freedom, and there are dangers to our freedom inherent in language too.

Among the many arts of expression which man has at his disposal by which to construct his self, one of the most important is the use of language. Merleau-Ponty also insists at great length on the body and gesture as media of expression (p, 174 ff.). In addition to the body's own expressive functions apart from language, it is clear that the body and gesture have importance in a theory of language at the level of situational context, for it is the body that delivers the speech and that gestures in the act of delivery, but our interest in this book is at the level of discourse, so we shall turn to this aspect of expression.

Since it is by language that I discover the Other and the world, and since the discovery of the Other and the world are indispensable foundations of my own being, it is clear that language is the instrumental root of my being. It is in this sense that Gusdorf can say that speaking gives man his reality (s, 38), that "language is one of the agents of our incarnation" (s, 80). Heidegger and Sartre put this thought even more strongly:

> In the intersubjectivity of the for-others, it is not necessary to invent language because it is already given in the recognition of the other. I *am* language. By the sole fact that whatever I may do, my acts freely conceived and executed, my projects launched towards my possibilities have outside of them a meaning which escapes me and which I experience. It is in this sense—and in this sense only—that Heidegger is right in declaring that *I am what I say*" (b, 455–56, his italics).

Since I am what I say, if I am alive I must always have something to say. Therefore Gusdorf can conclude:

> A living man, writer or not, always has something to say, as a contribution to the reality of the world in which his task is to declare himself (s, 70).

In this sense, death is simply the absolute silence.

Since it is by language that man finds both his self and his thoughts, and since self is emotionally grounded, it follows that all discourse is emotionally grounded. The reason for this is that man uses language to achieve the projects which he values, and the desire for the project has an emotional component. Every discourse, then, is, at the moment of delivery located in the field of the "situation," and is best understood only in the light of that unique historical moment. No adequate science of language can ignore this:

And each utterance is a free project of designation issuing from the choice of a personal for-itself and destined to be interpreted in terms of the global situation of this for-itself. What is primary is the situation in terms of which I understand the *meaning* of the sentence; this meaning is not in itself to be considered as a given but rather as an end chosen in a free surpassing of means. Such is the only *reality* which the working linguist can encounter (Sartre, b, 634; 630–38 are all relevant).

In this crucial sense, no discourse is autonomous, but the expressive component of any discourse, and especially expressive discourse, requires the context of the situation to be understood.

Because of being grounded in a situational context, all discourse is based on expression (Gusdorf, s, 56–57), and the discourse so interpreted must be understood as the totality of the text. The term that both Merleau-Ponty and Gusdorf use for this is adopted from the linguist Ferdinand de Saussure. It is de Saussure's *la parole* as distinct from *la langue,* a distinction that was used at the beginning of this book to establish the nature of discourse as distinct from language (see p. 22). By *parole,* Merleau-Ponty means exactly what has here consistently been termed "discourse":

> By word (*parole*), Merleau-Ponty does not mean the phonetic unit (*mot*) but a self-contained meaningful expressive structure, whether a single *mot* (Fire"), a whole poem, or an entire book (Langan, m, 134).

Each discourse (*parole*) is a "manifestation, a revelation of intimate being" (Merleau-Ponty, p, 196)). This derives from its existence in the situation:

> The word owes its efficacy to the fact that it is not an objective notation, but an index of value.... It crystallizes reality, it condenses it into a function of an attitude of the person.... In other words, each word is a situation-word (le mot de la situation), the word which sums up the state of the world as a function of my decision. Undoubtedly the objectivity of established language ordinarily hides this personal sense. However, the real world is much less an in-itself than a for-myself (s, 9).

Nonetheless, even in these more or less impersonal forms, the speaker or writer still retains some of his own personality, and therefore some of his own style, for style is individuality in language, as we established in the previous chapter in the discussion of literary style. If I am what I say, then if I have a personality, I will have style. If I have no personality, I have no style. Most of Gusdorf's final paragraphs to his chapter on expression are an eloquent commentary on this point:

The power of style, then, is not the privilege of the poet alone. The writer seems to us testimony to man in his enterprise to impose his mark on the environment. Style expresses the *thread of life,* the movement of a destiny according to its creative meaning. The celebrated words of Buffon: "style is the very man" must be understood in the fullest sense. Style establishes man, not simply the style of speaking or writing, but the style of living in general.... The struggle for style may here stand as a definition of the whole personality, since it is the undertaking of giving an appropriate value to each movement of self-affirmation.

*   *   *

Thus style is the peculiar expression of personality.... To be original is to be an origin, a beginning, and to stamp the situation with one's mark. That doesn't mean that it is enough, like the young fashion-plate, Alcibiades, to have one's dog's tail cut off, or to lisp in the manner of the dandies in the Directoire period. The virtue of originality does not consist in attracting attention to oneself by any means whatsoever. Originality is not turned outward, but inward. It corresponds to the concern for proper expression, to honesty in self-expression. In this sense, it behooves each one to give himself his language, his style.... The struggle for style is the struggle for consciousness (s, 75–76).

The symptom of true expression, then, is style. With this final characteristic, we are in a position to delineate the nature of self-expression. The self must be represented in its three basic dimensions and in the signal of its expression. The three basic dimensions are Being-for-Itself, Being-for-Others, and Being-in-the-World. The signal of self-expression is style. The diagram, therefore can be seen in Figure VI, 1:

Figure VI, 1: The Components of Self-Expression

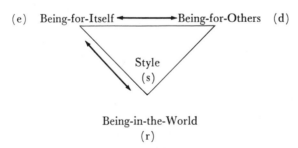

Being-in-the-World
(r)

The components obviously correspond to the components of the communications triangle: encoder (Being-for-Itself), decoder (Being-for-Others), reality (Being-in-the-World), and signal (style).

A person achieves personality and, therefore, true self-expression, when he has an authentic Being-for-Itself with an honest recognition and repudiation of his past, a vision of his future projects, an acceptance of his Being-for-Others, and a unillusioned picture of his Being-in-the-World. All of this will give him a unique style in his verbal expressions.

Certain corollaries follow from each of these axioms. They concern the Being-for-Itself, the Being-for-Others, and the Being-in-the-World. The For-Itself is always in the process of remaking its goals. It must be ready, at any given moment, to pull out of a commitment to one project and to engage in another (Sartre, b, 40–41; Langan, m, 121). This repudiation of a project, which then becomes past, is characteristic of the For-Itself. It must continually negate its past in order to envision a new future (Sartre, b, 533). There is always, in the face of the future, a certain anguish which the For-Itself feels, a diffidence and a suspicion that it will not achieve its projects. Repudiation of the past and anguish are inescapable aspects of the For-Itself.

The great danger of the For-Itself is the danger of bad faith with oneself. Bad faith consists in lying to oneself, hiding the truth from oneself, believing what one does not really believe, being convinced by evidence which the self knows is not really persuasive (Sartre, b, 59 ff., 83 ff.). It can take many forms: the self can deny its own past or part of it, or recognize itself only as its future projections, even to the point of being pathological (Sartre, b, 70 ff.); or it can make an objective *thing* (not a person) out of the self in one of its roles and *play* at professor or administrator or poet (Sartre, b, 72–73). The self of a student, for instance, can play at being a student:

> The attentive pupil who wishes to *be* attentive, his eyes riveted on the teacher, his ears open wide, so exhausts himself in playing the attentive role that he ends up by no longer hearing anything (Sartre, b, 73).

The self can pour itself into an emotion, such as sadness or bereavement so as to make it a thing, not *me* (Sartre, b, 74). The Being-for-Itself can refuse its own past or future and escape into the Being-for-Others' image of itself, or deny the image others have of it and escape into its past or future projections (Sartre, b, 70). The opposite of all of these tendencies is *sincerity;* sincerity is a basic characteristic of expression. It is not surprising, therefore, that "sincerity" was a cardinal characteristic of Romantic theories of poetry when they were based on the expressive theory (see p. 321).

With regard to the Being-for-Others, two important concerns have to do with expression. They might be summarized in the two words "reciprocity" and "love." The two concepts are closely related. Sartre's exposition of the nature of love is in terms of a project of the For-Itself. The

For-Itself wants to be more than a thing, more than an instrument. It wants to be an end, a purpose, a goal or center towards which or around which the world is oriented or revolved, a value and the criterion of all other values. This it can become if it is the object of love by the "Other":

> Thus to want to be loved is to want to be placed beyond the whole system of values posited by the other and to be the condition of all valorization and the objective foundation of all values. This demand is the usual theme of lovers' conversations...as the woman in love demands that the beloved in his acts should sacrifice traditional morality for her and is anxious to know whether the beloved would betray his friends for her, "would steal for her," "would kill for her," etc. (Sartre, b, 451).

Thus being the object of love makes the For-Itself the center of and the supreme value in the world. But the choice of my For-Itself as the love object of the Other must be a free choice; otherwise it is not true love and I am not really established as *the* value. I must therefore acknowledge the Other's freedom and must request his love given freely. I must therefore acknowledge the "Other" as a person and not just as a thing. To be the object of love without respect for the freedom and the person of the other is seduction, not love. Love is achieved only by my giving myself to the other, by a surrender of some of my freedom (cf. Sartre, b, 458 ff.). By so doing, I am loved and constitute myself as a value.

Love is based on reciprocity, therefore, and without reciprocity I am not an *objective value*. By love, therefore, I achieve another dimension of my being, "I assume myself as value" (Sartre b, 451). This love (and reciprocity) is another aspect of the foundation of the importance of the social in my quest of being. This finding of being in the social world is stressed by all of the thinkers whom we have been consolidating. Merleau-Ponty says pointedly,

> The For-Themselves—me for myself and the other for himself—must stand out against the background of the For-Others—I for the other and the other for me. My life must have a significance which I do not constitute; there must, strictly speaking, be an intersubjectivity (p, 448).

And, like Sartre, he emphasizes the necessity of not making a "thing" of the Other or of myself:

> Our relationship to the social is, like our relationship to the world, deeper than any expressed perception or any judgment. It is as false to place ourselves in society as an object among other objects, as it is to place society within ourselves as an object of thought, and in both cases, the mistake lies in treating the social as an object (p, 362).

Finally, Merleau-Ponty categorically concludes some observations on this topic as follows:

> In the absence of reciprocity there is no alter Ego, since the world of the one then takes in completely that of the other, so that one feels disinherited in favour of the other.... Co-existence [giving up a part of one's Ego to experience that of another] must in all cases be experienced on both sides (p, 357).

Cassirer, studying the ways by which mythical man achieved his ego, found this grounding of the self in society a constant element (cf. p, II, 63, 175–77, 192; p, III, 189; m, 141–43). Gusdorf is even more explicit: "An isolated self can truly be said to be only an abstraction" (s, 48, cf. also s, 85). He then applies the principle of reciprocity to speech and to teaching:

> To be open to the speech of others is to grasp it in its best sense, continually striving not to reduce it to banality, but to find in it something original. By doing this, moreover, by helping the other to use his own voice, one will stimulate him to discover his innermost need. Such is the task of the teacher, if, going beyond the monologue of instruction, he knows how to carry the pedagogical task into authentic dialogue where personality is developed. The great educator is he who spreads around himself the meaning of the honor of language as a concern for integrity in the relations with others and oneself (s, 125).

Finally, a few corollaries concerning the relationship of the For-Itself to the world will conclude the basic components of a healthy concept of expression. Because the world is viewed as the sum total of the instruments whereby I can achieve my projects, the world is viewed as more than just an object—it becomes a partner with me, both working to achieve myself. In this way I give meaning to the world, I "interiorize" the world, as Sartre remarks. I ask reality to help me, says Merleau-Ponty, "it can be literally said that our senses question things and things reply to them" (p, 319). So a kind of fertile dialogue between self and nature ensues. "To this extent, every perception is a communication or a communion, the taking up or completion by us of some extraneous intention, or, on the other hand, the complete expression outside ourselves of our perceptual powers and a coition, so to speak, of our body with things" (p, 320). By this coition, I establish the world as valuable and the world enables me to achieve my values. Such is the healthy respect of the farmer for his land, of the scientist for his specimens and reagents, of the artisan for his material. Reality also becomes more than object—it becomes a value.

This is the attitude of the mythical man towards reality. Again, Cassirer abundantly documents this component of mythical thought. The

"I" is formed by the "I's" taking possession of the world and by the I's influencing the world (p, II, 200). The "I" is formed by the process of creativity, and in the process the tools of creativity become an "organ projection" of the self (p, II, 215). "Over and over again we thus find confirmation of the fact that man can apprehend and know his own being only insofar as he can make it visible in the image of his gods" (p, II, 218; cf. also II, 38, 46; p, III, 72). In effect, this is a Wordsworthian view of nature, not a Tennysonian or Hardyan view of "Nature red in tooth and claw."

Analysis of an Example
of Expressive Discourse :
The " Declaration of Independence "

The "Declaration of Independence" has been analyzed from many points of view by experts in various fields. It is a momentous event in history, it embodies much political theory, it is important as a legal document, it even merits a full chapter in Tyler's *Literary History of the American Revolution*. The treatment here is not in competition with these views of the "Declaration." I do not wish to pose as a political theorist, a historian, a legal authority; nor would I ever attempt to treat the "Declaration" as a literary document, in the sense in which literature was defined in the preceding chapter. The "Declaration" is chosen for analysis here because, whatever else it is, it is also a piece of discourse with strong expressive components. It is from this point of view that it will be examined in this chapter.

Strange as it may seem at first, the "Declaration" is a very apt example of the nature of expressive discourse as outlined above in the theoretical section of this part of the chapter. Not that the "Declaration" did not have other important purposes; as was stated above, expressive discourse, possibly more than the others, tends to overlap with the other basic aims of discourse. It is a fact of history that the "Declaration" had some important persuasive purposes. By appealing to all the colonies and by incorporating their individual and collective grievances, it coalesced them into a unity that favored independence and confederation; by appealing to the world, it persuaded other nations to recognize the independence of the new nation and grant it the rights of a sovereign state; by appealing to the thoughtful and the groundlings on the basis of the universal rights of men, it justified, legally and morally, the move of the colonies; by using the familiar phraseology of English and colonial political development, it encouraged the majority of the colonists to join with the minority in Philadelphia; it was an attempt to be a factual documentation of what were thought, at the time, to be the immediate courses leading up to the separation; it was a move to enlist foreign, especially French support, in the war (cf. Friedenwald, d, 174 ff.; Becker, d, 203; Hazelton, d, 42–108, Hawke, t, 143). But the ultimate purpose of all the persuasive aims of the declaration was an expressive aim: to enable a new social personality to achieve self-determination. As we have seen above, this is always the purpose of expressive discourse. In this sense, the persuasive aims of the "Declaration" are subordinate to its expressive aim. Jefferson put this succinctly himself, in answer to a charge of a lack of "originality" in it made by John Adams:

> Not to find out new principles, or new arguments never before thought of, not merely to say things which had never been said before; but to place before mankind the common sense of the subject, in terms so plain and firm as to command their assent.... Neither aiming at originality of principles or sentiments, nor yet copied from any particular and previous writing, *it was intended to be an expression of the American mind....* All *its authority rests then on the harmonizing sentiments of the day,* whether expressed in conversation, in letters, printed essays, or the elementary books of public right, as Aristotle, Cicero, Locke, Sidney, etc. (*Works,* VII, 407, quoted in Becker, d, 25–26, my italics; cf. also Friedenwald, d, 158–59).

What Jefferson was attempting to do, therefore, was to outline to the world the grievances and aspirations of the colonists. That Jefferson was admirably prepared to do this most historians acknowledge. As Parrington remarks,

> Far more completely than any other American of his generation he embodied the idealisms of the great revolution—its faith in human nature, its economic individualism, its conviction that here in America, through the instrumentality of human democracy, the lots of the common man should somehow be made better (m, I, 343).

Jefferson, in effect, in the "Declaration" erected the American myth, with its idealism and possibly with some of its political unrealism. Both of these aspects will be given some consideration below. The myth was accepted enthusiastically in his time in America, as can be seen by the recital of the details of its reception in the various colonies (cf. Hazelton, d, 260 ff.). It has been accepted by most, though not all, Americans since that time. Even today, of the five full-length twentieth-century book treatments of it which I consulted, all were generally receptive to the myth (Hawke is the most critical, cf. d, 237). There have been sporadic severe critics of the "Declaration" in the eighteenth, nineteenth and twentieth centuries in America, as well as elsewhere.

To understand the basic aspirations of this myth as incorporated into the "Declaration of Independence," a sense of its over-all organization is useful. The details of the organization are given below, and, when necessary, the reader can refer to the outline there presented (see pp. 424–26).

The first paragraph of the "Declaration" immediately establishes the basic dimensions of the expressing self. Although this section is grammatically the most impersonal of the entire document, the three basic dimensions of the expressing self are prominent. It is evident that a For-Itself is repudiating an unsatisfactory past and envisages a desirable future: its previous political bands are being dissolved and its aspiration is to be recognized as an entity of separate and equal station among the other powers of the earth. It is also evident that the "Others" are considered and respected; indeed, "a decent Respect to the Opinions of Mankind" is the grammatical subject of the very first sentence. The For-Itself desires to be viewed by the others as an equal. Equality of men is said to be a self-evident truth. It is also clear that Being-in-the-World is relevant: the "Laws of *Nature* and *Nature's* God" are the basis for the selfhood which the new nation desires among the "powers of the *Earth*." The Being-for-Itself, the Being-for-Others, and the Being-in-the-World are all sustained aspects of the self throughout the "Declaration."

Fundamentally these *laws of nature* are the foundation for the second section on the philosophical and political bases of the "Declaration." The repudiation of the past is justified by the longest section of the "Declaration," the long train of abuses of the King and Parliament. Neither the King nor Parliament have acknowledged the right of the colonies to a Being-for-Others or a Being-for-Itself. The King has made of the colonies a despotic object, not a social person. The right to *freedom* of the For-Itself is reiterated again and again in the last and culminating paragraph ("Free and Independent States" is repeated and capitalized twice and "Independent States" is also capitalized). Further, freedom or liberty is one of the unalienable rights with which man is endowed. With this freedom, a new entity is created, and, for the first time in the official acts of the Continental Congress, a new name is used for the personality expressing itself: the "United States of America" (Dumbauld, d, 27). This free and new being asserts its Being-for-Others and its right to do what all free "Others" may do. These rights constitute its aspirations to the future: the powers to levy war, conclude peace, contract alliances, establish commerce "and to do all other acts and Things which INDEPENDENT STATES may of right do." These aspirations are its project for the future.

From the viewpoint of a phenomenologist examining the nature of a being expressing itself, all of the dimensions of the expressing self are dramatically present. Indeed, they structure the various parts of the "Declaration." In this sense, the "Declaration" is a distinctively expressive discourse. A more careful examination of some of these facets of the "Declaration" may make this clear.

Jefferson's use of the past in the "Declaration" is interesting. In a sense he steered between two extreme views of the past, that of John Adams and that of Thomas Paine (Hawke, t, 70). Jefferson carefully avoided both extremes. There is an almost nostalgic respect for the former self: it becomes *necessary* to dissolve these bands, this *necessity "constrains* them to alter their former Systems of Government," the English are still our "British Brethren," "we *must,* therefore, *acquiesce* in the *Necessity,* which *denounces* our Separation." Yet he used the past as an instrument. He employed the traditional structures and styles of the documents of British and American political development. The listing of the grievances and even the specific complaints of some of the grievances are effective echoes of the technique and content of the English Bill of Rights of 1689, presented to William and Mary, that denounced James II. The laws of nature on which Jefferson grounded his political theory are inheritances of the past, as he himself pointed out in the quotation used earlier. Despite this respect and use of the past, however, Jefferson repudiated it: "The past he looked upon as evil, and the record of experiences was a tale of injustice and bitter wrong. He would not have America follow the trodden paths, for whither they led he knew too well" (Parrington, m, 349).

The repudiation of the past makes for the most dramatic aspect of the "Declaration," the repudiation of the King and his governing policies in the past. The antagonist in the drama is the King, the protagonist is the "we," which is the subject of most of the main clauses of the "Declaration." This "we" is what Sartre calls the only real "we" which can lead to *personalization,* the we which is composed of an "I" in league with other "I's" against a third who makes of us an "object" (b, 507–33, especially 525). This kind of "we" is productive. It is clear that the "we" in the "Declaration" is the kind of united "I's" leagued against a third. The "We" technically is the "Representatives of the United States of America," but in reality it is the several "I" states opposed to George III. In the confrontation the King is represented as being "exclusively aggressive" and the colonists as "essentially submissive" (Becker, d, 207). The conflict in the "Declaration" becomes a primitive conflict of right and wrong. This is, of course, characteristic of myth; it is also characteristic of the legal pleas of an advocate in court, and Jefferson considered himself (as the author of the "Declaration") as the advocate of the colonies. It was up to the opposition to supply its own arguments (Friedenwald, d, 177; Tyler, l, I, 509). There emerges, therefore, almost a literary view of the struggle. As Santayana remarked, "But the Declaration of Independence was a piece of literature, a salad of illusions" (quoted in Hawke, t, 240–41). Of this mythical illusion, Hawke remarks,

> Part and parcel of this illusion is the simplistic notion of evil in the

Declaration. A tyrant, combining with a few others, had caused all of the trouble. Remove him from the scene and all would go well.

* * *

The illusion perpetrated in the Declaration, that politics is an endless drama between forces of good and evil, Jefferson knew, if only from the debates on independence, to be nonsensical in 1776, but he never ceased moralizing on great political issues (t, 242–43).

The conflict between the Tyrant and People also serves to supply another crucial ingredient to the discourse if it is to be viewed as expressive: it supplies the emotion of the discourse. There are differing views on the emotional character of the "Declaration." Becker, a serious student of the "Declaration," maintains that, on the whole, the "Declaration" is lacking in emotion (d, 221–22), that Jefferson had a French, eighteenth-century, studied lack of "enthusiasm," that, unlike Lincoln, he did not have a "profoundly emotional apprehension of experience," that he felt with his head as some people think with their hearts (d, 218). John Adams, on the other hand, felt that calling, George III a tyrant was too passionate, and Tyler calls the "Declaration" "an impassioned manifesto of one party" (cf. Tyler, l, I, 509). It is, indeed, an emotional document, though Jefferson might not have possessed Lincoln's profound emotional apprehension of experience. There is emotion in all of the sections, but the middle section on the abuses, though they are submitted as "facts" to a candid world, is the most heavily emotive. Of the twenty-six "long train of abuses," thirteen are stated in superlative terms: "Laws most wholesome and necessary," "immediate and pressing importance...utterly neglected," "a Right inestimable," "for the sole purpose," "exposed to all the dangers," "Judges dependent on his will alone," etc. Many of the remaining abuses were so emotionally laden, in the situation, that their mere enumeration evoked angered emotive connotations: "For imposing Taxes on us without our Consent" (notice the capitals), "For transporting us beyond Seas to be tried for pretended Offences." Others have emotional references in the very words: "He has plundered our Seas, ravaged our Coasts, burnt our Towns, and destroyed the Lives of our People," "He has constrained our fellow Citizens taken captive on the high Seas to bear Arms against their Country, to become the Executioners of their Friends and Brethren, or to fall themselves by their Hands," etc. Indeed, if this is feeling with his head, as Becker says it is, how would Jefferson have felt with his heart?

The other five sections are not quite so patently emotive as this section, but emotion is not lacking in them either. Section II, establishing the philosophic and moral bases of the revolution begins calmly enough, but works up to an emotional crisis, incorporating such phrases as "pursuing invariably...absolute Despotism," "patient sufferance," "repeated Injuries and Usurpations, all having in direct Object the Establishment of an absolute Tyranny over these States." This is hardly a cold intellectual appraisal of the situation. Section IV, on the answers to petitions for redress, concludes, "A prince, whose Character is thus marked for every Act which may define a Tyrant, is unfit to be the Ruler of a Free People." The section on redress from the British people is also heavily emotive. The final section declaring independence is punctuated throughout by superlatives and ends with, "And for the support of this Declaration, with a firm Reliance on the Protection of divine Providence, we mutually pledge to each other our Lives, our Fortunes, and our sacred Honor." This is a strongly emotive conclusion.

Actually, therefore, only the first paragraph is comparatively neutral, yet even here there are some hints of emotion. The document as a whole is an "impassioned manifesto," as Tyler called it. Each section is grounded in a deeply felt grievance or aspiration. It is considerably more emotional than the English Bill of Rights, the *Magna Carta,* and most of the *Communist Manifesto*—if comparisons can be made to similar types of documents in other times.

In addition to the emotion and drama which the opposition to the King gave to the "Declaration," there was also the important political reason for setting up the confrontation of the King and the colonies, grounded in the political theory of the Constitution. This assumes that the colonies were joined only to the King and that Parliament had no legislative power over them: only their own legislatures could legislate for them. That is why Parliament is not referred to in the "Declaration" (Becker, d, 19 ff.; Dumbauld, d, 120); but this issue is tangential to our present analysis.

The confrontation with the King is, in summary, an aspect of the Being-for-Others, just as the repudiation of the past is an aspect of the Being-for-Itself. Let us now take a brief look at the aspirations for the future, also an aspect of the Being-for-Itself. The aspirations can be divided into those viewed as goals and those viewed as means. The general aspirations viewed as goals are outlined in the fundamental second section which outlines the philosophic bases of the "Declaration." The specific aspirations viewed as means are outlined in the list of abuses and in the final paragraph proclaiming the rights of the free states. To these specific means we shall return in the section of this chapter entitled "Organization of Expressive Discourse." For the present let us turn our attention briefly to the aspirations viewed as goals.

These aspirations include "equality," and "life, liberty, and the pursuit of happiness." The relationship between equality and the consequent rights is seen more clearly, in my opinion, in Jefferson's original

"Rough Draft," before it was corrected by the Committee and Congress. The "Rough Draft" reads:

> We hold these truths to be sacred and undeniable; that all men are created equal and independent, that from that equal creation they derive rights inherent and inalienable, among which are the preservation of life & liberty, & the pursuit of happiness; that to secure these ends, governments are instituted among men, deriving their just powers from the consent of the governed (quoted in Dumbauld, d, 53).

Several points in this draft make the intent of the paragraph in the "Declaration" clearer. First, in Jefferson's mind, it is from the fact of "equal" creation that are derived the three rights of the preservation of life and liberty, and the pursuit of happiness. It is from the state of nature, from Being-in-the-World as equals, that the three rights derive. This makes clearer the phrases of the first paragraph: "the separate and equal Station to which the *Laws of Nature* and *Nature's God* entitle them." Second, it is clear from Jefferson's phrase that the preservation of life and liberty, and the pursuit of happiness are *ends* of existence (not just rights). It is also clear that the function of government is "to secure these ends."

The three ends of government as stated by Jefferson in the "Declaration" are actually a significant combination of some ideas from both English and French theories of government. Locke had used the phrases "life, liberty and fortune" and "life, liberty, and estates." In fact Locke, a true Whig, declared that "government has no other end but the preservation of property" (Dumbauld, d, 60). The phrase "life, liberty & property" had already been used by the First Continental Congress in its resolution of October 14, 1774; the same phrase had been used for the Massachusetts Council on January 25, 1773 (Dumbauld, d, 60). In George Mason's draft of a "Declaration of Rights for Virginia," written a few weeks previous to the drafting of the "Declaration of Independence," this phrasing was used: "life and liberty, with the means of acquiring and possessing property, and preserving and obtaining happiness and safety" (Hawke, t, 147). The same trilogy of "life, liberty, and property" was later used in the Fifth and Fourteenth Amendments to the Constitution. The important substitution of "pursuit of happiness" for "property" in these formulas reflected the influence of the French, rather than the English theorists on Jefferson, maintains Parrington:

> ...it was the substitution of a broader sociological conception; and it was the substitution that gave th document the note of idealism which was to make its appeal so perenr y human and vital (m, 344).

This substitution was consistent w efferson. Later, when Lafayette presented Jefferson with a draft of the "Declaration of the Rights of Man" at the time of the French Revolution, Jefferson suggested that the inalienable right to property be omitted (Hawke, t, 149). Jefferson did not intend to deny or denigrate the right to property, but he considered the right to the pursuit of happiness more fundamental and natural (Hawke, t, 61). Similarly, when it was a matter of determining the right to vote during the Constitutional Convention, Jefferson stressed residency as opposed to property and small property holdings as opposed to control by large property owners (cf. Parrington, m, 299 ff., 354).

All of these rights have been ridiculed by American and other critics (cf. Dumbauld, d, 61 f.; Hawke, t, 231 ff.). Reinhold Niebuhr feels that the "pursuit of happiness" has taken on almost totally materialistic connotations and that its slogan influence is almost a force of evil, that it represents a "kind of vulgarity" which is not found in Communist cultures (cf. Hawke, t, 240). Yet it need not be given such an interpretation. As it is stated in the "Declaration" it is nothing more nor less than the free right of an individual to pursue his own projects; as such, it is perfectly consistent with existential freedom and expression. Indeed it seems as good a phrase as Sartre's or anyone else's who is primarily interested in the individual, not the state; and the coordinate stress on liberty is also existential and individual.

It will be recalled that both liberty and pursuit of happiness (as well as preservation of life) were viewed by Jefferson as deriving from our "equal creation," from our existence in nature. This brings the discussion to a consideration of the Being-in-the-World aspect of the "Declaration" viewed as expressive discourse. The founding of the equality on the concept of Nature, the Laws of Nature, and Nature's God must be somewhat carefully interpreted, for "Nature" is one of those philosophic concepts which has been given a myriad of interpretations in theology, politics, literature, and other disciplines. Three aspects of Jefferson's notion of nature are particularly relevant to our concern here. In the first place, Jefferson, like most eighteenth-century minds, viewed "nature" in the context of the Newtonian natural philosophy so influential at this time. Becker considers this so important in interpreting the "Declaration of Independence" that he devotes some forty-three pages to clarifying it (d, 36–79). Nature, for the eighteenth century, was the objective world as interpreted to man by his reason. These laws of nature were obviously God's laws, and the only way we could get to know God's laws was to study nature:

> In the eighteenth century as never before, "Nature" had stepped in between man and God; so that there was no longer any way to know God's will except by discovering the "laws" of Nature, which would doubtless be the laws of "nature's god," as Jefferson said (Becker, d, 37).

The "Laws of Nature and Nature's God," the phrases occurring in the first paragraph of the "Declaration," then, are to be interpreted as one and the same thing. In fact, in the "Rough Draft" the references to the deity did not occur; Congress added them. Nature is also the source of the rights in the second paragraph, as we have already seen. Not that Jefferson disbelieved in the deity or even denied that the Creator did give these rights, rather the contrary (cf. Dumbauld, d, 58–59). The important point to grasp here is that for the eighteenth-century mind, Nature had practically been deified and all that one needed to know about God and his laws could be found in Nature (Becker, d, 40 ff.). Nature, then, is almost a person in the "Declaration," indeed almost a god.

Second, Nature for Jefferson was an ally, not an enemy. Here Jefferson adopted Locke's optimistic view of Nature, and not Hobbes' and John Adams' pessimistic view of Nature (Dumbauld, d, 64–65). Jefferson always was closely related to the "land," to the physical potential of America. He was the product of a rural society in Virginia and believed that from the economic freedom bestowed by the land came political freedom (Parrington, m, 345). He wanted an agrarian, not a capitalistic economy (Parrington, m, 347). He "lived in a world dominated by the land" (Hawke, t, 28). His home, Monticello, he felt, was the expression of his own personality and he worked at building and improving it for forty years (Hawke, t, 45–47). Nature, therefore, for Jefferson meant the sum total of the world's possibilities, viewed in a very physical way. Nature was almost god and was also a friendly god.

Third, Nature for Jefferson meant human Nature, in which Jefferson put more optimistic trust than either John Adams or Alexander Hamilton. His view of human Nature was as optimistic as his view of the world as Nature. Jefferson saw the real future of America in the potential of the common man to collaborate with the land. Consequently, as Hawke precisely expresses it, "America in the Declaration became a land of promise" (t, 170). It is certainly this aspiration which drew many of the immigrants to America before, during, and after Jefferson's day.

These triple dimensions of Nature must be kept in mind in reading the "Declaration of Independence." It is almost unnecessary to point out that such a view of reality is not far removed from the concept of Being-in-the-World of Sartre and Merleau-Ponty. The world, says Sartre, is the sum total of my instruments to achieve the aspirations of my For-Itself. Because the world is so viewed in the "Declaration," the land, the states, do achieve a personality. Being-in-the-World constitutes the possibility of a dialogue between man and Nature, in the sense spoken of by Merleau-Ponty.

In summary, then, the "Declaration of Independence" contains the fundamental components of the expressing self as outlined by the phenomenologists. There is a Being-for-Itself which of necessity repudiates its past and which has projects for a future; the colonies reject their colonial image and envisage a new land of promise. There is a Being-for-Others: the new nation wants to be accepted as a social entity by the other national entities of the world; and the several states league together in a "we" to attack King George III. There is a Being-in-the-World, for the new nation bases its rights on nature and pins its hopes on nature to achieve its goals.[1] Thus, the "Declaration of Independence" is, in a rather complete sense, the expression of a personality. In the "Declaration" a new social entity with three basic dimensions comes into being, and that is the function of expressive discourse—to beget and develop personality. The last component of expression, style, will be examined in the last section of this chapter.

The Logic of Expressive Discourse

Susanne Langer remarks that if there is a logic of expression, no one has yet discovered or formulated it (in Werner, o, 9); I am inclined to agree. However, I shall pass on some remarks or hints made by others in this general area, make a few original suggestions, and then admit that of all the logics of discourse, the expressive logic is practically a virgin forest.

Theory of Expressive Logic

There are some promising studies currently being done by psychologists interested in the process of creativity. The work of Getzels and Jackson (c) and, in language creativity, that of Torrance (g) will certainly have some particular relevance to expressive thought eventually. But creativity is not equivalent to expression, though it involves expression. There is creativity in gathering information in exploration, in science, in persuasion, in art; and, at present, there are no distinctions being made in these various kinds of creativity.

Furthermore, the analyses of mythical thought being made in anthropology and other disciplines might be relevant to an expressive logic, but it would be dangerous to equate mythical thought to expressive thought. It even seems dangerous to posit a rigid unity in mythical thought, as if mythical man made no distinctions among his primitive attempts at proof or exploration, his recorded representations of the universe, his persuasions,

---

[1] I am not at all trying to imply here that Being-in-the-World, as Sartre or Merleau-Ponty view it, is as restricted as Jefferson's in this case.

his art, and his declarations of aspirations. Cassirer reduces mythical thought to an almost monolithic sameness; possibly it is because of this that in his later works, especially in *The Myth of the State,* he really opposes mythical thought and fears it as a regression from rationality. Ultimately for Cassirer myth is the negative aspect of language; in myth lurks the danger of illogic and ambiguity; myth is a great illusion (m, 18, 19, 21). It is man's recourse in dangerous situations; and this is true of the primitive and of the sophisticate (m, 279, 298). For anyone attempting to relate mythical thought to expressive discourse, this is a discouraging climax to encounter in a lifetime of study often preoccupied with myth. It is to be hoped that other students of myth will not be so pessimistic.

The current sporadic interests among logicians and philosophers in a logic of value or will may turn up something that can be related to a logic of expression. Such studies seem promising, particularly in phenomenology (cf. Ricoeur, p). Finally, studies of the process of esthetic expression may provide substantial help for a general theory of expression. As has already been indicated (and the point will be considered below), expression does not take place solely in an artistic medium. Croce and Dewey do, it is true, reduce all expression to art, but the reduction tends to give us invalid theories of both art and expression. Nevertheless, it should prove profitable to make some extractions from the findings about literary expression to expression in general.

After this somewhat discouraging prelude, can anything positive be said? Some of the suggestions of Croce, Dewey, Cassirer, and the phenomenologists do seem to hint at the direction a logic of expression will take. For whatever it is worth, nearly all of these thinkers posit some kind of intuition as the basis of expression. Both Cassirer and Croce distinguish clearly from the rational procedures of science (or "thought") and the intuitive or emotional procedures of expression or myth. Croce makes the distinction quite categorically:

> Knowledge has two forms: it is either *intuitive* knowledge or *logical* knowledge; knowledge obtained through the *imagination* or knowledge obtained through the *intellect;* knowledge of the *individual* or knowledge of the *universal;* of *individual* things or of the *relations* between them; it is in fact, productive either of *images* or of *concepts* (a, 1, his italics; cf. a, 11, 26, 35–36, *passim*).

For Croce, in a given discourse, the two kinds of knowledge may overlap, but one will be subordinate to the other (a, 2–3). Croce specifies this intuitive knowledge and, in effect, equates it to emotion given a form: "The aesthetic fact, therefore, is form, and nothing but form" (a, 16). It is not simple emotion, it is emotion formalized:

Intuition or representation is distinguished as *form* from what is felt and suffered, from the flux or wave of sensation, or from psychic matter; and this form, this taking possession is expression. To intuite is to express, and nothing else (nothing more, but nothing less) than *to express* (a, 11, his italics; the spelling of "intuite" is the decision of Ainslie, the translator).

Cassirer makes somewhat different distinctions: "Art gives us a unity of intuition; science gives us a unity of thought; religion and myth give us a unity of feeling" (m, 37). These distinctions are repeated again and again throughout his works. Unlike Croce, Cassirer separates intuition from feeling; but these neat distinctions are not consistently maintained throughout much of his work. In the last volume of *The Philosophy of Symbolic Forms,* particularly, intuition is not restricted to art at all (cf. especially 162–90, 288, 346). Indeed, there is much discussion of discursive and mathematical intuition, as well as of mythical and esthetic intuition. In any case, it is not very clear just what is meant by intuition. Finally, for Cassirer, all of these—art, science, religion, and myth—are modalities of expression; consequently, there is no particular logic of expression as such: it can be intuitive, thoughtful, or emotive. Many of Croce's distinctions also seem dangerous—the equation of intuition to knowledge of the individual and the equation of this to art; but some elements can be salvaged from both of these authors. Finally, for Sartre all real knowledge is intuitive: "There is only intuitive knowledge" (b, 210); and Husserl also stresses the primacy of intuition (cf. Spiegelberg, p, I, 123 ff.).

This consistent refusal to allow myth or art or expression to be reduced to the rational and the willingness to posit an intuitive thinking behind them, and sometimes to equate intuitive thinking with feeling was part of the motivation for the conference at Clark University on the expressive aspects of language activity. The introductory paragraphs to the volume of the anthologized speeches make this clear:

A number of students from various fields concerned with language activity have recently challenged the modern logistic view that would divide language from its beginnings into two separate spheres: the conceptual and emotive. Many theorists have recognized a mode of apprehending language which transcends any bifurcation into cognitive and emotive—a mode of using language which involves a fusion of affective, motor, and conceptual components. They have urged that this mode of apprehending and employing language persists through ontogenetic development, modified in certain ways, unmodified in others; they have argued on the basis of phenomenological and experimental evidence that this type of language activity permeates not only poetic, religious and philosophical discourse, as well as the discourse of everyday life, but is also manifested in primordial forms of language activity such as are found in dreams and psychopathology.

The ubiquity of "expressive language" and its character imposes on those who desire to study it the acceptance of a truly interdisciplinary view (Werner, o, 1).

This passage makes it clear that whatever thought processes are going on in the expressive components of discourse or in discourse which is predominantly expressive, they should not be reduced to a simply conceptual or simply emotive component. The logic of expressive discourse must embody some emotional and some intellectual components, and maybe this unification can be called intuition—though there ought to be a better term for it.

Certainly the emotive component is partially supplied by the For-Itself which proposes a goal to itself. This goal is an object of desire and is therefore invested with an emotive dimension. Sartre, Merleau-Ponty, Dewey, and Cassirer all insist on the presence of a valued goal. An "experience" which will result in expression, says Dewey, must be one that is pursued through to an end, a fulfillment (a, 35). In myth, says Cassirer, all action is related to a *telos* (the Greek word for end, p, II, 121). We have already stressed the importance of the end or project in Sartre, Merleau-Ponty, and Gusdorf, insofar as the expressing self is concerned. The presence of an *emotionally valued goal* cannot be ignored in any analysis of the logic of expression. Whatever logic is implied in the process of positing a value is therefore a part of the logic of expression. In the next volume of this work, *The Modes of Discourse,* the logic peculiar to value judgments will be analyzed in considerable detail. There it will be shown that many theories of value incorporate a principle of operation towards a goal, the principle of finality or teleology, as it is usually called; the principle of finality is obviously a component of the logic of expression.

But the procedure of evaluation and that of expression are not equivalent. Expression involves value, but expressive discourse is not the same as evaluative discourse. To evaluate something is not quite the same thing as to express it. In fact, language balks at paralleling the two phrases. We *can* evaluate or describe, or classify, or narrate something—these are modes of discourse, but we cannot scientize or inform or persuade or literate it. These are aims of discourse. In the process of evaluative discourse, we make value judgments about something; in expressive discourse, we assume a valued something and work towards it. Evaluative discourse can, as a matter of fact, be strictly scientific or persuasive, etc., but expressive discourse, as such, is not scientific or persuasive or literary.

Assuming a valued goal, expressive discourse works towards its achievement. The technique of marshalling means to an end, the method of making a potential into an actual, constitutes another dimension to the logic of expression. Dewey continually returns to this technique of ordering means to ends. The selection and organization of the materials in order to achieve the desired purpose are an indispensable part of the act of expression, according to him (cf. Dewey, a, 66, 69). This part of the act of expression is rational, according to Dewey. Sartre's concept of value involving the actualizing of a possible sounds so close to Aristotle's notion of potency-act that he disavows an equivalence (b, 120), yet there is considerable similarity. Now the actualizing of a potential involves the principle of causality—nearly every analyst of change posits this, from Aristotle to Newton. Consequently besides the principle of formality, the principle of causality is also involved in the logic of expression.

Expressive Logic in the "Declaration of Independence"

It seems obvious enough that the principle of finality or purpose operates at several crucial levels in the "Declaration." The ultimate end of the "Declaration" is to secure the equal rights of the colonists to pursue happiness and to preserve life and liberty. The necessary penultimate end, a means to the achievement of the final end, is the establishment of a representative government which will secure these ends. Before this can be done, the present government by the King must be abolished because it is "destructive of these Ends," since it has for "Direct Object the Establishment of an Absolute Tyranny over these States." The facts that prove this are "submitted to a candid World." Once the new government is established it will (it is implied) rectify the abuses of the present government and engage in all the "Acts and Things which Independent States may of right do." The end of these acts and things, some of which are enumerated in the final paragraph, is to secure the basic rights of equality, preservation of life and liberty, and pursuit of happiness. The relationship of all of this hierarchy of purpose to the self of the social personality has already been established above, under "Nature of Expressive Discourse." Put somewhat differently, it might be said that equal station among the powers of this earth assures Being-for-Others and Being-in-the-World. The purpose of these is to secure selfhood to the Being-for-Itself, to enable it to repudiate its past and work out future projects of its own choosing. In terms of self-expression, the "Declaration" states succinctly a hierarchy of ends which the new self has in mind whereby it can achieve the full development of its selfhood. The first two sections and the last section determine these.

The three middle sections operate at more specific levels that orient means to ends. These, therefore, are the particular levels of causality whereby the possible will be actualized. Causality and finality are here, as every-where, reciprocally related (cf. Sartre, b, 151). Causality operates in two distinct ways in the "Declaration." First, there is the principle of causality viewed as operating in the past. The "Declaration" is very aware of this. The "causes which impel them to the Separation" must be declared to the World, says the first paragraph; and the second says, "Governments long established should not be changed for light and transient Causes." But the long train of abuses constitute weighty and sustained causes which have operated to deprive the colonists of basic freedoms. The effect of these causes has been to deprive the colonists of these basic freedoms and to reduce them to a state of near despotism.

By removing the government which fosters these causes to achieve its design, the colonists will be able to establish a government which will set in motion other causes to produce opposite effects. This is implied only. The specific setting in motion of legislative, judicial, and administrative powers which corrected these abuses came only with the "Articles of Con-federation" and the "Constitution." But it is clearly implied that the new government will correct these abuses and prescribe instruments to achieve their opposites. Some of these positive implications are discussed in the next section under "Organization of Expressive Discourse." A few of the specific instruments needed immediately are detailed in the last paragraph: power to levy war, conclude peace, contract alliances, establish commerce.

It is clear from this cursory examination that the principles of finality or purpose and causality or agency operate consistently throughout the "Declaration." There is some justification, therefore, to suggest that at least one aspect of the logic of expressive discourse includes the principles of finality and causality.

The Organization of Expressive Discourse

Theory

Given the individual character of expressive discourse, it might seem almost foolhardy to discuss any general organizational patterns. Croce believes this to be true in an important sense: since each expression is a species to itself, expression can not function as a genus (a, 68). For this reason, he is opposed to the idea of literary genres or types in literary theory (cf. Kinneavy, s, 2 ff., for a discussion of this attitude). One recalls the dicta of medieval Scholasticism: "The individual is ineffable" and "there can be no science of the individual." Yet because expressive discourse uses language, which is a medium whose very nature is conventional and inter-subjective, there must be some compromises between pure individualism and expression in language. Further, despite the fact that individuals do have different experiences, these experiences have some common character-istics. Langan affirms this point in explaining Merleau-Ponty's doctrine of expression: "Each act of linguistic expression is an event, creative in a limited, dependent way, a creation that depends on espousing the lines of force of what preceded, of a tradition" (m, 85). T. S. Eliot has reminded us of this problem in literature in his essay on "Tradition and the Individual Talent," and, with some qualifications, the principles he considered there also apply to expressive discourse. As will be seen, there is an operative readjustment of a tradition in the "Declaration of Independence." The more formal genres of expressive discourse, the confession, the utopia, the party platform, the club or national constitution, for example, are more heavily indebted to traditions than the less formal genres. Presumably, the social genres of expression are more conventional as a group than the personal genres. This would seem to hold especially for the legal and busi-ness genres.

All of the writers who have been considered as authorities on ex-pression agree that expression is characterized by some kind of form. Here they seem to oppose the progressive education concept that expression is without laws. For Croce, as has been shown, expression *is* form. But these writers differ radically on the form which such expression takes. For Dewey and Croce especially, all expression eventuates in esthetic form (cf. Croce, a, 12). Yet, it is clear that not all expressive form is esthetic form. The structures of expressive conversation, of cathartic interviews, of political manifestoes, of riots, and of many other genres of expressive discourse are certainly far from esthetic structures.

From the above listing it is clear that no single kind of principle of ordering is particularly native to modes of expressive discourse. In social situations, the kind of organizing principle may well be partially dictated by the implicit or explicit rules of procedure which the society has adopted to govern itself by, such as Roberts' rules of parliamentary procedure, or the form of legal documents, or international law. This principle of organization applies, in part, to the "Declaration of Independence," as will be shown in the next subsection.

Organization of the "Declaration of Independence"

For referral purposes in the subsequent discussion, an outline of the "Declaration" is here appended.

I *Necessity of Declaring Causes of Separation to Mankind*

II *Philosophic Bases of Independence*

   A All men are created with certain equal rights.

   B Governments are established to secure these rights.

   C A government which does not secure these rights should be abolished and replaced.

   D The government by King George III has denied these rights. Therefore it should be abolished and replaced. The proof follows.

III *List of Abuses*

   A Legislative Abuses
     1. Refused consent to wholesome and necessary laws.
     2. Refused to allow laws to be passed, or suspended them.
     3. Refused to allow laws to be passed unless representation relinquished.
     4. Required legislative bodies to meet at distant places.
     5. Dissolved representative houses.
     6. Refused reelections, after dissolutions.
     7. Obstructed laws of naturalization and immigration.

   B Judicial Abuses
     8. Refused to allow laws establishing judiciary.
     9. Made judges dependent on him.

   C Executive Abuses
     10. Erected many new offices and sent new officers.
     11. Maintained standing armies.
     12. Made military superior to civil power.

   D Abuses in Conjunction with Others (13)
     Police Army
     a. Quartered troops among us.
     b. Protected these troops by mock trials.
     Financial
     c. Cut off our trade with world.
     d. Taxed us without our consent.
     Judicial
     e. Deprived us of trial by jury.
     f. Transported us overseas for trials.
     Legislative
     g. Abolished free law in Canada, ultimately to threaten us.
     h. Took away Charters, abolished laws.
     i. Suspended our Legislatures, and said Parliament can legislate in any area.

   E Abuses Related to War
     14. Abolished governments, waged war.
     15. Plundered seas, coasts, towns, killed people.

16. Hired foreign mercenaries to fight us.
17. Forced colonists to fight against each other.
18. Excited domestic insurrections.

IV *Futility of Seeking Redress from King*

V *Futility of Seeking Redress from British People*

VI *Formal Declaration of Independence*

A United States of America declared free and independent states.

B Allegiance to King abolished.

C Political connection to Great Britian dissolved.

D Rights of United States asserted.

E Pledge made of lives, fortunes, and honor to support the declaration.

The "Declaration" is hardly a chaotic piece of discourse—there is evident form. The sequence of ideas is dictated by the purpose of the piece, stated in the first section: "a decent Respect to the Opinions of Mankind requires that" the representatives of the United States should declare the "causes which impel them to the separation." To establish the validity of these causes, an anthropological axiom is first enunciated: all men have certain inalienable rights. This entails a political axiom: governments are established to secure these rights. From these two axioms the large structure of the remainder of the declaration follows by a series of deductions: (1) When governments do not secure these rights, they should be abolished and replaced; this is a necessary conclusion from the purpose of governments; (2) the government by the King has not secured these rights; inductive evidence for this point is given in the list of abuses and is reinforced by the two following sections that show the futility of redress; (3) therefore the government of the colonies by the King should be abolished and the colonies should establish their own government (Section VI).

The large structure of the "Declaration" is therefore a deductive structure, a series of conclusions drawn from a stated purpose and two axioms. The microstructure of the bulk of the inductive proof given in Sections III, IV, and V, which places the present situation under the general rule that permits the abolishing of an existing government and the establishing of a new government, is not, however, deductively organized. Let us examine the patterns of sequence in these sections.

As can be seen in the outline, the first set of abuses is legislative (II A 1–7), the second is judicial (II B 8–9), the third is executive (II C 10–12). These are the abuses perpetrated by the King personally. There then follow the abuses perpetrated by the King in conjunction with Parliament. These concern the police army, and financial, judicial, and legislative affairs (III D 13 a–i). Lastly the specific abuses relating to war are listed (III E 14–18).

The abuses perpetrated by the King are listed in the order of the three functions of government, and primacy is here given to the legislative function over the judicial and executive. This is consonant with the theory of government implicit in the previous section of the philosophic bases. The sequence within the legislative abuses moves from the more centrally necessary to the somewhat peripheral. The King has not given assent to necessary and wholesome laws; or he has suspended them when they have been passed; or he has allowed them to be passed but deprived the colonies of representation; or he has forced legislative bodies to meet at distant places; or he has abolished representative legislative houses; and he has refused to allow reelections after such dissolutions. Finally, one specific set of necessary and wholesome laws is singled out: those concerning naturalization and migration. The judicial abuses again start with the basic issue, the right of the colonies to legislate concerning judiciary powers, and then move to the corollary, the right to have independent judges. The executive abuses start with the general (many new offices) and move to the specific, the rule by military power.

The abuses perpetrated by the King in conjunction with others follow the abuses perpetrated by the King personally because, as has been pointed out already, the "Declaration" operates under the colonial theory of government which related the colonies directly to the King without the intermediacy of Parliament. The "Declaration" assumes that the colonial charters were a contract between King and colony, and that each colony had its own legislative body and was not to be legislated to by Parliament. Consequently the King was primarily responsible for his actions by the mediacy of Parliament. Within this section, the order of abuses is directly the reverse of the personal abuses of the King. Here the military issue comes first, then the judicial, and finally the legislative (the financial, a specific executive abuse, is given particular attention along with the military). I can only speculate on the reasons for this reversal. Possibly, by placing the two military issues one after the other, he exploits the emotion which this issue connotated.

The immediate abuses relating to war are then detailed, beginning again with the most crucial: the King has "abdicated Government here." Particularly thorny complaints are then aired. Here, as throughout the "Declaration," specific complaints relating to one or several or all of the colonies are singled out for the purpose of uniting all of the colonies in the revolution. Standing armies, taxation without representation, the use of foreign mercenaries, forcing colonists to fight against each other are examples of such specific complaints.

The organization of the interior section of the "Declaration" contains a distinctive formal principle of ordering, partly classificatory and partly hierarchical. The abuses are not at all haphazardly listed. The "Declaration" is, therefore, both in its macrostructure and in its microstructures a very carefully ordered piece of discourse. It may or may not be typical of all expressive discourse in this respect, but it at least is meticulously organized. As Cassirer has remarked, mere facts never organize themselves (p, II, 32). In the "Declaration" the facts are partially organized by the conventions of similar declarations in the past, especially the English Bill of Rights of 1689. In addition, the custom of the Continental Congress to begin any important resolution with a "high-sounding preamble" is also adhered to (Hawke, t, 117); but this custom is used by Jefferson to establish the purpose of the "Declaration," and ultimately, therefore, to dictate its order and logic. However, all expressive discourse will not follow such a rigorous organizational ordering as that of the "Declaration of Independence."

The Style of
Expressive Discourse

Theory

Of all the aims of discourse, less has been written on expression than on any other; and, as might be expected, less has been written on the style of expressive discourse than on any other kind of style. One does not have to search very far for the reason: few people actually distinguish expression as a specific aim of discourse. When they do, as has been shown, there is a tendency to equate expressive with literary discourse. As far as I can ascertain, only a few stylistic analyses have been made of the specifically expressive aspects of this type of discourse either as it exists in a relatively pure state or even as it exists submerged as a secondary or tertiary aim in other kinds of discourse.

Indeed, it is probably hazardous, maybe erroneous, to entitle this section "The Style of Expressive Discourse." Just as there are many literary, many persuasive, and even many reference styles, so *a fortiori* would there seem to be many different expressive styles, rather than one style. Indeed, if Gusdorf's statement is correct, that one achieves individuality through style, and if expressive discourse is precisely that kind of discourse wherein a private or a social entity achieves individuality, then one should expect a certain ineffable idiosyncrasy to be found in the style of such discourse. This is partially true of very personal genres of expression; but the style of "The Apostles' Creed" or of the "Declaration of Independence" would not normally be termed ineffably idiosyncratic. The "Creed" and the "Declaration" have, in fact, proven effable, that is, expressible in speech. It may be, as the medieval scholastics had it, that the individual is ultimately ineffable; but on the other hand, it is only by expression that the individual achieves itself. The inexpressible must therefore partially express itself to achieve itself—this is part of the paradox of the style of expressive discourse. To express itself in language, the individual must adopt the conventional instrument of linguistic forms. The alternative is silence, and silence is the death or negation of the person.

Yet the wide variety of the genres of expressive discourse does indicate the wide variety of the styles. Contrast the style of ordinary conversation with that of the highly ritualistic Christian "Litany of the Saints," or the style of More's *Utopia* with that of the *Communist Manifesto,* or that of a Greek myth with that of the "Constitution of the United States." Yet these are all heavily expressive in aim. Only a few of these kinds of discourse have been analyzed for style; and the abstraction of the specifically expressive characteristics has not usually been made in such analyses. Northrop Frye, in *The Well-Tempered Critic,* returns again and again to the characteristics of the associative language, as he calls it; and Frye's associative language is very close to some simpler forms of expressive discourse. Frye's analysis of this kind of discourse does make the proper abstraction, and it will be drawn on at several instances in this chapter. Similarly, Osgood's analysis of suicide notes abstracts to a fairly pure consideration of expressive discourse as such, and it also will be drawn on sporadically. Osgood contrasts suicide notes to ordinary letters and then to pseudo-suicide notes and finds some significant variations in both contrasts (cf. Osgood, s, 298 ff.).

For purposes of consistency, the same format which was used to treat reference, persuasive, and literary styles will also be adopted here, even at the risk of displaying the meager information we now possess in most of these areas. Consequently, a few remarks will be made on the cultural and situational context features of expressive style, then a few on the discourse features, then a few on the semantic and grammatical aspects. Finally, a brief analysis of the style of the "Declaration of Independence" will be presented.

Cultural Context, Situational Context, and Discourse Features of Expressive Discourse

Dewey, Merleau-Ponty, and Gusdorf all insist on the necessity, in the expressive act, of removing oneself from "conventional associations," of establishing a fresh viewpoint (cf. Dewey, a, 95; Langan, m, 145–57). Gusdorf, who, it will be recalled, maintains that only in the discovery of a personal style does the individual find himself, makes it quite clear that such a discovery involves a divorce from conventions.

> The discipline of a style corresponds to a need for precision that removes the creator from all the ready-made formulas of the established language. He has had to pass from the common meaning to the particular meaning that is his, sometimes at the cost of an heroic struggle (s, 89).

This neolanguage carries with it the corollary, on the part of the receptor, to be willing to see new and unique meanings in the expressive discourse (Gusdorf, s, 89). The individual who does not revolt against conventional language does not really discover himself:

> In fact, the life of the mind ordinarily begins not with the acquisition of language, but with revolt against language, once it is acquired. The adolescent discovers values in the *revolt* against the language he had until then blindly trusted and which seems to him, in the light of the crisis, destitute of all authenticity. Every man worthy of the name has known that crisis in the appreciation of language which causes one to pass from naive confidence to doubt and denial (Gusdorf, s, 40).

Consequently, Gusdorf continually stresses the fact that, "Every spiritual or intellectual revolution demands a previous transformation of the established language" (s, 23). He analyzes some significant revolutions in thought as overthrows of various conceptions of language (cf. s, 22–33).

The particular cultural conventions of language are uprooted by the existential situation. In the moment of crisis for the individual or the group personality, aspects of the inherited conventions are seen as no longer meaningful or even as harmful, as Gusdorf has pointed out. The linguistic environment must be interpreted in the unique situation of the For-Itself. Consequently, Sartre maintains that there can be no universal symbolism in an existential psychoanalysis (b, 701–2). This dynamic and neologistic aspect of expressive discourse is reminiscent of the dynamic and changing attitude to meanings discussed above in both scientific and persuasive styles (see pp. 175–76, 289–90, 296).

There are a few discourse features that characterize expressive discourse. Some modes, media, and arts of discourse are more congenial to expressive discourse than others. Thus evaluation, as a mode, is more oriented to expressive discourse than the other three modes because of the necessary value elements implicit in all expressive discourse. Similarly, some media lend themselves better to expressive discourse than others: parliamentary procedure, interviews of all sorts, questionnaires, letters to editors of journals or personal letters, political and religious conventions, small conversations, counseling sessions, and similar media seem more adaptable to expression than some other kinds of media such as teaching machines, scholarly journals, academic conventions, language laboratories, and the like. Finally, the arts of discourse, speaking and writing (the so-called "expressive" arts) are more congenial to expression than are the receptive arts of listening and reading. Of the two, speaking would seem to be a more spontaneous and genuine art of expression than the art of writing, as Gusdorf maintains. In the speaking situation, the media of dialogue and conversation are better than the monologue, he also points out. Northrop Frye finds in ordinary conversation the most typical exemplification of his "associative" style:

> Ordinary speech is concerned mainly with putting into words what is loosely called the stream of consciousness: the daydreaming, remembering, worrying, associating, brooding and mooning that continually flow through the mind, and which, with Walter Mitty, we often speak of as thought. *Thus ordinary speech is concerned mainly with self-expression.* Whether from immaturity, pre-occupation, or the absence of a hearer, it is imperfectly aware of an audience. Full awareness of an audience makes speech rhetorical, and rhetoric means a conventionalized rhythm (w, 20, my italics).

Frye distinguishes the rhythm of rhetoric from the rhythm of the associative style—this will be returned to later. For the present, the point of the citation is to show that Frye sees much self-expression in the medium of conversation, and thus agrees with Gusdorf.

Semantic Features
of Expressive Style

In the field of semantic differentials, that is, meanings that differ from one encoder to another or one decoder to another, one would expect to find a significant characteristic of expressive style if what has been said above about the expressor's breaking with conventional meanings has any validity. If, as Sartre, Merleau-Ponty, and Gusdorf maintain, the expressor must give new meanings relevant to his unique existential situation to all words or even create new words, then expressive discourse should be characterized by an idiolect, a private dialect with some private meanings. And, just as the individual person creates his own idiolect, so also the social person creates its own dialect (or jargon, cant, argot). A social personality probably does not emerge until it has its own subdialect. Jargon, therefore, in the best meaning of the term, is a sign of a forming social personality. Cassirer became aware of this phenomenon when he analyzed the idiosyncratic German of the Nazis. He found that the German words which he had known had taken on entirely new meanings; he found new words, and he found new emotional charges injected into formerly neutral terms (m, 283).

In the area of reference (cf. Figure V, 2, see pp. 349–51), other semantic characteristics of expressive discourse can be discerned. The referents (kinds of realities referred to) of expressive discourse are usually highly subjective, embodied in images, and connotative rather than simply denotative. In myth, as Cassirer points out, there is a fusion of image, name, and object (p, II, 41–42; p, III, 85–86). In fact, in mythic expression the object and the image are often one and the same thing (p, III, 85–86), and the image of the object is often more important than the object itself (p, III, 69).

The particular referents of expressive discourse are normally one-sided. Langan, explaining Merleau-Ponty's position on this, says that elements in reality that do not function within the unity of expressive perception are "simply crossed out as unreal" (m, 59; cf. 79). Quoting Max Scheler, Langan says that such perception grasps everything "whose nature or *alteration* count *practically* for me" (m, 61, his italics). This, in part, explains the one-sided view of the colonial situation presented in the "Declaration of Independence." Persuasion and the adoption of an advocate approach also contribute to the one-sided picture of reality in the "Declaration."

Because of this essentially subjective view of referents, the terms referring to it carry heavy connotative and emotional associations. Werner, Kaplan, and Sperber, in the Clark anthology, *On Expressive Language,* all emphasize this feature of expressive discourse (cf. Werner, o, 13–15, 20, 39–40). Like persuasion, expression embodies those aspects of myth which Lasswell calls *miranda,* things to be admired (see p. 280 ff.); and the admiration embodies emotional associations.

One other characteristic of the expressive referents might be singled out: the distinct tendency to make classes all-inclusive. As Osgood points out in his analysis of suicide notes, there is a heavy preponderance of what he calls "allness" terms. Grammatically, this will be marked by superlatives. The "Declaration of Independence" also characteristically exemplifies this feature. Of course, persuasion also embodies this feature, as we have seen.

One important feature of the expressive discourse that does frequently differentiate it from persuasive (and literary and reference) discourse is the picture presented of the speaker, the I-narrator or the I-expositor. As has been shown in Chapter IV, the picture of the I presented in persuasion is an "image," a projection, often a deliberate distortion. In literature, it is largely, often totally fictional. In reference discourse the speaker generally does not intrude so noticeably. But in expressive discourse the authentic I emerges clearly, indeed he is partly born in the discourse

With regard to referends, the kinds of referring terms used, a few characteristics of expression have been pointed out by some writers. Precisely because object and speaker are so closely identified, particularly in myth, there is a distinct tendency to the personification of things and to the objectification of persons. These two nonliteral kinds of terms, then, are to be expected in myth and expression generally. Personifications, of course, in Greek myth even led to the deification of many of the forces of nature. The opposite tendency can also be seen and is illustrated by Asch in his essay in *On Expressive Language*. We speak of persons as deep, shallow, bright, dull (in Werner, o, 29–30); but these subjective connotations of objective attributes will often vary from culture to culture. "Hot," for example, symbolizes different attitudes in different cultures: "rage or wrath (Hebrew), enthusiasm (Chinese, Malaysian), sexual arousal (Thai), worry (Thai), energy (Hausa), or nervousness (Shilka)" (in Werner, o, 33). Even in a single culture, the term may polarize to a nearly opposite meaning; and "hot" and "cool" in American slang in this century have done something like this.

Finally, in the area of referral, the process of relating term to object, a few remarks can also be suggested. Expressive terms, like exploratory terms, are often ambiguous. As Merleau-Ponty remarks, there is a necessary ambiguity in the operations of freedom (p, 445); often the revolution cannot foresee the end. He instances the Russian revolution of 1917: "For example, it is doubtful whether the Russian peasants of 1917 expressly envisaged revolution and the transfer of property" (p, 445). Similarly, the ambiguities of the phrase of the "Declaration," "all men are created equal" have plagued American history for nearly 200 years. Does equality for all men include political equality for Negroes, or women, or nonpropertied residents; does it involve economic and educational and housing equality? Much of the work of the Supreme Court is a matter of clarifying the seemingly univocal phrases of Congress.

In the third area of semantics, technically called "meaning," some interesting studies have been made. "Meaning," in this context, is defined as the semantic implications of the grammar of a language. At the very beginning of the study of expressive discourse in the nineteenth century, much effort was expended by serious scholars to show that certain sounds or classes of sounds embodied rather distinct attitudes to reality. Humboldt maintained that "st" gives an impression of endurance and stability, that "l" expresses melting and fluid reality, that "v" gives an impression of evenness; Jacob Grimm felt that "k questions, calls; t shows, explains, answers;" Müller said that "a," "o," and "u" indicate greater distance, that "e" and "i" indicate lesser distance (cf. Cassirer, p, I, 192–93). Cassirer himself says that for children, "m" and "n" seem to indicate an inward direction, while "p," "b," and "t" indicate outwardness (p, I, 201). Many linguists in this century tend to deprecate such studies, but of late some of the more interesting studies in psycholinguistics have again evinced interest in such concepts, though the particular formulations of Humboldt or Grimm may not be accepted.

In addition to these interests, much of the concern over the Sapir-Whorf hypothesis about reciprocity between a culture's linguistic system and its attitude to reality, its *Weltanschauung,* is also relevant to expressive discourse. For if a culture's language system is conditioned by and also conditions its attitude to reality, then the language system will necessarily embody some of the aspirational attitudes of the group to reality. Its language is an expression of and a means of attaining its fundamental projects.

Grammatical Features of Expressive Discourse

I have encountered only a few scattered remarks relating to the syntax of expressive discourse. In the first place, it is of some significance that in many kinds of expressive discourse the listing or litany type of repetitive syntax is used. The longest part of the "Declaration" is a list of abuses. The same is true of the English Bill of Rights of 1689, the American Constitution, the Apostles' and Nicene Creeds, the Christian Litanies, the culminating proposals of the crucial Section II of the *Communist Manifesto,* etc. This is possibly due to the fact that before the For-Itself repudiates its past, there is usually an accumulation of dissatisfactions, culminating in a crisis. The expression of aspirations therefore embodies the counterparts of these accumulated dissatisfactions in what emerges as a litany or a list. The "Declaration" has been criticized stylistically as being monotonous. This is a criticism by literary norms; it really is no indictment of the basic purpose of the "Declaration," to list the abuses and implied counterpart aspirations. This kind of repetitiveness is no blemish on expressive discourse, any more than it is a blemish on informative discourse, where similar listings also occur. No one complains of the monotonous listings in the telephone directory or of the monotony of the tables in the latest edition of the *Handbook of Chemistry and Physics,* or of the monotony of the dictionary. Repetitiveness has also been found to occur in suicide notes (Osgood, s, 298, 305), but suicide notes are actually a particular case of expressive discourse. Just as there is good and bad literature, effective and ineffective persuasion, so also is there successful and unsuccessful expression. In a suicide note, obviously the future projects—except self-annihilation—of the For-Itself are abandoned; Being-for-Others is refused; and Being-in-the-World is relinquished, for the world is no longer viewed as a sum of possible means to future projects. In effect, all of the components of the self are denied and selfhood becomes meaningless. Suicide notes are almost the antithesis of successful expression; they are a perverted expression. They are to real expression what misinformation is to information. Nevertheless they belong to the genre of expressive discourse.

Morphemically, the most significant aspect of expressive discourse is the implicit or explicit omnipresence of the "I" or "we" pronoun forms or their equivalents. "We" is the subject of the main sentences in the philosophy section of the "Declaration;" "we" is the subject of the main sentences in each of the two paragraphs on redress; and "we" is the subject of the two sentences in the final paragraph declaring independence. Grammatically, "we" is the dominant word in the "Declaration of Independence." Similarly, "we" is the source of all of the affirmations of the Constitution: "We, the people of the United States...do ordain and establish this Constitution." "I" is the subject of all of the beliefs of the Apostles' and Nicene Creeds. The responses to each address in the litanies are "Pray for *us*" or "Deliver *us*, O Lord."

Cassirer points out that Humboldt and others interested in the expressive function of language

> ...have often attempted to demonstrate that the personal pronoun is, as it were, the "bedrock" of language formation, the most ancient and obscure, but also the firmest and most enduring component of languages (p, I, 250; cf. note 141 for references).

Without endorsing this position completely, Cassirer does point out the many aspects of language which manifest the I-feelings or I-attitudes, especially in verb formations: active, passive, and middle voices; the subjunctive mood indicating volitive or deliberative attitudes; the prospective and optative and imperative moods of most languages; the implorative, desiderative, and obligative moods in some American Indian languages; the reflexive and reciprocal forms in many languages; and in noun and pronoun forms, the possessive or genitive cases in many languages (Cassirer, p, I, 251–60). Obviously, interjections are a medium of expressing I-attitudes (Cassirer, p, I, 190; see note 22 for references).

As was pointed out earlier, the superlative form of adjectives and adverbs is a characteristic feature of much expressive discourse. Its ubiquity in the "Declaration of Independence" will be pointed out shortly.

Finally, at the phonemic level of style, the study of the rhythms of

expressive discourse by Northrop Frye gives some further information about
certain kinds of expressive discourse. Throughout *The Well-Tempered Critic*
Frye distinguishes between three basically different kinds of rhythm:

> There are, then, three primary rhythms of verbal expression. First,
> there is the rhythm of prose, of which the unit is the sentence. Second,
> there is an associative rhythm, found in ordinary speech and in various
> places in literature, in which the unit is a short phrase of irregular length
> and primitive syntax. Third, there is the rhythm of a regularly repeated
> pattern of accent or meter, often accompanied by other recurring features,
> like rhyme or alliteration (w, 24).

To clarify the notion of the associative rhythm of ordinary speech, Frye
had earlier given a sample, after some introductory remarks:

> If we listen to children talking, we do not hear prose: we hear a
> heavily accented speech rhythm with a good deal of chanting in it, or
> whining, depending on the mood of the child. If we get lost in a strange
> town and ask someone for directions, we do not get prose: we get pure
> Gertrude Stein, a speech rhythm that is prolix and repetitive, and in
> which the verbal unit is no more a prose sentence than it is a villanelle.
> The teenager issuing mating calls over a telephone is not speaking prose,
> although the speech rhythm he uses is as formalized as prayer, which it
> somewhat resembles. The lady screaming amiabilities at a crowded cock-
> tail party is not allowed to speak prose, for her hearers are not listening
> for sentences, but for a single rise and fall of the voice. The other day a
> student came to consult me about a failure in English, and what he said,
> as I recorded immediately after he left was this:
>
> > Y'know, I couldn' figure what happened, cause, jeez, well, I figured,
> > y'know, I had that stuff cold—I mean, like I say, I'd gone over the stuff
> > an I figured I knew it, and—well, jeez, I do' know.
>
> I submit that this is not prose, and I suspect he had failed because he
> had not understood the difficulties of translating his speech into prose (w,
> 19–20).

In the next paragraph, Frye states that "ordinary speech is concerned mainly
with self-expression" and points out that it is often made with not much
of an audience in mind (w, 20–21). This passage was cited in more complete
form earlier in Section **IV** of this chapter in another connection. The sample
of such discourse from the student, which Frye gives, is clearly an example
of this self-expression, almost without an audience in mind. It is, in fact,
a primitive form of confession, and its rhythm is clearly a phrasal and
repetitive kind of chant. It is obvious enough that this kind of rhythm also
characterizes a good deal of the simpler forms of expressive discourse:

prayer formulas, litanies, mob chants, sports rally cries, religious credos, or popular love songs. In more sophisticated forms of discourse, where prose is superficially adopted as the medium, the associative rhythm is sometimes extended to a somewhat longer unit, phrasal or sentential, also repeated cyclically (cf. Frye, w, 82). This happens in the "Declaration of Independence" in the list of abuses in Section III and in the list of aspirations in Section VI. There is no implication here, however, that such associative rhythms are the only kind of rhythms in expressive discourse, or that they characterize all expressive discourse, or that they are not found in other kinds of discourse. But they do seem to characterize some important kinds of expressive discourse.

These sporadic remarks on the style of expressive discourse make no pretense to comprehensiveness. They are only sketchy suggestions of areas that must be investigated in detail in future studies. Some of the suggestions seem possessed of a certain *a priori* validity; others seem at first somewhat questionable.

Some Aspects
of Expressive Style
in the " Declaration of Independence "

METALINGUISTIC
AND METALANGUAGE FEATURES

A good number of the stylistic qualities of the "Declaration" have already been alluded to in the previous subsection, in order to illustrate theoretical points. Without being repetitive here, I shall adduce a few additional characteristics of the "Declaration." Somewhat lengthy stylistic analyses of the document have already been made, particularly by Becker (d, 194–223) and by Tyler (l, 494–521); both approach it stylistically from a literary point of view. Becker's chapter is called "The Literary Qualities of the Declaration"; Tyler's purely stylistic considerations occur in a section called "Estimate of Its Purely Literary Character" and the whole volume is called *The Literary History of the American Revolution*. Both men have, however, a very broad view of the scope of literature.

One of the reasons Jefferson was designated in committee as the author of the first draft was because he had already acquired the reputation of a stylist. John Adams wrote that when Jefferson came to Congress,

> ...he brought with him a reputation for literature, science, and a happy talent for composition. Writings of his were handed about remarkable for the peculiar felicity of expression (quoted in Becker, d, 194).

Becker feels that these words, "peculiar felicity of expression," would perhaps sum up the "distinguishing characteristics of Jefferson's style" (d, 194). Becker also says that the "Declaration" is filled with "felicities of phrase which bear the stamp of Jefferson's mind" and he gives several examples (d, 196). Friedenwald, also writing in our century, has high praise for its style (d, 188–90).

On the other hand, Tyler, in summarizing the destructive attacks on the style of the "Declaration," uses the words "grandiose and vaporing style" (l, 499). And a British professor, Goldwin Smith, writing in the late nineteenth century, says much the same thing by remarking derogatorily that it was written in "a highly rhetorical strain" and that it opened "with sweeping aphorisms about the natural rights of man, at which political science now smiles" (quoted in Tyler, l, I, 502). He also feels that its veracity was largely as unreliable as the "general utterances" of the statesman who was its scribe (cf. Tyler, l, I, 502). Some of these criticisms, favorable and unfavorable, seem capable of verification in the text or against the background of the situational context. Others are metaphorical and vague; it would probably be difficult to provide evidence for its vaporous or its musical or its electrical qualities, attributes which Friedenwald uses (d, 178–80).

As with any piece of expressive discourse, it must first be placed within its own unique situational context. Jefferson almost certainly wrote it in a house on Market and Seventh Streets in Philadelphia on a small portable desk (Hazelton, d, 149). Generally Jefferson wrote quickly, though carefully, and with many corrections (Becker, d, 194–95). Jefferson later wrote that he did not use or consult any documents for reference at the time. But there are distinct analogues, even specific phrases, seemingly drawn from memory, from Jefferson's own "A Summary View of the Rights of British America," printed in 1774; from George Mason's draft for a "Declaration of Rights for Virginia"; from some French philosophers; from a pamphlet by James Otis; possibly even from a tragi-comedy by Aphra Behn; from a jury charge by Chief Justice Drayton in Charleston, delivered in April of 1776; and possibly also from a declaration of independence adopted by some citizens in Mecklenburg, North Carolina, in May, 1775 (cf. Hawke, t, 147 ff.; Tyler, l, I, 504). At any rate, Jefferson presumably himself made some fifteen changes in the first rough draft. Then the drafting committee made some thirty-one more changes. Finally, Congress made eighty-six changes. Some of these tended to tone down Jefferson's superlative exuberance; some concerned charges for which Congress felt there was not sufficient evidence; the several references to the deity were added; and, especially, Jefferson's long and violent diatribe against slavery was entirely deleted (cf. Hawke, t, 188–98).

The final document appeared as a broadside, printed by John

Dunlap of Philadelphia, on the night of July 4, 1776. A copy of this was inserted into the Journal of the Congress among the proceedings for the date of July 4. The secretary of the Congress, Charles Thomson, copied a version for the "corrected" journal; and the parchment copy, to which most of the signatures were appended on August 2, 1776, is also considered an official copy.

The "Declaration," therefore, is a document with several significant sources, carefully written, corrected first by Jefferson, then by the Committee, and then by Congress, in all a total of 132 times. It is not, clearly, the "spontaneous overflow of powerful feelings" which some writers seem to imply expressive discourse must be. In addition, as has already been pointed out, it draws on the legal and political conventions of format of Britain and the Continental Congress. In these senses, it is not only not spontaneous, it is also not original. The issue of originality, stylistic and conceptual, has received considerable attention.

There are, of course, those who point to the borrowed phrases coming from Locke and Mason and therefore question a stylistic or even a conceptual originality. Others go further, contending that in the situation at the time, the last thing wanted would have been originality. Jefferson himself seems to have endorsed this opinion. When John Adams, long after 1776, wrote that the "Declaration" "...contained no new ideas, that it is a commonplace compilation, its sentiments hackneyed in Congress for two years before, and its essence contained in Otis's pamphlet" (quoted in Tyler, l, I, 507–8), Jefferson replied that this might

> ...all be true: of that I am not to be the judge.... Whether I had gathered my ideas from reading or reflection, I do not know. I know only that I turned to neither book nor pamphlet while writing it. I did not consider it as any part of my charge to invent new ideas altogether, and to offer no sentiment which had ever been expressed before.
>
> *   *   *
>
> As for myself, I thought it a duty to be on that occasion, a passive auditor of the opinions of others (quoted in Tyler, t, 508; and Friedenwald, d, 158–59).

This last phrase, possibly, can give us a clue to what true originality the "Declaration" possessed. It may not have been an individual, but rather a social originality. The ideas and phrases may have been hackneyed aloud in Congress for two years; but their union in a single and forceful document which cut the umbilical cord from Great Britain and gave birth to a new social entity was an original *social* effort, unique in the annals of political history. The synthesis of British and French political thought to produce a political philosophy native to America was an original fusion, as Becker has carefully shown. The radical substitution of pursuit of happiness for the right to property in the British formula established a new moral foundation for government, one which had not, in these terms, been invoked before. The concept that a fledgling nation should justify its conduct because a "decent respect to the opinions of mankind" dictated it elevated social decorum to a hitherto unattained height. Finally, the coalescence of the aspirations of the newborn nation created a new political vision. It is because of these considerations that Parrington can say of Jefferson: "He was our first great leader to erect a political philosophy native to the economics and experience of America, as he was the first to break consciously with the past" (m, 355). This vision was, in fact, so new that many of the signers were probably not even aware of its vast implications. As Hawke says of Jefferson, "He evoked a private vision of America's past and present, and he anticipated a future that would have unsettled most leaders of the day if they had comprehended his vision" (t, 3). The vision has not yet been fully realized today. Political, educational, sexual, racial, economic, housing, and other equalities are still being fought for. Certainly this vision had not been hackneyed aloud in Congress for two years before the "Declaration."

The particular style of this original synthesis is described in very different terms by different critics. Becker finds Jefferson's style generally to be personal, felicitous, and possessed of the "genial urbanity of cultivated conversation" (d, 196). Jefferson was, it seems, much more at home in a pleasant conversational group or in front of a desk with a pen than he was in a formal speaking situation. Adams somewhat sarcastically wrote that Jefferson could compete with no one in elocution or public address (cf. Hazelton, d, 121). Jefferson rarely spoke in Congress.

Yet it seems difficult to make a case for the conversational style of the "Declaration." If anything, it would have to be a heightened conversation, and it would apply mostly to the style in the section on the abuses. Here the shortened sentences, the repetitiveness, the near disappearance of paragraphing, and the emotional aspect of the style do have elements in common with a kind of heightened, though one-sided conversation. Appropriately enough, the first printed version appeared in a broadside, the eighteenth-century version of a printed handout. In addition, it is written as a lawyer might write a brief for his side of the case. Finally, it survived committee meetings and a Congressional debate. These are the media of the "Declaration," and they partially account for its style.

In the sense that the "Declaration" achieves something, it is the kind of discourse that J. L. Austin would call "performative." In the sense that the "Declaration" causes a group of entities to cohere as a unity, it is the kind of discourse which some philosophers of language have called "cohesive." All *social* expressive discourses do this, from marriage contracts

to constitutions of states. Such are some of the discourse characteristics of
the style of the "Declaration." Let us now turn to the semantic features of
its style.

SEMANTIC FEATURES OF STYLE

Four significant semantic features of the style of the "Declaration"
have already been given considerable attention in other sections. It is distinctly a subjective and one-sided view of reality. It is a very emotional
view of reality. It is written in words drawn from the English language of
the day; but many of the words have been given radically new meanings
(cf. Hawke, t, 3 ff.). Thus it can be said to have its own idiolect. Finally,
many of the terms in the "Declaration," despite a seeming surface clarity,
have ambiguous referents. These four features are often characteristic of
expressive discourse generally.

Some other semantic features characterize the "Declaration." Imagery is not a dominating feature of most of the "Declaration." In all but one
section, the language tends to the abstract. Terms like law, God, Nature,
mankind, equality, rights, liberty, happiness, evil, prudence, and the like
heavily predominate in most of the discourse. But in the abuses relating to
war, there is a vivid shift. Here the concrete terms of imagistic language take
over: waged war, plundered seas, ravaged coasts, burnt towns, transported
armies, destroyed lives, etc.

Some kinds of nonliteral language also characterize the "Declaration." It is clear that the King has become a symbol of oppression; this
symbolism persists throughout the document, once it has been established.
It is also clear that the King has been made to carry all of the animus of
the colonists—the part has been consciously substituted for the whole.
Synedoche is thus a distinct feature of the style. Even the abuses of "others"
are ascribed to him. Attention has already been called to the use of hyperbole
in the "Declaration." Superlatives abound—the evidence for this has already
been presented. These are some of the semantic features of the style of
the "Declaration."

GRAMMATICAL FEATURES OF STYLE

There are a few interesting features of the syntax of the "Declaration" which have not yet been considered. In the first place, if one considers
the main clauses of the document, there is an almost monotonous preponderance of normal sentence word order over inverted order. Of forty
main clauses only six are in inverted order—but these six are located at
crucial spots. The first introduces the "Declaration;" the second introduces
the argument justifying independence generally; the third introduces the

long list of abuses; the fourth introduces the paragraph on redress to the King; the fifth introduces the paragraph on redress to the people of Britain; and the last is the concluding sentence of the "Declaration."

The most obvious aspect of the syntax of the "Declaration" is the abundant parallelism of syntactical units. The long list of abuses of the King follows a similar syntactic structure: He has...Once this is deviated from: He *is* transporting...The subordinate listing of abuses with others each begins "For..." The second paragraph and the final paragraph are syntactically very similar in the first long sentence:

> We hold these truths...
>> that all men are created...
>> that they are endowed...
>> that to secure these rights...
>> that whenever any form...

> We, therefore...do...publish and declare
>> that these United Colonies...
>> that they are absolved...
>> that all political...
>> that, as free...

Several of the crucial inversions begin with similar 'when" clauses:

> *When* in the course of
> ...that, *whenever* any form of government,...
> But *when* a long train of abuses

Participial parallelism is very noticeable, in addition to its occurrence in the main sections of the abuses. Thus in the paragraph on seeking redress from the British people the powerful participial repetition drives home the point: warned, reminded, appealed, conjured. Infinitive parallelisms occur at several instances: to harass...eat; to bear, to become, to fall...

Possibly the most interesting syntactic structure of the whole "Declaration" can be seen from a study of the subjects of the verbs in the main clauses. In the beginning of the "Declaration" there is considerable variety in the subjects: respect, we, prudence, experience, it, such, such, history, facts. But once the abuses begin a powerful monotony sets in: "he," the King, is the subject of nineteen clauses; once "the prince" is substituted for the pronoun; and once "they," the British people, is used. The villain is the grammatical subject of twenty-one out of forty main clauses. "We," the hero, is the subject of eleven main clauses (once "*our* petitions" is substituted for the personal pronoun). Grammatically the syntax dramatically shows the conflict. "We" introduces nearly all the main sections: the philosophy, the two redresses, the declaration, the conclusion.

Finally, a few interesting graphemic features of the style of the "Declaration" might be commented on. Possibly the first feature that the average student of today notices is the abundant use of capitals in the middle of the sentence. This was not a particular stylistic deviation of the "Declaration." Such rhetorical capitalization was common enough at the time. But there are surprising divergences in the various official or semi-official versions of the "Declaration." The version usually printed is the Dunlap broadside version. The two other official versions include the parchment version with the appended signatures, and the handwritten version done by the secretary of the Congress. Three versions in Jefferson's hand also exist: the rough draft, and two copies which he presumably sent to two of his friends and which are now kept respectively in the New York Public Library and in the Massachusetts Historical Society library in Boston. Finally, a draft of the "Declaration" in the handwriting of John Adams also exists.

The complete parallel rendition of all of these versions is given in Hazelton, d, 306–43. For the student interested in expressive discourse, some interesting facts emerge from a comparison and contrast of the various versions. First of all, the abundant capitalization within the sentence that is found in Dunlap's printed version does not at all exist in Jefferson's handwritten versions. In fact, there are 287 more intrasentence capitals in the Dunlap version than in Jefferson's version sent to Lee. This might be explained by the difference between the conventions of print and those of handwriting, were it not for the fact that Adams' handwritten version follows Dunlap very closely, though not entirely. The signed parchment version, a handwritten version, has 126 more intrasentence capitals than does Jefferson's version, though, as the records of the Journal of the Second Continental Congress note, the parchment version was compared, presumably, to the Dunlap and the secretary's versions, both in the Journal. Thomson's version, it might be added, agrees in all but two or three cases, in this matter, with Jefferson's. Jefferson, further, does not capitalize at the beginning of sentences; in Jefferson's prose, words, like men, are created equal and few wear crowns.

A comparison of some spelling differences is also revealing. First of all, Jefferson invariably avoids the old-fashioned "ſ", used for initial and intrasyllabic "s." All of the other versions use the "ſ," though some inconsistently. Second, Jefferson generally uses the "&" sign for "and," more consistently, it might be pointed out, in his finished versions than in his rough draft. Sometimes Thomson also does this, though much less frequently. The others never do (Adams does once). Third, Jefferson seems to have been among the innovators of whom Noah Webster speaks who preferred "honor," "endeavor," and "neighboring," to their older forms "honour," etc. We do know that Jefferson, some six or seven years later, met Noah Webster, and at that time he approved of the spelling and grammar book which Webster was trying to get published. But Webster, in 1783, still would not have approved of Jefferson's innovations in this matter. In that year he wrote: "Expunging the superfluous letters appears to arise from the same pedantic fondness for singularity that prompts the new fashions in pronunciation" (quoted in Warfel, n, 66). And Harry Warfel, his biographer, who is reporting this, adds, "even more surprising is his statement that innovating authors 'have omitted the letter that is sounded and retained one that is silent, for the words are pronounced *onur, favur*'" (Warfel n, 66).

Jefferson also uses lower case for "god" and "nature" (Thomson follows him in "nature," but not in "god"). Only Jefferson simplifies "unacknowledged" to "unacknoleged," in all three versions. Jefferson seems to vacilate between the "y" and "i" in "die," and "ties" (Adams still uses Tryal). He uses "paiment" consistently where the others use "payment." He would like a consistency of noun and pronoun in possessives, and therefore writes "it's" for the possessive. The others use "its," as we still do.

There are some minor differences in punctuation. Jefferson uses the colon more profusely and even permitted himself an "!" in the petition of redress to the British people (it was deleted by Congress). This seems to be the second instance of a more exuberant graphemic style that distinguished Jefferson from the others. Jefferson's habitually toned-down graphemic style deserted him in the violent section against slavery, which was deleted by Congress. Here he used underlinings, printing instead of cursives, and capitalized whole words. It seems evident from these considerations that Jefferson's versions of the "Declaration" are a sort of graphemic idiolect. He follows these characteristics in many of his writings. Some of these tendencies have been noticed by others (cf. Boyd, p, xxx), but an interesting study could be made of Jefferson's habits in these matters. He is partially declaring a linguistic independence based on nature and reason.

EXERCISES

I *Nature of Expressive Discourse*

1. Attempt to determine the rough percentage of expressive discourse in your own communication day over an average week.

2. Look for evidences of expressive discourse in some predominantly reference, persuasive, or literary discourse.

3. Analyze a Greek myth in order to find the embodiment of a significant cultural aspiration (Pandora, Apollo, etc.).

4. Contrast any patterns you can find in some common curse words in two or three different languages: e.g., obscenity and blasphemy in Latin American Spanish with the same elements in French or English curse words.

5. Analyze a religious autobiography for evidences of the Being-for-Itself, or the Being-for-Others, or Being-in-the-World.

6. Contrast two different cultures' concepts of the deity as reflections of the two cultures' aspirations.

7. Analyze one of the anthropological investigations of folklore in the 1966 volume of the *Journal of American Folklore* from the structural framework suggested in this chapter.

8. Analyze a more objective genre of expressive discourse, such as a business contract, for evidences of Being-for-Itself, Being-for-Others, and Being-in-the-World.

9. Write a piece of original expressive discourse, expressing your own global project and outlining the means of achievements as you envisage them.

II *The Logic of Expressive Discourse*

1. Analyze a business contract in teleological terms, i.e., establishing of means towards a goal.

2. Analyze the telic character of a Greek myth.

3. Analyze "The Apostles' Creed" in telelogical terms. Does the eschatology at the end of the Creed serve to give a telic unity to to the Creed?

4. Analyze the *Communist Manifesto* from the standpoint of a set of goals and the establishing of means to achieve them.

5. Analyze Wordsworth's "Preface to the *Lyrical Ballads*," for 1800, as a manifesto of Romanticism. Examine it for goals and means.

6. Examine the overall structure of the *Constitution of the United States* for its basic goal and fundamental means.

7. Analyze any religious prayer for its value assumptions.

8. Analyze any local minority statement (labor, race, religion, etc.) for its value assumptions.

III *The Organization of Expressive Discourse*

1. Tape an informal gripe session and then analyze the discourse in terms of its organization.

2. Comment on the statements:

> Myth is the part of language where the formula *traduttore, tradittore* [to translate is to be a traitor] reaches its lowest truth value. From that point of view it should be put in the whole

gamut of linguistic expressions at the end opposite to that of
poetry, in spite of all the claims which have been made to prove
the contrary. Poetry is a kind of speech which cannot be translated except at the cost of serious distortions; whereas the mythical value of the myth remains preserved, even through the worst
translation. Whatever our ignorance of the language and culture
of the people where it originated, a myth is still felt as a myth
by any reader throughout the world. Its substance does not lie
in its style, its original music, or its syntax, but in the *story*
which it tells (Claude Lévi-Strauss, in Sebeok, m, 85–96); and:
All expressive folklore works esthetically; that is, it engineers a
feeling of control by embodying the problem-situation in the
controlled context of the predictable work of art. Art involves
the creation of another 'world,' another 'reality'—this is a commonplace of literary criticism. This new world differs from that
which we encounter in everyday existence because it is excerpted
from life, removed, controlled by the shaping hand of the
artist. (Roger D. Abrahams, unpublished manuscript; the second
sentence begins another paragraph in Abrahams' text).

3. Analyze the organization of More's *Utopia*. If this is a lengthy
theme, relate the structure to the various interpretations of the
Utopia.

4. Analyze the structure of the constitution of some group you belong to.

5. Discuss the structure of "The Apostles' Creed," the "Litany of
the Saints," or any other religious credo or affirmation.

6. Compare and contrast the organizational patterns of the "Declaration of Independence" and the "Constitution."

7. Tape a conversation of yourself and some of your friends. Analyze
its thematic structure.

IV *The Style of Expressive Discourse*

1. Contrast a scientific with an expressive or persuasive or literary
treatment of the same topic. For example, contrast Aquinas'
treatment of death in the *Summa* with the "Dies Irae" of the
Mass of the Dead, or Aquinas' own poem-prayer "Pange Lingua
Gloriosi" with his treatment of a similar theme in the *Summa*.

2. Analyze a taped gripe session or a conversation for evidences of
Frye's associative rhythm.

3. Investigate a piece of expressive discourse for its "unconventional"
aspects, whether in situational context, medium, theme, style, etc.
What "norm" are you assuming as "conventional" to determine
deviation?

4. Investigate a piece of expressive discourse in an attempt to find its *semantic* deviations, i.e., the differences in meanings it gives to terms. Here a minority manifesto, or a statement of protest, etc., can be profitably used as a corpus.

5. Analyze a myth for its imagery structures.

6. Analyze a piece of expressive discourse for overt or covert evidences of its one-sidedness.

7. Analyze the use of superlative or all-inclusive terms in a piece of expressive discourse.

8. Analyze a piece of expressive discourse for the intrusion of the singular or plural personal pronoun.

9. Write a piece of original expressive discourse and then analyze it for evidences of your own style.

BIBLIOGRAPHY AND FOOTNOTE REFERENCES

Becker, Carl. *The Declaration of Independence: A Study in the History of Political Ideas.* New York: Peter Smith, 1933 (d).

Bühler, Karl. "Die Axiomatik der Sprachwissenschaften." *Kant-Studien,* XXXVIII (1933), 19–90 (a).

Cassirer, Ernst. *The Myth of the State.* New Haven: Yale University Press, 1946 (m).

———. *The Philosophy of Symbolic Forms.* Tr. Ralph Manheim. Vols. I, II, III. New Haven, Conn.: Yale University Press, 1953 (p).

Croce, Benedetto. *Aesthetic, As Science of Expression and General Linguistic.* Tr. Douglas Ainslie. New York: The Noonday Press, 1922 (a).

Dewey, John. *Art as Experience.* New York: Minton, Balch & Company, 1934 (a).

Dumbauld, Edward. *The Declaration of Independence and What It Means Today.* Norman, Okla.: University of Oklahoma Press, 1950 (d).

Eisenson, Jon, J. J. Auer, and J. Erwin. *The Psychology of Communication.* New York: Appleton Century Crofts, 1963 (p).

Friedenwald, H. *The Declaration of Independence.* New York: The Macmillan Company, 1904 (d).

Frye, Northrop. *The Well-Tempered Critic.* Bloomington, Ind.: Indiana University Press, 1963 (w).

Getzels, Jacob W. and Philip W. Jackson. *Creativity and Intelligence: Explorations with Gifted Students.* London: John Wiley, 1962 (c).

Gusdorf, Georges. *Speaking (La Parole)*. Tr. Paul T. Brockelman. Evanston, Ill.: Northwestern University Press, 1965 (s).

Hawke, David. *A Transaction of Free Men: The Birth and Course of the Declaration of Independence*. New York: Charles Scribner's Sons, 1964 (t).

Hazelton, John H. *The Declaration of Independence: Its History*. New York: Dodd, Mead and Company, 1906 (d).

Husserl, Edmund. *Cartesian Meditations*. Tr. Dorion Cairns. The Hague: Martinus Nijhoff, 1960 (c).

——. *Ideas*. Tr. W. R. Royce Gibson. New York: The Macmillan Company, 1931 (i).

Jefferson, Thomas. *The Papers of Thomas Jefferson*. Vol. I. Ed. Julian P. Boyd. Princeton, N. J.: Princeton University Press, 1950 (Boyd, p).

Kinneavy, James L. *A Study of Three Contemporary Theories of Lyric Poetry*. Washington, D. C.: Catholic University of America Press, 1956 (g).

Kockelmans, Joseph H., ed. *Phenomenology: The Philosophy of Edmund Husserl and Its Interpretation*. Garden City, N.Y.: Doubleday & Company, Inc., 1967 (p).

La Drière, J. Craig. "Expression." In *Dictionary of World Literature*, ed. Joseph T. Shipley. New York: Philosophical Library, 1943. Pp. 225–27 (e).

Langan, Thomas. *Merleau-Ponty's Critique of Reason*. New Haven, Conn.: Yale University Press, 1966 (m).

Langer, Susanne K. "On Cassirer's Theory of Language and Myth." In *The Philosophy of Ernst Cassirer*, ed. Paul A. Schilpp. New York: Tudor Publishing Company, 1949 (o).

Merleau-Ponty, Maurice. *Phenomenology of Perception*. Tr. Colin Smith. New York: Humanities Press, 1962 (p).

——. *The Primacy of Perception*. Ed. and tr., James M. Edel. Evanston, Ill.: Northwestern University Press, 1964 (pr).

——. *Sense and Non-Sense*. Tr. Hubert L. Dreyfus and Patricia A. Dreyfus. Evanston, Ill.: Northwestern University Press, 1964 (s).

——. *Signs*. Tr. Richard C. McCleary. Evanston, Ill.: Northwestern University Press, 1964 (si).

Osgood, Charles E. "Some Effects of Motivation on Style in Decoding." In *Style in Language*, ed. Thomas A. Sebeok. New York: John Wiley & Sons Inc., and the Technology Press of Massachusetts Institute of Technology, 1960. Pp. 293–306 (s).

Parrington, Vernon Louis. *Main Currents in American Thought*. Vol. I: *The Colonial Mind, 1620–1800*. New York: Harcourt, Brace and Company, 1927 (m).

Ricoeur, Paul. *La philosophie de la volonté*. Paris: Aubier, 1949 (p).

Sartre, Jean Paul. *Being and Nothingness: An Essay on Phenomenological Ontology*. Tr. Hazel E. Barnes. New York: Washington Square Press, 1953 (b).

Spiegelberg, Herbert. *The Phenomenological Movement: A Historical Introduction.* 2 Vols. Nos. 5 and 6 of *Phaenomenologica.* The Hague: Martinus Nijhoff, 1960 (p).

Torrance, Ellis Paul. *Guiding Creative Talent.* Englewood Cliffs, N. J.: Prentice-Hall, Inc., 1962 (g).

Tyler, Moses Coit. *The Literary History of the American Revolution, 1763–1783.* Vol. 1, 1763–1776. New York: G. P. Putnam's Sons, 1897 (l).

Warfel, Harry R. *Noah Webster: Schoolmaster to America.* New York: The Macmillan Company, 1936 (n).

Werner, Heinz, ed. *On Expressive Language: Papers Presented at the Clark University Conference on Expressive Language Behavior.* Worcester, Mass.: Clark University Press, 1955 (o).

Appendix

**An Example
of Reference Discourse:
The Effective Use
of Statistics**[1]

Common Sense and Statistics

1. Most of us pass through two stages in our attitudes toward statistical conclusions. At first we tend to accept them, and the interpretations placed on them, uncritically. In discussion or argument, we wilt the first time somebody quotes statistics, or even asserts that he has seen some. But then we are misled so often by skillful talkers and writers who deceive us with correct facts that we come to distrust statistics entirely, and assert that "statistics can prove anything"—implying, of course, that statistics can prove nothing.

2. He who accepts statistics indiscriminately will often be duped unnecessarily. But he who distrusts statistics indiscriminately will often be ignorant unnecessarily. A main objective of this book is to show that there is an accessible alternative between blind gullibility and blind distrust. It is possible to interpret statistics skillfully. In fact, you can do it yourself. The art of interpretation need not be monopolized by statisticians, though, of course, technical statistical knowledge helps. This book represents an attempt to illustrate the fact that many important ideas of technical statistics can be conveyed to the nonstatistician without distortion or dilution.

3. Statistical interpretation depends not only on statistical ideas, but also on "ordinary" clear thinking. Clear thinking is not only indispensable in interpreting statistics, but is often sufficient even in the absence of specific statistical knowledge. Before we turn to the main stream of our exposition of statistical ideas, we shall devote this chapter and the next one to a series of statistical examples which can be interpreted reasonably well without any statistical background.

4. In the next chapter we will consider misuses of statistics, but in this one we will consider effective uses. First we will give quick sketches of successful applications of statistics in World War II, in business, in the social sciences, in the bio-

---

[1] Selections from Chapter II of *Statistics: A New Approach,* by W. Allen Wallis and Harry V. Roberts. Glencoe, Ill.: The Free Press, 1956.

logical sciences, in the physical sciences, and in the humanities. Then we will take a closer, more detailed look at three examples, one each from the social, biological, and physical sciences.

5. One warning is needed before the examples are discussed. A receptive yet critical mind is essential. The rewards of open-minded skepticism are great, yet such skepticism is harder to apply than to advocate, especially when the problem in which statistical methods have been used is interesting. If one is interested in race relations in a community, in the effectiveness of an advertising campaign, or in the sexual habits of the population, it may seem tedious and pedantic to be critical about statistical methods. Statisticians are not much more immune to this attitude than anyone else, although they may be more consciously aware of it. One of the authors once recorded this reaction to an interesting book:

> When I first examined the volume, paying attention mostly to its fascinating substantive findings and scarcely at all to its methods, I was very favorably impressed indeed. When I diverted my attention to the general methods I began to note shortcomings; but I felt that these were technicalities—mere blemishes on the surface of the monument, which might modify some of the findings in detail but surely would not affect the broad conclusions. After all, many of (the) figures would still be important and interesting even if we had to allow for an error factor as large as two or even three. But when I spent some time studying the statistical methods in detail, I realized that my confidence in the basic significance of the findings cannot be securely buttressed by factual material included in the volume. In fact, it now seems to me that the inadequacies in the statistics are such that it is impossible to say that the book has much value beyond its role in opening a broad and important field.[2]

Even in the successful examples that follow, one should note potential flaws, and consider what effect they might have on special applications of the findings.

*   *   *

Three Detailed Examples

NATURE AND PURPOSE OF THE EXAMPLES

6. The remainder of this chapter is devoted to rather detailed examinations of three successful statistical studies, one each in the social, biological, and physical sciences. The first example, on long-term trends in the frequency of mental disease, involves a historical study in which the investigators had to rely on existing data and records, whereas the second example, on the effect of vitamins B and C on human endurance under severe physical stress in extreme cold, and the third, on

---

[2] W. Allen Wallis, "The Statistics of the Kinsey Report," *Journal of the American Statistical Association,* Vol. 44 (1949), p. 466.

making rain by "seeding" clouds, involve experiments arranged by the investigators for their specific purposes. The second and third examples, though completely different in subject matter, are in many respects similar statistically.

7. The purposes of presenting these three examples are: (1) to dispel any aura of magic that may have resulted from the brief summaries in the earlier part of the chapter; (2) to present a glimpse of the inner "works" of a statistical investigation; (3) to impart a feel for the necessity of caution, judgment, and detailed information in drawing conclusions from even the best research; and (4) to indicate the extent to which the over-all soundness of an investigation depends on care and skill with a large number of details. In these examples, therefore, instead of omitting details and focusing on the major methods and findings, we shall give particular attention to details, though it will be impractical to recapitulate the original studies in full detail.

8. It is not essential to study these examples intensively now; indeed, in a quick reading they could, if necessary, be omitted altogether. There are occasional references to them later, especially in Chapter 15, but nothing in later chapters depends on familiarity with the details of these examples.

* * *

VITAMINS AND ENDURANCE

THE PROBLEM 9. By 1952 there was a good deal of evidence that extremely large doses of certain vitamins might enable animals and possibly humans better to withstand severe physical and psychological stresses that exist under conditions of extreme cold. It had been reported, for example, that the ability of rats to continue swimming in very cold water (48° F.) was enhanced by vitamin supplementation of the diet. There was related, but less conclusive, evidence for human beings. On the basis of such evidence, the Canadian Army had decided upon vitamin supplementation for certain combat and survival rations. Supplementation on the scale needed (many times the normal requirements for the vitamins in question) was somewhat expensive, however, so the United States Army decided to conduct a special experiment involving simulation of battle conditions before supplementing its own combat rations. This experiment, which we shall describe in some detail, illustrates the care, persistence, and ingenuity needed to answer what at first appears to be a simple question, even though the investigators could specify what evidence they wanted, instead of being limited, as were Goldhamer and Marshall, to data that happened to have survived.

10. The objective of the experiment was "to determine the effect of supplementation with large amounts of ascorbic acid (vitamin C) and B-complex vitamins on the physical performance of soldiers engaging in a high-activity program in a cold environment, with and without caloric restriction." This objective is narrower that the original objective in two interesting and important ways. Originally, the intent was to ascertain the effect of supplementation on the physical performance of soldiers engaging in combat-type activity. The change to "a high-activity program" was necessary because of the near-impossibility of simulating combat conditions effectively; as we shall see later, this change was of considerable importance in interpreting the results of the experiment. Originally, also, the intent was to

ascertain the separate effects of ascorbic acid (vitamin C) and of B complex. The decision to narrow the objective to the study of the combined effect was dictated primarily by statistical considerations relating to the comparative smallness of the number of men available. We shall describe these considerations later.

11. The statistical problems of this investigation were anticipated in advance, when the study design could be molded to meet them. The scientific staff, though mostly M.D.'s and Ph.D.'s with specialization in physiology, were more conversant with statistical principles than are most research workers. Moreover, they worked closely with professional statisticians from the planning stage to the analysis and interpretation of the study.

STATISTICAL PLANNING 12. Initially, it appeared that about 100 soldiers would be available, all volunteers and almost all from a Medical Corps establishment in Texas. Ideally, as we shall see in succeeding chapters, a random sample drawn from all combat soldiers in the Army would have given a better basis for generalizations beyond the group participating in the experiment. Such a random sample was, however, impossible for administrative reasons. The scientists had to make an extra-statistical decision, namely, that results for the population sampled would apply to the target population of interest—that is, that the sampling process actually used was satisfactory for studying the physiological response to vitamin supplementation.

13. All the men were to be housed in relatively insubstantial barracks, unheated during the night, in a cold and lonely spot in Wyoming, called Pole Mountain, at an elevation of 8,310 feet. Their clothing would be inadequate except when they were quite active. For most of ten weeks in January, February, and March, 1953, they were to engage in strenuous outdoor activities: marches, forced marches, calisthenics, and sports. There were to be no leaves or passes. The diet was designed for monotony; the caloric total was ample at the start—4,100 calories— but a three-week period of short rations was scheduled for the end of the experiment, with only about 2,100 to 2,500 calories per day—about enough to maintain a stenographer's weight. It was anticipated that many of the men would collapse under the combination of strenuous activity and restricted diet, and the experiment would have to be terminated before the three-week period was over. Throughout the experiment there were to be periodic measurements of physical condition and performance, and also of psychological attitudes and aptitudes.

14. So much for the bleak regimen in store for the 100 volunteers. What about the statistical design? Your first reaction might be simply to give the vitamin supplements to everyone and see what happened. But when experiments are done that way, their findings are nearly valueless. The fatal defect is that no one knows how the men would have performed under these conditions in the absence of vitamin supplementation. The only way to find out what would happen without supplementation was to withhold the vitamins from some of the 100 soldiers. Then a comparison of performance could be made between those who did and those who did not receive the supplementation, the latter being called the "control group."

15. But which group of men should not receive the supplementation? The control and experimental groups should be such that, chance factors aside, both groups would react the same if treated the same. Then, if the supplemented group

did better than the unsupplemented group even after allowance for chance factors, a decision could be made in favor of the vitamin supplementation. There is, basically, only one method of separating the men into the two groups so that the experimenter can draw valid conclusions about the effect of the supplementation: the separation should make proper use of *random sampling*. For example, the names of the 100 men could be put on slips of paper, the slips shuffled thoroughly, and the names for the control group selected by a blindfolded person. Random selection of the control group has two advantages. First, it protects against any bias of selection, conscious or unconscious, that might tend to make the control group systematically different from the other group. Second, only when the selection is essentially random is it possible to measure the influence of chance on the differences between the two groups, and so decide whether or not the actual difference exceeds that which would be expected from chance alone. These advantages will be explained in later chapters.

16. An important technical contribution of the statisticians to the design came about in the following way. The scientists suggested dividing the men randomly into four groups of 25 each. One group was to receive both vitamins C and B. The second was to receive vitamin C but not vitamin B, the third was to receive vitamin B but not vitamin C, and the fourth group was to receive neither vitamin. An alternative suggestion was to divide the 100 men at random into two groups of 50 each, one receiving *both* C and B, the other receiving *neither*. The statisticians recommended the second suggestion. With this two-group design, a more adequate evaluation could be made of the combined effect of vitamins C and B, though at the cost of not learning about the separate effects. With the four-group design, it was more likely that important *true* effects of vitamin supplementation would be obscured by chance factors, in which case a promising line of experimentation would be wrongly abandoned. If a significant effect for vitamins B and C together were detected by the experiment, further experiments to refine the findings by isolating individual effects would be inevitable. This reasoning was reinforced by the arbitrariness of the designation "vitamin B complex," which includes many distinct elements, each potentially as important as vitamin C. Hence even the original four-group experiment could not show which specific B-complex component was responsible for any effects of vitamin B complex. Moreover, in terms of the immediate military problem, the cost of multiple-ingredient vitamin capsules for front-line troops would not be much greater than that of capsules which contained only the effective ingredient or ingredients, since the cost of distribution from manufacturer to the Army and then to the troops represented the bulk of the total cost. Thus, if the combined B-complex and C supplementation proved effective, interim action could be taken, and later experiments could investigate more carefully the specific source of the benefits.

17. There was one major qualification in the recommendation of the statisticians that the vitamins be studied only in combination. This would be disastrous if, in truth, vitamin C and vitamin B complex each had beneficial effects, but the two together tended to cancel each other. The extent of this danger had to be evaluated by the scientists on the basis of their knowledge of the physiological effects of vitamins. They decided that the danger was remote, and adopted the two-group design.

18. An important question was whether 100 men were enough to make the experiment worth performing at all. The basic approach to this question was as follows: Suppose that the vitamins really have an effect which, if it could be detected despite inevitable chance variations, would be worth knowing about. What would be the probability of detecting such an effect in an experiment with 100 men? To answer the question, the statisticians needed to know (1) how big a difference would be "worth knowing about," and (2) how great the chance variation among men treated alike was apt to be. Both of these questions were studied in terms of one of the proposed measures of physical performance, the Army Physical Fitness Test, which consisted of five exercises: pull-ups, squat-jumps, push-ups, sit-ups, and squat-thrusts. This test had been used in the Army for several years with a standardized scoring system. It was known that an average improvement of about 20 points on this test might be expected during six weeks of the basic training period. If the same amount of improvement could be achieved merely by vitamin supplementation, supplementation would seem worthwhile. Next, records of past performance on the test were procured for a group of soldiers at an eastern camp. These records gave some idea about variation of scores on this test among individuals, and also about the variation of scores for the same individual on different occasions. This information made possible an assessment of the probabilities that such variation would obscure a true average effectiveness of supplementation of 20 units in an experiment based on 80, 100, or indeed any number of men that might be contemplated. It turned out that 100 men was about the smallest number for which an experiment would probably give valuable information.

19. Between the completion of the plans and the start of the experiment, the number of soldiers available was reduced to 87. This jeopardized the success of the experiment, but it was felt still to be worth doing. The previous decision to use two groups rather than four now seemed especially desirable.

20. In the planning period, several other issues were discussed by the statisticians and scientists. Some of them may not at first appear statistical, but all were relevant to the design of the experiment and to subsequent analysis of its results.

21. (1) It was essential to the success of the experiment that the soldiers themselves not learn who was receiving the supplements. Such knowledge might influence perfomance by its effect on the morale of the participants. It had been decided, therefore, to give capsules to everyone. The capsules for the control group had no nutritive value except for a trivial amount of vitamin C—just enough for normal requirements in the low-calorie phase of the experiment. All capsules appeared identical in every respect but one: for ease of administration, capsules given to the supplemented group were colored orange while the others were colored brown. Thus, it would be known who was receiving the same treatment, although it would not be known what the treatments were. Even this knowledge could affect the experiment adversely. For example, one of the measures of physical performance was to be the ability to complete forced marches. Suppose that the first two men who fell out of a forced march turned out to be members of the group receiving capsules of the same color. Other men receiving capsules of this color might then suspect that they were not getting the superior treatment, and that they might soon have to drop out. Since, as the subsequent experiment con-

firmed, physical performance is very much influenced by attitude, falling out might become epidemic among those receiving capsules of the same color. Thus, what was really a matter of a few men being unable to continue would be exaggerated in the data because of psychological contagion. Moreover, all subsequent performance for the duration of the experiment might be strongly influenced by the memory of this one unhappy forced march. Unfortunately, it was not possible to correct this situation by making all capsules the same color. It was hoped that this defect in the design could be compensated by fostering strong inter-platoon competition in all the performance tests. Since each platoon contained men receiving capsules of both colors, men might identify themselves primarily with their own platoons rather than with their capsule colors.

22. (2) At the recommendation of the statisticians, all performance measurements were made once for each man before vitamin supplementation started. This permitted a more powerful analytical technique, based on the amount of improvement (or deterioration) of each man during the course of the experiment, rather than on his final performance alone. The importance of initial measurements of physical performance before supplementation was stressed by one of the statisticians in these words : "...failure to do so would be tantamount to removal of more than three quarters of the men from the experiment."

23. (3) The general strategy of the two-group design was modified to take into account the fact that the men were organized into four platoons, and that every effort would be made to foster inter-platoon competition. Instead of subdividing the entire group of men randomly into a supplemented and control group, a random subdivision was made within each platoon. This was as if four small experiments were performed instead of one big one, and there was reason to believe that the four small experiments combined would yield more reliable results than one big one.

24. (4) A still finer subdivision of the experiments by squads within platoons was considered and rejected.

EXECUTION OF THE EXPERIMENT 25. Complex administrative problems arose in carrying out the experiment. A staff of 47 people—officers, enlisted men, and civilians was needed, even though the subjects themselves handled the camp chores. The following jobs, among others, had to be done:

1. Menus had to be devised to give the desired caloric values along with as much monotony as could be injected without causing excessive rejection of the food.
2. The food had to be prepared with more than usual care in order that the theoretical caloric levels could actually be offered.
3. All food not eaten by each subject had to be sorted and weighed in order to estimate his caloric intake, both in total and for protein, fat, and carbohydrate separately.
4. The capsules had to be given to the right men, and it was necessary to be sure they were actually swallowed.
5. Uniforms and barrack temperatures had to be adjusted to the weather.
6. All activities and work details had to be scheduled properly.

7. All performance tests had to be carefully supervised and recorded. For example, records had to be kept of the time and distance at which each man fell out on a forced march. Alertness was needed to notice such things as that fewer men fell out on forced marches if they were picked up and brought home in an open truck rather than a heated ambulance, and that still fewer gave up if they had to walk home anyway at their own pace. Total physical exhaustion was rarely encountered. "Experience with the forced march as a measure of performance, and specifically endurance, demonstrated that the usual cause of dropping out was loss of the will to proceed. It is not proper to call a man a quitter if he stops after marching 20 miles uphill into a fierce wind, yet in only rare instances did men apparently reach the limit of their capacity to march."

8. Many special records had to be kept. For example, one Army enlisted man, trained as a meteorologist, kept detailed records of the weather.

9. Twelve technicians in the laboratory section were needed to make the various physical and biochemical determinations, such as blood pressure, body weight, skinfold thickness, blood glucose, blood and urinary ascorbic acid, hemoglobin, and the like.

ANALYSIS OF THE FINDINGS   26. As the experiment drew to a close, attention was focused more closely on the details of the analysis. The general nature of the analysis had been determined before the experiment had even started, but there were many detailed questions to be answered. There were also innovations and improvisations in the experiment itself that had not been anticipated.

27. As data were collected in the field, rough analyses had been made by the supervising scientists, partly out of curiosity to see if the answer was going to be obvious. The most striking finding to emerge from these rough analyses was that the average physical performance for the entire group, supplemented and controls combined, had improved steadily throughout the experiment. In the last three weeks, when the 2,100–2,500 calorie diet had been expected to cause the experiment to terminate, the men not only carried on but continued to show improvement on the physical tests. When they departed on their "convalescent" furloughs, they were actually in better physical condition than at the start of the experiment. The unanticipated improvement of the men during the entire experiment, and especially that during the short-ration period, might have been attributed to the vitamins had there not been a control group which showed similar improvement. This outcome of the experiment thus underscores our earlier comments about the need for a control group.[3]

---

[3] The need for controls is also illustrated by the experience of an elderly man who, having difficulty in hearing conversation, placed in his ear a plastic button with a cord long enough to run under his collar. Thereafter, he had no difficulty in hearing. People mistook the button and cord for a hearing aid, and talked louder. Had this man had a real hearing aid, he might have attributed all of the improvement in his hearing to the aid.

28. The answer to the basic question, then, was not obvious from the rough analysis. It would have been obvious only if the effect of the vitamin supplementation had been large and consistent. The actual differences were relatively small. Careful analysis was needed to decide whether the supplemented and control groups differed more than could reasonably be ascribed to chance.

29. As we have seen, there were many measures of physical status and performance. One of the most important was the Army Physical Fitness Test, described earlier. Initially, the combined fitness score—the sum of scores on the five components—was the focus for analysis. Before actual numerical work could begin, certain decisions about treatment of the data had to be made. The fitness test had been administered weekly during the experiment. A major problem arose because some of the subjects had missed an occasional test on account of injury or illness, or had participated when their physical conditions were below par for one of these reasons. When the latter occurred, a decision was typically made by the medical officers *before* the actual test whether or not the man's score would be included. However, six subjects presented more serious problems, and these were not finally resolved until the analysis was about to begin. To illustrate, we quote the description of two of these cases.

30. *Test Subject No.* 311: A thin, slight man of 22 developed an upper respiratory infection during the second week of capsule administration. . . . Soon thereafter, following vigorous physical exercise he developed a large hematoma in the right thigh. A pneumonitis ensued with fever, anorexia, vomiting, and 7-1/2 pounds weight loss. He was at bed rest and light activity for approximately one month, a week of which was spent in the F. E. Warren AFB Station Hospital. During this time he missed four consecutive weeks of physical and metabolic tests. Following this illness his performance was generally poor and he continued to lose weight on the restricted caloric diet. It was decided to eliminate all of his data from the experiment. (This was the only subject for whom all data were discarded.) *Test Subject No.* 432: This 30 year old platoon sergeant was granted emergency leave during the third week of the test. . . because of acute illness of several members of his family. He was absent from the test site for 10 days during which he administered nursing care to his family and continued to take capsules at the usual rate. No significant change of weight occurred during his absence, and tests of physical performance after his return showed no deterioration. It was decided to include all of the data collected from this man.

31. The final analysis, you will recall, was to be based essentially on improvement between the initial and final fitness test scores, and other performance measures. There were 44 men in the supplemented group and 40 in the control group for whom usable data were available for the first and last fitness tests. The results are shown in Table 54. The average score for the supplemented group was lower at the beginning and higher at the end; the average improvement was therefore greater for the supplemented group than for the controls.

32. On first glance, then, the supplementation appears effective. Actually, how-

ever, Table 54 shows only the over-all average for these two groups of 40 and 44 for the particular time period of the experiment. The table does not by itself tell whether these findings apply more generally. This question is what we had in mind earlier in our allusions to the effects of chance and the problem of allowing for those effects in interpreting the data. It is possible to analyze the original data from which Table 54 was computed in order to reach a decision as to whether the greater improvement shown for the supplemented group is more than we would ordinarily expect by chance alone. The analysis used, though not the idea underlying it, is too technical for this book. The conclusion was that differences at least as great as the ones observed in Table 54 would arise purely by chance about 17 times in 100, *even if the supplementation had no effect.* The italicized clause, to use again the technical terminology first introduced in our discussion of the study of the incidence of major psychoses, expressed the null hypothesis. The evidence of the experiment is not strong enough to warrant discarding the null hypothesis, at least so far as this analysis was concerned.

TABLE 54

Mean Physical Performance Scores of Soldiers, Initial and Final
Tests, Vitamin-Supplemented and Control Groups

Group	Initial Test	Final Test
Control	175.33	330.33
Supplemented	164.50	340.07

33. Several other analyses of the same type were made for other aspects of the fitness test data. For example, a separate analysis of each of the five component tests was made. In addition, analyses were devised which utilized not only the beginning and ending scores, but also the intermediate scores. None of these analyses provided convincing evidence against the null hypothesis.

34. The same analytical procedure was applied to several of the other physical and psychological tests. For some of these measures, the control, and for others the treated, group appeared slightly better. For the most part, the differences were readily ascribable to chance. On one type of test, however, the supplemented group appeared superior by a margin exceeding what would be expected by chance alone. The average drop in body temperature after periods of passive exposure to cold, both indoors and out, was less for the treated than for the control group. On the other hand, the loss of body weight during the experiment appeared significantly greater for the treated group.

35. Some of the measurements, such as performance on the forced marches, could not be analyzed by the approach just described because the data were qualitative (for example, a man did or did not fall out on a forced march) rather than quantitative (for example, scores on the fitness test). There was a variety of minor problems of analysis, but we shall report only the main conclusion: no convincing evidence in favor of supplementation.

36. This account may make the analysis sound tedious and complicated. It was. Moreover, many key questions arising during the analysis had to be handled by relatively crude statistical methods because more refined methods were not possi-

ble, given the then current state of statistical knowledge. There were a few interesting methodological by-products, statistical and medical, such as a better method for scoring the physical performance tests. Much was learned that would enable future experiments of this type to be more effectively conducted, and this was thoroughly discussed in the final report.

37. The most important criticism of the experiment was not a statistical one, but the problem of the meaning of *cold stress*. One crucial element of combat stress was missing: long, anxious, sleepless waiting in the cold. As the final report stated,

> The type and degree of cold stress should be precisely defined prior to the study and adhered to throughout...continued high energy activity is not compatible with body cooling despite the wearing of minimal uniforms. On the other hand, prolonged inactivity in the cold (simulating the fixed battlefield condition) is not compatible with high energy output....

38. Our description of the experiment has necessarily neglected many important phases, but perhaps we have gone far enough to give you an appreciation of what underlay the brief statement of conclusions and recommendations, which we quote in full:

> Under the conditions of this experiment, supplementation of an adequate diet with large amounts of ascorbic acid and B complex vitamins in men subjected to the stresses of high physical activity, residence in a cold environment and, during the later part of the experiment, caloric deficit, did not result in significantly better physical performance than that of unsupplemented men.
>
> Vitamin supplementation of the type used in this study resulted in a reduction in the fall in rectal temperature on exposure to cold.
>
> A caloric deficit of 1,200 calories per day for 22 days did not lead to detectable impairment of physical performance.
>
> The present study indicates that the current army minimal allowances of water-soluble vitamins are capable of supporting good physical performance under the conditions of this study.
>
> An ascorbic acid intake of about 60 mg per day (control group) resulted in whole blood ascorbic acid levels of 0.3 to 1.2 mg % with a mean value of 0.7 mg %.

RECOMMENDATIONS

1. That Army rations to be used in cold weather not be supplemented with ascorbic acid and B complex vitamins. This recommendation is subject to change if further studies should reveal benefits not detected in the present study.
2. That further studies be made on the effect of vitamin supplementation on the physiological and pathological response of human subjects to cold exposure while at rest.

*　　*　　*

Conclusion

39. Statistical methods are used effectively in the most diverse subjects, ranging from minor business and personal decisions to abstruse questions of pure science and scholarship.

40. Brief illustrations serve to indicate the range of applicability of statistics, but they can give only the barest hints about the way statistics enters into these applications. Statistics, when used effectively, becomes so intertwined in the whole fabric of the subject to which it is applied as to be an integral part of it. Full appreciation of the ways in which statistics enters into an investigation requires, therefore, a detailed analysis of the subject matter and of all the methods brought to bear on it.

INDEX

Boldface entries are items in bibliographies.